Introducing
Christian
Doctrine

Introducing Christian Doctrine

Millard J. Erickson

Edited by
L. Arnold Hustad

BAKER BOOK HOUSE
Grand Rapids, Michigan 49516

Copyright © 1992 by Baker Books
a division of Baker Book House Company
P.O. Box 6287, Grand Rapids, MI 49516-6287

Sixth printing, March 1997

Printed in the United States of America

For information about academic books, resources for Christian leaders,
and all new releases available from Baker Book House, visit our web
site:
                    http://www.bakerbooks.com/

Library of Congress Cataloging-in-Publication Data

Erickson, Millard J.
    Introducing Christian doctrine / Millard J. Erickson.
        p.   cm.
    Includes index.
    ISBN 0-8010-3215-6
    1. Theology, Doctrinal. I. Title.
    BT75.2.E76   1992
    230—dc20   92-16479

In memory of

Siri Mahal Erickson Inoferio
January 24–October 14, 1991

"Jesus said, 'Let the little children come to me,
and do not hinder them,
for the kingdom of heaven belongs to such as these'"
(Matthew 19:14, NIV)

Contents

Contents

Contents

Preface

For several years now, my book *Christian Theology* has served well the purpose for which it was designed: to be an introductory seminary-level textbook in systematic theology. The wide adoption and positive response by both instructors and students have been gratifying.

In addition, a number of instructors in Christian liberal-arts colleges and Bible colleges have been using *Christian Theology* as a textbook in courses surveying Christian doctrine. Some of them have expressed their desire for a briefer version of this book, which would eliminate some of the more technical portions. They have convinced me that there is a group of students who could benefit from a work of this type. It was to meet this need that the present volume was prepared.

Introducing Christian Doctrine is so designed as to provide a preparation for and transition to *Christian Theology*. It agrees in style and in perspective with that larger work, many sentences having been taken over unchanged from it. Students and others who desire more-extended discussions of some of the issues raised here, or treatments of some issues not addressed here, are encouraged to consult that larger work.

I am especially appreciative of the work of L. Arnold Hustad, professor of theology and philosophy at Crown College, who has served as editor of this project. It is always a source of satisfaction to an instructor to have a student of his calibre. He wrote his master of theology thesis under my direction and served as my teaching assistant during the 1972–73 academic year. His thesis on the doctrine of transcendence in the theology of Paul Tillich is one of the finest pieces of student scholarship I have had the privilege to read. It is a further source of gratification when one's student goes on to obtain his doctorate and enter a career of teaching and scholarship. An even greater satisfaction, however, comes when one is able to work with that former student as a colleague on a joint project such as this one. The process of condensation has been one in which he and I jointly decided upon the nature and extent of the changes to be made, largely at his suggestion. He then did the major work of deletion and condensation, and I rewrote some portions. So while the content is entirely mine, the form of that content, as compared with *Christian Theology*, is largely his. We then reviewed each other's work. He has shown excellent judgment, balance, and a sense of the needs of undergraduates, which is based upon his several years of experience teaching. He also gave the result of our joint labors a pilot test in his course in Christian theology at Crown College during the summer of 1991.

I am grateful for the suggestions of a number of undergraduate instructors. I am also especially appreciative of the students at Crown College who used a draft of this work as a textbook. Their comments and observations enabled us to make a number of improvements in the final product. The encouragement of Baker Book House, and especially of Allan Fisher, was also of great help in bringing this endeavor to fruition.

MILLARD J. ERICKSON

Part One

The Doing
of Theology

1

The Study of God

The Nature of Theology

Theology as the Study of Doctrine

To some readers, the word *doctrine* may prove somewhat frightening. It conjures up visions of very technical, difficult, abstract beliefs, perhaps propounded dogmatically. Doctrine is not that, however. Christian doctrine is simply statements of the most fundamental beliefs that the Christian has, beliefs about the nature of God, about his action, about us who are his creatures, and about what he has done to bring us into relationship with himself. Far from being dry or abstract, these are the most important types of truths. They are statements on the fundamental issues of life: namely, who am I, what is the ultimate meaning of the universe, where am I going? Christian doctrine is, then, the answers that the Christian gives to those questions that all human beings ask.

Doctrine deals with general or timeless truths about God and the rest of reality. It is not simply the study of specific historical events, such as what God has done, but of the very nature of the God who acts in history. The study of doctrine is known as theology. Literally, theology is the study of God. It is the careful, systematic study, analysis, and statement of Christian doctrine. Certain of its characteristics will help us understand the nature of the theological enterprise:

1. Theology is biblical. It takes its primary content from the Old and New Testament Scriptures. While additional insight may be

5. Theology is practical. Paul expounded doctrine not merely to inform his readers, so that they might have more data. Rather, he intended that the doctrine he expounded be applied to everyday life. The doctrine of the second coming of Christ can, of course, become the object of speculation—people attempt to ascertain when it will occur in relation to other events. Paul, however, in 1 Thessalonians 4:16–18 urges his readers to comfort one another with this truth. That the Lord will return and will resurrect all who have believed in him is a source of peace and encouragement in a world in which so much of value appears to be undergoing destruction.

The Necessity for the Study of Doctrine

Is there really a need to study doctrine? Isn't it sufficient if I simply love Jesus? In

---

Far from being dry or abstract, Christian doctrine deals with the most fundamental issues of life: who am I, what is the ultimate meaning of the universe, where am I going?

---

obtained by the study of God's creation, or what is sometimes referred to as the book of God's work, it is primarily God's Word that constitutes the content of theology.

2. Theology is systematic. It does not look at each of the books of the Bible separately, but attempts to draw together into one coherent whole what the entirety of Scripture says on a given topic, such as human sinfulness.

3. Theology is done in the context of human culture. Theology, particularly in its more advanced or technical sense, must relate the teachings of Scripture to data found in other disciplines that deal with the same subject matter.

4. Theology is contemporary. The aim of the theological enterprise is to restate timeless biblical truths in a form that is understandable to the people who are living today.

the view of some people, doctrine is not only unnecessary, it is undesirable, and may be divisive. There are, however, several reasons why such study is not optional:

1. Correct doctrinal beliefs are essential to the relationship between the believer and God. Thus, for example, the writer to the Hebrews said, "And without faith it is impossible to please him. For whoever would draw near to God must believe that he exists and that he rewards those who seek him" (Heb. 11:6). Also important for a proper relationship with God is belief in the humanity of Jesus; John wrote, "By this you know the Spirit of God: every spirit which confesses that Jesus Christ has come in the flesh is of God" (1 John 4:2). Paul emphasized the importance of belief in the resurrection of Christ: "If you confess with your mouth, 'Jesus is Lord,' and believe in your heart that God raised him from the dead, you will be

saved. For it is with your heart that you believe and are justified, and it is with your mouth that you confess and are saved" (Rom. 10:9–10, NIV).

2. Doctrine is important because of the connection between truth and experience. Our age is one in which immediate experience is very highly valued. Thus, many utilize drugs because of the excitement or stimulation which they provide. Fantasies supply satisfying experiences to some. Yet in the long run, our experience is affected by, indeed, depends upon reality. A person who falls from an upper story of a tall building may shout as he passes each window on the way down, "I'm doing fine," but eventually the facts will catch up with his experience. Simply feeling good about Jesus cannot be divorced from the question of whether he is genuinely the Son of God. Hope for the future depends upon whether his resurrection took place and ours will some day.

3. Correct understanding of doctrine is important because there are many secular and religious systems of thought that compete for our devotion these days. Marxism, the basis of communism, long claimed the allegiance of many. Popular self-help philosophies and psychologies abound. Among the religious options there are large numbers of sects and cults in addition to a great variety of Christian denominations. And alternative religions not only are found in foreign lands, but also claim significant numbers of devotees in the United States. It is, therefore, not simply a question of *whether* one shall believe, but *what* one shall believe.

It has been suggested that the way to deal with the numerous alternatives is a thoroughgoing refutation and systematic exposing of their shortcomings. A positive approach of teaching the views of the Christian faith would seem to be preferable, however. This approach provides a basis upon which to measure the alternative positions. Consider as an analogy that the United States Treasury Department trains agents to recognize counterfeit money not by showing them innumerable counterfeit bills, but by exposing them continually to genuine United States currency, until they know just what it feels and looks like. They will eventually be able to detect an imitation not merely by the presence of wrong features, but also by the absence of (or a variation in) the correct features.

Theology as Science

A question is sometimes raised regarding the legitimacy of the study of Christian doctrine in an institution of higher education. Is the teaching of theology not mere indoctrination? To be sure, there are limits to the teaching of Christian theology in a state institution, where there cannot be any official connection with a given form of religion. However, there is nothing prohibiting an objective, scientific study of Christianity as well as of other religions. In a private institution, and particularly one which has a commitment to Christianity, the study of Christian doctrine is quite appropriate. It need not in any way be inferior to the other disciplines studied.

To be a proper topic for study, theology must in some sense be a science. We do not mean to say that it must be a science in the narrow sense of the natural sciences.[1] Rather, it must have some of the traditional criteria of scientific knowledge: (1) a definite object of study; (2) a method for investigating the subject matter and for verifying assertions; (3) objectivity in the sense that the study deals with phenomena external to the immediate experience of the learner and therefore accessible to investigation by others; and (4) coherence among the propositions of the subject matter so that the content forms a definite body of knowledge rather than a series of unrelated or loosely connected facts.

Theology as we will be dealing with it meets these criteria. It also occupies com-

1. Here we are speaking of science in the broader European sense: the Germans, for example, speak of *Naturwissenschaften*, or sciences of nature, and *Geisteswissenschaften*, which are roughly what we would call behavioral sciences.

mon ground with the other sciences. (1) It accepts the same rules of logic as do the other disciplines. Where difficulties appear, theology does not simply invoke paradox or incomprehensibility. (2) It is communicable—it can be expressed in propositional verbal form. (3) To some extent, it employs methods used by other specific disciplines, particularly history and philosophy. (4) It shares some subject matter with other disciplines. Thus, there is the possibility of at least some of its propositions' being confirmed or refuted by other disciplines such as natural science, behavioral science, or history.

And yet theology has its own unique status. Some of its subject matter is unique to it, for example, God. It also deals with common objects but in a unique way; for example, it considers people in terms of their relationship to God. Thus, while Christian theology or the study of Christian doctrine is a science, it is a science with its own pecu-

what has been believed is made normative for what should be believed.
3. *The Scriptures.* The Bible is held to be the defining document or the constitution of the Christian faith. Thus, it specifies what is to be believed and what is to be done.
4. *Experience.* The religious experience of a Christian today is regarded as providing authoritative divine information.

We will follow the third approach. A similar practice can be found in various institutions and organizations which have some charter, constitution, or articles of incorporation defining what the institution is to be and the procedures it is to follow. Where there is a dispute between two claimants to be the true representative of such a group or movement, a court of law will ordinarily rule in favor of the party deemed to adhere to the basic charter. In our country, the Con-

> *The Bible is the constitution of the Christian faith: it specifies what is to be believed and what is to be done.*

liar status. It cannot be reduced to any other science, either natural or behavioral.

The Starting Point for the Study of Christian Doctrine

One of the questions that must immediately be faced when we study Christian doctrine is the source from which our knowledge will be drawn. Even in Christian circles, several answers have been given:

1. *Natural theology.* The created universe is studied to determine certain truths about God and about human nature. (This empirical approach to doctrine will be examined in ch. 3.)
2. *Tradition.* Inquiry is made into what has been held and taught by individuals and organizations identifying themselves as Christian. Thus,

stitution is binding. Indeed, any law that contradicts the Constitution will be declared invalid by a court.

In the case of Christianity, we also are dealing with a constitution, namely the Bible. Christians are those who continue in the teachings that Jesus Christ himself laid down. They cannot deny or modify that which was taught and practiced by Jesus, or by those whom he authorized. In theory, of course, it would be possible to amend the constitution. Note that in human dealings, however, only certain persons are eligible to make such an amendment; an external organization cannot alter the constitution. In the case of Christianity, its constitution, the Bible, was not created or formulated by the humans who make up the Christian church. Rather, it originated from God himself. That being the case, only God has the authority to change the standards of belief and practice. The Bible is the guideline that is to be followed since it possesses the right of defining correct belief and practice.

This is not to say that Christianity down through the ages has repeated and will continue to repeat the accounts of the Bible in exactly that form. Much of the Bible deals with specific cases and was written to specific situations in history. To repeat the same words in the same fashion would be to distort the meaning. Rather, what is to be done is to express for today what Jesus or Paul or Isaiah would say if he were addressing the present situation. This does not involve an alteration of the fundamental meaning, but a reexpression and reapplication of it.

The Method of Theology

We have said that theology is a science. That means in part that it has a definite procedure. While the steps we will describe need not be rigidly followed in sequence, there is a logical development to them.

1. Collection of the Biblical Materials

The first step will be to identify all the relevant biblical passages dealing with the topic being investigated and then to interpret them very carefully. This is the process known as exegesis. The exegete will want to use the very best of theological tools and methods. These tools include concordances, commentaries, and, for the person who knows the original languages, the biblical texts, grammars, and lexicons.

It is important even at this step to think carefully about the materials being used. We should consider the position of the author of a commentary, for example. We should at least be aware of the author's theological perspective so that presuppositions inconsistent with our own general orientation are not imported unknowingly. The potential problem here is like that which may occur when we use an instrument for navigation. A small error in a compass, for example, can, when we have traveled a long distance, result in our being far off course. Thus, careful evaluation of our interpretational tools is important.

At this point, the crucial consideration is to determine precisely what the author was saying to his particular audience. This will involve the study of biblical backgrounds so that we understand, as it were, the other partner in the dialogue. Reading a biblical passage is somewhat like hearing one-half of a telephone conversation. Paul, for example, wrote to specific groups and related to positions that they held. Unless we are familiar with those positions, it will be difficult to determine Paul's meaning.

Such biblical inquiry will involve examination of various types of biblical material. In some cases we will do word studies; for example, we might determine the meaning of "faith" by a study of all occurrences of the Greek noun *pistis* and the verb *pisteuō*. It will frequently prove profitable to examine didactic passages of Scripture in which an author addresses in forthright fashion some particular topic. Because the specific intent of these passages is to teach, the doctrinal significance is often quite overt. More difficult, but also extremely important, are the narrative passages. Here we have descriptions of divine and human actions rather than discourses on theological matters. These passages frequently serve as illustrations of doctrinal truths. In some cases, the author also gives an interpretation or an explanation in which the doctrinal import is evident.

2. Unification of the Biblical Materials

It is important to learn what a biblical author says in different settings about a given subject. Doctrine, however, is more than a mere description of what Paul, Luke, or John said; and so we must draw these several witnesses together into some sort of coherent whole. In this, the theologian is following a procedure that is not totally different from that of other disciplines. In psychology, for example, one would ordinarily look first at the points of agreement among psychologists of a given school of thought and then seek to ascertain whether or not apparent differences are actual disagreements.

This very endeavor, of course, assumes a unity and coherence among the several biblical materials and biblical witnesses. While that should not make us blind to unique emphases and nuances of meaning, it does mean that we will look for agreement rather than disagreement. As one New Testament scholar put it, "We interpret the 5 percent of materials in which the synoptic gospels [Matthew, Mark, and Luke] differ in light of the 95 percent in which there is clear agreement rather than the other way around."

3. Analysis of the Meanings of Biblical Teachings

When the doctrinal material has been collected into a coherent whole, we must ask what it *really* means. Part of the issue here is making certain that we do not read contemporary meanings into biblical references. It is also possible, when most of our conversation is with people who have long been familiar with a particular interpretation of Scripture, to simply assume that a concept such as being born again will be understood by everyone in the same way.

Theologians, therefore, must relentlessly press the question, "What does this really mean?" For if biblical concepts are to be accurately translated into a contemporary form, it is important that they be correctly understood. If they are not, there will be even greater imprecision at later points in the process as the ambiguity is compounded. As is commonly said, unless something is clear in the mind of the speaker, it will never be clear in the mind of the hearer. Likewise, unless something is clear in the mind of the theologian as exegete, it will not be clear in the mind of the theologian as preacher seeking in turn to communicate to others the results of exegesis.

4. Examination of Historical Treatments

One of the tools of theology is a study of church history. Here we are able to put our own interpretations in the context of how a particular doctrine has been viewed in the past. The purpose of this is not simply to formulate the lowest common denominator of what has been held at various points in the past, but to help us realize that frequently our interpretations or constructions are parallels of earlier ones. We can, therefore, often tell the implications of a current view by looking at the historical results of a similar view.

Another benefit of the study of historical theology is that we learn the doing of theology by observing how others have done it. As we see the way in which Augustine and Thomas Aquinas adapted the expression of the Christian message to a particular situation of their time, we may learn to do something similar for our own period.

5. Identification of the Essence of the Doctrine

Bearing in mind that the biblical teachings were written to specific situations and that our current cultural setting may be in some respects considerably different from that of the biblical writers, we must make sure that we not simply reexpress the biblical message in the same form. We must discover the underlying message behind all its specific forms of expression. We must ascertain, for instance, the common truth about salvation that is found in the Book of Deuteronomy and in the Book of Romans. If we fail to do this, one of two things may happen. We may insist upon preserving a particular form of a teaching. We might, for example, insist upon retention of the Old Testament sacrificial system. The other danger is that we will, in the process of attempting to declare the message, so alter it that it becomes in effect a different genus rather than a different species within the same genus. In the example of the sacrificial system, what is permanent and unchanging is not the form of the sacrifice, but the truth that there must be a vicarious sacrifice for the sins of humanity. This task of identifying the permanent truth within temporary forms of expression is so important that we will be devoting a large portion of the following chapter to this subject.

6. Illumination from Sources Beyond the Bible

We said earlier that the Bible is the primary source of our doctrinal construction. While it is the major source, it is not, however, the only one. God has revealed himself in a more general sense in his creation and in human history. Examination of that revelation will help us to understand more fully the special revelation preserved for us in the Bible.

An example is the question of the image of God in humankind. The Bible teaches us that God created humans in his own image and likeness. Though there are some general indications of its nature, we are not able to determine from Scripture what the image of God involves specifically. The behavioral sciences, on the other hand, may give us some insight into the image of God by enabling us to identify what is unique about the human among the various types of creatures.

It is worth noting that in the history of biblical interpretation some nonbiblical disciplines have in fact contributed to our theological knowledge—sometimes despite the reluctance of biblical exegetes and theologians. For example, the scholarly effort to determine whether the days referred to in Genesis 1 are to be thought of as twenty-four-hour periods, longer periods, or even nontemporal concepts has not been limited to biblical exegesis. Natural sciences, particularly geology, have contributed to our knowledge of what God did.

We need to make certain, however, that the Bible is the primary authority in our endeavor. We also need to be certain that we do not draw conclusions prematurely about the relationship between biblical and non-biblical materials. While the Bible, when completely understood, and the creation, when completely understood, are in perfect harmony with one another, we must recognize that we do not have a perfect understanding of either one. Accordingly, there may well be some tension at times in our treatment of them.

7. Contemporary Expression of the Doctrine

Once we have determined the abiding essence or permanent content of the doctrine, we must express it in a fashion that is reasonably accessible to persons of our day. One of the ways in which this may be done was first formulated by Paul Tillich and is known as the method of correlation. The first step is to inquire what questions are being asked by our age. By this we mean not simply the immediate existential issues that individuals face, but the whole way in which the general culture views reality. These questions then become the starting point for our presentation of the Christian message; that is, we relate the content of biblical theology to them. To be sure, we must not allow the non-Christian world to set the agenda completely, for in many cases it may not ask or even recognize the existence of the most important questions. Nonetheless, it is frequently helpful to ascertain what questions are being asked.

A number of themes will present themselves as fruitful for exploration as we seek to formulate a contemporary expression of the message. Although our age seems to be increasingly characterized by depersonalization and detachment, there are indications that there is a craving for a personal dimension in life to which the doctrine of the God who knows and cares about each one can be profitably related. And although there has been a confidence that modern technology could solve the problems of the world, there is a growing awareness that the problems are much larger and more frightening than realized and that humans are the greatest problem to themselves. Against this backdrop the power and providence of God have a new pertinence.

Today it is popular to speak of "contextualizing" the message. This term is frequently used in the realm of missiology, where there is a need to translate concepts from Western cultures to Third World cultures. There seem to be three dimensions of the contextualizing process. The first we may call length. This involves taking the message from biblical times to the present and re-expressing it.

The second dimension we may call breadth—Christianity may assume different forms of expression in different cultures. Western missionaries must be certain that they do not simply carry their own culture to other parts of the world. Little white chapels with spires have sometimes been built for Christian worship in the Orient. Church architecture is not the only realm where this problem occurs. It is imperative, for instance, that we find out the philosophical distinctives of the various cultures. It has been observed that increasingly the most important distinction culturally will be between North and South, rather than East and West, as the Third World grows in prominence. We must develop the ability to express concepts like sin and atonement in culturally relevant ways, for these concepts are of the essence of the Christian message.

There is also the dimension of height. A message can be expressed at different levels of complexity and sophistication. This may involve simply the age of the hearers. One should not, for example, communicate the Christian message in the same form to a child as to a university professor. Beyond that, there is the question of background in biblical and theological concepts. Frequently students will read the work of a professional theologian who is at a much more advanced level than are those to whom they in turn will bear testimony to the truth. The ability to express biblical truth at different times and places and to different audiences is vital.

8. Development of a Central Interpretive Motif

It is not always necessary for individual Christians to formulate a basic central characterization of their theology. Frequently, however, this is helpful. Sometimes this motif reflects one's denomination. For example, some persons of the Reformed tradition stress the sovereignty of God, whereas some Lutherans emphasize the grace of God and the role of faith. The way in which we characterize our theology is often related to our own personality and background. The customizing touch will make biblical truth more functional when we install it into our own lives.

9. Stratification of the Topics

It is important that we decide what are the major issues of theology and what are the subpoints or subissues. The more major a given point, the greater should be the degree of tenacity with which we insist upon it. Thus, while one may not as a condition of fellowship with another believer insist upon agreement as to whether the church will be removed from the world before or after the great tribulation, there must be agreement on the issue of whether Christ will return. In part, this is a matter of simply outlining our theology so that we determine what are major points, what are subpoints, and what topics are subordinate to the subpoints.

Having said this, however, we recognize that there is still a gradation among the major doctrines. For example, the doctrine of Scripture is fundamental because our understanding of all other doctrines is derived from it. Further, the doctrine of God is basic because it supplies the very framework within which all other theological construction is done. It also may be the case that at a given time a particular issue or topic requires more attention because it is under attack or because it receives special treatment in the world which we are addressing. Clearly, a careful consideration of the relative significance of theological topics is essential.

2

Contemporizing
the Christian Message

The Contemporary Context of Theology

The way in which theology is done has varied considerably throughout church history. There have been periods in which there was a considerable uniformity within theology, with an accompanying uniformity of method. The era of Roman Catholic Scholasticism is an example. Protestant theology has on occasion exhibited similar homogeneity. The period immediately following the Reformation was such a time in Lutheranism. Today, however, there is considerable diversity.

One characteristic of our time is the relatively short life-spans of theologies. In a sense, the great theological synthesis constructed by Augustine lasted approximately eight centuries. Thomas Aquinas formulated a theological system and methodology which endured for two-and-a-half centuries (and in Catholic circles for as much as seven centuries). John Calvin's theology prevailed for almost three centuries. When we come to Friedrich Schleiermacher, however, we find the liberalism which he inspired lasting little more than one century. Karl Barth's theology was supreme for only about twenty-five years, and Rudolf Bultmann's demythologization for only about a dozen years.

A further dimension of the present theological environment is the decline of great theological schools of thought. In the 1950s one could basically identify most theologians as belonging to a particular camp, whether neoorthodox, neoliberal, Bultmannian, or some other group. Now, however, there are often only individual theologians and theologies. While there may be general consensuses or clusterings of ideas, there are no strong commitments to systems of thought as such. Thus, one can no longer simply decide to espouse a ready-made system.

Concurrent with this decline is the fact that the theological giants have now passed from the scene. The early part of the twentieth century featured the thought of Karl Barth, Paul Tillich, and Reinhold Niebuhr. Recently, however, few have equaled their

There are certain lessons that we can learn from this quick glance at the contemporary theological environment. First, we must beware of identifying too closely with contemporary culture. Because culture is changing so rapidly with the explosion of knowledge and with shifting social factors, those theologies which align themselves too closely with contemporary developments will likely become obsolete. An analogy here is a piece of machinery: there must not be too much slack, lest there be excessive wear; on the other hand, if it is tightened too severely, the parts will break under the strain. Similarly, it is important to strike a balance between stating the timeless essence of Christian doctrine and contextualizing it to a specific situation. If in our endeavor we must favor one or the other, we will concentrate on the former.

Although there have been significant nuances in theological approach through the centuries, the evangelical's concern is simply to investigate what the Bible says on a given issue and coalesce that into some sort of coherent whole.

thought, and none has gathered a following such as they had. For the most part, it is every theologian for himself or herself.

To a considerable extent, evangelical or conservative theology has avoided decline. Because evangelicalism is clear that its source is the Bible, it does not suffer from fluctuations of opinion regarding the relative place of experience or of tradition, nor does it debate whether religion's primary focus is feelings or ethical activity. Although there have been significant nuances in theological approach through the centuries, the evangelical's concern is simply to investigate what the Bible says on a given issue and coalesce that into some sort of coherent whole. The methodology advocated in this chapter maintains that basic stance.

A second lesson from the contemporary scene is that a certain amount of eclecticism is possible in the doing of theology. This is not to suggest that we take inconsistent elements from different theologies and combine them uncritically. Rather, what we are saying is that no one system has an exclusive corner on the doctrinal market, and therefore it is possible to learn from several different theologies.

A third lesson is the importance of maintaining a certain degree of independence when one studies a particular theologian's ideas. While there is value in being, at least to some extent, a disciple of another, one must not fall into a discipleship that accepts uncritically whatever a theological master says. To do so is actually to make one's faith dependent upon that of another. Even in the case of those with whom one most closely agrees (and perhaps especially in such cases), it is essential to question what one reads. The decline of the great giants should, of course, contribute to creative and independent thinking. Although this makes the theological endeavor somewhat more difficult, it is worth the effort.

Approaches to Contemporizing the Christian Message

When we compare the present world and the world of biblical times, we notice some significant differences. Modes of transportation, for example, have changed tremendously. In biblical times it was common to walk or to ride a horse or a donkey. Thus, travel over vast distances was almost unheard of. Paul's journeys throughout the Mediterranean area were an experience that very few equaled. Most people lived and died within walking distance of their birthplace. Today, on the other hand, it is possible in one day to have meetings thousands of miles apart. Space travel has been achieved, and horizons are ever expanding. Communications are similarly revolutionary in that one may, through television satellites, observe at the very moment of occurrence something happening on the other side of the world, whereas in biblical times it could take weeks and even months to convey a message from Rome to Palestine.

Other aspects of culture have changed greatly as well. The way in which various concepts are understood is quite different today from biblical times. For example, in biblical times heaven and hell were thought of in terms of up and down: heaven was somewhere very high above the earth. Today we understand that such directions are relative. We do not live on a flat earth that lies beneath heaven. Rather, we understand the term *heaven* to connote that God is somehow different from and, in some nonspatial sense, far removed from us.

The problem is how to express biblical truths in imagery that makes sense today. In some cases the task is quite simple; for example, we can readily provide contemporary equivalents that will be understood by people not familiar with the images of a shepherd and sheep. More difficult, however, is the problem of making demon possession intelligible to persons who think of illness exclusively in terms of bacteria and viruses, and who simply cannot conceive of invisible spiritual beings.

There are different types of approaches to the task of contemporizing the Christian message. First is the approach that simply says we should present biblical concepts in biblical terminology. It is not the task of the Christian messenger to try to make the message intelligible. That is the work of the Holy Spirit. We, therefore, do not need to do any translating or interpreting of the message into contemporary expression, particularly since non-Christians and the spirit of the modern age are opposed to anything supernatural. To make the message intelligible and acceptable to such people would be to pervert it.

A contrasting extreme is the approach of the group sometimes referred to as transformers of the Christian message.[1] These people say that portions of the biblical view are obsolete and therefore must be eliminated. There is no way to make intelligible to contemporary persons ideas that carry over from an earlier period of human ignorance. For example, someone living on the basis of modern technology cannot be asked to believe in supernatural answers to prayer. That would call for a sacrifice of the intellect. Thus, certain portions of the Christian message must be surrendered. Belief in such antiquated ideas as angels, demons, and hell must be abandoned. In the process of restating the Christian message it may even on occasion be necessary to alter its essentials.

1. For a discussion of the differences between transformers and translators, see William Hordern, *New Directions in Theology Today*, vol. 1, *Introduction* (Philadelphia: Westminster, 1966), pp. 141–54.

A third position is midway between these two. It is that of the translators of the Christian message. These people are basically conservative in that they desire to retain the essential content of the biblical teaching. At the same time, however, they desire to restate it or translate it into more-modern concepts, to find contemporary equivalents for the concepts drawn from the biblical era. Translators endeavor to make the biblical message understandable to the modern mentality, but do not believe that it necessarily can or should be made acceptable on modern grounds. To do so would be to alter the very nature of the message, for it has a built-in dimension that will always be a cause of offense to sinful humans.

The Permanent Element in Christianity

We must now try to identify the unchangeable factor in Christianity. Various theories have been propounded:

One theory holds that the permanent element is institutional. This is the position of the Roman Catholic Church. What is permanent and persistent throughout time is the institution of the Catholic church. Its teaching, therefore, is what is to be maintained. In the Catholic view, an oral tradition which descended from the apostles has been entrusted to the Catholic church. Through its history, the church has made explicit what is implicit within that tradition and has promulgated it as doctrine. To the outsider this appears to be a propounding of new ideas; but in actuality, according to the Catholic church, these doctrines were present within the tradition from the beginning. They are verified by their connection with the institutional church that has been present from the very beginning of Christian history.

A second theory holds that the permanent element in Christianity is experience. Harry Emerson Fosdick suggests that Christianity is in essence abiding experiences which are expressed in changing categories. Accordingly, we need not believe in, say, the second coming of Christ. That is merely a temporary category that was used to express confidence in the ultimate triumph of God. Is there a modern-day category that will adequately express or evoke the same experience of confidence in ultimate triumph? Fosdick believes that there is, namely, the concept of progress. He does not necessarily mean automatic or invariable progress, but simply the idea that advance is being made within this world. A person who has this hope in the future, which resembles the hope of the early Christians, has retained the essential element of Christianity, even though the categories or doctrines have greatly changed.[2]

A third approach maintains that certain actions or a certain type of living constitutes the permanent element. One who held this view was Walter Rauschenbusch, perhaps the best-known exponent of the social gospel. Rauschenbusch insisted that it is the teachings of Jesus regarding ethical living and the kingdom of God that constitute the abiding or permanent factor.[3] Whether one happens to hold the particular conceptions of God, the world, and the afterlife that Jesus held is not the crucial question. Rather, it is whether one follows the moral teachings of Jesus and lives as Jesus and his disciples did. The permanent factor in Jesus' teaching, therefore, is to be found in "Love your neighbor as yourself" rather than in "I go and prepare a place for you, [and] I will come again and will take you to myself."

Finally, there are those who insist that the permanent element is to be found in doctrines. J. Gresham Machen vigorously argued this position. He pointed out that simply adopting the moral teachings of Jesus is not sufficient. Take, for example, the Golden Rule. It might actually not work for good but for evil. If, for instance, a recovering alcoholic's former drinking partners were to

2. Harry Emerson Fosdick, *The Modern Use of the Bible* (New York: Macmillan, 1933), pp. 104–10.
3. Walter Rauschenbusch, *Christianizing the Social Order* (New York: Macmillan, 1919), pp. 48–68.

do unto him as they would want done unto them, they would give him another drink. Thus, the Golden Rule depends for its effectiveness upon the moral and spiritual character of the person practicing it.[4]

There are other problems as well with trying to separate moral action from the doctrinal teachings of Jesus. One is that Jesus taught his ethical dictums in such a way that they are virtually inseparable from his teaching about himself. If we hold that he was not the Son of God but merely a teacher of morality, then we have a person who either spoke falsely about himself or was mentally deranged. In either case there would be little reason to follow his ethical teachings.

A similar problem occurs when we regard as the permanent element in Christianity experience independent of doctrine. We pointed out earlier (p. 17) that experience is very much tied up with doctrine. Furthermore, in the process of changing from belief in a supernatural establishment of the divine kingdom by the return of the Lord to belief in human progress, we are actually altering the experience. In the latter case our confidence is based upon an estimation of human capability, whereas in the former case it is based upon divine and supernatural working. Obviously, while doctrine may not be the whole of the permanent element within Christianity, it is an indispensable part of it.

The Nature of Contemporization

From our determination that doctrine is the unchangeable factor in Christianity, it should be apparent that we advocate the approach of the translators. It is true that God is the one who in the final analysis must give understanding and conviction regarding biblical truths, and that he does so through the working of his Holy Spirit. This does not mean, however, that he does not use our efforts to convey the meaning in a

4. J. Gresham Machen, *Christianity and Liberalism* (Grand Rapids: Eerdmans, 1923), pp. 34–38.

form as understandable as possible. Thus, what we must do is to retain the essential meaning of the biblical teaching while we apply it in a contemporary setting. This is a matter of changing the form but not the content of the teaching.

The process is not as simple, however, as finding twentieth-century equivalents for first-century concepts. Rather, we must determine the essence of the first-century doctrine. In doing so, we will be following a method often used in the teaching of languages. One approach is to teach what word in one language is equivalent to what word in another language. For example, English-speaking persons learning German are taught that *der Stuhl* = the chair. Such an approach, however, does not truly get students thinking in the other language. Better is the approach used in courses where the students do not speak the same language. The instructor will point to a chair and say *der Stuhl*, then touch the wall and say *die Wand*. The aim is to get the students thinking *der Stuhl* when they see a chair. The focus is on the common meaning which exists in all languages.

Similarly, we must distinguish between the permanent or abiding essence of a concept and its temporary forms of expression. To use the example cited earlier, the permanent essence of the concept that God dwells in heaven is the transcendence of God—he is other than and superior to us in many respects. This is the truth that must be retained from biblical times to the present. That God is high above us spatially is simply the form in which that idea was once expressed.

The Criteria of Permanence in Doctrine

Finally, we must ask ourselves what criteria will help us to distinguish between the permanent, timeless content or essence of doctrine and temporary expressions or forms of it. In some cases, this is not too difficult to do, for the essential doctrine may explicitly appear in a didactic passage in which its permanence is emphasized. An example is found in Psalm 100:5: "For the LORD is good; his steadfast love endures for ever, and his faithfulness to all generations." Here is an indication that we are dealing with an aspect of the nature and work of God which is timeless. In other cases, however, the task may be more difficult. It may involve extracting the timeless truth from a narrative passage or from a teaching written for a particular group or individual and dealing with a specific problem. In such cases, there are several criteria or measures that we may apply to help identify the permanent factor:

1. *Constancy across cultures.* We are generally aware of the variety of cultures that exist today and also of the difference in culture between our present time and biblical times. It is easy, however, to forget that within the biblical period there were also a variety of temporal, geographical, linguistic, and cultural settings. There was no uniform culture. Many centuries intervened between the writing of the first books of the Old Testament and the last books of the New. Geographical and cultural situations range from a pastoral setting in ancient Palestine to the urban setting of imperial Rome. While the differences between Hebrew and Greek culture and language have sometimes been exaggerated, they are nonetheless real. If, then, we can identify factors that are found in several of these settings, we may well be dealing with permanent or changeless elements in the message.

One example of such constancy across cultures is found in the principle of sacrificial atonement together with the rejection of any type of works-righteousness. This principle is found in the Old Testament sacrificial system and in the New Testament teaching regarding Christ's atoning death. Another example is the centrality of belief in Jesus Christ, which is emphasized in both Jewish and Gentile contexts. Peter, for example, preached it at Pentecost in Jerusalem to Jews from various cultures. Paul declared it in a Gentile setting to the Philippian jailer (Acts 16:31).

2. *Universal setting.* Some doctrines are taught in a fashion that makes clear that they apply universally. An example is baptism. There are, of course, various biblical references to specific situations where it was practiced, but baptism also plays a significant part in the universal setting of the Great Commission: "All authority in heaven

> *God uses our efforts to convey his truth in a form as understandable as possible. What we must do is to retain the essential meaning of the biblical teaching while we apply it in a contemporary setting.*

and on earth has been given to me. Therefore go and make disciples of all nations, baptizing them into the name of the Father and of the Son and of the Holy Spirit, and teaching them to obey everything I have commanded you. And surely I will be with you always, to the very end of the age" (Matt. 28:18–20, NIV). Note three respects in which this can be regarded as a universal setting. (1) Jesus' statement that *all* authority has been given to him suggests that as he transfers authority to his disciples, he has in mind a task which is to be carried out indefinitely. (2) The "all nations" suggests a universality of place and culture (cf. the commission of Acts 1:8—"You shall be my witnesses . . . to the end of the earth"). (3) Jesus would be with his disciples always, even to the end of the age. This suggests that the commission is to apply permanently. We may, on the basis of these considerations, conclude that baptism was not practiced at only a few times and places, but has universal applicability.

Another practice sometimes regarded as similarly permanent and universal is the footwashing described in John 13. Note, however, that there are no general or universal references here. While Jesus did say, "You also ought to wash one another's feet" (v. 14), he said nothing about the duration of the practice. While he did say that he had given his disciples an example, that they should "do as I have done to you" (v. 15), the underlying reason for his action is suggested by his statement that the servant is not greater than his master (v. 16). What Jesus was attempting to instill was the attitude of humility and willingness to subordinate oneself to others. In that particular culture, washing the feet of others symbolized such an attitude. In another culture, something else might be a much more effective expression of it. We do find humility taught elsewhere in Scripture without mention of footwashing (Matt. 20:27; 23:10–12; Phil. 2:3). We therefore conclude that the attitude of humility, not the particular act of footwashing, is the permanent component in Jesus' teaching.

3. *A recognized permanent factor as a basis.* Sometimes a particular teaching is based upon a recognized permanent factor. This may argue for the permanence of that particular teaching. For example, when Jesus teaches about marriage, he bases it upon the fact that God made humans as male and female and pronounced them to be one (Matt. 19:4–6, citing Gen. 2:24). This act of God was a once-for-all occurrence; his pronouncement about the uniting of male and female was intended to have permanent force. By citing God's act and pronouncement, Jesus is declaring the marriage relationship to be permanent.

Another example is the doctrine of the priesthood of all believers. The writer to the Hebrews bases it upon the fact that our great High Priest has once for all "gone through the heavens." We can therefore "approach the throne of grace with confidence" (Heb. 4:14–16, NIV). What Jesus did was done once and for all. There is, therefore, no reversing of the process and no need for renewing it. Furthermore, because Jesus is a High Priest forever (Heb. 7:21, 24), it is always the case that all who draw near to God through him are saved (v. 25).

4. *Indissoluble link with an essential experience.* In dealing with the resurrection, Rudolf Bultmann attempted to separate the question of whether Jesus actually was raised from the Christian's experience of renewal of hope and openness to the future. Paul, however, says in 1 Corinthians 15:17 that it is not possible to maintain the experience independently of the resurrection of Christ: "If Christ has not been raised, your faith is futile and you are still in your sins." On the other hand, if our experience of the resurrection is real and permanent, the resurrection of Christ must also be factual, permanent, and universal. Any alteration of this doctrine will result in a similar alteration of the experience.

5. *Final position within progressive revelation.* One of the reasons that some forms of expression were replaced is that they were but imperfect anticipations of the final work to be done by God in the New Testament era or under the new covenant. As God revealed himself more completely, the later forms elaborated upon and progressed beyond the earlier expressions. Thus, for example, Jesus frequently said, "You have heard that it was said . . . , but I say to you that. . . ." In these cases, Jesus was giving a final expression of a truth that had been incompletely stated earlier.

Another example pertains to the sacrificial work of Christ. Whereas in the Old Testament there were continual offerings of sacrifice in the court, twice-daily offerings of incense in the outer tent, and the annual sacrifice by the high priest in the inner place, the Holy of Holies (Heb. 9:1–10), Christ brought this process to an end by fulfilling it (v. 12). The offering of his own blood was once for all. The permanent factor here is the need for sacrificial atonement and the satisfaction of that need through the death of Christ. The earlier forms were simply anticipations or reflections of what was yet to come.

In some cases, the essence of a doctrine was not explicitly realized within biblical times. It was only approximated. For example, the status of women in society was elevated dramatically by Jesus. Similarly, Paul granted an unusual status to slaves. Yet the lot of these groups did not improve as much as it ultimately would. So to find the essence of how such persons should be treated, we must look to principles laid down or implied regarding their status, not to accounts of how they actually were treated in biblical times.

We will attempt to get at the basic essence of the message, recognizing that all revelation has a point. Sometimes this process has been compared to separating the kernel and the husk of grain. Adolf von Harnack advocated separating the kernel from the husk and then discarding the husk. We maintain, instead, that even the form of expression conveys something significant. Nor are we talking about "discarding the cultural baggage," as some anthropologically oriented interpreters of the Bible say. We are referring to finding the essential spiritual truth upon which a given portion of Scripture rests, and then making a contemporary application of it. Our aim is not to eliminate any portion of Scripture, but to find out the meaning of all of it.

It is common to observe (correctly) that very few Christians turn to the genealogies in Scripture for their personal devotions. Yet even these portions must have some significance. An attempt to go directly from "what a genealogy meant" to "what it means" will probably prove frustrating. Instead, we must ask, "What are the underlying truths?" Several possibilities come to mind: (1) all of us have a human heritage from which we derive much of what we are; (2) we have all, through the long process of descent, received our life from God; (3) God is at work providentially in human history, a fact of which we will be acutely aware if we study that history and God's dealings with humankind. These truths have meanings for our situations today. Similarly, the Old Testament rules of sanitation speak to us of God's concern for human health and well-being, and the importance of taking steps to preserve that well-being. Pollution control and wise dietary practices would be modern applications of the underlying truth. To some exegetes this will sound like allegorizing. But we are not looking for symbolism, spiritual meaning hidden in literal references. Rather, we are advocating that Christians ask themselves the real reason why a particular statement was spoken or written.

In doing all of this, we must be careful to recognize that our understanding and interpretation are influenced by our own circumstances in history, lest we mistakenly identify the form in which we state a biblical teaching with its permanent essence. If we fail to recognize this, we will absolutize our form, and be unable to update it when the situation changes. I once heard a Roman Catholic theologian trace the history of the formulation of the doctrine of revelation. He then attempted to describe the permanent essence of the doctrine, and stated very clearly and accurately a twentieth-century, neoorthodox, existentially oriented view of revelation!

It is important to note that finding the abiding essence is not a matter of studying historical theology in order to distill out the lowest common denominator from the various formulations of a doctrine. On the contrary, historical theology points out that all postbiblical formulations are conditional. It is the biblical statements themselves from which we must draw out the essence, and they are the continuing criteria of the validity of that essence.

Part Two

God's Revelation

3

God's Universal Revelation

The Nature of Revelation

Because humankind is finite and God is infinite, we cannot know God unless he reveals himself to us, that is, unless he manifests himself to humans in such a way that they can know and fellowship with him. There are two basic classifications of revelation. On the one hand, general revelation is God's communication of himself to all persons at all times and in all places. Special revelation, on the other hand, involves God's particular communications and manifestations of himself to particular persons at particular times, communications and manifestations which are available now only by consulting certain sacred writings.

General revelation refers to God's self-manifestation through nature, history, and the inner being of the human person. It is general in two aspects: its universal availability (it is accessible to all persons at all times) and the content of the message (it is less particularized and detailed than special revelation). A number of questions need to be raised. One concerns the genuineness of the revelation. Is it really there? Further, we need to ask regarding the efficacy of this revelation. If it exists, what can be made of it? Can one construct a "natural theology," a knowledge of God from nature?

The Modes of General Revelation

The traditional modes of general revelation are three: nature, history, and the constitution of the human being. Scripture itself proposes that there is a knowledge of God available through the created physical order. The psalmist says, "The heavens are telling the glory of God" (Ps. 19:1). And Paul says, "Ever since the creation of the world [God's] invisible nature, namely, his eternal power and deity, has been clearly perceived

tern. Some persons have found great significance in individual events of history, for instance, the evacuation of Dunkirk and the battle of Midway in World War II. Individual events, however, are more subject to differing interpretations than are the broader, longer-lasting trends of history, such as the preservation of God's special people.

The third mode of general revelation is God's highest earthly creation, humans themselves. Sometimes God's general revelation is seen in the physical structure and mental capacities of humans. It is, however, in their moral and spiritual qualities that God's character is best perceived. Humans make moral judgments, that is, judgments of what is right and wrong. This involves something more than our personal likes and dislikes, and something more than mere ex-

Because humankind is finite and God is infinite, we cannot know or fellowship with him unless he reveals himself to us.

in the things that have been made. So [humans] are without excuse" (Rom. 1:20). These and numerous other passages, such as the "nature psalms," suggest that God has left evidence of himself in the world he has created. The person who views the beauty of a sunset and the biology student dissecting a complex organism are exposed to indications of the greatness of God.

The second mode of general revelation is history. If God is at work in the world and is moving toward certain goals, it should be possible to detect the trend of his work in events that occur as part of history. An example often cited of God's revelation in history is the preservation of the people of Israel. This small nation has survived over many centuries within a basically hostile environment, often in the face of severe opposition. Anyone who investigates the historical records will find a remarkable pat-

pediency. We often feel that we ought to do something, whether it is advantageous to us or not, and that others have a right to do something which we may not personally like.

General revelation is also found in humankind's religious nature. In all cultures, at all times and places, humans have believed in the existence of a reality higher than themselves, and even of something higher than the human race collectively. While the exact nature of the belief and worship practice varies considerably from one religion to another, many see in this universal tendency toward worship of the holy the manifestation of a past knowledge of God, an internal sense of deity, which, although it may be marred and distorted, is nonetheless still present and operating in human experience.

The Reality and Efficacy of General Revelation

Natural Theology

Regarding the nature, extent, and efficacy of general revelation, there are some rather sharply contrasting views. One position which has had a long and conspicuous history within Christianity maintains not only that there is a valid, objective revelation of God in such spheres as nature, history, and human personality, but that it is actually possible to gain some true knowledge of God from these spheres—in other words, to construct a natural theology apart from the Bible.

Certain assumptions are involved in this view. One is, of course, that God actually has made himself known in nature and that patterns of meaning are objectively present even if no one perceives, understands, and accepts this revelation. Moreover, nature is basically intact—it has not been substantially distorted by anything that has occurred since the creation. In short, the world we find about us is basically the world as it came from the creative hand of God, and as it was intended to be.

A second major assumption of natural theology is the integrity of the person perceiving and learning from the creation. Neither the natural limitations of humanity nor the effects of sin and the fall prevent one from recognizing and correctly interpreting the handiwork of the Creator.

There are other assumptions as well. One is that there is a congruity between the human mind and the creation about us. The order of the human mind is basically the same as the order of the universe. The mind is capable of drawing inferences from the data it possesses, since the structure of its thinking processes coheres with the structure of what it knows. The validity of the laws of logic is also assumed. Natural theologians assiduously avoid paradoxes and logical contradictions, considering them something to be removed by a more complete logical scrutiny of the issues under consideration. They regard a paradox as a sign of intellectual indigestion; had it been more completely chewed, it would have disappeared.

The core of natural theology is the idea that it is possible, without a prior commitment of faith to the beliefs of Christianity, and without relying upon any special authority, such as an institution (the church) or a document (the Bible), to come to a genuine knowledge of God on the basis of reason alone. Reason here refers to the human capacity to discover, understand, interpret, and evaluate the truth.

Perhaps the outstanding example of natural theology in the history of the church is the massive effort of Thomas Aquinas. According to Thomas, all truth belongs to one of two realms. The lower realm is the realm of nature, the higher the realm of grace. While the claims pertaining to the upper realm must be accepted on authority, those pertaining to the lower realm may be known by reason.

Thomas contended that he could prove certain beliefs by pure reason: the existence of God, the immortality of the human soul, and the supernatural origin of the Catholic church. More-specific elements of doctrine—such as the triune nature of God—could not be known by unaided reason, but must be accepted on authority. These are truths of revelation, not truths of reason. Reason rules the lower level, while the truths on the upper level are matters of faith.

One of the traditional arguments for the existence of God is the cosmological proof. Thomas has three or possibly even four versions of this proof. The argument proceeds somewhat as follows: In the realm of our experience, everything that we know is caused by something else. There cannot, however, be an infinite regress of causes, for if that were the case, the whole series of causes would never have begun. There must, therefore, be some uncaused cause (unmoved mover) or necessary being. And this we (or all people) call God. Anyone looking honestly at the evidence must reach this conclusion.

Another argument frequently employed, and found in Thomas as well, is the teleological argument. This focuses particularly upon the phenomenon of orderliness or apparent purpose in the universe. Thomas observes that various parts of the universe exhibit behavior which is adaptive or which helps bring about desirable ends. When such behavior is displayed by human beings, we recognize that they have consciously willed and directed themselves toward that end. Some of the objects in our universe, however, cannot have done any purposive planning. Certainly rocks and atmosphere have not chosen to be as they are. Their ordering according to a purpose or design must come from somewhere else. Some intelligent being must, therefore, have ordered things in this desirable fashion. And this being, says Thomas, we call God.

Sometimes the whole universe is considered in the teleological argument. In such cases the universe is often compared to some mechanism. For example, if we were to find a watch lying on the sand, we would immediately recognize it as a watch, for all of its parts are ideally suited to the purpose of recording and displaying the time. We would certainly not say, "What a remarkable coincidence!" We would recognize that some able person(s) must have planned and brought about the amazing way in which each part fits in with the other parts. Similarly, the way in which each part of nature meshes so well with every other part cannot be dismissed as pure chance. Someone must have designed and constructed digestive systems, eyes, properly balanced atmospheres, and much else in our world. All of this argues for the existence of a supreme Designer, a wise and capable Creator. There must be a God.

These are two major arguments which have historically been employed in developing a natural theology. Two others which appear in the history of philosophy and theology, although perhaps less prominently

than the cosmological and the teleological arguments, are the anthropological and the ontological.

The anthropological argument sees some of the aspects of human nature as a revelation of God. In Immanuel Kant's formulation (in the *Critique of Practical Reason*) it appears somewhat as follows. We all possess a moral impulse or a categorical imperative. Following this impulse by behaving morally is sometimes not well rewarded within this life, however. Being good does not always pay! Why should one be moral then? There must be some basis for ethics and morality, some sort of reward, which in turn involves several factors—immortality and an undying soul, a coming time of judgment, and a God who establishes and supports values, and who rewards good and punishes evil. Thus, the moral order (as contrasted with the natural order) requires the existence of God.

All of these are empirical arguments. They proceed from observation of the universe by sense experience. The major *a priori* or rational argument is the ontological argument. This is a pure-thought type of argument. It does not require one to go outside one's own thinking. In the *Proslogion* Anselm formulated what is undoubtedly the most famous statement of the ontological argument: God is the greatest of all conceivable beings. Now a being which does not exist cannot be the greatest of all conceivable beings (for the nonexistent being of our conceptions would be greater if it had the *attribute* of existence). Therefore, by definition, God must exist.

There have been several responses to the ontological argument, many of which follow Kant's contention that, in effect, existence is not an attribute. A being that exists does not have some attribute or quality lacked by a similar being which does not exist. If I imagine a dollar and compare it with a real dollar, there is no difference in their essence, in what they are. The only difference is in whether they are. There is a logical difference between the sentence "God is good" (or loving, or holy, or just) and the sentence "God is." The former predicates some quality of God; the latter is a statement of existence. The point here is that existence is not a necessary predicate of the greatest of all conceivable beings. Such a being may exist—or it may not. In either case its essence is the same.

A Critique of Natural Theology

Despite natural theology's long and hallowed history, its present effects do not seem overly impressive. If the arguments are valid and are adequately presented, any rational person should be convinced. Yet numerous philosophers have raised criticisms against the proofs, and many theologians have joined them. Why should any Christian be opposed to an effort to convince non-Christians of the truth of Christianity, or at least of the existence of God? The answer is that use of these proofs may actually work to disadvantage if one's desire is to make the most effective presentation possible of the claims of Christ. If the proofs are inadequate, then the unbeliever, in rejecting the proofs, may also reject the Christian message, assuming that these proofs are the best grounds that can be offered for its acceptance.

Some of the problems with the arguments relate to assumptions which they contain. Thomas held as virtually an axiom, or a first truth known intuitively, that there cannot be an infinite regress of causes. But numerous persons today would disagree. A linear sequence of causes is not the only way to view causation. Some would question the necessity of asking about ultimate causation. Even if one does ask, however, there is the possibility of a circle of causes, with each cause within the closed system causing another. Similarly, the assumption that motion has to have a cause or explanation is not universally held today. Reality may well be dynamic rather than static.

There is also criticism of the procedure of extending the argument from the observable to that which goes beyond experience.

In the case of the watch found in the sand, we have something which can be verified by sense experience. We can actually check with the company whose name appears (coincidentally?) on the watch, and inquire as to whether they manufactured it. Furthermore, we recognize that the watch is similar to other watches which we have seen before. Thus, we can extrapolate from past experience. In the case of the world, however, we do not have something which can be so easily verified by other sense experience. How many worlds have we observed being created? The assumption is that the universe is a member of a class of objects (including such things as watches and cameras) to which we can compare it, and thus we can make rational judgments about its design. This, however, must be established, not assumed, if the argument from the analogy of the watch is to succeed.

A further problem was alluded to earlier. Suppose one succeeds in proving, by a valid argument, that this world must have had a cause. One cannot, however, conclude from this that such a cause must be infinite. One can affirm only that there was a cause sufficient to account for the effect.[1] That one can lift a 100-pound weight does not warrant the conclusion that he can lift any more than that. Similarly, one cannot prove the existence of an infinite Creator from the existence of a finite universe. A further argument is needed to prove that the sufficient cause of the universe is the God of Christianity and, indeed, that the gods which constitute the conclusions of Thomas's several arguments are all the same being. If we are to have a natural theology, this must be argued on the basis of our human reason (without resort to some other authority).

The teleological argument has come in for special criticism. Since Charles Darwin, the usual appeal to the intricacy and beauty of the organic realm has not carried a great

---

1. David Hume, *An Enquiry Concerning Human Understanding*, section 11; Gordon H. Clark, *A Christian View of Men and Things* (Grand Rapids: Eerdmans, 1952), p. 29.

deal of persuasiveness for those who accept the theory of organic evolution. They believe changes in characteristics have arisen through chance variations called mutations. Some of these were advantageous and some were disadvantageous. In the struggle for survival occasioned by the fecundity of nature, any characteristic which enables a species to survive will be transmitted, and those branches of the species which lack this characteristic will tend to die out. Thus, the process of natural selection has produced the remarkable qualities which the teleological argument claims point to a design and a Designer. To be sure, this criticism of the teleological argument has its shortcomings (e.g., natural selection cannot explain away the inorganic adaptation observed in the universe), but the point is simply that those persons who accept evolution disagree with Thomas's assertion that there is a compelling and necessary character to the teleological argument.

The teleological argument also encounters the problem of what might be termed the "dysteleological." If the argument is to be truly empirical, it must, of course, take into account the whole sweep of data. Now the argument proceeds on the basis of seeming indications of a wise and benevolent God controlling the creation. But there are some disturbing features of the world as well, natural catastrophes, diseases, and the cruelty and injustice inflicted by humans upon their fellows. If God is all-powerful and completely good, how can these things be? It is possible by emphasizing these features of the universe to construct an argument for either the nonexistence of God or the existence of a nongood God. Perhaps the teleological argument would then turn out to be an argument, not for the existence of God, but of the devil. When these considerations are taken into account, the teleological argument appears less than impressive.

Examination of Relevant Passages

We need now to examine more closely several key passages dealing with the issue of general revelation, and attempt to see exactly what they say. We will then draw the meanings of these several passages together into a coherent position on the subject.

Of the many nature psalms, all conveying the same basic meaning, Psalm 19 is perhaps the most explicit:

1. The heavens declare the glory of God;
   the skies proclaim the work of his hands.
2. Day after day they pour forth speech;
   night after night they display knowledge.
3. There is no speech or language
   where their voice is not heard.
4. Their voice goes out into all the earth,
   their words to the ends of the world.
   [NIV]

These verses clearly assert that created nature tells forth God's glory.

Romans 1–2 is the other major passage dealing with general revelation. The particularly significant portion of chapter 1 is verses 18–32, which emphasizes the revelation of God in nature, whereas 2:14–16 seems especially to elaborate the general revelation in human personality. The theme of the epistle is enunciated in 1:16–17: in the gospel the righteousness of God is revealed from faith to faith. This righteousness of God in providing salvation, however, presupposes the wrath of God revealed from heaven against all human ungodliness and wickedness (v. 18). Paul is concerned to indicate how this wrath of God can be just. The answer is that the people on whom God's wrath is visited have the truth but suppress it by their unrighteousness (v. 18b). God has plainly shown them what can be known about him. This self-manifestation has continued since the creation of the world, being perceived in the things that God has made. God's invisible qualities of eternal power and divinity are clearly perceived, and consequently the wicked are without excuse (v. 20). They had known God but did not honor or thank him; rather, their minds were darkened and they became futile in their thinking (vv. 21–22).

The language of this passage is clear and strong. It is hard to interpret expressions like "what can be known about God" and "has shown" (v. 19) as pointing to anything other than an objectively knowable truth about God. Similarly, "although they knew God" (v. 21) and "the truth about God" (v. 25) indicate possession of genuine and accurate knowledge.

The second chapter continues the argument. The point here seems to be that all, Gentile and Jew alike, are condemned: the Jews because they fail to do what they know the law to require; the Gentiles because, even without having the law, they also know enough to make them responsible to God for their actions, yet they disobey. When they do by nature what the law requires, they are showing that what the law requires

The final passage of particular significance for our purposes is Acts 17:22–31. Here Paul appears before a group of philosophers—the Athenian Philosophical Society as it were—on the Areopagus. Two points are of particular significance in Paul's presentation. First, Paul had noticed an altar "to an unknown god" in the Athenians' place of worship. He proceeded to proclaim this god to them. The god whom they sensed from their speculations, without having had special revelation, was the same God whom he knew from special manifestation. Second, he quoted an Athenian poet (v. 28). The significant item here is that a pagan poet had been able to come to a spiritual truth without God's special revelation.

General Revelation, But Without Natural Theology

When we begin to draw these several passages together, the position proposed by

> *God has given us an objective, valid, rational revelation of himself in nature, history, and human personality. It is there for anyone who wants to observe it.*

is written on their hearts (vv. 14–15). Thus, whether having heard the law or not, all people know God's truth.

Acts 14:15–17 also deals with the issue of general revelation. The people of Lystra had thought Paul and Barnabas were gods. They began to worship them. In attempting to divest the people of this idea, Paul pointed out that they should turn to the God who had made heaven and earth. Paul then observed that even while God had allowed the nations to walk in their own ways, he had left a witness of himself to all peoples, by doing good, providing rain and fruitful seasons, and satisfying their hearts with food and gladness. The argument appears to relate to God's witness to himself in nature and (perhaps even more so) in history.

John Calvin appears most reasonable. Basically, this is the view that God has given us an objective, valid, rational revelation of himself in nature, history, and human personality. It is there for anyone who wants to observe it. General revelation is not something read into nature by those who know God on other grounds; it is already present, by the creation and continuing providence of God.

Paul asserts, however, that humankind does not clearly perceive God in the general revelation. Sin—we are thinking here of both the fall of the human race and our continuing evil acts—has a double effect upon the efficacy of the general revelation. On the one hand, sin has marred the witness of the general revelation. The created order is now under a curse (Gen. 3:17–19). Paul speaks in

Romans 8:18–25 about the creation's having been subjected to futility (v. 20); it waits for its liberation (vv. 19, 21, 23). As a result, its witness is somewhat refracted. While it is still God's creation and thus continues to witness to him, it is not quite what it was when it came from the hand of the Maker. It is a spoiled creation. The testimony to the Maker is blurred.

The more serious effect of sin and the fall is upon humans themselves. Scripture speaks in several places of the blindness and darkness of human understanding. In Romans 1:21 Paul says that people knew God but rejected this knowledge, and blindness followed. In 2 Corinthians 4:4 Paul attributes this blindness to the work of Satan: "In their case the god of this world has blinded the minds of the unbelievers, to keep them from seeing the light of the gospel of the glory of Christ, who is the likeness of God." Although Paul is here referring to ability to see the light of the gospel, this blindness would doubtless affect the ability to see God in the creation as well.

General revelation evidently does not enable the unbeliever to come to the knowledge of God. Paul's statements about general revelation (Rom. 1–2) must be viewed in the light of what he says about sinful human beings (Rom. 3—all are under sin's power; none is righteous) and the urgency of telling people about Christ (10:14): "But how are men to call upon him in whom they have not believed? And how are they to believe in him of whom they have never heard? And how are they to hear without a preacher?" Thus in Paul's mind the possibility of constructing a full-scale natural theology seems seriously in question.

What is necessary, then, is what Calvin calls "the spectacles of faith." Calvin draws an analogy between the condition of the sinner and persons who have a sight problem.[2] When the latter look at an object, they see it but indistinctly. It is blurry to them. But

when they put on spectacles, they can see clearly. Similarly, sinners do not recognize God in the creation. But when they put on the spectacles of faith, their sight improves, and they can see God in his handiwork. When we are exposed to the special revelation found in the gospel and respond, our mind is cleared through the effects of regeneration, enabling us to see distinctly what is there. We then are able to recognize in nature what we have more clearly seen in the special revelation.

It is worth noting that Scripture nowhere suggests that the evidences within the general revelation constitute a formal argument for the existence of God. There is an assertion that God is seen in his handiwork, but this is scarcely a formal proof of his existence. And it is notable that when Paul made his presentation and appeal to the Athenians, some believed, some rejected, and some expressed interest in hearing more on another occasion (Acts 17:32–34). Thus the conclusion that there is an objective general revelation, but that it cannot be used to construct a natural theology, seems to fit best the full data of Scripture on the subject.

General Revelation and Human Responsibility

But what of the condemnation of humankind, spoken of by Paul in Romans 1–2? If it is just for God to condemn human beings, and if they can become guilty without having known God's special revelation, does that mean that humans without special revelation can do what will enable them to avoid the condemnation of God? In Romans 2:14 Paul says: "When Gentiles who have not the law do by nature what the law requires, they are a law to themselves, even though they do not have the law." Is Paul suggesting that they could have fulfilled the requirements of the law? But that is not possible even for those who have the law (see Gal. 3:10–11 as well as Rom. 3). Paul also makes clear in Galatians 3:23–24 that the law was not a means of justifying us, but a

2. John Calvin, *Institutes of the Christian Religion,* book 1, chapter 6, section 1.

guide to make us aware of our sin and to lead us to faith by bringing us to Christ.

Now the internal law which the unbeliever has performs much the same function as does the law which the Jew has. From the revelation in nature (Rom. 1), a person ought to conclude that there exists a powerful eternal God. And from the revelation within (Rom. 2), a person should realize that one does not live up to the standard. The content of the moral code held will vary in different cultural situations. All persons, however, have an inner compulsion that there is something to which they ought to adhere; and they should reach the conclusion that they are not fulfilling that standard. In other words, the knowledge of God which all humans have, if they do not suppress it, should bring them to the conclusion that they are guilty in relationship to God.

What if we were to throw ourselves upon the mercy of God, not knowing on what basis that mercy was provided? Would we not then in a sense be in the same situation as were the Old Testament believers? The doctrine of Christ and his atoning work had not been fully revealed to them. Yet they knew that there was provision for the forgiveness of sins, and that they could not be accepted on the merits of any works of their own. They had the form of the gospel without its full content. And they were saved. Now if the god known in nature is the same as the God of Abraham, Isaac, and Jacob (as Paul seems to assert in Acts 17:23), then it would seem that persons who come to a belief in a single powerful God, who despair of any works-righteousness to please this holy God, and who throw themselves upon the mercy of this good God, would be accepted as were the Old Testament believers. The basis of acceptance would be the work of Jesus Christ, even though the persons involved are not conscious that this is how provision has been made for their salvation.[3] We should note

that the basis of salvation was apparently the same in the Old Testament as in the New. Salvation has always been appropriated by faith (Gal. 3:6–9); this salvation rests upon Christ's deliverance of us from the law (vv. 10–14, 19–29).

What inference are we to draw, then, from Paul's statement in Romans 2:1–16? Is it conceivable that one can be saved by faith without having the special revelation? Paul seems to be laying open this theoretical possibility. Yet it is merely a theoretical possibility. That anyone actually experiences salvation without having special revelation is highly questionable. Paul suggests in Romans 3 that no one does. And in chapter 10 he urges the necessity of preaching the gospel (the special revelation) so that people may believe. Thus it is apparent that in failing to respond to the light of general revelation which they have, people are fully responsible, for they have truly known God, but have willfully suppressed that truth. Thus in effect the general revelation serves, as does the law, merely to make guilty, not to make righteous.

Implications of General Revelation

1. There is a common ground or a point of contact between the believer and the nonbeliever, or between the gospel and the thinking of the unbeliever. All persons have a knowledge of God. Although it may be suppressed to the extent of being unconscious or unrecognizable, it is nonetheless there, and there will be areas of sensitivity to which the message may be effectively directed as a starting point. It is therefore neither necessary nor desirable to fire the message at the hearer in an indiscriminate fashion.

2. There is a possibility of some knowledge of divine truth outside the special revelation. We may understand more about the specially revealed truth by examining the general revelation. This should be considered a supplement to, not a substitute for, special revelation. Sin's distortion of human

3. For a fuller statement of this possibility, see Millard J. Erickson, "Hope for Those Who Haven't Heard? Yes, but . . . ," *Evangelical Missions Quarterly* 2 (1975): 122–26.

understanding of the general revelation is greater the closer one gets to the relationship between God and humankind. Thus, sin produces relatively little obscuring effect upon the understanding of matters of physics, but a great deal with respect to matters of psychology and sociology. Yet it is at those places where the potential for distortion is greatest that the most complete understanding is possible.

3. God is just in condemning those who have never heard the gospel in the full and formal sense. No one is completely without opportunity. All have known God; their not having effectually perceived him is a result of their having suppressed the truth. Thus all are responsible. This increases the motivation of missionary endeavor, for no one is innocent.

4. General revelation serves to explain the worldwide phenomenon of religion and religions. All persons are religious, because all have a type of knowledge of God. From this indistinct and perhaps even unrecognizable revelation have been constructed religions which unfortunately are distortions of the true biblical religion.

5. Since both creation and the gospel are intelligible and coherent revelations of God, there are harmony between the two and a mutual reinforcement of one by the other. The biblical revelation is not totally distinct from what is known of the natural realm.

6. Genuine knowledge and genuine morality in unbelieving (as well as believing) human beings are not their own accomplishment. Truth arrived at apart from special revelation is still God's truth. Knowledge and morality are not so much discovery as they are "uncovery" of the truth God has structured into his entire universe, both physical and moral.

God's Particular Revelation

The Definition and Necessity of Special Revelation

By special revelation we mean God's manifestation of himself to particular persons at definite times and places, enabling those persons to enter into a redemptive relationship with him. The Hebrew word for "reveal" is *gālāh*. A common Greek word for "reveal" is *apokalyptō*. Both express the idea of uncovering what was concealed. The Greek *phaneroō*, which especially conveys the idea of manifesting, is also frequently used.

Why was special revelation necessary? The answer lies in the fact that humans had lost the relationship of favor which they had with God prior to the fall. It was necessary for them to come to know God in a fuller way if the conditions of fellowship were once again to be met. This knowledge had to go beyond the initial or general revelation which was still available to them, for now in addition to the natural limitation of human finiteness, there was also the moral limitation of human sinfulness. After the fall humankind was turned away from God and in rebellion against him; their understanding of spiritual matters was obscured. So their situation was a more complicated matter than had originally been the case, and more complete instruction was consequently needed.

Note that the objective of special revelation was relational. The primary purpose of this revelation was not to enlarge the general scope of knowledge. The knowledge *about* was for the purpose of knowledge *of*. Information was to lead to acquaintance; consequently, the information revealed was often quite selective. For example, we know relatively little about Jesus from a biographical standpoint. We are told nothing about his appearance, his characteristic activities, his interests, or his tastes. Details such as are ordinarily found in biographies were omitted, because they are not significant for faith. The merely curious are not accommodated by the special revelation of God.

A further introductory word is needed regarding the relationship of special to general revelation. It is commonly assumed that special revelation is a postfall phenomenon necessitated by human sinfulness. It is frequently considered *remedial*.[1] Of course, it is not possible for us to know the exact status of the relationship between God and humankind before the fall. We simply are not told much about it. Adam and Eve may have had such an unclouded consciousness of God that they were constantly aware of him everywhere, in their own internal experience and in their perception of nature. If so, this consciousness of him could be thought of as general revelation. There is no indication that such was the case, however. The account of God's looking for Adam and Eve in the Garden subsequent to their sin (Gen. 3:8) gives the impression that this was one in a series of special encounters which occurred. Further, the instructions given to humankind (Gen. 1:28) regarding their

> ## Special revelation was necessary because the human race had lost the relationship of favor which they had with God prior to the fall.

place and activity in the creation suggest a particular communication from Creator to creature; it does not seem that these instructions were merely read off from observation of the created order. If this is the case, special revelation antedated the fall.

When sin entered the human race, however, the need for special revelation became more acute. The direct presence of God, the most immediate and complete form of special revelation, was lost. In addition, God now had to speak regarding matters which were previously not of concern. The problems of sin, guilt, and depravity had to be resolved; means of atonement, redemption, and reconciliation had to be provided. And now sin diminished human comprehension of general revelation, thus lessening its efficacy. Therefore, special revelation had to become remedial with respect to both human knowledge of and relationship to God.

It is common to point out that general revelation is inferior to special revelation, both in the clarity of the treatment and the range of subjects considered. The insufficiency of general revelation therefore re-

---

1. Benjamin B. Warfield, "The Biblical Idea of Revelation," in *The Inspiration and Authority of the Bible*, ed. Samuel G. Craig (London: Marshall, Morgan and Scott, 1951), p. 74.

quired the special revelation. The special revelation, however, requires the general revelation as well.[2] Without the general revelation, we would not possess the concepts regarding God which enable us to know and understand the God of the special revelation. Special revelation builds upon general revelation. The relationship between them is in some ways parallel to that which Immanuel Kant found between the categories of understanding and sense perception: "Concepts without percepts are empty; percepts without concepts are blind." The two are harmonious. Only if the two are developed in isolation from one another does there seem to be any conflict between them. They have a common subject matter and perspective, yielding a harmonious and complementary understanding.

The Style of Special Revelation

The Personal Nature of Special Revelation

We need to ask about the style of special revelation, the nature or fashion of it. It is, first of all, personal. A personal God presents himself to persons. This is seen in a number of ways. God reveals himself by telling his name. Nothing is more personal than one's name. When Moses asked who he should say had sent him to the people of Israel, Jehovah responded by giving his name, "I AM WHO I AM [or I WILL BE WHO I WILL BE]" (Exod. 3:14). Moreover, God entered into personal covenants with individuals (Noah, Abraham) and with the nation of Israel. The Psalms contain numerous testimonies of personal experience with God. And the goal of Paul's life was a personal acquaintance with God: "that I may know him and the power of his resurrection, and may share his sufferings, becoming like him in his death" (Phil. 3:10).

The whole of Scripture is personal in nature. What we find is not a set of universal truths, like the axioms of Euclid in geometry, but rather a series of specific or particular statements about concrete occurrences and facts. Neither is Scripture a formal theological presentation, with arguments and counterarguments, such as one would find in a theological textbook. Nor are there systematized creedal statements. There are elements of creedal affirmation, but not a thoroughgoing intellectualization of Christian belief.

There is little information about matters not directly concerned with God's redemptive working and his relationship with humankind. Cosmology, for example, does not receive the scrutiny sometimes found in other religions. The Bible does not digress into matters of merely historical concern. It does not fill in gaps in the knowledge of the past. It does not concentrate on biographical details. What God reveals is primarily himself as a person, and especially those dimensions of himself that are particularly significant for faith.

The Anthropic Nature of Special Revelation

The God who is revealed is, however, a transcendent being. He lies outside our sensory experience. The Bible claims that God is unlimited in his knowledge and power; he is not subject to the confines of space and time. Consequently the revelation must involve a condescension on God's part (in the good sense of that word). We cannot reach up to investigate God and would not understand even if we could. So God has revealed himself by a revelation in *anthropic* form. This should not be thought of as anthropomorphism as such, but as simply a revelation coming in human language and human categories of thought and action.[3]

This anthropic character entails the use of human languages common at the time. Koine Greek was once believed to be a special, divinely created language since it is so different from classical Greek. We now know, of course, that it was simply the ver-

2. Ibid., p. 75.

3. Bernard Ramm, *Special Revelation and the Word of God* (Grand Rapids: Eerdmans, 1961), pp. 36–37.

nacular language. Idioms of the day appear in the Scripture. And it utilizes ordinary ways of describing nature, of measuring time and distance, and so on.[4]

The revelation is also anthropic in the sense that it often came in forms which are part of ordinary, everyday human experience. Dreams, for example, were a frequent means used by God to reveal himself. Yet few experiences are as common to humankind as are dreams. It was not the particular type of experience employed, but rather the unique content supplied and the unique utilization of this experience which distinguished revelation from the ordinary and natural. The same is true of the incarnation. When God came to earth, he used the modality of an ordinary human being. Sometimes artists have tried to set Jesus' humanity apart from that of other persons by portraying him with a halo or some other visible sign of distinctiveness. But apparently Jesus carried no visible sign of distinctiveness. Most persons took him for an ordinary, average human being, the son of Joseph the carpenter. He came as a human, not an angel or a being clearly recognizable as a god.

To be sure, there were revelations which clearly broke with typical experience. The voice of the Father speaking from heaven (John 12:28) was one of these. The miracles were striking in their effect. Yet much of the revelation was in the form of natural occurrences.

The Analogical Nature of Special Revelation

God draws upon those elements in our universe of knowledge that can serve as a likeness of or partially convey the truth in the divine realm. His revelation employs analogical language. When a term is used analogically in two clauses, there is always at least some univocal element (i.e., the meaning of the term is in at least one sense the same in both clauses), but there are differ-

ences as well, as when we say that Jeff runs the 100-yard dash and that the Chicago and Northwestern commuter train runs between Chicago and Elmhurst.

Whenever God has revealed himself, he has selected elements which are univocal in his universe and ours. Langdon Gilkey has pointed out that, in the orthodox view, when we say that God acts, we have the very same meaning in mind as when we say that a human acts.[5] When we say that God stopped the Jordan River, we have the very same thing in mind as when we say that the Army Corps of Engineers stopped a river from flowing. The acts of God are occurrences within a space-time universe. The death of Jesus was an event observably the same as that of James, John, Peter, Andrew, or any other human. And when the Bible says that God loves, it means just the same sort of qualities that we refer to when we speak of humans loving (in the sense of *agapē*): a steadfast, unselfish concern for the welfare of the other person.

As we are here using the term *analogical*, we mean "qualitatively the same"; in other words, the difference is one of degree rather than of kind or genus. God is powerful as humans are powerful, but much more so. When we say that God knows, we have the same meaning in mind as when we say that humans know—but while humans know something, God knows everything. We cannot grasp how much more of each of these qualities God possesses, or what it means to say that God has our knowledge amplified to an infinite extent. Having observed only finite forms, we find it impossible to grasp infinite concepts. In this sense, God always remains *incomprehensible*. It is not that we do not have knowledge of him, and genuine knowledge at that. Rather, the shortcoming lies in our inability to encompass him within our knowledge. Although *what* we know of him is the same as his knowledge of

---

4. Ibid., p. 39.

5. Langdon Gilkey, "Cosmology, Ontology, and the Travail of Biblical Language," *Journal of Religion* 41 (1961): 196.

himself, the degree of our knowledge is much less.

What makes this analogical knowledge possible is that it is God who selects the components which he uses. Unlike human beings, God is knowledgeable of both sides of the analogy. If humans by their own natural unaided reason seek to understand God by constructing an analogy involving God and humankind, the result is always some sort of conundrum, for they are in effect working with an equation containing two unknowns. For instance, if one were to argue that God's love is to our love what God's being is to our being, it would be tantamount to saying $^x/2 = \ ^y/5$. Not knowing the relationship between God's being (or nature, or essence) and that of humanity, we cannot construct a meaningful analogy. God, on the other hand, knowing all things completely, therefore knows which elements of human knowledge and experience are sufficiently similar to the divine truth that they can be used to help construct a meaningful analogy.

The Modes of Special Revelation

We now turn to examine the actual modes or means or modalities by which God has revealed himself: historical events, divine speech, and the incarnation.

Historical Events

The Bible emphasizes a whole series of divine events by which God has made himself known. From the perspective of the people of Israel, a primary event was the call of Abraham, to whom they looked as the father of their nation. The Lord's provision of Isaac as an heir, under most unlikely conditions, was another significant divine act. God's provision in the midst of the famine during the time of Joseph benefited not only the descendants of Abraham, but the other residents of the whole area as well. Probably the major event for Israel, still celebrated by Jews, was the deliverance from Egypt through the series of plagues culminating in

the Passover and the crossing of the Red Sea. The conquest of the Promised Land, the return from captivity, even the captivity itself, were God's self-manifestation. The birth of Jesus, his wondrous acts, his death and particularly his resurrection, were God at work. In the creation and expansion of the church God was also at work bringing his people into being.

All of these are acts of God and thus revelations of his nature. Those which we have cited here are spectacular or miraculous. The acts of God are not limited to such events, however. God has been at work both in these greater occurrences and also in the more mundane events of the history of his people.

Divine Speech

The second major modality of revelation is God's speech. A very common expression in the Bible and especially in the Old Testament is the statement, "The word of the LORD came to me, saying, . . ." (e.g., Jer. 18:1; Ezek. 12:1, 8, 17, 21, 26; Hos. 1:1; Joel 1:1; Amos 3:1). The prophets had a consciousness that their message was not of their own creation, but was from God. In writing the Book of Revelation, John was attempting to communicate the message which God had given to him. The writer to the Hebrews noted that God had spoken often in times past, and now had particularly spoken through his Son (Heb. 1:1–2). God does not merely demonstrate through his actions what he is like; he also speaks, telling us about himself, his plans, his will.

We may be inclined to think that God's speech is really not a modality at all. It seems so direct. Yet we should note that it is necessarily a modality, for God is spiritual and thus does not have bodily parts. Since speech requires certain bodily parts, it cannot be an unmediated communication from God. Furthermore, it always comes in some human language, the language of the prophet or apostle, whether that is Hebrew, Aramaic, or Greek. Yet God presumably does not have a language in which he speaks. Thus, the use of language is an indication that God's speech is mediated rather than direct revelation.[6]

Divine speech may take several forms.[7] It may be an audible speaking. It may be a silent, inward hearing of God's message, like the subvocal process in which slow readers engage (they "hear" in their heads the words they are reading). It is likely that in many cases this was the mode used. Often this inaudible speech was part of another modality, such as a dream or vision. In these instances, the prophet heard the Lord speaking to him, but presumably anyone else present at the time heard nothing. Finally, there is "concursive" inspiration—revelation and inspiration have merged into one. As the authors of Scripture wrote, God placed within their minds the thoughts that he wished communicated. This was not a case of the message's already having been revealed, and the Holy Spirit's merely bringing these matters to remembrance, or directing the writers to thoughts with which they were already familiar. God created thoughts in the minds of the writers as they wrote. The writers could have been either conscious or unconscious of what was happening. In the latter case, they may have felt that the ideas were simply dawning upon them. Although Paul occasionally indicates that he "thinks" he has the Spirit of God (e.g., 1 Cor. 7:40), there are other times when he is more definite that he has received his message from the Lord (e.g., 1 Cor. 11:23). There are also some cases, such as the letter to Philemon, where Paul does not indicate that he is conscious of God's directing his writing, although God was doubtless doing so.

Quite frequently, the spoken word of God was the interpretation of an event. While this event was usually something past or contemporary with the writing, there were times when the interpretation preceded the event, as in predictive prophecy. The contention being advanced here, despite some strong recent disagreements, is that not only the event but also the interpretation was revelation from God; the interpretation was not merely the insight or product of the reflection of a biblical writer. Without this specially revealed interpretation, the event itself would often be opaque and thus quite mute. It would be subject to various interpretations, and the explanation given by the Scripture might then be merely an erroneous human speculation. Take such a central event as the death of Jesus. If we knew that this event had occurred, but its meaning had not been divinely revealed to us, we might understand it in widely differing ways, or find it simply a puzzle. It might be regarded as a defeat, which is the position the disciples apparently held immediately after Jesus' death. Or it might be considered a sort of moral victory, a martyr dying for his principles. Without the revealed word of explanation we could only guess that Jesus' death was an atoning sacrifice. We must conclude that the interpretation of certain events is a modality of revelation as genuine as that of God's acts in history.

The Incarnation

The most complete modality of revelation is the incarnation. The contention here is that Jesus' life and speech were a special revelation of God. We may again be inclined to think that this is not a modality at all, that God was directly present in unmediated form. But since God does not have human form, Christ's humanity must represent a mediation of the divine revelation. This is not to say that his humanity concealed or obscured the revelation. Rather, it was the means by which the revelation of deity was conveyed. Scripture specifically states that God has spoken through or in his Son. Hebrews 1:1–2 contrasts this with the earlier forms of revelation, and indicates that the incarnation is superior.

Here revelation as event most fully occurs. The pinnacle of the acts of God is to be found in the life of Jesus. The miracles, his

6. Ramm, *Special Revelation*, p. 54.
7. Ibid., pp. 59–60.

death, and the resurrection are redemptive history in its most condensed and concentrated form. Here too is revelation as divine speech, for the messages of Jesus surpassed those of the prophets and apostles. Jesus even dared to place his message over against what was written in the Scriptures, not as contradicting, but as going beyond or fulfilling them (Matt. 5:17). When the prophets spoke, they were bearers of a message from God and about God. When Jesus spoke, it was God himself speaking.

Revelation also took place in the very perfection of Jesus' character. There was a godlikeness about him which could be discerned. Here God was actually living among humans and displaying his attributes to them. Jesus' actions, attitudes, and affections did not merely mirror the Father. They showed that God was actually living on earth. The centurion at Calvary, who presumably had seen many persons die of crucifixion, apparently saw something different in Jesus, which caused him to exclaim, "Truly this was the Son of God!" (Matt. 27:54). Peter, after the miraculous catch of fish, fell on his knees and said, "Depart from me, for I am a sinful man, O Lord" (Luke 5:8). These were people who found in Jesus a revelation of the Father.

Here revelation as act and revelation as word come together. Jesus both spoke the Father's word and demonstrated the Father's attributes. He was the most complete revelation of God, because he was God. John could make the amazing statement, "That which was from the beginning . . . we have heard . . . we have seen with our eyes . . . we have looked upon and touched with our hands" (1 John 1:1). And Jesus could say, "He who has seen me has seen the Father" (John 14:9).

Special Revelation: Propositional or Personal?

It is necessary at this point to speak briefly of neoorthodoxy, which views revelation not as the communication of information (or propositions), but as God's presentation of himself. According to neoorthodoxy, God does not tell us anything about himself; rather, we come to know him through encounter with him. Revelation, then, is not propositional; it is personal. To a large extent, our view of faith will reflect our understanding of revelation.[8] If we regard revelation as the communication of propositional truths, we will view faith as a response of assent, of believing those truths. If, on the other hand, we regard revelation as the presentation of a person, we will correspondingly view faith as an act of personal trust or commitment. According to this latter view, theology is not a set of doctrines that have been revealed. It is the church's attempt to express what it has found in God's revelation of himself.

The neoorthodox approach presents at least a couple of problems. The first is to establish a basis upon which faith can rest. Advocates of both views—that revelation is personal, and that it is propositional—recognize the need for some basis of faith. The question is whether the nonpropositional view of revelation provides a sufficient basis for faith. Can the advocates of this view be sure that what they encounter is really the God of Abraham, Isaac, and Jacob? In order to trust someone, we must have some knowledge about that person.

That there must be belief before there can be trust is evident from our own experiences. Suppose I have to make a bank deposit in cash, but am unable to do so in person. I must ask someone else to do this for me. But whom will I ask? To whom will I entrust myself, or at least a portion of my material possessions? I will trust or commit myself to someone whom I believe to be honest. Believing *in* that person depends upon believing something *about* him. I will probably select a good friend whose integrity I do not question. Similarly, how can we trust that it is the Christian God whom we

8. John Baillie, *The Idea of Revelation in Recent Thought* (New York: Columbia University Press, 1956), pp. 85–108.

are encountering unless he tells us who he is and what he is like?

Another problem is the problem of theology itself. Those who maintain that revelation is personal are nevertheless very concerned about correctly defining belief, or stating correct doctrinal understandings, while of course insisting that faith is not belief in doctrinal propositions. Karl Barth and Emil Brunner, for example, argued over such issues as the nature and status of the image of God in humankind, as well as the virgin birth and the empty tomb. Presum-

vealing, then the Bible is not revelation. Revelation is something that occurred long ago. If, however, it is also the product, the result or the *revealed*, then the Bible may also be termed revelation.

A larger issue is the nature of revelation. If revelation is propositional and hence can be preserved, then the question of whether the Bible is in this derivative sense a revelation is a question of whether it is inspired, of whether it indeed preserves what was revealed. This will be the subject of the next chapter.

Special revelation is both personal and propositional: God reveals himself by telling us something about himself.

---

ably, each felt he was trying to establish the true doctrine in these areas. But how are these doctrinal propositions related to, or derived from, the nonpropositional revelation? There is a problem here.

This is not to suggest that there cannot be a connection between nonpropositional revelation and propositions of truth, but that this connection has not been adequately explicated by neoorthodoxy. The problem derives from making a disjunction between propositional and personal revelation. Revelation is not *either* personal *or* propositional; it is *both/and*. What God primarily does is to reveal *himself*, but he does so at least in part by telling us something *about* himself.

Scripture as Revelation

If revelation includes propositional truths, then it is of such a nature that it can be preserved. It can be written down or *inscripturated*. And this written record, to the extent that it is an accurate reproduction of the original revelation, is also by derivation revelation and entitled to be called that.

The definition of revelation becomes a factor here. If revelation is defined as only the actual occurrence, the process or the *re-*

We should also note that this revelation is *progressive*. Some care needs to be exercised in the use of this term, for it has sometimes been used to represent the idea of a gradual evolutionary development. This is not what we have in mind. That approach, which flourished under liberal scholarship, regarded sections of the Old Testament as virtually obsolete and false; they were only very imperfect approximations of the truth. The idea which we are here suggesting, however, is that later revelation builds upon earlier revelation. It is complementary and supplementary to it, not contradictory. Note the way in which Jesus elevated the teachings of the law by extending, expanding, and internalizing them. He frequently prefaced his instruction with the expression, "You have heard . . . but I say to you." In a similar fashion, the author of Hebrews points out that God, who in the past spoke by the prophets, has in these last days spoken by a Son, who reflects the glory of God and bears the very stamp of his nature (Heb. 1:1–3). The revelation of God is a process even as is redemption, and a process which moved to an ever more complete form.[9]

---

9. Ramm, *Special Revelation*, pp. 161–87.

We have seen that God has taken the initiative to make himself known to us in a more complete way than general revelation, and has done so in a fashion appropriate to our understanding. This means that lost and sinful humans can come to know God and then go on to grow in understanding of what he expects of and promises to his children. Because this revelation includes both the personal presence of God and informational truth, we are able to identify God, to understand something about him, and to point others to him.

5 The Preservation of the Revelation: Inspiration

Definition of Inspiration

By inspiration of the Scripture we mean that supernatural influence of the Holy Spirit upon the Scripture writers which rendered their writings an accurate record of the revelation or which resulted in what they wrote actually being the Word of God.

If, as we have contended in the preceding chapter, revelation is God's communication to humankind of truth that they need to know in order to relate properly to him, then it should be apparent why inspiration also is necessary. While revelation benefits those who immediately receive it, that value might well be lost for those beyond the immediate circle of revelation. Since God does not repeat his revelation for each person, there has to be some way to preserve it. It could, of course, be preserved by oral retelling or by being fixed into a definite tradition, and this certainly was operative in the period which sometimes intervened between the occurrence of the initial revelation and its inscripturation. Certain problems attach to this, however, when long periods of time are involved, for oral tradition is subject to erosion and modification. Anyone who has ever played the parlor game in which the first person whispers a story to the second, who whispers it to the next person, and so on until the story has been retold to all the players, has a good idea of how easily oral tradition can be corrupted. And so does anyone who has observed the way in which rumors spread. While the unusual tenacity of the Oriental memory and the storyteller's determination to be faithful to the tradition should not be underestimated, it is apparent that something more than oral retelling is needed.

While revelation is the communication of divine truth from God to humankind, inspiration relates more to the relaying of that truth from the first recipient(s) of it to other

makes this very point in John 21:25, when he says that if everything that Jesus did were written down, "I suppose that the world itself could not contain the books that would be written." If, as we asserted in the previous chapter, all of Jesus' words and actions were the words and actions of God, the Spirit was apparently very selective in what he inspired the biblical authors to report.

The Fact of Inspiration

We begin by noting that throughout Scripture there is the assumption or even the claim of its divine origin, or of its equivalency with the actual speech of the Lord. This point is sometimes spurned on the grounds of its being circular. There is a dilemma which any theology (or any other

---

Throughout Scripture there is the assumption of its equivalency with the actual speech of the Lord.

---

persons, whether then or later. Thus, revelation might be thought of as a vertical action, and inspiration as a horizontal matter. We should note that although revelation and inspiration are usually thought of together, it is possible to have one without the other. There were cases of inspiration without revelation. The Holy Spirit in some instances moved Scripture writers to record the words of unbelievers, words which certainly were not divinely revealed. Some Scripture writers may well have written down matters which were not specially revealed to them, but were pieces of information readily available to anyone who would make the inquiry. The genealogies, both in the Old Testament and in the New Testament (the listing of Jesus' lineage), may well be of this character. There also was revelation without inspiration: instances of revelation which went unrecorded because the Holy Spirit did not move anyone to write them down. John

system of thought for that matter) faces when dealing with its basic authority. Either it bases its starting point upon itself, in which case it is guilty of circularity, or it bases itself upon some foundation other than that upon which it bases all its other articles, in which case it is guilty of inconsistency. Note, however, that we are guilty of circularity only if the testimony of Scripture is taken as settling the matter. But surely the Scripture writer's own claim should be taken into consideration as part of the process of formulating our hypothesis of the nature of Scripture. Other considerations will of course be consulted when we evaluate the hypothesis. What we have here is somewhat like a court trial. Defendants are permitted to testify in their own behalf. This testimony is not taken as settling the matter, however; that is, after hearing the defendant's plea of "not guilty," the judge will not immediately rule, "I find the defendant not guilty." Additional testimony is called for and evaluated, in order to determine credibility. But the defendant's testimony is admitted.

One other item needs to be observed in answering the charge of circularity. In consulting the Bible to determine the authors' view of Scripture, one is not necessarily presupposing its inspiration. One may consult it merely as a historical document which informs us that its authors considered it the inspired Word of God. In this case one is not viewing the authority of the Bible as its own starting point. There is circularity only if one begins with the assumption of the inspiration of the Bible, and then uses that assumption as a guarantee of the truth of the Bible's claim to be inspired. One is not guilty of circularity if the Scripture writers' claim is not presented as final proof. It is permissible to use the Bible as a historical document and to allow it to plead its own case.

There are several ways in which the Bible gives witness of its divine origin. One of these is the view of New Testament authors regarding the Scriptures of their day, which we would today term the Old Testament. Second Peter 1:20–21 is a cardinal instance: "First of all you must understand this, that no prophecy of scripture is a matter of one's own interpretation, because no prophecy ever came by the impulse of man, but men moved by the Holy Spirit spoke from God." Here Peter is affirming that the prophecies of the Old Testament were not produced by the will or decision of a human being. Rather they were moved by the Spirit of God. The impetus which led to the writing was from the Holy Spirit.

A second reference is that of Paul in 2 Timothy 3:16: "All scripture is inspired by God and profitable for teaching, for reproof, for correction, and for training in righteousness." This is part of a passage in which Paul is exhorting Timothy to continue in the teachings which he has received. Paul assumes Timothy is familiar with the "sacred writings" (v. 15) and urges him to continue in them since they are divinely inspired (or more correctly, "God-spired" or "God-

breathed"). The impression here is that they are divinely produced, just as God breathed the breath of life into humankind (Gen. 2:7). They therefore carry value for building up believers into maturity so that they may be "complete, equipped for every good work" (2 Tim. 3:17).

When we turn to the early church's preaching, we find a similar understanding of the Old Testament. In Acts 1:16 Peter says, "Brethren, the scripture had to be fulfilled, which the Holy Spirit spoke beforehand by the mouth of David. . . ," and then proceeds to quote from Psalms 69:25 and 109:8 regarding the fate of Judas. It is notable here that Peter not only regards the words of David as authoritative, but actually affirms that God spoke by the mouth of David. David was God's "mouthpiece," so to speak. The same thought, that God spoke by the mouth of the prophets, is found in Acts 3:18, 21, and 4:25. The earliest preaching of the church, then, identifies "it is written in the scripture" with "God has said it."

This fits well with the testimony which the prophets themselves gave. Again and again they declared, "Thus says the LORD." Jeremiah said: "These are the words which the LORD spoke concerning Israel and Judah" (30:4). Amos declared: "Hear this word that the LORD has spoken against you, O people of Israel" (3:1). And David said: "The Spirit of the LORD speaks by me, his word is upon my tongue" (2 Sam. 23:2). Statements like these, which appear over and over again in the prophets, indicate that they were aware of being "moved by the Holy Spirit" (2 Peter 1:21).

Finally, we note the position that our Lord himself held regarding the Old Testament writings. In part, we may infer this from the way he related to the view of the Bible held by his dialogical opponents, the Pharisees. (This was also the view held by most Jews of that day.) He never challenged or corrected their view of the nature of the Scripture. He merely disagreed with them regarding the interpretations which they had placed upon the Bible, or the traditions which they had added to the content of the Scriptures themselves. In his discussions and disputes with his opponents, he repeatedly quoted from the Scriptures. In his threefold temptation, he responded to Satan each time with a quotation from the Old Testament. He spoke of the authority and permanence of the Scripture: "scripture cannot be broken" (John 10:35); "till heaven and earth pass away, not an iota, not a dot, will pass from the law until all is accomplished" (Matt. 5:18). Two objects were regarded as sacred in the Israel of Jesus' day, the temple and the Scriptures. He did not hesitate to point out the transiency of the former, for not one stone would be left upon another (Matt. 24:2). There is, therefore, a striking contrast between his attitude toward the Scriptures and his attitude toward the temple.[1] Clearly, he regarded the Scriptures as inspired, authoritative, and indestructible.

Theories of Inspiration

We may conclude from the foregoing that the uniform testimony of the Scripture writers is that the Bible has originated from God and is his message to humanity. This is the fact of the Bible's inspiration; we must now ask what it means. It is here that differences in view begin to occur.

1. The intuition theory makes inspiration largely a high degree of insight. Inspiration is the functioning of a special gift, perhaps almost like an artistic ability, but nonetheless a natural endowment, a permanent possession. The Scripture writers were religious geniuses. Yet their inspiration was essentially no different from that of other great religious and philosophical thinkers, such as Plato, Buddha, and others. The Bible then is great religious literature reflecting the spiritual experiences of the Hebrew people.[2]

2. The illumination theory maintains that there was an influence of the Holy Spirit upon the authors of Scripture, but that it involved only a heightening of their normal powers, an increased sensitivity and perceptivity with regard to spiritual matters. It was not unlike the effect of stimulants sometimes taken by students to heighten their awareness or amplify the mental processes. Thus, the work of inspiration is different only in degree, not in kind, from the Spirit's work with all believers. The result of this type of inspiration is increased ability to discover truth.[3]

3. The dynamic theory emphasizes the combination of divine and human elements in the process of inspiration and of the writing of the Bible. The work of the Spirit of God was in directing the writer to the thoughts or concepts he should have, and allowing the writer's own distinctive personality to come into play in the choice of words and expressions. Thus, the person writing gave expression to the divinely directed thoughts in a way that was uniquely characteristic of him.[4]

4. The verbal theory maintains that the influence of the Holy Spirit extended beyond the direction of thoughts to the selection of words used to convey the message. The work of the Holy Spirit was so intense that each word is the exact word which God wants used at that point to express the message. Ordinarily, great care is taken to insist that this is not dictation, however.[5]

5. The dictation theory is the teaching that God actually dictated the Bible to the writers. Passages where the Spirit is depicted as telling the author precisely what to write are regarded as applying to the entire Bible. This means that there is no distinctive style attributable to the different authors of the biblical books. The number of people

1. Abraham Kuyper, *Principles of Sacred Theology* (Grand Rapids: Eerdmans, 1954), p. 441.
2. James Martineau, *A Study of Religion: Its Sources and Contents* (Oxford: Clarendon, 1889), pp. 168–71.
3. Auguste Sabatier, *Outlines of a Philosophy of Religion* (New York: James Pott, 1916), p. 90.
4. Augustus H. Strong, *Systematic Theology* (Westwood, N.J.: Revell, 1907), pp. 211–22.
5. J. I. Packer, *Fundamentalism and the Word of God* (Grand Rapids: Eerdmans, 1958), p. 79.

who actually hold this view is considerably smaller than the number to whom it is ascribed—most adherents of the verbal view do take great pains to dissociate themselves from the dictation theorists. There are, however, some who accept this designation of themselves.[6]

The Extent of Inspiration

We must now pose the question of the extent of inspiration, or, to put it somewhat differently, of what is inspired. Is the whole of the Bible to be thus regarded, or only certain portions?

One easy solution would be to cite 2 Timothy 3:16, "All scripture is inspired by God and profitable. . . ." There is a problem, however, in that there is an ambiguity in the first part of this verse. The Greek text may be translated, "All scripture is God-breathed and profitable," or, "All God-breathed scripture is also profitable." If the former rendering is adopted, the inspiration of all Scripture would be affirmed. If the latter is followed, the sentence would emphasize the profitability of all God-breathed Scripture. From the context, however, one cannot really determine what Paul intended to convey. (What does appear from the context is that Paul had in mind a definite body of writings known to Timothy from his childhood. It is unlikely that Paul was attempting to make a distinction between inspired and uninspired Scripture within this body of writings.)

Can we find additional help on this issue in two other texts previously cited—2 Peter 1:19–21 and John 10:34–35? At first glance this seems not to succeed, since the former refers specifically to prophecy and the latter to the law. It appears from Luke 24:25–27, however, that "Moses and all the prophets" equals "all the scriptures," and from Luke 24:44–45 that "the law of Moses and the prophets and the psalms" equals "the scriptures." In John 10:34, when Jesus refers to the law, he actually quotes from Psalm 82:6. And Peter refers to the "prophetic word" (2 Peter 1:19) and every "prophecy of scripture" (v. 20) in such a way as to lead us to believe that the whole of the collection of writings commonly accepted in that day is in view. It appears that "law" and "prophecy" were often used to designate the whole of the Hebrew Scriptures.

Can this understanding of inspiration be extended to cover the books of the New Testament as well? This problem is not so easily solved. We do have some indications of belief that what these writers were doing was of the same nature as what the writers of the Old Testament had done. One explicit reference of a New Testament author to the writings of another is 2 Peter 3:16. Here Peter refers to the writings of Paul and alludes to the difficulty of understanding some things in them, which, he says, "the ignorant and unstable twist to their own destruction, *as they do the other scriptures*." Thus Peter groups Paul's writings with other books, presumably familiar to the readers, which were regarded as Scripture. Moreover, John identified what he was writing with God's word: "We are of God. Whoever knows God listens to us, and he who is not of God does not listen to us. By this we know the spirit of truth and the spirit of error" (1 John 4:6). He makes his own words the standard of measurement. Paul wrote that the gospel received by the Thessalonians had come by the Holy Spirit (1 Thess. 1:5), and had been accepted by them as what it really was, the word of God (2:13). It should be clear that these New Testament writers regarded the Scripture as being extended from the prophetic period to their own time.

The Intensiveness of Inspiration

We must next ask about the matter of the intensiveness of the inspiration. Was it only a general influence, perhaps involving the suggesting of concepts, or was it so thorough-

6. John R. Rice, *Our God-breathed Book—The Bible* (Murfreesboro, Tenn.: Sword of the Lord, 1969), pp. 192, 261–80. Rice accepts the term *dictation* but disavows the expression *mechanical dictation*.

going that even the choice of words reflects God's intention?

When we examine the New Testament writers' use of the Old Testament, an interesting feature appears. We sometimes find indication that they regarded every word, syllable, and punctuation mark as significant. At times their whole argument rests upon a fine point in the text that they are consulting. For example, in Matthew 22:32, Jesus' quotation of Exodus 3:6, "I am the God of Abraham, and the God of Isaac, and

tation. Evidently, in the mind of Jesus anything that the Old Testament said was what God said.

In addition to these specific references, we should note that Jesus often introduced his quotations of the Old Testament with the formula, "It is written." Whatever the Bible said he identified as having the force of God's own speech. It was authoritative. This, of course, does not speak specifically to the question of whether the inspiring work of the Holy Spirit extended to the

Jesus and the New Testament writers regarded every word, syllable, and punctuation mark of the Old Testament as significant.

the God of Jacob," the point depends upon the tense of the verb, which leads him to draw the conclusion, "He is not God of the dead, but of the living." In verse 44, the point of the argument hangs upon a possessive suffix, "The Lord said to *my* Lord." In this case Jesus expressly says that when David spoke these words, he was "inspired by the Spirit." Apparently David was led by the Spirit to use the particular forms he did, even to the point of a detail as minute as the possessive in "*my* Lord."

One other argument regarding the intensiveness of inspiration is the fact that New Testament writers attribute to God statements in the Old Testament which in the original form are not specifically ascribed to him. A notable example is Matthew 19:4–5, where Jesus asks, "Have you not read that he who made them from the beginning made them male and female, and said . . .?" He then proceeds to quote from Genesis 2:24. In the original, however, the statement is not attributed to God. It is just a comment on the event of the creation of woman from man. But the words of Genesis are cited by Jesus as being what God said; Jesus even puts these words in the form of a direct quo-

choice of words, but it does indicate a thoroughgoing identification of the Old Testament writings with the word of God. One would infer that the inspiration of the Scripture was so intense that it extended even to the choice of particular words.

A Model of Inspiration

When formulating a theory of inspiration, it is necessary to recognize the two basic methods which may be employed. The first method is a didactic approach which places its primary emphasis upon what the biblical writers actually say about the Bible and the view of it which is revealed in the way they use it. This method is represented in the writings of Benjamin B. Warfield and the "Princeton School" of theology.[7] The second approach is to look at what the Bible is like, to analyze the various ways in which the writers report events, to compare parallel accounts. This characterizes the method of Dewey Beegle, who developed a theory of

7. Benjamin B. Warfield, "The Biblical Idea of Inspiration," in *The Inspiration and Authority of the Bible*, ed. Samuel G. Craig (London: Marshall, Morgan and Scott, 1951), pp. 131–65.

Figure 1. Levels of Specificity

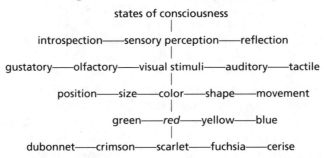

states of consciousness
|
introspection——sensory perception——reflection
|
gustatory——olfactory——visual stimuli——auditory——tactile
|
position——size——color——shape——movement
|
green——*red*——yellow——blue
|
dubonnet——crimson——scarlet——fuchsia——cerise

inspiration based primarily upon the phenomena of Scripture.[8]

If we are to maintain both methods, it will be necessary to find some way of integrating them. We will give primary consideration to the didactic material. This means concluding that inspiration extends even to the choice of words (i.e., inspiration is verbal). We will define just what that choice of words means, however, by examining the phenomena.

We suggest that what the Spirit may do is to direct the thoughts of the Scripture writer. The direction effected by the Spirit, however, is quite precise. God being omniscient, it is not gratuitous to assume that his thoughts are precise, more so than ours. This being the case, there will be within the vocabulary of the writer one word that will most aptly communicate the thought God is conveying (although that word in itself may be inadequate). By creating the thought and stimulating the understanding of the Scripture writer, the Spirit will lead him in effect to use one particular word rather than any other.

While God directs the writer to use particular words (precision) to express the idea, the idea itself may be quite general or quite specific. This is what linguist Kenneth Pike has called the dimension of magnification.[9] One cannot expect that the Bible will always

display maximum magnification or a great deal of detail. It will, rather, express just that degree of detail or specificity that God intends, and, on that level of magnification, just that concept which he intends. This accounts for the fact that sometimes Scripture is not so detailed as we might expect or desire. Indeed, there have been occasions when the Holy Spirit, to serve the purpose of a new situation, moved a Scripture writer to reexpress a concept on a more specific level than its original form.

Figure 1 will help to illustrate what we have in mind. This figure depicts various levels of specificity or detail or magnification. The dimension of specificity involves vertical movement on the chart. Suppose the concept under consideration is the color red. This idea has a particular degree of specificity, no more and no less. It is neither more specific (e.g., scarlet) nor less specific (color). It occurs in a particular location on the chart—both vertically on the generality-specificity axis, and horizontally on its given level of specificity (i.e., red, versus yellow or green). In another instance one may have either more or less detail in a picture (a higher or lower degree of magnification, in Pike's terminology), and a sharper or fuzzier focus. At a less precise focus, of course, the detail will become blurry or even get lost. These two dimensions (detail and focus) should not be confused, however. If the idea is sufficiently precise, then only one word in a given language, or in the vocabulary of a

8. Dewey Beegle, *Scripture, Tradition, and Infallibility* (Grand Rapids: Eerdmans, 1973), pp. 175–97.

9. Kenneth L. Pike, "Language and Meaning: Strange Dimensions of Truth," *Christianity Today*, 8 May 1961, p. 28.

given writer, will adequately communicate and express the meaning.

It is our contention here that inspiration involved God's directing the thoughts of the writers, so that they were precisely the thoughts that he wished expressed. At times these thoughts were very specific; at other times they were more general. It is also our contention that inspiration was verbal, extending even to the choice of words. It was not merely verbal, however, for at times thoughts may be more precise than the words available. Such, for example, was probably the case with John's vision on Patmos, which produced the Book of Revelation.

At this point the objection is generally raised that inspiration extending to the choice of words necessarily becomes dictation. Answering this charge will force us to theorize regarding the process of inspiration. Here we must note that the Scripture writers, at least in every case where we know their identity, were not novices in the faith. They had known God, learned from him, and practiced the spiritual life for some time. God therefore had been at work in their lives for some time, preparing them through a wide variety of family, social, educational, and religious experiences for the task they were to perform. In fact, Paul suggests that he was chosen even before his birth (Gal. 1:15). And through all of the experiences of, say, the fisherman Peter, God was creating the kind of personality and worldview that would later be employed in the writing of Scripture. Luke's vocabulary resulted from his education and his whole broad sweep of experience; in all of this God had been at work preparing him for his task.

It was possible, therefore, for a Scripture writer who had been given only a suggestion of a new direction, but who had known God for a long time, to "think the thoughts of God." To give a personal example: a secretary had been with a church for many years. At the beginning of my pastorate there, I dictated letters to her. After a year or so, I could tell her the general tenor of my thinking and she could write my letters, using my style. By the end of the third year I could simply hand her a letter which I had received and ask her to reply, since we had discussed so many issues connected with the church that she actually knew my thinking on most of them. It is possible—without dictation—to know just what another person wants to say. Note, however, that this assumes a closeness of relationship and a long period of acquaintance. So a Scripture writer, given the circumstances which we have described, could—without dictation—write God's message just as God wanted it recorded.

Inspiration is herein conceived of as applying to both the writer and the writing. In the primary sense, it is the writer who is the object of the inspiration. As the writer pens the Scripture, however, the quality of inspiredness is communicated to the writing as well. It is inspired in a derived sense.[10] This is much like the definition of revelation as both the revealing and the revealed (see p. 50). We have observed that inspiration presupposes an extended period of God's working with the writer. This involves not only the preparation of the writer, but also the preparation of the material for his use. While inspiration in the strict sense probably does not apply to the preservation and transmission of this material, the providence which guides this process should not be overlooked.

Because the Bible has been inspired, we can be confident of having divine instruction. The fact that we did not live when the revelatory events and teachings first came does not leave us spiritually or theologically deprived. We have a sure guide. And we are motivated to study it intensively, since its message is truly God's word to us.

10. It should be observed that 2 Peter 1:20–21 refers to the authors, while 2 Timothy 3:16 refers to what they wrote. Thus the dilemma of whether inspiration pertains to the writer or the writing is shown to be a false issue.

6

The Dependability of God's Word: Inerrancy

The inerrancy of Scripture has recently been a topic of heated debate among conservative Christians. This is the doctrine that the Bible is fully truthful in all of its teachings. To those in the broader theological community, this seems an irrelevant issue, a carry-over from an antiquarian view of the Bible. To many evangelicals, however, it is an exceedingly important and even crucial issue. It therefore requires a careful examination. In a real sense, it is the completion of the doctrine of Scripture. For if God has given special revelation of himself and inspired servants of his to record it, we will want assurance that the Bible is indeed a dependable source of that revelation.

Various Conceptions of Inerrancy

The term *inerrancy* means different things to different people. As a matter of fact, there is frequent contention over which position properly deserves to be called by that name. It is therefore important to summarize briefly some of the current positions on the matter of inerrancy.

1. Absolute inerrancy holds that the Bible, which includes rather detailed treatment of matters both scientific and historical, is fully true. The impression is conveyed that the biblical writers intended to give a considerable amount of exact scientific and historical data. Thus, apparent discrepancies can and must be explained. For example, the description of the molten sea in 2 Chronicles 4:2 indicates that its diameter was 10 cubits while the circumference was 30 cubits. However, as we all know, the circumference of a circle is π (3.14159) times the diameter. If, as the biblical text says, the molten sea was circular, there is a discrepancy here, and an explanation must be given.[1]

2. Full inerrancy also holds that the Bible is completely true. While the Bible does not primarily aim to give scientific and historical data, such scientific and historical assertions as it does make are fully true. There is no essential difference between this position and absolute inerrancy in terms of their view of the religious/theological/spiritual message. The understanding of the scientific and historical references is quite different, however. Full inerrancy regards these references as phenomenal; that is, they are reported the way they appear to the human eye. They are not necessarily exact; rather, they are popular descriptions, often involving general references or approximations. Yet they are correct. What they teach is essentially correct in the way they teach it.[2]

3. Limited inerrancy also regards the Bible as inerrant and infallible in its salvific doctrinal references. A sharp distinction is drawn, however, between nonempirical, revealed matters on the one hand, and empirical, natural references on the other. The scientific and historical references in the Bible reflect the understanding current at the time the Bible was written. The Bible writers were subject to the limitations of their time. Revelation and inspiration did not raise the writers above ordinary knowledge. God did not reveal science or history to them. Consequently, the Bible may well contain what we would term errors in these areas. This, however, is of no great consequence. The Bible does not purport to teach science and history. For the purposes for which the Bible was given, however, it is fully truthful and inerrant.[3]

The Importance of Inerrancy

Why should the church be concerned about inerrancy at all? Some suggest that inerrancy is an irrelevant, false, or distracting issue. For one thing, "inerrant" is a negative term. It would be far better to use a positive term to describe the Bible. Further, inerrancy is not a biblical concept. In the Bible, erring is a spiritual or moral matter rather than intellectual. Inerrancy distracts us from the proper issues. By focusing our attention upon minutiae of the text and spurring us to expend energy in attempts to resolve minor discrepancies, this concern for inerrancy distracts us from hearing what the Bible is really trying to tell us about our relationship to God. Finally, this issue is harmful to the church. It creates disunity among those who otherwise have a great deal in common. It makes a major issue out of what should be a minor matter at most.[4]

In view of these considerations, would it not be better to disregard the issue of inerrancy and "get on with the matters at hand"? In answer we note that there is a very practical concern at the root of much of the discussion about inerrancy. A seminary student who was serving as student pastor of a small rural church summarized well the

1. Harold Lindsell, *The Battle for the Bible* (Grand Rapids: Zondervan, 1976), pp. 165–66.

2. Roger Nicole, "The Nature of Inerrancy," in *Inerrancy and Common Sense*, ed. Roger Nicole and J. Ramsey Michaels (Grand Rapids: Baker, 1980), pp. 71–95.

3. Daniel P. Fuller, "Benjamin B. Warfield's View of Faith and History," *Bulletin of the Evangelical Theological Society* 11 (1968): 75–83.

4. David Hubbard, "The Irrelevancy of Inerrancy," in *Biblical Authority*, ed. Jack Rogers (Waco, Tex.: Word, 1977), pp. 151–81.

concern of his congregation when he said, "My people ask me, 'If the Bible says it, can I believe it?'" Whether the Bible is fully truthful is a matter which is of importance to us theologically, historically, and epistemologically.

Theological Importance

Jesus, Paul, and other major New Testament figures regarded and employed details of the Scripture as authoritative. This argues for a view of the Bible as completely inspired by God, even to the selection of details within the text. If this is the case, certain implications follow. If God is omniscient, he must know all things. He cannot be ignorant of or in error on any matter. Further, if he is omnipotent, he is able to so affect the biblical author's writing that nothing erroneous enters into the final product. And being a truthful or veracious being, he will certainly desire to utilize these abilities in such a way that humans will not be misled by the Scriptures. Thus, our view of inspiration logically entails the inerrancy of the Bible. Inerrancy is a corollary of the doctrine of full inspiration. If, then, it should be shown that the Bible is not fully truthful, our view of inspiration would also be in jeopardy.

Historical Importance

The church has historically held to the inerrancy of the Bible. While there has not been a fully enunciated theory until modern times, nonetheless there was, down through the years of the history of the church, a general belief in the complete dependability of the Bible. Whether this belief entailed precisely what contemporary inerrantists mean by the term *inerrancy* is not immediately apparent. Whatever the case, we do know that the general idea of inerrancy is not a recent development.

We should note what have tended to be the implications for other areas of doctrine whenever biblical inerrancy has been abandoned. There is evidence that where a theologian, a school, or a movement begins by regarding biblical inerrancy as a peripheral or optional matter and abandons this doctrine, it frequently then goes on to abandon or alter other doctrines which the church has ordinarily considered quite major, such as the deity of Christ or the Trinity. Since history is the laboratory in which theology tests its ideas, we must conclude that the departure from belief in complete trustworthiness of the Bible is a very serious step, not only in terms of what it does to this one doctrine, but even more in terms of what happens to other doctrines as a result.[5]

Epistemological Importance

The epistemological question is simply, How do we know? Since our basis for knowing and holding to the truth of any theological proposition is that the Bible teaches it, it is of utmost importance that the Bible be found truthful in all of its assertions. If we should conclude that certain propositions (historical or scientific) taught by the Bible are not true, the implications for theological propositions are far-reaching. To the extent that evangelicals abandon the position that everything taught or affirmed by Scripture is true, other bases for doctrine will be sought. This might well be either through the resurgence of a philosophy of religion or, what is more likely given the current "relational" orientation, through basing theology upon behavioral sciences, such as psychology of religion. But whatever the form that such an alternative grounding takes, there will probably be a shrinking of the list of tenets, for it is difficult to establish the Trinity or the virgin birth of Christ upon either a philosophical argument or the dynamics of interpersonal relationships.

Inerrancy and Phenomena

Our belief in the inerrancy of the Scriptures is not based on an examination of the nature of all of the Bible, but on the teaching

5. Richard Lovelace, "Inerrancy: Some Historical Perspectives," in *Inerrancy and Common Sense*, ed. Nicole and Michaels, pp. 26–36.

of the biblical authors regarding its inspiration. That teaching tells us only that the Bible is fully truthful. It does not tell us just exactly what the nature of its errorlessness is, or in exactly what way the Bible teaches errorlessly. For that, we must look at the actual phenomena of Scripture.

There are a number of types of problematic passages. For instance, the biblical account contains apparent discrepancies with references in secular history and with the claims of science. There are also contradictions between parallel passages in Scripture, such as in the books of Samuel, Kings, and Chronicles in the Old Testament, and in the Gospels in the New Testament. These contradictions include matters of chronology, numbers, and other details. There are even seeming ethical discrepancies at points. An idea of the various kinds of problems can be gained by comparing Mark 6:8 with Matthew 10:9–10 and Luke 9:3; Acts 7:6 with Exodus 12:40–41; 2 Samuel 10:18 with 1 Chronicles 19:18; 2 Samuel 24:1 with 1 Chronicles 21:1; and James 1:13 with 1 Samuel 18:10.

How are these problems to be dealt with? Several different approaches have been taken. Benjamin B. Warfield, among others, maintained that the doctrinal teaching of biblical inerrancy is in itself such a strong consideration that the phenomena can virtually be ignored.[6] Some theologians, such as Dewey Beegle, contend that the problematic phenomena require us to abandon belief in biblical inerrancy.[7] Yet others, such as Louis Gaussen, attempt to eliminate the troublesome phenomena by harmonizing all the differences;[8] some of their explanations seem to be rather artificial.

None of these approaches is fully satisfactory as a solution. Rather, we would be wisest to follow the way of moderate harmonization.[9] In such an approach, the problems are resolved where available information yields a plausible explanation. With respect to some of the problems, however, we simply lack sufficient information to understand completely. Yet we can continue to hold to inerrancy on the basis of the Bible's own claims, knowing that if we had all the data, the problems would vanish.

Defining Inerrancy

We may now state our understanding of inerrancy: The Bible, when correctly interpreted in light of the level to which culture and the means of communication had developed at the time it was written, and in view of the purposes for which it was given, is fully truthful in all that it affirms. This definition reflects the position of full inerrancy, which, as we pointed out in the opening portion of this chapter, lies between absolute inerrancy and limited inerrancy. It is now necessary to elaborate and expound upon this definition. It is not our intention here to attempt to deal with all of the problems. Rather, we will note some principles and some illustrations which will help us to define inerrancy more specifically and to remove some of the difficulties.

1. Inerrancy pertains to what is affirmed or asserted rather than what is merely reported. The Bible reports false statements made by ungodly persons. The presence of these statements in the Scripture does not mean they are true; it only guarantees that they are correctly reported. The same judgment can be made about certain statements of godly men who were not speaking under the inspiration of the Holy Spirit. Stephen, in his speech in Acts 7, may not have been inspired, although he was filled with the Holy Spirit. Thus, his chronological statement in verse 6 is not necessarily free from error. It appears that even Paul and Peter may on occasion have made incorrect state-

6. Benjamin B. Warfield, "The Real Problem of Inspiration," in *The Inspiration and Authority of the Bible*, ed. Samuel G. Craig (London: Marshall, Morgan and Scott, 1951), pp. 219–20.

7. Dewey Beegle, *Scripture, Tradition, and Infallibility* (Grand Rapids: Eerdmans, 1973), pp. 195–97.

8. Louis Gaussen, *The Inspiration of the Holy Scriptures* (Chicago: Moody, 1949).

9. Everett Harrison, "The Phenomena of Scripture," in *Revelation and the Bible*, ed. Carl Henry (Grand Rapids: Baker, 1959), pp. 237–50.

ments. When, however, something is taken by a biblical writer, from whatever source, and incorporated in his message as an affirmation, not merely a report, then it must be judged as truthful. This does not guarantee the canonicity of the book quoted. Nonbelievers, without special revelation or inspiration, may nonetheless be in possession of the truth. Just because one holds that everything within the Bible is truth, it is not necessary to hold that all truth is within the Bible. Thus, Jude's references to two noncanonical books (vv. 9, 14–15) do not necessarily create a problem, for one is not required thereby to believe either that Jude affirmed error, or that Enoch and the Assumption of Moses are divinely inspired books which ought to be included within the canon of the Old Testament.

The question arises, Does inerrancy have any application to moods other than the indicative? The Bible contains questions, wishes, and commands as well as assertions. These, however, are not ordinarily susceptible to being judged either true or false. Thus inerrancy seems not to apply to them. However, within Scripture there are assertions or affirmations (expressed or implied) that someone asked such a question, expressed such a wish, or uttered such a command. While the statement, "Love your enemies!" cannot be said to be either true or false, the assertion, "Jesus said, 'Love your enemies!'" is susceptible to being judged true or false. And as an assertion of Scripture, it is inerrant.

2. We must judge the truthfulness of Scripture in terms of what the statements meant in the cultural setting in which they were expressed. We should judge the Bible in terms of the forms and standards of its own culture. For example, we should not expect that the standards of exactness in quotation to which our age of the printing press and mass distribution is accustomed would have been present in the first century. We ought also to recognize that numbers were often used symbolically in ancient times, much more so than is true in our culture today. The names parents chose for their children also carried a special meaning; this is rarely true today. The word *son* has basically one meaning in our language and culture. In biblical times, however, it was broader in meaning, almost tantamount to "descendant." There is a wide diversity, then, between our culture and that of biblical times. When we speak of inerrancy, we mean that what the Bible affirms is fully true in terms of the culture of its time.

3. The Bible's assertions are fully true when judged in accordance with the purpose for which they were written. Here the exactness will vary (the specificity of which we wrote earlier) according to the intended use of the material. Suppose a hypothetical case in which the Bible reported a battle in which

> *The Bible's assertions are fully true when judged in accordance with the purpose for which they were written.*

9,476 men were involved. What then would be a correct (or infallible) report? Would 10,000 be accurate? 9,000? 9,500? 9,480? 9,475? Or would only 9,476 be a correct report? The answer is that it depends upon the purpose of the writing. If the report was an official military document which an officer was to submit to his superior, the number must be exact. That would be the only way to ascertain whether there were any deserters. If, on the other hand, the intent of the account was simply to give some idea of the size of the battle, then a round number like 10,000 would be adequate, and in this setting correct. The same is true regarding the molten sea of 2 Chronicles 4:2. If the aim in giving the dimensions was to provide a plan from which an exact duplicate could be constructed, then it is important to know whether it was built with a diameter of 10 cubits or a circumference of 30 cubits. But if the purpose was merely to communicate an idea of the size of the object, then the approximation given by the chronicler is sufficient and may be judged fully true. We often find such approximations in the Bible.

Giving approximations is a common practice in our own culture. Suppose that a person's actual gross income last year was $50,118.82. And suppose that he is asked what his gross income for last year was and he replies, "Fifty thousand dollars." Has he told the truth, or has he not? That depends upon the situation and setting. If the question is asked by a friend in an informal social discussion of the cost of living, he has told the truth. But if the question is asked by an Internal Revenue agent conducting an audit, then he has not told the truth.

That the purpose of writing must be considered when judging whether something is true applies not only to the use of numbers, but also to such matters as the chronological order in historical narratives, which was occasionally modified in the Gospels. In some cases a change in words was necessary in order to communicate the same meaning to different persons. Thus Luke has "Glory in the highest" where Matthew and Mark have "Hosanna in the highest"; the former would make better sense to Luke's Gentile readership than would the latter. Even expansion and compression, which are used by preachers today without their being charged with unfaithfulness to the text, were practiced by biblical writers.

4. Reports of historical events and scientific matters are in phenomenal rather than technical language. That is, the writer reports how things appear to the eye. A commonly noted instance of this practice has to do with the matter of the sun rising. When the weatherman on the evening news says that the sun will rise the next morning at 6:37, he has, from a strictly technical standpoint, made an error, for it has been known since the time of Copernicus that the sun does not move—the earth does. Yet there is no problem with this popular expression. Indeed, even in scientific circles the term *sunrise* has become something of an idiom; though scientists regularly use the term, they do not take it literally. Similarly, biblical reports make no effort to be scientifically exact; they do not attempt to theorize over just what actually occurred when, for example, the walls of Jericho fell, or the Jordan River was stopped, or the axhead floated. The writer simply reported what was seen, how it appeared to the eye.

5. Difficulties in explaining the biblical text should not be prejudged as indications of error. It has already been suggested that we should not attempt to set forth a definite solution to problems too soon. It is better to wait for the remainder of the data to come in, with the confidence that if we had all the data, the problems could be resolved. In some cases, the data may never come in. There is encouragement to be found, however, in the fact that the trend is toward the resolution of difficulties as more data come in. Some of the severe problems of a century ago, such as the unknown Sargon mentioned by Isaiah (20:1), have been satisfactorily explained, and without artificial contortions. And even the puzzle of the death of Judas seems now to have a workable and reasonable solution.

According to Matthew 27:5, Judas committed suicide by hanging himself; Acts 1:18, however, states that "falling headlong he burst open in the middle and all his bowels gushed out." The specific Greek word in Acts that caused the difficulty regarding the death of Judas is *prēnēs*. For a long period of time it was understood to mean only "falling headlong." Twentieth-century investigations of ancient papyri, however, have revealed that this word has another meaning in Koine Greek. It also means "swelling up."[10] It is now possible to hypothesize an end of Judas's life which seems to accommodate all of

10. G. Abbott-Smith, *A Manual Greek Lexicon of the New Testament* (Edinburgh: T. and T. Clark, 1937), p. 377.

the data. Having hanged himself, Judas was not discovered for some time. In such a situation the visceral organs begin to degenerate first, causing a swelling of the abdomen characteristic of cadavers that have not been properly embalmed (and even of those which have been embalmed, if the process is not repeated after several days). And so, "swelling up [Judas] burst open in the middle and his bowels gushed out." While there is no way of knowing whether this is what actually took place, it seems to be a workable and adequate resolution of the difficulty. We must continue to work at resolving all such tensions in our understanding of the Bible.

Ancillary Issues

1. Is inerrancy a good term, or should it be avoided? There are certain problems which attach to it. One is that it tends to carry the implication of extreme specificity, which words like correctness, truthfulness, trustworthiness, dependability, and, to a lesser extent, accuracy do not connote. However, because the term *inerrancy* has become common, it probably is wise to use it. On the other hand, it is not sufficient simply to use the term, since, as we have seen, radically different meanings are attached to it by different persons. The statement of William Hordern is appropriate here as a warning: "To both the fundamentalist and the nonconservative, it often seems that the new conservative is trying to say, 'The Bible is inerrant, but of course this does not mean that it is without error.'"[11] We must carefully explain what we mean when we use the term so there is no misunderstanding.

2. We must also define what we mean by error. If this is not done, the meaning of inerrancy will be lost. If there is an "infinite coefficient of elasticity of language," so that the

word *truth* can simply be stretched a bit more, and a bit more, and a bit more, eventually it comes to include everything, and therefore nothing. We must be prepared, then, to indicate what would be considered an error. Statements in Scripture which plainly contradict the facts (or are contradicted by them) must be considered errors. If Jesus did not die on the cross, if he did not still the storm on the sea, if the walls of Jericho did not fall, if the people of Israel did not leave their bondage in Egypt and depart for the Promised Land, then the Bible is in error.

3. The doctrine of inerrancy applies in the strict sense only to the originals, but in a derivative sense to copies and translations, that is, to the extent that they reflect the originals. This view is often ridiculed as a subterfuge, and it is pointed out that no one has seen the inerrant autographs.[12] Yet, as Carl Henry has pointed out, no one has seen the errant originals either.[13] We must reaffirm that the copies and the translations are also the Word of God, to the degree that they preserve the original message. When we say they are the Word of God, we do not have in mind, of course, the original process of the inspiration of the biblical writer. Rather, they are the Word of God in a derivative sense which attaches to the product. So it was possible for Paul to write to Timothy that all Scripture is inspired, although undoubtedly the Scripture that he was referring to was a copy and probably also a translation (the Septuagint) as well.

In a world in which there are so many erroneous conceptions and so many opinions, the Bible is a sure source of guidance. For when correctly interpreted, it can be fully relied upon in all that it teaches. It is a sure, dependable, and trustworthy authority.

11. William Hordern, *New Directions in Theology Today*, vol. 1, *Introduction* (Philadelphia: Westminster, 1966), p. 83.

12. Beegle, *Scripture, Tradition, and Infallibility*, pp. 156–59.

13. Reported in Harrison, "Phenomena of Scripture," p. 239.

The Power of God's Word: Authority

Religious Authority

By authority we mean the right to command belief and/or action. This is a subject arousing considerable controversy in our society today. External authority is often refused recognition and obedience in favor of accepting one's own judgment as final. There is even a strong antiestablishmentarian mood in the area of religion, where individual judgment is often insisted upon. For example, many Roman Catholics are questioning the traditional view of papal authority as being infallible.

On the subject of religious authority, the crucial question is, Is there some person, institution, or document possessing the right to prescribe belief and action in religious matters? In the ultimate sense, if there is a Supreme Being higher than humans and everything else in the created order, he has the right to determine what we are to believe and how we are to live. This volume proposes that God is the ultimate authority in religious matters. He has the right, both by virtue of who he is and what he does, to establish the standard for belief and practice. With respect to major issues he does not exercise authority in a direct fashion, however. Rather, he has delegated that authority by creating a book, the Bible. Because it conveys his message, the Bible carries the same weight God himself would command if he were speaking to us personally.

The Internal Working of the Holy Spirit

Revelation is God's making his truth known to humankind. Inspiration guarantees that what the Bible says is just what God would say if he were to speak directly. One other element is needed in this chain, however. For the Bible to function as if it is

The second reason the special working of the Holy Spirit is needed is that we require certainty with respect to divine matters. On the subject of (spiritual and eternal) life and death, it is necessary to have more than mere probability. Our need for certainty is in direct proportion to the importance of what is at stake; in matters of eternal consequence, we need a certainty that human reasoning cannot provide. If one is deciding what automobile to purchase, or what kind of paint to apply to his home, listing the advantages of each of the options will usually suffice. (The option with the most advantages frequently proves to be the best.) If, however, the question is whom or what to

As the expression of God's will, the Bible possesses the right to define what we are to believe on religious matters and how we are to conduct ourselves.

God speaking to us, the Bible reader needs to understand the meaning of the Scriptures, and to be convinced of their divine origin and authorship. This is accomplished by an internal working of the Holy Spirit, illumining the understanding of the hearer or reader of the Bible, bringing about comprehension of its meaning, and creating a certainty of its truth and divine origin.

There are a number of reasons why the illumination or witness of the Holy Spirit is needed if we are to understand the meaning of the Bible and be certain of its truth. (Neither the church nor human reason will do.) First, there is the ontological difference between God and humans. God is transcendent; he goes beyond our categories of understanding. He can never be fully grasped within our finite concepts or by our human vocabulary. He can be understood, but not comprehensively. These limitations are inherent in human beings. They are not a result of the fall or of individual human sin, but of the Creator-creature relationship.

believe with respect to one's eternal destiny, the need to be certain is far greater.

A third reason for the internal working of the Holy Spirit is the limitations which result from the sinfulness of the human race. In Matthew 13:13–15 and Mark 8:18 Jesus speaks of those who hear but never understand and see but never perceive. Their condition is depicted in vivid images throughout the New Testament. Their hearts have grown dull, their ears are heavy of hearing, and their eyes they have closed (Matt. 13:15). They know God but do not honor him as God, and so they have become futile in their thinking and their senseless minds are darkened (Rom. 1:21). Romans 11:8 attributes their condition to God, who "gave them a spirit of stupor, eyes that should not see and ears that should not hear." Consequently, "their eyes are darkened" (v. 10). All of these references, as well as numerous other allusions, argue for the need of some special work of the Spirit to enhance human perception and understanding.

In 1 Corinthians 2:14 Paul tells us that the unregenerate person (one who neither perceives nor understands) has not received the gifts of the Spirit of God. In the original we find the word *dechomai*, which signifies not merely to "receive" something, but rather to "accept" something, to welcome it, whether a gift or an idea.[1] The unregenerate do not accept the gifts of the Spirit because they find the wisdom of God foolish, and are unable to understand it because it must be spiritually discerned or investigated. The problem, then, is not merely that unbelievers are unwilling to accept the gifts and wisdom of God, but that, without the help of the Holy Spirit, the unregenerate are unable to understand them.

In the context of 1 Corinthians 2:14 there is corroborating evidence that we cannot understand without the Spirit's aid. Verse 11 says that only the Spirit of God comprehends the things of God. Paul also indicates in 1:20–21 that the world cannot know God through its wisdom, for God has made foolish the wisdom of this world. Indeed, the wisdom of the world is folly to God (3:19). The gifts of the Spirit are imparted in words taught not by human wisdom but by the Spirit (2:13). From all of these considerations it appears that Paul is not saying that unspiritual persons understand but do not accept. Rather, they do not accept, at least in part, because they do not understand.

But this condition is overcome when the Holy Spirit begins to work within us. Paul speaks of having the eyes of the heart enlightened—the verb form used here suggests that something has been done and remains in effect (Eph. 1:18). In 2 Corinthians 3 he speaks of the removal of the veil placed upon the mind (v. 16) so that one may behold the glory of the Lord (v. 18). The New Testament refers to this enlightenment in various other ways: circumcision of the heart (Rom. 2:29), being filled with spiritual wisdom and understanding (Col. 1:9), the

gift of understanding to know Jesus Christ (1 John 5:20), hearing the voice of the Son of God (John 10:3). What previously had seemed to be foolish (1 Cor. 1:18; 2:14) and a stumbling block (1 Cor. 1:23) now appears to the believer as the power of God (1 Cor. 1:18), as secret and hidden wisdom of God (1:24; 2:7), and as the mind of Christ (2:16).

What we have been describing here is a one-time work of the Spirit—regeneration. It introduces a categorical difference between the believer and the unbeliever. There is also, however, a continuing work of the Holy Spirit in the life of the believer, a work particularly described and elaborated by Jesus in his message to his followers in John 14–16:

1. The Holy Spirit will teach believers all things and bring to their remembrance all that Jesus had taught them (14:26).
2. The Holy Spirit will witness to Jesus. The disciples will also be witnesses to Jesus, because they have been with him from the beginning (15:26–27).
3. The Holy Spirit will convict (*elenchō*) the world of sin, righteousness, and judgment (16:8). This particular word implies rebuking in such a way as to bring about conviction, as contrasted with *epitimaō*, which may suggest simply an undeserved (Matt. 16:22) or ineffectual (Luke 23:40) rebuke.[2]
4. The Holy Spirit will guide believers into all the truth. He will not speak on his own authority, but will speak whatever he hears (John 16:13). In the process, he will also glorify Jesus (16:14).

Note in particular the designation of the Holy Spirit as the Spirit of truth (14:17). John's account of what Jesus said does not refer to the Holy Spirit as the true Spirit, but the Spirit of truth. This may represent nothing more than the literal translation of an Aramaic expression into Greek, but more

---

1. William F. Arndt and F. Wilbur Gingrich, eds., *A Greek-English Lexicon of the New Testament*, 4th ed. (Chicago: University of Chicago Press, 1957), p. 176.

2. Richard Trench, *Synonyms of the New Testament* (Grand Rapids: Eerdmans, 1953), pp. 13–15.

likely signifies that the very nature of the Spirit is truth. He is the one who communicates truth. The world is not able to receive (*lambanō*, simple reception, as opposed to *dechomai*, acceptance) him, because it neither sees him nor knows him. Believers, on the other hand, know him, because he abides with them and will be in them.

Let us summarize the role of the Spirit as depicted in John 14–16. He guides into truth, calling to remembrance the words of Jesus, not speaking on his own, but speaking what he hears, bringing about conviction, witnessing to Christ. This work seems to be not so much a new ministry, or the addition of new truth not previously made known, but rather an action of the Holy Spirit in relationship to truth already revealed. Thus the Holy Spirit's ministry involves elucidating the truth, bringing belief and persuasion and conviction, but not new revelation.

Objective and Subjective Components of Authority

There is, then, as illustrated in Figure 2, what Bernard Ramm has called a *pattern* of authority.[3] The objective Word, the written, inspired Scripture, together with the subjective word, the inner illumination and conviction of the Holy Spirit, constitutes the authority for the Christian.

Figure 2. The Pattern of Authority

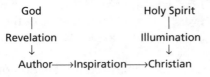

Scholastic orthodoxy of the seventeenth century virtually maintained that the authority is the Bible alone. In some cases this also has been the position of American fundamentalism of the twentieth century.

3. Bernard Ramm, *The Pattern of Religious Authority* (Grand Rapids: Eerdmans, 1968).

Those who hold this position see an objective quality in the Bible that automatically brings one into contact with God. Reading the Bible daily is thought to confer a value, in and of itself. The old adage, "an apple a day keeps the doctor away," has a theological parallel: "a chapter a day keeps the devil away." A potential danger here is that the Bible may become almost a fetish.[4]

On the other hand, there are some groups which regard the Holy Spirit as the chief authority for the Christian. Certain charismatic groups, for example, believe that special prophecy is occurring today. New messages from God are being given by the Holy Spirit. In most cases these messages are regarded as explaining the true meaning of certain biblical passages. Thus, the contention is that while the Bible is authoritative, in practice its meaning would often not be found without special action by the Holy Spirit.[5]

Actually, it is the combination of these two factors that constitutes authority. Both are needed. The written Word, correctly interpreted, is the objective basis of authority. The inward illuminating and persuading work of the Holy Spirit is the subjective dimension. Together, the two yield a maturity that is necessary in the Christian life—a cool head and warm heart (not a cold heart and hot head). As one pastor put it in a rather crude fashion: "If you have the Bible without the Spirit, you will dry up. If you have the Spirit without the Bible, you will blow up. But if you have both the Bible and the Spirit together, you will grow up."

4. A. C. McGiffert, *Protestant Thought Before Kant* (New York: Harper, 1961), p. 146.
5. In one church a decision was to be made on two proposed plans for a new sanctuary. One member insisted that the Lord had told him that the church should adopt the plan calling for the larger sanctuary. His basis was that the ratio between the number of seats in the larger plan and the number in the smaller plan was five to three, exactly the ratio between the number of times that Elisha told Joash he should have struck the ground and the number of times he actually struck it (2 Kings 13:18–19). The church eventually separated over disagreement on this and similar issues.

The Bible and Reason

At this point arises a question concerning the relationship between biblical authority and reason. Is there not the possibility of some conflict here? Ostensibly the authority is the Bible, but various means of interpretation are brought to bear upon the Bible to elicit its meaning. If reason is the means of interpretation, is not reason, rather than the Bible, the real authority, since it in effect comes to the Bible from a position of superiority?

Here a distinction must be drawn between legislative authority and judicial authority. In the federal government, the houses of Congress produce legislation, but the judiciary (ultimately the Supreme Court) decides what the legislation means. They are separate branches of government, each with its own appropriate authority.

This seems to be a good way to think of the relationship between Scripture and reason. Scripture is our supreme legislative authority. It gives us the content of our belief and of our code of behavior and practice. Reason does not tell us the content of our belief. It does not discover truth. When we come to determine what the Scripture means, however, and, at a later stage, assess whether it is true, we must utilize the power of reasoning. We must employ the best methods of interpretation or hermeneutics. And then we must decide whether the Christian belief system is true by rationally examining and evaluating the evidences. This we term apologetics. While there is a dimension of the self-explanatory within Scripture, Scripture alone will not give us the meaning of Scripture. There is therefore no inconsistency in regarding Scripture as our supreme authority in the sense that it tells us what to do and believe, and employing various hermeneutical and exegetical methods to determine its meaning.

Historical and Normative Authoritativeness

One other distinction needs to be drawn and elaborated. It concerns the way in which the Bible is authoritative for us. The Bible is certainly authoritative in telling us what God's will was for certain individuals and groups within the biblical period. The question being considered here is, Is what was binding upon those people also binding upon us?

It is necessary to distinguish between two types of authority: historical and normative. The Bible informs us as to what God commanded of the people in the biblical situation and what he expects of us. Insofar as the Bible teaches us what occurred and what the people were commanded in biblical times, it is historically authoritative. But is it also normatively authoritative? Are we bound to carry out the same actions as were expected of those people? Here one must be careful not to identify too quickly God's will for those people with his will for us. It will be necessary to determine what is the permanent essence of the message, and what is the temporary form of its expression. It is quite possible for something to be historically authoritative without being normatively authoritative.

> *The objective Word, the written, inspired Scripture, together with the subjective word, the inner illumination and conviction of the Holy Spirit, constitutes the authority for the Christian.*

The Nature of God

The Doctrine of God

The doctrine of God is the central point for much of the rest of theology. One's view of God might even be thought of as supplying the whole framework within which one's theology is constructed and life is lived. It lends a particular coloration to one's style of ministry and philosophy of life.

Problems or difficulties on two levels make it evident that there is a need for a correct understanding of God. First is the popular or practical level. In his book *Your God Is Too Small*, J. B. Phillips has pointed out some common distorted understandings of God.[1] Some people think of God as a kind of celestial police officer who looks for opportunities to pounce upon erring and straying persons. A popular country song enunciates this view: "God's gonna get you for that; God's gonna get you for that. Ain't no use to run and hide, 'cuz he knows where you're at!" Insurance companies, with their references to "acts of God"—always catastrophic occurrences—seem to have a powerful, malevolent being in mind. The opposite view, that God is grandfatherly, is also prevalent. Here God is conceived of as an

1. J. B. Phillips, *Your God Is Too Small* (New York: Macmillan, 1961).

indulgent, kindly old gentleman who would never want to detract from humans' enjoyment of life. These and many other false conceptions of God need to be corrected if our spiritual lives are to have any real meaning and depth.

Problems on a more sophisticated level also point out the need for a correct view of God. The biblical understanding of God has often been problematic. In the early church, the doctrine of the Trinity created special tension and debate. While that particular topic has not totally ceased to present difficulty, other issues have become prominent in our day. One of these concerns God's relationship to the creation. Is he so separate and removed from the creation (transcendent) that he does not work through it, and hence nothing can be known of him from it? Or is he to be found within human society and the processes of nature (immanent)? These and other issues call for clear thinking and careful enunciation of the understanding of God.

Many errors have been made in attempts to understand God, some of them opposite in nature. One is an excessive analysis, in which God is submitted to a virtual autopsy. The attributes of God are laid out and classified in a fashion similar to the approach taken in an anatomy textbook.[2] It is also possible to make the study of God an excessively speculative matter; and in that case the speculative conclusion itself, instead of a closer relationship with him, becomes the end. This should not be so. Rather, the study of God's nature should be seen as a means to a more accurate understanding of him and hence a closer personal relationship with him.

The Immanence and Transcendence of God

An important pair of emphases which we must make certain we preserve is the doc-

trines of God's immanence within his creation and his transcendence of it. Both truths are taught in Scripture. Jeremiah 23:24, for example, stresses God's presence everywhere within the universe, "'Can anyone hide in secret places so that I cannot see him?' declares the LORD. 'Do not I fill heaven and earth?' declares the LORD" (NIV). In this very context, however, both immanence and transcendence appear together: "'Am I only a God nearby,' declares the LORD, 'and not a God far away?'" (v. 23). Paul told the philosophers on Mars' Hill in Athens, "He is not far from each one of us. 'For in him we live and move and have our being.' As some of your own poets have said, 'We are his offspring'" (Acts 17:27b–28, NIV).

On the other hand, in Isaiah 55:8–9 we read that God's thoughts and ways transcend ours: "For my thoughts are not your thoughts, neither are your ways my ways, says the LORD. For as the heavens are higher than the earth, so are my ways higher than your ways and my thoughts than your thoughts." In Isaiah 6:1–5 God is depicted as seated on a throne, high and exalted, and seraphs call, "Holy, holy, holy is the LORD of hosts." Isaiah is very conscious of his own uncleanness and unworthiness. Yet here there is also witness to God's immanence, for the seraphs sing, "The whole earth is full of his glory" (v. 3).

The meaning of immanence is that God is present and active within his creation, and within the human race, even those members of it that do not believe in or obey him. His influence is everywhere. He is at work in and through natural processes. The meaning of transcendence is that God is not merely a quality of nature or of humanity; he is not simply the highest human being. He is not limited to our ability to understand him. His holiness and goodness go far beyond, infinitely beyond ours, and this is true of his knowledge and power as well.

It is important to keep these two doctrines together, but it is not always easy to do so, for there are problems in knowing how to view them. The traditional way of

2. E.g., Stephen Charnock, *Discourses upon the Existence and Attributes of God* (Grand Rapids: Baker, 1979 reprint).

thinking about God's transcendence has been spatial in nature: God is in heaven, high above the world. This is the picture found in the Bible, but we now realize that "up" and "down" do not really apply to a spirit, who is not located at some specific place within the universe. Further, with our understanding of the earth as a sphere, "up" and "down" are not meaningful terms. Are there other images which can be used to convey accurately the truth of God's transcendence and immanence?

I find helpful the concept of different levels or realms of reality. For example, several realities can coexist within the same space

45:1). He uses technology and human skill and learning. Yet it is important to bear in mind the truth that God is transcendent. He is infinitely more than any natural or human event. If we emphasize immanence too much, we may identify everything that happens as God's will and working, as did the German Christians who in the 1930s regarded Adolf Hitler's policies as God's working in the world. We must bear in mind that there is a separation between God's holiness and much of what happens in the world. If we emphasize transcendence too much, however, we may expect God to work miracles at all times, while he may purpose in-

God's holiness and goodness go far beyond, infinitely beyond ours, and this is true of his knowledge and power as well.

and yet be independent in such a way that they cannot be accessed from one another. Indeed, several different instances of the same general type of reality can nonetheless be separated from one another in certain ways. We are told by physicists that more than one universe might occupy the same space. An illustration here is the phenomenon of sound. There are many different sounds present (immanent) which we do not hear. The reason is that they occur at a frequency which the unaided human ear cannot pick up. If, however, we have a radio receiver, those sounds become audible. In a similar fashion, many visual images are present but unseen unless we have a television receiver. God is present and active within his creation, yet he is also transcendent to it, for he is a totally different type of being. He is divine.

We have noted the importance of maintaining both emphases. Immanence signifies that God does much of his work through natural means. He is not restricted to miracles. He even uses ordinary unbelieving humans such as Cyrus, whom he described as his "shepherd," his "anointed" (Isa. 44:28;

stead to work through our effort. We may tend to mistreat the creation, forgetting that he himself is present and active there. We may depreciate the value of what non-Christians do, or their possession of some degree of sensitivity to the message of the gospel, forgetting that God is at work in and in touch with them.

Implications of Immanence

Divine immanence of the limited degree taught in Scripture carries several implications:

1. God is not limited to working directly to accomplish his purposes. While it is very obviously a work of God when his people pray and a miraculous healing occurs, it is also God's work when through the application of medical knowledge and skill a physician is successful in bringing a patient back to health. Medicine is part of God's general revelation, and the work of the doctor is a channel of God's activity.

2. God may use persons and organizations that are not avowedly Christian. In biblical times, God did not limit himself to working through the covenant nation of Is-

rael or through the church. He even used Assyria, a pagan nation, to bring chastening upon Israel. He is able to use secular or nominally Christian organizations. Even non-Christians do some genuinely good and commendable things.

3. We should have an appreciation for all that God has created. The world is God's, and he is present and active within it. While it has been given to humankind to be used to satisfy their legitimate needs, they ought not to exploit it for their own pleasure or out of greed. The doctrine of divine immanence therefore has ecological application. It also has implications regarding our attitudes to other people. God is genuinely present within everyone (although not in the special sense in which he indwells Christians). Therefore, no one is to be despised or treated disrespectfully.

4. We can learn something about God from his creation. All that is has been brought into being by God and, further, is actively indwelt by him. We may therefore detect clues about what God is like by observing the behavior of the created universe. For example, a definite pattern of logic seems to apply within the creation. There is an orderliness, a regularity, about it. Those who believe that God is sporadic, arbitrary, or whimsical by nature and that his actions are characterized by paradox and even contradiction either have not taken a close look at the behavior of the world or have assumed that God is in no sense operating there.

5. God's immanence means that there are points at which the gospel can make contact with the unbeliever. If God is to some extent present and active within the whole of the created world, he is present and active within humans who have not made a personal commitment of their lives to him. Thus, there are points at which they will be sensitive to the truth of the gospel message, places where they are already in touch with God's working. Evangelism aims to find those points and direct the message to them.

Implications of Transcendence

The doctrine of transcendence has several implications which will affect our other beliefs and our practices.

1. There is something higher than human beings. Good, truth, and value are not determined by the shifting flux of this world and human opinion. There is something which gives value to humankind from above.

2. God can never be completely captured in human concepts. This means that all of our doctrinal ideas, helpful and basically correct though they may be, cannot fully exhaust God's nature. He is not limited to our understanding of him.

3. Our salvation is not our achievement. We are not able to raise ourselves to God's level by fulfilling his standards for us. Even if we were able to do so, it still would not be our accomplishment. The very fact that we know what he expects of us is a matter of his self-revelation, not our discovery. Even apart from the additional problem of sin, then, fellowship with God would be strictly a matter of his gift to us.

4. There will always be a difference between God and human beings. The gap between us is not merely a moral and spiritual disparity which originated with the fall. It is metaphysical, stemming from creation. Even when redeemed and glorified, we will still be his human creatures. We will never become God.

5. Reverence is appropriate in our relationship with God. Some worship, rightfully stressing the joy and confidence that the believer has in relationship to a loving heavenly Father, goes beyond that point to an excessive familiarity treating him as an equal, or worse yet, as a servant. If we have grasped the fact of the divine transcendence, however, this will not happen. While there are room and need for enthusiasm of expression, and perhaps even an exuberance, that should never lead to a loss of respect. Our prayers will also be characterized by reverence. Rather than making demands, we will pray as Jesus did, "Not my will, but thine, be done."

6. We will look for genuinely transcendent working by God. Thus we will not expect that only those things which can be accomplished by natural means will come to pass. While we will use every available technique of modern learning to accomplish God's ends, we will never cease to be dependent upon his working. We will not neglect prayer for his guidance or for his special intervention.

As with the matter of God's immanence, so also with transcendence we must guard against the dangers of excessive emphasis. We will not look for God merely in the religious or devotional; we will also look for him in the "secular" aspects of life. We will not look for miracles exclusively, but we will not disregard them either. Some of the divine attributes, such as holiness, eternity, omnipotence, are expressive of the transcendent character of God. Others, such as omnipresence, are expressive of the immanent. If all these aspects of God's nature are given the emphasis and attention that the Bible assigns to them, a fully rounded understanding of God will be the result. While God is never fully within our grasp since he goes far beyond our ideas and forms, yet he is always available to us when we turn to him.

The Nature of Attributes

If we are to understand the relationship of God to the creation, it is important to understand his nature. When we speak of the attributes of God, we are referring to those qualities of God which constitute what he is. They are the very characteristics of his nature. Note that we are not referring here to the acts which he performs, such as creating, guiding, and preserving, nor to the corresponding roles he plays—Creator, Guide, Preserver.

The attributes are qualities of the entire Godhead. They should not be confused with properties, which, technically speaking, are the distinctive characteristics of the various persons of the Trinity. Properties are functions (general), activities (more specific), or acts (most specific) of the individual members of the Godhead.

The attributes are permanent qualities. They cannot be gained or lost. They are intrinsic. Thus, holiness is not an attribute (a permanent, inseparable characteristic) of Adam, but it is of God. God's attributes are essential and inherent dimensions of his very nature. While our understanding of God is undoubtedly filtered through our own mental framework, his attributes are not our conceptions projected upon him. They are objective characteristics of his nature.

The attributes are inseparable from the being or essence of God. Some earlier theologies thought of the attributes as somehow adhering to or being at least in some way distinguishable from the underlying substance or being or essence.[3] In many cases, this idea was based upon the Aristotelian conception of substance and attribute. Some other theologies have gone to the opposite extreme, virtually denying that God has an essence. Here the attributes are pictured as a sort of collection of qualities. They are thought of as fragmentary parts or segments of God.[4] It is better to conceive of the attributes of God as his nature, not as a collection of fragmentary parts nor as something in addition to his essence. Thus, God is his love, holiness, and power. These are but different ways of viewing the unified being, God. God is richly complex, and these conceptions are merely attempts to grasp different objective aspects or facets of his being.

When we speak of the incomprehensibility of God, then, we do not mean that there is an unknown being or essence beyond or behind his attributes. Rather, we mean that we do not know his qualities or his nature completely and exhaustively. We know God only as he has revealed himself. While his self-revelation is doubtless consistent with

3. William G. T. Shedd, *Dogmatic Theology* (Grand Rapids: Zondervan, 1971 reprint), vol. 1, p. 158.
4. Charnock, *Existence and Attributes of God.*

his full nature and accurate, it is not an exhaustive revelation. Further, we do not totally understand or know comprehensively that which he has revealed to us of himself. Thus there is, and always will be, an element of mystery regarding God.

Classifications of Attributes

In attempts to better understand God, various systems of classifying his attributes have been devised. With some modifications, the classification adopted for this study is that of natural and moral attributes. The moral attributes are those which in the human context would relate to the concept of rightness (as opposed to wrongness). Holiness, love, mercy, and faithfulness are examples. Natural attributes are the nonmoral superlatives of God, such as his knowledge and power.[5] Instead of natural and moral, however, we will speak of attributes of *greatness* and attributes of *goodness*. We turn first, in the following chapter, to the qualities of greatness, which include spirituality, life, personality, infinity, and constancy.

5. Edgar Y. Mullins, *The Christian Religion in Its Doctrinal Expression* (Philadelphia: Judson, 1927), p. 222.

The Greatness of God

Spirituality

Among the most basic of God's attributes of greatness is the fact that he is spirit; that is, he is not composed of matter and does not possess a physical nature. This is most clearly stated by Jesus in John 4:24, "God is spirit, and those who worship him must worship in spirit and truth." It is also implied in various references to his invisibility (John 1:18; 1 Tim. 1:17; 6:15–16).

One consequence of God's spirituality is that he does not have the limitations involved with a physical body. For one thing, he is not limited to a particular geographical or spatial location. This is implicit in Jesus' statement, "The hour is coming when neither on this mountain nor in Jerusalem will you worship the Father" (John 4:21). Consider also Paul's statement in Acts 17:24: "The God who made the world and everything in it, being Lord of heaven and earth, does not live in shrines made by man." Furthermore, he is not destructible, as is material nature.

There are, of course, numerous passages which suggest that God has physical features such as hands or feet. How are we to regard these references? It seems most helpful to treat them as anthropomorphisms, attempts to express the truth about God through human analogies. There also are cases where God appeared in physical form, particularly in the Old Testament. These should be understood as theophanies, or temporary manifestations of God. It seems best to take the clear statements about the spirituality and invisibility of God at face value and interpret the anthropomorphisms and theophanies in the light of them. Indeed, Jesus himself clearly indicated that a spirit does not have flesh and bones (Luke 24:39).

In biblical times, the doctrine of God's spirituality was a counter to the practice of idolatry and of nature worship. God, being spirit, could not be represented by any physical object or likeness. That he is not restricted by geographical location also countered the idea that God could be contained and controlled. In our day, the Mormons maintain that not only God the Son, but also the Father has a physical body, although the Holy Spirit does not. Indeed, Mormonism contends that an immaterial body cannot exist.[1] This is clearly contradicted by the Bible's teaching on the spirituality of God.

Life

Another attribute of greatness is the fact that God is alive. He is characterized by life. This is affirmed in Scripture in several different ways. It is found in the assertion that he *is*. His very name "I AM" (Exod. 3:14) indicates that he is a living God. It is also significant that Scripture does not argue for his existence. It simply affirms it or, more often, merely assumes it. Hebrews 11:6 says that everyone who "would draw near to him must believe that he exists and that he re-

wards those who seek him." Thus, existence is considered a most basic aspect of his nature.

This characteristic of God is prominent in the contrast frequently drawn between him and other gods. He is depicted as the living God, as contrasted with inanimate objects of metal or stone. Jeremiah 10:10 refers to him as the true God, the living God, who controls nature. "The gods who did not make the heavens and the earth," on the other hand, "shall perish from the earth and from under the heavens" (v. 11). First Thessalonians 1:9 draws a similar contrast between the idols from which the Thessalonians had turned and the "living and true God."

Not only does this God have life, but he has a kind of life different from that of every other living being. While all other beings have their life in God, he does not derive his life from any external source. He is never depicted as having been brought into being. John 5:26 says that he has life in himself. The adjective *eternal* is applied to him frequently, implying that there never was a time when he did not exist. Further, we are told that "in the beginning," before anything else came to be, God was already in existence (Gen. 1:1). Thus, he could not have derived his existence from anything else.

Moreover, the continuation of God's existence does not depend upon anything outside of himself. All other beings, insofar as they are alive, need something—nourishment, warmth, protection—to sustain that life. With God, however, there is no indication of such a need. On the contrary, Paul denies that God needs anything or is served by human hands (Acts 17:25).

While God is independent in the sense of not needing anything else for his existence, this is not to say that he is aloof, indifferent, or unconcerned. God relates to us, but it is by his choice that he thus relates, not because he is compelled by some need. He has acted and continues to act out of *agapē*, unselfish love, rather than out of need.

---

1. James E. Talmage, *A Study of the Articles of Faith*, 36th ed. (Salt Lake City: Church of Jesus Christ of Latter-day Saints, 1957), p. 48.

Sometimes the life of God is described as self-caused. It is preferable to refer to him as the uncaused one. His very nature is to exist. It is not necessary for him to will his own existence. For God not to exist would be logically contradictory.

A proper understanding of this aspect of God's nature should free us from the idea that God needs us. God has chosen to use us to accomplish his purposes, and in that sense he now needs us. He could, however, if he so chose, have bypassed us. It is to our gain that he permits us to know and serve him, and it is our loss if we reject that opportunity.

Personality

In addition to being spiritual and alive, God is personal. He is an individual being, with self-consciousness and will, capable of feeling, choosing, and having a reciprocal relationship with other personal and social beings.

That God has personality is indicated in several ways in Scripture. One is the fact that God has a name. He has a name which he assigns to himself and by which he reveals himself. In biblical times names were not mere labels to distinguish one person from another. In our impersonal society, this may seem to be the case. Names are seldom chosen for their meaning; rather, parents choose a name because they happen to like it, or it is currently popular. The Hebrew approach was quite different, however. A name was chosen very carefully, and with attention to its significance.[2] When Moses wonders how he should respond when the Israelites will ask the name of the God who has sent him, God identifies himself as "I AM" or "I WILL BE" (Yahweh, Jehovah, the Lord—Exod. 3:14). By this he demonstrates that he is not an abstract, unknowable being, or a nameless force. Nor is this name used merely to refer to God or to describe

2. Walther Eichrodt, *Theology of the Old Testament* (Philadelphia: Westminster, 1967), vol. 2, pp. 40–45.

him. It is also used to address him. Genesis 4:26 indicates that humans began to call upon the name of the Lord. Psalm 20 speaks of boasting in the name of the Lord (v. 7) and calling upon him (v. 9). The name is to be spoken and treated respectfully, according to Exodus 20:7. The great respect accorded to the name is indicative of the personality of God.

A further indication of the personal nature of God is the activity in which he engages. He is depicted in the Bible as knowing and communing with human persons. In the earliest picture of his relationship with them (Gen. 3), God comes to and talks with Adam and Eve; the impression is given that this had been a regular practice. Although this representation of God is undoubtedly anthropomorphic, it nonetheless teaches that he is a person who related to persons as such. He is depicted as having all of the capacities associated with personality: he knows, he feels, he wills, he acts.

There are a number of resulting implications. Because God is a person, the relationship we have with him has a dimension of warmth and understanding. God is not a machine or a computer that automatically supplies the needs of people. He is a knowing, loving, good Father.

Further, our relationship with God is not merely a one-way street. God is, to be sure, an object of respect and reverence. But he does not simply receive and accept what we offer. He is a living, reciprocating being. He is not merely one of whom we hear, but one whom we meet and know. Accordingly, God is to be treated as a being, not an object or force. He is not something to be used or manipulated.

God is an end in himself, not a means to an end. He is of value to us for what he is in himself, not merely for what he *does*. The rationale for the first commandment, "You shall have no other gods before me" (Exod. 20:3), is given in the preceding verse: "I am the LORD your God, who brought you out of the land of Egypt." We misread the passage if we interpret it as meaning that the Israelites were to put God first because of what he had done—that out of gratitude they were to make him their only God. Rather, what he had done was the proof of what he is; it is because of what he is that he is to be loved and served, not only supremely but exclusively. God as a person is to be loved for what he is, not for what he can do for us.

Infinity

God is infinite. This means not only that God is unlimited, but that he is unlimitable. In this respect, God is unlike anything we experience. Even those things that common sense once told us are infinite or boundless are now seen to have limits. Energy at an earlier time seemed inexhaustible. We have in recent years become aware that the types of energy with which we are particularly familiar have rather sharp limitations, and we are approaching those limits considerably more rapidly than we imagined. The infinity of God, however, speaks of a limitless being.

Space

The infinity of God may be thought of from several angles. We think first in terms of space. Here we have what has traditionally been referred to as immensity and omnipresence. God is not subject to limitations of space. By this we do not mean merely the limitation of being in a particular place—if an object is in one place it cannot be in another. Rather, it is improper to think of God as present in space at all. All finite objects have a location. They are somewhere. This necessarily prevents their being somewhere else. With God, however, the question of whereness or location is not applicable. God is the one who brought space (and time) into being. He was before there was space. He cannot be localized at a particular point. Consider here Paul's statement that God does not dwell in manmade shrines, because he is the Lord of heaven and earth; he made the world and everything in it (Acts 17:24–25).

Another aspect of God's infinity in terms of space is that there is no place where he cannot be found. We are here facing the tension between the immanence of God (he is everywhere) and the transcendence (he is not any*where*). The point here is that nowhere within the creation is God inaccessible. Jeremiah quotes God as saying, "Am I a God at hand, . . . and not a God afar off?" (Jer. 23:23). The implication seems to be that being a God at hand does not preclude his being afar off as well. He fills the whole heaven and earth (v. 24). Thus, we cannot

God is unlimited and unlimitable in terms of space, time, knowledge, and power.

hide "in secret places" so that we cannot be seen. The psalmist found that he could not flee from the presence of God—wherever the psalmist went, God would be there (Ps. 139:7–12). Jesus himself carried this concept a step further. In giving the Great Commission, he commanded his disciples to go as witnesses everywhere, even to the end of the earth, and he would be with them to the end of the age (Matt. 28:19–20; Acts 1:8). Thus, he in effect indicated that he is not limited either by space or by time.

Time

That God is not limited by time means that time does not apply to him. He was before time began. The question, How old is God? is simply inappropriate. He is no older now than a year ago, for infinity plus one is no more than infinity.

God is the one who always is. He was, he is, he will be. Psalm 90:1–2 says, "LORD, thou hast been our dwelling place in all generations. Before the mountains were brought forth, or ever thou hadst formed the earth and the world, from everlasting to everlasting thou art God." Jude 25 says, "To the only God, our Savior through Jesus Christ our Lord, be glory, majesty, dominion, and authority, before all time and now and for ever." A similar thought is found in Ephesians 3:21. The use of expressions such as "the first and the last" and the "Alpha and Omega" serve to convey the same idea (Isa. 44:6; Rev. 1:8; 21:6; 22:13).

The fact that God is not bound by time does not mean that he is not conscious of the succession of points of time. He is aware that events occur in a particular order. Yet he is equally aware of all points of that order simultaneously. This transcendence over time has been likened to a person who sits on a steeple while he watches a parade. He sees all parts of the parade at the different points on the route rather than only what is going past him at the moment. He is aware of what is passing each point of the route. So God also is aware of what is happening, has happened, and will happen at each point in time. Yet at any given point within time he is also conscious of the distinction between what is now occurring, what has been, and what will be.[3]

Knowledge

The infinity of God may also be considered with respect to objects of knowledge. His understanding is immeasurable (Ps. 147:5). Jesus said that not a sparrow can fall to the ground without the Father's will (Matt. 10:29), and that even the hairs of the disciples' heads are all numbered (v. 30). We are all completely transparent before God (Heb. 4:13). He sees and knows us totally.

3. See James Barr, *Biblical Words for Time* (Naperville, Ill.: Alec R. Allenson, 1962), especially his criticism of Oscar Cullmann, *Christ and Time: The Primitive Christian Conception of Time and History* (Philadelphia: Westminster, 1950).

And he knows all genuine possibilities, even when they seem limitless in number.

A further factor, in the light of this knowledge, is the wisdom of God. By this is meant that when God acts, he takes all of the facts and correct values into consideration. Knowing all things, God knows what is good. In Romans 11:33 Paul eloquently assesses God's knowledge and wisdom: "O the depth of the riches and wisdom and knowledge of God! How unsearchable are his judgments and how inscrutable his ways!" The psalmist describes God's works as having all been made in wisdom (Ps. 104:24).

God has access to all information. So his judgments are made wisely. He never has to revise his estimation of something because of additional information. He sees all things in their proper perspective; thus he does not give anything a higher or lower value than what it ought to have. One can therefore pray confidently, knowing that God will not grant something that is not good.

Power

Finally, God's infinity may also be considered in relationship to what is traditionally referred to as the omnipotence of God. By this we mean that God is able to do all things which are proper objects of his power. This is taught in Scripture in several ways. There is evidence of God's unlimited power in one of his names, *'el Shaddai*. When God appeared to Abraham to reaffirm his covenant, he identified himself by saying, "I am God Almighty" (Gen. 17:1). We also see God's omnipotence in his overcoming apparently insurmountable problems. The promise in Jeremiah 32:15 that fields will once again be bought and sold in Judah seems incredible in view of the impending fall of Jerusalem to the Babylonians. Jeremiah's faith, however, is strong: "Ah Lord GOD! . . . Nothing is too hard for thee" (v. 17). And after speaking of how hard it is for a rich man to enter the kingdom of God, Jesus responds to his disciples' question as to who can then be saved: "With men this is impossible, but with God all things are possible" (Matt. 19:26).

This power of God is manifested in several different ways. References to the power of God over nature are common, especially in the Psalms, often with an accompanying statement about God's having created the whole universe. God's power is also evident in his control of the course of history. Paul spoke of God's "having determined allotted periods and the boundaries of their habitation" for all peoples (Acts 17:26). Perhaps most amazing in many ways is God's power in human life and personality. The real measure of divine power is not the ability of God to create or to lift a large rock. In many ways, changing human personality, turning sinners to salvation, is far more difficult.

There are, however, certain qualifications of this all-powerful character of God. He cannot arbitrarily do anything whatsoever that we may conceive of. He can do only those things which are proper objects of his power. Thus, he cannot do the logically absurd or contradictory. He cannot make square circles or triangles with four corners. He cannot undo what happened in the past, although he may wipe out its effects or even the memory of it. He cannot act contrary to his nature—he cannot be cruel or unconcerned. He cannot fail to do what he has promised. In reference to God's having made a promise and having confirmed it with an oath, the writer to the Hebrews says: "So that through two unchangeable things, in which it is impossible that God should prove false, we . . . might have strong encouragement" (Heb. 6:18). All of these "inabilities," however, are not weaknesses, but strengths. The inability to do evil or to lie or to fail is a mark of positive strength rather than of failure.

Another aspect of the power of God is that he is free. While God is bound to keep his promises, he was not initially under any compulsion to make those promises. On the contrary, it is common to attribute his decisions and actions to the "good pleasure of his will." God's decisions and actions are not determined by consideration of any factors outside himself. They are simply a matter of his own free choice.

Constancy

In several places in Scripture, God is described as unchanging. In Psalm 102, the psalmist contrasts God's nature with the heavens and the earth: "They will perish, but thou dost endure; . . . they pass away; but thou art the same, and thy years have no end" (vv. 26–27). God himself says that although his people have turned aside from his statutes, "I the LORD do not change" (Mal. 3:6). James says that with God "there is no variation or shadow due to change" (James 1:17).

This divine constancy involves several aspects. There is first no quantitative change. God cannot increase in anything, because he is already perfection. Nor can he decrease, for if he were to, he would cease to be God. There also is no qualitative change. The nature of God does not undergo modification. Therefore, God does not change his mind, plans, or actions, for these rest upon his nature, which remains unchanged no matter what occurs. Indeed, in Numbers 23:19 the argument is that since God is not human, his actions must be unalterable. Further, God's intentions as well as his plans are always consistent, simply because his will does not change. Thus, God is ever faithful to his promises, for example, his covenant with Abraham.

What, then, are we to make of those passages where God seems to change his mind, or to repent over what he has done? These passages can be explained in several ways:

1. Some of them are to be understood as anthropomorphisms and anthropopathisms. They are simply descriptions of God's actions and feelings in human terms, and from a human perspective. Included here are representations of God as experiencing pain or regret.

2. What may seem to be changes of mind may actually be new stages in the working out of God's plan. An example of this is the offering of salvation to the Gentiles. Although a part of God's original plan, it represented a rather sharp break with what had preceded.

3. Some apparent changes of mind are changes of orientation that result when humans move into a different relationship with God. God did not change when Adam sinned; rather, humankind had moved into God's disfavor. This works the other way as well. Take the case of Nineveh. God said, "Forty days and Nineveh will be destroyed, *unless they repent.*" Nineveh repented and was spared. It was humans who had changed, not God's plan.

Some interpretations of the doctrine of divine constancy, expressed as immutability, have actually drawn heavily upon the Greek idea of immobility and sterility. This makes God inactive. But the biblical view is not that God is static but stable. He is active and dynamic, but in a way which is stable and consistent with his nature. What we are dealing with here is the dependability of God. He will be the same tomorrow as he is today. He will act as he has promised. He will fulfil his commitments. The believer can rely upon that (Lam. 3:22–23; 1 John 1:9).

God is a great God. The realization of this fact stirred biblical writers such as the psalmists. And this realization stirs believers today, causing them to join with the songwriter in proclaiming:

O Lord my God! When I in awesome wonder
Consider all the worlds Thy hands have made,
I see the stars, I hear the rolling thunder,
Thy power throughout the universe displayed!
  Then sings my soul, my Savior God, to Thee:
  How great Thou art! How great Thou art!
  Then sings my soul, my Savior God, to Thee:
  How great Thou art! How great Thou art!*

(Stuart K. Hine, 1953)

10 The Goodness of God

Moral Qualities

If the qualities of greatness we described in the preceding chapter were God's only attributes, he might conceivably be an immoral or amoral being, exercising his power and knowledge in a capricious or even cruel fashion. But what we are dealing with is a good God, one who can be trusted and loved. He has attributes of goodness as well as greatness. In this chapter we will consider his moral qualities, that is, the characteristics of God as a moral being. For convenient study, we will classify his basic moral attributes as purity, integrity, and love.

Moral Purity

By moral purity we are referring to God's absolute freedom from anything wicked or evil. His moral purity includes the dimensions of (1) holiness, (2) righteousness, and (3) justice.

1. Holiness

There are two basic aspects to God's holiness. The first is his uniqueness. He is totally separate from all of creation. This is what Louis Berkhof called the "majesty-holiness" of God.[1] The uniqueness of God is affirmed in Exodus 15:11: "Who is like thee, O Lord, among the gods? Who is like thee, majestic in holiness, terrible in glorious deeds, doing wonders?" Isaiah saw the Lord "sitting upon a throne, high and lifted up." The foundations of the thresholds shook, and the house was filled with smoke. The seraphs cried out, "Holy, holy, holy is the Lord of hosts" (Isa. 6:1–4). The Hebrew word for "holy" (*qādōsh*) means "marked off" or "withdrawn from common, ordinary use." The verb from which it is derived suggests "to cut off" or "to separate." Whereas in the religions of the peoples around Israel the adjective *holy* was freely applied to objects, actions, and personnel involved in the worship, in Israel's covenant worship it was very freely used of the Deity himself.

The other aspect of God's holiness is his absolute purity or goodness. This means that he is untouched and unstained by the evil in the world. He does not in any sense participate in it. Note the way in which Habakkuk 1:13 addresses God: "Thou who art of purer eyes than to behold evil and canst not look on wrong." James 1:13 says that God cannot be tempted with evil. In this respect God is totally unlike the gods of other religions. Those gods frequently engaged in the same type of sinful acts as did their followers. Jehovah, however, is free from such acts.

God's perfection is the standard for our moral character and the motivation for religious practice. The whole moral code follows from his holiness. The people of Israel were told, "For I am the Lord your God; consecrate yourselves therefore, and be holy, for I am holy. You shall not defile yourselves with any swarming thing that crawls upon the earth. For I am the Lord who brought you up out of the land of Egypt, to be your God; you shall therefore be holy, for I am holy" (Lev. 11:44–45).

It is a point of repeated emphasis in the Bible that the believer is to be like God. Thus, because God is holy, they who are his followers are also to be holy. God not only is personally free from any moral wickedness or evil. He is unable to tolerate the presence of evil. He is, as it were, allergic to sin and evil. Isaiah, upon seeing God, became very much aware of his own impurity. He despaired, "Woe is me! For I am lost; for I am a man of unclean lips, and I dwell in the midst of a people of unclean lips; for my eyes have seen the King, the Lord of hosts!" (Isa. 6:5). Similarly, Peter, on the occasion of the miraculous catch of fish, realizing who and what Jesus was, said, "Depart from me, for I am a sinful man, O Lord" (Luke 5:8). When one measures one's holiness, not against the standard of oneself or of other humans, but against God, the need for a complete change of moral and spiritual condition becomes apparent.

2. Righteousness

The second dimension of God's moral purity is his righteousness. This is, as it were, the holiness of God applied to his relationships to other beings. The righteousness of God means, first of all, that the law of God, being a true expression of his nature, is as perfect as he is. Psalm 19:7–9 puts it this way: "The law of the Lord is perfect, reviving the soul; the testimony of the Lord is sure, making wise the simple; the precepts of the Lord are right, rejoicing the heart; the commandment of the Lord is pure, enlightening the eyes; the fear of the Lord is clean, enduring for ever; the ordinances of the Lord are true, and righteous altogether." In other

---

1. Louis Berkhof, *Systematic Theology* (Grand Rapids: Eerdmans, 1953), p. 73.

words, God commands only what is right, and what will therefore have a positive effect upon the believer who obeys.

The righteousness of God also means that his actions are in accord with the law which he himself has established. Thus, God in his actions is described as doing right. For example, Abraham says to Jehovah, "Far be it from thee to do such a thing, to slay the righteous with the wicked, so that the righteous fare as the wicked! Far be that from thee! Shall not the Judge of all the earth do right?"

dard of right and wrong, a standard which is part of the very structure of reality. But that standard to which God adheres is not external to God—it is his own nature. He decides in accordance with reality, and that reality is himself.

3. Justice

We have noted that God himself acts in conformity with his law. He also administers his kingdom in accordance with his law. That is, he requires that others conform to it. The righteousness described in the pre-

---

Because God has attributes of goodness as well as greatness, he can be trusted and loved.

(Gen. 18:25). Because God is righteous, measuring up to the standard of his law, we can trust him. He is honest in his dealings.

A question which has been a topic of debate down through the history of Christian thought is, What makes certain actions right and others wrong? In medieval times one school of thought, the realists, maintained that God chooses the right because it is right.[2] What he calls good could not have been designated otherwise, for there is an intrinsic good in kindness and an inherent evil in cruelty. Another school of thought, the nominalists, asserted that it is God's choice which makes an action right. God does not choose an action because of some intrinsic value in it.[3] Rather, it is his sovereign choice of that action which makes it right. He could have chosen otherwise; if he had done so, the good would be quite different from what it is. Actually, the biblical position falls between realism and nominalism. The right is not something arbitrary, so that cruelty and murder would have been good if God had so declared. In making decisions, God does follow an objective stan-

ceding section is God's personal or individual righteousness. His justice is his official righteousness, his requirement that other moral agents adhere to the standards as well. God is, in other words, like a judge who as a private individual adheres to the law of society, and in his official capacity administers that same law, applying it to others.

The Scripture makes clear that sin has definite consequences. These consequences must eventually come to pass, whether sooner or later. In Genesis 2:17 we read God's warning to Adam and Eve: "Of the tree of the knowledge of good and evil you shall not eat, for in the day that you eat of it you shall die." Similar warnings recur throughout the Scripture, including Paul's statement that "the wages of sin is death" (Rom. 6:23). God will eventually punish sin, for sin intrinsically deserves to be punished.

The justice of God means that he is fair in the administration of his law. He does not show favoritism or partiality. Who we are is not significant. What we have done or not done is the only consideration in the assigning of consequences or rewards. Evidence of God's fairness is that he condemned those judges in biblical times who, while charged to serve as his representatives, accepted

2. E.g., Anselm *Cur Deus homo?* 1.12.
3. William of Ockham, *Reportatio*, book 3, questions 13C, 12CCC.

bribes to alter their judgments (e.g., 1 Sam. 8:3; Amos 5:12). The reason for their condemnation was that God himself, being just, expected the same sort of behavior from those who were to administer his law.

As was the case regarding holiness, God expects his followers to emulate his righteousness and justice. We are to adopt as our standard his law and precepts. We are to treat others fairly and justly (Amos 5:15, 24; James 2:9) because that is what God himself does.

Integrity

The cluster of attributes which we are here classifying as integrity relates to the matter of truth. There are three dimensions of truthfulness: (1) genuineness—being true; (2) veracity—telling the truth; and (3) faithfulness—proving true. Although we think of truthfulness primarily as telling the truth, genuineness is the most basic dimension of truthfulness. The other two derive from it.

1. Genuineness

The basic dimension of the divine integrity is God's genuineness. In contrast to the many false or spurious gods that Israel en-

---

God is true, he tells the truth, and he proves true.

---

countered, their Lord is the true God. In Jeremiah 10, the prophet describes with considerable satire the objects which some people worship. They construct idols with their own hands, and then proceed to worship them, although these products of their own making are unable to speak or walk (v. 5). Of the Lord, however, it is said, "But the LORD is the true God; he is the living God and the everlasting King" (v. 10). In John 17:3, Jesus addresses the Father as the only true God. There are similar references in 1 Thes-

salonians 1:9; 1 John 5:20; and Revelation 3:7 and 6:10.

God is real; he is not fabricated or constructed or imitation, as are all the other claimants to deity. God is what he appears to be. This is a large part of his truthfulness. The vice-president for public affairs at a Christian college used to say, "Public relations is nine-tenths being what you say you are, and one-tenth modestly saying it." God does not simply seem to embody the qualities of greatness and goodness which we are examining. He actually is those attributes.

2. Veracity

Veracity is the second dimension of God's truthfulness. God represents things as they really are. Samuel said to Saul, "The Glory of Israel will not lie or repent; for he is not a man, that he should repent" (1 Sam. 15:29). Paul speaks of the God "who never lies" (Titus 1:2). And in Hebrews 6:18 we read that when God added his oath to his promise, there were "two unchangeable things, in which it is impossible that God should prove false." We should note that these passages are affirming more than that God does not and will not lie. God *cannot* lie. Lying is contrary to his very nature.

God has appealed to his people to be honest in all situations. They are to be truthful both in what they formally assert and in what they imply. Thus, for example, the Israelites were to have only one set of weights in their bag. While there were some people who had two sets of weights, one of which they used when they were making purchases and the other when they were selling, God's people were to use the same set for both types of dealings (Deut. 25:13–15). God's people are to be thoroughly honest in the presentation of the gospel message as well. While some might rationalize that the significance of the end justifies use of the means of misrepresentation, Paul makes clear that "we have renounced disgraceful, underhanded ways; we refuse to practice cunning or to tamper with God's word, but by the open statement of the truth we would commend ourselves to every man's conscience in the sight of God" (2 Cor. 4:2). A God of truth is best served by presentation of the truth.

3. Faithfulness

If God's genuineness is a matter of his being true and veracity is his telling of the truth, then his faithfulness means that he proves true. God keeps all his promises. He never has to revise his word or renege on a promise. As Balaam said to Balak, "God is not man, that he should lie, or a son of man, that he should repent. Has he said, and will he not do it? Or has he spoken, and will he not fulfil it?" (Num. 23:19). Paul is more concise: "He who calls you is faithful, and he will do it" (1 Thess. 5:24). Similar descriptions of God as faithful are to be found in 1 Corinthians 1:9; 2 Corinthians 1:18–22; 2 Timothy 2:13; and 1 Peter 4:19.

The faithfulness of God is demonstrated repeatedly throughout the pages of Scripture. God proved himself to be a God who always fulfils what he has said he will do. His promise to Abraham of a son came when Abraham and Sarah were seventy-five and sixty-five years of age respectively. Sarah was already past the age of childbearing and had proved to be barren. Yet God showed himself faithful—the son whom he had promised (Isaac) was born.

As is the case with his other moral attributes, the Lord expects believers to emulate his truthfulness. God's people are not to give their word thoughtlessly. And when they do give their word, they are to remain faithful to it (Eccles. 5:4–5). They must keep not only the promises made to God (Pss. 61:5, 8; 66:13) but those made to their fellow humans as well (Josh. 9:16–21).

Love

When we think in terms of God's moral attributes, perhaps what comes first to mind is the cluster of attributes we are here classifying as love. Many regard it as the basic attribute, the very nature or definition of God. There is some scriptural basis for this. For example, in 1 John 4:8 and 16 we read: "He who does not love does not know God; for God is love. . . . So we know and believe the love God has for us. God is love, and he who abides in love abides in God, and God abides in him." In general, God's love may be thought of as his eternal giving or sharing of himself. As such, love has always been present among the members of the Trinity. Jesus said, "But I do as the Father has commanded me, so that the world may know that I love the Father" (John 14:31). The triunity of God means that there has been an eternal exercise of God's love, even before there were any created beings. The basic dimensions of God's love to us are: (1) benevolence, (2) grace, (3) mercy, and (4) persistence.

1. Benevolence

Benevolence is a basic dimension of God's love. By this we mean the concern of God for the welfare of those whom he loves. He unselfishly seeks our ultimate welfare. Of numerous biblical references, John 3:16 is probably the best known. Statements of God's benevolence are not restricted to the New Testament. For example, in Deuteronomy 7:7–8 we read, "It was not because you were more in number than any other people that the LORD set his love upon you and chose you, for you were the fewest of all peoples; but it is because the LORD loves you, and is keeping the oath which he swore to your fathers, that the LORD has brought you out with a mighty hand."

God's love is an unselfish interest in us for our sake. It is *agapē*, not *erōs*. In John 15 Jesus draws a contrast between a master-servant (or employer-employee) relationship and a friend-to-friend relationship. It is the latter type of relationship which is to characterize the believer and the Savior. He is concerned with our good for our own sake, not for what he can get out of us. God does not need us. He is all-powerful, all-sufficient. He can accomplish what he wishes without us, although he has chosen to work through us.

This self-giving, unselfish quality of the divine love is seen in what God has done. God's love in sending his Son to die for us was not motivated by our prior love for him. The apostle John says, "In this is love, not that we loved God but that he loved us and sent his Son to be the expiation for our sins" (1 John 4:10). The whole of Romans 5:6–10 elaborates upon the same theme. Note especially verse 8 ("But God shows his love for us in that while we were yet sinners Christ died for us") and verse 10 ("while we were enemies we were reconciled to God"). This divine love not only took the initiative in creating the basis of salvation by sending Jesus Christ, but it also continuously seeks us out. The three parables of Jesus in Luke 15 emphasize this strongly.

God's benevolence, the actual caring and providing for those he loves, is seen in numerous ways. God even cares for and provides for the subhuman creation. Jesus taught that the Father feeds the birds of the air and clothes the lilies of the field (Matt. 6:26, 28; see also Ps. 145:16). The principle that God is benevolent in his provision and protection is extended to his human children as well (Matt. 6:25, 30–33). While we may tend to take these promises somewhat exclusively to ourselves as believers, the Bible indicates that God is benevolent to the whole human race. In the sense of benevolence, God's love is extended to all humankind. He "makes his sun rise on the evil and on the good, and sends rain on the just and on the unjust" (Matt. 5:45). So we see that God inherently not only feels in a particular positive way toward the objects of his love, but he acts for their welfare. Love is an active matter.

2. Grace

Grace is another attribute which is part of the manifold of God's love. By this we mean that God deals with his people not on the basis of their merit or worthiness, what they deserve, but simply according to their need; in other words, he deals with them on the basis of his goodness and generosity. This grace is to be distinguished from the benevolence (unselfishness) that we just described. Benevolence is simply the idea that God does not seek his own good, but rather that of others. It would be possible for God to love unselfishly, with a concern for others, but still to insist that this love be deserved, thus requiring each person to do something or offer something that would earn the favors received or to be received. Grace, however, means that God supplies us with undeserved favors. He requires nothing from us.

The graciousness of God is, of course, prominent in the New Testament. Some have suggested that the Old Testament picture of God is quite different, however. Yet numerous passages in the Old Testament speak of the graciousness of God. In Exodus 34:6, for example, God says of himself: "The LORD, the LORD, a God merciful and gracious, slow to anger, and abounding in steadfast love and faithfulness." In the New Testament there are passages which explicitly relate salvation to the extravagant gift of God's grace. For example, Paul says in Ephesians 2:8–9: "For by grace you have been saved through faith; and this is not your own doing, it is the gift of God—not because of works, lest any man should boast" (cf. Titus 2:11; 3:4–7). Salvation is indeed the gift of God. Sometimes the justice of God is impugned on the grounds that some receive this grace of God and others do not. That any are saved at all is, however, the amazing thing. If God gave to all what they deserve, none would be saved. Everyone would be lost and condemned.

3. Mercy

God's mercy is his tenderhearted, loving compassion for his people. It is his tenderness of heart toward the needy. If grace contemplates humans as sinful, guilty, and condemned, mercy sees them as miserable and needy. The psalmist said, "As a father pities his children, so the LORD pities those who fear him" (Ps. 103:13). Similar ideas are found in Deuteronomy 5:10; Psalm 57:10;

and Psalm 86:5. The attribute of mercy is seen in the compassion which Jesus felt when people suffering from physical ailments came to him (Mark 1:41). Their spiritual condition also moved him (Matt. 9:36). Sometimes both kinds of needs are involved. Thus, in describing the same incident, Matthew speaks of Jesus' having compassion and healing the sick (Matt. 14:14), while Mark speaks of his having compassion and teaching many things (Mark 6:34). Matthew elsewhere combines the two ideas. When Jesus saw the crowds were helpless like sheep without a shepherd, he had compassion on them. So he went about "teaching in their synagogues and preaching the gospel of the kingdom, and healing every disease and every infirmity" (Matt. 9:35–36).

4. Persistence

A final dimension of the love of God is persistence. We read of God's persistence in Psalm 86:15; Romans 2:4; 9:22; 1 Peter 3:20; and 2 Peter 3:15. In all of these verses God is pictured as withholding judgment and continuing to offer salvation and grace over long periods of time.

God's long-suffering was particularly apparent with Israel; this was, of course, an outflow of his faithfulness to them. The people of Israel repeatedly rebelled against Jehovah, desiring to return to Egypt, rejecting Moses' leadership, setting up idols for worship, falling into the practices of the people about them, and intermarrying with them. There must have been times when the Lord was inclined to abandon his people. A large-scale destruction of Israel on the fashion of the flood would have been most appropriate, yet the Lord did not cut them off.

But God's patience was not limited to his dealings with Israel. Peter even suggests (1 Peter 3:20) that the flood was delayed as long as it was in order to provide opportunity of salvation to those who ultimately were destroyed. In speaking of the future day of great destruction, Peter also suggests that the second coming is delayed because of God's forbearance. He does not wish "that any should perish, but that all reach repentance" (2 Peter 3:9).

On one occasion Peter came to Jesus (on behalf of the disciples, no doubt) and asked how often he should forgive a brother who sinned against him: as many as seven times? Jesus' reply to Peter, which has been interpreted as either "77 times" or "490 times," indicates the persistent, relentless nature of the love that is to be characteristic of a follower of the Lord. Jesus himself demonstrated such persistent love with Peter. Though Peter denied Jesus three times, Jesus forgave him, just as he had with so many other shortcomings. As a matter of fact, the angel at the tomb instructed the three women to go tell the disciples *and Peter* that Jesus was going to Galilee where they would see him (Mark 16:7). God's faithfulness and forbearance were also manifested in his not casting off other believers who had sinned and failed him: Moses, David, Solomon, and many more.

God's Love and Justice— A Point of Tension?

We have looked at many characteristics of God, without exhausting them by any means. But what of the interrelationships among them? Presumably, God is a unified, integrated being whose personality is a harmonious whole. There should be, then, no tension among any of these attributes. But is this really so?

The one point of potential tension usually singled out is the relationship between the love of God and his justice. On one hand, God's justice seems so severe, requiring the death of those who sin. This is a fierce, harsh God. On the other hand, God is merciful, gracious, forgiving, long-suffering. Are not these two sets of traits in conflict with one another? Is there, then, internal tension in God's nature?[4]

4. Nels Ferré, *The Christian Understanding of God* (New York: Harper and Brothers, 1951), pp. 227–28.

If we begin with the assumptions that God is an integrated being and the divine attributes are harmonious, we will define the attributes in the light of one another. Thus, justice is loving justice and love is just love. The idea that they conflict may have resulted from defining these attributes in isolation from one another. While the conception of love apart from justice, for example, may be derived from outside sources, it is not a biblical teaching. What we are saying is that love is not fully understood unless we see it as including justice. If love does not include justice, it is mere sentimentality.

Actually, love and justice have worked together in God's dealing with humanity. God's justice requires that there be payment of the penalty for sin. God's love, however, desires that we be restored to fellowship with him. The offer of Jesus Christ as the atonement for sin means that both the justice and the love of God have been maintained. And there really is no tension between the two. There is tension only if one's view of love requires that God forgive sin without any payment being made. But that is to think of God as different from what he really is. Moreover, the offer of Christ as atonement shows a greater love on God's part than would simply indulgently releasing people from the consequences of sin. To fulfil his just administration of the law, God's love was so great that he gave his Son for us. Love and justice are not two separate attributes competing with one another. God is both righteous and loving, and has himself given what he demands.[5]

5. William G. T. Shedd, *Dogmatic Theology* (Grand Rapids: Zondervan, 1971 reprint), vol. 1, pp. 377–78.

11 God's Three-in-Oneness: The Trinity

In the doctrine of the Trinity, we encounter one of the truly distinctive doctrines of Christianity. Among the religions of the world, the Christian faith is unique in making the claim that God is one and yet there are three who are God. In so doing, it presents what seems on the surface to be a self-contradictory doctrine. Furthermore, this doctrine is not overtly or explicitly stated in Scripture. Nevertheless, devout minds have been led to it as they sought to do justice to the witness of Scripture.

The doctrine of the Trinity is crucial for Christianity. It is concerned with who God is, what he is like, how he works, and how he is to be approached. Moreover, the question of the deity of Jesus Christ, which has historically been a point of great tension, is very much wrapped up with one's understanding of the Trinity. The position we take on the Trinity will have profound bearing on our Christology.

The position we take on the Trinity will also answer several questions of a practical nature. Whom are we to worship—Father only, Son, Holy Spirit, or the Triune God? To whom are we to pray? Is the work of each to be considered in isolation from the work of the others, or may we think of the atoning death of Jesus as somehow the work of the Father as well? Should the Son be thought of as the Father's equal in essence, or should he be relegated to a somewhat lesser status?

We will begin our study of the Trinity by examining the biblical basis of the doctrine. It will be important to note the type of wit-

who brought you out of the land of Egypt, out of the house of bondage. You shall have no other gods before me [or besides me]" (Exod. 20:2–3).

The prohibition of idolatry, the second commandment (v. 4), also rests upon the uniqueness of Jehovah. He will not tolerate any worship of objects made by human hands, for he alone is God. The rejection of polytheism runs throughout the Old Testament. God repeatedly demonstrates his superiority to other claimants to deity.

A clearer indication of the oneness of God is the *Shema* of Deuteronomy 6, the great

The Christian faith is unique in making the claim that God is one and yet there are three who are God.

ness in the Scripture which led the church to formulate and propound this strange doctrine. Then we will examine various early attempts to deal with the biblical data, including the orthodox formulation. Finally, we will note the essential elements of the doctrine and search for analogies that may help us to understand it somewhat better.

The Biblical Teaching

We begin with the biblical data bearing upon the doctrine of the Trinity. There are three separate but interrelated types of evidence: evidence for the unity of God—that God is one; evidence that there are three persons who are God; and finally, indications or at least intimations of the three-in-oneness.

The Oneness of God

The religion of the ancient Hebrews was a rigorously monotheistic faith, as indeed the Jewish religion is to this day. The unity of God was revealed to Israel at several different times and in various ways. The Ten Commandments, for example, begin with the statement, "I am the LORD your God,

truths of which the people of Israel were commanded to absorb themselves and to inculcate into their children. They were to meditate upon these teachings ("these words . . . shall be upon your heart," v. 6). They were to talk about them—at home and on the road, when lying down and when arising (v. 7). They were to use visual aids to call attention to them—wearing them on their hands and foreheads, and writing them on the doorframes of their houses and on their gates. And what are these great truths that were to be emphasized so? One is an indicative, a declarative statement: "The LORD our God is one LORD" (v. 4). The second great truth God wanted Israel to learn and teach is a command based on his uniqueness: "Love the LORD your God with all your heart, and with all your soul, and with all your might" (v. 5). Because he is one, there was to be no division of Israel's commitment.

The teaching regarding the oneness of God is not restricted to the Old Testament. James 2:19 commends belief in one God, while noting its insufficiency for justification. Paul writes as he discusses the eating of meat which had been offered to idols:

"We know that an idol is nothing at all in the world, and that there is . . . but one God, the Father, from whom all things came and for whom we live; and there is but one Lord, Jesus Christ, through whom all things came and through whom we live" (1 Cor. 8:4, 6, NIV). Here Paul, like the Mosaic law, excludes idolatry on the grounds that there is only one God.

The Deity of Three

All this evidence, if taken by itself, would no doubt lead us to a basically monotheistic belief. What, then, moved the church beyond this evidence? It was the additional biblical witness to the effect that three persons are God. The deity of the first, the Father, is scarcely in dispute. In addition to the references in 1 Corinthians 8:4, 6, and 1 Timothy 2:5–6, we may note the cases where Jesus refers to the Father as God. In Matthew 6:26, for example, he indicates that "your heavenly Father feeds [the birds of the air]." In a parallel statement which follows shortly thereafter, he indicates that "God . . . clothes the grass of the field" (v. 30). It is apparent that, for Jesus, "God" and "your heavenly Father" are interchangeable expressions. And in numerous other references to God, Jesus obviously has the Father in mind (e.g., Matt. 19:23–26; 27:46; Mark 12:17, 24–27).

Somewhat more problematic is the status of Jesus as deity, yet Scripture also identifies him as God. A key reference to the deity of Christ Jesus is found in Philippians 2. In verses 5–11 Paul has taken what was in all likelihood a hymn of the early church and used it as the basis of an appeal to his readers to practice humility. He notes that "though [Jesus] was in the form of God, [he] did not count equality with God a thing to be grasped" (v. 6). The word here translated "form" is *morphē*. This term in classical Greek as well as in biblical Greek means "the set of characteristics which constitutes a thing what it is." Denoting the genuine nature of a thing, *morphē* contrasts with *schēma*, which is also generally translated "form," but in the sense of shape or superficial appearance rather than substance. The use of *morphē* in this passage, which reflects the faith of the early church, suggests a deep commitment to the full deity of Christ.

Another significant passage is Hebrews 1. The author, whose identity is unknown to us, is writing to a group of Hebrew Christians. He (or she) makes several statements which strongly imply the full deity of the Son. In the opening verses the writer argues that the Son is superior to the angels, and notes that God has spoken through the Son, appointed him heir of all things, and made the universe through him (v. 2). The author then describes the Son as the "radiance of God's glory" (NIV) and the "exact representation of his being." While it could perhaps be maintained that this affirms only that God revealed himself through the Son, rather than that the Son *is God*, the context suggests otherwise. In addition to identifying himself as the Father of the one whom he here calls Son (v. 5), God is quoted in verse 8 (from Ps. 45:6) as addressing the Son as "God" and in verse 10 as "Lord" (from Ps. 102:25). The writer concludes by noting that God said to the Son, "Sit at my right hand" (from Ps. 110:1). It is significant that the Scripture writer addresses Hebrew Christians, who certainly would be steeped in monotheism, in ways which undeniably affirm the deity of Jesus and his equality with the Father.

A final consideration is Jesus' own self-consciousness. We should note that Jesus never directly asserted his deity. He never said simply, "I am God." Yet several threads of evidence suggest that this is indeed how he understood himself. He claimed to possess what properly belongs only to God. He spoke of the angels of God (Luke 12:8–9; 15:10) as his angels (Matt. 13:41). He regarded the kingdom of God (Matt. 12:28; 19:14, 24; 21:31, 43) and the elect of God (Mark 13:20) as his own. Further, he claimed to forgive sins (Mark 2:8–10). The Jews recognized that only God can forgive sins, and they consequently accused Jesus of blasphemy. He also claimed the power to judge the world (Matt. 25:31) and to reign over it (Matt. 24:30; Mark 14:62).

There also are biblical references which identify the Holy Spirit as God. Here we may note that there are passages where references to the Holy Spirit occur interchangeably with references to God. One example of this is Acts 5:3–4. Ananias and Sapphira held back a portion of the proceeds from the sale of their property, misrepresenting what they laid at the apostles' feet as the entirety. Here, lying to the Holy Spirit (v. 3) is equated with lying to God (v. 4). The Holy Spirit is also described as having the qualities and performing the works of God. It is the Holy Spirit who convicts the world of sin, righteousness, and judgment (John 16:8–11). He regenerates or gives new life (John 3:8). In 1 Corinthians 12:4–11, we read that it is the Spirit who conveys gifts to the church, and who exercises sovereignty over who receives those gifts. In addition, he receives the honor and glory reserved for God.

In 1 Corinthians 3:16–17, Paul reminds believers that they are God's temple and that his Spirit dwells within them. In chapter 6, he says that their bodies are a temple of the Holy Spirit within them (vv. 19–20). "God" and "Holy Spirit" seem to be interchangeable expressions. Also there are several places where the Holy Spirit is put on an equal footing with God. One is the baptismal formula of Matthew 28:19; a second is the Pauline benediction in 2 Corinthians 13:14; finally, there is 1 Peter 1:2, where Peter addresses his readers as "chosen and destined by God the Father and sanctified by the Spirit for obedience to Jesus Christ and for sprinkling with his blood."

Three-in-Oneness

On the surface, these two lines of evidence—God's oneness and threeness—seem contradictory. As the church began to reflect upon doctrinal issues, it concluded that God must be understood as three-in-one or, in other words, triune. At this point we must pose the question whether this doctrine is explicitly taught in the Bible, is suggested by the Scripture, or is merely an inference drawn from other teachings of the Bible.

One text which has traditionally been appealed to as documenting the Trinity is 1 John 5:7, that is, as it is found in earlier versions such as the King James: "For there are three that bear record in heaven, the Father, the Word, and the Holy Ghost: and these three are one." Here is, apparently, a clear and succinct statement of the three-in-oneness. Unfortunately, however, the textual basis is so weak that some recent translations (e.g., NIV) include this statement only in an italicized footnote, and others omit it altogether (e.g., RSV). If there is a biblical basis for the Trinity, it must be sought elsewhere.

The plural form of the noun for the God of Israel, *ĕlōhîm*, is sometimes regarded as an intimation of a trinitarian view. This is a generic name used to refer to other gods as well. When used with reference to Israel's God, it is generally, but not always, found in the plural. Some would argue that here is a hint of the plural nature of God.

There are other plural forms as well. In Genesis 1:26, God says, "Let us make man in our image." Here the plural appears both in the verb "let us make" and in the possessive suffix "our." When Isaiah was called, he heard the Lord saying, "Whom shall I send, and who will go for us?" (Isa. 6:8). What is significant, from the standpoint of logical analysis, is the *shift* from singular to plural. Genesis 1:26 actually says, "Then God said [singular], 'Let us make [plural] man in our [plural] image.'" God is quoted as using a plural verb with reference to himself. Similarly Isaiah 6:8 reads: "Whom shall I send [singular], and who will go for us [plural]?"

The teaching regarding the image of God in humankind has also been viewed as an intimation of the Trinity. Genesis 1:27 reads:

So God created man in his own image,
in the image of God he created him;
male and female he created them.

Some would argue that what we have here is a parallelism not merely in the first two, but in all three lines. Thus, "male and female he created them" is equivalent to "So God created man in his own image" and to "in the image of God he created him." On this basis, the image of God in man (generic) is to be found in the fact that man has been created male and female (i.e., plural).[1] This means that the image of God must consist in a unity in plurality, a characteristic of both the ectype and the archetype. According to Genesis 2:24, man and woman are to become one (*'echād*); a union of two separate entities is entailed. It is significant that the same word is used of God in the *Shema:* "The LORD our God is one [*'echād*] LORD" (Deut. 6:4). It seems that something is being affirmed here about the nature of God—he is an organism, that is, a unity of distinct parts.

In several places in Scripture the three persons are linked together in unity and apparent equality. One of these is the baptismal formula as prescribed in the Great Commission (Matt. 28:19–20): baptizing in (or into) the name of the Father and of the Son and of the Holy Spirit. Note that "name" is singular although there are three persons included. Yet another direct linking of the three names is the Pauline benediction in 2 Corinthians 13:1—"The grace of the Lord Jesus Christ and the love of God and the fellowship of the Holy Spirit be with you all." Here again is a linkage of the three names in unity and apparent equality.

It is in the Fourth Gospel that the strongest evidence of a coequal Trinity is to be found. The threefold formula appears again and again: 1:33–34; 14:16, 26; 16:13–15; 20:21–22 (cf. 1 John 4:2, 13–14). The interdynamics among the three persons comes through repeatedly, as George Hendry has observed.[2] The Son is sent by the Father (14:24) and comes forth from him (16:28). The Spirit is given by the Father (14:16), sent from the Father (14:26), and proceeds from the Father (15:26). Yet the Son is closely involved in the coming of the Spirit: he prays for his coming (14:16); the Father sends the Spirit in the Son's name (14:26); the Son will send the Spirit from the Father (15:26); the Son must go away so that he can send the Spirit (16:7). The Spirit's ministry is understood as a continuation and elaboration of that of the Son. He will bring to remembrance what the Son has said (14:26); he will bear witness to the Son (15:26); he will declare what he hears from the Son, thus glorifying the Son (16:13–14).

The prologue of the Gospel also contains material rich in significance for the doctrine of the Trinity. John says in the first verse of the book: "The Word was with God, and the Word was God." Here is an indication of the divinity of the Word. Here also we find the idea that while the Son is distinct from the Father, yet there is fellowship between them, for the preposition *pros* ("with") does not connote merely physical proximity to the Father, but an intimacy of fellowship as well.

There are other ways in which this Gospel stresses the closeness and unity between the Father and the Son. Jesus says, "I and the Father are one" (10:30), and "he who has seen me has seen the Father" (14:9). He prays that his disciples may be one as he and the Father are one (17:21).

Our conclusion from the data we have just examined: Although the doctrine of the Trinity is not expressly asserted, the Scripture, particularly the New Testament, contains so many suggestions of the deity and unity of the three persons that we can understand why the church formulated the doctrine, and conclude that they were right in so doing.

1. Paul King Jewett, *Man as Male and Female* (Grand Rapids: Eerdmans, 1975), pp. 33–40, 43–48; Karl Barth, *Church Dogmatics* (Edinburgh: T. and T. Clark, 1958), vol. 3, part 1, pp. 183–201.

2. George S. Hendry, *The Holy Spirit in Christian Theology* (Philadelphia: Westminster, 1956), p. 31.

Historical Constructions

During the first two centuries A.D. there was little conscious attempt to wrestle with the theological and philosophical issues of what we now term the doctrine of the Trinity. Such thinkers as Justin and Tatian stressed the unity of essence between the Word and the Father and used the imagery of the impossibility of separating light from its source, the sun. In this way they illustrated that, while the Word and the Father are distinct, they are not divisible or separable.[3]

The "Economic" View of the Trinity

In Hippolytus and Tertullian, we find the development of an "economic" view of the Trinity. There was little attempt to explore the eternal relations among the three; rather, there was a concentration on the ways in which the Triad were manifested in creation and redemption. While creation and redemption showed the Son and the Spirit to be other than the Father, they were also regarded as inseparably one with him in his eternal being. Like the mental functions of a human being, God's reason, that is, the Word, was regarded as being immanently and indivisibly with him.

By way of a quick evaluation, we note that there is something of a vagueness about this view of the Trinity. Any effort to come up with a more exact understanding of just what it means will prove disappointing.

Dynamic Monarchianism

In the late second and third centuries, two attempts were made to come up with a precise definition of the relationship between Christ and God. Both of these views have been referred to as monarchianism (literally, "sole sovereignty"), since they stress the uniqueness and unity of God, but only the latter claimed the designation for itself.

Dynamic monarchianism maintained that God was dynamically present in the life of the man Jesus. There was a working or force of God upon or in or through the man Jesus, but there was no real presence of God within him. The originator of dynamic monarchianism, Theodotus, asserted that prior to baptism Jesus was an ordinary, though completely virtuous man. At the baptism, the Spirit, or Christ, descended upon him, and from that time on he performed miraculous works of God. These ideas of dynamic monarchianism never became widespread.[4]

Modalistic Monarchianism

By contrast, modalistic monarchianism was a fairly widespread, popular teaching. Whereas dynamic monarchianism seemed to deny the doctrine of the Trinity, modalism appeared to affirm it. Both varieties of monarchianism desired to preserve the doctrine of the unity of God. Modalism, however, was also strongly committed to the full deity of Jesus. Since the term *Father* was generally regarded as signifying the Godhead itself, any suggestion that the Word or Son was somehow other than the Father upset the modalists. It seemed to them to be a case of bitheism, belief in two gods.

The essential idea of this school of thought is that there is one Godhead which may be variously designated as Father, Son, or Spirit. The terms do not stand for real distinctions, but are merely names which are appropriate and applicable at different times. Father, Son, and Holy Spirit are identical—they are successive revelations of the same person. The modalistic solution to the paradox of threeness and oneness was, then, not three persons, but one person with three different names, roles, or activities.[5]

It must be acknowledged that in modalistic monarchianism we have a genuinely unique, original, and creative conception, and one which is in some ways a brilliant breakthrough. Both the unity of the Godhead and the deity of all three—Father, Son,

---

3. Justin Martyr *Dialogue with Trypho* 61.2; 128.3–4.

4. Athanasius *On the Decrees of the Nicene Synod (Defense of the Nicene Council)* 5.24; *On the Councils of Ariminum and Seleucia* 2.26; Eusebius *Ecclesiastical History* 7.30.

5. Athanasius *Four Discourses Against the Arians* 3.23.4.

and Holy Spirit—are preserved. Yet the church in assessing this theology deemed it lacking in some significant respects. In particular, the fact that the three occasionally appear simultaneously upon the stage of biblical revelation proved to be a major stumbling block to this view. The baptismal scene, where the Father speaks to the Son, and the Spirit descends upon the Son, is an example. Some of the trinitarian texts noted earlier also proved troublesome.

The Orthodox Formulation

The orthodox doctrine of the Trinity was enunciated in a series of debates and councils which were in large part prompted by the controversies sparked by such movements as monarchianism and Arianism. It was at the Council of Constantinople (381) that there emerged a definitive statement in which the church made explicit the beliefs which had been held implicitly. The view which prevailed was basically that of Athanasius (293–373), as it was elaborated and refined by the Cappadocian theologians—Basil, Gregory of Nazianzus, and Gregory of Nyssa.

The formula which expresses the position of Constantinople is "one *ousia* [substance] in three *hypostases* [persons]." The emphasis often seems to be more on the latter part of the formula, that is, on the separate existence of the three persons rather than on the one indivisible Godhead. The one Godhead exists simultaneously in three modes of being or hypostases. The Godhead exists "undivided in divided persons." There is an "identity of nature" in the three hypostases.

The Cappadocians attempted to expound the concepts of common substance and multiple separate persons by the analogy of a universal and its particulars—the individual persons of the Trinity are related to the divine substance in the same fashion as individual humans are related to the universal human (or humanity). Each of the individual hypostases is the ousia of the Godhead distinguished by the characteristics or properties peculiar to him, just as individual humans have unique characteristics which distinguish them from other individual human persons. These respective properties of the divine persons are, according to Basil, paternity, sonship, and sanctifying power or sanctification.[6]

It is clear that the orthodox formula protects the doctrine of the Trinity against the danger of modalism. Has it done so, however, at the expense of falling into the opposite error—tritheism? On the surface, the danger seems considerable. Two points were made, however, to safeguard the doctrine of the Trinity against tritheism.

First, it was noted that if we can find a single activity of the Father, Son, and Holy Spirit which is in no way different in any of the three persons, we must conclude that there is but one identical substance involved. And such unity was found in the divine activity of revelation. Revelation originates in the Father, proceeds through the Son, and is completed in the Spirit. It is not three actions, but one action in which all three are involved.

Second, there was an insistence upon the concreteness and indivisibility of the divine substance. Much of the criticism of the Cappadocian doctrine of the Trinity focused on the analogy of a universal manifesting itself in particulars. To avoid the conclusion that there is a multiplicity of Gods within the Godhead just as there is a multiplicity of humans within humanity, Gregory of Nyssa suggested that, strictly speaking, we ought not to talk about a multiplicity of humans, but a multiplicity of the one universal human. Thus the Cappadocians continued to emphasize that, while the three members of the Trinity can be distinguished numerically as persons, they are indistinguishable in their essence or substance. They are distinguishable as persons, but one and inseparable in their being.

It should be reiterated here that ousia is not abstract, but a concrete reality. Further, this divine essence is simple and indivisible.

6. Basil *Letters* 38.5; 214.4; 236.6.

Following the Aristotelian doctrine that only what is material is quantitatively divisible, the Cappadocians at times virtually denied that the category of number can be applied to the Godhead at all. God is simple and incomposite. Thus, while each of the persons is one, they cannot be added together to make three entities.

Essential Elements of a Doctrine of the Trinity

It is important to pause here to note the salient elements which must be included in any doctrine of the Trinity.

1. We begin with the unity of God. God is one, not several. The unity of God may be compared to the unity of husband and wife, but we must keep in mind that we are dealing with one God, not a joining of separate entities.

2. The deity of each of the three persons, Father, Son, and Holy Spirit, must be affirmed. Each is qualitatively the same. The Son is divine in the same way and to the same extent as is the Father, and this is true of the Holy Spirit as well.

well, orthodoxy deals with the problem by suggesting that the way in which God is three is in some respect different from the way in which he is one. The fourth-century thinkers spoke of one ousia and three hypostases. Now comes the problem of determining what these two terms mean, or more broadly, what the difference is between the nature of God's oneness and that of his threeness.

4. The Trinity is eternal. There have always been three, Father, Son, and Holy Spirit, and all of them have always been divine. One or more of them did not come into being at some point in time, or at some point become divine. The Triune God is and will be what he always has been.

5. The function of one member of the Trinity may for a time be subordinate to one or both of the other members, but that does not mean he is in any way inferior in essence. Each of the three persons of the Trinity has had, for a period of time, a particular function unique to himself. This is to be understood as a temporary role for the purpose of accomplishing a given end, not a change in his status or essence. In human

---

We will someday understand God better than we do now, yet even then we will not totally comprehend him.

---

3. The threeness and the oneness of God are not in the same respect. Although the orthodox interpretation of the Trinity seems contradictory (God is one and yet three), the contradiction is not real, but only apparent. A contradiction exists if something is A and not A at the same time and in the same respect. Modalism attempted to deal with the apparent contradiction by stating that the three modes or manifestations of God are not simultaneous; at any given time, only one is being revealed. Orthodoxy, however, insists that God is three persons at every moment of time. Maintaining his unity as

experience, there is functional subordination as well. Several equals in a business or enterprise may choose one of their number to serve as the captain of a task force or the chairperson of a committee for a given time, but without any change in rank. In like fashion, the Son did not during his earthly incarnation become less than the Father, but he did subordinate himself functionally to the Father's will. Similarly, the Holy Spirit is now subordinated to the ministry of the Son (see John 14–16) as well as to the will of the Father, but this does not imply that he is less than they are.

6. The Trinity is incomprehensible. We cannot fully understand the mystery of the Trinity. When someday we see God, we shall see him as he is, and understand him better than we do now. Yet even then we will not totally comprehend him.

The Search for Analogies

The problem in constructing a statement of the doctrine of the Trinity is not merely to understand the terminology. That is in itself hard enough; for example, it is difficult to know what "person" means in this context. More difficult yet is to understand the interrelationships among the members of the Trinity. The human mind occasionally seeks analogies which will help in this effort.

On a popular level, analogies drawn from physical nature have often been utilized. A widely used analogy, for example, is the egg: it consists of yolk, white, and shell, all of which together form one whole egg. Another favorite analogy is water: it can be found in solid, liquid, and vaporous forms. At times other material objects have been used as illustrations. One pastor, in instructing young catechumens, attempted to clarify the threeness yet oneness by posing the question, "Is (or are) trousers singular or plural?" His answer was that trousers is singular at the top, and they are plural at the bottom.

Note that these analogies and illustrations, as well as large numbers of similar analogies drawn from the physical realm, tend to be either tritheistic or modalistic in their implications. On one hand, the analogies involving the egg and the trousers seem to suggest that the Father, the Son, and the Holy Spirit are separate parts of the divine nature. On the other hand, the analogy involving the various forms of water has modalistic overtones, since ice, liquid water, and steam are modes of existence. A given quantity of water does not simultaneously exist in all three states.

One of the most creative minds in the history of Christian theology was Augustine. In *De trinitate*, which may be his greatest work, he turned his prodigious intellect to the problem of the nature of the Trinity. The major contribution of Augustine to the understanding of the Trinity is his analogies drawn from the realm of human personality. He argued that since humankind is made in the image of God, who is triune, it is therefore reasonable to expect to find, through an analysis of human nature, a reflection, however faint, of God's triunity. With this thought in mind, let us examine two analogies drawn from the realm of human experience.

The first analogy is drawn from the realm of individual human psychology. As a self-conscious person, I may engage in internal dialogue with myself. I may take different positions and interact with myself. I may even engage in a debate with myself. Furthermore, I am a complex human person with multiple roles and responsibilities in dynamic interplay with one another. As I consider what I should do in a given situation, the husband, the father, the seminary professor, and the United States citizen that together constitute me may mutually inform one another.

One problem with this analogy is that in human experience it is most clearly seen in situations where there is tension or competition, rather than harmony, between the individual's various positions and roles. The discipline of abnormal psychology affords us with extreme examples of virtual warfare between the constituent elements of the human personality. But in God, by contrast, there are always perfect harmony, communication, and love.

The other analogy is from the sphere of interpersonal human relations. Take the case of identical twins. In one sense, they are of the same essence, for their genetic makeup is identical. An organ transplant from one to the other can be accomplished with relative ease, for the recipient's body will not reject the donor's organ as foreign; it will accept it as its very own. Identical twins are very close in other ways as well.

They have similar interests and tastes. Although they have different spouses and different employers, a close bond unites them. And yet they are not the same person. They are two, not one.

These two analogies emphasize different aspects of the doctrine of the Trinity. The former puts major stress upon the oneness. The latter illustrates more clearly the threeness. From a logical standpoint, both cannot be true simultaneously, at least as far as we can understand. May it not be that what we have here is a mystery? We must cling to both, even though we cannot see the exact relationship between the two.

Perhaps this mystery which we must cling to in order to preserve the full data is, as Augustus Strong puts it, "inscrutable." Yet theologians are not the only ones who must retain two polarities as they function. Physicists have never finally and perfectly resolved the question of the nature of light. One theory says that it is waves. The other says it is quanta, little bundles of energy as it were. Logically it cannot be both. Yet, to account for all the data, one must hold both theories simultaneously.

The doctrine of the Trinity is a crucial ingredient of our faith. Each of the three, Father, Son, and Holy Spirit, is to be worshiped, as is the Triune God. And, keeping in mind their distinctive work, it is appropriate to direct prayers of thanks and of petition to each of the members of the Trinity, as well as to all of them collectively. Furthermore, the perfect love and unity within the Godhead model for us the oneness and affection that should characterize our relationships within the body of Christ.

It appears that Tertullian was right in affirming that the doctrine of the Trinity must be divinely revealed, not humanly constructed. It is so absurd from a human standpoint that no one would have invented it. We do not hold the doctrine of the Trinity because it is self-evident or logically cogent. We hold it because God has revealed that this is what he is like. As someone has said of this doctrine:

> Try to explain it, and you'll lose your mind;
> But try to deny it, and you'll lose your soul.

The Work of God

12 God's Plan

Where is history going, and why? What if anything is causing the pattern of history to develop as it is? These are questions which confront all thinking persons and which crucially affect their way of life. Christianity's answer is that God has a plan which includes everything that occurs, and that he is now at work carrying out that plan.

Key Definitions

We may define the plan of God (which is often referred to as his decrees) as his eternal decision rendering certain all things which shall come to pass. There are analogies which, though necessarily insufficient, may help us to understand this concept.

The plan of God is like the architect's plans, drawn first in her mind and then on paper according to her intention and design, and only afterward executed in an actual structure. Or God may be thought of as being like a general who has carefully conceived a battle plan for his army to carry out.

It is necessary at this point to clarify certain terminology. Many theologians use the terms *predestinate* and *foreordain* virtually synonymously. For our purposes, however, we shall use them somewhat differently. "Predestinate" carries a somewhat narrower connotation than does "foreordain." Since it literally suggests the destiny of someone or something, it is best used of God's plan as it relates in particular to the eternal condition of moral agents. We will use the term *foreordain* in a broader sense, that is, to refer to the decisions of God with respect to any matters within the realm of cosmic history. "Predestination" will be reserved for the matter of eternal salvation or condemnation. Within predestination, "election" will be used of God's positive choice of individuals, nations, or groups to eternal life and fellowship with him, while "reprobation" will refer to negative predestination or God's choice of some to suffer eternal damnation or lostness. The use of "predestination" is limited in this volume to either election or reprobation or both; "foreordination," on the other hand, while it also may refer to election, reprobation, or both, has a far broader range of meaning.

The Biblical Teaching

The Old Testament Teaching

In the Old Testament presentation, the planning and ordaining work of God is very much tied up with the covenant which the Lord made with his people. As we read of all that God did in choosing and taking personal care of his people, two truths about him stand out. On one hand, God is supremely powerful, the creator and sustainer of all that is. On the other hand is the loving, caring, personal nature of the Lord. He is not mere abstract power, but is thought of as a loving person.[1]

For the Old Testament writers, it was virtually inconceivable that anything could happen independently of the will and working of God. As evidence of this, consider that common impersonal expressions like "It rained" are not found in the Old Testament. For the Hebrews, rain did not simply happen; God sent the rain. They saw him as the all-powerful determiner of everything that occurs. God himself comments, for example, concerning the destruction inflicted by the king of Assyria: "Have you not heard that I determined it long ago? I planned from days of old what now I bring to pass, that you should make fortified cities crash into heaps of ruins" (Isa. 37:26). Even something as seemingly trivial as the building of reservoirs is described as having been planned long before (Isa. 22:11). Furthermore, there is in God's plan a special concern for the welfare of the nation of Israel, and of every one of God's children (Pss. 27:10–11; 37; 65:3; 91; 121; 139:16; Dan. 12:1; Jon. 3:5).

The Old Testament also enunciates belief in the efficaciousness of God's plan. What is now coming to pass is doing so because it is (and has always been) part of God's plan. What he has promised, he will do. In fact, in Isaiah 14:24–27 we read not only of God's faithfulness to his avowed purpose, but also of the futility of opposing it: "For the LORD of hosts has purposed, and who will annul it? His hand is stretched out, and who will turn it back?" (v. 27; cf. Job 42:2; Jer. 23:20; Zech. 1:6).

It is particularly in the wisdom literature and the prophets that the idea of an all-inclusive divine purpose is most prominent.[2] God has from the beginning, from all eternity, had an inclusive plan encompassing the whole of reality and extending even to the minor details of life. "The LORD has made everything for its purpose, even the

---

1. Benjamin B. Warfield, "Predestination," in *Biblical Doctrines* (New York: Oxford University Press, 1929), pp. 7–8.
2. Ibid., p. 15.

wicked for the day of trouble" (Prov. 16:4; cf. 3:19–20; Job 38, especially v. 4; Isa. 40:12; Jer. 10:12–13). We humans may not always understand as God works out his purpose in our lives. This was the experience of Job throughout the book that bears his name; it is articulated particularly in 42:3, "'Who is this that hides counsel without knowledge?' Therefore I have uttered what I did not understand, things too wonderful for me, which I did not know." Thus, in the view of the Old Testament believer, God had created the world, he was directing history, and all this was but the unfolding of a plan prepared in eternity and related to his intention of fellowship with his people.

The New Testament Teaching

The plan and purpose of God is also prominent in the New Testament. Jesus affirmed that God had planned not only the large, complex events, such as the fall and destruction of Jerusalem (Luke 21:20–22), but details as well, such as the apostasy of and betrayal by Judas, and the faithfulness of the remaining disciples (Matt. 26:24; Mark 14:21; Luke 22:22; John 17:12; 18:9). The fulfilment of God's plan and Old Testament prophecy is a prominent theme in the writing of Matthew (1:22; 2:15, 23; 4:14; 8:17; 12:17; 13:35; 21:4; 26:56) and of John (12:38; 19:24, 28, 36). While critics may object that some of these prophecies were fulfilled by people who knew about them and may have had a vested interest in seeing them fulfilled (e.g., Jesus fulfilled Ps. 69:21 by saying, "I thirst" [John 19:28]), it is notable that other prophecies were fulfilled by persons who had no desire to fulfil them and probably had no knowledge of them, such as the Roman soldiers in their casting lots for Jesus' garment and not breaking any of his bones.[3] Even where there was no specific prophecy to be fulfilled, Jesus conveyed a sense of necessity concerning future events. For example, he said to his disciples, "And when you hear of wars and rumors of wars, do not be alarmed; this must take

place, but the end is not yet. . . . And the gospel must first be preached to all nations" (Mark 13:7, 10).

The apostles also laid emphasis upon the divine purpose. Peter said in his speech at Pentecost, "This Jesus, delivered up according to the definite plan and foreknowledge of God, you crucified and killed by the hands of lawless men" (Acts 2:23). In writing the Book of Revelation the apostle John gave us a particularly striking example of belief in the divine plan. The note of certainty pervading the whole book, the entire series of events predicted there, derives from belief in God's plan and foreordination.

It is in Paul's writings that the divine plan according to which everything comes to pass is made most explicit. Everything that occurs is by God's choice and in accordance with his will (1 Cor. 12:18; 15:38; Col. 1:19). The very fortunes of nations are determined by him (Acts 17:26). God's redemptive work unfolds in accordance with his intended purpose (Gal. 3:8; 4:4–5). The choice of individual and nation to be his own and the consequent events are God's sovereign doing (Rom. 9–11). One might well take the image of the potter and the clay, which Paul uses in a specific and somewhat narrow reference (Rom. 9:20–23), and see it as expressive of his whole philosophy of history. Paul regards "all things" that happen as part of God's intention for his children (Eph. 1:11–12). Thus Paul says that "in everything God works for good for those who are called according to his purpose" (Rom. 8:28), his purpose being that we might be "conformed to the image of his Son" (v. 29).

The Nature of the Divine Plan

We now need to draw together, from these numerous and varied biblical references, some general characteristics of God's plan. This will enable us to understand more completely what the plan is like and what we can expect from God.

3. Bernard Ramm, *Protestant Christian Evidences* (Chicago: Moody, 1953), p. 88.

1. God's plan is from all eternity. The psalmist spoke of God's having planned all of our days before there were any of them (Ps. 139:16). Paul in Ephesians indicates that God "chose us in [Christ] before the foundation of the world" (1:4). Such decisions are not made as history unfolds and events occur. God manifests his purpose within history (2 Tim. 1:10), but his decisions have been made from all eternity, from before the beginning of time (see also Isa. 22:11).

Being eternal, the plan of God does not have any chronological sequence within it. There is no before and after within eternity.

they are not a matter of internal compulsion either. That is to say, although God's decisions and actions are quite consistent with his nature, they are not constrained by his nature. God did not have to create. He had to act in a loving and holy fashion in whatever he did, but he was not required to create. He freely chose to create for reasons not known to us.

3. In the ultimate sense, the purpose of God's plan is God's glory. Paul indicates that God chose us in Christ and destined us "according to the purpose of his will, to the praise of his glorious grace" (Eph. 1:5–6). What God does, he does for his own name's

> *God is now at work carrying out his plan, which is from all eternity and includes everything that occurs.*

There is, of course, a logical sequence (e.g., the decision to let Jesus die on the cross logically follows the decision to send him to the earth), and there is a temporal sequence in the enacting of the events which have been decreed; but there is no temporal sequence to God's willing. It is one coherent simultaneous decision.

2. The plan of God and the decisions contained therein are free on God's part. This is implied in expressions like "the good pleasure of his will." It is also implicit in the fact that no one has advised him (for that matter, there is no one who could advise him). Isaiah 40:13–14 says, "Who has directed the Spirit of the LORD, or as his counselor has instructed him? Whom did he consult for his enlightenment, and who taught him the path of justice, and taught him knowledge, and showed him the way of understanding?" Paul quotes this very passage as he concludes his great statement on the sovereignty and inscrutability of God's workings (Rom. 11:34).

Not only do God's decisions not stem from any sort of external determination,

sake (Isa. 48:11; Ezek. 20:9). Jesus said that his followers were to let their lights so shine that others would see their good works and glorify their Father in heaven (Matt. 5:16; cf. John 15:8).

This is not to say that there are no secondary motivations behind God's plan and resultant actions. He has provided the means of salvation in order to fulfil his love for humankind and his concern for their welfare. This, however, is not an ultimate end, but only a means to the greater end, God's own glory.

4. The plan of God is all-inclusive. This is implicit in the great variety of items which are mentioned in the Bible as parts of God's plan. Beyond that, however, are explicit statements of the extent of God's plan. Paul speaks of God as the one who "accomplishes all things according to the counsel of his will" (Eph. 1:11). The psalmist says that "all things are thy servants" (Ps. 119:91). While all ends are part of God's plan, all means are as well. And although we tend at times to think of sacred and secular areas of life, no such division exists from God's standpoint.

There are no areas that fall outside the purview of his concern and decision.

5. God's plan is efficacious. What he has purposed from eternity will surely come to pass. The Lord says, "As I have planned, so shall it be, and as I have purposed, so shall it stand. . . . For the LORD of hosts has purposed, and who will annul it? His hand is stretched out, and who will turn it back?" (Isa. 14:24, 27). He will not change his mind, nor will he discover hitherto unknown considerations which will cause him to alter his intentions.

6. God's plan relates to his actions rather than his nature. It pertains to his decisions regarding what he shall do, not to his personal attributes. God does not have to choose to be loving and powerful; indeed, he could not choose to be otherwise. Thus, the decisions of God relate to objects, events, and processes external to the divine nature, not to what he is or what transpires within his person.[4]

7. The plan of God relates primarily to what God himself does in terms of creating, preserving, directing, and redeeming. It also involves human willing and acting, but only secondarily, that is, as means to the ends he purposes, or as results of actions which he takes. Note that God's role here is to decide that certain things will take place in our lives, not to lay down commands to act in a certain way. The plan of God does not force us to act in particular ways, but renders it certain that we will *freely* act in those ways.

8. Thus, while the plan of God relates primarily to what God does, human actions are also included. Jesus noted, for example, that the responses of individuals to his message were a result of the Father's decision (John 6:37, 44; cf. 17:2, 6, 9). Luke said in Acts 13:48 that "as many as were ordained to eternal life believed."

God's plan includes what we ordinarily call good acts. On the other hand, the evil actions of individuals, which are contrary to

4. Augustus H. Strong, *Systematic Theology* (Westwood, N.J.: Revell, 1907), pp. 353–54.

God's law and moral intentions, are also seen in Scripture as part of God's plan, as foreordained by him. The betrayal, conviction, and crucifixion of Jesus are a prominent instance of this (Luke 22:22; Acts 2:23; 4:27–28).

9. The plan of God in terms of its specifics is unchangeable. God does not change his mind or alter his decisions regarding specific determinations. This may seem strange in light of the seeming alteration of his intentions with regard to Nineveh (Jonah), and his apparent repentance for having made human beings (Gen. 6:6). The statement in Genesis 6, however, should be regarded as an anthropomorphism, and Jonah's announcement of impending destruction should be viewed as a warning used to effect God's actual plan for Nineveh. We must keep in mind here that constancy is one of the attributes of God's greatness.

Logical Priority: God's Plan or Human Action?

We must now consider whether God's plan or human action is logically prior. While Calvinists and Arminians are agreed that human actions are included in God's plan, they disagree as to what is the cause and what is the result. Do people do what they do because God has decided that this is exactly how they are going to act, or does God first foresee what they will do and then on that basis make his decision as to what is going to happen?

1. Calvinists believe that God's plan is logically prior and that human decisions and actions are a consequence. With respect to the particular matter of the acceptance or rejection of salvation, God in his plan has chosen that some shall believe and thus receive the offer of eternal life. He foreknows what will happen because he has decided what is to happen. This is true with respect to all the other decisions and actions of human beings as well. God is not dependent upon what humans decide. It is not the case, then, that God determines that what we are

going to do will come to pass, nor does he choose to eternal life those who he foresees will believe. Rather, God's decision has rendered it certain that every individual will act in a particular way.[5]

2. Arminians, on the other hand, place a higher value upon human freedom. God allows and expects human beings to exercise the will they have been given. If this were not so, we would not find the biblical invitations to choose God, the "whosoever will" passages, such as "Come to me, all who labor and are heavy-laden, and I will give you rest" (Matt. 11:28). The very offering of such invitations implies that one can either accept or reject them. This, however, seems inconsistent with the position that God's decisions have rendered the future certain. If they had, there would be no point in issuing invitations, for God's decisions as to what would happen would come to pass regardless of what we do. The Arminians therefore look for some other way of regarding the decisions of God.

The key lies in understanding the role of God's foreknowledge in the formation and execution of the divine plan. In Romans 8:29 Paul says, "Whom he foreknew he also predestined." From this verse the Arminian draws the conclusion that God's choice or determination of each individual's destiny is a result of foreknowledge. Thus, those who God foreknew would believe are those he decided would be saved. A similar statement can be made of all human actions, of all other aspects of life for that matter. God knows what all of us are going to do. He therefore wills what he foresees will happen.[6] So one might say that in the Arminian view this aspect of God's plan is conditional upon human decision; in the Calvinistic view, on the other hand, God's plan is unconditional.

A Moderately Calvinistic Model

The Unconditional Nature of God's Plan

Despite difficulties in relating divine sovereignty to human freedom, we nonetheless come to the conclusion on biblical grounds that the plan of God is unconditional rather than conditional upon human choice. There simply is nothing in the Bible to suggest that God chooses humans because of what they are going to do on their own. The Arminian concept of foreknowledge (*prognōsis*), appealing though it is, is not borne out by Scripture. The word means more than simply having advance knowledge or precognition of what is to come. It appears to have in its background the Hebrew concept of *yāda'*, which often meant more than simple awareness. It suggested a kind of intimate knowledge—it was even used of sexual intercourse.[7] When Paul says that God foreknew the people of Israel, he is not referring merely to an advance knowledge which God had. Indeed, it is clear that God's choice of Israel was not upon the basis of advance knowledge of a favorable response on their part. Had God anticipated such a response, he would certainly have been wrong. Note that in Romans 11:2 Paul says, "God has not rejected his people whom he foreknew," and that a discussion of the faithlessness of Israel follows. Certainly in this passage foreknowledge must mean something more than advance knowledge. In Acts 2:23, foreknowledge is linked with the will of God. Moreover, in 1 Peter 1 we read that the elect are chosen according to the foreknowledge of God (v. 2) and that Christ was foreknown from before the foundation of the world (v. 20). To suggest that foreknowledge here means nothing more than previous knowledge or acquaintance is to virtually deprive these verses of any real meaning. We must conclude that foreknowledge as used in Ro-

5. J. Gresham Machen, *The Christian View of Man* (Grand Rapids: Eerdmans, 1947), p. 78.

6. Henry C. Thiessen, *Introductory Lectures in Systematic Theology* (Grand Rapids: Eerdmans, 1949), p. 157.

7. Francis Brown, S. R. Driver, and Charles A. Briggs, *Hebrew and English Lexicon of the Old Testament* (New York: Oxford University Press, 1955), pp. 393–95.

mans 8:29 carries with it the idea of favorable disposition or selection as well as advance knowledge.

Furthermore, there are passages where the unconditional nature of God's selecting plan is made quite explicit. This is seen in Paul's statement regarding the choice of Jacob over Esau: "Though they were not yet born and had done nothing either good or bad, in order that God's purpose of election might continue, not because of works but because of his call, she [Rebekah] was told, 'The elder will serve the younger.' As it is written, 'Jacob I loved, but Esau I hated'" (Rom. 9:11–13). Paul seems to be taking great pains to emphasize the unmerited or unconditional nature of God's choice of Jacob. Later in the same chapter Paul comments, "So then he has mercy upon whomever he wills, and he hardens the heart of whomever he wills" (v. 18). The import of the subsequent image of the potter and the clay is very difficult to escape (vv. 20–24). Similarly, Jesus told his disciples, "You did not choose me, but I chose you and appointed you that you should go and bear fruit and that your fruit should abide" (John 15:16). Because of these and similar considerations, we must conclude that the plan of God is unconditional rather than conditional upon human actions which he has foreseen.

The Meaning of Human Freedom

At this point we must raise the question of whether God can create genuinely free beings and yet render certain all things that are to come to pass, including the free decisions and actions of those beings. The key to unlocking the problem is the distinction between rendering something certain and rendering it necessary. The former is a matter of God's decision that something *will* happen; the latter would be a matter of his decreeing that it *must* occur. In the former case, the human being will not act in a way contrary to the course of action which God has chosen; in the latter case, the human being cannot act in a way contrary to what

God has chosen. What we are saying is that God renders it certain that a person who could act (or could have acted) differently does in fact act in a particular way (the way that God wills).[8]

What does it mean to say that I am free? It means that I am not under constraint. Thus, I am free to do whatever pleases me. But am I free with respect to what pleases me and what does not? To put it differently, I may choose one action over another because it holds more appeal for me. But I am not fully in control of the appeal which each of those actions holds for me. That is quite a different matter. I make all my decisions, but those decisions are in large measure influenced by certain characteristics of mine which I am not capable of altering by my own choice. If, for example, I am offered for dinner a choice between liver and steak, I am quite free to take the liver, but I do not desire to do so. I have no conscious control over my dislike of liver. That is a given that goes with my being the person I am. In that respect my freedom is limited. I do not know whether it is my genes or environmental conditioning which has caused my dislike of liver, but it is apparent that I cannot by mere force of will alter this characteristic of mine.

There are, then, limitations upon who I am and what I desire and will. I certainly did not choose the genes that I have; I did not select my parents nor the exact geographical location and cultural setting of my birth. My freedom, therefore, is within these limitations. And here arises the question: Who set up these factors? The theistic answer is, "God did."

I am free to choose among various options. But my choice will be influenced by who I am. Therefore, my freedom must be understood as my ability to choose among options in light of who I am. And who I am

8. I hold what Antony Flew has called "compatibilistic freedom": human freedom is compatible with (in this case) God's having rendered certain everything which occurs—"Compatibilism, Free Will, and God," *Philosophy* 48 (1973): 231–32.

is a result of God's decision and activity. God is in control of all the circumstances that bear upon my situation in life. He may bring to bear (or permit to be brought to bear) factors which will make a particular option appealing, even powerfully appealing, to me. Through all the factors that have come into my experience in time past he has influenced the type of person I now am. Indeed, he has affected what has come to pass by willing that it was I who was brought into being.

Whenever a child is conceived, there are an infinite number of possibilities. A countless variety of genetic combinations may emerge out of the union of sperm and ovum. We do not know why a particular combina-

answer to the question, "But would he have?" is no. In our understanding, for human freedom to exist, only the first question need be answered in the affirmative. But others would argue that human freedom exists only if both questions can be answered in the affirmative; that is, if the individual not only could have chosen differently, but could also have desired to choose differently. In their view freedom means total spontaneity, random choice. We would point out to them that when it comes to human decisions and actions, nothing is completely spontaneous or random. There is a measure of predictability with respect to human behavior; and the better we know an individual, the better we

The plan of God does not force us to act in particular ways, but renders it certain that we will freely act in those ways.

tion actually results. But now, for the sake of argument, let us consider the possibility of a hypothetical individual whose genetic combination differs infinitesimally from my own. He is identical to me in every respect; in every situation of life he responds as I do. But at one particular point he will choose to move his finger to the left whereas I will move mine to the right. I am not compelled to move my finger to the right, but I freely choose to do so. Now by making sure that it was I, and not my hypothetical double, who came into existence, and setting the circumstances of my life, God rendered it certain that at that one particular point I would freely move my finger to the right.

God's Will and Human Freedom

Is God's having rendered human decisions and actions certain compatible with human freedom? How we respond depends on our understanding of freedom. According to the position we are espousing, the answer to the question, "Could the individual have chosen differently?" is yes, while the

can anticipate his or her responses. For example, a good friend or relative might say, "I knew you were going to say that." We conclude that if by freedom is meant random choice, human freedom is a practical impossibility. But if by freedom is meant ability to choose between options, human freedom exists and is compatible with God's having rendered our decisions and actions certain.

It should be noted that if certainty of outcome is inconsistent with freedom, divine foreknowledge, as the Arminian understands that term, presents as much difficulty for human freedom as does divine foreordination. For if God knows what I will do, it must be certain that I am going to do it. If it were not certain, God could not know it; he might be mistaken (I might act differently from what he expects). But if what I will do is certain, then surely I will do it, whether or not I know what I will do. It will happen! But am I then free? In the view of those whose definition of freedom entails the implication that it cannot be certain that a particular event will occur, presumably I am not free.

In their view, divine foreknowledge is just as incompatible with human freedom as is divine foreordination.

It might seem that the divine choice we have argued for is the same as the Arminian idea of foreknowledge. There is a significant difference, however. In the Arminian understanding, there is a foreknowledge of actual existing entities. God simply chooses to confirm, as it were, what he foresees real individuals will decide and do. In our scheme, however, God has a foreknowledge of possibilities. God foresees what possible beings will do if placed in a particular situation with all the influences that will be present at that point in time and space. On this basis he chooses which of the possible individuals will become actualities and which circumstances and influences will be present. He foreknows what these individuals will freely do, for he in effect made that decision by choosing them in particular to bring into existence.

God's Wish and God's Will

Our position that God has rendered certain everything that occurs raises another question: Is there not a contradiction at certain points between what God commands and says he desires and what he actually wills? For example, sin is universally prohibited, yet apparently God wills for it to occur. Certainly murder is prohibited in Scripture, and yet the death of Jesus by execution was apparently willed by God (Luke 22:22; Acts 2:23). Further, we are told that God is not willing that any should perish (2 Peter 3:9), yet apparently he does not actually will for all to be saved, since not everyone is saved. How are we to reconcile these seemingly contradictory considerations?

We must distinguish between two different senses of God's will, which we will refer to as God's "wish" ($will_1$) and God's "will" ($will_2$). The former is God's general intention, the values with which he is pleased. The latter is God's specific intention in a given situation, what he decides shall actually occur. There are times, many of them,

when God wills to permit, and thus to have occur, what he really does not wish. This is the case with sin. God does not desire sin to occur. There are occasions, however, when he simply says, in effect, "So be it," allowing a human to choose freely a sinful course of action.

We are reminded here of the way parents sometimes treat their children. A mother may wish for her son to avoid a particular type of behavior, and may tell him so. Yet there are situations in which she may, though seeing her son about to engage in the forbidden action, choose not to intervene to prevent it. Here is a case in which the parent's wish is clearly that the child not engage in certain behavior, yet her will is that he do what he has willed to do. By choosing not to intervene to prevent the act, the mother is actually willing that it take place. Perhaps this is the way we should understand Joseph's treatment at the hands of his brothers. It did not please God; it was not consistent with what he is like. God did, however, will to permit it; he did not intervene to prevent it. And interestingly enough, God used their action to produce the very thing it was intended to prevent—Joseph's ascendancy.

God's Will and the Need for Human Action

Another issue that must be examined concerns whether our view of the all-encompassing plan of God removes incentives for activity on our part. If God has already rendered certain what is to occur, is there any point in our seeking to accomplish his will? Does what we do really make any difference in what happens? This issue relates particularly to evangelism. If God has already chosen (elected) who will be saved and who will not, what difference does it make whether we (or anyone else for that matter) seek to propagate the gospel? Nothing can change the fact that the elect will be saved and the nonelect will not.

Two points should be made by way of response. One is that if God has rendered certain the end, his plan also includes the means to that end. His plan may well include that our witness is the means by which an elect person will come to saving faith. Thus it is foreordained by God that we should witness to that person. The other consideration is that we do not know in detail what God's plan is. So we must proceed on the basis of what God has revealed of his wish. Accordingly, we must witness. This may mean that some of our time is spent on someone who will not ultimately enter the kingdom of heaven. But that does not mean that our time has been wasted. It may well have been the means to fulfilling another part of God's plan. And ultimately it is faithfulness, not success, that is God's measure of our service.

Various Understandings of History

As we noted at the beginning of this chapter, Christianity's doctrine of the divine plan responds specifically to the questions of where history is going and what is moving it. Some understandings of the movement of history are quite negative. This is particularly true of cyclical views, which do not see history as progressing, but as simply repeating the same pattern, albeit in somewhat different fashion. The Eastern religions tend to be of this type, particularly Hinduism, with its emphasis upon reincarnation. One goes through cycles of death and rebirth, with the status of one's life in each new incarnation largely determined by one's conduct in the previous life. Salvation, if we may term it that, consists in Nirvana, escape from the repeated process.

Doomsday philosophies abound in our time. It is believed that history will soon come to a disastrous end as a result of either an economic collapse, an ecological crisis involving massive pollution of the environment, or an outbreak of nuclear warfare.[9] Humankind is doomed because we have failed to manage the world about us wisely.

Another prominent twentieth-century pessimistic philosophy is existentialism. The idea of the absurdity of the world, of the paradoxical and the ironic in reality, of the blind randomness of much that occurs, leads to despair. Since there is no discernible pattern in the events of history, one must create one's own meaning by a conscious act of free will.

On the other hand, there have been a number of quite optimistic views, especially in the latter half of the nineteenth century. Darwinism was extended from the biological realm to other areas, particularly to society. In the thought of Herbert Spencer it became an all-inclusive philosophy entailing the growth, progress, and development of the whole of reality. Although this view proved rather unrealistic, it had considerable influence in its time. In more recent years, utopianisms employing the methods of the behavioral sciences have sought to restructure society or at least individual lives.[10]

Perhaps the most militant philosophy of history on a global scale has been dialectical materialism, the philosophy upon which communism is based. Adapting Georg Hegel's philosophy, Karl Marx replaced its idealistic metaphysic with a materialistic view. The forces of material reality are impelling history to its end. Through a series of steps, the economic order is being changed. Each stage of the process is characterized by a conflict between two antithetical groups or movements. The prevailing means of production is changing from feudalism to capitalism to a final socialistic stage where there will be no private ownership. In the classless society, the dialectic which has moved history through the rhythmical process of thesis-antithesis-synthesis will cease, and all evil will wither away. Note that this trust is in an impersonal force. Consequently, many of the people who have lived under commu-

9. E.g., Barry Commoner, *The Closing Circle* (New York: Alfred A. Knopf, 1971); Paul R. Ehrlich, *The Population Bomb* (New York: Ballantine, 1976).

10. E.g., B. F. Skinner, *Walden Two* (New York: Macmillan, 1948).

nism found it neither personally satisfying nor societally effective.

Finally, there is the Christian doctrine of the divine plan, which affirms that an all-wise, all-powerful, good God has from all eternity planned what is to occur and that history is carrying out his intention. There is a definite goal toward which history is progressing. History is not, then, merely chance happenings. And the force causing its movements is not impersonal atoms or blind fate. It is, rather, a loving God with whom we can have a personal relationship. We may look forward with assurance, then, toward the attainment of the telos of the universe. And we may align our lives with what we know will be the outcome of history.

13 God's Originating Work: Creation

The plan of God may be thought of as being like the architect's plans and drawings for a building that is to be constructed. But the plan was not merely a scheme in the mind of God. It has been translated into reality by God's actions. At this point in our study we turn to these various works of God. In this part we will concentrate on those works which are attributed especially, although not exclusively, to God the Father. The first of these is creation. By creation we mean the work of God in bringing into being, without the use of any preexisting materials, everything that is.

Reasons for Studying the Doctrine of Creation

1. There are several reasons for giving careful study to the doctrine of creation. First is the fact that the Bible places great significance upon it. The very first statement of the Bible is, "In the beginning God created the heavens and the earth" (Gen. 1:1).

Creation is likewise one of the first assertions in the Gospel according to John, the most theologically oriented of the New Testament Gospels (John 1:1–3). Clearly, the creative work of God plays a prominent role in the Bible's presentation of him.

2. The doctrine of creation has been a significant part of the church's faith; it has been a highly important aspect of its teaching and preaching. The first article of the Apostles' Creed says, "I believe in God the Father Almighty, Maker of heaven and earth." Although this particular element (i.e., the phrase dealing with creation) was not in the earliest form of the creed, but

root there are similarities between Christianity and Hinduism, for example, a close examination reveals that the Christian doctrine of God and creation is quite different from Hinduism's Brahma-Atman teaching.

5. The study of the doctrine of creation is one point of potential dialogue between Christianity and natural science. At times the dialogue has been quite furious. The great evolution debate of the early twentieth century makes it clear that while theology and science run in parallel courses most of the time, not intersecting in a common topic, the issue of the origin of the world is one point where they do encounter one an-

The whole of what now exists was begun by God's act of bringing it into existence—he did not fashion and adapt something which already existed independently of him.

added somewhat later, nonetheless, it is significant that in a formulation as brief as the Apostles' Creed, creation was rather early thought important enough to be included.

3. Our understanding of the doctrine of creation is important because of its effect upon our understanding of other doctrines. Humans were created by God as separate beings; they did not emanate from him. Because they came from the hand of a good God who pronounced the whole of his creation good, there is no inherent evil in being material rather than spiritual. These various facets of the doctrine of creation tell us a great deal about the status of humans. Moreover, since the universe is God's doing rather than a mere chance happening, we are able to discern something about the nature and the will of God from an examination of creation. Alter the doctrine of creation at any point, and you have also altered these other aspects of Christian doctrine.

4. The doctrine of creation helps differentiate Christianity from other religions and worldviews. While some might think that at

other. It is important to understand just what the Christian and biblical position is upon this subject, and what is at stake.

6. There needs to be a careful understanding of the doctrine of creation because there sometimes have been sharp disagreements within Christian circles. In the modernist-fundamentalist controversy of the early twentieth century, the struggle was on a large scale—evolution versus creation. Today, by contrast, there seem to be internal disputes within evangelicalism between the theory of progressive creationism and the view that the earth is only a few thousand years old. A careful look must be taken at precisely what the Bible does teach on this subject.

Elements of the Biblical Teaching on Creation

Creation out of Nothing

We begin our examination of the doctrine of creation by noting that it is creation out of nothing (*ex nihilo*), or without the use of preexisting materials. This does not mean that all of God's creative work was direct and immediate, occurring at the very beginning of time. (Certainly there was immediate or direct creation, the bringing into being of all reality; but there has also been mediate or derivative creation, God's subsequent work of developing and fashioning what he had originally brought into existence.) Rather, what we are here affirming is that the whole of what now exists was begun by God's act of bringing it into existence—he did not fashion and adapt something which already existed independently of him.

Although the language in the Old Testament is not conclusive, the idea of *ex nihilo* creation can be found in a number of New Testament passages where the aim is not primarily to make a statement about the nature of creation. In particular, there are numerous references to the beginning of the world or the beginning of creation:

"from [since, before] the foundation of the world" (Matt. 13:35; 25:34; Luke 11:50; John 17:24; Eph. 1:4; Heb. 4:3; 9:26; 1 Peter 1:20; Rev. 13:8; 17:8)

"from the beginning" (Matt. 19:4, 8; John 8:44; 2 Thess. 2:13; 1 John 1:1; 2:13–14; 3:8)

"from the beginning of the world" (Matt. 24:21)

"from the beginning of the creation" (Mark 10:6; 2 Peter 3:4)

"from the beginning of creation which God created" (Mark 13:19)

"since the creation of the world" (Rom. 1:20)

"Thou, Lord, didst found the earth in the beginning" (Heb. 1:10)

"the beginning of God's creation" (Rev. 3:14)

Regarding these several expressions Werner Foerster says, "These phrases show that creation involves the beginning of the existence of the world, so that there is no pre-existent matter."[1]

In the New Testament we can find several more-explicit expressions of the idea of creating out of nothing. We read that God calls things into being by his word. Paul says that God "calls into existence the things that do not exist" (Rom. 4:17). God said, "Let light shine out of darkness" (2 Cor. 4:6). This surely suggests the effect occurred without the use of any antecedent material cause. God created the world by his word "so that what is seen was made out of things which do not appear" (Heb. 11:3).

From these biblical references we can draw several conclusions. For one, God has the power simply to will situations to be, and they immediately come to pass exactly as he has willed. Second, creation is an act of his will, not an act to which he is driven by any force or consideration outside himself. Further, God does not involve himself, his own being, in the process. Creation is not something made out of him. It is not a part of him or an emanation from his reality.

Its All-inclusive Nature

God did not create merely a certain part of reality, with the remainder attributable to some other origin. The entirety of reality has come into being through his act. In the opening statement of Genesis ("In the beginning God created the heavens and the earth"), the expression "the heavens and the earth" is not intended to designate those items alone. It is an idiom referring to everything that is. It is an affirmation that the whole universe came into being through this act of God. John 1:3 makes the same point most emphatically and explicitly in both positive and negative terms: "all things were made through him, and without him was not anything made that was made." Here are an affirmation of the creaturehood of all

---

1. Werner Foerster, κτίζω, in *Theological Dictionary of the New Testament*, ed. Gerhard Kittel and Gerhard Friedrich, trans. Geoffrey W. Bromiley, 10 vols. (Grand Rapids: Eerdmans, 1964–76), vol. 3, p. 1029.

that is, and a rejection of the notion that something might have been made by someone or something other than God.

The Work of the Triune God

Creation is the work of the Triune God. A large number of the Old Testament references to the creative act attribute it simply to God, rather than to the Father, Son, or Spirit, for the distinctions of the Trinity had not yet been fully revealed (e.g., Gen. 1:1; Ps. 96:5; Isa. 37:16; 44:24; 45:12; Jer. 10:11–12). In the New Testament, however, we find differentiation. First Corinthians 8:6, which appears in a passage where Paul discusses the propriety of eating food which had been offered to idols, is particularly instructive. In contrasting God with idols, Paul says, "Yet for us there is one God, the Father, from whom are all things and for whom we exist, and one Lord, Jesus Christ, through whom are all things and through whom we exist." Paul is including both the Father and the Son in the act of creation and yet also distinguishing them from one another. The Father apparently has the more prominent part; he is the source from whom all things come. The Son is the means or the agent of the existence of all things. There is a similar affirmation in John 1:3 and Hebrews 1:10. In addition, there are references which seem to indicate the Spirit of God was active in creating as well—Genesis 1:2; Job 26:13; 33:4; Psalm 104:30; and Isaiah 40:12–13. In some of these cases, however, it is difficult to determine whether the reference is to the Holy Spirit or to God's working by means of his breath, since the Hebrew word *rûach* can be used for either one.

There may seem to be a conflict between attributing creation to the Father, the Son, and the Holy Spirit, and maintaining that each member of the Trinity has his own distinctive work. Yet this is not a problem, unless we think that there is but one form of causation. When a house is built, who actually builds it? In one sense, it is the architect who designs it and creates the plans from which it is constructed. In another sense,

however, it is the contractor who actually carries out the plan, and yet it is the construction workers who in fact build the house. But certainly the owners, although they may not drive a single nail, are also in a sense the ones who build the house, since they sign the legal papers authorizing its construction, and will make the mortgage payments each month. Each one, in a different way, is the cause of the house. A similar statement can be made about creation. It appears from Scripture that it was the Father who brought the created universe into existence. But it was the Spirit and the Son who fashioned it, who carried out the details of the design. While the creation is *from* the Father, it is *through* the Son and *by* the Holy Spirit.

Its Purpose: God's Glory

While God did not have to create, he did so for good and sufficient reasons. He had a purpose in bringing reality into being. And the creation fulfils that purpose of God. In particular, the creation glorifies God by carrying out his will. The inanimate creation glorifies him (Ps. 19:1); the animate creatures obey his plan for them. In the story of Jonah, we see this in rather vivid fashion. Everyone and everything (except Jonah initially) obeyed God's will and plan: the storm, the dice, the sailors, the great fish, the Ninevites, the east wind, the gourd, and the worm. Each part of creation is capable of fulfilling God's purposes for it, but each obeys in a different way. The inanimate creation does so mechanically, obeying natural laws which govern the physical world. The animate creation does so instinctively, responding to impulses within. Humans alone are capable of obeying God consciously and willingly, and thus glorify God most fully.

The Theological Meaning of the Doctrine

We turn now to examine the theological meaning of the doctrine of creation. What really is being affirmed by this teaching?

And, perhaps just as important for our purposes, what is being rejected or contradicted?

1. The doctrine of creation is first and rather obviously a statement that everything that is not God has derived its existence from him. To put it another way, the idea that there is any ultimate reality other than God is rejected. There is no room for dualism. In a dualism, as the word would indicate, there are two ultimate principles. In one form of dualism there is the Lord, the Creator, the Maker. And there is what the Creator utilizes, or what he works upon, the material that he employs in creating. But this is not what the Christian doctrine affirms. God did not work with something which was in existence. He brought into existence the very raw material which he employed. If this were not the case, God would not really be infinite.

2. The original act of divine creation is unique. It is unlike human "creative" acts, which involve fashioning, using the materials at hand. In producing works of art, artists must work within the limitations of the medium employed, for example, the reflective characteristics of oil paint. Moreover, even the concepts artists express are dependent upon their previous experience. Their work will be either an expression of an idea they have directly experienced or a combination of elements previously experienced into some new whole; a genuinely novel idea, totally new and fresh, is very rare indeed. God, however, is not bound by anything external to himself. His only limitations are those of his own nature and the choices he has made.

3. The doctrine of creation also means that nothing made is intrinsically evil. Everything has come from God, and the creation narrative says five times that he saw that it was good (Gen. 1:10, 12, 18, 21, 25). Then, when he completed his creation of man, we are told that God saw everything he had made, and it was very good (v. 31). There was nothing evil within God's original creation.

In any type of dualism, by contrast, there tends to be a moral distinction between the higher and the lower principles or elements.[2] Since the higher realm is divine and the lower is not, the former is thought of as more real than the other. Eventually this metaphysical difference tends to be regarded as a moral difference as well—the higher is good and the lower is evil. If, however, the whole of reality owes its existence to God, and if what God made was "good" throughout, we cannot think of matter as inherently or intrinsically evil.[3]

4. The doctrine of creation also thrusts a responsibility upon humankind. We cannot justify our evil behavior by blaming the evil realm of the material. The material world is not inherently evil. Our sin must be an exercise of our own freedom. Nor can we blame society. Human society was also part of what God made, and it was very good. To regard society as the cause of sin is therefore an inaccurate and misleading ploy.

5. The doctrine of creation also guards against depreciating the incarnation of Christ. If the material world were somehow inherently evil, it would be very difficult to accept the fact that the Second Person of the Trinity took on human form, including a physical body. On the other hand, a correct understanding of the doctrine of creation—what God made was good—enables us to affirm the full meaning of the incarnation of Jesus Christ, his taking of human flesh upon himself.

6. The doctrine of creation also restrains us from asceticism. Believing that the physical nature is evil has led some, including Christians, to shun the human body and any type of physical satisfaction. Spirit, being more divine, is the proper realm of the good and the godly. Thus, meditation is pursued, and an austere diet and abstinence from sex are regarded as conditions of spirituality. But the doctrine of creation affirms that God has made all that is and has made it good. It is therefore redeemable. Salvation and spirituality are to be found, not by fleeing from or

2. Langdon Gilkey, *Maker of Heaven and Earth* (Garden City, N.Y.: Doubleday, 1965), p. 48.

3. Ibid., pp. 58–59.

avoiding the material realm, but by sanctifying it.

7. If all of creation has been made by God, there are a connection and an affinity among the various parts of it. I am a brother to all other people, for the same God created us and watches over us. Since inanimate material also comes from God, I am, at base, one with nature, for we are members of the same family.

8. While the doctrine of creation excludes any dualism, it also excludes the type of monism that regards the world as an emanation from God. In monism, what we have is an outflow or emanation from God's nature, a part of him separated from his essence as it were. There is a tendency to regard this emanation as still divine; hence the end result of this view is usually pantheism. It is a change of status, rather than a beginning of being, that is conceived of here.

Christianity's doctrine of creation out of nothing rejects all of this. The individual elements of the world are genuine creatures dependent upon God their Creator. Clearly separate from him (i.e., they are not emanations from his nature), they are finite dependent creatures.

9. Further, the doctrine of creation points out the inherent limitations of creaturehood. No creature or combination of creatures can ever be equated with God. Thus there is no basis whatsoever for idolatry—for worshiping nature or for revering human beings. God has a unique status, so that he alone is to be worshiped (Exod. 20:2–3).

We sometimes think of the great metaphysical gap in the universe as a quantitative gap falling between humans and the rest of the creation. In reality, however, the great metaphysical gap is quantitative *and* qualitative, and falls between God on one side and all else on the other.[4] He is to be the object of worship, praise, and obedience. All other existents are to be subjects who offer these acts of submission to him.

4. Francis Schaeffer, *The God Who Is There* (Downers Grove, Ill.: Inter-Varsity, 1968), pp. 94–95.

The Creation Doctrine and Its Relation to Science

Science and the Bible

For many years, theology was the "queen of the sciences." It was the foremost source of authority in the West, and the teachings of the Bible and the church were the standard against which claims to truth were measured. In the modern period, however, the rise of science produced friction between theology and science. Christians who believed fully that the Bible is inspired and authoritative, and that God created the world and gave it order and meaning, had a natural desire to see theology and science interrelate, since both derive from God and point to him. Instead, open and violent conflict at times erupted. In the early stages, theology's quarrel was primarily with natural science; later on the behavioral sciences presented the major problem.

> *The great metaphysical gap falls between God on one side and all else on the other.*

In recent years the controversy has taken on added intensity, with court cases to decide the teaching of evolution and creationism. The conflict has led many people to one extreme or the other. Some, thinking that there is an irreconcilable conflict between the scientific evidence for evolution and the biblical teaching regarding creation, have abandoned faith in Christianity. Others have virtually abandoned trust in the scientific method, believing that it rests upon false assumptions. In many cases, however, they continue to use the modern technology which science has helped to develop.

A related area of disagreement is the nature of the Bible. Some believe that the Bible has a great deal to say about such scientific matters as the origin of the universe, life, and the human race, and says it in fairly technical fashion. Others, asserting that the Bible is not a science textbook, treat it as quite irrelevant to any scientific matters, maintaining that its message is purely religious. Both conceptions are wrong. The Bible must be understood in light of its purpose: to make it possible for humans to be savingly related to God. It was not given to satisfy our curiosity, or to supply us with information which might be obtained by study of God's creation, his general revelation to us. Scripture describes matters of nature, not in the technical language which scientists use, but in the language of ordinary conversation, which reflects how the world appears to the eye. On the other hand, the fact that a book is not a formal text on a particular subject (few books are) does not mean that it says nothing bearing upon that subject. In reality, the Bible makes assertions or affirmations about nature and God's relationship to it which have implications for science. Its religious affirmations are in some cases so tied up with statements about nature that they cannot be separated. We must take seriously both of God's books: the book of his Word and the book of his works.

The Age and Development of the Earth

Apart from the issues relating specifically to the origin and nature of human beings, there are two problems which have caused concern over the years: the age of the earth, and development within the creation. The conflict regarding the age of the earth pits the understanding that the Bible teaches that God created everything about six thousand years ago (4004 B.C. was the exact calculation produced by Archbishop James Ussher) against the indications of geology that the earth is several billion years old. Attempted resolutions have usually taken the form of adjusting either the scientific or the biblical indications of age, or, in some cases, both.

Those who maintain that the earth is relatively young frequently challenge the validity of the scientific methods of dating, especially those involving radioactive materials. Some of them argue that at the time of the flood the earth was subjected to unusual geological forces which so altered it that it appears much older than it actually is. One ingenious theory holds that God created the world six thousand years ago, but made it as if it were already billions of years old. On the other hand, those who believe the earth is billions of years old point out that the genealogies in the Bible were never intended to be used to calculate the beginning of time. Furthermore, the Hebrew word translated "day" in Genesis 1 can have several different meanings, including a long period of time. Some hold that the "days" are not time periods at all, but simply figures of speech. The most satisfactory approach appears to me to be that which holds that God created in a series of acts which involved long periods, and which took place an indefinite time ago. This does full justice to both the scientific and the biblical data.

The other major issue regarding creation and science is the question of development. Evolutionists hold that life originated through a set of chance factors, and that through a process known as natural selection all the species which now exist derived from one simple organism. Fiat creationists insist that God directly created at the beginning every species that would ever be, and that there has been no evolution. Theistic evolutionists hold that God created the first organism and placed within his universe the process by which life then developed in accordance with scientific laws, perhaps aided at some points by God's intervention (e.g., the changing of a higher primate into the first human).

We must note the significant evidence for the arising of new species through natural development: the resemblance between some different forms, and the existence of some transitional forms; the restriction of certain species to isolated areas (e.g., Australia); the existence of vestigial organs (e.g., the coccyx in humans). The biblical record, however, as understood from the perspective on inspiration and authority that we have espoused in this book, seems to teach that God created in a series of acts. The best combination of these considerations is found in what is sometimes called progressive creationism. This notes that the Hebrew word translated "kind(s)" in Genesis 1 cannot be made more specific than that. It is simply a word for subdivisions, and thus does not require the interpretation that God directly created every species. According to this view, God would create the first member of a group of creatures (say, the first horse); over a long period of time other forms closely related evolved therefrom. Then God created other kinds, quite different in nature, so that birds did not evolve from fish, for example. This fits well both the biblical data and the scientific data, for, significantly, there are systematic deficiencies in the fossil record. So one can take seriously both science and theology.

Sometimes Christians are intimidated by the theory of evolution, forgetting that it is simply a theory, although one built on many data. But when science goes beyond describing the facts and offering explanations of specific occurrences to give an overall explanation of the universe, it is going beyond its competence. It has then become philosophy, and specifically cosmology, which intellectual integrity requires should not be presented without pointing out that there are other explanatory theories. Among the alternatives, of course, is the view that there is a higher being who has brought into existence all that is.

Implications of the Doctrine of Creation

What are the implications of belief in creation? The doctrine has a significant impact upon how we view and treat life and the world.

1. Everything that is has value. It was a wise plan that brought into being just what there is within the creation. Each part has its place, which is just what God intended for it to have. God loves all of his creation, not just certain parts of it. Thus we should also have concern for all of it, to preserve and guard and develop what God has made.

2. God's creative activity includes not only the initial creative activity, but also his later indirect workings. Creation does not preclude development within the world; it includes it. Thus God's plan involves and utilizes the best of human skill and knowledge in the genetic refinement of the creation. Such endeavors are our partnership with God in the ongoing work of creation. Yet, of course, we must be mindful that the materials and truth we employ in those endeavors come from God.

3. There is justification for scientifically investigating the creation. Science assumes that there is within the creation some sort of order or pattern which it can discover. If the universe were random and, consequently, all the facts scientists gather about it were merely a haphazard collection, no real understanding of nature would be possible. But by affirming that everything has been made in accordance with a logical pattern, the doctrine of creation substantiates science's assumption. It is significant that historically science developed earliest and most rapidly in European culture, where there was a belief in a single God who had created according to a rational plan, rather than in some other culture where there was a belief in several gods who engage in conflicting activities.[5] Knowing that there is an intelligent pattern to the universe, the Christian is motivated to seek for it.

4. Nothing other than God is self-sufficient or eternal. Everything else, every object and every being, derives its existence from him. It exists to do his will. Although we will highly respect the creation, since it has been made by him, we will always maintain a clear distinction between God and it.

5. Alfred North Whitehead, *Science and the Modern World* (New York: Macmillan, 1925), p. 12.

14 God's Continuing Work: Providence

While creation is God's originating work with respect to the universe, providence is his continuing relationship to it. By providence we mean the continuing action of God by which he preserves in existence the creation which he has brought into being, and guides it to his intended purposes for it. In terms of the daily dynamics of our lives, therefore, providence has in many ways more actual pertinence than does the doctrine of creation. The word derives from the Latin *providere*, which literally means to foresee. But more than merely knowing about the future is involved. The word also carries the connotation of acting prudently or making preparation for the future.

Providence in certain ways is central to the conduct of the Christian life. It means that we are able to live in the assurance that God is present and active in our lives. We are in his care and can therefore face the future confidently, knowing that things are not happening merely by chance. We can pray, knowing that

God hears and acts upon our prayers. We can face danger, knowing that he is not unaware and uninvolved.

Providence may be thought of as having two aspects. One aspect is God's work of preserving his creation in existence, maintaining and sustaining it; this is generally called preservation or sustenance. The other is God's activity in guiding and directing the course of events to fulfil the purposes which he has in mind. This is termed government or providence proper. Preservation and government should not be thought of as sharply separate acts of God, but as distinguishable aspects of his unitary work.

Providence as Preservation

Preservation is God's maintaining his creation in existence. It involves God's protection of his creation against harm and destruction, and his provision for the needs of the elements or members of the creation.

Biblical Teaching on Preservation

Numerous biblical passages speak of God's preserving the creation as a whole. In Nehemiah 9:6 Ezra says, "Thou art the LORD, thou alone; thou hast made heaven, the heaven of heavens, with all their host, the earth and all that is on it, the seas and all that is in them; and thou preservest all of them; and the host of heaven worships thee." After a statement about the role of Christ in creation, Paul links him to the continuation of the creation as well: "He is before all things, and in him all things hold together" (Col. 1:17). The writer to the Hebrews speaks of the Son as "upholding the universe by his word of power" (1:3).

The Scripture writers see the preserving hand of God everywhere. In particular, the psalmists' hymns of praise emphasize God's preserving work throughout nature. An outstanding example is Psalm 104. God has set the earth on its foundations, so that it should never be shaken (v. 5). He sends the streams into the valleys (v. 10) and waters the mountains (v. 13). He makes the darkness so that the beasts of prey can seek their sustenance (vv. 20–21). All of the creatures of God receive their food from him (vv. 24–30). The import of the passages we have just cited is to deny that any part of the creation is self-sufficient. Both the origination and the continuation of all things are a matter of divine will and activity.

God's presence is particularly evident in the preservation of Israel as a nation. For example, the hand of God was present in providing for the needs of his people at the time of the great famine. God had brought Joseph to Egypt to make provision for feeding the people in the time of shortage. The sparing of the people in the time of Moses is also particularly noteworthy. The children of Israel were enabled to pass through the Red Sea on dry land, while the pursuing Egyptians were engulfed in the waters and drowned. God's chosen people then received miraculous provision in their wanderings through the wilderness, and they were given victories in battle, sometimes against great odds, as they sought to take the land promised to them.

In the Book of Daniel, God's work of preservation is again very striking. Shadrach, Meshach, and Abednego were condemned to be burned in the fiery furnace for failure to worship the golden image that had been set up. Yet they emerged unharmed from the furnace, while those who cast them in were destroyed by the heat. Daniel, because he prayed to his God, was thrown into a den of lions, yet he also emerged unharmed. Certainly God's preserving of his people was never clearer.

Jesus has also given clear teaching regarding the Father's work of preservation. The disciples were concerned about the necessities of life—what they would eat and what they would wear. Jesus reassured them that the Father feeds the birds of the air and clothes the flowers of the fields. He would surely do the same for them. While God provides for the lesser members of his creation, humans are of more value than birds (Matt. 6:26) and flowers (v. 30). It therefore is not necessary for humans to be anxious about food and clothing, for if they seek God's kingdom and righteousness, all these things will be added to them (vv. 31–33). This is a reference to God's provision. A similar teaching occurs in Matthew 10:28–32.

The Theological Dimensions of Preservation

An important emphasis of both Jesus' and Paul's teaching on preservation is the inseparability of God's children from his love and keeping. In John 10, Jesus draws a contrast between his sheep and the unbelievers who had just asked for a plain statement about his messiahship. His sheep recognize and respond to his voice. They shall never perish. No one shall snatch them out of his hand; no one is able to snatch

> *God's children cannot be separated from his love and keeping; though not spared from trial or danger, they are preserved within it.*

them out of the Father's hand (vv. 27–30). Paul strikes a similar note when he asks, "Who shall separate us from the love of Christ?" (Rom. 8:35). After rehearsing the various possibilities, all of which he rejects, he summarizes by saying, "For I am sure that neither death, nor life, nor angels, nor principalities, nor things present, nor things to come, nor powers, nor height, nor depth, nor anything else in all creation, will be able to separate us from the love of God in Christ Jesus our Lord" (vv. 38–39).

One salient dimension of God's preserving us and supplying us with what we need is that the believer is not spared from danger or trial, but preserved within it. There is no

promise that persecution and suffering will not come. The promise is that they will not prevail over us. Paul rejoiced that God will supply all of our needs according to his riches in glory in Christ Jesus (Phil. 4:19). Writing those words from prison, Paul indicated that he had learned to be content in any state in which he found himself (v. 11). He had learned the secret of facing either plenty and abundance or hunger and want (v. 12); he could do all things through Christ who strengthened him (v. 13).

Another concept excluded by the biblical teaching on the divine work of preservation is the deistic idea that God has simply made the world, established its patterns of action so that whatever is needed by each member of the creation will be automatically provided, and then allowed the world to go on its way.[1] Given this model, the creation will remain unless God acts to terminate it. Given the biblical model, however, creation would cease to be if God did not continuously will it to persist. God is directly and personally concerned about and involved with the continuation of his creation.

An image to help us correctly understand God's work of preservation can be drawn from the world of mechanics. We can start a manual electric drill by engaging the switch and then activate a locking device which will keep the drill running until definite action is taken to release the lock. The drill will remain on indefinitely if simply left by itself. This is like the deistic view of God's work of preservation. There are other tools, such as power saws, which do not have built-in locking devices. Such tools require continuous application of pressure to the switch. This is like the "dead man's switch" in a railroad locomotive. If the person operating the machine fails for whatever reason to continue to apply pressure, it comes to a halt. Such machines can serve as metaphors of the biblical view of preservation.

1. G. C. Joyce, "Deism," in *Encyclopedia of Religion and Ethics*, ed. James Hastings (New York: Scribner, 1955), vol. 4, pp. 5–11.

One other idea of preservation or sustenance needs to be avoided. This is the idea that God is like a celestial repairman: The creation has been established and ordinarily functions as God intends. At times, however, it is necessary for God to intervene to make an adjustment before something goes amiss, or perhaps to make a repair after something has gone wrong. In this view, God is not needed when things are going as they were designed to; he merely observes, approvingly. However, the Bible pictures a much more active involvement by God on a continuing basis.[2] God is immanently at work in his creation, constantly willing it to remain.

The biblical writers who understood the divine work of preservation had a definite sense of confidence. For example, Psalm 91 describes the Lord as our refuge and fortress. The psalmist had learned the lesson that Jesus was to teach his disciples—not to fear the one who can destroy the body but cannot touch the soul (Matt. 10:28). This is not to say that death cannot touch the believer, for death comes to all (Heb. 9:27). Rather, it is the confidence that physical death is not the most significant factor, that even death cannot separate one from God's love. So while the doctrine of God's work of preservation is no justification for foolhardiness or imprudence, it is a guard against terror or even anxiety.

God's work of preservation also means that we can have confidence in the regularity of the created world. It is possible to plan and to carry out our lives accordingly because there is a constancy to our environment. We take this fact for granted, yet it is essential to any sort of rational functioning in the world. The basis of the Christian's belief at this point is not a material or impersonal ground of reality, but an intelligent, good, and purposeful being who continues to will the existence of his creation, so that ordinarily no unexpected events occur.

2. G. C. Berkouwer, *The Providence of God* (Grand Rapids: Eerdmans, 1952), p. 74.

Providence as Government

The Extent of God's Governing Activity

By the government of God we mean his activity in the universe so that all its events fulfil his plan for it. As such, the governing activity of God of course broadly includes the matter which we have referred to as preservation. Here, however, the emphasis is more fully upon the purposive directing of the whole of reality and the course of history to the ends that God has in mind. It is the actual execution, within time, of his plans devised in eternity.

This governing activity of God extends over a large variety of areas. God is described as controlling nature. Particularly dramatic evidence of God's power over nature can be seen in the case of Elijah, who told Ahab that it would not rain except by the word of God, and it did not rain for three-and-a-half years, and who prayed at Mount Carmel for God to send down lightning from heaven, and it was done. Jesus' power over nature was part of what caused the disciples to recognize that he was God (Mark 4:39–41). (For similar expressions of the Lord's governance of the forces of nature, see Job 9:5–9; 37; Pss. 104:14; 147:8–15; Matt. 6:25–30.)

Scripture tells us that God guides and directs the animal creation. In Psalm 104:21–29, the beasts, from the young lions to the teeming sea creatures, are depicted as carrying out his will and as depending upon him for their provisions. Incapable of conscious choice, animals instinctively obey God's command.

Further, God's government involves human history and the destiny of the nations. A particularly vivid expression of this is found in Daniel 2:21: "He changes times and seasons; he removes kings and sets up kings." And there is a dramatic illustration in Daniel 4:24–25. The Lord uses Assyria to accomplish his purposes with Israel, and then in turn brings destruction upon Assyria as well (Isa. 10:5–12). (For similar expressions of

God's direction of human history, see Job 12:23; Pss. 47:7–8; 66:7.)

The Lord is also sovereign in the circumstances of the lives of individual persons. Hannah, inspired by the miraculous answer to her prayer (the Lord had given her a son, Samuel), expressed her praise: "The Lord kills and brings to life; he brings down to Sheol and raises up. The Lord makes poor and makes rich; he brings low, he also exalts" (1 Sam. 2:6–7). Paul asserts that even before he was born God had set him apart for his task (Gal. 1:15–16). David found comfort in the fact that God was sovereign in his life: "But I trust in thee, O Lord, I say, 'Thou art my God.' My times are in thy hand; deliver me from the hand of my enemies and persecutors!" (Ps. 31:14–15).

God is sovereign even in what are thought of as the accidental occurrences of life. Proverbs 16:33 says, "The lot is cast into the lap, but the decision is wholly from the Lord." When the early believers sought someone to replace Judas within the circle of the apostles, they in effect nominated two, and prayed that God would show them which of the two, Barsabbas or Matthias, was his choice. They then cast lots; and when the lot fell on Matthias, they enrolled him with the eleven apostles (Acts 1:23–26).

God's governing activity is to be thought of in the widest possible setting. The psalmist says, "The Lord has established his throne in the heavens, and his kingdom rules over all." The psalmist then proceeds to call upon all the angels, all the hosts of the Lord, the ministers that do his will, all his works, in all the places of his dominion, to bless him (Ps. 103:19–22). The free actions of humans are included in God's governmental working. When Ezra was refurbishing the temple, King Artaxerxes of Persia provided resources out of his nation's funds. Ezra comments: "Blessed be the Lord, the God of our fathers, who put such a thing as this into the heart of the king, to beautify the house of the Lord which is in Jerusalem" (Ezra 7:27). Even the sinful actions of humans are part of God's providential working. Probably the most notable instance of this is the crucifixion of Jesus, which Peter attributed to both God and sinful men: "This Jesus, delivered up according to the definite plan and foreknowledge of God, you crucified and killed by the hands of lawless men" (Acts 2:23).

The Relationship Between God's Governing Activity and Sin

At this point we must address the difficult problem of the relationship between God's working and the committing of sinful acts by humans. It is necessary to distinguish between God's normal working in relation to human actions and his working in relation to sinful acts. The Bible makes quite clear that God is not the cause of sin (James 1:14). But if sinful actions are not caused by God, what do we mean when we say that they are within his governing activity? There are several ways in which God can and does relate to sin: he can (1) prevent it; (2) permit it; (3) direct it; or (4) limit it.[3] Note that in each case God is not the cause of human sin, but acts in relationship to it.

1. God can prevent sin. At times he deters or precludes people from performing certain sinful acts. David prayed that God would keep him from sin: "Keep back thy servant also from presumptuous sins; let them not have dominion over me!" (Ps. 19:13).

2. God does not always prevent sin. At times he simply wills to permit it. Although it is not what he would wish to happen, he acquiesces in it. By not preventing the sin we determine to do, God renders it *certain* that we will indeed commit it; but he does not cause us to sin, or render it *necessary* that we act in this fashion. This is probably put most clearly by the Lord in Psalm 81:12–13: "So I gave them over to their stubborn hearts, to follow their own counsels. O that my people would listen to me, that Israel would walk in my ways!"

3. God can also direct sin. That is, while permitting some sins to occur, God none-

3. Augustus H. Strong, *Systematic Theology* (Westwood, N.J.: Revell, 1907), pp. 423–25.

theless directs them in such a way that good comes out of them. Peter saw that God had used the crucifixion of Jesus for good: "Let all the house of Israel therefore know assuredly that God has made him both Lord and Christ, this Jesus whom you crucified" (Acts 2:36; see also Rom. 11:13–15, 25). God is like a judo expert who redirects the evil efforts of sinful people and Satan in such a way that they become the very means of doing good.

4. Finally, God can limit sin. There are times when he does not prevent evil deeds, but nonetheless restrains the extent or effect of what evil people and the devil and his demons can do. A prime example is the case of Job. God permitted Satan to act, but limited what he could do: "Behold, all that he has is in your power; only upon himself do not put forth your hand" (Job 1:12). Later the Lord said, "Behold, he is in your power; only spare his life" (2:6).

The Major Features and Implications of God's Governing Activity

We need now to summarize the major features and the implications of the doctrine of divine government.

1. God's governing activity is universal. It extends to all matters, that which is obviously good and even that which seemingly is not good. Paul wrote, "We know that in everything God works for good with those who love him, who are called according to his purpose" (Rom. 8:28).

2. God's providence does not extend merely to his own people. While there is a special concern for the believer, God does not withhold his goodness entirely from the rest of humankind. Jesus said this quite openly in Matthew 5:45: "he makes his sun to rise on the evil and on the good, and sends rain on the just and on the unjust." This goes contrary to an opinion held by some Chris-

tians, an opinion which was expressed humorously a few years ago in a comic strip entitled "The Reverend." One day the Reverend, attired in his clerical garb, was leaving on vacation. His neighbor offered to water his lawn while he was gone. "Thank you for your thoughtfulness," replied the Reverend, "but I've made other arrangements." In the last panel, rain was pouring down on the Reverend's lawn, but not on the adjacent yards. That, says Jesus, is *not* how God ordinarily works. The unbeliever as well as the believer benefits from the Father's goodness. My father was a Christian; the man whose farm was next to ours was a non-Christian who worked seven days a week. But when it rained, it usually rained on both farms alike.

3. God is good in his government. He works for the good, sometimes directly bringing it about, sometimes countering or deflecting toward good the efforts of evil individuals. That God is good in his government should produce in the believer a confidence in the ultimate outcome of the events of life. God is not only in control; he is directing matters according to the goodness and graciousness of his character.

4. God is personally concerned about those who are his. He cares about the one lost sheep (Luke 15:3–7). This personal di-

> *God is not only in control; he is directing matters according to the goodness and the graciousness of his character.*

mension of God's government speaks significantly to the contemporary situation. With growing automation and computerization has also come increased depersonalization. We are only cogs in the machinery, faceless robots, numbers on file, punches in computer cards, or entries on tape. A brilliant English major, applying to graduate school, was assigned a number by one institution and told that it would not be necessary to use his name in future correspondence; the number would be sufficient. He chose a different university, one which still uses names. The doctrine of the providence of God assures us that his personal relationship to us is important. He knows each of us, and each one matters to him.

5. Our activity and the divine activity are not mutually exclusive. We have no basis for laxity, indifference, or resignation in the face of the fact that God is at work accomplishing his goals. As we have seen, his providence includes human actions. Sometimes humans are conscious that their actions are fulfilling divine intention, as when Jesus said that he must do the Father's will (e.g., Matt. 26:42). At other times there is an unwitting carrying out of God's plan. Little did Caesar Augustus know when he made his decree (Luke 2:1) that the census he was ordering would make possible the fulfilment of the prophecy that the Messiah would be born in Bethlehem, but he helped fulfil it nonetheless.

The increasing sophistication of human activity and the corresponding decrease in the need for spectacular divine intervention should not lead to any loss of belief in the providence of God. Many members of today's secular society see little place for God in this world. They know, for example, what makes a person ill (at least in many cases), and medical science can prevent or cure the illness. Prayers for healing seem inappropriate (except in critical or hopeless cases). God's providence appears to be a foreign concept.[4] Yet we have seen that providence includes the immanent working of God; thus, God is providentially at work as much in the cure wrought by the physician as in a miraculous healing.

6. God is sovereign in his government. This means that he alone determines his plan and knows the significance of each of his actions. It is not necessary for us to know where he is leading. We need to be careful, then, to avoid dictating to God what he should do to give us direction. Sometimes the Christian is tempted to tell God, "If you want me to do A, then show me by doing X." It would be far better, Gideon's fleece (Judg. 6:36–40) notwithstanding, if we simply allow God to illumine us—if he so wishes and to the extent he wishes—as to the significance of his working. To suppose that we should be able to understand the significance of all of God's leading and that he will spell it out for us through some means akin to Gideon's fleece is superstition, not piety.

7. We need to be careful as to what we identify as God's providence. The most notable instance of a too ready identification of historical events with God's will is probably the "German Christians'" 1934 endorsement of the action of Adolf Hitler as God's working in history. The words of their statement are sobering to us who now read them: "We are full of thanks to God that He, as Lord of history, has given us Adolf Hitler, our leader and savior from our difficult lot. We acknowledge that we, with body and soul, are bound and dedicated to the German state and to its *Führer*. This bondage and duty contains for us, as evangelical Christians, its deepest and most holy significance in its obedience to the command of God."[5] From our perspective, the folly of such a statement seems obvious. But are there perhaps some pronouncements we are making today which will be seen as similarly mistaken by those who come a few decades after us? While we need not necessarily go so far as did Karl Barth in rejecting a natural theology based upon the developments of history, in his condemnation of the German Christians' action there is a word of caution that is instructive to us.

Providence and Prayer

One problem that has concerned thoughtful Christians when considering the nature of providence is the role of prayer. The dilemma stems from the question of what

4. Karl Heim, *Christian Faith and Natural Science* (New York: Harper and Row, 1957), p. 15.

5. Quoted in Berkouwer, *Providence of God*, pp. 176–77.

prayer really accomplishes. On the one hand, if prayer has any effect upon what happens, then it seems that God's plan was not fixed in the first place. Providence is in some sense dependent upon or altered by whether and how much someone prays. On the other hand, if God's plan is established and he is going to do what he is going to do, then does it matter whether we pray?

We should note that this is simply one particular form of the larger issue of the relationship between human effort and divine providence. Two facts are noteworthy here: (1) Scripture teaches that God's plan is definite and fixed—it is not subject to revision; and (2) we are commanded to pray and taught that prayer has value (James 5:16). But how do these two facts relate to each other?

It appears from Scripture that in many cases God works in a sort of partnership with humans. God does not act if they do not play their part. Thus, when Jesus ministered in his hometown of Nazareth, he did not perform any major miracles. All he did was to heal a few sick people. That Jesus "marveled because of their unbelief" (Mark 6:6) suggests that the people of Nazareth simply did not bring their needy ones to him for healing. It is clear that in many cases the act of faith was necessary for God to act—and such faith was lacking in Nazareth. On the other hand, when Jesus walked on the water (Matt. 14:22–33), Peter asked to be bidden to go to Jesus on the water and was enabled to do so. Presumably Jesus could have enabled all of the disciples to walk on the water that day, but only Peter did because only he asked. The centurion bringing his request for the healing of a servant (Matt. 8:5–13) and the woman with the hemorrhage (Matt. 9:18–22), clinging to Jesus' garment, are examples of faith which, demonstrated in petition, resulted in God's working. When God wills the end (in these cases, healing), he also wills the means (which includes a request to be healed, which in turn presupposes faith). That is, God wills the healing in part by willing that those in need should bring their entreaties. Thus, prayer does not change what he has purposed to do. It is the means by which he accomplishes his end. It is vital, then, that a prayer be uttered, for without it the desired result will not come to pass.

This means that prayer is more than self-stimulation. It is not a method of creating a positive mental attitude in ourselves so that we are able to do what we have asked to have done. Rather, prayer is in large part a matter of creating in ourselves a right attitude with respect to God's will. Jesus taught his disciples and us to pray, "Thy kingdom come, thy will be done," before "Give us this day our daily bread." Prayer is not so much getting God to do our will as it is demonstrating that we are as concerned as is God that his will be done. Moreover, Jesus taught us persistence in prayer (Luke 11:8–10—note that the grammatical forms used in the original Greek suggest continuous action: keep asking, keep seeking, keep knocking). It takes little faith, commitment, and effort to pray once about something and then cease. Persistent prayer makes it apparent that our petition is important to us, as it is to God.

We do not always receive what we ask for. Jesus asked three times for the removal of the cup (death by crucifixion); Paul prayed thrice for the removal of his thorn in the flesh. In each case, the Father granted instead something that was more needful (e.g., 2 Cor. 12:9–10). The believer can pray confidently, knowing that our wise and good God will give us, not necessarily what we ask for, but what is best. For as the psalmist put it, "No good thing does the LORD withhold from those who walk uprightly" (Ps. 84:11).

Providence and Miracles

What we have been examining thus far are matters of ordinary or normal providence. While they are supernatural in origin, they are relatively common and hence not too conspicuous or spectacular. We must, however, examine one additional species of providence—miracles. Here we are referring to those striking or unusual workings by God which are clearly supernatural. By miracle we mean those special supernatural works of God's providence which are not explicable on the basis of the usual patterns of nature.

One of the important issues regarding miracles involves their relationship to natural laws or the laws of nature. To some, miracles have been, not an aid to faith, but an obstacle, since they are so contrary to the usual patterns of occurrence as to appear very unlikely or even incredible. Thus, the question of how these events are to be thought of in relationship to natural law is of great importance. There are at least three views of the relationship between miracles and natural laws.

The first conception is that miracles are actually the manifestations of little-known or virtually unknown natural laws. If we fully knew and understood nature, we would be able to understand and even predict these events. Whenever the rare circumstances which produce a miracle reappear in that particular combination, the miracle will reoccur.[6] Certain biblical instances seem to fit this pattern, for example, the miraculous catch of fish in Luke 5. According to this view, Christ did not create fish for the occasion, nor did he somehow drive them from their places in the lake to where the net was to be let down. Rather, unusual conditions were present so that the fish had gathered in a place where they would not ordinarily be expected. Thus, Jesus' miracle was not so much a matter of omnipotence as of omniscience. The miracle came in his knowing where the fish would be. Similarly, some of the healings of Jesus could well have been psychosomatic healings, that is, cases of powerful suggestion removing hysterical symptoms. He simply used his extraordinary knowledge of psychosomatics to accomplish these healings.

There is much about this view that is appealing, particularly since some of the biblical miracles fit this scheme quite well; it may well be that some of them were of this nature. There are certain problems with adopting this view as an all-inclusive explanation, however. There are some miracles that are very difficult to explain in terms of this view. For example, was the man born blind (John 9) a case of psychosomatic *congenital* blindness? Now of course none of us knows what laws there may be that we do not know. But it is reasonable to assume that we should have at least some hint of what those unknown laws might be. The very vagueness of the theory is at once its strength and its weakness. To say, without further argument, that there are laws of nature which we do not know can never be either confirmed or refuted.

A second conception is that miracles break the laws of nature. In the case of the axhead that floated, for example (2 Kings 6:6), this theory suggests that for a brief period of time, in that cubic foot or so of water, the law of gravity was suspended. In effect, God turned off the law of gravity until the axhead was retrieved, or he changed the density of the axhead or of the water. This view of miracles has the virtue of seeming considerably more supernatural than the preceding one. But there are certain drawbacks attaching to it. For one thing, such suspending or breaking of the laws of nature usually introduces complications requiring a whole series of compensating miracles. In the story of Joshua's long day (Josh. 10:12–14), for example, numerous adjustments would have to be made, of which there is no hint in the narrative, if God actually stopped the revolution of the earth on its axis. While this is certainly possible for an almighty God, there is no indication of it in the astronomical data.[7] There are

---

6. Patrick Nowell-Smith, "Miracles," in *New Essays in Philosophical Theology*, ed. Antony Flew and Alasdair MacIntyre (New York: Macmillan, 1955), pp. 245–48.

7. Bernard Ramm, *The Christian View of Science and Scripture* (Grand Rapids: Eerdmans, 1954), pp. 156–61. A simpler explanation is that a miracle of refraction resulted in a prolongation of daylight.

two other problems, one psychological and one theological. Psychologically, the apparent disorderliness introduced into nature by the view that miracles are violations of natural law unnecessarily predisposes scientists to be prejudiced against them. As a matter of fact, there are those who categorically reject miracles strictly on the basis of this definition.[8] And, theologically, this view seems to make God work against himself, thus introducing a form of self-contradiction.

A third conception is the idea that when miracles occur, natural forces are countered by supernatural force. In this view, the laws of nature are not suspended. They continue to operate, but supernatural force is introduced, negating the effect of the natural law.[9] In the case of the axhead, for instance, the law of gravity continued to function in the vicinity of the axhead, but the unseen hand of God was underneath it, bearing it up, just as if a human hand were lifting it. This view has the advantage of regarding miracles as being genuinely supernatural or extranatural, but without being antinatural, as the second view makes them to be. To be sure, in the case of the fish, it may have been the conditions in the water which caused the fish to be there, but those conditions would not have been present if God had not influenced such factors as the water flow and temperature. And at times there may have been acts of creation as well, as in the case of the feeding of the five thousand.

At this point we should mention the purposes of miracles. There are at least three. The most important is to glorify God. This means that when miracles occur today, we should credit God, who is the source of the miracle, not the human agent who is the channel. In biblical times, a second purpose

of miracles was to establish the supernatural basis of the revelation which often accompanied them. That the Greek word *sēmeia* ("signs") frequently occurs in the New Testament as a term for miracles underscores this dimension. We note, too, that miracles often came at times of especially intensive revelation. This can be seen in the ministry of our Lord (e.g., Luke 5:24). Finally, miracles occur to meet human needs. Our Lord frequently is pictured as moved with compassion for the needy, hurting people who came to him. He healed them to relieve the suffering caused by such maladies as blindness, leprosy, and hemorrhaging. He never performed miracles for the selfish purpose of putting on a display.

We have seen that the doctrine of providence is not an abstract conception. It is the believer's conviction that he or she is in the hands of a good, wise, and powerful God who will accomplish his purposes in the world.

Be not dismayed whate'er betide,
God will take care of you;
Beneath His wings of love abide,
God will take care of you.

Through days of toil when heart doth fail,
God will take care of you;
When dangers fierce your path assail,
God will take care of you.

No matter what may be the test,
God will take care of you;
Lean, weary one, upon His breast,
God will take care of you.

God will take care of you, through every day, o'er all the way;
He will take care of you,
God will take care of you.

(Civilla Durfee Martin, 1904)

8. E.g., David Hume, *An Enquiry Concerning Human Understanding*, section 10, part 1.
9. C. S. Lewis, *Miracles* (New York: Macmillan, 1947), pp. 59–61.

15 Evil and God's World: A Special Problem

The Nature of the Problem

We have spoken of the nature of God's providence and have noted that it is universal: God is in control of all that occurs. He has a plan for the entire universe and all of time, and is at work bringing about that good plan. But a shadow falls across this comforting doctrine: the problem of evil.

The problem may be stated in a simple or a more complex fashion. David Hume put it succinctly when he wrote of God: "Is he willing to prevent evil, but not able? then is he impotent. Is he able, but not willing? then is he malevolent. Is he both able and willing: whence then is evil?"[1] The existence of evil can also be seen as presenting a problem for the mealtime prayer that many

1. David Hume, *Dialogues Concerning Natural Religion*, part 10.

children have been taught to pray: "God is great, God is good. Let us thank him for our food." For if God is great, then he is able to prevent evil from occurring. If God is good, he will not wish for evil to occur. But there is rather evident evil about us. The problem of evil then may be thought of as a conflict involving three concepts: God's power, God's goodness, and the presence of evil in the world. Common sense seems to tell us that all three cannot be true.

The evil that precipitates this dilemma is of two general types. On one hand, there is what is usually called natural evil. This is evil that does not involve human willing and acting, but is merely an aspect of nature which seems to work against human welfare. The destructive forces of nature include hurricanes, earthquakes, tornadoes, and the suffering and loss of human lives caused by diseases such as cancer, cystic fibrosis, and multiple sclerosis. The other type of evil is termed moral evil. These are evils which can be traced to the choice and action of free moral agents. Here we find war, crime, cruelty, class struggles, discrimination, slavery, and injustices too numerous to mention. While moral evils can to some extent be removed from our consideration here by blaming them upon the exercise of human free will, natural evils cannot be dismissed from our consideration.

The problem of evil takes differing forms. In general, the religious form of the problem of evil occurs when some particular aspect of one's experience has had the effect of calling into question the greatness or goodness of God, and hence threatens the relationship between the believer and God. The theological form of the problem is concerned with evil in general. It is not a question of how a specific concrete situation can exist in light of God's being what and who he is, but of how any such problem could possibly exist. It is important to note these distinctions. For as Alvin Plantinga has pointed out, the person for whom some specific evil is presenting a religious difficulty may need pastoral care rather than help in working out

intellectual problems.[2] Similarly, to treat one's genuine intellectual struggle as merely a matter of feelings will not be very helpful. Failure to recognize the religious form of the problem of evil will appear insensitive; failure to deal with the theological form will appear intellectually insulting. Particularly where the two are found together it is important to recognize and distinguish the respective components.

Types of Solutions

There have been many different types of theodicies, that is, attempts to show that God is not responsible for evil. For the most part, (our analysis here is somewhat oversimplified) these attempted solutions work at reducing the tension by modifying one or more of the three elements which in combination have caused the dilemma: the greatness of God, his goodness, and the presence of evil.

One way of solving the tension of the problem which we have been describing is to abandon the idea of God's omnipotence. This approach, which is called finitism, is often found in dualisms such as Zoroastrianism or Manichaeism. These dualisms propose that there are two ultimate principles in the universe: God and the power of evil. God is attempting to overcome evil, and would if he could, but he is simply unable to do so.

A second way of lessening the tensions of the problem is to modify the idea of God's goodness. While few if any who call themselves Christian would deny the goodness of God, there are those who, at least by implication, suggest that the goodness must be understood in a sense that is slightly different from what is usually meant. One who falls into this category is Gordon H. Clark.

A staunch Calvinist, Clark does not hesitate to use the term *determinism* to depict God's causing of all things, including human

2. Alvin Plantinga, *God, Freedom, and Evil* (New York: Harper and Row, 1974), pp. 63–64.

acts. In regard to the relationship of God to certain evil actions of human beings, he even states, "I wish very frankly and pointedly to assert that if a man gets drunk and shoots his family, it was the will of God that he should do it."[3] Because God is the sole ultimate cause of everything, and whatever God causes is good, Clark concludes that it is good and right that God (ultimately) causes such evil acts as a drunken man's shooting his family, although God does not sin and is not responsible for this sinful act. Clearly, in this solution to the problem of evil the term *goodness* has undergone such transformation as to be quite different from what is usually meant by the goodness of God.

A third proposed solution to the problem of evil rejects the reality of evil, rendering unnecessary any account of how it can coexist with an omnipotent and good God. We find this viewpoint in various forms of pantheism. The philosophy of Benedict Spinoza, for example, maintains that there is just one substance and all distinguishable things are modes or attributes of that substance. Everything is deterministically caused; God brings everything into being in the highest perfection.[4] A more popularly held, but considerably less sophisticated version of this solution to the problem of evil is to be found in Christian Science, which affirms that evil in general, and particularly disease, is an illusion; it has no reality.[5]

Themes for Dealing with the Problem of Evil

A total solution to the problem of evil is beyond human ability. So what we will do here is to present several themes which in combination will help us to deal with the problem. These themes will be consistent with the basic tenets of the theology espoused in this writing. This theology can be characterized as a mild Calvinism which gives primary place to the sovereignty of God, while seeking to relate it in a positive way to human freedom and individuality. This theology is a dualism in which the second element is contingent upon or derivative from the first. That is, there are realities distinct from God which have a genuine and good existence of their own, but which ultimately received their existence from him by creation (not emanation). This theology also affirms the sin and fall of the human race and the consequent sinfulness of each human; the reality of evil and of personal demonic beings headed by the devil; the incarnation of the Second Person of the Triune God, who became a sacrificial atonement for humanity's sins; and an eternal life beyond death. It is in the context of this theological structure that the following themes are presented as helps in dealing with the problem of evil:

Evil as a Necessary Accompaniment of the Creation of Humankind

There are some things God cannot do. God cannot be cruel, for cruelty is contrary to his nature. He cannot lie. He cannot break his promise. There are some other things that God cannot do without certain inevitable results. For example, God cannot make a circle, a true circle, without all points on the circumference being equidistant from the center. Similarly, God cannot make a human without certain accompanying features.

Humans would not be human if they did not have free will. Whether humans are free in the sense assumed by Arminians or free in a sense not inconsistent with God's having rendered certain what is to happen, God's having made humans as he purposed means that we have certain capacities (e.g., the capacities to desire and to act) which we could not fully exercise if there were no such thing as evil. If God had prevented evil, he

---

3. Gordon H. Clark, *Religion, Reason, and Revelation* (Philadelphia: Presbyterian and Reformed, 1961), p. 221; for Clark's argument see pp. 221–41.

4. Benedict Spinoza, *Ethics*, part 1, proposition 33, note 2.

5. Mary Baker Eddy, *Science and Health with Key to the Scriptures* (Boston: Trustees under the will of Mary Baker Eddy, 1934), p. 348.

would have had to make us other than we are. To be truly human, we must have the ability to desire to have and do things some of which will not be what God wants us to have and to do. Evil, then, was a necessary accompaniment of God's good plan to make us fully human.

Another dimension of this theme is that for God to make the physical world as it is required certain concomitants. Apparently, for humans to have a genuine moral choice with the possibility of genuine punishment for disobedience meant that they would be capable of dying. Further, the sustenance of life required conditions which could lead to death instead. So, for example, we need

A Reevaluation of What Constitutes Good and Evil

Some of what we term good and evil may not actually be that. It is therefore necessary to take a hard look at what constitutes good and evil.

First, we must consider the divine dimension. Good is not to be defined in terms of what brings personal pleasure to humans in a direct fashion. Good is to be defined in relationship to the will and being of God. Good is that which glorifies him, fulfils his will, conforms to his nature. The promise of Romans 8:28 is sometimes quoted rather glibly by Christians: "We know that in everything God works for good with those who

---

Though a total solution to the problem is beyond human ability, evil may be a necessary accompaniment of God's plan to make us fully human or the means to a greater good.

---

water to live. But the same water which we drink can in other circumstances enter our lungs, cutting off our supply of oxygen, and thus cause us to drown. The water which is necessary to sustain life can also cut it off.

At this point someone might raise the question, "If God could not create the world without the accompanying possibility of evil, why did he create at all, or why did he not create the world without humans?" In a sense, we cannot answer that question since we are not God, but it is appropriate to note here that God chose the greater good. He decided to create rather than not create, and to create human beings rather than something lesser. He decided to create beings who would fellowship with and obey him, beings who would choose to do so even in the face of temptations to do otherwise. This was evidently a greater good than to introduce "humankind" into a totally antiseptic environment from which even the logical possibility of desiring anything contrary to God's will would have been excluded.

love him, who are called according to his purpose." But what is this good? Paul gives us the answer in verse 29: "For those whom he foreknew he also predestined to be conformed to the image of his Son, in order that he might be the firstborn among many brethren." This then is the good: not personal wealth or health, but being conformed to the image of God's Son. It is not the short-range comfort, but the long-range welfare of humanity as determined by the superior knowledge and wisdom of God.

Second, we must consider the dimension of time or duration. Some of the evils which we experience are actually very disturbing on a short-term basis, but in the long term work a much larger good. The pain of the dentist's drill and the suffering of postsurgical recovery may seem like quite severe evils, but they are in actuality rather small in light of the long-range effects that flow from them. Scripture encourages us to evaluate our temporary suffering in the light of eternity. Paul said, "I consider that the sufferings of this present time are not worth comparing with the glory that is to be revealed to us" (Rom. 8:18; see also 2 Cor. 4:17; Heb. 12:2; 1 Peter 1:6–7). A problem is often magnified by its proximity to us now, so that it becomes disproportionate to other pertinent matters. A good question to ask regarding any apparent evil is, "How important will this seem to me a year from now? five years? a million years?"

Third, there is the question of the extent of the evil. We tend to be very individualistic in our assessment of good and evil. But this is a large and complex world, and God has many persons to care for. The Saturday rainfall that spoils a family picnic or round of golf may seem like an evil to me, but be a much greater good to the farmers whose parched fields surround the golf course or park, and ultimately to a much larger number of people who depend upon the farmers' crops, the price of which will be affected by the abundance or scarcity of supply.

Part of what we are saying here is that what appears to be evil may actually in some cases be the means to a greater good. Though we may not understand them, God's plans and actions are always good and lead invariably to good consequences. Note, however, that God's plans and actions are not made good by their consequences. Rather, what makes God's plans and actions good is the fact that he has willed them.

Evil in General as the Result of Sin in General

A cardinal doctrine of the theology being developed in this book is the fact of racial sin. By this we do not mean the sin of race against race, but rather the fact that the entire human race has sinned and is now sinful. In its head, Adam, the entire human race violated God's will and fell from the state of innocence in which God had created humanity. Consequently, all of us begin life with a natural tendency to sin. The Bible tells us that with the fall, humankind's first sin, a radical change took place in the universe. Death came upon humankind (Gen.

2:17; 3:2–3, 19). God pronounced a curse upon them which is represented by certain specifics: anguish in childbearing (3:16), male domination over the wife (v. 16), toilsome labor (v. 17), thorns and thistles (v. 18). It seems likely that these are merely a sample of the actual effects upon the creation. Paul in Romans 8 says that the whole creation has been affected by the sin of humanity, and is now in bondage to decay. It waits for its redemption from this bondage. Thus, it appears likely that a whole host of natural evils may also have resulted from the sin of humankind.

More serious and more obvious, however, is the effect of the fall in the promotion of moral evil, that is, evil which is related to human willing and acting. There is no question that much of the pain and unhappiness of human beings is a result of structural evil within society. For example, power may reside in the hands of a few who use it to exploit others. Selfishness on a collective scale may keep a particular social class or racial group in painful or destitute conditions.

There is an important question that must be asked here; namely, how could sin have happened in the first place? Part of the answer is that humans must have an option if they are to be genuinely free. The choice is to obey or disobey God. In the case of Adam and Eve, the tree of the knowledge of good and evil symbolized that choice (Gen. 2:17). When they disobeyed God, their relationship to him was distorted, and sin became a reality. Humans have been greatly affected by sin: their attitudes, values, and relationships have changed. In the case of Adam and Eve, this change was reflected in their new awareness of their nakedness, in their fear of God, and in their unwillingness to accept responsibility for their sin.

It is clear, then, that God did not create sin. He merely provided the options necessary for human freedom, options which could result in sin. It is humans who sinned, not God.

Specific Evil as the Result of Specific Sins

Some specific evils are the result of specific sins or at least imprudences. Some of the evil occurrences in life are caused by the sinful actions of others. Murder, child abuse, theft, and rape are evils tied in with the exercise of sinful choices by sinful individuals. In some cases, the victim is innocent of the evil which occurs. In other cases, however, the "victim" contributes to or provokes the evil action.

In a fair number of cases, we bring evil upon ourselves by our own sinful or unwise actions. We must be very careful here. Job's friends tended to attribute his misfortunes solely to his sins (e.g., Job 22). But Jesus indicated that tragedy is not always the result of a specific sin. When his disciples asked concerning a man who had been born blind, "Rabbi, who sinned, this man or his parents, that he was born blind?" Jesus replied, "It was not that this man sinned, or his parents, but that the works of God might be made manifest in him" (John 9:2–3). Jesus was not saying that the man and his parents had not sinned; rather, he was refuting the idea that the blindness was the result of a specific sin. It is unwise to attribute misfortunes automatically to one's own sin.

But having given this warning, we need to note that there are instances of sin bringing unfortunate results upon the individual sinner. A case in point is David, whose sin with Bathsheba and murder of Uriah resulted in the death of the child of David and Bathsheba as well as conflict in David's own household. This perhaps should be thought of more in terms of the effects of certain acts than in terms of punishment from God. We do not know what was involved, but it may well be that certain conditions pertaining at the time of the act of adultery resulted in a genetic defect in the child. And David's sense of guilt may have led to indulgence with his own children, which in turn led to their sins. Much of the evil recounted in Scripture came upon people as a result of their own sin, or that of someone close to them.

Paul said, "Do not be deceived; God is not mocked, for whatever a man sows, that he will also reap. For he who sows to his own flesh will from the flesh reap corruption; but he who sows to the Spirit will from the Spirit reap eternal life" (Gal. 6:7–8). While Paul was probably thinking primarily of the eternal dimension of sin's consequences, the context (the earlier part of ch. 6) seems to indicate that he had temporal effects in mind as well. Whoever violates the law against adultery (Exod. 20:14) may find that the result is the destruction of relationships of trust, not only with one's spouse, but with one's children as well. The habitual drunkard may well destroy his health with cirrhosis of the liver. God is not attacking him; rather, the drunkard's sin has brought about the disease. This is not to say, however, that God may not use the natural results of sin to chasten people.

God as the Victim of Evil

That God took sin and its evil effects upon himself is a unique contribution by Christian doctrine to the solution of the problem of evil.[6] It is remarkable that, while knowing that he himself was to become a victim (indeed, the major victim) of the evil resulting from sin, God allowed sin to occur anyway. The Bible tells us that God was grieved by the sinfulness of humankind (Gen. 6:6). While there is certainly anthropomorphism here, there nonetheless is indication that the sin of humanity is painful or hurtful to God. But even more to the point is the fact of the incarnation. The Triune God knew that the Second Person would come to earth and be subject to numerous evils: hunger, fatigue, betrayal, ridicule, rejection, suffering, and death. He did this in order to negate sin and thus its evil effects. God is a fellow sufferer with us of the evil in this world, and consequently is able to deliver us from evil. What a measure of love this is! Anyone who would impugn the goodness of God for allowing sin and consequently evil must measure that

6. C. S. Lewis, *The Problem of Pain* (New York: Macmillan, 1962), pp. 119–20.

charge against the teaching of Scripture that God himself became the victim of evil so that he and we might be victors over evil.

The Life Hereafter

There is no question that in this life there are what seem to be rather clear instances of injustice and innocent suffering. If this life were all that there is, then surely the problem of evil would be unresolvable. But Christianity's doctrine of the life hereafter teaches that there will be a great time of judgment—every sin will be recognized and the godly will also be revealed. The judgment will be thoroughly just. Punishment for evil will be administered, and the final dimension of eternal life will be granted to all who have responded to God's loving offer. Thus the complaint of the psalmist regarding how the evil prosper and the righteous suffer will be satisfied in the light of the life hereafter.

16 God's Special Agents: Angels

When we come to the discussion of angels, we are entering upon a subject which in some ways is the most unusual and difficult of all of theology. Karl Barth, who has given the most extensive treatment of the subject to be found in recent theology textbooks, described the topic of angels as the "most remarkable and difficult of all."[1] It is, therefore, a topic which it is tempting to omit or neglect. Yet the teaching of Scripture is that God has created these spiritual beings and has chosen to carry out many of his acts through them. Therefore, if we are to be faithful students of the Bible, we have no choice but to speak of these beings.

By angels we mean those spiritual beings that God created higher than humankind, some of whom have remained obedient

---

1. Karl Barth, *Church Dogmatics* (Edinburgh: T. and T. Clark, 1961), vol. 3, part 3, p. 369.

to God and carry out his will, and others of whom disobeyed, lost their holy condition, and now oppose and hinder his work.

One reason for the difficulty of the subject is that while there are abundant references to angels in the Bible, they are not treated in themselves. When they are mentioned, it is always in order to inform us further about God, what he does, and how he does it.

Good Angels

Terminology

The primary Hebrew term for angel is *mal'āk*; the corresponding Greek word is *angelos*; in each case, the basic meaning is messenger. The two terms are used both of human messengers and of angels. When used of angels, the terms emphasize their message-bearing role. Other Old Testament terms for angels are "holy ones" (Ps. 89:5, 7) and "watchers" (Dan. 4:13, 17, 23). Collectively, they are referred to as "the council" (Ps. 89:7), "the assembly" (Ps. 89:5), and "host" or "hosts," as in the very common expression "LORD [or LORD God] of hosts," which is found more than sixty times in the Book of Isaiah alone. New Testament expressions believed to refer to angels are "heavenly host" (Luke 2:13), "spirits" (Heb. 1:14), and in varying combinations, "principalities," "powers," "thrones," "dominions," and "authorities" (see especially Col. 1:16; also Rom. 8:38; 1 Cor. 15:24; Eph. 6:12; Col. 2:15). The term *archangel* appears in two passages, 1 Thessalonians 4:16 and Jude 9. In the latter, Michael is named as an archangel.

Their Origin, Nature, and Status

It is not explicitly stated in Scripture that angels were created, nor are they mentioned in the creation account (Gen. 1–2). That they were created is, however, clearly implied in Psalm 148:2, 5: "Praise him, all his angels, praise him, all his host! . . . Let them praise the name of the LORD! For he commanded and they were created."

Jews and Christians have long believed and taught that angels are immaterial or spiritual beings. Here, as with the matter of their creation, explicit evidence is not abundant. Indeed, one might conclude that angels and spirits are being distinguished from one another in Acts 23:8–9, although angels may be part of the genus of spirits. The clearest statement regarding the spiritual nature of angels is found in Hebrews 1:14, where the writer, obviously referring to angels (see vv. 5, 13), says, "Are they not all ministering spirits sent forth to serve, for the sake of those who are to obtain salvation?" It seems safe to conclude that angels are spiritual beings; they do not have physical or material bodies. Physical manifestations recorded in Scripture must be regarded as appearances assumed for the occasion (angelophanies).

There have at times been tendencies to exalt angels unduly, giving them worship and reverence due only to the Deity. The most extended passage on angels, Hebrews 1:5–2:9, however, makes a particular point of establishing that Christ is superior to the angels. Although he was made for a brief time a little lower than the angels, he is in every way superior to them. And while they in turn are superior to humans in many of their abilities and qualities, angels are still part of the class of created and thus finite beings.

There are large numbers of angels. Scripture has various ways of indicating their numbers: "ten thousands" (Deut. 33:2); "twice ten thousand, thousands upon thousands" (Ps. 68:17); "twelve legions" (36,000 to 72,000—the size of the Roman legion varied between 3,000 and 6,000) (Matt. 26:53); "innumerable angels in festal gathering" (Heb. 12:22); "thousands upon thousands, and ten thousand times ten thousand" (Rev. 5:11, NIV). While there is no reason to take any of these figures as exact numbers, particularly in view of the symbolic significance of the numbers used (12 and 1,000), it is clear that the angels are a very large group.

Their Capacities and Powers

The angels are represented as personal beings. They can be interacted with. They have intelligence and will (2 Sam. 14:20; Rev. 22:9). They are moral creatures, some being characterized as holy (Matt. 25:31; Mark 8:38; Luke 1:26; Acts 10:22; Rev. 14:10), while others, who have fallen away, are described as lying and sinning (John 8:44; 1 John 3:8–10).

In Matthew 24:36 Jesus implies that angels have superhuman knowledge, but at the same time expressly asserts that this knowledge is not unlimited: "But of that day and hour no one knows, not even the angels of heaven, nor the Son, but the Father only." Just as the angels possess great knowledge but not omniscience, so they also have great and superhuman power, but not omnipotence. This great power is derived from God, and the angels remain dependent upon his favorable will to exercise it. They are restricted to acting within the limits of his permission. This is true even of Satan, whose

2. Angels reveal and communicate God's message to humans. This activity is most in keeping with the meaning of the word *angel*. Angels were particularly involved as mediators of the law (Acts 7:53; Gal. 3:19; Heb. 2:2). Although they are not mentioned in Exodus 19, Deuteronomy 33:2 says, "The LORD came from Sinai, . . . from the ten thousands of holy ones." This obscure passage may be an allusion to the mediation of angels. While they are not said to have performed a similar function with respect to the new covenant, the New Testament frequently depicts them as conveyers of messages from God. Gabriel appeared to Zechariah (Luke 1:13–20) and to Mary (Luke 1:26–38). Angels also spoke to Philip (Acts 8:26), Cornelius (Acts 10:3–7), Peter (Acts 11:13; 12:7–11), and Paul (Acts 27:23).

3. Angels minister to believers. This includes protecting believers from harm. In the early church it was an angel that delivered the apostles (Acts 5:19) and later Peter (Acts 12:6–11) from prison. The psalmist ex-

---

The good angels praise God continually, communicate his message to us, minister to us, execute judgment on his enemies, and will participate in the second coming.

---

ability to afflict Job was circumscribed by the will of the Lord (Job 1:12; 2:6). God's angels act only to carry out God's commands. There is no instance of their acting independently. Only God does the miraculous (Ps. 72:18). As creatures, angels are subject to all the limitations of creaturehood.

Their Activities

1. Angels continually praise and glorify God (Job 38:7; Pss. 103:20; 148:2; Rev. 5:11–12; 7:11; 8:1–4). While this activity usually takes place in God's presence, on at least one occasion it took place on earth—at the birth of Jesus the angels sang, "Glory to God in the highest" (Luke 2:13–14).

perienced the angels' care (Pss. 34:7; 91:11). The major ministry is to spiritual needs, however. Angels take a great interest in the spiritual welfare of believers, rejoicing at their conversion (Luke 15:10) and serving them in their needs (Heb. 1:14). Angels are spectators of our lives (1 Cor. 4:9; 1 Tim. 5:21), and are present within the church (1 Cor. 11:10). At death, the believer is conveyed to the place of blessedness by angels (Luke 16:22).

4. Angels execute judgment upon the enemies of God. The angel of the Lord brought death to 185,000 Assyrians (2 Kings 19:35), and to the children of Israel until the Lord told him to stay his hand at Jerusalem

(2 Sam. 24:16). It was an angel of the Lord that killed Herod (Acts 12:23). The Book of Revelation is full of prophecies regarding the judgment to be administered by angels (8:6–9:21; 16:1–17; 19:11–14).

5. The angels will be involved in the second coming. They will accompany the Lord at his return (Matt. 25:31), just as they were present at other significant events of Jesus' life, including his birth, temptation, and resurrection. They will separate the wheat from the weeds (Matt. 13:39–42). Christ will send forth his angels with a loud trumpet call to gather the elect from the four winds (Matt. 24:31; see also 1 Thess. 4:16–17).

What of the concept of guardian angels, the idea that all persons or at least all believers have a specific angel assigned to care for them and to accompany them in this life? This idea was part of popular Jewish belief at the time of Christ and has carried over in some Christian thinking.[2] Two biblical texts are cited as evidence of guardian angels. Upon calling a child and placing him in the midst of the disciples, Jesus said: "See that you do not despise one of these little ones; for I tell you that in heaven their angels always behold the face of my Father who is in heaven" (Matt. 18:10). When the maid Rhoda told the others in the house that Peter was at the gate, they said, "It is his angel!" (Acts 12:15). These verses seem to indicate that angels are specially assigned to individuals.

We should note, however, that elsewhere in the Bible we read that not just one, but many angels accompanied, protected, and provided for believers. Elisha was surrounded by many horses and chariots of fire (2 Kings 6:17); Jesus could have called twelve legions of angels; several angels carried Lazarus's soul to Abraham's bosom (Luke 16:22). Moreover, Jesus' reference to the angels of the little ones specifies that they are in the presence of the Father. This suggests that they are angels who worship in

2. A. J. Maclean, "Angels," in *Dictionary of the Apostolic Church*, ed. James Hastings (New York: Scribner, 1916), vol. 1, p. 60.

God's presence rather than angels who care for individual humans in this world. The reply to Rhoda reflects the Jewish tradition that guardian angels resemble the persons to whom they are assigned. But a report indicating that certain disciples believed in guardian angels does not invest the belief with authority. Some Christians still had mistaken or confused beliefs on various subjects. In the absence of definite didactic material, we must conclude that there is insufficient evidence for the concept of guardian angels.

Evil Angels

The Origin of Demons

The Bible has little to say about how evil angels came to have their current moral character, and even less about their origin. We may derive something about their origin by noting what is said about their moral character. There are two closely related passages which inform us regarding the fall of the evil angels. Second Peter 2:4 says that "God did not spare the angels when they sinned, but cast them into hell and committed them to pits of nether gloom to be kept until the judgment." Jude 6 says that "the angels that did not keep their own position but left their proper dwelling have been kept by him in eternal chains in the nether gloom until the judgment of the great day." The beings described in these two verses are clearly identified as angels who sinned and came under judgment. They must, then, like all the other angels, be created beings.

A problem presented by these verses is the fact that the evil angels are said to have been cast into nether gloom to be kept until the judgment. This has led some to theorize that there are two classes of fallen angels, those who are imprisoned, and those who are free to carry on their evil in the world. Another possibility is that these two verses describe the condition of all demons. That the latter is correct is suggested by the remainder of 2 Peter 2. In verse 9 Peter says that "the Lord knows how to rescue the godly from trial, and to keep the unrighteous under punishment until the day of judgment." This language is almost identical to that used in verse 4. Note that the remainder of the chapter (vv. 10–22) is a description of the continued sinful activity of these people who are being kept under punishment. We conclude that, likewise, though cast into nether gloom, the fallen angels have sufficient freedom to carry on their evil activities.

Demons, then, are angels created by God and thus were originally good; but they sinned and thus became evil. Just when this rebellion took place we do not know, but it must have occurred between the time when God completed the creation and pronounced it all "very good," and the temptation and fall of humankind (Gen. 3).

The Chief of the Demons

The devil is the name given in Scripture to the chief of these fallen angels. He is also known as Satan, which means to be or act as an adversary.[3] The most common Greek word for him is *diabolos* (devil, adversary, accuser). Several other terms are used of him less frequently: tempter (Matt. 4:3; 1 Thess. 3:5), Beelzebub (Matt. 12:24, 27; Mark 3:22; Luke 11:15, 19), enemy (Matt. 13:39), evil one (Matt. 13:19, 38; 1 John 2:13; 3:12; 5:18), Belial (2 Cor. 6:15), adversary (1 Peter 5:8), deceiver (Rev. 12:9), great dragon (Rev. 12:3), father of lies (John 8:44), murderer (John 8:44), sinner (1 John 3:8). All of these convey something of the character and activity of the devil.

The devil is, as his name indicates, engaged in opposing God and the work of Christ. He does this especially by tempting humans. This is shown in the temptation of Jesus, the parable of the weeds (Matt. 13:24–30), and the sin of Judas (Luke 22:3). (See also Acts 5:3; 1 Cor. 7:5; 2 Cor. 2:11; Eph. 6:11; 2 Tim. 2:26.)

3. Francis Brown, S. R. Driver, and Charles A. Briggs, *Hebrew and English Lexicon of the Old Testament* (New York: Oxford University Press, 1955), p. 966.

One of the primary means used by Satan is deception. Paul tells us that Satan disguises himself as an angel of light, and that his servants disguise themselves as servants of righteousness (2 Cor. 11:14–15). His use of deception is also mentioned in Revelation 12:9 and 20:8, 10. He has "blinded the minds of the unbelievers, to keep them from seeing the light of the gospel of the glory of Christ, who is the likeness of God" (2 Cor. 4:4). He opposes and hinders (1 Thess. 2:18) Christians in their service, even using physical ailments to that end (so, probably, 2 Cor. 12:7).

For all of his power, Satan is limited. As we have already mentioned, he could do nothing to Job that God did not expressly permit. He can be successfully resisted, and will flee (James 4:7; see also Eph. 4:27). He can be put to flight, however, not by our strength, but only by the power of the Holy Spirit (Rom. 8:26; 1 Cor. 3:16).

Activities of Demons

As Satan's subjects, demons carry out his work in the world. It may therefore be assumed that they engage in all the forms of temptation and deception which he employs. They inflict disease: dumbness (Mark 9:17), deafness and dumbness (Mark 9:25), blindness and deafness (Matt. 12:22), convulsions (Mark 1:26; 9:20; Luke 9:39), paralysis or lameness (Acts 8:7). And most particularly, they oppose the spiritual progress of God's people (Eph. 6:12).

Demon Possession

Incidents of demon possession are given prominent attention in the biblical accounts. The technical expression is to "have a demon" or to "be demonized." Sometimes we find expressions like "unclean spirits" (Acts 8:7) or "evil spirits" (Acts 19:12).

The manifestations of demon possession are varied. We have already noted some of the physical ailments demons inflict. The person possessed may have unusual strength (Mark 5:2–4), may act in bizarre ways such as wearing no clothes and living among the tombs rather than in a house (Luke 8:27), or may engage in self-destructive behavior (Matt. 17:15; Mark 5:5). There evidently are degrees of affliction, since Jesus spoke of the evil spirit who "goes and brings with him seven other spirits more evil than himself" (Matt. 12:45). In all of these cases is the common element that the person involved is being destroyed, whether that be physically, emotionally, or spiritually. It appears that the demons were able to speak, presumably using the vocal equipment of the person possessed (e.g., Matt. 8:29, 31). It appears that demons can also inhabit animals (see the parallel accounts of the incident involving the swine—Matt. 8; Mark 5; Luke 8).

It is noteworthy that the biblical writers did not attribute all illness to demon possession. Luke reports that Jesus distinguished between two types of healing: "Behold, I cast out demons and perform cures today and tomorrow" (Luke 13:32). Nor was epilepsy mistaken for demon possession. We read in Matthew 17:15–18 that Jesus cast out a demon from an epileptic, but in Matthew 4:24 epileptics (as well as paralytics) are distinguished from demoniacs. In the case of numerous healings no mention is made of demons. In Matthew, for example, no mention is made of demon exorcism in the case of the healing of the centurion's servant (8:5–13), or of the woman with the hemorrhage of twelve years' duration (9:19–20).

Jesus cast out demons without pronouncing an elaborate formula. He merely commanded them to come out (Mark 1:25; 9:25). He attributed the exorcism to the Spirit of God (Matt. 12:28) or the finger of God (Luke 11:20). Jesus invested his disciples with the authority to cast out demons (Matt. 10:1). But the disciples needed faith if they were to be successful (Matt. 17:19–20). Prayer is also mentioned as a requirement for exorcism (Mark 9:29). Sometimes faith on the part of a third party was a requirement (Mark 9:23–24; cf. 6:5–6). At times demons were expelled from someone who had expressed no wish to be healed.

There is no reason to believe that demon possessions are restricted to the past. There are cases, especially but not exclusively in less developed cultures, which seem to be explainable only on this basis. The Christian should be alert to the possibility of demon possession occurring today. At the same time, one should not too quickly attribute aberrant physical and psychical phenomena to demon possession. Even as Jesus and the biblical writers distinguished cases of possession from other ailments, so should we, testing the spirits.

In recent years there has been a flare-up of interest in the phenomenon of demon possession. As a consequence, some Christians may come to regard this as the primary manifestation of the forces of evil. In actuality, Satan, the great deceiver, may be encouraging interest in demon possession in hopes that Christians will become careless about other more subtle forms of influence by the powers of evil.

The Role of the Doctrine of Angels

Obscure and strange though this belief in good and evil angels may seem to some, it has a significant role to play in the life of the Christian. There are several benefits to be drawn from our study of this topic:

1. It is a comfort and an encouragement to us to realize that there are powerful and numerous unseen agents available to help us in our need. The eye of faith will do for the believer what the vision of the angels did for Elisha's servant (2 Kings 6:17).

2. The angels' praise and service of God give us an example of how we are to conduct ourselves now, and what our activity will be in the life beyond in God's presence.

3. It sobers us to realize that even angels who were close to God succumbed to temptation and fell. This is a reminder to us to "take heed lest [we] fall" (1 Cor. 10:12).

4. Knowledge about evil angels serves to alert us to the danger and the subtlety of temptation which can be expected to come from satanic forces, and gives insight into some of the devil's ways of working. We need to be on guard against two extremes.

We should not take him too lightly, lest we disregard the dangers. Nor, on the other hand, should we have too strong an interest in him.

5. We receive confidence from the realization that powerful though Satan and his accomplices are, there are definite limits upon what they can do. We can, therefore, by the grace of God, resist him successfully. And we can know that his ultimate defeat is certain, for Satan and his angels will be cast into the lake of fire and brimstone forever (Matt. 25:41; Rev. 20:10).

Part Five

Humanity

17 Introduction to the Doctrine of Humanity

Images of Humankind

The doctrine of humanity is a particularly opportune one for us to study and utilize in our dialogue with the non-Christian world. It is an area in which contemporary culture is perpetually asking questions to which the Christian message can offer answers. Because so many different disciplines deal with human nature, there are many different images of humankind. It will be helpful to us, in developing our Christian theological conception, to be aware of at least three of the more prevalent ones.

Humans as Machines

One prevalent perspective on humans is in terms of what they are able to do. The employer, for example, is interested in the human being's strength and energy, the skills or capabilities pos-

155

sessed. On this basis, the employer "rents" the employee for a certain number of hours a day (although some employers think that they own some of their employees, controlling almost all areas of their lives).

The chief concern of those who have this conception will be to satisfy those needs which will keep the human being (the machine) functioning effectively. The health of the worker is of interest not because illness might mean personal distress, but because it might result in loss of working efficiency. If the work can be done better by a machine, or by the introduction of more-advanced techniques, there will be no hesitation to adopt such measures, for the work is the primary goal and concern. In addition, the worker is paid no more than is absolutely necessary to get the task accomplished.[1]

In this approach, persons are basically regarded as things, as means to ends rather than as ends in themselves. They are of value as long as they are useful. They may be moved around like chess pieces, as some large corporations do with their management personnel. They are manipulated if necessary, so that they accomplish their intended function.

Humans as Animals

Another view sees humans primarily as members of the animal kingdom and as derivations from some of its higher forms. They have come into being through the same sort of process as have all other animals, and will have a similar end. There is no qualitative difference between human beings and the other animals. The only difference is one of degree.

This view of humankind is perhaps most fully developed in behavioristic psychology. Here human motivation is understood primarily in terms of biological drives. Knowledge of humans is gained not through introspection, but by experimentation upon animals. For example, conclusions about humans are drawn from the discovery that

if water is poured into a rat's throat but prevented from running into its stomach, it will have relief from its feelings of thirst relatively quickly, but the relief will not last as long as it would if, bypassing the throat, the water were poured directly into the stomach.[2]

Human behavior can be affected by processes similar to those used on animals. Just as Pavlov's dog learned to salivate when a bell was rung, human beings can also be conditioned to react in certain ways. Positive reinforcement (rewards) and, less desirably, negative reinforcement (punishment) are the means of control and training.

Humans as Pawns of the Universe

Among certain existentialists particularly, but also in a broader segment of society, we find the idea that humans are at the mercy of forces in the world which control their destiny but have no real concern for them. These are seen as blind forces, forces of chance in many cases. Sometimes they are personal forces, but even then they are forces over which humans have no control, and upon which they have no influence, such as political superpowers. This is basically a pessimistic view which pictures humans as being crushed by a world which is either hostile or at best indifferent to their welfare and needs. The result is a sense of helplessness, of futility.

Albert Camus has captured this general idea in his reworking of the classical myth of Sisyphus. Sisyphus had died and gone to the nether world. He had, however, been sent back to earth. When recalled to the nether world, he refused to return, for he thoroughly enjoyed the pleasures of life. As punishment he was brought back and sentenced to push a large rock up to the top of a hill. When he got it there, however, it rolled back

1. "The Robot Invasion Begins to Worry Labor," *Business Week*, 29 March 1982, p. 46.

2. On behavioristic psychology see, e.g., Paul Young, *Motivation of Behavior: The Fundamental Determinants of Human and Animal Activity* (New York: John Wiley and Sons, 1936). For a novel depicting an ideal society built upon the use of behavioristic conditioning, see B. F. Skinner, *Walden Two* (New York: Macmillan, 1948).

down. He trudged his way to the bottom of the hill and again pushed the rock to the top only to have it roll back down. He was doomed to repeat this process endlessly. For all his efforts there was no permanent result.[3] Whether immersed in fearful thoughts about death, the forthcoming natural extinction of the planet, or nuclear destruction, or merely in the struggle against those who control the political and economic power, all those who hold that humans are basically pawns at the mercy of the universe are gripped by a similar sense of helplessness and resignation.

The Christian View of Humanity

By contrast, the Christian view of humanity is that we are creatures of God, made in the image of God. This means, first, that humanity is to be understood as having originated not through a chance process of evolution, but through a conscious, purposeful act by God. Thus there is a reason for human existence, a reason which lies in the intention of the Supreme Being. Second, the image of God is intrinsic to humankind. We would not be human without it. Of all creation, we alone are capable of having a conscious personal relationship with the Creator and of responding to him.

Humans also have an eternal dimension. They had a finite point of beginning in time. But they were created by an eternal God, and they have an eternal future. Thus, when we ask what is the good for human beings, we must not answer only in terms of temporal welfare or physical comfort. There is another (and in many senses more important) dimension which must be fulfilled. Yet humans, to be sure, as a part of the physical creation and the animal kingdom, have the same needs as do the other members of those groups. Our physical welfare is important. It is of concern to God, and should therefore be of concern to us as well.

3. Albert Camus, "The Myth of Sisyphus," in *Existentialism from Dostoevsky to Sartre*, ed. Walter Kaufmann (Cleveland: World, 1956), pp. 312–15.

Because humans are God's creation, they cannot discover their real meaning by regarding themselves and their happiness as the highest of all values, nor can they find happiness, fulfilment, or satisfaction by going out in search of it. Their value has been conferred upon them by a higher source, and they are fulfilled only when serving and loving that higher being.

It is our contention that many of the questions being asked directly or implicitly by contemporary culture are answered by the Christian view of humanity. In addition, this view gives the individual a sense of identity. The image of humans as machines, for example, leads to the feeling that we are insignificant cogs, unnoticed and unimportant. The Christian view, however, looks to the Bible, which indicates that everyone is valuable and is known to God: every hair of our head is numbered (Matt. 10:28–31). Moreover, the Christian view accounts for the full range of human phenomena more completely and with less distortion than does any other view. And this view more than any other approach to life enables us to function in ways that are deeply satisfying to us in the long run.

The Biblical Account of Human Creation

When we speak of the origin of humanity, we are speaking of something more than merely their beginning. "Beginning" refers simply to the fact of coming into being. Theology, however, does not ask merely how humans came to be on the face of the earth, but why, or what purpose lies behind their presence here. The biblical picture is that an all-wise, all-powerful, and good God created the human race to love and serve him, and to enjoy a relationship with him.

Genesis contains two accounts of God's creation of humanity. The first, in 1:26–27, simply records (1) God's decision to make human beings in his own image and likeness, and (2) God's action implementing this decision. Nothing is said about the materials or method used. The first account places more emphasis upon the purpose or reason for the creation of humankind; namely, they were to be fruitful and multiply and have dominion over the earth (v. 28). The second account, Genesis 2:7, is quite different: "Then the LORD God formed man of dust from the ground, and breathed into his nostrils the breath of life; and man became a living being." Here the emphasis seems to be upon the way in which God created.

Direct Human Creation in Scripture

The biblical picture of the creation of the human race by God certainly appears to conflict sharply with the evolutionary account of humans' having come into existence through the work of natural forces. In fact, the disputes that have taken place be-

A major factor in determining our answer to the question of whether all of human nature was a *de novo* (new) creation, or some of it was derived from the process of evolution, is the hermeneutical approach which we take to the opening chapters of Genesis. One approach is to maintain that the passage does not say anything specific that would bear upon scientific questions about the origin of the human. This seems unduly extreme and unwarranted. A more reasonable approach is to ask what type of literary material we are dealing with in the first three chapters of Genesis.

It certainly appears that in Genesis 1–3 not every object is to be understood as merely that object. For example, the tree of which Adam and Eve were forbidden to eat was not merely a tree, but "the tree of the

We are creatures of God, made in the image of God.

tween the church and science over evolution have centered mostly upon the origin of the human race. Perhaps the most pertinent issue here is the extent to which we view the creation of humans as direct. Did God directly create the entirety of Adam's makeup, both physical and psychological, or did he simply take an existing higher primate and modify it, conferring upon it the image of God, so that it became a living human being? This issue separates theistic evolution (God created the first organism and then worked within the process of evolution, occasionally intervening, however, to modify what was emerging [e.g., he infused the human soul into a previously existent physical form]) from both fiat creationism (God created every species in a brief period of time) and progressive creationism (God directly created each of the various "kinds," including humans; these separate creations constituted a series of steps over a long period of time).

knowledge of good and evil." The serpent appears to have been not merely a speaking serpent, but the evil one himself. Is it not therefore quite possible that the "dust" used to form Adam (Gen. 2:7) was something more than physical particles of earth? Could it represent or symbolize the inanimate building blocks from which organic matter and hence life came? Or could it, as theistic evolutionists sometimes suggest, represent a prehuman life form?

One issue which must be faced is whether the symbolism is consistent. The word *dust* appears not only in Genesis 2:7, but also in 3:19 ("you are dust, and to dust you shall return"). If we interpret it in 2:7 to mean some previously existing life form, we are faced with two choices: either the meaning of the term must be different in 3:19 (as well as in 3:14), or we have the rather ludicrous situation that upon death a human being first degenerates to a high primate and then decomposes. Even in cases of severe human degeneration, however, where a person becomes virtually subhuman, the change occurs prior to actual death, and there is no transformation of the person's physical makeup and appearance. It would be better, then, to interpret the less clear reference to dust (in 2:7) in light of the clearer (3:19).

A second problem for the theistic evolutionist is the expression "and man became a living being" (Gen. 2:7). The very words translated "living being" are also used to describe the other creatures which God had made earlier (1:20, 21, 24). This seems to indicate that Adam became a living being at the point of God's special activity in 2:7, which contradicts the theistic evolutionary view that he was already a living being (though of a different sort) prior to this time. In light of such considerations, we conclude that the biblical data favor the view that humans were directly created in their entirety by God.

Direct Human Creation and Science

What of the scientific data, however? How do they fit with progressive creationism? Do they preclude direct creation? We note that evolutionists have long been seeking the missing link between humans and the highest primate. Nothing has been found which can be clearly identified as such; indeed, it is unlikely that such a linkage could ever be proved. Progressive creationism, then, would seem to be the best interpretation of both the biblical and the scientific data.

One question which frequently is raised is, "Where does Adam fit on the fossil record?" A Christian anthropologist used to answer this question semifacetiously, "If you will tell me just exactly what Adam looked like, I will tell you." This points up the fact that we are given very little detail about the physical characteristics of Adam. It also underscores the fact that physical appearance is not the major criterion of humanity. So to answer the question, we must first ask what defines humanity, not theologically, but anthropologically.

Among the suggestions as to the distinguishing mark of humanity are tool-making, burial of the dead, and the use of complex symbolism or, more specifically, language. Tool-making of an elementary fashion, however, has been found among chimpanzees. James Murk argues that burial of the dead presupposes only fear of the unknown, which in turn requires only imagination, not moral sense.[4] The third suggestion, the use of language, seems to have the fewest difficulties. This would correlate Adam (and thus the beginning of humanity) with a great outburst of culture about 30,000 to 40,000 years ago, which was the time of Cro-Magnon man. There are some difficulties with this date, however, especially in view of Neolithic elements (e.g., agriculture) found in Genesis 4. Since the Neolithic period began about 10,000 to 8,000 years ago, we have the problem of a gap of 20,000 years between generations. Several possible solutions for this problem have been proposed. However, this is an area in which there are insufficient data to make any categorical statements; it will require much additional study.

The Theological Meaning of Human Creation

Now that we have briefly looked at the Christian view of human creation, we must determine its theological meaning. Several points need special attention and interpretation.

1. That humans were created means that they have no independent existence. They came into being because God willed that they should exist, and acted to bring them into being. This should cause us to ask the reason for our existence. Why did God put us here, and what are we to do in light of that purpose? Since we would not be alive but for God, everything we have and are derives from him. So stewardship does not

4. James W. Murk, "Evidence for a Late Pleistocene Creation of Man," *Journal of the American Scientific Affiliation* 17.2 (June 1965): 37–49.

mean giving God a part of what is ours, some of our time or some of our money. All of our life is rightfully his, by virtue of our origin and his continued ownership of us.

This means that we humans are not the ultimate value. Our value is derived from, and conferred upon us by, a higher value, God. Thus the essential question in evaluating anything is not whether it contributes to our pleasure and comfort, but whether it contributes to God's glory and the fulfilment of his plan.

2. Humankind is part of the creation. As different as we are from God's other created beings, we are not so sharply distinguished from the rest of them as to have no relationship with them. We are part of the sequence of creation, as are the other beings. The origin of humans on one of the days of creation links us far more closely with all the other created beings than with the God who did the creating. This means that there should be harmony between us and the rest of the creatures.

When taken seriously, our kinship with the rest of creation has a definite impact. Ecology takes on a rich meaning. The word

tures. Animals are all said to be made "according to their kind." Humans, on the other hand, are described as made in the image and likeness of God. They are placed over the rest of the creation, to have dominion over it. This means that humans are not fulfilled when all of their animal needs have been satisfied. The transcendent element designated by the unique way in which humanity is described and thus distinguished from the various other creatures must be kept in mind.

4. There is a common bond among human beings. The doctrine of creation and of the descent of the entire human race from one original pair means that we are all related to one another. The negative side of our common descent is that in the natural state all persons are rebellious children of the heavenly Father and thus are estranged from him and from one another. We are all like the prodigal son. But if the bond between us is fully understood and acted upon, it should produce a concern and empathy for other people. We will rejoice with those who rejoice and weep with those who weep, even if they are not fellow Christians.

By virtue of our origin, we have a kinship with the rest of God's creation, and in particular with the entire human race.

---

derives from the Greek *oikos*, which means "house." Thus, "ecology" points up the idea that there is one great household. What we humans do to one part of it affects other parts as well, a truth that is becoming painfully clear as we find pollution harming human lives, and the destruction of certain natural predators leaving pests a relatively unhampered opportunity.

3. Humanity, however, has a unique place in the creation. As we have noted, humans are creatures and thus share much with the rest of the creatures. But there is an element which makes people unique, which sets them apart from the rest of the crea-

5. There are definite limitations upon humanity. Humans are creatures, not God, and have the limitations that go with being finite. Our finiteness means that our knowledge will always be incomplete and subject to error. This should impart a certain sense of humility to all our judgments, as we realize that it is always possible that we might be wrong, no matter how impressive our fund of facts may seem. Finiteness also pertains to our lives. Humans are not inherently immortal. And, as presently constituted, they must face death (Heb. 9:27). Even in humanity's original state, any possi-

bility of living forever depended on God. Only God is inherently eternal; all else dies.

Finiteness means that there are practical limitations to all of our accomplishments. While humans have made great progress in such matters as physical feats, the progress is not unlimited. Athletes now execute high jumps of seven feet, but it is unlikely that anyone will, within our atmosphere, ever jump a thousand feet without the aid of some sort of propulsion equipment. Other areas of accomplishment, whether intellectual, physical, or whatever, have similar practical limitations upon them.

6. Limitation is not inherently bad. There is a tendency to bemoan the fact of human finiteness. Some, indeed, maintain that this is the cause of human sin. If we were not limited, we would always know what is right, and would do it. But the Bible indicates that having made humans with the limitations which go with creaturehood, God looked at the creation and pronounced it "very good" (Gen. 1:31). Finiteness may well lead to sin if we fail to accept our limitation and to live accordingly. But the mere fact of our limitation does not inevitably produce sin. Rather, improper responses to that limitation either constitute or result in sin.

There are those who feel that the sinfulness of humankind is a carry-over from earlier stages of our evolution but is gradually being left behind. As our knowledge and ability increase, we will become less sinful. That, however, does not prove true. In actual practice, increases in sophistication seem instead to give opportunity for more ingenious means of sinning. One might think that the tremendous growth in computer technology, for example, would result in solutions to many basic human problems and thus in a more righteous human being. While such technology is indeed often used for beneficial purposes, human greed has also led to new and ingenious forms of theft

of both money and information by the use of computer. Reduction of our limitations, then, does not lead inevitably to better human beings. The conclusion is obvious: human limitations are not evil in themselves.

7. Humans are something wonderful. Although creatures, we are the highest among them, the only ones made in the image of God. We are not simply a chance production of a blind mechanism, or a by-product or scraps thrown off in the process of making something better. We are an expressly designed product of God.

Sometimes Christians have felt it necessary to minimize the ability and accomplishments of humans in order to give greater glory to God. To be sure, we must put human achievements in their proper context relative to God. But it is not necessary to protect God against competition from his highest creature. Human greatness can glorify God the more.

Humans are great, but what makes them great is that God has created them. The name *Stradivari* speaks of quality in a violin; its maker was the best. Even as we admire the instrument, we are admiring all the more the giftedness of the maker. Of humans it can be said that they have been made by the best and wisest of all beings, God. A God who could make such a wondrous creature is a great God indeed.

> Know that the LORD is God!
>> It is he that made us, and we are his;
>> we are his people, and the sheep of his
>> pasture.
>
> Enter his gates with thanksgiving,
>> and his courts with praise!
>> Give thanks to him, bless his name!
>
> For the LORD is good;
>> his steadfast love endures for ever,
>> and his faithfulness to all generations.
>> [Ps. 100:3–5]

18 The Image of God in the Human

As important as our answer to the question "Where did humans come from?" is to understanding who and what they are, it does not tell us all we need to know. We still must ask just what it is that God brought into being when he created humankind.

If we investigate the Bible's depiction of humanity, we find that people today are actually in an abnormal condition. The real human is not what we now find in human society. The real human is the being that came from the hand of God, unspoiled by sin and the fall. In a very real sense, the only true human beings were Adam and Eve before the fall, and Jesus. All the others are twisted, distorted, corrupted samples of humanity. It therefore is necessary to look at humans in their original state and at Christ if we would correctly assess what it means to be human.

A key expression used in describing the original form of humanity is that God made humankind in his own image and likeness. This distinguished human beings from all the other creatures, for only of humans is this expression used. There has been a great amount of discussion on the subject; in fact, some would say it has been discussed too much. Actually, however, the concept is critical because the image of God is what makes us human.[1]

In this chapter we will examine the salient biblical passages. Then we will look at some representative interpretations of what the expression "the image of God" means. These are attempts to draw the several biblical passages together into a construct. Finally, we will attempt to formulate an understanding which is faithful to the full biblical witness, and to spell out the contemporary significance of the concept.

The Relevant Scripture Passages

Several biblical passages speak of the image of God. The best-known is probably Genesis 1:26–27: "Then God said, 'Let us make man in our image, after our likeness; and let them have dominion over the fish of the sea, and over the birds of the air, and over the cattle, and over all the earth, and over every creeping thing that creeps upon the earth.' So God created man in his own image, in the image of God he created him; male and female he created them." Verse 26 is God's statement of intention; it includes the terms *ṣelem* and *dĕmûth*, which are translated, respectively, "image" and "likeness." The former term is repeated twice in verse 27. In Genesis 5:1 we have a recapitulation of what God had done: "When God created man, he made him in the likeness of God." The writer adds in verse 2: "Male and female he created them, and he blessed them and named them Man when they were created." The term used here is *dĕmûth*. In Genesis 9:6 murder is prohibited on the grounds that humankind was created in God's image: "Whoever sheds the blood of

1. Gerhard von Rad, "εἰκών—The Divine Likeness in the OT," in *Theological Dictionary of the New Testament*, ed. Gerhard Kittel, trans. Geoffrey W. Bromiley (Grand Rapids: Eerdmans, 1964), vol. 2, pp. 390–92; Walther Eichrodt, *Theology of the Old Testament* (Philadelphia: Westminster, 1967), vol. 2, p. 122.

man, by man shall his blood be shed; for God made man in his own image." This statement governing our behavior in relation to others was clearly made after the fall. Sinful humans, then, continued to bear the image.

In the New Testament two passages refer to the image of God in connection with the creation of humanity. In 1 Corinthians 11:7 Paul says, "For a man ought not to cover his head, since he is the image and glory of God; but woman is the glory of man." Paul does not say that woman is the image of God, but merely points out that she is the glory of man as man is the glory of God. And in James 3:9, on the grounds that humans are made in the likeness of God, the author condemns use of the tongue to curse others: "With [the tongue] we bless the Lord and

> *The image of God distinguishes humans from all other creatures; it is what makes us human.*

Father, and with it we curse men, who are made in the likeness of God." There is also something of a suggestion of the image of God in Acts 17:28, although the term is not actually used: "'In him we live and move and have our being'; as even some of your poets have said, 'For we are indeed his offspring.'"

In addition there are several passages in the New Testament which refer to the image of God in connection with what believers are becoming through the process of salvation. Romans 8:29 notes that they are being conformed to the image of the Son: "For those whom he foreknew he also predestined to be conformed to the image of his Son, in order that he might be the first-born among many brethren." In 2 Corinthians 3:18 we read, "And we all, with unveiled face, beholding the glory of the Lord, are being changed into his likeness from one degree of glory to another; for this comes from the Lord who is the Spirit" (see also Eph. 4:23–24; Col. 3:10).

Views of the Image

It is necessary to come up with some sort of definition of the image of God. This process will involve not only interpreting individual references, but endeavoring to formulate an integrative understanding of the concept as it is found in the several overt statements as well as in various allusions in Scripture. There are three general ways of viewing the nature of the image. Some consider the image to consist of certain characteristics within the very nature of humankind, characteristics which may be physical or psychological/spiritual. This view we will call the *substantive* view of the image. Others regard the image not as something inherently or intrinsically present in humanity, but as the experiencing of a relationship between humans and God, or between two or more humans. This is the *relational* view. Finally, some consider the image to be, not something that humans are or experience, but something that they do. This is the *functional* view.

The Substantive View

The substantive view has been dominant during most of the history of Christian theology. The common element in the several varieties of this view is that the image is identified as some definite characteristic or quality within the makeup of the human. Some have considered the image of God to be an aspect of our physical or bodily makeup. Although this form of the view has never been widespread, it has persisted even to this day. It may be based upon a literal reading of the Hebrew word *ṣelem*, which in its most concrete sense means "statue" or "form."[2] Given this reading, Genesis 1:26 would actually mean something like, "Let us make men who look like us." The Mormons are probably the most prominent current advocates of the position that the image of God is physical.

More-common substantive views of the image of God isolate it in terms of some psychological or spiritual quality in human nature. Here the favorite candidate has been reason. There has been a long history of regarding reason as the unique feature which distinguishes humans from the other creatures. Indeed, humans are classified biologically as *Homo sapiens*, the thinking being.

It is not surprising that reason has been singled out by theologians as the most significant aspect of human nature, for theologians are the segment of the church charged with intellectualizing or reflecting on their faith. Note that in so doing, however, not only have they isolated but one aspect of human nature for consideration, but they have also concentrated their attention upon but one facet of God's nature. This may result in a misapprehension. To be sure, omniscience and wisdom constitute a significant dimension of the nature of God, but they are by no means the very essence of divinity!

Although substantive views differ widely in their conceptions of the nature of the image of God, they agree in one particular: the location of the image. It is located within humans; it is a quality or capacity resident in their nature.

The Relational View

Many modern theologians do not conceive of the image of God as something resident within human nature. Indeed, they do not ordinarily ask what a human is, or what sort of a nature a human may have. Rather, they think of the image of God as the experiencing of a relationship. We are said to be in the image or to display the image when we stand in a particular relationship. In fact, that relationship *is* the image.

Two theologians who held this view are Emil Brunner and Karl Barth. Although there was at one point a sharp disagreement between them, an accord gradually developed.[3] These two representatives of the rela-

---

2. Charles Ryder Smith, *The Bible Doctrine of Man* (London: Epworth, 1956), pp. 29–30, 94–95.

3. Emil Brunner, "The New Barth," *Scottish Journal of Theology* 4.2 (June 1951): 124–25.

tional approach came to share several basic tenets:

1. The image of God and human nature are best understood through a study of the person of Jesus, not of human nature per se.
2. We obtain our understanding of the image from the divine revelation.
3. The image of God is not to be understood in terms of any structural qualities within humanity; it is not something humans are or possess. Rather, the image is a matter of one's relationship to God; it is something one experiences. Thus, it is dynamic rather than static.
4. The relationship of humans to God, which constitutes the image of God, is paralleled by the relationship of one human to another. Barth makes much more of the male-female relationship; Brunner tends to emphasize the larger circle of human relationships, that is, society.
5. The image of God is universal; it is found in all humans at all times and places. Therefore, it is present in sinful humanity. There is always a relationship, either positive or negative.
6. No conclusion can or need be drawn as to what there might be in humans that would constitute them able to have such a relationship. Brunner and Barth never ask what if anything is required structurally for the image of God to be present in humankind.

Thus, for Brunner and Barth, the image of God is not an entity which we possess so much as the experience which is present when a relationship is active.

The Functional View

We come now to a third type of view of the image, which has had quite a long history and has recently enjoyed an increase in popularity. This is the idea that the image is not something present in the makeup of humankind, nor is it the experiencing of relationship with God or with fellow humans. Rather, the image consists in something we do. It is a function which we perform, the most frequently mentioned being the exercise of dominion over the creation.

In Genesis 1:26, "Let us make man in our image, after our likeness," is followed immediately by "and let them have dominion over the fish of the sea. . . ." A close connection between these two concepts is found not only in this verse, where God expresses his intention to create, but also in verses 27–28, where we read that God did in fact create humanity in the image of God and issue to the man and woman a command to have dominion.[4] Some regard the juxtaposition of these two concepts as more than coincidental. The exercise of dominion is considered to be the content of the image of God.

A second passage in which a close connection is seen between the image of God in humankind and the exercise of dominion is Psalm 8:5–6: "Yet thou hast made him little less than God, and dost crown him with glory and honor. Thou hast given him dominion over the works of thy hands; thou hast put all things under his feet." According to Norman Snaith, "commentators generally are satisfied that Psalm 8 is largely dependent on Genesis 1." One of their proofs is the catalog of creatures in Psalm 8:7–8: beasts of the field, birds of the air, and fish of the sea.[5] The conclusion is then drawn that verse 5 is equivalent to the statements in Genesis 1 that humanity was created in God's image.

Perhaps the most extensive recent interpretation of the image of God as the exercise of dominion is Leonard Verduin's *Somewhat Less than God*, which makes the point quite strongly: "The idea of dominion-having stands out as the central feature. That man is a creature meant for dominion-

---

4. Leonard Verduin, *Somewhat Less than God: The Biblical View of Man* (Grand Rapids: Eerdmans, 1970), p. 27.
5. Norman Snaith, "The Image of God," *Expository Times* 86.1 (Oct. 1974): 24.

having and that as such he is in the image of his Maker—this is the burden of the creation account given in the book of Genesis, the Book of Origins. It is the central point the writer of this account wanted to make."[6] This perspective has given rise to a strong emphasis upon what is sometimes called in Reformed circles the cultural mandate. Just as Jesus sent his apostles forth into the world and commissioned them to make disciples of all persons, so God here sent his highest creatures, human beings, out into creation, and commissioned them to rule over it. In this commission it is implied that we are to make full use of our ability to learn about the whole creation. For by coming to understand the creation, we will be able to predict and control its actions. These activities are not optional, but are part of the responsibility that goes with being God's highest creature.

Evaluation of the Views

We need now to do some evaluating of the three general views of the image of God. We will begin with the less traditional views, the conceptions of the image as relationship and as a function.

The relational view has correctly seized upon the truth that humans alone, of all of the creatures, know and are consciously related to God. The portrayals of Adam and Eve in the Garden of Eden suggest that God and they customarily communed together. It is significant that both in the Old Testament law (the Ten Commandments in Exod. 20) and in Jesus' statement of the two great commandments (Matt. 22:36–40; Mark 12:28–31; Luke 10:26–27), the thrust of God's will for humanity (which presumably embodies or expresses his intention for us) concerns relationship to God and to other people.

There are certain problems, however, with the view that the image of God is totally a relational matter. One of them is the uni-

versality of the image. In what sense can it be said that those who are living in total indifference to God, or even in hostile rebellion against him, are (or are in) the image of God? Another problem surfaces when we ask what it is about humans that enables them to have this relationship which no other creature is able to have. Certainly there are some prerequisite factors if relationship is to occur.

We must conclude that Barth and Brunner were led astray by their wholeheartedly antisubstantialist presuppositions, which stemmed from existentialism. This leads to the position that human uniqueness must be formal rather than substantive. But the exact basis of our formal constitution as a being capable of relationship is never delineated.

When we turn to the functional view, we again see an insightful seizing upon one of the major elements in the biblical picture of the image of God, namely, that God's act creating human beings is immediately followed by the command to have dominion. There certainly is, at the very least, a very close connection between the image and the exercise of dominion. There is also, to be sure, a parallel between Genesis 1 and Psalm 8 (i.e., in the description of the domain over which humans are to have dominion). Yet there are difficulties with this view as well.

One difficulty concerns the connection between Psalm 8 and Genesis 1. It is notable that the terms *image* and *likeness* do not appear in Psalm 8. If the psalm is indeed dependent upon Genesis 1, where we do find specific reference to the image, and if exercising dominion over the creatures mentioned in verses 7–8 of the psalm does indeed constitute the image of God, then one would expect in this passage as well some specific reference to the image.

Further, in Genesis 1 there is no clear equation of the image of God with the exercise of dominion. On the contrary, there are some indications that they are distinguishable. God is said to create humankind in his

---

6. Verduin, *Somewhat Less than God*, p. 27.

own image; then God gives the command to have dominion. In other words, humans are spoken of as being in God's image before they are ordered to practice dominion. In verse 26 the use of two hortative expressions—"Let us make man in our image, after our likeness," and "let them have dominion"—seems to distinguish the two concepts. Walther Eichrodt points out that a blessing is given when humanity is created, but that a second blessing is necessary before dominion over the creatures can be exercised.[7] It appears, then, that the functional view may have taken a consequence of the image and equated it with the image itself.

We must now look carefully at the substantive or structural view. It is significant that the text of Scripture itself never identifies what qualities within humans might be the image. The criticism that, in misguided attempts to identify such qualities, a number of advocates of the structural view have actually suggested nonbiblical concepts (e.g., the ancient Greek notion of reason) is justified.[8] Further, the structural view often is narrowed to one aspect of human nature and, particularly, to the intellectual dimension of humankind. This in turn implies that the image of God varies with different human beings. The more intellectual a person is, the greater the extent to which the image of God is present. And then there is the additional problem of determining just what happened when humanity fell into sinfulness. It does not seem to be the case that the fall affected intelligence or reason in general. Moreover, some unbelievers are more intelligent and perceptive than are some highly sanctified Christians.

Conclusions Regarding the Nature of the Image

Having noted that there are difficulties with each of the general views, we must now attempt to form some conclusions as to just what the image of God is. The existence of a wide diversity of interpretations is an indication that there are no direct statements in Scripture to resolve the issue. Our conclusions, then, must necessarily be reasonable inferences drawn from what little the Bible does have to say on the subject:

1. The image of God is universal within the human race. The first and universal man, Adam, not merely a portion of the human race, was made in the image of God.

2. The image of God has not been lost as a result of sin or specifically the fall. This being the case, the image of God is not something accidental or external to human nature. It is something inseparably connected with humanity.

3. There is no indication that the image is present in one person to a greater degree than in another. Superior natural endowments, such as high intelligence, are not evidence of the presence or degree of the image.

4. The image is not correlated with any variable. For example, there is no direct statement correlating the image with development of relationships, nor making it dependent upon the exercise of dominion. The statements in Genesis 1 simply say that God resolved to make man in his own image and then did so. This seems to antedate any human activity.

5. In light of the foregoing considerations, the image should be thought of as primarily substantive or structural. The image is something in the very nature of humans, in the way in which they were made. It refers to something we *are* rather than something we *have* or *do*. By contrast the focus of the relational and functional views is actually on consequences or applications of the image rather than on the image itself.

6. The image refers to the elements in the makeup of human beings which enable the fulfilment of their destiny. The image is the powers of personality which make each human, like God, a being capable of inter-

7. Eichrodt, *Theology of the Old Testament*, vol. 2, p. 127.
8. David Cairns, *The Image of God in Man* (New York: Philosophical Library, 1953), p. 57.

acting with other persons, of thinking and reflecting, and of willing freely.

God's creation was for definite purposes. Humans were intended to know, love, and obey God. They were to live in harmony with others, as the story of Cain and Abel indicates. And they were certainly placed here upon earth to exercise dominion over the rest of creation. But these relationships and this function presuppose something else. We are most fully human when we are active in these relationships and perform this function, for we are then fulfilling our *telos*, God's purpose for us. But these are the consequences or the applications of the image. The image itself is that set of qualities of God which, reflected in humans, make relationships and the exercise of dominion possible.

Beyond this matter of what the image of God consists of, we must ask why humans are made in God's image. What is God's intention for them within life? It is here that the other views of the image are of special help to us, for they concentrate upon consequences or manifestations of the image. The character and actions of Jesus will be a particularly helpful guide in this matter, since he was the perfect example of what human nature is intended to be:

1. Jesus had perfect fellowship with the Father. While on earth he communed with and frequently spoke to the Father. Their fellowship is most clearly seen in the high-priestly prayer in John 17. Jesus spoke of how he and the Father are one (vv. 21–22). He had glorified and would glorify the Father (vv. 1, 4), and the Father had glorified and would glorify him (vv. 1, 5, 22, 24).

2. Jesus obeyed the Father's will perfectly. In the Garden of Gethsemane, Jesus prayed, "Father, if thou art willing, remove this cup from me; nevertheless not my will, but thine, be done" (Luke 22:42). Indeed, throughout his ministry his own will was subordinate (John 4:34; 5:30; 6:38).

3. Jesus always displayed a strong love for humans. Note, for example, his concern for the lost sheep of Israel (Matt. 9:36; 10:6), his

compassion for the sick (Mark 1:41) and the sorrowing (Luke 7:13), his patience with and forgiveness for those who failed.

It is God's intention that a similar sense of fellowship, obedience, and love characterize our relationship to God, and that humans be bound together with one another in love. We are completely human only when manifesting these characteristics.

Implications of the Doctrine

1. We belong to God. Dorothy Sayers has noted and David Cairns has argued that although the expression "image of God" does not appear, it is crucial to a full understanding of Mark 12:13–17.[9] The issue was whether to pay taxes to Caesar. Having been brought a coin, Jesus asked whose image appeared on it. When the Pharisees and Herodians correctly answered, "Caesar's," Jesus responded, "Render to Caesar the things that are Caesar's, and to God the things that are God's." What are "the things that are God's"? Presumably, whatever bears the image of God. Jesus then was saying, "Give your money to Caesar; it has his image on it, and thus it belongs to him. But give yourselves to God. You bear his image, and you belong to him." Commitment, devotion, love, loyalty, service to God—all of these are proper responses for those who bear the image of God.

2. We should pattern ourselves after Jesus, who is the complete revelation of what the image of God is. He is the full image of God, and he is the one person whose humanity was never spoiled by sinning (Heb. 4:15).

3. We experience full humanity only when we are properly related to God. No matter how cultured and genteel, no one is fully human unless a redeemed disciple of God. There is room, then, in our theology for humanism, that is, a Christian and biblical humanism which is concerned to bring

9. Dorothy Sayers, *The Man Born to Be King* (New York: Harper, 1943), p. 225; Cairns, *Image of God*, p. 30.

others into proper relationship with God. The New Testament makes clear that God will restore the damaged image, and perhaps even build upon and go beyond it (2 Cor. 3:18).

4. There is goodness in learning and work. The exercise of dominion is a consequence of the image of God. We are to gain an understanding and control of the creation as well as to exercise dominion over our own personalities and abilities. Note that the exercise of dominion was part of God's original intention for humankind; it preceded the fall. Work, then, is not a curse. It is part of God's good plan.

5. The human is valuable. The sacredness of human life is an extremely important principle in God's scheme of things. Even after the fall, murder was prohibited; the

one possesses the potential for fellowship with God and will be incomplete unless it is realized.

Because all are in the image of God, nothing should be done which would encroach upon another's legitimate exercise of dominion. Freedom must not be taken from a human who has not forfeited this right by abusing it (the list of those who have abused their freedom would include murderers, thieves, etc.). This means, most obviously, that slavery is improper. Beyond that, however, it means that depriving someone of freedom through illegal means, manipulation, or intimidation is improper. Everyone has a right to exercise dominion, a right which ends only at the point of encroaching upon another's right to exercise dominion.

The image of God is the powers of personality which make us capable of interacting with other persons, of thinking and reflecting, and of willing freely.

reason given was that humans, though sinners, are still made in the image of God (Gen. 9:6).

6. The image is universal in humankind. It is found in all categories of people. Both sexes possess the image of God. Genesis 1:27 and 5:1–2 make it clear that the image was borne by both male and female. Similarly, all races are included in God's family and thus are objects of his love. People of all ages, of all economic and marital statuses, are included as well.

The universality of the image means that there is a dignity to being human. Each individual is something beautiful, even though a distortion of what God originally intended humankind to be. The universality of the image also means that all persons have points of sensitivity to spiritual things. Although at times these points may be deeply buried and difficult to identify, every-

One other issue that has far-reaching implications, particularly for ethics, concerns the status of the unborn or, more specifically, of the fetus still in the mother's uterus. Is the fetus to be regarded as human, or merely as a mass of tissue within the mother's body? If the former, abortion is indeed the taking of a human life and has serious moral consequences. If the latter, abortion is simply a surgical procedure involving the removal of an unwanted growth like a cyst or a tumor.

While no passage of Scripture demonstrates conclusively that the fetus is a human in God's sight, nevertheless, various texts (e.g., Ps. 139:13–15; Luke 1:41–44; Heb. 7:9–10), when taken as a whole, do give us enough evidence to render that conclusion very likely. And where one is dealing with an issue as momentous as the possible destruction of a human life, prudence dictates that a conservative course be followed. If one is driving and sees what may be either a pile of rags or a child lying in the street, one will assume that it is a human. And a conscientious Christian will treat a fetus as human, since it is highly likely that God regards a fetus as a person capable of (at least potentially) that fellowship with God for which humanity was created.

Every human being is God's creature made in God's own image. God endowed each of us with the powers of personality that make worship and service of our Creator possible. When we are using those powers to those ends, we are most fully what God intended us to be. It is then that we are most completely human.

19 The Constitutional Nature of the Human

When we ask what humankind is, we are asking several different questions. One, which we have already addressed, is the question of where humans came from—how did they come into being? We are also asking what humanity's function or purpose is—what are they intended to do? That might lead us to the question of where humans are going—what is their ultimate destiny? Human makeup is yet another issue raised by the question of what we are. Are we a unitary whole, or made up of two or more components? And if made up of multiple components, what are they?

Basic Views of the Human Constitution

Trichotomism

A view rather popular in conservative Protestant circles has been termed the "trichotomist" view. Humans are composed of three elements. The first element is the physical body. A physical nature is something we have in common with animals and plants. The difference is one of degree, as humans have a more complex physical structure. The second part of the human person is the soul. This is the psychological element, the basis of reason, of emotion, of social interrelatedness and the like. Animals are thought to have a rudimentary soul. Possession of a soul is what distinguishes humans and animals from the plants. What distinguishes humanity from the animals is not that we have a more complex and advanced soul, but that we possess a third element, namely, a spirit. This religious element enables the human to perceive spiritual matters and respond to spiritual stimuli. It is the seat of the spiritual qualities of the individual, whereas the personality traits reside in the soul.[1]

A goodly portion of trichotomism is indebted to ancient Greek metaphysics. Except for an occasional explicit reference, however, the influence of the Greek philosophers is not readily apparent. Actually the major foundation of trichotomism is certain Scripture passages which either enumerate three components of human nature or distinguish between the soul and the spirit. A primary text is 1 Thessalonians 5:23: "May the God of peace himself sanctify you wholly; and may your spirit and soul and body be kept sound and blameless at the coming of our Lord Jesus Christ" (see also Heb. 4:12). Beyond that, a threefold division seems to be implied in 1 Corinthians 2:14–3:4, where Paul classifies human persons as "of the flesh" (*sarkikos*), "unspiritual" (*psychikos*—literally, "of the soul"), or "spiritual" (*pneumatikos*). These terms seem to refer to different functions or orientations, if not to different components of human beings.

Trichotomism became particularly popular among the Alexandrian fathers of the early centuries of the church. Although the form varies somewhat, trichotomism is found in Clement of Alexandria, Origen, and Gregory of Nyssa. It fell into a certain amount of disrepute after Apollinarius made use of it in constructing his Christology, which the church determined to be heretical. Although some of the Eastern fathers continued to hold it, it suffered a general decline in popularity until it was revived in the nineteenth century by English and German theologians.[2]

Dichotomism

Probably the most widely held view through most of the history of Christian thought has been that humans are composed of two elements, a material aspect, the body, and an immaterial component, the soul or spirit. Dichotomism was commonly held from the earliest period of Christian thought. Following the Council of Constantinople in 381, however, it grew in popularity to the point where it was virtually the universal belief of the church.

Recent forms of dichotomism maintain that the Old Testament presents a unitary view of human nature. In the New Testament, however, this unitary view is replaced by a dualism: humans are composed of body and soul. The body is the physical part; it is the part which dies. The soul, on the other hand, is the immaterial part, the part which survives death. It is this immortal nature which sets humanity apart from all other creatures.[3]

Many of the arguments for dichotomism are, in essence, arguments against the trichotomist conception. The dichotomist objects to trichotomism on the grounds that if one follows the principle that each of the separate references in verses like 1 Thessalonians 5:23 represents a distinct entity, difficulties arise with some other texts. For example, in Luke 10:27 Jesus says, "You shall love the Lord your God with all your heart, and with all your soul, and with all your strength, and with all your mind." Here we have not three but four entities, and these

---

1. Franz Delitzsch, *A System of Biblical Psychology* (Grand Rapids: Baker, 1966), pp. 116–17.

2. Louis Berkhof, *Systematic Theology* (Grand Rapids: Eerdmans, 1953), pp. 191–92.
3. Ibid., pp. 192–95.

four hardly match the three in 1 Thessalonians. Indeed, only one of them is the same, namely, the soul. Further, "spirit" as well as "soul" is used of the brute creation. For example, Ecclesiastes 3:21 refers to the spirit of the beast. The terms *spirit* and *soul* often seem to be used interchangeably. Note, for example, Luke 1:46–47, which is in all likelihood an example of parallelism: "My soul magnifies the Lord, and my spirit rejoices in God my Savior." Here the two terms seem virtually equivalent. There are many other instances. The basic components of human nature are designated body and soul in Matthew 6:25 and 10:28, but body and spirit in Ecclesiastes 12:7 and 1 Corinthians 5:3, 5. Death is described as giving up the soul (Gen. 35:18; 1 Kings 17:21; Acts 15:26) and as giving up the spirit (Ps. 31:5; Luke 23:46). At times the word *soul* is used in such a way as to be synonymous with one's self or life: "For what will it profit a man, if he gains the whole world and forfeits his life [literally, soul]?" (Matt. 16:26). There are references to being troubled in spirit (Gen. 41:8; John 13:21) and to being troubled of soul (Ps. 42:6; John 12:27).

Although liberal theologians quite clearly distinguished the soul and the body as virtually two different substances, and some of them, notably Harry Emerson Fosdick, substituted immortality of the soul for the traditional doctrine of resurrection of the body, conservatives have not taken the dualistic view this far. While believing that the soul is capable of surviving death, living on in a disembodied state, conservatives also look forward to a future resurrection. It is not resurrection of the body versus survival of the soul.[4] Rather, it is both of them as separate stages in humankind's future.

Monism

The points of agreement between the trichotomist and the dichotomist views exceed their differences. They both agree that humans are complex or compound, that they are made up of separable parts. In contrast are various forms of the view that humans are indivisible. Monism insists that we are not to be thought of as in any sense composed of parts or separate entities, but rather as a radical unity. In the monistic understanding, the Bible does not view the human being as body, soul, and spirit, but simply as a self. The terms sometimes used to distinguish parts of human nature are actually to be taken as basically synonymous.

According to monism, to be human is to be or have a body. The idea that a human can somehow exist apart from a body is unthinkable. Consequently, there is no possibility of postdeath existence in a disembodied state. Immortality of the soul is quite untenable. Not only, then, is there no possibility of a future life apart from bodily resurrection, but any sort of intermediate state between death and resurrection is ruled out as well.

Monism, which arose in part as a reaction against the liberal idea of immortality of the soul, was popular in neoorthodoxy and in the biblical-theology movement. Their approach was largely through a word-study method. One prominent example is *The Body*, John A. T. Robinson's study in Pauline theology.[5] This volume draws on H. Wheeler Robinson's discussion of the Old Testament terminology for humans and their nature, according to which the expression "body and soul" is not to be understood as making a distinction between the two, or dividing human nature into components. Rather, it should be considered an exhaustive description of human personality. In the Old Testament conception, the human being is a psychophysical unity, flesh animated by soul. As a now classic sentence of H. Wheeler Robinson has it, "The Hebrew idea of personality is an animated body, and not an incarnated soul."[6] Given this unitary

---

4. Augustus H. Strong, *Systematic Theology* (Westwood, N.J.: Revell, 1907), pp. 998–1003, 1015–23.

5. John A. T. Robinson, *The Body* (London: SCM, 1952).
6. H. Wheeler Robinson, "Hebrew Psychology," in *The People and the Book*, ed. Arthur S. Peake (Oxford: Clarendon, 1925), p. 362.

view of human nature, Hebrew has no explicit word for the body: "it never needed one so long as the body was the man."[7]

To summarize the modern monistic argument as typified by John A. T. Robinson: The biblical data picture humans as unitary beings. Hebrew thought knows no distinction within human personality. Body and soul are not contrasting terms, but interchangeable synonyms.

Biblical Considerations

We must now evaluate monism in the light of the whole of the biblical data. As we take a closer look, we will find that the absolute monistic view of humankind has overlooked or obscured some of the significant data.

Certain passages seem to indicate an intermediate state between death and resurrection, a state in which the individual lives on in conscious personal existence. One of these passages is Jesus' statement to the thief on the cross, "Truly, I say to you, today you will be with me in Paradise" (Luke 23:43). Another is the parable of the rich man and Lazarus (Luke 16:19–31). Some have thought that this is not a parable but the record of an actual event, since it would be unique among parables in naming one of the characters within the story. We are told that a rich man and a poor man died. The rich man went to Hades, where he was in great torment in the flame, while the poor man, Lazarus, was taken to Abraham's bosom. Both were in a state of consciousness. A third consideration pointing to an intermediate state is Paul's reference to being away from the body and at home with the Lord (2 Cor. 5:8). The apostle expresses a dread of this state of nakedness (vv. 3–4), desiring rather to be reclothed (v. 4). Finally, there are some references in the Scripture where the distinction between body and soul is difficult to dismiss. A prominent instance is Jesus' statement in Matthew 10:28:

7. Ibid., p. 366.

"And do not fear those who kill the body but cannot kill the soul; rather fear him who can destroy both soul and body in hell."

It appears, from the foregoing considerations, that it is by no means necessary to conclude that the biblical teaching rules out the possibility of some type of compound character, or at least some sort of divisibility, within the human makeup.

An Alternative Model: Conditional Unity

We must now attempt to draw together some conclusions and form a workable model. We have noted that in the Old Testament, the human individual is regarded as a unity. In the New Testament the body-soul terminology appears, but it cannot be precisely correlated with the idea of embodied and disembodied existence. While body and soul are sometimes contrasted (as in Jesus' statement in Matt. 10:28), they are not always so clearly distinguished. Furthermore, Scripture seems to picture humans for the most part as unitary beings. Seldom is their spiritual nature addressed independently of or apart from the body.

Having said this, however, we must also recall those passages which point to an immaterial aspect of human beings which is separable from their material existence. Scripture indicates that there is an intermediate state involving personal conscious existence between death and resurrection. This concept of an intermediate state is not inconsistent with the doctrine of resurrection. For the intermediate (i.e., immaterial or disembodied) state is clearly incomplete or abnormal (2 Cor. 5:2–4). In the coming resurrection (1 Cor. 15) the person will receive a new or perfected body.

The full range of the biblical data can best be accommodated by the view which we will term "conditional unity." According to this view, our normal state is as a materialized unitary being. It is significant that Scripture nowhere urges us to flee or escape from the body, as if it were somehow inherently evil.

This monistic condition can, however, be broken down, and at death it is, so that the immaterial aspect lives on even as the material decomposes. At the resurrection, however, there will be a return to a material or bodily condition. The person will assume a body which has some points of continuity with the old body, but is also a new or reconstituted or spiritual body. The solution to the variety of data in the biblical witness is not, then, the immortality of the soul *or the* resurrection of the body. In keeping with what has been the orthodox tradition within the church, it is *both/and.*

What sort of analogy can we employ to help us understand this idea or complex of ideas? One that is sometimes used is the chemical compound as contrasted with a mixture of elements. In a mixture the atoms of each element retain their distinctive characteristics because they retain their separate identities. If human nature were a mixture,

We might think of each human being as a unitary compound of a material and an immaterial element. The spiritual and the physical elements are not always distinguishable, for the human is a unitary subject; there is no struggle between the material and immaterial nature. The compound is dissolvable, however; dissolution takes place at death. At the resurrection a compound will again be formed, with the soul (if we choose to call it that) once more becoming inseparably attached to a body.

Implications of Conditional Unity

What are the implications of contingent monism, that is, the view that human nature is a conditional unity?

1. Each human is to be treated as a unity. One's spiritual condition cannot be dealt with independently of physical and psychological condition, and vice versa. Psycho-

Since we are unitary beings, our spiritual condition cannot be dealt with independently of our physical and psychological condition, and vice versa.

then the spiritual and physical qualities would somehow be distinguishable, and one could act as either a spiritual or a physical being. On the other hand, in a compound the atoms of all the elements involved enter into new combinations to form molecules. These molecules have characteristics or qualities which are unlike those of any of the elements of which they are composed. In the case of simple table salt (the compound sodium chloride), for example, one cannot detect the qualities of either sodium or chlorine. It is possible, however, to break up the compound, whereupon one again has the original elements with their distinctive characteristics. These characteristics would include the poisonous nature of chlorine, whereas the compound product is nonpoisonous.

somatic medicine is proper. So also is psychosomatic ministry (or should we term it pneumopsychosomatic ministry?). The Christian who desires to be spiritually healthy will give attention to such matters as diet, rest, and exercise. Any attempt to deal with spiritual condition apart from physical condition and mental and emotional state will be less than completely successful, as will any attempt to deal with human emotions apart from one's relationship to God.

2. Humans are complex beings. Their nature is not reducible to a single principle.

3. The different aspects of human nature are all to be attended to and respected. There is to be no depreciating of the body, emotions, or intellect. The gospel is an appeal to the whole person. It is significant that Jesus in his incarnation became fully

human, for he came to redeem the whole of what we are.

4. Religious development or maturity does not consist in subjugating one part of human nature to another. There is no part of human nature that is evil per se. Total depravity means that sin infects all of what a human is, not merely the body or mind or emotions. Thus, the Christian should not aim at bringing the body (which many erroneously regard as the only evil part of human nature) under the control of the soul. Similarly, sanctification is not to be thought of as involving only one part of human nature, for no one part is the exclusive seat of good or of righteousness. God is at work renewing the whole of what we are. Consequently, asceticism, in the sense of denying one's natural bodily needs simply for its own sake, is not to be practiced.

5. Human nature is not inconsistent with the scriptural teaching of a personal conscious existence between death and resurrection. We will examine this doctrine at greater length in our treatment of eschatology (pp. 366–71).

Part Six

Sin

20 The Nature and Source of Sin

The Difficulty of Discussing Sin

As important as the doctrine of sin is, it is not an easy topic to discuss in our day. There are several reasons for this. One is that sin, like death, is not a very pleasant or enjoyable subject. It depresses us. We do not like to think of ourselves as bad or evil persons. Yet the doctrine of sin teaches us that this is what we are by nature. Not only do individuals react against this negative teaching, but there is abroad in our society an emphasis on having a positive mental attitude. This emphasis has almost become a new type of legalism, the major prohibition of which is, "Thou shalt not speak anything negative."[1]

Another reason it is difficult to discuss sin is that to many people it is a foreign concept. Not only are the problems of society blamed on an unwholesome environment rather than on sinful humans, but there has been a corresponding loss of a sense of

1. Róbert H. Schuller, *Self-Esteem*: *The New Reformation* (Waco, Tex.: Word, 1982).

guilt. We have in mind here the fact that a sense of objective guilt has become relatively uncommon in certain circles. In part through the influence of Freudianism, guilt is understood as an irrational feeling that one ought not to have. Without a transcendent, theistic reference point, there is no one other than oneself and other human beings to whom one is responsible or accountable. Thus, if no one is harmed by our actions, there is no reason to feel guilt.[2]

Further, many people are unable to grasp the concept of sin. The idea of *sin* as an inner force, an inherent condition, a controlling power, is largely unknown. People today think more in terms of *sins*, that is, individual wrong acts. Sins are something external and concrete; they are logically separable from the person. On this basis, people who have done nothing wrong (generally conceived of as an external act) consider themselves good; there is no thought of sin.

Biblical Perspectives on the Nature of Sin

Although many people today are ignorant of or uncomfortable with the topic of sin, it is imperative that we discuss this doctrine. The Bible presents a number of perspectives on the nature of sin:

1. Sin is an inward inclination. Sin is not merely wrong acts, but sinfulness as well. It is an inherent inner disposition inclining us to wrong acts. Here motives are virtually as important as actions. So Jesus condemned anger and lust as vehemently as he did murder and adultery (Matt. 5:21–22, 27–28). It is not simply that we are sinners because we sin; we sin because we are sinners. We offer, then, this definition of sin: "Sin is any lack of conformity, active or passive, to the moral law of God. This may be a matter of act, of thought, or of inner disposition or state." Sin is failure to live up to what God expects of us in act, thought, and being.

2. Sin is rebelliousness and disobedience. The Bible assumes that all persons are in contact with the truth of God. Paul notes that this includes even the Gentiles, who, though they do not have God's special revelation, have the law of God written on their hearts (Rom. 2:14–15). Failure to believe the message, particularly when openly and specially presented, is disobedience or rebellion against God. A prime example is the sin of Adam and Eve. Though they were permitted to eat of any tree in the Garden of Eden, God commanded them not to eat from the tree of

> *Sin is any lack of conformity, active or passive, to the moral law of God. This may be a matter of act, thought, or inner disposition.*

the knowledge of good and evil (Gen. 2:16–17). Adam and Eve rejected God's prerogative to say what was right and wrong for them. They rebelled against God's authority, and thus disobeyed him.

3. Sin entails spiritual disability. It alters our inner condition, our character. In sinning we become twisted or distorted as it were. The image of God in which we were created is disturbed. In Romans 1, Paul describes this process. Having refused to acknowledge God, sinners became futile in their thinking, and their senseless minds were darkened (v. 21). God gave them over to a base mind (v. 28), actually an unqualified or disqualified mind. When left to itself, the human mind is not adequate to properly inform and direct our conduct.[3] The results of this spiritual disability are the sins listed in verses 29–31. Only through a renewal of the mind by God can the individual be re-

---

2. On the loss of a sense of guilt, see, e.g., Karl Menninger, *Whatever Became of Sin?* (New York: Hawthorn, 1973).

3. James D. G. Dunn, *Romans 1–8*, vol. 38 of *Word Biblical Commentary* (Dallas: Word, 1988), p. 75.

stored to an undistorted, spiritually healthy condition (Rom. 12:2).

4. Sin is incomplete fulfilment of God's standards. A common element running through all of the biblical characterizations of sin is the idea that the sinner has failed to fulfil God's law. There are various ways in which we fail to meet his standard of righteousness. We may simply fall short of the norm that is set, or not do at all what God commands and expects. Saul failed to follow through on God's command to destroy the Amalekites and all they possessed. Because Saul spared King Agag and the best livestock, God rejected Saul as king of Israel (1 Sam. 15:23). Sometimes we may do the right thing, but for the wrong reason, thus fulfilling the letter of the law, but not its spirit. In Matthew 6, Jesus condemns good acts done primarily out of a desire to obtain the approval of other people rather than to please God (vv. 2, 5, 16).

5. Sin is displacement of God. Placing something else, anything else, in the supreme place which belongs to God is sin. Choosing any finite object over God is wrong, no matter how selfless such an act might seem. This contention is supported by major texts in both the Old and New Testaments. The Ten Commandments begin with the command to give God his proper place. "You shall have no other gods before me" (Exod. 20:3) is the first prohibition in the law. Similarly, Jesus affirmed that the first and great commandment is, "You shall love the Lord your God with all your heart, and with all your soul, and with all your mind, and with all your strength" (Mark 12:30). Proper recognition of God is primary. Idolatry in any form, not pride, is the essence of sin.

The Source of Sin

Various Conceptions

We have mentioned several biblical perspectives on sin. Now we need to ask regarding the source of sin, the cause of or occasion leading to sin. This is vital because the cure for sin will necessarily involve identifying and negating the cause.

Frederick Tennant held that the source of sin is our animal nature. Sin is simply the persistence of normal instincts and patterns of behavior from our animal ancestry into the period when humans acquired moral consciousness.[4] In this case, the cure cannot be a simple reversal to an earlier innocent stage. Rather, it will be a matter of completely freeing ourselves from those older instincts, or of learning to control and direct them properly. This conception of the cure for sin embraces the optimistic belief that the evolutionary process is carrying the human race in the right direction.

In Reinhold Niebuhr's view, the source of sin is the anxiety caused by human finiteness, the attempt to overcome through self-efforts the tension between our limitations and our aspirations.[5] The cure will involve accepting our limitations and placing our confidence in God. But this cure is a matter of altering our attitude, not of real conversion.

Paul Tillich related sin to existential estrangement from the ground of all being (Tillich's definition of God), from other beings, and from oneself, a condition which seems to be virtually a natural accompaniment of creaturehood.[6] Here, too, the fundamental cure is a matter of changing one's attitude, not of real conversion. The solution entails becoming increasingly aware of the fact that one is part of being, or that one participates in the ground of being. The result will be the end of one's alienation from the ground of being, other beings, and self.

According to liberation theology, the source of sin is economic struggle.[7] The so-

4. Frederick R. Tennant, *The Origin and Propagation of Sin* (Cambridge: Cambridge University Press, 1902), pp. 90–91.
5. Reinhold Niebuhr, *The Nature and Destiny of Man* (New York: Scribner, 1941), vol. 1, pp. 180–82.
6. Paul Tillich, *Systematic Theology* (Chicago: University of Chicago Press, 1957), vol. 2, p. 44.
7. See Gustavo Gutierrez, *A Theology of Liberation*, trans. Sister Caridad Inda and John Eagleson (Maryknoll, N.Y.: Orbis, 1973); James H. Cone, *A Black Theology of Liberation* (Philadelphia: Lippincott, 1970).

lution is to eliminate oppression and inequities in possessions and power. Rather than evangelizing individuals, our chief pursuit should be economic and political action aimed at altering the structure of society.

Harrison Sacket Elliott viewed individualistic competitiveness as the source of sin. Since sin is learned through education and social conditioning, it must be eliminated the same way.[8] The antidote is education that stresses noncompetitive endeavor toward common goals.

The Biblical Teaching

From the evangelical perspective, the problem lies in the fact that humans are sinful by nature and live in a world in which powerful forces seek to induce them to sin. It is important to note first that sin is not caused by God. James very quickly disposes of this idea, which would probably be quite appealing to some: "Let no one say when he is tempted, 'I am tempted by God'; for God cannot be tempted with evil and he himself tempts no one" (James 1:13). Nor is any encouragement given for the idea that sin inevitably results from the very structure of reality. Rather, responsibility for sin is placed squarely at the door of the individual: "Each person is tempted when he is lured and enticed by his own desire. Then desire when it has conceived gives birth to sin; and sin when it is full-grown brings forth death" (James 1:14–15). By analyzing this and other passages, both didactic and narrative, we can determine what the Bible teaches to be the basis or cause of sin.

We all have certain desires. These, at root, are legitimate. In many cases their satisfaction is indispensable to the survival of the individual or the race. For example, hunger is the desire for food. Without the satisfaction of this desire or drive, we would starve to death. Similarly, the sexual drive seeks gratification. Were it to go unsatisfied, there would be no human reproduction and hence no preservation of the human race.

Without attempting to deal here with the question of the propriety of eating for enjoyment or of sex for pleasure, we may assert that these drives were given by God, and that there are situations in which their satisfaction is not only permissible but may even be mandatory.

We note, further, human capability. Humans are able to choose among alternatives; these alternatives may include options which are not immediately present. Humans alone of all the creatures are capable of transcending their location in time and space. Through memory they are able to relive the past, and to accept or repudiate it. Through anticipation they are able to construct scenarios regarding the future, and choose among them. They can envision themselves occupying a different position in society, or married to a different partner. Thus, they may desire not only what is actually available to them, but also what is not proper or legitimate for them. This capability expands greatly the possibilities of sinful action and/or thoughts.[9]

Every human has a number of natural desires which, while good in and of themselves, are potential areas for temptation and sin:[10]

1. *The desire to enjoy things.* God has implanted certain needs in each of us. Not only is the satisfaction of those needs essential, but it can also bring enjoyment. For example, the need for food and drink must be satisfied because life is impossible without them. At the same time food and drink may also be legitimately desired as a source of enjoyment. When food and drink are pursued, however, merely for the pleasure of consumption, and in excess of what is needed, the sin of glut-

---

8. See Harrison S. Elliott, *Can Religious Education Be Christian?* (New York: Macmillan, 1940).

9. Reinhold Niebuhr, *The Self and the Dramas of History* (London: Faber and Faber, 1956), pp. 35–37.

10. M. G. Kyle, "Temptation, Psychology of," in *International Standard Bible Encyclopedia,* ed. James Orr (Grand Rapids: Eerdmans, 1952), vol. 5, pp. 2944–2944B.

tony is being committed. The sex drive, while not necessary for the preservation of the life of the individual, is essential for sustaining and continuing the human race. We may legitimately desire satisfaction of this drive because it is essential and also because it brings pleasure. When, however, the drive is gratified in ways which transcend natural and proper limitations (i.e., when it is satisfied outside of marriage), it becomes the basis of sin. Any improper satisfaction of a natural desire is an instance of "the lust of the flesh" (1 John 2:16).

2. *The desire to obtain things.* There is a role in God's economy for the obtainment of possessions. This is implicit in the command to have dominion over the world (Gen. 1:28) and in the stewardship parables (e.g., Matt. 25:14–30). Further, material possessions are regarded as legitimate incentives to encourage industriousness. When, however, the desire to acquire worldly goods becomes so compelling that it is satisfied at any cost, even by exploiting or stealing from others, then it has degenerated into "the lust of the eyes" (1 John 2:16).

3. *The desire to do things.* The stewardship parables also depict the desire to achieve as both natural and appropriate. It is part of what God expects of humankind. When, however, this urge transgresses proper limitations and is pursued at the expense of others, it has degenerated into "the pride of life" (1 John 2:16).

There are proper ways to satisfy each of these desires, and there are also divinely imposed limits. Failure to accept these desires as they have been constituted by God and therefore to submit to divine control is sin. In such cases, the desires are not seen in the context of their divine origin and as means to the end of pleasing God, but as ends in themselves.

Note that in the temptation of Jesus, Satan appealed to legitimate desires. The desires which Satan bade Jesus fulfil were not wrong per se. Rather, the suggested time and manner of fulfilment constituted the evil. Jesus had fasted for forty days and nights and consequently was hungry. This was a natural need which had to be satisfied if life was to be preserved. It was right for Jesus to be fed, but not through some miraculous provision, and probably not before the completion of his trial. It was proper for Jesus to desire to come down safely from the pinnacle of the temple, but not to require a miraculous display of power by the Father. It was right for Jesus to lay claim to all the kingdoms of the earth, for they are his. He had created them (John 1:3) and even now sustains them (Col. 1:17). But it was not right to seek to establish this claim by worshiping the chief of the forces of evil.

Oftentimes temptation involves inducement from without. This was true in the case of Jesus. In the case of Adam and Eve, the serpent did not directly suggest that they eat of the forbidden tree. Rather, he raised the question whether the fruit of all the trees was off limits to them. Then he asserted, "You will not die . . . [but] will be like God" (Gen. 3:4–5). While the desire to eat of the tree or to be like God may have been present naturally, there was also an external inducement of satanic origin. In some cases another human entices one to overstep the divinely imposed bounds upon behavior. In the final analysis, however, *sin is the choice of the person who commits it.* The desire to do what is done may be present naturally, and there may be external inducement as well. But the individual is ultimately responsible. Adam and Eve chose to act upon impulse and suggestion; Jesus chose not to.

In addition to natural desire and temptation, there must of course be an opportunity for sin as well. Initially, Adam could not have been tempted to infidelity to his wife, nor could Eve have been jealous of other women. For those of us who live after the fall, and are not Jesus, there is a further complicating factor. There is something termed "the flesh," which strongly influences what we do. Paul speaks of it in numerous passages, for example, Romans 7:18: "For I know that nothing good dwells within me, that is, in my flesh. I can will what is right, but I cannot do it." In Galatians 5:16–24 he speaks vividly of the opposition between the flesh and the Spirit, and of the works of the flesh, which constitute a whole catalog of evils. By "flesh" Paul does not mean the physical nature of the human being. Rather, the term designates the self-centered life, denial or rejection of God. This is something that has become a part of human nature—a bent, a tendency, a bias toward sin and away from doing God's will. Accordingly, we today are less able to choose the right than were the original humans. It is even conceivable that as a consequence of the fall natural desires, which are good in themselves, may have undergone alteration.

What does the biblical teaching on the source of sin tell us about the cure? The cure must come through a supernaturally produced alteration of one's human nature and also through divine help in countering the power of temptation. It is individual conversion and regeneration that will alter the person and bring him or her into a relationship to God that will make successful Christian living possible.

21 The Results of Sin

One emphasis that runs through both Testaments is that sin is a very serious matter with very serious consequences. In the next chapter we will be looking at the corporate effects of sin, that is, the impact of Adam's sin on the whole of his posterity. In this chapter, however, we will be concerned with the individual effects of one's sin as they are illustrated in Scripture (particularly in the account of Adam and Eve) and found in our own experience.

The impact of sin has several dimensions. There are effects upon the sinner's relationships with God and fellow humans. And sin also affects the sinner himself or herself. Some of the results of sin might be termed "natural consequences," that is, they follow from the sin in virtually an automatic cause-and-effect sequence. Others are specifically ordained and directed by God as a penalty for sin.

Results Affecting the Relationship with God

Sin produced an immediate transformation in the relationship which Adam and Eve had with God. They had evidently been on close and friendly terms with God. They trusted and obeyed him, and on the basis of Genesis 3:8 it can be concluded that they had customarily had fellowship with God. Now, however, all of this was changed. Because they had violated the trust and the command of God, the relationship became quite different. They had placed themselves on the wrong side of God, and had in effect become his enemies. It was not God who had changed or moved, but Adam and Eve.

Divine Disfavor

It is notable how the Bible characterizes God's relationship to sin and the sinner. In two instances in the Old Testament, God is said to hate sinful Israel. In Hosea 9:15 God says, "Every evil of theirs is in Gilgal; there I began to hate them. Because of the wickedness of their deeds I will drive them out of my house. I will love them no more; all their princes are rebels." This is a very strong expression. A similar sentiment is expressed in Jeremiah 12:8. On two other occasions God is said to hate the wicked (Pss. 5:5; 11:5). Much more frequent, however, are passages in which he is said to hate wickedness (e.g., Prov. 6:16–17; Zech. 8:17). The hate is not one-sided on God's part, however, for the wicked are described as those who hate God (Exod. 20:5; Deut. 7:10) and, more commonly, as those who hate the righteous (Pss. 18:40; 69:4; Prov. 29:10). In those few passages where God is said to hate the wicked, it is apparent that he does so because they hate him and have already committed wickedness.

That God looks with favor upon some and with disfavor or anger upon others, and that he is sometimes described as loving Israel and at other times as hating them, are not signs of change, inconsistency, or fickleness in God. Rather, it is part of his holy nature to be categorically opposed to sinful actions. When we engage in such actions, we have moved into the territory of God's disfavor. The Old Testament frequently describes those who sin and violate God's law as enemies of God. Yet only very rarely does the Bible speak of God as their enemy (Exod. 23:22; Isa. 63:10; Lam. 2:4–5). Ryder Smith comments: "In the Old Testament, 'enmity,' like hatred, is rare with God, but common with man."[1] By rebelling against God, it is humanity, not God, that breaks the relationship.

In the New Testament there is a particular focus on the enmity and hatred of unbelievers and the world toward God and his people. To sin is to make oneself an enemy of God. In Romans 8:7 and Colossians 1:21 Paul describes the mind that is set on the flesh as being "hostile to God." In James 4:4 we read that "whoever wishes to be a friend of the world makes himself an enemy of God." God, however, is not the enemy of anyone; he loves all and hates none. He loved enough to send his Son to die for us while we were yet sinners and at enmity with him (Rom. 5:8–10). He epitomizes what he commands. He loves his enemies.

Although God is not the enemy of sinners nor does he hate them, it is also quite clear that God is angered by sin. Scripture not merely refers to God's present reaction to sin, but also suggests certain divine actions

1. Charles Ryder Smith, *The Bible Doctrine of Sin and of the Ways of God with Sinners* (London: Epworth, 1953), p. 43.

to come. In John 3:36, for example, Jesus says, "He who believes in the Son has eternal life; he who does not obey the Son shall not see life, but the wrath of God rests upon him." There are several passages which teach that while the anger of God presently rests upon sin and those who commit it, this anger will be converted into action at some future time. Romans 1:18 teaches that "the wrath of God is revealed from heaven against all ungodliness and wickedness of men who by their wickedness suppress the truth." Romans 2:5 speaks of "storing up wrath" for the day of judgment. God's wrath is a very real and present matter, but will not

guilt. These feelings are often thought of as irrational, and indeed they sometimes are. That is, a person may not have done anything objectively wrong so as to be deserving of punishment, but nonetheless may have these feelings. What we are referring to here, however, is the objective state of having violated God's intention for humankind and thus being liable to punishment. It is this aspect of guilt that deserves our special attention.

To clarify what we mean by "guilt," it will be helpful for us to comment briefly on two words which may occur in one's definition of sin, namely, "bad" and "wrong." On the

By sinning, we have placed ourselves on the wrong side of God and in effect become his enemies.

be fully revealed, or manifested in action, until some later point.

From the foregoing it is evident that God looks with disfavor upon sin, indeed, that sin occasions anger or wrath or displeasure within him. Two additional comments should be made, however. The first is that anger is not something that God chooses to feel. His disapproval of sin is not an arbitrary matter, for his very nature is one of holiness; it automatically rejects sin. The second comment is that we must avoid thinking of God's anger as being excessively emotional. It is not as if he is seething with anger, his temper virtually surging out of control. He is capable of exercising patience and long-suffering, and does so. Nor is God to be thought of as somehow frustrated by our sin. Disappointment is perhaps a more accurate way of characterizing his reaction.

Guilt

Another result of our sins which affects our relationship with God is guilt. This word needs some careful explication, for in today's world the usual meaning of the term is guilt feelings, or the subjective aspect of

one hand, we may define sin as that which is intrinsically bad rather than good. It is impure, repulsive, hated by God simply because it is the opposite of the good. There is a problem here, however. The statement that sin is bad may be understood only in aesthetic terms—sin is ugly, twisted, spoiled action which comes short of the perfect standard of what God intended.

On the other hand, however, we may define sin as involving not merely the bad, but the wrong as well. In the former case, sin might be likened to a foul disease which healthy people shrink from in fear. But in the latter case, we are thinking of sin not merely as a lack of wholeness or of perfection, but as moral wrong, as a deliberate violation of what God has commanded, and thus as deserving of punishment.

This distinction can be illustrated by thinking of an athlete executing a particular play poorly; for example, a basketball player who shoots at the basket but misses it completely. Poorly executed, the play results in no score, but it is not an infraction of the rules, and no foul will be called. On the other hand, if in the process of shooting, the player charges into a stationary defensive player, then a rule has been broken and a foul will be called. Now when we speak of guilt, we mean that the sinner, like the basketball player who commits a foul, has violated the law and, accordingly, is liable to punishment.

At this point we must look into the precise nature of the disruption which sin and guilt produce in the relationship between God and humans. God is the almighty, eternal one, the only independent or noncontingent reality. Everything that is has derived its existence from him. And humans, the highest of all of the creatures, have the gifts of life and personhood only because of God's goodness and graciousness. As the master, God has placed us in charge of the creation and commanded us to rule over it (Gen. 1:28). As the almighty and completely holy one, God has asked our worship and obedience in return for his gifts. But we have failed to do God's bidding. Entrusted with the wealth of the creation, humans have used it for their own purposes, like an employee who embezzles from his employer. In addition, like a citizen who treats contemptuously a monarch or a high elected official, a hero or a person of great accomplishment, we have failed to treat with respect the highest of all beings. Further, we are ungrateful for all that God has done for us and given to us (Rom. 1:21). And finally, humankind has spurned God's offer of friendship and love, and, in the most extreme case, the salvation accomplished through the death of God's own Son. These offenses are magnified by who God is: he is the almighty Creator infinitely above us. Whenever the creature deprives the Creator of what is rightfully his, the balance is upset, for God is not being honored and obeyed. Were such wrong, such disruption, to go uncorrected, God would virtually cease to be God. Therefore, sin and the sinner deserve and even need to be punished.

Punishment

Liability to God's punishment, then, is another result of our sin. It is important for us to ascertain the basic nature and intent of God's punishment of the sinner. Is it remedial, intended to correct the sinner? Is it deterrent, a pointing out of the consequences to which sin leads and hence a warning to others against wrongdoing? Or is it retributive, designed simply to give sinners what they deserve?

There is today a rather widespread feeling of opposition to the idea that God's punishment of the sinner is retribution. Retribution is regarded as primitive, cruel, a mark of hostility and vindictiveness, which is singularly inappropriate in a God of love who is a Father to his earthly children.[2] Yet despite this feeling, which may reflect a permissive society's conception of what a loving father is, there is definitely a dimension of divine retribution in the Bible, particularly in the Old Testament. Certainly, the death penalty was not intended to be rehabilitative, being terminal in nature. And while it also had a deterrent effect, the direct connection between what had been done to the victim and what was to be done to the offender is clear. This is seen particularly in a passage like Genesis 9:6: "Whoever sheds the blood of man, by man shall his blood be shed; for God made man in his own image."

The idea of retribution is also seen quite clearly in the Hebrew term *nāqam*. This word, which (including its derivatives) appears about eighty times in the Old Testament, is frequently rendered "avenge, revenge, take vengeance." While the terms *vengeance* and *revenge* are appropriate translations in designating Israel's actions against her neighbors, there is something inappropriate about applying them to God's actions.[3] "Vengeance" or "revenge" carries the idea of retaliation, of gaining satisfaction (psychologically) to compensate for

2. Nels Ferré, *The Christian Understanding of God* (New York: Harper and Brothers, 1951), p. 228.
3. Smith, *Doctrine of Sin*, p. 47.

what was done, rather than the idea of obtaining and administering justice. God's concern, however, is the maintenance of justice. Thus, in connection with God's punishment of sinners, "retribution" is a better translation than is "vengeance."

There are numerous references, particularly in the Major Prophets, to the retributive dimension of God's punishment of sinners. Examples are to be found in Isaiah 1:24; 61:2; 63:4; Jeremiah 46:10; and Ezekiel 25:14. In Psalm 94:1 God is spoken of as the "God of vengeance." In these cases, as in most instances in the Old Testament, the punishment envisioned is to take place within historical time rather than in some future state. The idea of retribution is found not only in didactic material, but also in numerous narrative passages. For example, the flood (Gen. 6) was not sent to deter anyone from sin, for the only survivors, Noah and his family, were already righteous people. And it certainly could not have been sent for any corrective or rehabilitative reason, since the wicked were all destroyed.

Although less frequently than in the Old Testament, the idea of retributive justice is also found in the New Testament. Here the reference is more to future rather than temporal judgment. Paraphrases of Deuteronomy 32:35 are found in both Romans 12:19 and Hebrews 10:30—"Vengeance is mine, I will repay, says the Lord."

While God's punishment of sinners definitely has a retributive character, we should not overlook its two other dimensions or functions. The stoning of Achan and his family was partly retribution for what he had done, but it was also a means of dissuading others from a similar course of conduct. For this reason the punishment of evildoers was frequently administered publicly.

There is also the disciplinary effect of punishment. Punishment was administered to convince sinners of the error of their ways and to turn them from it. Psalm 107:10–16 indicates that the Lord had punished Israel for their sins and they had consequently turned from their wrongdoing, at least temporarily. The writer to the Hebrews tells us, "For the Lord disciplines him whom he loves, and chastises every son whom he receives" (Heb. 12:6). In the Old Testament there is even a bit of the idea of purification from sin through punishment. This is at least hinted at in Isaiah 10:20–21. Assyria will be used of God to punish his people; as a result of this experience a remnant of Israel will learn to lean upon the Lord. "A remnant will return, the remnant of Jacob, to the mighty God."

Death

One of the most obvious results of sin is death. This truth is first pointed out in God's statement forbidding Adam and Eve to eat of the fruit of the tree of the knowledge of good and evil: "for in the day that you eat of it you shall die" (Gen. 2:17). It is also found in clear didactic form in Romans 6:23: "The wages of sin is death." Paul's point is that, like wages, death is a fitting return, a just recompense for what we have done. This death which we have deserved has several different aspects: (1) physical death, (2) spiritual death, and (3) eternal death.

Physical Death

The mortality of all humans is both an obvious fact and a truth taught by Scripture. Hebrews 9:27 says, "It is appointed for men to die once, and after that comes judgment." Paul in Romans 5:12 attributes death to the original sin of Adam. Yet while death entered the world through Adam's sin, it spread to all humans because all sinned.

This raises the question of whether humans were created mortal or immortal. Would they have died if they had not sinned? Calvinists have basically taken the negative position, arguing that physical death entered with the curse (Gen. 3:19).[4] The Pelagian view, on the other hand, is that humankind was created mortal. The princi-

---

4. Louis Berkhof, *Systematic Theology* (Grand Rapids: Eerdmans, 1953), p. 260. Arminians generally tend to agree with Calvinists rather than Pelagians on this point. See H. Orton Wiley, *Christian Theology* (Kansas City, Mo.: Beacon Hill, 1958), vol. 1, pp. 34–37, 91–95.

ple of death and decay is a part of the whole of creation.[5] The Pelagians point out that if the Calvinist view is correct, then it was the serpent who was right and Jehovah was wrong in saying, "In the day that you eat of it you shall die," for Adam and Eve were not struck dead on the day of their sin.[6] Physical death, in the Pelagian view, is a natural accompaniment of being human. The biblical references to death as a consequence of sin are understood as references to spiritual death, separation from God, rather than physical death.

The problem is not as simple as it might at first appear. The assumption that mortality began with the fall, and that Romans 5:12 and similar New Testament references to death are to be understood as references to physical death, may not be warranted. A roadblock to the idea that physical mortality is a result of sin is the case of Jesus. Not only did he not sin himself (Heb. 4:15), but he was not tainted by the corrupted nature of Adam. Yet he died. How could mortality have affected someone who, spiritually, stood where Adam and Eve did before the fall? We have conflicting data here. Is it possible somehow to slip between the horns of the dilemma?

First, we must observe that physical death is linked to the fall in some clear way. Genesis 3:19 would seem to be not a statement of what is the case and has been the case from creation, but a pronouncement of a new situation: "In the sweat of your face you shall eat bread till you return to the ground, for out of it you were taken; you are dust, and to dust you shall return." Further, it seems difficult to separate the ideas of physical death and spiritual death in the writings of Paul, particularly in 1 Corinthians 15. Paul's theme is that physical death has been defeated through Christ's resurrection. His resurrection does not mean that humans no longer die, but that the finality of death has been removed. Paul attributes to sin the power which physical death possesses in the absence of resurrection. But with Christ's overcoming of physical death, sin itself (and thus spiritual death) is defeated (vv. 55–56). Apart from Christ's resurrection from physical death, we would remain in our sins, that is, we would remain spiritually dead (v. 17). Louis Berkhof appears to be correct when he says, "The Bible does not know the distinction, so common among us, between a physical, a spiritual, and an eternal death; it has a synthetic view of death and regards it as separation from God."[7]

On the other hand, there are the considerations that Adam and Eve died spiritually but not physically the moment or the day that they sinned, and that even the sinless Jesus was capable of dying. How is all of this to be untangled?

I would suggest the concept of *conditional immortality* as the state of Adam before the fall. He was not inherently able to live forever, but he need not have died.[8] Given the right conditions, he could have lived on forever. This may be the meaning of God's words when he decided to expel Adam and Eve from Eden and from the presence of the tree of life: "and now, lest he put forth his hand and take also of the tree of life, and eat, and live for ever" (Gen. 3:22). The impression is given that Adam, even after the fall, could have lived forever if he had eaten the fruit of the tree of life. What happened at the time of expulsion from Eden was that the man and woman, who formerly could have either lived forever or died, were now separated from those conditions which made eternal life possible, and thus it became inevitable that they die. Previously they *could* die; now they *would* die. This also means that Jesus was born with a body that was subject to death. He had to eat to live;

5. See Augustine, *A Treatise on the Merits and Forgiveness of Sins, and the Baptism of Infants* 1.2.

6. Dale Moody, *The Word of Truth: A Summary of Christian Doctrine Based on Biblical Revelation* (Grand Rapids: Eerdmans, 1981), p. 295.

7. Berkhof, *Systematic Theology*, pp. 258–59.

8. Augustine makes a similar point in distinguishing between being "mortal" and being "subject to death" (*Merits and Forgiveness of Sins* 1.3).

had he failed to eat, he would have starved to death.

We should note that there were other changes as a result of sin. In Eden, Adam and Eve had bodies which could become diseased; after the fall there were diseases for them to contract. The curse, involving the coming of death to humankind, also included a whole host of ills which would lead to death. Paul tells us that someday this set of conditions will be removed, and the whole creation delivered from this "bondage to decay" (Rom. 8:18–23).

To sum up: the potential of death was within the creation from the beginning. But the potential of eternal life was also there. Sin, in the case of Adam and each of us, means that death is no longer merely potential but actual.

Spiritual Death

Spiritual death is both connected with physical death and distinguished from it. Spiritual death is the separation of the person, in the entirety of his or her nature, from God. God, as a perfectly holy being, cannot look upon sin or tolerate its presence. Thus, sin is a barrier to the relationship between God and human beings. It brings them under his judgment and condemnation.

In addition to this objective aspect of spiritual death, there is also a subjective aspect. There are numerous statements in the Bible to the effect that humans apart from Christ are dead in trespasses and sins. This means, at least in part, that sensibility to spiritual matters and the ability to act and respond spiritually, to do good things, are absent or severely impaired. On the other hand, the newness of life which is now ours through Christ's resurrection and symbolized in baptism (Rom. 6:4), while not precluding physical death, most certainly involves a death to the sin which has afflicted us. It produces a new spiritual sensitivity and vitality.

Eternal Death

Eternal death is in a very real sense the extending and finalizing of the spiritual death of which we have just written. If one comes to physical death still spiritually dead, separated from God, that condition becomes permanent. As eternal life is both qualitatively different from our present life and unending, so eternal death is separation from God which is both qualitatively different from physical death and everlasting in character.

In the last judgment the persons who appear before God's judgment seat will be di-

> *"The wages of sin is death"—physical, spiritual, and eternal.*

vided into two groups. Those who are judged righteous will be sent into eternal life (Matt. 25:34–40, 46b). Those judged to be unrighteous will be sent into eternal punishment or eternal fire (vv. 41–46a). In Revelation 20 John writes of a "second death." The first death is physical death, from which the resurrection gives us deliverance, but not exemption. Although all will eventually die the first death, the important question is whether in each individual case the second death has been overcome. Those who participate in the first resurrection are spoken of as "blessed and holy." Over such the second death is said to have no power (v. 6). In the latter part of the chapter, death and Hades are cast into the lake of fire (vv. 13–14), into which the beast and the false prophet were earlier cast (19:20). This is spoken of as the second death (20:14). Anyone whose name is not found written in the book of life will be cast into the lake of fire. This is the permanent state of what the sinner chose in life.

We have examined the results which sin has upon our relationship with God. We should bear them in mind whenever we hear the argument that certain actions are not wrong, provided they are performed by consenting adults and no one is harmed. Such rationalizing disregards the fact that sin is primarily wrong against God, and its primary effects are upon the relationship between the sinner and God.

Effects on the Sinner

Enslavement

Although the primary effects of sin are on our relationship with God, it is vital that we investigate the other dimensions that are affected by sin. Sin has consequences for the person who commits it. One of the effects of sin is its enslaving power. Sin becomes a habit or even an addiction. One sin leads to another sin. For example, after killing Abel, Cain felt constrained to lie when God asked him where his brother was.

What some people consider freedom to sin, freedom from the restrictions of obedience to the will of God, is actually the enslavement which sin produces. In some cases sin gains so much control and power that a person cannot escape it. Paul recalls that the Roman Christians "were once slaves of sin" (Rom. 6:17). But sin's grip on the individual is loosed by the work of Christ: "For the law of the Spirit of life in Christ Jesus has set me free from the law of sin and death" (Rom. 8:2).

Flight from Reality

Sin also results in an unwillingness to face reality. The harsh dimensions of life, and especially the consequences of our sin, are not faced realistically. In particular, society avoids thinking about the stark fact that sooner or later everyone must die (Heb. 9:27). A suppressed realization that death is the wages of sin (Rom. 6:23) may underlie many of our attempts to avoid thinking about it.

Denial of Sin

Accompanying our denial of death is a denial of sin. There are various ways of denying sin. It may be relabeled, so that it is not acknowledged as sin at all. It may be considered a matter of sickness, deprivation, ignorance, or perhaps social maladjustment at worst.

Another way of denying our sin is to admit the wrongness of what we have done, but to decline to take responsibility for it. We see this dynamic at work in the case of the very first sin. When confronted by the Lord's question, "Who told you that you were naked? Have you eaten of the tree of which I commanded you not to eat?" (Gen. 3:11), Adam responded by shifting the blame: "The woman whom thou gavest to be with me, she gave me fruit of the tree, and I ate" (v. 12). Adam's immediate reaction was to deny personal responsibility—he had eaten only at the inducement of Eve. Note that he even tried to shift the blame to God.

Attempting to shift responsibility from oneself is a common practice. For deep down there is often a sense of guilt which one desperately wants to eradicate. But trying to shift responsibility compounds the sin and makes repentance more unlikely. All of the excuses and explanations which we offer for our actions are signs of the depth of our sin.

Self-Deceit

Self-deceit is the underlying problem when we deny our sin. Jeremiah wrote, "The heart is deceitful [slippery, crooked] above all things, and desperately corrupt; who can understand it?" (17:9). The hypocrites of whom Jesus often spoke probably fooled themselves before they tried to fool others. He pointed to the ludicrous lengths to which self-deceit can go: "Why do you see the speck that is in your brother's eye, but do not notice the log that is in your own eye?" (Matt. 7:3).

Insensitivity

Sin also produces insensitivity. As we continue to sin and to reject God's warnings and condemnations, we become less and less responsive to the promptings of conscience. Whereas there may initially be a tenderness when one does wrong, the eventual effect of sin is that we are no longer stirred by the Word and the Spirit. In time even gross sins can be committed with no compunction. A clear example of insensitivity to God's truth is the case of the Pharisees who, having seen Jesus' miracles and heard his teaching, attributed what was the work of the Holy Spirit to Beelzebub, the prince of the demons.

Self-Centeredness

An increasing self-centeredness also results from sin. In many ways sin is a turning in upon oneself which is confirmed with practice. We call attention to ourselves, and to our good qualities and accomplishments, and minimize our shortcomings. We seek special favors and opportunities in life, wanting an extra little edge that no one else has. We display a certain special alertness to our own wants and needs, while we ignore those of others.

Restlessness

Finally, sin often produces restlessness. There is a certain insatiable character about sin. Complete satisfaction never occurs. Although some sinners may have a relative stability for a time, sin eventually loses its ability to satisfy. It is alleged that in answer to the question, "How much money does it take to satisfy a man?" John D. Rockefeller responded, "Just a little bit more."

Effects on the Relationship to Other Humans

Competition

Sin also has massive effects upon the relationships between humans. One of the most significant is the proliferation of competition. Since sin makes one increasingly self-centered and self-seeking, there will inevitably be conflict with others. We wish the same position, the same marriage partner, or the same piece of real estate that another has. Whenever someone wins, someone else loses. The most extreme and large-scale version of human competition is war, with its wholesale destruction of property and human lives. James is quite clear as to the major factors that lead to war: "What causes wars, and what causes fightings among you? Is it not your passions that are at war in your members? You desire and do not have; so you kill. And you covet and cannot obtain; so you fight and wage war" (James 4:1–2).

Inability to Empathize

Inability to empathize with others is a major consequence of sin. Being concerned about our personal desire, reputation, and opinion, we see only our own perspective. This is the opposite of what Paul commended to his readers: "Do nothing from selfishness or conceit, but in humility count others better than yourselves. Let each of you look not only to his own interests, but also to the interests of others. Have this mind among yourselves, which you have in Christ Jesus" (Phil. 2:3–5).

Rejection of Authority

Rejection of authority is often a social ramification of sin. If we find security in our own possessions and accomplishments, then any outside authority is threatening. It restricts our doing what we want. It must be resisted or ignored, so that we might be free to do as we will. In the process, of course, many others' rights may be trampled.

Inability to Love

Finally, sin results in inability to love. Since other people stand in our way, representing competition and a threat to us, we cannot really act for the ultimate welfare of others if our aim is self-satisfaction. And so suspicions, conflicts, bitterness, and even hatred issue from the self-absorption or the pursual of finite values that has supplanted God at the center of the sinner's life.

Sin is a serious matter; it has far-reaching effects—upon our relationship to God, to ourselves, and to other humans. Accordingly, it will require a cure with similarly extensive effects.

22 The Magnitude of Sin

Having seen something of the nature of sin, its source, and its effects, we must now ask regarding its magnitude. There are two facets to this question: (1) How extensive, how common is sin? (2) How intensive, how radical is it?

The Extent of Sin

To the question of who sins, the answer is apparent: sin is universal. It is not limited to a few isolated individuals or even to a majority of the human race. All humans, without exception, are sinners.

The Old Testament Teaching

The universality of sin is taught in several ways and places in Scripture. In the Old Testament, we do not usually find general statements about all people at all times, but about all the people who were living at the time being written about. In the time of Noah, the sin of the race was so great and so extensive that God resolved to destroy everything (with the exception of Noah, his family, and the animals taken on board the ark). The description is vivid: "The LORD saw that the wickedness of man was great in the earth, and that every imagination of the thoughts of his heart was only evil continually" (Gen. 6:5). God regretted having made humankind and resolved to blot out the entire human race, together with all other living things, for the corruption was worldwide.

Even after the flood destroyed the wicked of the earth, God still characterized "the imagination of man's heart [as being] evil from his youth" (Gen. 8:21). A categorical statement about the sinfulness of humanity is found in 1 Kings 8:46: "for there is no man who does not sin" (cf. Rom. 3:23). David makes a similar statement when he asks for mercy from God: "Enter not into judgment with thy servant; for no man living is righteous before thee" (Ps. 143:2; see also Ps. 130:3; Eccles. 7:20).

These statements of the universal sinfulness of the human race should be regarded as qualifying all the scriptural references to perfect or blameless persons (e.g., Ps. 37:37; Prov. 11:5). Even those who are specifically described as perfect have shortcomings. David was a man after God's own heart (1 Sam. 13:14). Yet his sins were grievous and occasioned the great penitential psalm (Ps. 51). Isaiah 53:6 takes pains to universalize its metaphorical description of sinners: "All we like sheep have gone astray; we have turned every one to his own way; and the LORD has laid on him the iniquity of us all."

The New Testament Teaching

The New Testament is even clearer concerning the universality of human sin. The most famous passage is, of course, Romans 3, where Paul quotes and elaborates upon Psalms 14 and 53, as well as 5:9; 140:3; 10:7; 36:1; and Isaiah 59:7–8. He asserts that "all men, both Jews and Greeks, are under the power of sin" (v. 9), and then heaps up a number of descriptive quotations beginning with, "None is righteous, no, not one; no one understands, no one seeks for God. All have turned aside, together they have gone wrong; no one does good, not even one" (vv. 10–12). None will be justified by works of the law (v. 20). The reason is clear: "all have sinned and fall short of the glory of God" (v. 23). Paul also makes it plain that he is talking not only about unbelievers, those outside the Christian faith, but believers as well, including himself (Eph. 2:3). It is apparent that there are no exceptions to this universal rule.

Not only does the Bible frequently assert that all are sinners, it also assumes it everywhere. Note, for example, that the commands to repent relate to everyone. In his Mars' Hill address Paul said, "The times of ignorance God overlooked, but now he commands all men everywhere to repent" (Acts 17:30). It is apparent that in the New Testament each person, by virtue of being human, is regarded as a sinner in need of repentance and new birth. Sin is universal. As Ryder Smith puts it, "The universality of sin is taken as matter of fact. On examination, it will be found that every speech in Acts, even Stephen's, and every Epistle just assumes that men have all sinned. This is also the assumption of Jesus in the Synoptic Gospels. . . . Jesus deals with everyone on the assumption, 'Here is a sinner.'"[1]

An additional proof of the universality of sin is that all persons are subject to the penalty for sin, namely, death. Except for those

---

1. Charles Ryder Smith, *The Bible Doctrine of Sin and of the Ways of God with Sinners* (London: Epworth, 1953), pp. 159–60.

alive when Christ returns, everyone will succumb to death. Romans 3:23 ("all have sinned and fall short of the glory of God") and 6:23 ("the wages of sin is death") are interconnected. The universality of the death spoken of in the latter is evidence of the universality of sin of which the former verse speaks. Between these two verses comes Romans 5:12: "Therefore as sin came into the world through one man and death through sin, and so death spread to all men because all men sinned—." Here, too, sin is considered universal.

The Intensiveness of Sin

Having seen that the extent of sin is universal, we turn now to the issue of its intensiveness. How sinful is the sinner? How deep is our sin? Are we basically pure, with a positive inclination toward the good, or are we totally and absolutely corrupt? We must look carefully at the biblical data and then seek to interpret and integrate them.

The Old Testament Teaching

The Old Testament for the most part speaks of sins rather than of sinfulness, of sin as an act rather than as a state or disposition. Yet a distinction was drawn between sins on the basis of the motivation involved. The right of sanctuary for manslayers was reserved for those who had killed accidentally rather than intentionally (Deut. 4:42). The motive was fully as important as the act itself. In addition, inward thoughts and intentions were condemned quite apart from external acts. An example is the sin of covetousness, an internal desire which is deliberately chosen.[2]

There is yet a further step in the Old Testament understanding of sin. Particularly in the writings of Jeremiah and Ezekiel sin is depicted as a spiritual sickness which afflicts the heart. Our heart is wrong and must be changed, or even exchanged. We do not merely do evil; our very inclination is evil.

2. Ibid., p. 34.

Jeremiah says that "the heart is deceitful above all things, and desperately corrupt; who can understand it?" (Jer. 17:9). In the Book of Ezekiel God asserts that the hearts of the people need change: "And I will give them one heart [or a new heart], and put a new spirit within them; I will take the stony heart out of their flesh and give them a heart of flesh" (Ezek. 11:19).

Psalm 51, the great penitential psalm, most fully expresses the idea of sinfulness or a sinful nature. We note here a strong emphasis upon the idea of sin as an inward condition or disposition, and the need of purging the inward person. David speaks of his having been brought forth in iniquity and conceived in sin (v. 5). He speaks of the Lord's desiring truth in the inward parts, and the need of being taught wisdom in the secret heart (v. 6). The psalmist prays to be washed and cleansed (v. 2), purged and washed (v. 7), and asks God to create in him a clean heart and to put a new and right (or steadfast) spirit within him (v. 10). One can scarcely find anywhere in religious literature stronger conscious expressions of need for change of disposition or inner nature. It is unmistakably clear that the psalmist does not think of himself merely as one who commits sins, but as a sinful person.

The New Testament Teaching

The New Testament is even clearer and more emphatic on these matters. Jesus spoke of the inward disposition as evil. Sin is very much a matter of the inward thoughts and intentions. It is not sufficient not to commit murder; he who is angry with his brother is liable to judgment (Matt. 5:21–22). It is not enough to abstain from committing adultery. If a man lusts after a woman, he has in his heart already committed adultery with her (Matt. 5:27–28).

Paul's own self-testimony also is a powerful argument that it is the corruption of human nature that produces individual sins. He recalls that "while we were living in the flesh, our sinful passions, aroused by the law, were at work in our members to bear fruit for death" (Rom. 7:5). He sees "in my members another law at war with the law of my mind and making me captive to the law of sin which dwells in my members" (v. 23). In Paul's thinking, then, as in Jesus', sins are the result of human nature. In every human being there is a strong inclination toward evil, an inclination with definite effects.

Sin and Total Depravity

The adjective *total* is often attached to the idea of depravity. Very early in the Bible we read, "The LORD saw that the wickedness of man was great in the earth, and that every imagination of the thoughts of his heart was only evil continually" (Gen. 6:5). But the expression *total depravity* must be carefully used. For it has sometimes been interpreted as conveying (and on occasion has even been intended to convey) an understanding of human nature which our experience belies.[3]

We do not mean by total depravity that the unregenerate person is totally insensitive in matters of conscience, of right and wrong. For Paul's statement in Romans 2:15 says that the Gentiles have the law written on their hearts, so that "their conscience also bears witness and their conflicting thoughts accuse or perhaps excuse them." Further, total depravity does not mean that the sinful person is as sinful as one can possibly be. There are unregenerate persons who are genuinely altruistic, who show kindness, generosity, and love to others, who are good, devoted spouses and parents. Finally, the doctrine of total depravity does not mean that the sinner engages in every possible form of sin.

What then do we mean, positively, by the idea of total depravity? First, sin is a matter of the entire person.[4] The seat of sin is not merely one aspect of the person, such as the body or the reason. Certainly several refer-

ences make clear that the body is affected (e.g., Rom. 6:6, 12; 7:24; 8:10, 13). Other verses tell us that the mind or the reason is involved (e.g., Rom. 1:21; 2 Cor. 3:14–15; 4:4). That the emotions also are involved is amply attested (e.g., Rom. 1:26–27; Gal. 5:24; and 2 Tim. 3:2–4, where the ungodly are described as being lovers of self and pleasure rather than lovers of God). Finally, it is evident that the will is also affected. Unregenerate persons do not have a truly free will. They are slaves to sin (Rom. 6:17).

Further, total depravity means that even the unregenerate person's altruism always contains an element of improper motive. The good acts are not done entirely or even primarily out of perfect love for God. In each case there is another factor, whether the preference of one's own self-interest or of some other object less than God. The Pharisees who so often dialogued with Jesus did many good things (Matt. 23:23), but they had no real love for God. So he said to them, "You search the scriptures [this of course was good], because you think that in them you have eternal life; and it is they that bear witness to me; yet you refuse to come to me that you may have life. I do not receive glory from men. But I know that you have not the love of God within you" (John 5:39–42).

Finally, total depravity means that sinners are completely unable to extricate themselves from their sinful condition.[5] The goodness they do is tainted by less than perfect love for God and therefore cannot serve to justify them in God's sight. But apart from that, good and lawful actions cannot be maintained consistently. Sinners cannot alter their lives by a process of determination, will power, and reformation. Sin is inescapable. This fact is depicted in Scripture's frequent references to sinners as "spiritually dead" (Eph. 2:1–2, 5). This does not mean that sinners are absolutely insensitive and unresponsive to spiritual stimuli, but, rather, that they are unable to do what they ought. Unregenerate individuals are

---

3. Augustus H. Strong, *Systematic Theology* (Westwood, N.J.: Revell, 1907), pp. 637–38; Louis Berkhof, *Systematic Theology* (Grand Rapids: Eerdmans, 1953), p. 246.

4. Berkhof, *Systematic Theology*, p. 247.

5. Strong, *Systematic Theology*, pp. 640–46.

incapable of genuinely good, redeeming works; whatever they do is dead or ineffective in relationship to God. Salvation by works is absolutely impossible (Eph. 2:8–9).

Whoever has attempted to live a perfect life in one's own strength has discovered what Paul is talking about here. Such endeavors eventually end in frustration at best. A seminary professor has described his personal attempt. He listed thirty characteristics of the Christian life. Then he assigned each one to a different day of the month. On the first day, he worked very hard on the first attribute. With a great deal of concentration, he managed to live up to his goal the entire day. On the second day of the month, he shifted to the second area, and mastered it. Then he moved on to the third area, successively mastering each in turn, until on the final day he perfectly realized the characteristic assigned to it. But just as he was reveling in the sense of victory, he looked back at the first day's goal to see how he was doing. To his chagrin, he discovered that he had completely lost sight of the goal of the first day—and of the second, third, and fourth days. The professor's experience is an empirical study of what the Bible teaches us: "There is none that does good, no, not one" (Pss. 14:3b; 53:3b; Rom. 3:12). The Bible also gives the reason for this: "They are all alike corrupt [depraved]" (Pss. 14:3a; 53:3a). We are totally unable to do genuinely meritorious works sufficient to qualify for God's favor.

Theories of Original Sin

All of us, apparently without exception, are sinners. By this we mean not merely that all of us sin, but that all of us have a depraved or corrupted nature which so inclines us toward sin that it is virtually inevitable. How can this be? What is the basis of this amazing fact? Must there not be some common factor at work in all of us? It is as if some antecedent or *a priori* factor in life

> *Total depravity means that sin affects every aspect of our person, that our good acts are not done entirely out of love for God, and that we are completely unable to extricate ourselves from this sinful condition.*

leads to universal sinning and universal depravity. But what is this common factor, which is often referred to as original sin?[6] Whence is it derived, and how is it transmitted or communicated?

We find the answer in Romans 5: "Therefore as sin came into the world through one man and death through sin, and so death spread to all men because all men sinned—" (v. 12). This thought is repeated in several different ways in the succeeding verses (vv. 15–19). In Paul's mind there is some sort of causal connection between what Adam did and the sinfulness of all humans throughout all time. But just what is the nature of this influence exerted by Adam upon all humanity, and by what means does it operate?

There have been a number of attempts to understand and elucidate this Adamic influence. In the following pages, we will examine several of these efforts. We will then attempt to construct a model which does justice to the various dimensions of the biblical witness and is also intelligible within the contemporary context.

Pelagianism

The first and in some ways the most interesting of the views of the relationship between individual humans and the first sin of

6. By "original sin" we mean the dimension of sin with which we begin life, or the effect which the sin of Adam has upon us as a precondition of our lives.

Adam is that of Pelagius. A British monk (although there is some question as to whether he actually was a monk) who had moved to Rome to teach,[7] Pelagius was a moralist: his primary concern was for people to live good and decent lives. It seemed to him that an unduly negative view of human nature was having an unfortunate effect upon human behavior. Coupled with an emphasis upon the sovereignty of God, the estimation of human sinfulness seemed to remove all motivation to exert an effort to live a good life.[8]

To counteract these tendencies, Pelagius laid heavy emphasis upon the idea of free will. Unlike the other creatures, humans were created free of the controlling influences of the universe. Furthermore, they are free of any determining influence from the fall. Holding to a creationist view of the origin of the soul, Pelagius maintained that the soul, created by God specially for every person, is not tainted by any supposed corruption or guilt.[9] The influence, if any, of Adam's sin upon his descendants is merely that of a bad example. Other than this there is no direct connection between Adam's sin and the rest of the human race.

If Adam's sin has no direct effect upon every human being, there is no need for a special working of God's grace within the heart of each individual. Rather, the grace of God is simply something which is present everywhere and at every moment.[10] We can, by our own efforts, perfectly fulfil God's commands without sinning.[11] There is no natural inclination toward sin at the beginning of life; whatever inclination in that direction there might be in later life comes only through the building up of bad habits. A salvation by works is thus quite possible, although that is something of a misnomer. Since we are not really sinful, guilty, and

condemned, this process is not a matter of salvation from something which presently binds us. It is rather a preservation or maintenance of our right status and good standing. By our own accomplishment we keep from falling into a sinful condition.

Arminianism

A more moderate view is the Arminian. James Arminius was a Dutch Reformed pastor and theologian who modified considerably the theological position in which he had been trained.[12] According to Arminianism, we receive from Adam a corrupted nature. We begin life without righteousness. Thus, all humans are unable, without special divine help, to fulfil God's spiritual commands. This inability is physical and intellectual, but not volitional.

Although some Arminians say that "guilt" is also part of original sin, they do not mean actual culpability, but merely liability to punishment. For whatever culpability and condemnation may have accrued to us through Adam's sin have been removed through prevenient grace. Prevenient grace, a universal benefit of the atoning work of Christ, nullifies the judicial consequences of Adam's sin. Orton Wiley says: "Man is not now condemned for the depravity of his own nature, although that depravity is of the essence of sin; its culpability, we maintain, was removed by the free gift of Christ." This prevenient grace is extended to everyone, and in effect neutralizes the corruption received from Adam.[13]

Calvinism

Calvinists have given more attention to the question of original sin than have most other schools of theology. In general terms, the Calvinist position on this matter is that

7. John Ferguson, *Pelagius* (Cambridge: W. Heffer, 1956), p. 40.

8. Ibid., p. 47.

9. Robert F. Evans, *Pelagius: Inquiries and Reappraisals* (New York: Seabury, 1968), pp. 82–83.

10. Augustine *On the Grace of Christ and on Original Sin* 1.3.

11. Augustine *On the Proceedings of Pelagius* 16.

12. The tradition that Arminius was a convinced Calvinist who was assigned to defend the Reformed faith and in the process of defending it was "converted" to the contradictory view is highly suspect. See Carl Bangs, *Arminius: A Study in the Dutch Reformation* (Nashville: Abingdon, 1971), pp. 138–41.

13. H. Orton Wiley, *Christian Theology* (Kansas City, Mo.: Beacon Hill, 1958), vol. 2, pp. 121–28. The quotation is from p. 135.

there is a definite connection between Adam's sin and all persons of all times. In some way, his sin is not just the sin of an isolated individual, but is also our sin. Because we participate in that sin, we all, from the beginning of life, perhaps even from the point of conception, receive a corrupted nature along with a consequent inherited tendency toward sin. Furthermore, all persons are guilty of Adam's sin. Death, the penalty for sin, is upon all people, having been transmitted from Adam; that is evidence of everyone's guilt. Thus, whereas in the Pelagian view God imputes neither a corrupted nature nor guilt to humankind, and in the Arminian view God imputes a corrupted nature but not guilt (in the sense of culpability), in the Calvinist scheme he imputes to us both a corrupted nature and guilt. The Calvinist position is based upon a very serious and quite literal understanding of Paul's statements in Romans 5:12–19 that sin entered the world through Adam and death through that sin, and so death passed to all individuals because all sinned. Through one man's sin all became sinners.

A question arises concerning the nature of the connection or relationship between Adam and us, and thus also between Adam's first sin and our sinfulness. Numerous attempts have been made to answer this question. The two major approaches see the relationship in terms of federal headship and natural headship.

The approach that sees Adam's connection with us in terms of a federal headship is generally related to the creationist view of the origin of the soul. This is the view that humans receive their physical nature by inheritance from their parents, but that the soul is specially created by God for each individual and united with the body at birth (or some other suitable moment). Thus, we were not present psychologically or spiritually in any of our ancestors, including Adam. Adam, however, was our representative. The consequences of his actions have been passed on to his descendants as well. Adam was on probation for all of us as it

were; and because Adam sinned, all of us are treated as guilty and corrupted. Bound by the covenant between God and Adam, we are treated as if we have actually and personally done what he as our representative did.

The other major approach sees Adam's connection with us in terms of a natural (or realistic) headship. This approach is related to the traducianist view of the origin of the soul, according to which we receive our souls by transmission from our parents, just as we do our physical natures. So we were present in germinal or seminal form in our ancestors; in a very real sense, we were there in Adam. His action was not merely that of one isolated individual, but of the entire human race. Thus, there is nothing unfair or improper about our receiving a corrupted nature and guilt from Adam, for we are receiving the just results of our sin. This is the view of Augustine.[14]

Original Sin: A Biblical and Contemporary Model

The key passage for constructing a biblical and contemporary model of original sin is Romans 5:12–19. Paul is arguing that death is the consequence of sin. The twelfth verse is particularly determinative: "Therefore as sin came into the world through one man and death through sin, and so death spread to all men because all men sinned—." Whatever be the exact meaning of these words, Paul certainly is saying that death originated in the human race because of Adam's sin. He is also saying that death is universal and the cause of this is the universal sin of humankind. Later, however, he says that the cause of the death of all is the sin of the one man, Adam—"many died through one man's trespass" (v. 15); "because of one man's trespass, death reigned through that one man" (v. 17). The problem is how to relate the statements that the uni-

14. Augustine *A Treatise on the Merits and Forgiveness of Sins, and the Baptism of Infants* 1.8–11.

versality of death came through the sin of Adam to the statement that it came through the sin of all.

It has been suggested that in the last clause of verse 12 Paul is speaking of the personal sin(s) of all. All of us sin individually and thereby incur through our own action the same personal guilt that Adam incurred through his action. The clause would then be rendered, "so also death spread to all men because all men sin." In keeping with the principle of responsibility for one's personal actions and for them alone, the meaning would be that all die because all are guilty, and all are guilty because each one has sinned individually.

There are several problems with this interpretation. One is the word *sinned* in verse 12. Were this interpretation correct, the word would properly be "sin," the present tense denoting something continually going on. Further, the sin referred to in "all men sin" would be different from that referred to in "sin came into the world through one man," as well as from that referred to in verses 15 and 17. And, in addition, the latter two clauses would still need to be explained.

There is another way of understanding the last clause in verse 12, a way that avoids these problems and makes some sense out of verses 15 and 17. The Greek verb translated "sinned" is in the aorist tense, which most commonly refers to a single past action. Had Paul intended to refer to a continued process of sin, other tenses (the present and imperfect) were available to him. But he chose the aorist, and it should be taken at face value. Indeed, if we regard the sin of all persons and the sin of Adam as the same, the problems we have pointed to become considerably less complex. There is then no conflict between verse 12 and verses 15 and 17. Further, the potential problem presented by verse 14, where we read that "death reigned from Adam to Moses, even over those whose sins were not like the transgression of Adam," is resolved, for it is not imitation or repetition of Adam's sin, but participation in it, that counts.

The last clause in verse 12 tells us that we were involved in some way in Adam's sin; it was in some sense also our sin. But what is meant by this? On the one hand, it may be understood in terms of federal headship—Adam acted on behalf of all persons. There was a sort of contract between God and Adam as our representative, so that what Adam did binds us. Our involvement in Adam's sin might better be understood in terms of natural headship, however. The position adopted in this volume is that the entirety of our human nature, both physical and spiritual, material and immaterial, has been received from our parents and more distant ancestors by way of descent from the first pair of humans. On that basis, we were actually present within Adam, so that we all sinned in his act. There is no injustice, then, to our condemnation and death as a result of original sin.

There is one additional problem here, however: the condition of infants and children. If the reasoning that precedes is correct, then all begin life with both the corrupted nature and the guilt that are the consequences of sin. Does this mean that should these little ones die before making a conscious decision to "receive the abundance of grace and the free gift of righteousness" (v. 17), they are lost and condemned to eternal death?

While the status of infants and those who never reach moral competence is a difficult question, it appears that our Lord did not regard them as basically sinful and guilty. Indeed, he held them up as an example of the type of person who will inherit the kingdom of God (Matt. 18:3; 19:14). David had confidence that he would again see his child that had died (2 Sam. 12:23). On the basis of such considerations, it is difficult to maintain that children are to be thought of as sinful, condemned, and lost.

To summarize the major tenets of the doctrine as we have outlined it: We have argued that the Bible, particularly in the writings of Paul, maintains that because of Adam's sin all persons receive a corrupted nature and are guilty in God's sight as well. We have, further, espoused the Augustinian view (natural headship) of the imputation of original sin. We were all present in undifferentiated form in the person of Adam, who along with Eve was the entire human race. Thus, it was not merely Adam but humankind who sinned. We were involved, although not personally, and are responsible for the sin. In addition, we have argued that the biblical teaching is that children are not under God's condemnation for this sin, at least not until attaining an age of responsibility in moral and spiritual matters. We must now ask whether the doctrine of original sin can be conceived of and expressed in a way which will somehow do justice to all of these factors.

The parallelism that Paul draws in Romans 5 between Adam and Christ in their of Christ makes it effective in our lives. But if this is the case, then would not the imputation of guilt based upon the action of Adam, albeit Adam as including us, require some sort of volitional choice as well? If there is no "unconscious faith," can there be "unconscious sin"? And what are we to say of infants who die? Despite having participated in that first sin, they are somehow accepted and saved. Although they have made no conscious choice of Christ's work (or of Adam's sin for that matter), the spiritual effects of the curse are negated in their case.

The current form of my understanding is as follows: We all were involved in Adam's sin, and thus receive both the corrupted nature that was his after the fall, and the guilt and condemnation that attach to his sin. With this matter of guilt, however, just as with the imputation of Christ's righteous-

We become responsible for and guilty of Adam's sin when we accept or approve of our own corrupt nature.

relationship to us is impressive. He asserts that in some parallel way what each of them did has its influence on us (as Adam's sin leads to death, so Christ's act of righteousness leads to life). What is this parallel? If, as we might be inclined to think, the condemnation and guilt of Adam are imputed to us without there being on our part any sort of conscious choice of his act, the same would necessarily hold true of the imputation of Christ's righteousness and redeeming work. But does his death justify us simply by virtue of his identification with humanity through the incarnation and independently of whether we consciously and personally accept his work? And do all people have the grace of Christ imputed to them, just as all have Adam's sin imputed to them? The usual answer of evangelicals is no; there is abundant evidence that there are two classes of persons, the lost and the saved, and that only a decision to accept the work ness, there must be some conscious and voluntary decision on our part. Until this is the case, there is only a conditional imputation of guilt. Thus, there is no condemnation until one reaches the age of responsibility. If a child dies before he or she is capable of making genuine moral decisions, there is only innocence, and the child will experience the same type of future existence with the Lord as will those who have reached the age of moral responsibility and had their sins forgiven as a result of accepting the offer of salvation based upon Christ's atoning death.

What is the nature of the voluntary decision which ends our childish innocence and constitutes a ratification of the first sin, the fall? One position on this question is that there is no final imputation of the first sin until we commit a sin of our own, thus ratifying Adam's sin. Unlike the Arminian view, this position holds that at the moment of our first sin we become guilty of both our own sin *and the original sin as well*. There is another position, however, one which is preferable in that it more fully preserves the parallelism between our accepting the work of Christ and the action of Adam, and at the same time it more clearly points out our responsibility for the first sin. We become responsible and guilty when we accept or approve of our corrupt nature. There is a time in the life of each one of us when we become aware of our own tendency toward sin. At that point we may abhor the sinful nature that has been there all the time. We would in that case repent of it and might even, if there is an awareness of the gospel, ask God for forgiveness and cleansing. At the very least there would be a rejection of our sinful makeup. But if we acquiesce in that sinful nature, we are in effect saying that it is good. In placing our tacit approval upon the corruption, we are also approving or concurring in the action in the Garden of Eden so long ago. We become guilty of that sin without having to commit a sin of our own. This view seems to fit best the various factors in the biblical presentation of the doctrine of original sin.

The Person of Christ

23 The Deity of Christ

We have seen that humans were created to love, serve, and fellowship with God. We have also seen that they fail to fulfil this divine intention; in other words, all humans sin. Because God loved us, however, he chose to act through Christ to restore us to the intended condition and relationship. Thus, our understanding of the person and work of Christ grows directly out of the doctrines of humanity and of sin.

When we come to the study of the person and work of Christ, we are at the very center of Christian theology. For since Christians are by definition believers in and followers of Christ, their understanding of Christ must be central and determinative of the very character of the Christian faith. All else is secondary to the question of what one thinks of Christ. This being the case, particular care and precision are especially in order in the doing of our Christology.

One of the most controversial topics here is the deity of Christ. It is at the same time one of the most crucial. It lies at the heart of our faith. For our faith rests on Jesus' actually being God in human flesh, and not simply an extraordinary human, albeit the most unusual person who ever lived.

The Biblical Teaching

We begin our inquiry at the point where all of our doctrinal construction must begin: the witness of Scripture. Here we find a wide variety of material and emphases, but not a divergence of opinion. While it is not possible to investigate every reference which bears on this consideration, we may at least sample the data.

Jesus' Self-Consciousness

In looking at the biblical evidence for the deity of Christ, we begin with Jesus' own self-consciousness. What did Jesus think and believe about himself? There have been those who argue that Jesus did not himself make any claim to be God. His message was entirely about the Father, not about himself. We are therefore called to believe *with* Jesus, not *in* Jesus.[1] How do the actual evidences of Scripture square with this contention?

We should note that Jesus did not make an explicit and overt claim to deity, saying in so many words, "I am God." What we do find, however, are claims which would be inappropriate if made by someone who is less than God. For example, Jesus said that he would send "his angels" (Matt. 13:41); elsewhere they are spoken of as "the angels of God" (Luke 12:8-9; 15:10). That reference is particularly significant, for in it he also speaks of the kingdom of God as "his kingdom."

More significant yet are the prerogatives which Jesus claimed. In particular, his claim

to forgive sins resulted in a charge of blasphemy against him. When the paralytic was lowered through the roof by his four friends, Jesus did not respond with a comment about the man's physical condition or his need of healing. Rather, his initial comment was, "My son, your sins are forgiven" (Mark 2:5). The reaction of the scribes indicates the meaning they attached to his words: "Why does this man speak thus? It is blasphemy! Who can forgive sins but God alone?" (v. 7). Robert Stein notes that their reaction shows that they interpreted Jesus' comment "as the exercising of a divine prerogative, the power to actually forgive sins."[2] Jesus claimed other prerogatives as well. In Matthew 25:31-46 he speaks of judging the world. He will sit on his glorious throne and divide the sheep from the goats. Certainly only God can exercise this power.

The authority which Jesus claimed and exercised is also clearly seen with respect to the Sabbath. The sacredness of the Sabbath had been established by God (Exod. 20:8-11). Only God could abrogate or modify this regulation. Yet consider what happened when Jesus' disciples picked heads of grain on the Sabbath, and the Pharisees objected that the Sabbath regulations (at least their version of them) were being violated. Jesus responded by pointing out that David had violated one of the laws by eating of the bread reserved for the priests. Then, turning directly to the situation at hand, Jesus asserted: "The sabbath was made for man, not man for the sabbath; so the Son of man is lord even of the sabbath" (Mark 2:27-28). He was clearly claiming the right to redefine the status of the Sabbath, a right which belongs only to someone virtually equal to God.

We see Jesus also claiming an unusual relationship with the Father, particularly in the sayings reported in John. For example, Jesus claims to be one with the Father (John 10:30), and that to see and know him is to

---

1. Adolf von Harnack, *What Is Christianity?* (New York: Harper and Brothers, 1957), p. 144.

2. Robert H. Stein, *The Method and Message of Jesus' Teaching* (Philadelphia: Westminster, 1978), p. 114.

see and know the Father (John 14:7–9). There is a claim to preexistence in his statement in John 8:58, "Truly, truly, I say to you, before Abraham was, I am." Note that rather than saying, "I was," he says, "I am." Leon Morris suggests that there is an implied contrast here between "a mode of being which has a definite beginning" and "one which is eternal."[3] It is also quite possible that Jesus is alluding to the "I AM" formula by which the Lord identified himself in Exodus 3:14–15. For in this case, as in Exodus, the "I am" is a formula denoting existence. While some of the statements which Jesus made may seem rather vague to us, there is no doubt as to how they were interpreted by his opponents. After his statement claiming that he existed before Abraham, the immediate reaction of the Jews was to take up stones to throw at him (John 8:59). Certainly this is an indication that they thought him guilty of blasphemy, for stoning was the prescription for blasphemy (Lev. 24:16). If they attempted to stone him merely because they were angered by his unfavorable references to them, they would, in the eyes of the law, have been guilty of attempted murder.

In some respects, the clearest indication of Jesus' self-understanding is found in connection with his trial and condemnation. The charge, according to John's account, was that "he has made himself the Son of God" (John 19:7). Matthew reports the high priest to have said at the trial, "I adjure you by the living God, tell us if you are the Christ, the Son of God" (Matt. 26:63). Jesus replied, "You have said so. But I tell you, hereafter you will see the Son of man seated at the right hand of Power, and coming on the clouds of heaven." This is as clear a declaration of his deity as one can find in the Gospels.

Not only did Jesus not dispute the charge that he claimed to be God, but he also accepted the attribution of deity to him by his disciples. The clearest case of this is his re-

sponse to Thomas's statement, "My Lord and my God!" (John 20:28). Here was an excellent opportunity to correct a misconception, if that is what it was, but Jesus did not do so.

There are additional indications of Jesus' self-estimation. One is the way in which he juxtaposes his own words with the Old Testament, the Scripture of his day. Time and again he says, "You have heard that it was said, . . . but I say to you . . ." (e.g., Matt. 5:21–22, 27–28). Here Jesus presumes to place his word on the same level as Old Testament Scripture. Jesus is claiming to have the power in himself to lay down teaching as authoritative as that given by the Old Testament prophets.

Jesus also by implication, direct statement, and deed indicates that he has power over life and death. In John 5:21 he asserts, "For as the Father raises the dead and gives them life, so also the Son gives life to whom he will." Perhaps the most emphatic statement is found in his words to Martha, "I am the resurrection and the life; he who believes in me, though he die, yet shall he live" (John 11:25).

Jesus specifically applied to himself expressions which conveyed his self-understanding. One of these is "Son of God." While the title is capable of various meanings, Jesus "poured into it a new content to describe His own unique person and relationship to God."[4] It signified that Jesus had a relationship to the Father distinct from that of any other human. That Jesus was thereby claiming a unique sonship differing "not merely quantitatively but qualitatively, not merely in degree but in kind,"[5] was understood by the Jews. We read in John 5:2–18, for example, that they reacted with great hostility when, in defense of his having healed on the Sabbath, Jesus linked his work with that of the Father. As John explains, "This was why the Jews sought all the more to kill him, because he not only

3. Leon Morris, *The Gospel According to John: The English Text with Introduction, Exposition, and Notes* (Grand Rapids: Eerdmans, 1971), p. 473.

4. George E. Ladd, *The New Testament and Criticism* (Grand Rapids: Eerdmans, 1967), p. 177.

5. Stein, *Method and Message*, p. 132.

broke the sabbath but also called God his Father, making himself equal with God" (v. 18). From all of the foregoing, it seems difficult, except on the basis of a certain type of critical presupposition, to escape the conclusion that Jesus understood himself as equal with the Father, and as possessing the right to do things which only God has the right to do.

The Gospel of John

When we examine the whole of the New Testament, we find that what its writers say about Jesus is thoroughly consistent with his own self-understanding and claims about

priests (4:14–5:10). He is superior for he is not merely a human or an angel, but something higher, namely, God.

Paul

Paul frequently witnesses to a belief in the deity of Jesus. In Colossians 1:15–20 Paul writes that the Son is the image of the invisible God (v. 15); he is the one in whom and through whom and for whom all things hold together (v. 17). In verse 19 Paul brings this line of argument to a conclusion: "For in him all the fulness of God was pleased to dwell." In Colossians 2:9 he states a very

Jesus understood himself as equal with the Father, and as possessing the right to do things which only God has the right to do.

himself. The Gospel of John is, of course, noted for its references to the deity of Jesus. The prologue particularly expresses this idea. John says, "In the beginning was the Word, and the Word was with God, and the Word was God." He has both identified the Word as divine and distinguished the Word from God. It is not a simple monotheism or a modalistic monarchianism that he is describing here. The remainder of the Gospel supports and amplifies the thrust of the prologue.

Hebrews

The Book of Hebrews is also most emphatic regarding Jesus' divinity. In the opening chapter the author speaks of the Son as the radiance of the glory of God and the exact representation of his nature (Heb. 1:3). This Son, through whom God created the world (v. 2), also upholds (or carries) all things by his word of power (v. 3). In verse 8, which is a quotation of Psalm 45:6, the Son is addressed as "God." The argument here is that the Son is superior to angels (1:4–2:9), Moses (3:1–6), and the high

similar idea: "For in him the whole fulness of deity dwells bodily."

Paul also confirms some of the claims which Jesus had earlier made. Judgment is in the Old Testament ascribed to God. Although Paul on occasion refers to the judgment of God (e.g., Rom. 2:3), he also speaks of "Christ Jesus who is to judge the living and the dead" (2 Tim. 4:1) and of the judgment seat of Christ (2 Cor. 5:10).

Philippians 2:5–11, a passage we discussed earlier (p. 98), is a clear assertion of the deity of Christ Jesus. It speaks of him as being or existing in the "form" (*morphē*) of God (v. 6). In biblical and classical Greek this term refers to "the set of characteristics which constitutes a thing what it is." The whole passage, as Reginald Fuller maintains, presents a "threefold christological pattern": Jesus, being God, emptied himself, became human, and then was again exalted to the status of deity or of equality with the Father.[6]

6. Reginald H. Fuller, *The Foundations of New Testament Christology* (New York: Scribner, 1965), p. 232.

210

The Term "Lord"

There is a more general type of argument for the deity of Christ. The New Testament writers ascribe the term *kyrios* ("Lord") to Jesus, particularly in his risen and ascended state. While the term can most certainly be used without any high christological connotations, there are several considerations which argue that the term signifies divinity when applied to Jesus. First, in the Septuagint (the Greek translation of the Old Testament) *kyrios* is the usual translation of the name *Jehovah* and of the reverential *Ădōnāi* which was ordinarily substituted for it. Further, several New Testament references to Jesus as "Lord" are quotations of Old Testament texts employing one of the Hebrew names for God (e.g., Acts 2:20–21 and Rom. 10:13 [cf. Joel 2:31–32]; 1 Peter 3:15 [cf. Isa. 8:13]). These references make it clear that the apostles meant to give Jesus the title *Lord* in its highest sense. Finally, *kyrios* is used in the New Testament to designate both God the Father, the sovereign God (e.g., Matt. 1:20; 9:38; 11:25; Acts 17:24; Rev. 4:11), and Jesus (e.g., Luke 2:11; John 20:28; Acts 10:36; 1 Cor. 2:8; Phil. 2:11; James 2:1; Rev. 19:16). William Childs Robinson comments that when Jesus "is addressed as the exalted Lord, he is so identified with God that there is ambiguity in some passages as to whether the Father or the Son is meant (e.g., Acts 1:24; 2:47; 8:39; 9:31; 11:21; 13:10–12; 16:14; 20:19; 21:14; cf. 18:26; Rom. 14:11)."[7] For the Jews particularly, the term *kyrios* suggested that Christ was equal with the Father.

The Evidence of the Resurrection

To some, the approach we have been taking in our effort to demonstrate Jesus' deity may appear to be uncritical in nature, to use the Bible without taking into consideration the findings of the more radical methods of biblical investigation. There is, however, another way to establish Jesus' deity, a way which will not enmesh us in contesting critical issues point for point. We turn to the Christology of Wolfhart Pannenberg, especially as it is developed in his book *Jesus—God and Man*. His Christology rests very heavily upon the resurrection of Jesus.

Pannenberg's argument can be understood only in light of his view of revelation and of history. To Pannenberg, the whole of history is revelatory. Thus, revelation can be said to have fully taken place only when history has run its course, because it is only then that we can see where it has been going. One would therefore expect that history has no revelatory value for us now, since we have only incomplete parts, like the pieces of a jigsaw puzzle. The resurrection, however, because it is the end of history, having taken place proleptically, does give us revelation, even within time.[8]

Pannenberg holds that the resurrection must be understood from the viewpoint of the historical traditions of which it is a part. Whereas it has become commonplace to regard an event as a constant and its interpretation as a variable changing with time, he unites the two. The meaning of an event is the meaning attached to it by the persons into whose history it comes. Pannenberg points out that, to Jews of Jesus' time, his resurrection would have signified divinity. We must, then, ask about the evidence for it. Pannenberg points to the emergence of Christianity, which Paul traced back to the appearances of the resurrected Christ. If the emergence of Christianity can be understood "only if one examines it in the light of the eschatological hope for a resurrection from the dead, then that which is so designated is a historical event, even if we do not know anything more particular about it."[9]

Pannenberg agrees with Paul Althaus that the proclamation of the resurrection in

7. William Childs Robinson, "Lord," in *Baker's Dictionary of Theology*, ed. Everett F. Harrison (Grand Rapids: Baker, 1960), pp. 328–29.

8. Wolfhart Pannenberg, "Dogmatic Theses on the Doctrine of Revelation," in *Revelation as History*, ed. Wolfhart Pannenberg (New York: Macmillan, 1968), p. 134.

9. Wolfhart Pannenberg, *Jesus—God and Man* (Philadelphia: Westminster, 1968), p. 98.

Jerusalem so soon after Jesus' death is very significant. Within the earliest Christian community there must have been a reliable testimony to the empty tomb. Pannenberg also observes that in the Jewish polemic against the Christian message of Jesus' resurrection there is no claim at all that Jesus' grave was not empty.[10] Therefore, we have adequate evidence to establish the historicity of the resurrection, which is proof in itself of Jesus' deity.[11]

Historical Departures from Belief in the Full Deity of Christ

As the church struggled to understand who and what Jesus is, and particularly how he is related to the Father, some heretical views arose.

Ebionism

The Ebionites, a sect of heretical Jewish Christians, denied the real or ontological deity of Jesus. Jesus was, according to the Ebionites, an ordinary man possessed of unusual but not superhuman or supernatural gifts of righteousness and wisdom. They rejected the virgin birth, maintaining that Jesus was born to Joseph and Mary in normal fashion.[12] The baptism was the significant event in Jesus' life, for it was then that the Christ descended in the form of a dove upon Jesus. This was understood more as the presence of God's power and influence within the man Jesus than as a personal, metaphysical reality. Near the end of Jesus' life, the Christ withdrew from him. Thus Jesus was primarily a man, albeit a man in whom, at least for a time, the power of God was present and active to an unusual degree.

The Ebionite view of Jesus had the virtue of resolving the tension between belief in the deity of Jesus and the monotheistic view of God. However, Ebionism had to ignore or deny a large body of scriptural material: all of the references to the preexistence, the vir-

gin birth, and the qualitatively unique status and function of Jesus. In the view of the church, this was far too great a concession.

Arianism

The teaching of an Alexandrian presbyter named Arius became the first major threat to the views implicitly held by the church regarding Jesus' deity. Although condemned by the church at the Council of Nicea in 325 and at subsequent councils, Arianism lingers on to our day in various forms. One large and aggressive variety of Arianism in popular form is the movement known as Jehovah's Witnesses.

A central conception in the Arian understanding of Jesus is the absolute uniqueness and transcendence of God.[13] God is the one source of all things, the only uncreated existent in the whole universe. He alone possesses the attributes of deity. Everything other than God has come into being through an act of creation by which he called it into existence out of nothing. Only God (by which Arius meant the Father) is uncreated and eternal. The Word is therefore a created being, although the first and highest of the beings. While the Word is a perfect creature, not really in the same class with the other creatures, he is not self-existent.

The Arians based their view upon a rather extensive collection of biblical references.[14] These include texts which seem to imply that Christ is inferior to the Father (e.g., John 14:28, where Jesus says, "The Father is greater than I") and texts which attribute to the Son such imperfections as weakness, ignorance, and suffering (e.g., Mark 13:32—"But of that day or that hour no one knows, not even the angels in heaven, nor the Son, but only the Father"). Somewhat less extreme were the semi-Arians, who stressed the similarity rather than the dissimilarity between the Word and the Father. They were willing to say that the Word is similar in nature (or essence) to the Father (*homoi-*

10. Ibid., pp. 100–101.
11. Ibid., p. 89.
12. Justin Martyr *Dialogue with Trypho* 47.

13. Athanasius *On the Councils of Ariminum and Seleucia* 16.
14. Athanasius *Four Discourses Against the Arians*.

ousios), but not that he is of the same essence as the Father (*homoousios*).

There are two major responses to Arian theology. One is to note that the types of evidence appealed to earlier in this chapter, in substantiating the deity of Christ, are either ignored or inadequately treated by the Arians. The other is to take a closer look at the passages appealed to in support of the Arian view. In general, it must be said that the Ari-

> *To know the love, the holiness, the power of God, we need only look at Christ.*

ans have misconstrued various biblical statements referring to the Son's subordination during his incarnation. Descriptions of his temporary functional subordination to the Father have been misinterpreted as statements about the essence of the Son.

Functional Christology

Not all modifications of the doctrine of the full deity of Jesus are found in the first centuries of the history of the church. One of the interesting christological developments of the twentieth century has been the rise of "functional Christology." By this is meant an emphasis upon what Jesus did rather than upon what he is. In general, functional Christology claims to be based purely on the New Testament rather than on the more metaphysical or speculative categories of a later period of reflection, which are viewed as rooted in Greek thought.[15] However, because functional Christology overlooks some features of the biblical witness and distorts others, it is not an adequate Christology for today. It is question-

15. E.g., Oscar Cullmann, *The Christology of the New Testament*, rev. ed. (Philadelphia: Westminster, 1963).

able whether, as functional Christologists claim, the New Testament puts far more stress on Jesus' function or work than on his person or nature. Ontological concepts are implicit if not explicit in the New Testament. Any Christology to be fully adequate must address and integrate ontological and functional matters.

Implications of the Deity of Christ

There are several significant implications of the doctrine of Christ's deity:

1. We can have real knowledge of God. Jesus said, "He who has seen me has seen the Father" (John 14:9). Whereas the prophets came bearing a message from God, Jesus was God. If we would know what the love of God, the holiness of God, the power of God are like, we need only look at Christ.

2. Redemption is available to us. The death of Christ is sufficient for all sinners who have ever lived, for it was not merely a finite human, but an infinite God who died. He, the Life, the Giver and Sustainer of life, who did not have to die, died.

3. God and humankind have been reunited. It was not an angel or a human who came from God to us, but God himself crossed the chasm created by sin.

4. Worship of Christ is appropriate. He is not merely the highest of the creatures, but he is God in the same sense and to the same degree as the Father. He is as deserving of our praise, adoration, and obedience as is the Father.

One day everyone will recognize who and what Jesus is. Those who believe in the deity of Christ already recognize who he is and act accordingly:

> Beautiful Savior!
> Lord of the nations!
> Son of God and Son of Man!
> Glory and honor,
> Praise, adoration,
> Now and forevermore be Thine!
>
> (*Münster Gesangbuch*, 1677)

24 The Humanity of Christ

The topic of the humanity of Jesus Christ does not, in some ways, arouse quite the attention and controversy that his deity does. It seems on first glance to be something of a self-evident matter, for whatever Jesus was, he most surely must have been human. In this century Jesus' humanity has not received the close and extensive attention paid to his deity, which has been a major topic of dispute between fundamentalists and modernists. For what is not disputed tends not to be discussed, at least not in as much depth as are major controversies. Yet, historically, the topic of Jesus' humanity has played at least as important a role in theological dialogue as has his deity, particularly in the earliest years of the church. And in practical terms, it has in some ways posed a greater danger to orthodox theology.

The Importance of the Humanity of Christ

The importance of Jesus' humanity cannot be overestimated, for our salvation is at stake. The basic problem we face is the gap between ourselves and God. This gap is, to be sure, ontological. God is high above us, so much so that he cannot be known by unaided human reason. If he is to be known, God must take some initiative to make himself known to us. But the problem is not merely ontological. There also is a spiritual and moral gap between God and us, a gap created by human sin. We are unable by our own moral effort to counter our sin, to elevate ourselves to the level of God. If we are to have fellowship with God, we have to be united with him in some other way. This, it is traditionally understood, has been accomplished by the incarnation, in which deity and humanity were united in one person. If, however, Jesus was not really one of us, humanity has not been united with deity, and we cannot be saved. For the validity of the work accomplished in Christ's death, or at least its applicability to us as human beings, depends upon the reality of his humanity, just as the efficacy of it depends upon the genuineness of his deity.

Furthermore, Jesus' intercessory ministry is dependent upon his humanity. If he was truly one of us, experiencing all of the temptations and trials of human existence, then he is able to understand and empathize with us in our struggles as humans. On the other hand, if he was not human, or only incompletely human, he cannot effect the kind of intercession that a priest must make on behalf of those whom he represents.

The Biblical Evidence

Physical Human Nature

There is ample biblical evidence that the man Jesus was a fully human person, not lacking any of the essential elements of humanity that are found in each of us. The first item to be noted is that he had a fully human body. He was born. He did not descend from heaven and suddenly appear upon earth, but was conceived in the womb of a human mother and nourished prenatally like any other child. Although his conception was unique in that it did not involve a male human, the process from that point on was apparently identical to what every human fetus experiences. Jesus also had a typical family tree, as is indicated by the genealogies in Matthew and Luke. He had ancestors and presumably received genes from them, just as every other human being receives genes from his or her forebears.

Not only Jesus' birth, but also his life indicates that he had a physical human nature. We are told that he increased "in wisdom and in stature, and in favor with God and man" (Luke 2:52). He grew physically, nourished by food and water. He did not have unlimited physical strength. Yet his body may have been more nearly perfect in some respects than ours, because there was in him none of the sin (neither original sin nor the personal sin common to every human) that affects health. Whatever the case, Jesus certainly was subject to the same physical limitations as other human beings, for he had the same physiology. Thus he experienced hunger when he fasted (Matt. 4:2). He also experienced thirst (John 19:28). In addition, he experienced fatigue when he traveled (John 4:6), and presumably on many other occasions as well.

Finally, Jesus suffered physically and died, just like everyone else. This is evident in the entire crucifixion story, but perhaps most clearly in John 19:34, where we read that a spear was thrust into his side, and water and blood mingled came out, indicating that he had already died. Surely he had felt physical suffering (as genuinely as would you or I) when he was beaten, when the crown of thorns was placed on his head, and when the nails were driven through his hands (or wrists) and feet.

A further indication of Jesus' humanity is his use of the word *man* in reference to himself. A clear statement is found in John 8:40, where Jesus says to the Jews, "Now you seek to kill me, a man who has told you the truth which I heard from God." Others also use the word *man* in reference to Jesus. Paul, in his argument regarding original sin, compares Jesus and Adam and uses the expression "one man" of Jesus three times (Rom. 5:15, 17, 19). We find a similar thought and expression in 1 Corinthians 15:21, 47–49.

Scripture also refers to Christ's taking on flesh, that is, becoming human. John said, "And the Word became flesh and dwelt between the perceiver and the object perceived. Thus, when John speaks of having "touched with our hands," he is emphasizing just how thoroughly physical was the manifestation of Jesus.

Psychological Human Nature

If Jesus was a true human being in the physical sense, he also was fully and genuinely human in the psychological sense. This is seen in the fact that Scripture attributes to him the same sort of emotional and intellectual qualities that are found in other humans. He thought, reasoned, and felt the full gamut of human emotions. He

In addition to a physical nature, Jesus had the same sort of emotional and intellectual qualities that all humans have— he thought, reasoned, and experienced the full gamut of human feelings.

among us" (John 1:14). John was particularly emphatic on this matter in his first letter, one of the purposes of which was to combat a heresy which denied that Jesus had been genuinely human: "By this you know the Spirit of God: every spirit which confesses that Jesus Christ has come in the flesh is of God, and every spirit which does not confess Jesus is not of God" (1 John 4:2–3a).

That Jesus had a physical body is evident in the fact that his contemporaries had a genuine physical perception of him. John puts it very vividly in 1 John 1:1: "That which was from the beginning, which we have heard, which we have seen with our eyes, which we have looked upon and touched with our hands, concerning the word of life—." John is here establishing the reality of the human nature of Jesus. He actually heard, saw, and touched Jesus. Touch was thought by the Greeks to be the most basic and most reliable of the senses, for it is a direct perception—no medium intervenes

loved, of course. One of his disciples is referred to as the disciple "whom Jesus loved" (John 13:23). Jesus had compassion or pity on those who were hungry, ill, or lost (Matt. 9:36; 14:14; 15:32; 20:34). The Greek word used here to denote his reaction literally means "to be moved in one's internal or visceral organs"—Jesus was internally moved by human predicaments. He could be sorrowful and troubled, as he was just before his betrayal and crucifixion (Matt. 26:37). He also experienced joy (John 15:11; 17:13; Heb. 12:2). He could be angry and grieved with people (Mark 3:5), and even indignant (Mark 10:14).

It should be borne in mind, of course, that some of these emotions do not in themselves prove that Jesus was human. For God certainly feels love and compassion, as we observed in our discussion of his nature, as well as anger and indignation toward sin. Some of Jesus' reactions, however, are uniquely human. For example, he shows astonishment in response to both positive and negative situations. He marvels at the faith of the centurion (Luke 7:9) and the unbelief of the residents of Nazareth (Mark 6:6). Instructive as well are the references to Jesus' being troubled. Here we see his peculiarly human reaction to a variety of situations, especially his sense of the death to which he had to go. In the Garden of Gethsemane, he was obviously in struggle and in stress, and apparently did not want to be left alone (Mark 14:32–42). At the cross, his outcry, "My God, my God, why hast thou forsaken me?" (Mark 15:34), was a very human expression of loneliness.

One of Jesus' most human reactions occurred at the death of Lazarus. Seeing Mary and her companions weeping, Jesus "was deeply moved in spirit and troubled" (John 11:33); he wept (v. 35); at the tomb he was "deeply moved again" (v. 38). The description here is very vivid, for to depict Jesus' groaning in the spirit, John chose a term that is used of horses snorting. Obviously Jesus possessed a human nature capable of feeling sorrow and remorse as deeply as we do.

When we turn to the subject of Jesus' intellectual qualities, we find that he had some rather remarkable knowledge. He knew the past, present, and future to a degree not available to ordinary human beings. For example, he knew the thoughts of both his friends (Luke 9:47) and his enemies (Luke 6:8). He knew that the Samaritan woman had had five husbands and was presently living with a man to whom she was not married (John 4:18). He knew that Lazarus was already dead (John 11:14).

Yet this knowledge was not without limits. Jesus frequently asked questions, and the impression given by the Gospels is that he asked because he did not know. There are, to be sure, some persons, particularly teachers, who ask questions the answers to which they already know. But Jesus seemed to ask because he needed information which he did not possess.[1] For example, he asked

the father of the epileptic boy, "How long has he had this?" (Mark 9:21). Apparently Jesus did not know how long the boy had been afflicted, information which was necessary if the proper cure was to be administered.

The biblical witness goes even further. There is at least one case where Jesus expressly declared that he did not know a particular matter. In discussing the second coming, he said, "But of that day or that hour no one knows, not even the angels in heaven, nor the Son, but only the Father" (Mark 13:32). This is a straightforward declaration of ignorance on the subject.

We must note also the "human religious life" of Jesus. While that may sound strange and perhaps even a bit blasphemous to some, it is nonetheless accurate. He attended worship in the synagogue, and did so on a regular or habitual basis (Luke 4:16). His prayer life was a clear indication of human dependence upon the Father. Jesus prayed regularly. At times he prayed at great length and with great intensity, as in the Garden of Gethsemane. Before the important step of choosing his twelve disciples, Jesus prayed all night (Luke 6:12). It is evident that Jesus felt himself dependent upon the Father for guidance, for strength, and for preservation from evil.

It is apparent, then, that for the disciples and the authors of the New Testament books, there was no question about Jesus' humanity. The point was not really argued, for it was scarcely disputed (with the exception of the situation to which 1 John was addressed). Those who were closest to Jesus, who lived with him every day, regarded him as being as fully human as themselves. They were able to verify for themselves that he was human; and when, on one occasion after Jesus' resurrection, there was some question as to whether he might be a spirit, he invited them to ascertain the genuineness of his humanity for themselves: "See my hands and my feet, that it is I myself; handle me, and see; for a spirit has not flesh and

1. Leon Morris, *The Lord from Heaven: A Study of the New Testament Teaching on the Deity and Humanity of Jesus* (Grand Rapids: Eerdmans, 1958), p. 45.

bones as you see that I have" (Luke 24:39). He did everything they did, except sin and pray for forgiveness. He ate with them, he bled, he slept, he cried. If Jesus was not human, then surely no one ever has been.

Early Heresies Regarding the Humanity of Jesus

Docetism

Early in the life of the church, however, there came several departures from the understanding of Jesus as fully human. We see such a departure already in the situation which John's first letter vigorously opposed. In addition to a specific group of Christians known as Docetists, a basic denial of Jesus' humanity permeated many other movements within Christianity, including Gnosticism and Marcionism.[2]

Docetism takes its name from the Greek verb *dokeō*, which means "to seem or appear." Its central thesis is that Jesus only seemed to be human. God could not really have become material, since all matter is evil, and he is perfectly pure and holy. The transcendent God could not possibly have united with such a corrupting influence. Being impassible and unchangeable, God could not have undergone the modifications in his nature which would necessarily have occurred with a genuine incarnation. He could not have exposed himself to the experiences of human life. The humanity of Jesus, his physical nature, was simply an illusion, not a reality. Jesus was more like a ghost, an apparition, than a human being.[3]

This particular Christology resolved the tension in the idea that deity and humanity were united in one person. It did so by saying that while the deity was real and complete, the humanity was only appearance. But the church recognized that this solution had been achieved at too great a price, the loss of Jesus' humanity and thus of any real connection between him and us. It is difficult today to find pure instances of Docetism, although docetic tendencies occur in many and varied schemes of thought.

Apollinarianism

Apollinarius, a fourth-century bishop from Syria, was very concerned to maintain the unity of the Son, Jesus Christ. Now if Jesus, reasoned Apollinarius, had two complete natures, he must have had a human *nous* (soul, mind, reason) as well as a divine *nous*. Apollinarius thought this duality absurd. So he constructed a Christology based upon an extremely narrow reading of John 1:14 ("the Word became flesh")—flesh was the only aspect of human nature involved.[4] According to Apollinarius, Jesus was a compound unity; part of the composite (some elements of Jesus) was human, the rest divine. What he (the Word) took was not the whole of humanity, but only flesh, that is, the body. This flesh could not, however, be animated by itself. There had to be a "spark of life" animating it. This was the divine Logos; it took the place of the human soul. Thus Jesus was human physically, but not psychologically. He had a human body, but not a human soul. His soul was divine.[5]

Therefore, Jesus, although human, was a bit different from other human beings. Jesus did not have a human will. Consequently, he could not sin, for his person was fully controlled by his divine soul.[6] Loraine Boettner draws the analogy of a human mind implanted into the body of a lion; the resulting being is governed, not by lion or animal psychology, but by human psychology. That is a rough parallel to the Apollinarian view of the person of Jesus.[7]

2. Tertullian *On the Flesh of Christ* 5.

3. J. F. Bethune-Baker, *An Introduction to the Early History of Christian Doctrine* (London: Methuen, 1903), p. 80.

4. J. N. D. Kelly, *Early Christian Doctrines* (New York: Harper and Row, 1960), p. 291.

5. Ibid., p. 292. There is a dispute as to whether Apollinarius was a dichotomist or trichotomist. For purposes of simplicity, we will treat him here as a dichotomist.

6. Ibid., p. 293.

7. Loraine Boettner, *Studies in Theology* (Grand Rapids: Eerdmans, 1947), p. 263.

Apollinarianism proved to be an ingenious but unacceptable solution to the problem. The dual nature of Jesus tended to become one nature in practice, the divine soul swallowing up the human body. Consequently, the Apollinarian doctrine was condemned at the Council of Constantinople in 381.

The Virgin Birth

Next to the resurrection, the most debated and controversial event of Jesus' life is the virgin birth, the means through which Christ took on human form. In the late nineteenth century and early twentieth century, the virgin birth was at the forefront of debate between the fundamentalists and modernists. The fundamentalists insisted upon the doctrine as an essential belief. The modernists either rejected it as unessential or untenable, or reinterpreted it in some nonliteral fashion. To the former it was a guarantee of the qualitative uniqueness and deity of Christ, while to the latter it seemed to shift attention from his spiritual reality to a biological issue.[8]

What we are speaking of here is really the "virgin conception." By this we mean that Jesus' conception in the womb of Mary was not the result of sexual relationship. Mary was a virgin at the time of the conception, and continued so up to the point of birth, for the Scripture indicates that Joseph did not have sexual intercourse with her until after the birth of Jesus (Matt. 1:25). Mary became pregnant through a supernatural influence of the Holy Spirit upon her, but that does not mean that Jesus was the result of copulation between God and Mary. It also does not mean that there was not a normal birth.

Biblical Evidence

The doctrine of the virgin birth is based upon just two explicit biblical references—Matthew 1:18–25 and Luke 1:26–38. There are other passages in the New Testament which some have argued refer to or at least allude to or presuppose the virgin birth, and there is the prophecy of Isaiah 7:14 which is cited by Matthew (1:23). But even when these passages are taken into consideration, the number of relevant references is quite few. That the Bible affirms the virgin birth not once but twice, however, is sufficient proof. Since we believe that the Bible is inspired and authoritative, Matthew 1 and Luke 1 convince us that the virgin birth is fact.

The Theological Significance

There are disagreements as to the importance of the virgin birth, even among those who insist that belief in the doctrine must be maintained. On one level, of course, the virgin birth is important simply because we are told that it occurred. Whether or not we can see a necessity for the virgin birth, if the Bible tells us that it happened, it is important to believe that it did, because not to do so is a tacit repudiation of the authority of the Bible. But, we must ask, is not the virgin birth important in some more specific way?

Some have argued that the doctrine is indispensable to the incarnation. Without the virgin birth there would have been no union of God and humanity.[9] If Jesus had been simply the product of a normal sexual union of man and woman, he would have been only a human being, not a God-man. But is this really true? Could he not have been God

8. Harry Emerson Fosdick, *The Man from Nazareth as His Contemporaries Saw Him* (New York: Harper and Brothers, 1949), pp. 158–60.

9. Tertullian *Adversus Marcionem* 4.10. Carl Henry comes close to this position when he says, "It may be admitted, of course, that the Virgin Birth is not flatly identical with the Incarnation, just as the empty tomb is not flatly identical with the Resurrection. The one might be affirmed without the other. Yet the connection is so close, and indeed indispensable, that were the Virgin Birth or the empty tomb denied, it is likely that either the Incarnation or the Resurrection would be called in question, or they would be affirmed in a form very different from that which they have in Scripture and historic teaching. The Virgin Birth might well be described as an essential, historical indication of the Incarnation, bearing not only an analogy to the divine and human natures of the Incarnate, but also bringing out the nature, purpose, and bearing of this work of God to salvation" ("Our Lord's Virgin Birth," *Christianity Today*, 7 Dec. 1959, p. 20).

and man if he had had two human parents, or none? Just as Adam was created directly by God, so Jesus could also have been a direct special creation. And accordingly, it should have been possible for Jesus to have two human parents and to have been fully the God-man nonetheless. What God did, however, was to supply by a special creation both the human component ordinarily contributed by the male (and thus we have the virgin birth) and, in addition, a divine factor (and thus we have the incarnation). The virgin birth requires only that a normal human being was brought into existence without a human male parent. This could have occurred without an incarnation, and there could have been an incarnation without a virgin birth. The point here is that Jesus' being both God and human did not depend on the virgin birth.

A second suggestion frequently made is that the virgin birth was indispensable to the sinlessness of Jesus.[10] If he had possessed both that which the mother contributes and what the father ordinarily contributes, he would have had a depraved and hence sinful nature, like the rest of us. But this argument seems to suggest that we too would be sinless if we did not have a male parent. And this in turn would mean one of two things: either (1) the father, not the mother, is the source of depravity, a notion which in effect implies that women do not have a depraved nature (or if they do, they do not transmit it), or (2) depravity comes not from the nature of our parents, but from the sexual act by which reproduction takes place. But there is nothing in the Scripture to support the latter alternative. The statement in Psalm 51:5, "in sin did my mother conceive me," simply means that the psalmist was sinful from the very beginning of life. It does not mean that the act of conception is sinful in and of itself. Unfortunately, this

misapprehension that the reproductive act is intrinsically sinful has led some Christians to have unhealthy attitudes about sex.

We are left, then, with the former alternative, namely, that the transmission of sin is related to the father. But this does not have any scriptural grounding either. While some support might be found in Paul's statement that it was the sin of *Adam* (Rom. 5:12) which made all people sinners, Paul also indicates that Eve, not Adam, "was deceived and became a transgressor" (1 Tim. 2:14). There are no signs of greater sinfulness among men than among women.

The question arises, If all of the human race is tainted by the original sin, would not Mary have contributed some of its consequences to Jesus? It has been argued that Jesus did have a depraved nature, but he committed no *actual* sin.[11] We would point out in reply that the angel said to Mary, "The Holy Spirit will come upon you, and the power of the Most High will overshadow you; therefore the child to be born will be called holy, the Son of God" (Luke 1:35). It seems likely that the influence of the Holy Spirit was so powerful and sanctifying in its effect that there was no conveyance of depravity or of guilt from Mary to Jesus. Without that special sanctifying influence, he would have possessed the same depraved nature that all of us have. Now if the Holy Spirit prevented corruption from being passed from Mary to Jesus, could not he have prevented it from being passed on by Joseph as well? We conclude that Jesus' sinlessness was not dependent upon the virgin conception.

A third suggestion is that while the virgin birth was not essential to the incarnation or the sinlessness of Christ, it has great value in terms of symbolizing the reality of the incarnation.[12] It is an evidential factor in much

10. James Orr, *The Virgin Birth of Christ* (New York: Scribner, 1907), pp. 190–201; Hans von Campenhausen, *The Virgin Birth in the Theology of the Ancient Church* (Naperville, Ill.: Alec R. Allenson, 1964), pp. 79–86.

11. Karl Barth appears to have held the position that Jesus took upon himself the same fallen nature which we now possess; his sinlessness consisted in his never committing actual sin (*Church Dogmatics* [Edinburgh: T. and T. Clark, 1956], vol. 1, part 2, pp. 151–55).

12. Edward J. Carnell, "The Virgin Birth of Christ," *Christianity Today*, 7 Dec. 1959, pp. 9–10.

the same way that the other miracles and particularly the resurrection function to certify the supernaturalness of Christ. On this basis, the virgin birth was not necessary ontologically, that is, the virgin birth was not necessary for Christ to be God. It is, however, necessary epistemologically, that is, in order for us to know that he is God.

Support for this third suggestion lies in the fact that the virgin birth is not mentioned in the evangelistic sermons in the Book of Acts. It may well be, then, that it is not one of the first-level doctrines (i.e., indispensable to salvation). It is a subsidiary or supporting doctrine; it helps create or sustain belief in the indispensable doctrines, or reinforces truths which are found in other doctrines:

1. The doctrine of the virgin birth is a reminder that our salvation is supernatural. John stated that those who believe and receive authority to become children of God are born "not of blood nor of the will of the flesh nor of the will of man, but of God" (John 1:13). The emphasis is that salvation does not come through our effort, nor is it our accomplishment. So also the virgin birth points to the helplessness of humans to initiate even the first step in the process. Not only are humans unable to secure their own salvation, but they could not even introduce the Savior into their society.

2. The virgin birth is also a reminder that God's salvation is fully a gift of grace. There was nothing particularly deserving about Mary. Certainly Mary manifested qualities which God could use, such as faith and dedication (Luke 1:38, 46–55). But she really had nothing special to offer, not even a husband. That someone apparently incapable of having a child should be chosen to bear God's Son is a reminder that salvation is not a human accomplishment but a gift from God, and an undeserved one at that.

3. The virgin birth is evidence of the uniqueness of Jesus the Savior. Although there could have been an incarnation without a virgin birth, the miraculous nature of the birth (or at least the conception) serves to show that Jesus was, at the very least, a highly unusual man singled out by God in particular ways.

4. Here is another evidence of the power and sovereignty of God over nature. On several occasions (e.g., the births of Isaac, Samuel, and John the Baptist) God had provided a child when the mother was barren or past the age of childbearing. Surely these were miraculous births. Even more amazing, however, was this birth. That God was able to work the seemingly impossible in the matter of the virgin birth is symbolic of his ability to accomplish the seemingly impossible task of granting a new birth to sinners. As Jesus himself said in regard to salvation: "With men this is impossible, but with God all things are possible" (Matt. 19:26).

The Sinlessness of Jesus

One further important issue concerning Jesus' humanity is the question of whether he sinned or, indeed, whether he could have sinned. The Bible is quite clear upon this matter. The writer to the Hebrews says that Jesus "in every respect has been tempted as we are, yet without sinning" (Heb. 4:15). Jesus is described as "a high priest, holy, blameless, unstained, separated from sinners, exalted above the heavens" (7:26), and as "without blemish" (9:14). Peter, who of course knew Jesus well, declared him to be "the Holy One of God" (John 6:69), and taught that Jesus "committed no sin; no guile was found on his lips" (1 Peter 2:22). John said, "In him there is no sin" (1 John 3:5). Paul also affirmed that Christ "knew no sin" (2 Cor. 5:21).

Jesus himself both explicitly and implicitly claimed to be righteous. He asked his hearers, "Which of you convicts me of sin?" (John 8:46); no one replied. He taught his disciples to confess their sins and ask for forgiveness, but there is no report of his ever confessing sin and asking forgiveness in his own behalf. Other than blasphemy, no charge of sin was brought against him; and, of course, if he was God, then what he did (e.g., his declaring sins to be forgiven) was not blasphemy. While not absolute proof of Jesus' sinlessness, there are ample testimonies of his innocence of the charges for which he was crucified. Pilate's wife warned, "Have nothing to do with that righteous man" (Matt. 27:19); the thief on the cross said, "This man has done nothing wrong" (Luke 23:41); and even Judas said, "I have sinned in betraying innocent blood"

Jesus is not only as human as we are; he is more human.

(Matt. 27:4). We must conclude that the Bible uniformly witnesses to the sinlessness of Jesus.[13]

But could Jesus have sinned? Scripture tells us that God does no evil and cannot be tempted (James 1:13). Was it really possible, then, for Jesus, inasmuch as he is God, to sin? And if not, was his temptation genuine? Here we are encountering one of the great mysteries of the faith, the relationship between Jesus' two natures, which will be more closely examined in our next chapter. Nonetheless, it is fitting for us to point out here that while he *could* have sinned, it was certain that he *would* not.[14] There were genuine struggles and temptations, but the outcome was always certain.

Does a person who does not succumb to temptation really feel it, or does he not? Leon Morris argues that the person who resists knows the full force of temptation. Sinlessness points to a more intense rather than

less intense temptation. "The man who yields to a particular temptation has not felt its full power. He has given in while the temptation has yet something in reserve. Only the man who does not yield to a temptation[,] who, as regards that particular temptation, is sinless, knows the full extent of that temptation."[15]

But the question remains, "Is a person who does not sin truly human?" If we say no, we are maintaining that sin is part of the essence of human nature. Such a view must be considered a serious heresy by anyone who believes that humankind has been created by God, since God would then be the cause of sin, the creator of a nature which is essentially evil. Inasmuch as we hold that, on the contrary, sin is not part of the essence of human nature, instead of asking, "Is Jesus as human as we are?" we might better ask, "Are we as human as Jesus?" For the type of human nature that each of us possesses is not pure human nature. The true humanity created by God has in our case been corrupted and spoiled. There have been only three pure human beings: Adam and Eve (before the fall), and Jesus. All the rest of us are but broken, corrupted versions of humanity. Jesus is not only as human as we are; he is more human. Our humanity is not a standard by which we are to measure his. His humanity, true and unadulterated, is the standard by which we are to be measured.

Implications of the Humanity of Jesus

The doctrine of the full humanity of Jesus has great significance for Christian faith and theology:

1. The atoning death of Jesus can truly avail for us. It was not some outsider to the human race who died on the cross. He was one of us, and thus could truly offer a sacrifice on our behalf. Just like the Old Testa-

---

13. There are, of course, those who contend that Jesus did sin. Among them is Nels Ferré, who detects in Jesus' behavior a lack of perfect trust in the Father, which constitutes the sin of unbelief. But Ferré's exegesis is faulty, and his view of sin heavily influenced by existential, rather than biblical, concepts. See *Christ and the Christian* (New York: Harper and Row, 1958), pp. 110–14.

14. This is reminiscent of our discussion of free will—while we are free to choose, God has already rendered our choice certain (see pp. 115–17).

15. Morris, *Lord from Heaven*, pp. 51–52.

ment priest, Jesus was a man who offered a sacrifice on behalf of his fellows.

2. Jesus can truly sympathize with and intercede for us. He has experienced all that we might undergo. When we are hungry, weary, lonely, he fully understands, for he has gone through it all himself (Heb. 4:15).

3. Jesus manifests the true nature of humanity. While we are sometimes inclined to draw our conclusions as to what humanity is from an inductive examination of ourselves and those around us, these are but imperfect instances of humanity. Jesus has not only told us what perfect humanity is, he has exhibited it.

4. Jesus can be our example. He is not some celestial superstar, but one who has lived where we live. We can therefore look to him as a model of the Christian life. The biblical standards for human behavior, which seem to us to be so hard to attain, are seen in him to be within human possibility. Of course, there must be full dependence upon the grace of God. The fact that Jesus found it necessary to pray and depend upon the Father is indication that we must be similarly reliant upon him.

5. Human nature is good. When we tend toward asceticism, regarding human nature, and particularly physical nature, as somehow inherently evil or at least inferior to the spiritual and immaterial, the fact that Jesus took upon himself our full human nature is a reminder that to be human is not evil, it is good.

6. God is not totally transcendent. He is not so far removed from the human race. If he could actually live among us at one time as a real human person, it is not surprising that he can and does act within the human realm today as well.

With John we rejoice that the incarnation was real and complete: "And the Word became flesh and dwelt among us, full of grace and truth; we have beheld his glory, glory as of the only Son from the Father" (John 1:14).

25 The Unity of the Person of Christ

The Importance and Difficulty of the Issue

Having concluded that Jesus was fully divine and fully human, we still face a large issue: the relationship between these two natures in the one person, Jesus. This is one of the most difficult of all theological problems, ranking with the Trinity and the paradox of human free will and divine sovereignty. It is also an issue of the greatest importance. We have already explained that Christology in general is important because the incarnation involved a bridging of the metaphysical, moral, and spiritual gap between God and humans. The bridging of this gap depended upon the unity of deity and humanity within Jesus Christ. For if Jesus was both God and a human being but the two natures were not united, then, although smaller, the gap remains. The separation of God and human beings is still a difficulty that has not been overcome. If the redemption accomplished on the cross is to avail for humankind, it must be the work of the human Jesus. But if it is to have the infinite value necessary to atone for the sins of all human beings in relationship to an infinite and perfectly holy God, then it must be the work of the divine Christ as well. If the death of the Savior is not the work of a unified God-man, it will be deficient at one point or the other.

The doctrine of the unification of divine and human within Jesus is difficult to comprehend because it posits the combination of two natures which by definition have contradictory attributes. As deity, Christ is infinite in knowledge, power, presence. If he is God, he must know all things. If he is God, he can do all things which are proper objects of his power. If he is God, he can be everywhere at once. But, on the other hand, if he was human, he was limited in knowledge. He could not do everything. And he certainly was limited to being in one place at a time. For one person to be both infinite and finite simultaneously seems impossible.

The issue is further complicated by the relative paucity of biblical material with which to work. We have in the Bible no direct statements about the relationship of the two natures. What we must do is draw inferences from Jesus' self-concept, his actions, and various didactic statements about him.

The Biblical Material

We begin by noting the absence of any references to duality in Jesus' thought, action, and purpose. There are, by contrast, indications of multiplicity within the Godhead as a whole, for example, in Genesis 1:26, "Then God said [singular], 'Let us make [plural] man in our [plural] image.'" Similar references, without a shift in number, are found in Genesis 3:22 and 11:7. There are instances of one member of the Trinity addressing another, in Psalms 2:7 and 40:7–8 as well as Jesus' prayers to the Father. Yet Jesus always spoke of himself in the singular. This is particularly notable in the prayer in John 17, where Jesus says that he and the Father are one (vv. 21–22), yet makes no ref-

> *The bridging of the metaphysical, moral, and spiritual gap between God and humans—and hence our very salvation—depends on the unity of deity and humanity within Jesus Christ.*

erence to any type of complexity within himself.

There are texts in Scripture which allude to both the deity and humanity of Jesus, yet clearly refer to a single subject. Among these are John 1:14 ("And the Word became flesh and dwelt among us, full of grace and truth"); Galatians 4:4 ("God sent forth his Son, born of woman, born under the law"); and 1 Timothy 3:16 ("He was manifested in the flesh, vindicated in the Spirit, seen by angels, preached among the nations, believed on in the world, taken up in glory"). The last text is particularly significant, for it refers to both Jesus' earthly incarnation and his presence in heaven before and after.

There are other references which focus upon the work of Jesus in such a way as to make it clear that it is the function not of either the human or the divine exclusively, but of one unified subject. For example, in reference to the work of Christ, John says, "But if any one does sin, we have an advocate with the Father, Jesus Christ the righteous; and he is the expiation for our sins, and not for ours only but also for the sins of the whole world" (1 John 2:1–2). This work of Jesus, which assumes both his humanity (4:2) and deity (4:15; 5:5), is the work of one person, who is described in the same epistle as the Son whom the Father has sent as the Savior of the world (4:14). One unified person whose acts presuppose both humanity and deity is in view.

Further, several passages in which Jesus is designated by one of his titles are highly revealing. We have situations in Scripture where a divine title is used in a reference to Jesus' human activity. For example, Paul says, "None of the rulers of this age understood this [the secret and hidden wisdom of God]; for if they had, they would not have crucified the Lord of glory" (1 Cor. 2:8). In Colossians 1:13–14, Paul writes, "[The Father] has delivered us from the dominion of darkness and transferred us to the kingdom of his beloved Son, in whom we have redemption, the forgiveness of sins." Here the kingly status of the Son of God is juxtaposed with the redemptive work of his bodily crucifixion and resurrection. Conversely, the title "Son of man," which Jesus often used of himself during his earthly ministry, appears in passages pointing to his heavenly status; for instance, in John 3:13, "No one has ascended into heaven but he who descended from heaven, the Son of man." Nothing in any of these references contradicts the position that the one person, Jesus Christ, was both earthly man and preexistent divine being who became incarnate. Nor is there any suggestion that these two natures took turns directing his activity.[1]

Early Misunderstandings

Reflection upon the relationship between the two natures arose comparatively late in church history. Logically prior were the discussions about the genuineness and completeness of the two natures. Once the church had settled these questions, at the councils of Nicea (325) and Constantinople

(381), it was appropriate to inquire into the precise relationship between the two natures. In effect, the matter at issue was, "What is really meant by declaring that Jesus was fully God and fully human?" In the process of suggesting and examining possible answers, the church rejected some of them as inadequate.

Nestorianism

One theologian who offered an answer was Nestorius, the patriarch of Constantinople. It is clear that the view condemned by the church as Nestorian fell short of the full orthodox position, and was probably held by some of Nestorius's followers.[2] It is the judgment of leading scholars, however, that Nestorius himself was not a "Nestorian," but that some poorly chosen terminology, coupled with an aggressive opposition, led to an unjust condemnation of his views.[3]

Soon after Nestorius was installed as patriarch in 428, he was obliged to rule upon the suitability of referring to Mary as *theotokos* ("God-bearing"). This Nestorius was reluctant to do, unless *theotokos* was accompanied by the term *anthrōpotokos* ("human-bearing"). While his ideas were not unique in that time, the choice of some rather unfortunate language caused problems for Nestorius. He observed that God cannot have a mother, and certainly no creature could have generated a member of the Godhead. Mary, therefore, did not bear God; she bore a man who was a vehicle for God. Although Nestorius would later profess to agree with the Chalcedonian formulation (two natures united in one person), he preferred to think in terms of a "conjunction" rather than a union. Perhaps the best possible summation of Nestorius is to say that while he did not consciously hold nor overtly

1. G. C. Berkouwer, *The Person of Christ* (Grand Rapids: Eerdmans, 1955), p. 293.

2. J. F. Bethune-Baker, *An Introduction to the Early History of Christian Doctrine* (London: Methuen, 1903), pp. 274–75.
3. Friedrich Loofs, *Nestorius and His Place in the History of Christian Doctrine* (New York: Lenox Hill, 1975), pp. 41, 60–61; J. F. Bethune-Baker, *Nestorius and His Teaching* (Cambridge: Cambridge University Press, 1908), pp. 82–100.

teach that there was a split in the person of Christ, what he said seemed to imply it.[4] From the statements of Nestorius and the reactions to his views came the traditional picture of Nestorianism as a heresy which split the God-man into two distinct persons. This heresy was condemned at the Council of Ephesus (431).

Eutychianism

Eutyches (ca. 375–454) was the archimandrite of a monastery in Constantinople. It is not easy to ascertain exactly what Eutyches' doctrine was. He declared that the Lord Jesus Christ after his birth possessed only one nature, that of God made flesh and become human. While rejecting the idea of two natures as contrary to the Scripture and to the opinions of the Fathers, Eutyches did, however, subscribe to the virgin birth and affirmed that Christ was simultaneously perfect God and perfect human. His basic contention seems to have been that there were two natures before the incarnation, one after.[5]

Eutyches' views constituted the foundation of a movement which taught that the humanity of Jesus was so absorbed into the deity as to be virtually eliminated. In effect, Eutychianism was a form of Docetism. There was a variant interpretation that Jesus' deity and humanity were fused into something quite different, a third substance, a hybrid as it were. It may be that this is what Eutyches himself held, although his thought was confused (at least in the way he expressed it).

Other Attempts to Solve the Problem

Adoptionism

An early and recurrent attempt to solve the problem of two natures in one person is adoptionism. Put in its simplest form, this is the idea that Jesus of Nazareth was merely a human during the early years of his life. At some point, however, probably Jesus' baptism (or perhaps his resurrection), God "adopted" him as his Son. This was more a case of a human's becoming God than of God's becoming human.[6] In support of their position, adoptionists concentrate on the scriptural idea that Jesus was begotten by God (e.g., John 3:16). Those who take seriously the full teaching of Scripture, however, are aware of major obstacles to this view, including the preexistence of Christ, the prebirth narrative, and the virgin birth.

Kenoticism

In the nineteenth century, it was suggested that the key to understanding the incarnation is to be found in the expression "[Jesus] emptied himself" (Phil. 2:7). According to this view, which is called kenoticism (the Greek word for "to empty" is *kenoō*), what Jesus emptied himself of was the form of God (v. 6). The Second Person of the Trinity laid aside his distinctly divine attributes (omnipotence, omnipresence, etc.) and took on human qualities instead. In effect, the incarnation consisted of an exchange of part of the divine nature for human characteristics.[7] His moral qualities, such as love and mercy, were maintained. Kenoticism also holds that Jesus is not God and human simultaneously, but successively. With respect to certain attributes, he is God, then he is human, then God again. While this view solves some of the difficulty, it does not account for the evidence we cited earlier to the effect that the biblical writers regarded Jesus as both God and human. Moreover, the indications of an apparent continuing incarnation (see, e.g., 1 Tim. 3:16) militate against the maintenance of this theory, innovative though it be.

4. A. B. Bruce, *The Humiliation of Christ in Its Physical, Ethical, and Official Aspects*, 2d ed. (New York: A. C. Armstrong and Son, 1892), pp. 50–51.

5. Jaroslav Pelikan, *The Christian Tradition* (Chicago: University of Chicago Press, 1971), vol. 1, pp. 262–63.

6. Robert L. Ottley, *The Doctrine of the Incarnation* (London: Methuen, 1896), vol. 2, pp. 151–61.

7. Hugh Ross Mackintosh, *The Doctrine of the Person of Jesus Christ* (New York: Scribner, 1914), pp. 463–90.

The Doctrine of Dynamic Incarnation

A final attempt to resolve the problem of two natures in one person might be termed the doctrine of dynamic incarnation. This holds that the presence of God in the God-man was not in the form of a personal hypostatic union between the Second Person of the Trinity and an individual human being, Jesus of Nazareth. Rather, the incarnation should be thought of as the active presence of the power of God within the man Jesus.[8] Given this interpretation of the incarnation, the difference between Christ and us is only quantitative, not qualitative. But, it must be noted, this interpretation conflicts with several emphases of Scripture: the fullness of God dwelling in Jesus bodily (Col. 2:9); the preexistence of Christ (John 1:18; 8:58); and the uniqueness of his sonship (John 3:16).

Basic Tenets of the Doctrine of Two Natures in One Person

We have reviewed several attempts to resolve the difficult christological problem of two natures in one person. The classic statement of this doctrine, the standard for all of Christendom, was formulated at the Council of Chalcedon in 451. This statement speaks of

> one and the same Christ, Son, Lord, Only-begotten, to be acknowledged in two natures, *inconfusedly, unchangeably, indivisibly, inseparably;* the distinction of natures being by no means taken away by the union, but rather the property of each nature being preserved, and concurring in one Person (*prosōpon*) and one Subsistence (*hypostasis*), not parted or divided into two persons, but one and the same Son, and only begotten, God the Word, the Lord Jesus Christ, as the prophets from the beginning [have declared] concerning him, and the Lord Jesus Christ himself has taught us, and the Creed of the holy Fathers has handed down to us.[9]

8. For a recent form of this view see Donald Baillie, *God Was in Christ* (New York: Scribner, 1948).

9. Philip Schaff, *The Creeds of Christendom* (New York: Harper and Brothers, 1919), vol. 2, p. 62.

Both the unity of the person and the integrity and separateness of the two natures are insisted upon within this statement. But this only serves to heighten the tension. For what is the precise relationship between the two natures? How can both be maintained without splitting Jesus into two persons, each having a separate and unique set of attributes? And how can we maintain that Jesus is one person, with one center of consciousness, without fusing the two natures into a mixture or hybrid? The Chalcedonian conclusion, unfortunately, is essentially negative—"*inconfusedly, unchangeably, indivisibly, inseparably.*" It tells us what "two natures in one person" does not mean. In a sense, Chalcedon is not the answer; it is the question. We must ask further, What are the essential principles of the doctrine of the incarnation, and how are they to be understood? Several crucial points will help us understand this great mystery.

1. The incarnation was more a gaining of human attributes than a giving up of divine attributes. Philippians 2:6–7 is often conceived of as meaning that Jesus emptied himself of some of his divine attributes, perhaps even his deity itself. According to this interpretation, he became human by becoming something less than God. In our interpretation of Philippians 2:6–7, however, what Jesus emptied himself of was not the divine *morphē*, the nature of God. At no point does this passage say that he ceased to possess the divine nature. This becomes clearer when we take Colossians 2:9 into account: "For in him the whole fulness of deity dwells bodily." What does it mean, then, to say that Jesus "emptied himself"?

Some have suggested that Jesus emptied himself by pouring his divinity into his humanity, as one pours the contents of one cup into another. This, however, fails to identify the vessel from which Jesus poured out his divine nature when he emptied it into his humanity. A better approach to Philippians 2:6–7 is to think of the participial phrase "taking the form of a servant" as a circumstantial explanation of the kenosis. We would render the first part of verse 7, "he emptied himself by taking the form of a servant." The participial phrase is an explanation of how Jesus emptied himself, or what he did that constituted kenosis. While the text does not specify what he emptied himself of, it is noteworthy that "the form of a servant" contrasts sharply with "equality with God" (v. 6). We conclude that it is equality with God, not the form of God, of

sprinter, their time will be much slower than if they competed separately.

This is like the situation of the incarnate Christ. Just as the runner could unloose the tie, but chooses to restrict himself for the duration of the event, so Christ's incarnation was a voluntary, self-chosen limitation. He did not have to take on humanity, but he chose to do so for the period of the incarnation.

While Jesus did not cease to be in nature what the Father was, he became functionally subordinated to the Father for the period of the incarnation.

---

which Jesus emptied himself. While he did not cease to be in nature what the Father was, he became functionally subordinated to the Father for the period of the incarnation.

2. The union of the two natures meant that they did not function independently. Jesus did not exercise his deity at times and his humanity at other times. His actions were always those of divinity-humanity. This is the key to understanding the functional limitations which the humanity imposed upon the divinity. For example, he still had the power to be everywhere (omnipresence). However, as an incarnate being, he was limited in the exercise of that power by possession of a human body. This should not be considered a reduction of the power and capacities of the Second Person of the Trinity, but rather a circumstance-induced limitation on the exercise of his power and capacities.

Picture the following analogy. The world's fastest sprinter is entered in a three-legged race, where he must run with one of his legs tied to a leg of a partner. Although his physical capacity is not diminished, the conditions under which he exercises it are severely circumscribed. Even if his partner in the race is the world's second fastest

3. In thinking about the incarnation, we must begin not with the traditional conceptions of humanity and deity, but with the recognition that the two are most fully known in Jesus Christ. We sometimes approach the incarnation with an antecedent assumption that it is virtually impossible. We know what humanity is and what deity is, and they are, of course, by definition incompatible. They are, respectively, the finite and the infinite. But this is to begin in the wrong place. Our understanding of human nature has been formed by an inductive investigation of both ourselves and other humans as we find them about us. But none of us is humanity as God intended it to be, or as it came from his hand. Humanity was spoiled and corrupted by the sin of Adam and Eve. When we say that in the incarnation Jesus took on humanity, we are not talking about this kind of humanity. For the humanity of Jesus was not the humanity of sinful human beings, but the humanity possessed by Adam and Eve from their creation and before their fall. The question is not whether Jesus was fully human, but whether we are. He was not merely as human as we are; he was more human than we are. He was, spiritually, the type of humanity that we will possess when we are glorified. Jesus

most fully reveals the true nature of humanity.

Jesus Christ is also our best source for knowledge of deity. We assume that we know what God is really like. But it is in Jesus that God is most fully revealed and known. As John said, "No one has ever seen God; the only Son, who is in the bosom of the Father, he has made him known" (John 1:18). Thus, our picture of what deity is like comes primarily through the revelation of God in Jesus Christ.

In connection with the possibility of unity between deity and humanity, we need to bear in mind the distinctive picture of humanity given us in the Bible. As the image of God, humans are already the creatures most like him. It is quite possible that God's purpose in making humans in his own image was to facilitate the incarnation which would someday take place.

4. It is important to think of the initiative of the incarnation as coming from above, as it were, rather than from below. Part of our problem in understanding the incarnation lies in the fact that we are in effect asking ourselves how a human being could ever be God, as if it were a matter of a human being's becoming God or somehow adding deity to his humanity. For God to become human (or, more correctly, to add humanity to his deity), however, is not impossible. He is unlimited and therefore is able to condescend to the lesser whereas the lesser cannot ascend to the greater or higher. The fact that a human did not ascend to divinity, nor did God elevate a human to divinity but, rather, God condescended to take on humanity, facilitates our ability to conceive of the incarnation.

5. It is also helpful to think of Jesus as a very complex person. Of the people whom we know, some are relatively simple. Other persons, on the other hand, have much more complex personalities. They may have a wider range of experience, a more varied educational background, or a more complex emotional makeup. Now if we imagine complexity expanded to an infinite degree, then we have a bit of a glimpse into the "personality of Jesus" as it were, his two natures in one person. For Jesus' personality included the qualities and attributes which constitute deity. To be sure, there is a problem here, for these qualities differ from the human not merely in degree, but in kind. This point serves to remind us that the person of Jesus was not simply an amalgam of human and

Figure 3. The Six Basic Heresies Regarding the Person of Christ

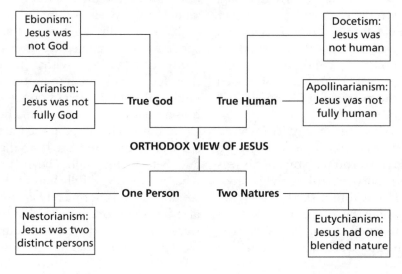

divine qualities merged into some sort of *tertium quid*. Rather, his was a personality that in addition to the characteristics of divine nature had all the qualities or attributes of perfect, sinless human nature as well.

We have noted several dimensions of biblical truth which will help us better understand the incarnation. Someone has said that there are only seven basic jokes, and every joke is merely a variation on one of them. A similar statement can be made about heresies regarding the person of Christ. There are basically six, and all of them appeared within the first four Christian centuries. As Figure 3 illustrates, they either deny the genuineness (Ebionism) or the completeness (Arianism) of Jesus' deity, deny the genuineness (Docetism) or the completeness (Apollinarianism) of his humanity, divide his person (Nestorianism), or confuse his natures (Eutychianism). Every departure from the orthodox doctrine of the person of Christ is simply a variation of one of these heresies. While we may have difficulty specifying exactly the content of this doctrine, full fidelity to the teaching of Scripture will carefully avoid each of these distortions.

Part Eight

The Work of Christ

26

Introduction to the Work of Christ

It has been important to make a thorough study of Christ's person, his deity and humanity, so that we might better understand what his unique nature enabled him to do for us. He always was, of course, the eternal Second Person of the Trinity. He became incarnate, however, because of the task that he had to accomplish—saving us from our sin. While some have argued that Jesus would have become incarnate whether humanity sinned or not, that seems rather unlikely.

We have been told in the biblical revelation who and what Jesus Christ is; we do not have to deduce his nature from the ministry that he performed. This gives us certain advantages. For without prior understanding of the person and nature of Jesus Christ, one cannot fully understand the work which he did. Who he was especially fitted him for what he was to do. With this knowledge we are in a much better position to understand Christ's work than if we had to interpret from our mere human perspective all that he has done.

The Stages of Christ's Work

As we survey Jesus' work, we find that it was done in two basic stages, which are traditionally referred to as the state of his humiliation and the state of exaltation. Each of these stages in turn consists of a number of steps. What we have are two steps down from his glory (incarnation and death), then a series of steps back up to his previous glory, and even something beyond that.

The Humiliation

Incarnation

The fact of Jesus' incarnation is sometimes stated in straightforward fashion, as in John 1:14 where the apostle says simply, "The Word became flesh." At other times there is emphasis upon either what Jesus left behind or what he took upon himself. An instance of the former is Philippians 2:6–7: Jesus Christ "did not count equality with God a thing to be grasped, but emptied himself, taking the form of a servant, being born in the likeness of man." An example of the latter is Galatians 4:4: "God sent forth his Son, born of woman, born under the law."

What Jesus gave up in coming to earth was immense. From a position of "equality with God," which entailed the immediate presence of the Father and the Holy Spirit as well as the continuous praise of the angels, he came to earth, where he had none of these. Even if Christ had come to the highest splendor that earth could afford, the descent would still have been immense. But it was not to the highest of human circumstances that he came. Rather, he took the form of a servant, a slave. He came into a very common family. He was born in the very obscure little town of Bethlehem. And even more striking, he was born in the very humble setting of a stable and laid in a manger.

He was born under the law. He who had originated the law, who was the Lord of it, became subject to the law, fulfilling all of it. It was as if an official, having enacted a statute which those under him had to follow, himself stepped down to a lower position where he too had to obey. Jesus' stepping down and becoming subject to the law were complete. Thus he was circumcised at the age of eight days, and at the proper time he was brought to the temple for the rite of the mother's purification (Luke 2:21–39). By becoming subject to the law, says Paul, Jesus was able to redeem those who are under the law (Gal. 4:5).

What of the attributes of deity during the period of the humiliation? We have already suggested (pp. 228–29) that the Second Person of the Trinity emptied himself of equality with God by adding or taking on humanity. In doing so, Jesus gave up the independent exercise of his divine attributes. This does not mean that he surrendered some (or all) of his divine attributes, but that he voluntarily gave up the ability to exercise them on his own. He could exercise them only in dependence upon the Father and in connection with possession of a fully human nature.[1] Both wills, the Father's and his, were necessary for him to utilize his divine attributes. A fair analogy is a safe-deposit box; two keys are necessary if it is to be opened—the bank's and the depositor's. In like manner, if Jesus was to exercise divine power, both wills had to agree upon an action for it to take place. There was, then, an immeasurable humiliation involved in assuming human nature. He could not freely and inde-

1. Augustus H. Strong, *Systematic Theology* (Westwood, N.J.: Revell, 1907), pp. 703–04.

pendently exercise all of the capabilities which he had when he was in heaven.

Death

The ultimate step downward in Jesus' humiliation was his death. He who was "the life" (John 14:6), the Creator, the giver of life and of the new life which constitutes victory over death, became subject to death. He who had committed no sin suffered death, which is the consequence or "wages" of sin. By becoming human, Jesus became subject to the possibility of death, that is, he became mortal; and death was not merely a possibility, but it became an actuality.

And what is more, Jesus suffered not only death, but a humiliating one at that! He experienced a type of execution reserved by the Roman Empire for grievous criminals. It was a slow, painful death, virtually death by torture. Add to this the ignominy of the circumstances. The mockery and taunting by the crowds, the abuse by the religious leaders and the Roman soldiers, compounded the humiliation. Death seemed to be the end of his mission; he had failed in his task. His voice was stilled, so that he could no longer preach and teach, and his body was lifeless, unable to heal, raise from the dead, and quiet the storms.

The Exaltation

Resurrection

The death of Jesus was the low point in his humiliation; the overcoming of death through the resurrection was the first step back in the process of his exaltation. The resurrection is particularly significant, for inflicting death was the worst thing that sin and the powers of sin could do to Christ. In the inability of death to hold him is symbolized the totality of his victory. What more can the forces of evil do if someone whom they have killed does not stay dead?

Because the resurrection is so important, it has occasioned a great deal of controversy. There were, of course, no human witnesses to the actual resurrection, since Jesus was alone in the tomb when it took place. We do find, however, two types of evidence.

First, the tomb in which Jesus had been laid was empty, and the body was never produced. Second, a great variety of persons testified that they had seen Jesus alive. The most natural explanation of these testimonies is that Jesus was indeed alive again. Moreover, there is no other (or, at least, better) way of accounting for the transformation of the disciples from frightened, defeated persons to militant preachers of the resurrection.[2]

One question that needs special attention is the nature of the resurrection body. There seems to be conflicting evidence on this matter. On the one hand, we are told that flesh and blood are not going to inherit the kingdom of God, and there are other indications that we will not have a body in heaven. On the other hand, Jesus ate after the resurrection, and apparently he was recognizable. Furthermore, the marks of the nails in his hands and the spear wound in his side suggest that he still had a material body (John 20:25–27). If we are to reconcile this seeming conflict, it is important to bear in mind that Jesus was at this point resurrected, but not ascended. At the time of our resurrection our bodies will be transformed in one step. In the case of Jesus, however, the two events, resurrection and ascension, were separated rather than collapsed into one. So the body that he had at the point of resurrection was yet to undergo a more complete transformation at the point of the ascension. It was yet to become the "spiritual body" of which Paul speaks in 1 Corinthians 15:44.

But even though Jesus' postresurrection body may have been more physical in nature than his postascension being, his resurrection, like the virgin birth, should not be thought of as essentially a biological matter or a physical fact. Rather, it was the triumph of Jesus over sin and death and all of the attendant ramifications. It was the fundamen-

2. Daniel Fuller, *Easter Faith and History* (Grand Rapids: Eerdmans, 1965), pp. 181–82; cf. Wolfhart Pannenberg, *Jesus—God and Man* (Philadelphia: Westminster, 1968), pp. 96–97.

tal step in his exaltation—he was freed from the curse brought on him by his voluntary bearing of the sin of the entire human race.

Ascension and Session at the Father's Right Hand

The first step in Jesus' humiliation involved giving up the status which he had in heaven and coming to the conditions of earth; the second step in the exaltation involved leaving the conditions of earth and reassuming his place with the Father. Jesus himself on several occasions foretold his return to the Father (John 6:62; 14:2, 12; 16:5, 10, 28; 20:17). Luke gives the most extended accounts of the actual ascension (Luke 24:50–51; Acts 1:6–11). Paul also writes regarding the ascension (Eph. 1:20; 4:8–10; 1 Tim. 3:16), as does the writer of the letter to the Hebrews (1:3; 4:14; 9:24).

In premodern times the ascension was usually thought of as a transition from one place (earth) to another (heaven). We now know, however, that space is such that heaven is not merely upward from the earth, and it also seems likely that the difference between earth and heaven is not merely geographical. One cannot get to God simply by traveling sufficiently far and fast in a rocket ship of some kind. God is in a different dimension of reality, and the transition from here to there requires not merely a change of place, but of state. Jesus' ascension, then, was not merely a physical and spatial change, but spiritual as well. At that time Jesus underwent the remainder of the metamorphosis begun with the resurrection of his body.

The significance of the ascension is that Jesus left behind the conditions associated with life on this earth. Thus the pain, both physical and psychological, of earth is no longer his. The opposition, hostility, unbelief, and unfaithfulness which he encountered have been replaced by the praise of the angels and the immediate presence of the Father. What a contrast to the abuse and insults he endured here!

There were definite reasons why Jesus had to leave the earth. One was in order to prepare a place for our future abode (John 14:2–3). Another reason he had to go is that the Holy Spirit, the Third Person of the Trinity, might come (John 16:7). The sending of the Holy Spirit was essential, for whereas Jesus could work with the disciples only through external teaching and example, the Holy Spirit could work within them (John 14:17). As a result, the believers would be able to do the works which Jesus did, and even greater ones (John 14:12). And through the ministry of the Holy Spirit, the Triune God would be present with them; thus Jesus could say that he would be with them forever (Matt. 28:20).

Jesus' ascension means that he is now seated at the right hand of the Father (see Matt. 26:64; Acts 2:33–36; 5:31; Eph. 1:20–22; Heb. 10:12; 1 Peter 3:22; and Rev. 3:21; 22:1). The right hand is the place of distinction and power. Recall how James and John desired to sit at Christ's right hand, and at his left as well (Mark 10:37–40). Jesus' sitting at the right hand of God should not be interpreted as signifying rest or inactivity. It is a symbol of authority and active rule. The right hand is also the place where Jesus is ever making intercession with the Father on our behalf (Heb. 7:25).

Second Coming

One dimension of the exaltation remains. Scripture indicates clearly that Christ will return at some point in the future; the exact time is unknown to us. Then his victory will be complete. He will be the conquering Lord, the judge over all. At that point his reign, which at present is in some ways only potential, and which many do not accept, will be total. He himself has said that his second coming will be in glory (Matt. 25:31). The one who came in lowliness, humility, and even humiliation, will return in complete exaltation. Then, indeed, every knee will bow and every tongue confess that Jesus Christ is Lord (Phil. 2:10–11).

The Functions of Christ

Historically, it has been customary to categorize the work of Christ in terms of three "offices": prophet, priest, and king. It is important to retain the truths that Jesus reveals God to humankind, reconciles God and us to one another, and rules and will rule over the whole of the creation, including human beings. These truths, if not the exact titles, must be maintained if we are to recognize the whole of what Christ accomplishes in his ministry. We have chosen to speak of the three *functions* of Christ—revealing, ruling, and reconciling. It is appropriate to think of these aspects of Christ's work as his commission, for Jesus was the Messiah, the anointed one.

The Revelatory Role of Christ

Many references to the ministry of Christ stress the revelation which he gave of the Father and of heavenly truth. And indeed, Jesus clearly understood himself to be a prophet in that he was sent from God. Yet there was a significant difference between him and them. He had come from the very presence of God. His preexistence with the Father was a major factor in his ability to reveal the Father, for he had been with him. So it is said by John, "No one has ever seen God; the only Son, who is in the bosom of the Father, he has made him known" (John 1:18).

The uniqueness of Jesus' prophetic ministry notwithstanding, there were a number of respects in which it was similar to the work of the Old Testament prophets. His message in many ways resembled theirs. There was declaration of doom and judgment, and there was proclamation of good news and salvation. In Matthew 23 Jesus pronounces judgments upon the scribes and Pharisees, calling them hypocrites, serpents, vipers. Certainly the prophetic message of condemnation of sin was prominent in his preaching. But Jesus also proclaimed good news.

As prophet, Jesus reveals the Father and heavenly truth; as king, Jesus rules over all of the universe; as priest, he makes our salvation possible.

prophet, for when his ministry in Nazareth was not received, he said, "A prophet is not without honor except in his own country and in his own house" (Matt. 13:57). That he was a prophet was recognized by those who heard him preach, at least by his followers. Moreover, at the time of his triumphal entry into Jerusalem the crowds said, "This is the prophet Jesus of Nazareth of Galilee" (Matt. 21:11).

That Jesus was a prophet was in itself a fulfilment of prophecy. Peter specifically identifies him with Moses' prediction in Deuteronomy 18:15: "The Lord God will raise up for you a prophet from your brethren as he raised me up" (Acts 3:22). Jesus' prophetic ministry was like that of the other Among the Old Testament prophets, Isaiah in particular had spoken of the good tidings from God (Isa. 40:9; 52:7). Similarly, in Matthew 13 Jesus describes the kingdom of heaven in terms which make it indeed good news: the kingdom of heaven is like a treasure hidden in a field (v. 44) and like a pearl of great price (v. 46).

Christ's revealing work covers a wide span of time and forms. He first functioned in a revelatory fashion even before his incarnation. As the Logos, he is the light which has enlightened everyone coming into the world; thus, in a sense all truth has come from and through him (John 1:9). A second and most obvious period of Jesus' revelatory work was, of course, his prophetic ministry during his incarnation and stay upon earth. Here two forms of revelation come together. He spoke the divine word of truth. Beyond that, however, he was the truth and he was God, and so what he did was a showing forth, not merely a telling, of the truth and of the reality of God. There is, third, the continuing revelatory ministry of Christ through his church.[3] He promised them his presence in the ongoing task (Matt. 28:20). He made clear that in many ways his ministry would be continued and completed by the Holy Spirit. The Spirit would be sent in Jesus' name, and would teach his followers all things and bring to remembrance all that he had said to them (John 14:26). In a very real sense, then, Jesus was to continue his revelatory work through the Holy Spirit. Perhaps this is why Luke makes the somewhat puzzling statement that his first book pertained to all that Jesus "began to do and teach" (Acts 1:1). We conclude that when the apostles proclaimed the truth, Jesus was continuing his work of revelation through them.

The final and most complete revelatory work of Jesus lies in the future. There is a time coming when he will return; one of the words for the second coming of Christ is "revelation" (*apokalypsis*).[4] At that time we will see clearly and directly (1 Cor. 13:12). When he appears, we shall see him as he is (1 John 3:2). Then all barriers to a full knowledge of God and of the truths of which Christ spoke will be removed.

The Rule of Christ

The Gospels picture Jesus as a king, the ruler over all of the universe. Isaiah had anticipated a future ruler who would sit upon David's throne (Isa. 9:7). The writer to the Hebrews applies Psalm 45:6–7 to the Son of God: "Thy throne, O God, is for ever and ever, the righteous scepter is the scepter of thy kingdom" (Heb. 1:8). Jesus himself said

that in the new world the Son of man would sit on a glorious throne (Matt. 19:28). He claimed that the kingdom of heaven was his (Matt. 13:41).

There is a tendency to think of Jesus' rule as being almost exclusively in the future. For as we look about us at the present time, it seems that his rule is not being very actively enforced. Yet we need to note that, on the contrary, there is abundant evidence that Christ is ruling today. In particular, the natural universe obeys him. Since Christ is the one through whom all things came into being (John 1:3) and through whom all things continue (Col. 1:17), he is in control of the natural universe. But is there evidence of a reign of Christ over modern-day humans? Indeed there is. The kingdom of God, over which Christ reigns, is present in the church. He is the head of the body, the church (Col. 1:18). When he was on earth, his kingdom was present in the hearts of his disciples. And wherever believers today are following the lordship of Christ, the Savior is exercising his ruling or kingly function.

In light of the foregoing, we can see that the rule of Jesus Christ is not a matter merely of his final exaltation, as some have thought to be the case. It is, however, in connection with the final step in his exaltation, when he returns in power, that his rule will be complete. The hymn in Philippians 2 emphasizes that Christ has been given a "name which is above every name, that at the name of Jesus every knee should bow, in heaven and on earth and under the earth, and every tongue confess that Jesus Christ is Lord, to the glory of God the Father" (vv. 9–10). There is a time coming when the reign of Christ will be complete; then all will be under his rule, whether willingly and eagerly, or unwillingly and reluctantly.

The Reconciling Work of Christ: Intercession and Atonement

One aspect of Christ's work as reconciler is his intercessory ministry. The Bible records numerous instances of Jesus' interceding for his disciples while he was here upon the

---

3. Charles Hodge, *Systematic Theology* (Grand Rapids: Eerdmans, 1952), vol. 2, p. 463.
4. See George E. Ladd, *The Blessed Hope* (Grand Rapids: Eerdmans, 1956), pp. 65–67.

earth. The most extended is his high-priestly prayer for the group (John 17). Here Jesus prayed that they might have his joy fulfilled in themselves (v. 13). He did not pray that they be taken out of the world, but that they be kept from the evil one (v. 15). He also prayed that they might all be one (v. 21). In addition this last prayer was for those who would believe through the word of the disciples (v. 20).

What Jesus did for his followers while he was on earth, he continues to do for all believers during his heavenly presence with the Father. In Romans 8:33–34 Paul raises the question of who might be condemning us or bringing a charge against us. Surely it cannot be Christ, for he is at the right hand of God, interceding for us. In Hebrews 7:25 we are told that he ever lives to make intercession for those who draw near to God through him, and in 9:24 we are told that he appears in the presence of God on our behalf.

What is the focus of this intercession? On the one hand, Jesus presents his righteousness to the Father for our justification. He also pleads the cause of his righteousness for believers who, while previously justified, continue to sin. And finally, it appears, particularly from the instances during his earthly ministry, that Christ beseeches the Father that believers might be sanctified and kept from the power of the evil tempter.

There is another, even more fundamental aspect of Christ's reconciling work, the aspect upon which his intercession is based. It is in the atonement that we come to the crucial point of Christian faith. The doctrine of the atonement is most critical for us, because it is the point of transition, as it were, from the objective to the subjective aspects of Christian theology. Here we shift our focus from the nature of Christ to his active work in our behalf; here systematic theology has direct application to our lives. The atonement has made our salvation possible. It is also the foundation of major doctrines which await our study: the doctrine of the church deals with the collective aspects of

salvation, the doctrine of the last things with its future aspects.

Our doctrines of God and of Christ will color our understanding of the atonement. For if God is a very holy, righteous, and demanding being, then humans will not be able to satisfy him easily, and it is quite likely that something will have to be done in their behalf to satisfy him. If, on the other hand, God is an indulgent, permissive Father who says, "We have to allow humans to have a little fun sometimes," then it may be sufficient simply for him to give us a little encouragement and instruction. If Christ was merely human, then the work that he did serves only as an example; he was not able to offer anything in our behalf beyond his perfect example of doing everything he was required to do, including dying on the cross. If, however, he is God, his work for us went immeasurably beyond what we are able to do for ourselves; he served not only as an example but as a sacrifice for us. The doctrine of humanity, broadly defined to include the doctrine of sin, also affects the picture. If human beings are basically spiritually intact, they probably can, with a bit of effort, fulfil what God wants of them. Thus, instruction, inspiration, and motivation constitute what humans need and hence the essence of the atonement. If, however, they are totally depraved and consequently unable to do what is right no matter how much they wish to or how hard they try, then a more radical work had to be done in their behalf.

The Manifold Theories of the Atonement

The meaning and impact of the atonement are rich and complex. Consequently, various theories of the atonement have arisen. Given the abundance of biblical testimony to the fact of atonement, different theologians choose to emphasize different texts. Their choice of texts reflects their views on other areas of doctrine. We will examine several of the theories, thus gaining an appreciation for the complexity of the meaning of the atonement. At the same time we will come to see the incompleteness and inadequacy of each one of them by itself.

The Socinian Theory: The Atonement as Example

Faustus and Laelius Socinus, who lived in the sixteenth century, developed a teaching which is best represented today by the Unitarians. They rejected any idea of vicarious satisfaction.[5] The Socinians pointed instead to 1 Peter 2:21: "For to this you have been called, because Christ also suffered for you, leaving you an example, that you should follow in his steps." From the Socinian perspective the death of Jesus fills two human needs. First, it fills the need for an example of that total love for God which we must display if we are to experience salvation. Second, the death of Jesus gives us inspiration. The ideal of total love for God is so lofty as to seem virtually unattainable. The death of Jesus is proof that such love does lie within the sphere of human accomplishment. What he could do, we can also!

The Socinian view, however, must come to grips with the fact that numerous portions of Scripture dealing with Jesus' death speak of ransom, sacrifice, priesthood, sin bearing, and the like. Note, in fact, the statement which follows just three verses after the favorite text of the Socinians (1 Peter 2:21): "He himself bore our sins in his body on the tree, that we might die to sin and live to righteousness. By his wounds you have been healed" (v. 24). How is such a statement to be understood? The usual reply of the Socinians and others of their conviction is that atonement is only a metaphorical concept.[6] All that is necessary for us to be restored to the intended relationship with God is personal adoption of both the teachings of Jesus and the example he set in life and especially in death.

The Moral-Influence Theory: The Atonement as a Demonstration of God's Love

The moral-influence theory sees Christ's death as a demonstration of God's love. First developed by Peter Abelard, this theory did not receive much support until it was popularized by Horace Bushnell (1802–1876) in the United States, and by Hastings Rashdall in Great Britain. In their view, God's nature is essentially love. They minimize such qualities as justice, holiness, and righteousness. Accordingly, they conclude that we need not fear God's justice and punishment. Thus, our basic problem is not that we have violated God's law and God will (indeed, must) punish us. Rather, our problem is that our own attitudes keep us apart from God.

This separation and alienation from God may take many different forms. We may not realize that our disobedience is a source of pain to God. Or we may not realize that despite all that has transpired, God still loves us. We may fear God, or we may blame him for the problems in our relationship with him, or even for the problems of the world in general. If we were to repent and turn to God in trust and faith, however, there would be reconciliation, for the difficulty does not lie with God's ability to forgive. The difficulty lies in us.[7] Bushnell regards sin as *a type of sickness from which we must be healed*. It is to correct this defect in us that Christ came. His dying demonstrates the full extent of God's love for us. Awareness of such love serves to heal our ignorance and fear of God.

The Governmental Theory: The Atonement as a Demonstration of Divine Justice

The preceding views of the atonement have pictured God as basically a sympathetic, indulgent being. They hold that in order to be restored to God's favor, it is necessary only to do one's best or to respond to God's love. According to the governmental

---

5. Faustus Socinus *De Jesu Christo servatore* 1.1.
6. Ibid., 1.3.

7. Hastings Rashdall, *The Idea of Atonement in Christian Theology* (London: Macmillan, 1920), p. 26.

theory, however, the law of God is a serious matter, and violation or disregard of it is not to be taken lightly.

The major proponent of the governmental view was Hugo Grotius (1583–1645), by training a lawyer rather than a clergyman. Grotius understood God as a very holy and righteous being who has established certain laws. Sin is a violation of those laws. God as ruler has the right to punish sin, for sin is inherently deserving of punishment.[8] The actions of God must be understood, however, in light of his dominant attribute, namely, love.

According to Grotius, although God has the right to punish sin, it is not necessary or mandatory that he do so. It is possible for God to relax the law so that he need not exact a specific punishment or penalty for each violation. He has, however, acted in such a way as to maintain the interests of government. It is important to understand that the role of God here is as a ruler rather than as a creditor or a master. A creditor may cancel a debt if he so chooses. A master may punish or not punish, according to his will. A ruler, however, may not simply ignore or overlook violations of the rules. God must, rather, act with a view to the best interests of those under his authority.[9] It was necessary, therefore, to have an atonement which would provide grounds for forgiveness and simultaneously retain the structure of moral government. Christ's death served to accomplish both ends.

In Grotius's view, Christ's death was not a penalty inflicted on him as a substitute for the penalty which should have attached to the sins of humanity. Rather, Grotius saw the death of Christ as a substitute for a penalty.[10] What God did through Christ's death was to demonstrate what God's justice will require us to suffer if we continue in sin. The spectacle of the sufferings Christ bore is enough to deter us from sin. And if we turn from sin, we can be forgiven and God's moral government preserved. Because of Christ's death, then, it is possible for God to forgive sins without a breakdown of the moral fiber of the universe.

One of the things that strike us as we examine the governmental theory is its lack of explicit scriptural basis. Rather, we see the lawyer's mind at work, focusing on general principles of Scripture and drawing certain inferences from them. The one verse that is cited as a direct support of the theory that the death of Christ was demanded by God's concern to preserve his moral government and law as he forgives sin is Isaiah 42:21: "The LORD was pleased, for his righteousness' sake, to magnify his law and make it glorious." But this verse does not deal with the idea of atonement in itself. Thus, whereas other theories take an explicit biblical statement concerning the nature of the atonement and emphasize it more than others, the governmental theory works inferentially from some of the general teachings and principles of Scripture.

The Ransom Theory: The Atonement as Victory over the Forces of Sin and Evil

The theory with the greatest claim to having been the standard view in the early history of the church is probably the so-called ransom theory. Gustaf Aulen has called it the classic view,[11] and in many ways that designation is correct, for in various forms it dominated the church's thinking until the time of Anselm and Abelard. It was even the primary way in which Augustine understood the atonement, and thus it enjoyed the immense prestige that his name accorded.

The major early developer of the ransom theory was Origen. Origen saw biblical history as the depiction of a great cosmic drama. In the cosmic struggle between the forces of good and evil, Satan established

8. Hugo Grotius *Defensio fidei catholicae de satisfactione Christi adversus Faustum Socinum* 5.
9. Ibid., 2–3.
10. Ibid., 5.

11. Gustaf Aulen, *Christus Victor: An Historical Study of the Three Main Types of the Idea of the Atonement,* trans. A. G. Hebert (New York: Macmillan, 1931), p. 20.

control over humankind. Satan now is the governing power in the world. As world ruler, his rights cannot simply be set aside, for God will not stoop to using techniques employed by the devil; God will not "steal" humanity back, as it were. The text on which Origen and others who hold the ransom theory rely most heavily is Jesus' statement that he had come to offer his life as a ransom for many (Matt. 20:28; Mark 10:45). To whom was this ransom paid? Certainly not to God. He would not pay a ransom to himself. Rather, it must have been paid to the evil one, for it was he who held us captive until the ransom, namely, the soul of Jesus, was paid.[12] According to Origen, Satan thought that he could be the lord of the soul of Jesus; Jesus' resurrection proved otherwise. Origen also suggests that the devil did not perceive that humankind, partially freed by Christ's teachings and miracles, would be completely delivered by his death and resurrection. So Satan released humanity, only to find that he could not hold Christ, whom he had accepted in exchange for humankind.[13]

However, Scripture does not teach that it was the payment of a ransom to Satan that ensured his defeat and the triumph of God, but Christ's taking our place to free us from the curse of the law (Rom. 6:6–8; Gal. 3:13). By bearing the penalty of our sin and thus satisfying once and for all the just requirements of the law, Christ nullified Satan's control over us at its root—the power to bring us under the curse and condemnation of the law. Christ's death, then, was indeed God's triumph over the forces of evil, but only because it was a substitutionary sacrifice.

The Satisfaction Theory: The Atonement as Compensation to the Father

Of all of the theories that we are examining in this chapter, the one that most clearly regards the major effect of Christ's death as objective is usually termed the commercial or satisfaction theory. It emphasizes that Christ died to satisfy a principle in the very nature of God the Father. Thus the atonement did not involve any sort of payment to Satan.

Anselm deals with the atonement in his major work, *Cur Deus homo?* (*Why God Human?*). The title indicates the basic direction of the treatise. Anselm attempts to discover why God became human in the first place. Anselm's understanding of the atonement (and the incarnation) builds fundamentally upon his doctrine of sin. Sin is basically failure to render God his due, taking from God what is rightfully his and dishonoring him. We sinners must restore to God what we have taken from him. But it is

> *Christ died to satisfy a principle in the very nature of God the Father.*

not sufficient merely to restore to God what we have taken away. For in taking from God what is his, we have injured him; and even after what we have taken has been returned, there must be some additional compensation or reparation for the injury that has been done.[14] A good comparison is modern judicial rulings which stipulate that a thief, in addition to restoring his victim's property, must pay punitive damages or serve a prison sentence.

God's violated honor can be put right again either by his punishing us humans (condemning us) or by accepting satisfaction made in our behalf.[15] How was this satisfaction to be accomplished? We could not possibly have rendered satisfaction in our own behalf, for even if we were to do our best, that would be nothing more than giv-

---

12. Origen, *Commentary on Matthew* 13:28.
13. Ibid.

14. Anselm *Cur Deus homo?* 1.11.
15. Ibid., 1.13.

ing God his due. To be effective, the satisfaction rendered had to be greater than what all created beings are capable of doing, since they can do only what is already required of them. So only God could make satisfaction. However, if it was to avail for us humans in relationship to God, it had to be made by a human being. Therefore, the satisfaction had to be rendered by someone who is both God and human. Consequently, the incarnation is a logical necessity.[16]

Christ, being both God and sinless human, did not deserve death. Therefore, his offering his life to God in behalf of the human race of which he was a part went beyond what was required of him. Thus, it could serve as a genuine satisfaction to God for human sins. Was the payment enough? Yes, it was. For the death of the God-man himself, inasmuch as he, being God, had power over his own life (John 10:18) and did not have to die, has infinite value. Indeed, for his body to have suffered even the slightest harm would have been a matter of infinite value.[17]

16. Ibid., 2.8.
17. Ibid., 2.10.

We have seen that Christ's death is interpreted in a wide variety of ways. Each of the theories we have examined seizes upon a significant aspect of his work. While we may have major objections to some of the theories, we recognize that each one possesses a dimension of the truth. In his death Christ (1) gave us a perfect example of the type of dedication God desires of us, (2) demonstrated the great extent of God's love, (3) underscored the seriousness of sin and the severity of God's righteousness, (4) triumphed over the forces of sin and death, liberating us from their power, and (5) rendered satisfaction to the Father for our sins. All of these things we as humans needed done for us, and Christ did them all. Now we must ask, Which of these is the most basic? Which one makes the others possible? We will turn to that question in the next chapter. As we do so, it will be with a profound appreciation for the full measure of what Christ did to bring us into fellowship with the Father.

27 The Central Theme of Atonement

In examining the several theories of the atonement in the preceding chapter, we noted that each seizes upon a significant aspect of Christ's atoning work. We must now ask which of those aspects is the primary or most basic dimension of that work, the one to which the others adhere, or upon which they depend.

Background Factors

Our views on other doctrines necessarily have a strong influence on our conclusions regarding the atonement. So we begin by reviewing the background against which we will construct our understanding of that doctrine.

The Nature of God

Just as biblical passages appear in contexts, so also do doctrines. In every matter for theological study, the broadest context is, of course, the doctrine of God. This is particularly the case when we are dealing with matters involving a relationship in which one of the parties is God. Now the nature of God is perfect and complete holiness. This is not optional or arbitrary; it is the way God is by nature. Nothing more need or can be said. It is useless to ask, "Why is God this way?" He simply is so. Being contrary to God's nature, sin is repulsive to him. He is allergic to sin, so to speak. He is compelled to turn away from it.

Status of the Law

The second major factor to be considered as we construct our theory of the atonement is the status of God's moral and spiritual law. The law should be seen as the expression of God's person and will. He does not command love and forbid murder simply because he decides to do so. His very nature

obeyed for its own sake—is unacceptable. Rather, the law is to be understood as a means of relating to a personal God.

A further point to be borne in mind is that violation of the law, whether by transgressing or by failing to fulfil it, carries the serious consequences of liability to punishment, and especially death. Adam and Eve were told that in the day that they ate of the fruit of the tree they would surely die (Gen. 2:15–17). According to Paul, "the wages of sin is death" (Rom. 6:23), and "he who sows to his own flesh will from the flesh reap corruption" (Gal. 6:8). There is a definite link between sin and liability to punishment. Particularly in the last of the citations (Gal. 6:7–8) a virtual cause-effect connection between sin and punishment is in evidence. In each case, however, it is understood that punishment is an inevitability rather than a possibility.

The Human Condition

Another crucial factor in our understanding of the atonement is the nature and condition of humanity. We noted earlier (pp. 197–98) the fact of total depravity, by which we meant not that humans are as wicked as they can possibly be, but rather that they are utterly unable to do anything to save them-

---

Jesus' humanity means that his atoning death is applicable to human beings; his deity means that his death can serve to atone for the sins of all humankind.

---

issues in his enjoining certain actions and prohibiting others. God pronounces love good because he himself is love. Lying is wrong because God himself cannot lie.

This means that, in effect, the law is something of a transcript of the nature of God. So then, disobeying the law is serious, not because the law has some inherent value or dignity which must be preserved, but because disobeying it is actually an attack upon the very nature of God himself. Thus, legalism—the attitude that the law is to be

selves or to extricate themselves from their condition of sinfulness. Since this is true, it follows that the atonement, to accomplish for us what needed to be done, had to be made by someone else on our behalf.

Christ

Our understanding of Christ's nature is crucial here. We earlier stated that Christ is both God and a human being (chs. 23–25). Jesus' humanity means that his atoning death is applicable to human beings. He was not an outsider attempting to do something for us. He was a genuine human being representing the rest of us. What he took upon himself he could redeem. This is implied in what Paul says in Galatians 4:4–5: "God sent forth his Son . . . born under the law, to redeem those who were under the law." His death is of sufficient value to atone for the entire human race. Of course, the death of an ordinary human could scarcely have sufficient value to cover his own sins, let alone those of the whole race. But Jesus' death is of infinite worth. As God, Jesus did not have to die. Because he was sinless, he did not have to die in payment for his own sins. Inasmuch as he is an infinite being who did not have to die, his death can serve to atone for the sins of all of humankind.

The Old Testament Sacrificial System

The atoning death of Christ must also be seen against the background of the Old Testament sacrificial system. Before Christ's atoning death it was necessary for sacrifices to be regularly offered to compensate for the sins which had been committed. These sacrifices were necessary, not to work a reformation in the sinner, nor to deter the sinner or others from committing further sin, but to atone for the sin, which was inherently deserving of punishment. There had been offense against God's law and hence against God himself, and this had to be set right.

The Hebrew word most commonly used in the Old Testament for the various types of atonement is *kāphar* and its derivatives. The word literally means "to cover."[1] Sinners were delivered from punishment by the interposing of something between their sin and God. God then saw the atoning sacrifice rather than the sin. The covering of the sin meant that the penalty no longer had to be exacted from the sinner.[2] Several factors

were necessary for the sacrifice to accomplish this intended effect. The sacrificial animal had to be spotless, without blemish. The one for whom atonement was being made had to present the animal and lay hands upon it (Lev. 1:3–4). The laying on of hands symbolized a transfer of the guilt from the sinner to the victim.[3] Then the offering or sacrifice was accepted by the priest.

While the legal portions of the Old Testament typify with considerable clarity the sacrificial and substitutionary character of Christ's death, the prophetic passages go even further. They establish the connection between the Old Testament sacrifices and Christ's death. Isaiah 53 is the clearest of all. Having described the person of the Messiah and indicated the nature and extent of the iniquity of sinners, the prophet makes an allusion to Christ's sacrifice: "All we like sheep have gone astray; we have turned every one to his own way; and the LORD has laid on him the iniquity of us all" (v. 6). The iniquity of sinners is to be transferred to the Suffering Servant, just as in the Old Testament rites the sins were transferred to the sacrificial animal. The laying on of hands was an anticipation of the believer's active acceptance of Christ's atoning work.

The New Testament Teaching

The Gospels

The New Testament is much more detailed on the subject of Christ's atonement. We will look first at our Lord's own testimony regarding the nature and purpose of his death. Although Jesus did not have a great deal to say about his death during the first part of his ministry, toward the end he began to speak about it quite explicitly.

Jesus had a profound sense that the Father had sent him, and that he had to do the Father's work. He declares in John 10:36 that the Father had sent him into the world.

1. Francis Brown, S. R. Driver, and Charles A. Briggs, *Hebrew and English Lexicon of the Old Testament* (New York: Oxford University Press, 1955), pp. 497–98.

2. R. Laird Harris, כָּפַר, in *Theological Wordbook of the Old Testament*, ed. R. Laird Harris (Chicago: Moody, 1980), vol. 1, pp. 452–53.

3. Gustave F. Oehler, *Theology of the Old Testament* (Grand Rapids: Zondervan, 1950), p. 274.

The apostle John expressly relates the sending by the Father to the Son's redemptive and atoning work: "For God sent the Son into the world, not to condemn the world, but that the world might be saved through him" (John 3:17). The purpose of the coming was atonement, and the Father was personally involved in that work, for the penalty fell on his own Son, whom he had voluntarily sent.

Jesus had a powerful conviction that his life and death constituted a fulfilment of Old Testament prophecies. In particular, he interpreted his own life and death as a clear fulfilment of Isaiah 53. At the Last Supper he said, "For I tell you that this scripture must be fulfilled in me, 'And he was reckoned with transgressors'; for what is written about me has its fulfilment" (Luke 22:37). He was citing Isaiah 53:12, thus identifying himself as the Suffering Servant. His frequent references to his suffering make it clear that he saw his death as the primary reason for his having come. For example, he plainly told his disciples that the Son of man must suffer many things, be rejected by the religious authorities, and be killed (Mark 8:31).

Jesus saw his death as constituting a *ransom*. Without specifying to whom the ransom was to be paid, or from whose control the enslaved were to be freed, Jesus indicated that his giving of his life was to be the means by which many would be freed from bondage (Matt. 20:28; Mark 10:45).

Christ also saw himself as our *substitute*. This concept is particularly prominent in the Gospel of John. Jesus said, "Greater love has no man than this, that a man lay down his life for his friends" (John 15:13). He was, of course, stating a principle of broad application. But inasmuch as he was speaking on the eve of his crucifixion, there can be little doubt of what was on his mind. Also pertinent here is Caiaphas's sneering remark to the Sanhedrin: "You know nothing at all; you do not understand that it is expedient for you that one man should die for the people, and that the whole nation should not perish" (John 11:49–50). The point of inter-

est is not the attitude of Caiaphas, but the deep truth which Caiaphas had unknowingly spoken. Jesus would die not merely in the place of the nation, but of the entire world. It is noteworthy that John calls attention to this remark of Caiaphas a second time (18:14).

There are also indications that Jesus saw himself in the role of a *sacrifice*. He said in his great high-priestly prayer, "And for their sake I consecrate myself, that they also may be consecrated in truth" (John 17:19). The verb here is common in sacrificial contexts. The statement of John the Baptist at the beginning of Jesus' ministry carries similar connotations—"Behold, the Lamb of God, who takes away the sin of the world!" (John 1:29).

Jesus had a profound sense that he was the source and giver of true life. He says in John 17:3, "And this is eternal life, that they know thee the only true God, and Jesus Christ whom thou hast sent." The giving of eternal life is here linked to both the Father and the Son. We can receive this life through an especially close relationship to the Son, which he also symbolically referred to as eating his flesh (John 6:52–58).

To sum up what Jesus and the Gospel writers said about his death: Jesus saw a close identification between himself and his Father. He spoke regularly of the Father's having sent him. He and the Father are one, and so the work that the Son did was also the work of the Father. Jesus came for the purpose of giving his life as a *ransom*, a means of liberating those people who were enslaved to sin. He offered himself as a *substitute* for them. Paradoxically, his death gives life; we obtain it by taking him into ourselves. His death was a *sacrifice* typified by the Old Testament sacrificial system. These various motifs are vital elements in our construction of the doctrine of the atonement.

The Pauline Writings

When we turn to the writings of Paul, we find a rich collection of teaching on the atonement, teaching which conforms with what the Gospels say on the subject. Paul also identifies and equates Jesus' love and working with the love and working of the Father. Among the numerous texts which can be cited are "God was in Christ reconciling the world to himself" (2 Cor. 5:19), and "God shows his love for us in that while we were yet sinners Christ died for us" (Rom. 5:8). Thus, like the Gospel writers and Jesus himself, Paul does not view the atonement as something Jesus did independently of the Father; it is the work of both. Furthermore, what Paul says of the Father's love, he also says of the Son's: "For the love of Christ controls us, because we are convinced that one has died for all; therefore all have died" (2 Cor. 5:14; see also Eph. 5:2). The love of the Father and that of the Son are interchangeable. George Ladd comments: "The idea that the cross expresses the love of Christ for us while he wrings atonement from a stern and unwilling Father, perfectly just, but perfectly inflexible, is a perversion of New Testament theology."[4]

Having said this, however, we must note that the theme of divine wrath upon sin is also prominent in Paul. It is important to realize, for example, that Romans 3:21–26, which is a passage about the redemption which God has provided in Jesus Christ, is the culmination of a process of reasoning which began with the pronouncement of God's wrath against sin: "For the wrath of God is revealed from heaven against all ungodliness and wickedness of men" (Rom. 1:18). The holiness of God requires that there be atonement if the condemned condition of sinners is to be overcome. The love of God provides that atonement.

Paul frequently thought of and referred to the death of Christ as a sacrifice. In 1 Corinthians 5:7 he writes, "For Christ, our paschal lamb, has been sacrificed." His numerous references to Christ's blood are also suggestive of a sacrifice: "we are now justified by his blood" (Rom. 5:9); "in him we have redemption through his blood" (Eph. 1:7); he has reconciled to himself all things, "making peace by the blood of his cross" (Col. 1:20). Ladd has pointed out, however, that there was very little actual shedding of Christ's blood as such.[5] While there was a loss of blood when the crown of thorns was put on his head and when the nails were driven into his flesh, it was not until after he had died that blood (mixed with water) gushed forth (John 19:34). So the references to Christ's blood are not to his actual physical blood per se, but to his death as a sacrificial provision for our sins.

The apostle Paul also maintains that Christ died for us or in our behalf. God "did not spare his own Son but gave him up for us all" (Rom. 8:32); "Christ loved us and gave himself up for us" (Eph. 5:2); he became a "curse for us" (Gal. 3:13; see also Rom. 5:8; 1 Thess. 5:10).

Finally, Paul regards the death of Christ as propitiatory, that is, Christ died to appease God's wrath against sin. This point has been questioned, especially by C. H. Dodd in his book *The Bible and the Greeks*. Dodd bases his argument upon the way in which the verb *hilaskomai* and its cognates are used in the Septuagint. He contends that it is not propitiation but expiation that is in view in verses like Romans 3:25.[6] God was not appeased by the death of Christ. Rather, what Christ accomplished in dying was to cleanse sinners of their sin, to cover their sin and uncleanness.

It appears questionable, however, whether Dodd's conclusions, influential though they have been, are accurate.[7] His conclusions may well have resulted from an inaccurate conception that the wrath of the Father and the love of the Son constitute an irresolvable contradiction within the Trinity. This mis-

---

4. George E. Ladd, *A Theology of the New Testament* (Grand Rapids: Eerdmans, 1974), p. 424.

5. Ibid., p. 425.
6. C. H. Dodd, *The Bible and the Greeks* (London: Hodder and Stoughton, 1935), p. 94.
7. See Ladd, *Theology*, pp. 429–30. For a more extensive refutation of Dodd's view see Roger Nicole, "C. H. Dodd and the Doctrine of Propitiation," *Westminster Theological Journal* 17 (1955): 117–57.

conception betrays itself in Dodd's failure to take very seriously the evidence in such passages as Zechariah 7:2; 8:22; and Malachi 1:9, where a cognate of the verb *hilaskomai* refers to propitiation or appeasing God.

In contradiction to Dodd, we note also that there are passages in Paul's writings which cannot be satisfactorily interpreted if we deny that God's wrath needed to be appeased. This is particularly true of Romans 3:25–26. In the past, God had left sins unpunished. He could conceivably be accused of overlooking sin since he had not required punishment for it. Now, however, he has put forth Jesus as a "propitiation" (KJV; the Greek word is *hilastērion*). This proves both that God is just (his wrath required the sacrifice) and that he is the justifier of those who have faith in Jesus (his love provided the sacrifice for them).

The numerous passages that speak of the wrath of God against sin are evidence that Christ's death was necessarily propitiatory. We read of the wrath of God against sin in Romans 1:18; 2:5, 8; 4:15; 5:9; 9:22; 12:19; 13:4–5; Ephesians 2:3; 5:6; Colossians 3:6; and 1 Thessalonians 1:10; 2:16; 5:9. So then, Paul's idea of the atoning death (Christ as *hilastērion*) is not simply that it covers sin and cleanses from its corruption (expiation), but that the sacrifice also appeases a God who hates sin and is radically opposed to it (propitiation).

The Basic Meaning of Atonement

Having reviewed the Bible's direct teaching on the subject of the atonement, we need now to concentrate on its basic motifs.

Sacrifice

We have already noted several references to the death of Christ as a sacrifice. We will now supplement our understanding of this concept by noting particularly what the Book of Hebrews says on the subject. In Hebrews 9:6–15 the work of Christ is likened to the Old Testament Day of Atonement. Christ is depicted as the high priest who entered into the Holy Place to offer sacrifice. But the sacrifice which Christ offered was not the blood of goats and calves, but his own blood (v. 12). Thus he secured "an eternal redemption." A vivid contrast is drawn between the sacrifice of animals, which had only a limited effect, and of Christ, whose death has eternal effect. Whereas the Mosaic sacrifices had to be offered repeatedly, Christ's death is a once-for-all atonement for the sins of all humankind (v. 28).

A similar thought is expressed in Hebrews 10:5–18. Here again the idea is that instead of burnt offerings, the body of Christ was sacrificed (v. 5). This was a once-for-all offering (v. 10). Instead of the daily offering by the priest (v. 11), Christ "offered for all time a single sacrifice for sins" (v. 12). In chapter 13, the writer likens the death of Christ to the sin offering of the Old Testament. He died in order to sanctify the people through his blood. We are therefore exhorted to go to him outside the camp, and bear the abuse he endured (vv. 10–13).

What is unique about Christ's sacrifice, and very important to keep in mind, is that Christ is both the victim and the priest who offers it. What were two parties in the Levitical system are combined in Christ. The mediation which Christ began with his death continues even now in the form of his priestly intercession for us.

Propitiation

In our discussion of the Pauline material on the atonement, we noted the controversy over whether Christ's death was propitiatory. Here we must note that the concept of propitiation is not limited to Paul's writings. In the Old Testament sacrificial system, the offering was made before the Lord and there it took effect as well: "The priest shall burn it on the altar, upon the offerings by fire to the LORD; and the priest shall make atonement for [the sinner] for the sin which he has committed, and he shall be forgiven" (Lev. 4:35). Can there be any doubt, especially in view of God's anger against sin, that this verse points to an appeasement of God?

How else can we interpret the statement that the offering should be made to the Lord and forgiveness would follow?

Substitution

We observed that Christ died for our sake or in our behalf. But is it proper to speak of his death as substitutionary, that is, did he actually die in our place?

Several considerations indicate that Christ did indeed take our place. First there is a whole set of passages which tell us that our sins were "laid upon" Christ, he "bore" our iniquity, he "was made sin" for us. One prominent instance is in Isaiah 53: "All we like sheep have gone astray; we have turned every one to his own way; and the LORD has laid on him the iniquity of us all" (v. 6); he "was numbered with the transgressors; yet he bore the sin of many, and made intercession for the transgressors" (v. 12b). On seeing Jesus, John the Baptist exclaimed, "Behold, the Lamb of God, who takes away the sin of the world!" (John 1:29). Paul said, "For our sake he made him to be sin who knew no sin, so that in him we might become the righteousness of God" (2 Cor. 5:21). And evidently having Isaiah 53:5–6, 12, in mind, Peter wrote, "He himself bore our sins in his body on the tree, that we might die to sin and live to righteousness. By his wounds you have been healed" (1 Peter 2:24). The common idea in these several passages is that Jesus bore our sins—they were laid on him or transferred from us to him. The idea of substitution is unmistakable.

A further line of evidence is the Greek prepositions used to designate the precise relationship between Christ's work and us. The preposition which most clearly suggests substitution is *anti*. This word in nonsoteriological contexts clearly means "instead of" or "in the place of." For example, Jesus asked, "What father among you, if his son asks for a fish, will instead of a fish give him a serpent?" (Luke 11:11). When we look at passages where the preposition *anti* is used to specify the relationship between Christ's

death and sinners, this same idea of substitution is clearly present. Thus, just as substitution is in view in the "eye for an eye" statement of Matthew 5:38, it is also in view in cases like Matthew 20:28: "The Son of man came not to be served but to serve, and to give his life as a ransom for many." A. T. Robertson says that important doctrinal passages like Matthew 20:28 "teach the substitutionary conception of Christ's death, not because *anti* of itself means 'instead,' which is not true, but because the context renders any other resultant idea out of the question."[8]

The other pertinent preposition is *hyper*. It has a variety of meanings, including "instead of." It has been asserted, however, that *anti* literally means "instead of" and *hyper* means "in behalf of." G. B. Winer counters, "In most cases one who acts in behalf of another appears for him (1 Tim. 2:6; 2 Cor. 5:15), and hence *hyper* sometimes borders on *anti, instead of*."[9] In some biblical passages, for example, Romans 5:6–8; 8:32; Galatians 2:20; and Hebrews 2:9, *hyper* may be taken in the sense of "in behalf of," although it probably means "instead of." In several other passages, however, notably John 11:50; 2 Corinthians 5:15; and Galatians 3:13, the meaning is obviously "instead of." It is not necessary that the meaning "instead of" be overt in every instance. For there is sufficient scriptural evidence that Christ's death was substitutionary.

Reconciliation

The death of Christ also brings to an end the enmity and estrangement which exist between God and humankind. Our hostility toward God is removed. The emphasis in Scripture is usually that we are reconciled to God, that is, he plays the active role; he reconciles us to himself. On this basis, the ad-

8. A. T. Robertson, *A Grammar of the Greek New Testament in the Light of Historical Research*, 2d ed. (New York: George H. Doran, 1915), p. 573.

9. G. B. Winer, *A Treatise on the Grammar of New Testament Greek, Regarded as a Sure Basis for New Testament Exegesis*, 3d ed. rev. (9th English ed.) (Edinburgh: T. and T. Clark, 1882), p. 479.

vocates of the moral-influence theory have contended that reconciliation is strictly God's work.[10] Are they right?

To answer, we need to note, first, that when the Bible entreats someone to be rec-

> *By substituting himself for us, Jesus actually bore the punishment due us, appeased the Father, and effected a reconciliation between God and humankind.*

onciled to another, the hostility does not necessarily lie with the person who is being addressed.[11] Jesus' statement in Matthew 5:23–24 bears out this contention: "So if you are offering your gift at the altar and there remember that your brother has something against you, leave your gift there before the altar and go; first be reconciled to your brother, and then come and offer your gift." Note that the brother is the one who feels wronged and bears the animosity; there is no indication that the one who is offering the gift feels any such hostility. Yet it is the latter who is urged to be reconciled to the brother. Similarly, although God is not the one bearing animosity, it is he who works to bring about reconciliation.

Another notable biblical reference in this regard is the word of Paul in Romans 11:15. The reconciliation of the world is now possible because of the casting off of the Jews. Note that in casting off the Jews, God takes the initiative, rejecting Israel from divine favor and the grace of the gospel. The reconciliation of the world (Gentiles) stands in contrast to the rejection of Israel. Reconciliation, then, is presumably God's act as well,

his act of receiving the world into his favor and of dealing specially with them. As important as it is for us to turn to God, the process of reconciliation is primarily God's turning in favor toward us.

Objections to the Penal-Substitution Theory

Obviously, of the several theories examined in the preceding chapter, it is the satisfaction theory which best expresses the essential aspect of Christ's atoning work. Christ died to satisfy the justice of God's nature. This view has commonly been referred to as the penal-substitution theory. By substituting himself for us, Jesus actually bore the punishment that should have been ours, appeased the Father, and effected a reconciliation between God and humankind. Although the relevant Scripture passages point clearly in the direction of this theory of the atonement, several objections have been raised.

The Objection to the Concept of the Necessity of Atonement

The first objection questions the necessity of the atonement. Why does God not simply forgive sins? If we humans are capable of forgiving one another simply by an act of good will, should not God be able to do the same?[12] This fails to consider, however, that God is not merely a private person who has been wronged, but also the official administrator of the judicial system. For God to remove or ignore the guilt of sin without requiring a payment would, in effect, destroy the very moral fiber of the universe, the distinction between right and wrong. An additional consideration is that when someone sins against us, we are aware that the fault may at least in part be ours, and that we have on numerous other occasions sinned against others. But with God, who does not tempt or do wrong, there is no such

10. Peter Abelard *Commentary on the Epistle to the Romans* 5:5.

11. John Murray, *Redemption—Accomplished and Applied* (Grand Rapids: Eerdmans, 1955), pp. 34–38.

12. Faustus Socinus *De Jesu Christo servatore* 1.1.

element of imperfection to make our sin seem less dreadful.

The Objection to the Concept of Substitution

The second objection suggests that the Father's substituting his Son to bear our penalty smacks of unfairness and injustice. To use a courtroom analogy: suppose that a judge, upon finding a defendant guilty, proceeds to punish not the defendant, but an innocent party. Would this not be improper?[13]

There are two answers to this objection. One is the voluntary character of the sacrifice (see John 10:17–18). Jesus was not compelled by the Father to lay down his life. He did so voluntarily, and thus pleased the Father. The second answer is that the Father and the Son are one, and thus the work of Jesus Christ in giving of his life also involved the Father. God is both the judge and the person paying the penalty. In terms of our courtroom analogy, it is as if the judge passes sentence upon the defendant, then removes his robes and goes off to serve the sentence in the defendant's place.

The Objection to the Concept of Propitiation

Another objection relates to the concept of propitiation. That the loving Son wins over the Father from his anger and wrath against sin to a loving, forgiving spirit is seen as an indication of internal conflict between the persons of the Trinity.[14]

In answering this objection it is helpful to recall the numerous references indicating that the Father sent the Son to atone for sin. Christ was sent by the *Father's* love. So it is not the case that the propitiation changed a wrathful God into a loving God. The love that prompted God to send his Son was al-ways there. This is indicated quite clearly in 1 John 4:10: "Herein is love, not that we loved God, but that he loved us, and sent his Son to be the propitiation for our sins" (KJV).

The Objection to the Concept of the Imputation of Christ's Righteousness

A further objection is to the idea that Christ's righteousness can be imputed to us. One person cannot be good in another's stead. Transferring credit, as it were, from one person to another is a very external and formal type of transaction inappropriate in the matter of our spiritual standing before God.

However, our relationship with Christ is not detached. The individual believer is actually united with him. With regard to my spiritual status, a new entity, so to speak, has come into being. It is as if Christ and I have been married or merged to form a new corporation. The imputation of Christ's righteousness is not, then, so much a matter of transferring something from him to me, as it is of bringing the two of us together so that we hold all things in common. In Christ I died on the cross, and in him I was resurrected. Thus, his death is not only in my place, but with me.

The Implications of Substitutionary Atonement

The substitutionary theory of the atoning death of Christ, when grasped in all its complexity, is a rich and meaningful truth. It carries several major implications for our understanding of salvation:

1. The penal-substitution theory confirms the biblical teaching of the total depravity of all humans. God would not have gone so far as to put his precious Son to death if it had not been absolutely necessary. We are totally unable to meet our need.

2. God's nature is not one-sided, nor is there any tension between its different aspects. He is not merely righteous and demanding, nor merely loving and giving. He is righteous, so much so that sacrifice for sin

13. *Racovian Catechism*, trans. Thomas S. Rees (London: Longman, Hurst, Rees, Orme, and Brown, 1818; Lexington, Ky.: American Theological Library Association, 1962), sec. 5, ch. 8.

14. Albrecht Ritschl, *The Christian Doctrine of Justification and Reconciliation* (Edinburgh: T. and T. Clark, 1900), vol. 3, p. 473.

had to be provided. He is loving, so much so that he provided that sacrifice himself.

3. There is no other way of salvation but by grace, and specifically, the death of Christ. It has an infinite value and thus covers the sins of all humanity for all time. A finite sacrifice, by contrast, cannot even fully cover the sins of the individual offering it.

4. There is security for the believer in his or her relationship to God. For the basis of the relationship, Christ's sacrificial death, is complete and permanent. Although our feelings might change, the ground of our relationship to God remains unshaken.

5. We must never take lightly the salvation which we have. Although it is free, it is also costly, for it cost God the ultimate sacrifice. We must therefore always be grateful for what he has done; we must love him in return and emulate his giving character.

"This is love: not that we loved God, but that he loved us and sent his Son as an atoning sacrifice for our sins" (1 John 4:10, NIV).

He paid a debt He did not owe,
I owed a debt I could not pay.
I needed someone to wash my sins away,
And now I sing a brand new song,
Amazing grace the whole day long,
For Jesus paid a debt that I could never
pay.

The Holy Spirit

The Person of the Holy Spirit

As we come to the concluding parts of our survey of systematic theology, it is well to place in their proper context those matters which are to be examined. We began with an examination of God, the Supreme Being, and of his work in planning, creating, and caring for all that is. We then examined the highest of the creatures, the human race, in terms of their divinely intended destiny and their departure from that divine plan. We saw as well the consequences which came upon the human race and the provision that God made for their redemption and restoration. Creation, providence, and the provision of salvation are the objective work of God. We come now to the subjective work of God—the application of his divine saving work to humans. We will be examining the actual character of the salvation received and experienced by human beings. Next we will investigate the collective form which faith takes, that is, the church. And we will be looking, finally, at the completion of God's plan, that is, the last things.

One other way of viewing our survey of systematic theology is to see it as focusing upon the work of the different members of the Trinity. The Father is highlighted in the work of creation and providence (parts 1–4), the Son has effected redemption for sinful humanity (parts 5–8), and the Holy Spirit applies this redemptive work to God's creature, thus making salvation real (parts 9–11). It is therefore important that we spend some time studying the Third Person of the Trinity before going on to the products of his endeavors.

The Importance of the Doctrine of the Holy Spirit

There are several reasons why the study of the Holy Spirit is of special significance for us. One is that the Holy Spirit is the point at which the Trinity becomes personal to the believer. We generally think of the Father as transcendent and far off in heaven; similarly, the Son seems far removed in history

we must become acquainted with the Holy Spirit's activity.

A third reason for the importance of the doctrine of the Holy Spirit is that current culture stresses the experiential, and it is primarily through him that we experience God. It is through the Holy Spirit's work that we feel God's presence within and the Christian life is given a special tangibility. Consequently, it is vital for us to understand the Holy Spirit.

Difficulties in Understanding the Holy Spirit

While study of the Holy Spirit is especially important, our understanding is often more incomplete and confused here than with most of the other doctrines. Among the reasons for this is that we have less explicit revelation in the Bible regarding the Holy

The Holy Spirit is the point at which the Trinity becomes personal to the believer.

and thus also relatively unknowable. But the Holy Spirit is active within the lives of believers; he is resident within us. The Holy Spirit is the particular person of the Trinity through whom the entire Triune Godhead works in us.

A second reason why the study of the Holy Spirit is especially important is that we live in the period in which the Holy Spirit's work is more prominent than that of the other members of the Trinity. The Father's work was the most conspicuous within the Old Testament period, as was the Son's within the period covered by the Gospels and up to the ascension. The Holy Spirit has occupied the center of the stage from the time of Pentecost on, that is, the period covered by the Book of Acts and the Epistles, and the ensuing periods of church history. If we are to be in touch with God today, then,

Spirit than we find about the Father and the Son. Perhaps this is due in part to the fact that a large share of the Holy Spirit's ministry is to declare and glorify the Son (John 16:14). Unlike other doctrines there are no systematic discussions regarding the Holy Spirit. Virtually the only extended treatment is Jesus' discourse in John 14–16. On most of the occasions when the Holy Spirit is mentioned, it is in connection with another issue.

A further problem is the lack of concrete imagery. God the Father is understood fairly well because the figure of a father is familiar to everyone. The Son is not hard to conceptualize, for he actually appeared in human form and was observed and reported upon. But the Spirit is intangible and difficult to visualize. Complicating this matter is the unfortunate terminology of the King James and other older English translations in referring to the Holy Spirit as the "Holy Ghost." Many persons who grew up using these versions of the Bible conceive the Holy Spirit as something inside a white sheet.

In addition, a problem arises from what Scripture reveals concerning the nature of the Holy Spirit's ministry in relationship to that of the Father and the Son. During the present era, the Spirit performs a ministry of serving the Father and Son, carrying out their will (which of course is also his). In this respect, we are reminded of the Son's earthly ministry, during which he was subordinate in function to the Father. Now this temporary subordination of function—the Son's during his earthly ministry and the Spirit's during the present era—must not lead us to draw the conclusion that there is an inferiority in essence as well. Yet in practice many of us have an unofficial theology which looks upon the Spirit as being of a lower essence than are the Father and the Son. In effect the Trinity is visualized as FATHER, SON, and holy spirit. This error is similar to that of the Arians. From the biblical passages which speak of the Son's subordination to the Father during his earthly ministry, they concluded that the Son is of a lesser status and essence than is the Father.

In the last half of the twentieth century, there has been considerable controversy regarding the Holy Spirit. As a result, there has been some reluctance to discuss the Spirit, for fear that such discussion might lead to dissension. Since Pentecostalists make so much of the Holy Spirit, certain non-Pentecostalists, anxious that they not be mistaken for Pentecostalists, avoid speaking of him altogether. Indeed, while in certain circles "charismatic Christian" is a badge of prestige, in others it is a stigma.

The Nature of the Holy Spirit

The Deity of the Holy Spirit

We now need to examine closely the nature of the Holy Spirit. We begin with his deity. The deity of the Holy Spirit is not as easily established as is that of the Father and

the Son. There are, however, several bases on which one may conclude that the Holy Spirit is God in the same fashion and to the same degree as are the Father and the Son.

First, we should note that various references to the Holy Spirit are interchangeable with references to God. A prominent instance is found in Acts 5. Ananias and Sapphira had sold a piece of property. Bringing a portion of the proceeds to the apostles, they represented it as the whole of what they had received. Peter spoke harsh words of condemnation to each of them, and both were struck dead. In rebuking Ananias, Peter asked, "Ananias, why has Satan filled your heart to lie to the Holy Spirit and to keep back part of the proceeds of the land?" (v. 3). In the next verse he asserts, "You have not lied to men but to God." It seems that in Peter's mind "lying to the Holy Spirit" and "lying to God" were interchangeable expressions.

Another passage where "Holy Spirit" and "God" are used interchangeably is Paul's discussion of the Christian's body. In 1 Corinthians 3:16 he writes, "Do you not know that you are God's temple and that God's Spirit dwells in you?" In 6:19 he uses almost identical language: "Do you not know that your body is a temple of the Holy Spirit within you, which you have from God?" It is clear that, to Paul, to be indwelt by the Holy Spirit is to be inhabited by God. By equating the phrase "God's temple" with the phrase "a temple of the Holy Spirit," Paul makes it clear that the Holy Spirit is God.

Further, the Holy Spirit possesses the attributes or qualities of God. One of these is omniscience. Paul writes in 1 Corinthians 2:10–11: "For the Spirit searches everything, even the depths of God. For what person knows a man's thoughts except the spirit of the man which is in him? So also no one comprehends the thoughts of God except the Spirit of God." And Jesus promises in John 16:13 that his followers will be guided into all truth by the Spirit.

The power of the Holy Spirit is also spoken of prominently in the New Testament.

In Luke 1:35, a reference to the virgin conception, the phrases "the Holy Spirit" and "the power of the Most High" are in parallel or synonymous construction. Paul acknowledged that the accomplishments of his ministry were achieved "by the power of signs and wonders, by the power of the Holy Spirit" (Rom. 15:19). Moreover, Jesus attributed to the Holy Spirit the ability to change human hearts and personalities: it is the Spirit who works conviction (John 16:8–11) and regeneration (John 3:5–8) within us. While these texts do not specifically affirm that the Spirit is omnipotent, they certainly indicate that he has power which presumably only God has.

Yet another attribute of the Spirit which brackets him with the Father and the Son is his eternality. In Hebrews 9:14 he is spoken of as "the eternal Spirit" through whom Jesus offered himself up. Only God, however, is eternal (Heb. 1:10–12), all creatures being temporal. So the Holy Spirit must be God.

In addition to having divine attributes, the Holy Spirit performs certain works which are commonly ascribed to God. He was and continues to be involved with the creation, both in the origination of it and in the providential keeping and directing of it. The psalmist says, "When thou sendest forth thy Spirit, they [all the parts of the creation previously enumerated] are created; and thou renewest the face of the ground" (Ps. 104:30).

The most abundant biblical testimony regarding the role of the Holy Spirit concerns his spiritual working upon or within humans. We have already noted Jesus' attribution of regeneration to the Holy Spirit (John 3:5–8). This is confirmed by Paul in Titus 3:5. In addition, the Spirit raised Christ from the dead and will also raise us, that is, God will raise us through the Spirit (Rom. 8:11).

Giving the Scriptures is another divine work of the Holy Spirit. In 2 Timothy 3:16 Paul writes, "All scripture is inspired by God [literally, 'God-breathed' or 'God-spirited']

and profitable for teaching, for reproof, for correction, and for training in righteousness." Peter also speaks of the Spirit's role in giving us the Scriptures, but emphasizes the influence upon the writer rather than the end product: "no prophecy ever came by the impulse of man, but men moved by the Holy Spirit spoke from God" (2 Peter 1:21). Thus the Holy Spirit inspired the writers and through them the writings.

Our final consideration arguing for the deity of the Holy Spirit is his association with the Father and the Son on a basis of apparent equality. One of the best-known evidences is the baptismal formula prescribed in the Great Commission: "Go therefore and make disciples of all nations, baptizing them in the name of the Father and of the Son and of the Holy Spirit" (Matt. 28:19). The Pauline benediction in 2 Corinthians 13:14 is another evidence, as is 1 Corinthians 12:4–6, where Paul in discussing spiritual gifts coordinates the three members of the Godhead. Peter likewise, in the salutation of his first epistle, links the three together, noting their respective roles in the process of salvation: "[To the exiles of the dispersion] chosen and destined by God the Father and sanctified by the Spirit for obedience to Jesus Christ and for sprinkling with his blood" (1 Peter 1:2).

The Personality of the Holy Spirit

In addition to the deity of the Holy Spirit it is important that we also note his personality. We are not dealing here with an impersonal force. This point is especially important at a time in which pantheistic tendencies are entering our culture through the influence of Eastern religions. The Bible makes clear in several ways that the Holy Spirit is a person and possesses all the qualities which that implies.

The first evidence of the Spirit's personality is the use of the masculine pronoun in representing him. Since the Greek word *pneuma* ("spirit") is neuter, and since pronouns are to agree with their antecedents in person, number, and gender, we would expect the neuter pronoun to be used to represent the Holy Spirit. Yet in John 16:13–14 Jesus' description of the Holy Spirit's ministry uses a masculine pronoun where we would expect a neuter pronoun. The only possible antecedent in the immediate context is "Spirit of truth" (v. 13). Either John in reporting Jesus' discourse made a grammatical error at this point (this is unlikely since we do not find any similar error elsewhere in the Gospel), or he deliberately chose to use the masculine to convey to us the fact that Jesus is referring to a person, not a thing.

A second line of evidence of the Holy Spirit's personality is a number of passages where his work is, in one way or another, reminiscent of the work of someone else who is clearly a personal agent. The term *paraklētos* ("counselor, advocate") is applied to the Holy Spirit in John 14:26; 15:26; and 16:7. In each of these contexts it is obvious that it is not some sort of abstract influence which is in view, for Jesus is also expressly spoken of as a *paraklētos* (1 John 2:1). Most significant are his words in John 14:16, where he says that he will pray to the Father, who will give the disciples another *paraklētos*. The word for "another" means "another of the same kind."[1] In view of Jesus' statements linking the Spirit's coming with his own going away (e.g., 16:7), it is clear that the Spirit is a replacement for Jesus and will carry on the same role. The similarity in their function is an indication that the Holy Spirit, like Jesus, must be a person.

Another function which both Jesus and the Holy Spirit perform, and which, accordingly, serves as an indication of the Spirit's personality, is that of glorifying another member of the Trinity. In John 16:14 Jesus says that the Spirit "will glorify me, for he will take what is mine and declare it to you." A parallel is found in John 17:4, where in his high-priestly prayer Jesus states that during his ministry on earth he glorified the Father.

The most interesting groupings of the Holy Spirit with personal agents are those in which he is linked with both the Father and the Son. Among the best known once again are the baptismal formula in Matthew 28:19 and the benediction in 2 Corinthians 13:14. Jude enjoins, "But you, beloved, build yourselves up on your most holy faith; pray in the Holy Spirit; keep yourselves in the love of God; wait for the mercy of our Lord Jesus Christ unto eternal life" (vv. 20–21). Peter addresses his readers as those who are "chosen and destined by God the Father and sanctified by the Spirit for obedience to Jesus Christ and for sprinkling with his blood" (1 Peter 1:2). The Holy Spirit is also linked with the Father and the Son in various events of Jesus' ministry. One such occurrence is the baptism of Jesus (Matt. 3:16–17), where all three persons of the Trinity were present. Another is his casting out of demons (Matt. 12:28). The conjunction of the Holy Spirit with the Father and the Son in these events is an indication that he is personal, just as are they.

The Spirit's possession of certain personal characteristics is our third indication of his personality. Among the most notable of these characteristics are intelligence, will, and emotions, traditionally regarded as the three fundamental elements of personhood. Of various references to the Spirit's intelligence and knowledge we cite here John 14:26, where Jesus promises that the Spirit "will teach you all things, and bring to your remembrance all that I have said to you." The will of the Spirit is attested in 1 Corinthians 12:11, which states that the recipients of the various spiritual gifts are "inspired by one and the same Spirit, who apportions to each one individually as he wills." That the Spirit has emotions is evident in Ephesians 4:30, where Paul warns against grieving the Spirit.

The Holy Spirit can also be affected as is a person, thus displaying personality passively. It is possible to lie to the Holy Spirit, as Ananias and Sapphira did (Acts 5:3–4). Paul speaks of the sins of grieving the Holy

1. Richard Trench, *Synonyms of the New Testament* (Grand Rapids: Eerdmans, 1953), pp. 357–61.

Spirit (Eph. 4:30) and quenching the Spirit (1 Thess. 5:19). Stephen accuses his adversaries of always resisting the Holy Spirit (Acts 7:51). While it is possible to resist a mere force, one cannot lie to or grieve something which is impersonal. And then, most notably, there is the sin of blasphemy against the Holy Spirit (Matt. 12:31; Mark 3:29). This sin, which Jesus suggests is more serious than blasphemy against the Son, surely cannot be committed against what is impersonal.

In addition, the Holy Spirit engages in moral actions and ministries which can be performed only by a person. Among these activities are teaching, regenerating, searching, speaking, interceding, commanding, testifying, guiding, illuminating, revealing. One interesting and unusual passage is Romans 8:26, where Paul says, "Likewise the Spirit helps us in our weakness; for we do not know how to pray as we ought, but the Spirit himself intercedes for us with sighs too deep for words." Surely, Paul has a person in view. And so does Jesus whenever he speaks of the Holy Spirit, as, for example, in John 16:8: "And when he comes, he will convince the world of sin and of righteousness and of judgment."

All of the foregoing considerations lead to one conclusion. The Holy Spirit is a person, not a force, and that person is God, just as fully and in the same way as are the Father and the Son.

Implications of the Doctrine of the Holy Spirit

A correct understanding of who and what the Holy Spirit is carries certain implications:

1. The Holy Spirit is a person, not a vague force. Thus, he is someone with whom we can have a personal relationship, someone to whom we can and should pray.

2. The Holy Spirit, being fully divine, is to be accorded the same honor and respect that we give to the Father and the Son. It is appropriate to worship him as we do them. He should not be thought of as in any sense inferior in essence to them, although his role may sometimes be subordinated to theirs.

3. The Holy Spirit is one with the Father and the Son. His work is the expression and execution of what the three of them have planned together. There is no tension among their persons and activities.

4. God is not far off. In the Holy Spirit, the Triune God comes close, so close as to actually enter into each believer. God is even more intimate with us now than in the incarnation. Through the operation of the Spirit he has truly become Immanuel, "God with us."

> Praise ye the Spirit! Comforter of Israel,
> Sent of the Father and the Son to bless us;
> Praise ye the Father, Son and Holy Spirit,
> Praise ye the Triune God.

The Work of the Holy Spirit

The work of the Holy Spirit is of special interest to Christians, for it is particularly through this work that God is personally involved and active in the life of the believer. Moreover, in the recent past this facet of the doctrine has been the subject of the greatest controversy regarding the Holy Spirit. This controversy centers on certain of his more spectacular special gifts. In actuality, however, the topic of these special gifts is too narrow a basis on which to construct our discussion here. The controversial issues must be seen against the backdrop of the Spirit's more general activity.

The Work of the Holy Spirit in the Old Testament

It is often difficult to identify the Holy Spirit within the Old Testament, for it reflects the earliest stages of progressive revelation. In fact, the term "Holy Spirit" is rarely employed here. Rather, the usual expression is "the Spirit of God." Most Old Testament references to the Third Person of the Trinity consist of

265

the two nouns *Spirit* and *God*. It is not apparent from this construction that a separate person is involved. The expression "Spirit of God" could well be understood as being simply a reference to the will, mind, or activity of God.[1] There are, however, some cases where the New Testament makes it clear that an Old Testament reference to the "Spirit of God" is a reference to the Holy Spirit. One of the most prominent of these New Testament passages is Acts 2:16–21, where Peter explains that what is occurring at Pentecost is the fulfilment of the prophet Joel's statement, "I will pour out my Spirit upon all flesh" (2:28). Surely the events of Pentecost were the realization of Jesus' promise, "You shall receive power when the Holy Spirit has come upon you" (Acts 1:8). In short, the Old Testament "Spirit of God" is synonymous with the Holy Spirit.[2]

There are several major areas of the Holy Spirit's working in Old Testament times. First is the creation: "The earth was without form and void, and darkness was upon the face of the deep; and the Spirit of God was moving over the face of the waters" (Gen. 1:2). God's continued working with the creation is attributed to the Spirit. Job says, "By his wind [or spirit] the heavens were made fair; his hand pierced the fleeing serpent" (26:13).

Another general area of the Spirit's work is the giving of prophecy and Scripture.[3] The Old Testament prophets testified that their speaking and writing were a result of the Spirit's coming upon them. Ezekiel offers the clearest example: "And when he spoke to me,

the Spirit entered into me and set me upon my feet; and I heard him speaking to me" (2:2; cf. 8:3; 11:1, 24; see also 2 Peter 1:21).

Yet another work of the Spirit of God in the Old Testament was in conveying certain necessary skills for various tasks.[4] For example, we read that in appointing Bezalel to construct and furnish the tabernacle, God said, "I have filled him with the Spirit of God, with ability and intelligence, with knowledge and all craftsmanship, to devise artistic designs, to work in gold, silver, and bronze, in cutting stones for setting, and in carving wood, for work in every craft" (Exod. 31:3–5). Administration also seems to have been a gift of the Spirit. Even Pharaoh recognized the Spirit's presence in Joseph: "And Pharaoh said to his servants, 'Can we find such a man as this, in whom is the Spirit of God?'" (Gen. 41:38). In the time of the judges, administration by the power and gifts of the Holy Spirit was especially dramatic.[5] This was a time when there was very little national leadership. Much of what was done was accomplished by what we would today call "charismatic leadership." The description of the call of Gideon reads, "But the Spirit of the LORD took possession of Gideon; and he sounded the trumpet, and the Abiezrites were called out to follow him" (Judg. 6:34). It is noteworthy that the Spirit's working at the time of the judges consisted largely of granting skill in waging war. The Spirit also endowed the early kings of Israel with special capabilities. We are told, for example, that David's anointing was accompanied by the coming of the Spirit of God (1 Sam. 16:13).

The Spirit is seen not only in dramatic incidents, however. In addition to the qualities of national leadership and the heroics of war, he was present in Israel's spiritual life. In this connection he is referred to as a "good Spirit." Addressing God, Ezra reminded the people of Israel of the provision made for their ancestors in the wilderness: "Thou gavest thy good Spirit to instruct them, and didst

1. J. H. Raven claims that the Old Testament references to the "Spirit of God" do not pertain specifically to the Holy Spirit: "There is here no distinction of persons in the Godhead. The Spirit of God in the Old Testament is God himself exercising active influence"— *The History of the Religion of Israel* (Grand Rapids: Baker, 1979), p. 164.

2. For the view that passages like Psalm 104:30 are personal references to the Holy Spirit, see Leon Wood, *The Holy Spirit in the Old Testament* (Grand Rapids: Zondervan, 1976), pp. 19–20.

3. Eduard Schweizer, *The Holy Spirit*, trans. Reginald H. and Ilse Fuller (Philadelphia: Fortress, 1980), pp. 10–19.

4. Wood, *Holy Spirit*, pp. 42–43.

5. Ibid., p. 41.

not withhold thy manna from their mouth, and gavest them water for their thirst" (Neh. 9:20). The goodness of the Spirit is seen also in references to him as a "holy Spirit." Asking that his sins be blotted out, David prays, "Take not thy holy Spirit from me" (Ps. 51:11). The Old Testament depicts the Holy Spirit as producing the moral and spiritual qualities of holiness and goodness in the person upon whom he comes or in whom he dwells. We should note, however, that while in some cases this internal working of the Holy Spirit seems to be permanent, in other cases, such as in the Book of Judges, his presence seems to be intermittent and related to a particular activity or ministry which is to be carried out.

There is within the Old Testament witness to the Spirit an anticipation of a coming time when the ministry of the Spirit is to be more complete.[6] Part of this relates to the coming Messiah, upon whom the Spirit is to rest in an unusual degree and fashion. Jesus quotes the opening verses of Isaiah 61 ("The Spirit of the Lord is upon me, because he has anointed me to preach good news to the poor . . ."), and indicates that they are now being fulfilled in him (Luke 4:18–21). There is a more generalized promise, however, one which is not restricted to the Messiah. This is found in Joel 2:28–29: "And it shall come to pass afterward, that I will pour out my spirit on all flesh; your sons and your daughters shall prophesy, your old men shall dream dreams, and your young men shall see visions. Even upon the menservants and maidservants in those days, I will pour out my spirit." At Pentecost Peter quoted this prophecy, indicating that it had now been fulfilled.

The Work of the Holy Spirit in the Life of Jesus

When we examine Jesus' life, we find a pervasive and powerful presence and activity of the Spirit throughout. Even the very beginning of his incarnate existence was a work of the Holy Spirit.[7] After informing Mary that she was to have a child, the angel explained, "The Holy Spirit will come upon you, and the power of the Most High will overshadow you; therefore the child to be born will be called holy, the Son of God" (Luke 1:35). The announcement of Jesus' ministry by John the Baptist also highlights the place of the Holy Spirit. John emphasized that, unlike his own baptism, which was merely with water, Jesus would baptize with the Holy Spirit (Mark 1:8).

The Spirit is present in dramatic form from the very beginning of Jesus' public ministry, if identified with his baptism, for there was a perceivable coming of the Holy Spirit upon him at that time (Matt. 3:16; Mark 1:10; Luke 3:22; John 1:32). Immediately afterward, Jesus was "full of the Holy Spirit" (Luke 4:1). The direct result was the major temptation, or series of temptations, at the inception of the public ministry.[8] Jesus was led by the Holy Spirit into the situation where the temptation took place. Mark's statement is forceful: "The Spirit immediately drove him out into the wilderness" (1:12). Jesus is virtually "expelled" by the Spirit. What is noteworthy here is that the presence of the Holy Spirit in Jesus' life brings him into direct and immediate conflict with the forces of evil. It seems that the antithesis between the Holy Spirit and the evil in the world had to be brought to light.

The rest of the ministry of Jesus as well was conducted in the power and by the direction of the Holy Spirit. This was obviously true of Jesus' teaching.[9] Luke tells us that following the temptation "Jesus returned in the power of the Spirit into Galilee" (4:14). He proceeded then to teach in all the synagogues.

What is true of Jesus' teaching is also true of his miracles, particularly his exorcism

6. George Smeaton, *The Doctrine of the Holy Spirit* (London: Banner of Truth Trust, 1958), pp. 33–35.

7. Karl Barth, *Dogmatics in Outline* (New York: Philosophical Library, 1949), p. 95.

8. Schweizer, *Holy Spirit*, p. 51.

9. Dale Moody, *Spirit of the Living God* (Nashville: Broadman, 1976), pp. 40–41.

of demons. On one occasion when Jesus healed a demoniac, the Pharisees maintained that Jesus cast out demons by the prince of demons. Jesus pointed out the internal contradiction within this statement (Matt. 12:25–27) and then countered, "But if it is by the Spirit of God that I cast out demons, then the kingdom of God has come upon you" (v. 28). His condemnation of the Pharisees' words as "blasphemy against the Spirit" (v. 31) and his warning that "whoever speaks against the Holy Spirit will not be forgiven" (v. 32) are evidence that what he had just done was done by the power of the Holy Spirit.

Not only his teaching and miracles, but Jesus' whole life at this point was "in the Holy Spirit." When the seventy returned from their mission and reported that even the demons were subject to them in Jesus' name (Luke 10:17), "in that same hour he rejoiced in the Holy Spirit" (v. 21). Even his emotions were "in the Holy Spirit."

It is noteworthy that there is no evidence of growth of the Holy Spirit's presence in Jesus' life. There is no series of experiences of the coming of the Holy Spirit, just the conception and the baptism. What there does seem to be, however, is a growing implementation of the Spirit's presence. Nor does one find any evidence of ecstatic phenomena in Jesus' life or any teaching of his on the subject. In light of the problems encountered by the church in Corinth, and the phenomena of Pentecost and later experiences recorded in Acts, it is surprising that neither the Savior's personal life nor his teaching gives any hint of such charismata.

The Work of the Holy Spirit in the Life of the Christian

The Beginning of the Christian Life

In Jesus' teaching we find an especially strong emphasis upon the work of the Holy Spirit in initiating persons into the Christian life. Jesus taught that the Spirit's activity is essential in both conversion, which from our perspective is the beginning of the

Christian life, and regeneration, which from God's perspective is its beginning.

Conversion is the individual's turning to God. It consists of a negative and a positive element: repentance, that is, abandonment of sin; and faith, that is, acceptance of the promises and the work of Christ. Jesus spoke especially of repentance, and specifically of conviction of sin, which is the prerequisite of repentance. He said, "And when [the Counselor] comes, he will convince the world of sin and of righteousness and of judgment: of sin, because they do not believe in me; of righteousness, because I go to the Father, and you will see me no more; of judgment, because the ruler of this world is judged" (John 16:8–11). Without this work of the Holy Spirit, there can be no conversion.

Regeneration is the miraculous transformation of the individual and implantation of spiritual energy. Jesus made very clear to Nicodemus that regeneration, which is essential to our acceptance by the Father, is a supernatural occurrence, and the Holy Spirit is the agent who produces it (John 3:5–6). The flesh (i.e., human effort) is not capable of effecting this transformation. Nor can this transformation even be comprehended by the human intellect. Jesus in fact likened this work of the Spirit to the blowing of the wind: "The wind blows where it wills, and you hear the sound of it, but you do not know whence it comes or whither it goes; so it is with every one who is born of the Spirit" (v. 8).[10]

The Continuation of the Christian Life

The work of the Spirit is not completed when one becomes a believer; on the contrary, it is just beginning. There are a number of other roles which he performs in the ongoing Christian life.

1. One of the Spirit's other roles is empowering. Jesus probably left his disciples

10. For a discussion of Jesus' words to Nicodemus, see Henry B. Swete, *The Holy Spirit in the New Testament: A Study of Primitive Christian Teaching* (London: Macmillan, 1909), pp. 130–35.

flabbergasted when he said, "Truly, truly, I say to you, he who believes in me will also do the works that I do; and greater works than these will he do, because I go to the Father" (John 14:12). It probably seemed incredible to the disciples, who by now were very much aware of their own weaknesses and shortcomings, that they would do greater works than the Master himself had done. Yet Peter preached on Pentecost Sunday and three thousand believed. Jesus himself never had that type of response, as far as we know. Perhaps he did not gather that many genuine converts in his entire minis-

topic developed at greater length in chapter 7. This ministry of the Holy Spirit was not merely for that first generation of disciples, but obviously also includes helping believers today to understand the Scripture.

4. Another point of particular interest is the intercessory work of the Holy Spirit. We are familiar with the intercession which Jesus, as the High Priest, makes in our behalf. Paul also speaks of an intercessory prayer in which the Holy Spirit engages in our behalf: "Likewise the Spirit helps us in our weakness; for we do not know how to pray as we ought, but the Spirit himself

We are initiated into the Christian life through the Spirit's activity in our conversion and regeneration.

try! The key to the disciples' success was not in their abilities and strengths, however. Jesus had told them to wait for the coming of the Holy Spirit (Acts 1:4–5). He explained that this coming of the Spirit would give them the power that he had promised, the ability to do the things that he had predicted (v. 8). This enablement by the Spirit is a resource still available today to any Christian wishing to serve the Lord.

2. Another element of Jesus' promise was that the Holy Spirit would indwell the believer (John 14:16–17). Part of the efficacy of the Spirit's work is a result of its internality. Jesus had been a teacher and leader, but his influence was that of external word and example. The Spirit, however, is able to affect us more intensely because, dwelling within, he can get to the very center of our thinking and emotions. By indwelling believers, the Spirit can lead them into all truth, as Jesus promised (John 16:13–14).

3. The Spirit evidently has a teaching role. Earlier in the same discourse we read that he would bring to mind and clarify for the disciples the words which Jesus had already given to them (John 14:26). Here we have the idea of illumination by the Holy Spirit, a

intercedes for us with sighs too deep for words. And he who searches the hearts of men knows what is the mind of the Spirit, because the Spirit intercedes for the saints according to the will of God" (Rom. 8:26–27). Thus believers have the assurance that when they do not know how to pray, the Holy Spirit wisely intercedes for them that the Lord's will be done.

5. The Holy Spirit also works sanctification in the life of the believer. By sanctification is meant the continued transformation of moral and spiritual character so that the life of the believer actually comes to mirror the standing which he or she already has in God's sight. While justification is an instantaneous act giving the individual a righteous standing before God, sanctification is a process making the person holy or good. In Romans 8:1–17, Paul dwells on this work of the Holy Spirit.

Life in the Spirit is what God intends for the Christian. Paul in Galatians 5 contrasts life in the Spirit with life in the flesh. He instructs his readers to walk by the Spirit instead of gratifying the desires of the flesh (v. 16). If they heed this instruction, the Spirit will produce in them a set of qualities which are collectively referred to as the "fruit of the Spirit" (vv. 22–23). These qualities cannot in their entirety be produced in human lives by unaided self-effort. They are a supernatural work. They are opposed to the works of the flesh—a list of sins in verses 19–21—just as the Spirit himself is in opposition to the flesh. The work of the Holy Spirit in sanctification, then, is not merely the negative work of mortification of the flesh (Rom. 8:13), but also the production of a positive likeness to Christ.

6. The Spirit also bestows certain special gifts upon believers within the body of Christ. In Paul's writings there are three different lists of such gifts; there is also a brief one in 1 Peter (see Figure 4). Certain observations need to be made regarding these lists. First, while all of them have reference to the gifts of the Spirit, their basic orientations differ. Ephesians 4:11 is really a listing of various offices in the church, or of persons who are God's gifts to the church as it were. Romans 12:6–8 and 1 Peter 4:11 actually catalog several basic functions which are performed in the church. The list in 1 Corinthians is more a matter of special abilities. It is likely that when these passages speak of the "gifts of the Spirit," they have different meanings in view. Hence no attempt should be made to reduce this expression to a unitary concept or definition. Sec-

ond, it is not clear whether these gifts are endowments from birth, special enablements received at some later point, or a combination of the two. Third, some gifts, such as faith and service, are qualities or activities expected of every Christian; in such cases it is likely that the writer has in mind an unusual capability in that area. Fourth, since none of the four lists includes all of the gifts found in the other lists, it is quite conceivable that collectively they do not exhaust all possible gifts of the Spirit. These lists, then, individually and collectively, are illustrative of the various gifts with which God has endowed the church.

It is also important at this point to note several observations which Paul made regarding both the nature of the gifts and the way in which they are to be exercised. These observations appear in 1 Corinthians 12 and 14.

1. The gifts are bestowed on the body (the church). They are for the edification of the whole body, not merely for the enjoyment or enrichment of the individual members possessing them (12:7; 14:5, 12).
2. No one person has all the gifts (12:14–21), nor is any one of the gifts bestowed on all persons (12:28–30). Con-

Figure 4. The Gifts of the Spirit

Romans 12:6–8	1 Corinthians 12:4–11	Ephesians 4:11	1 Peter 4:11
prophecy	wisdom	apostles	speaking
service	knowledge	prophets	service
teaching	faith	evangelists	
exhortation	healing	pastors and	
liberality	working of miracles	teachers	
giving aid	prophecy		
acts of mercy	ability to distinguish spirits		
	various tongues		
	interpretation of tongues		

sequently, the individual members of the church need each other.

3. Although not equally conspicuous, all gifts are important (12:22–26).
4. The Holy Spirit apportions the various gifts to whom and as he wills (12:11).

The Miraculous Gifts Today

Certain of the more spectacular gifts have attracted particular attention and stirred considerable controversy in recent years. These are sometimes referred to as remarkable gifts, miraculous gifts, special gifts, sign gifts, or charismatic gifts, the last being a somewhat redundant expression, since *charismata* basically means gifts. Most frequently mentioned are faith healing, exorcism of demons, and especially glossolalia or speaking in tongues. The question that has occasioned the most controversy is whether the Holy Spirit is still dispensing these gifts in the church today, and if so, whether they are normative (i.e., whether every Christian can and should receive and exercise them).

Charismatic groups appeared early in church history. The most prominent of these groups was the Montanists, who flourished in the latter half of the second century. At his baptism Montanus spoke in tongues and began prophesying. He declared that the Paraclete, the Holy Spirit promised by Jesus, was giving utterance through him. Montanus and two of his female disciples as well were believed to be spokespersons of the Holy Spirit. The Montanists taught that their prophecies clarified the Scriptures and that Spirit-inspired prophets would continue to arise within the Christian community.[11]

Groups like the Montanists did not have a lasting effect on the church. For centuries there was relatively little emphasis on the Holy Spirit and his work. At the close of the nineteenth century, however, there came a development which was to give the Holy Spirit, in some circles at least, virtually the preeminent role in theology. There were some outbursts of glossolalia in North Carolina as early as 1896. In Topeka, Kansas, Charles Parham, the head of a small Bible school, found it necessary to be gone for a period of time, during which the students focused on the topic of the baptism of the Holy Spirit. When Parham returned, their unanimous conclusion was that the Bible teaches that there is to be a baptism of the Holy Spirit subsequent to conversion and new birth, and that speaking in tongues is the sign that one has received this gift.[12]

The real outbreak of Pentecostalism, however, occurred in meetings organized by a black holiness preacher, William J. Seymour. These meetings were held in a former Methodist church at 312 Azusa Street in Los Angeles, and have consequently come to be referred to as the Azusa Street meetings.[13] From this beginning, the Pentecostal phenomenon spread throughout the United States and to other countries, most notably Scandinavia. In recent years, Pentecostalism of this type has become a powerful force in Latin America and other Third World countries.

For many years the Pentecostal movement was a relatively isolated factor within Christianity, however. It was found mostly in denominations composed heavily of persons from the lower social and economic classes. But in the early 1950s, this began to change. In some hitherto unlikely places, glossolalia began to be practiced. In Episcopal, Lutheran, and even Catholic churches, there was an emphasis on special manifestations of the Holy Spirit's work. There are significant differences between this movement, which could be called neo-Pentecostal or charismatic, and the old-line Pentecostalism which had sprung up at the beginning of the twentieth century and continues to this day. Neo-Pentecostalism is more of a trans-

11. Tertullian *On the Resurrection of the Flesh* 63.

12. Klaude Kendrick, *The Promise Fulfilled: A History of the Modern Pentecostal Movement* (Springfield, Mo.: Gospel, 1961), pp. 48–49, 52–53.

13. Ibid., pp. 64–68.

denominational movement, drawing many of its participants from the middle and upper-middle classes.[14] The two groups also differ in the way in which they practice their charismatic gifts. In the old-line Pentecostal groups, a number of members might speak or pray aloud at once. Such is not the case with charismatic Christians, some of whom use the gift only in their own private prayer time. Public manifestations of the gift are usually in special groups rather than in the plenary worship service of the congregation.

We need to examine both sides of the issue of special gifts if it is to be correctly understood and dealt with. Because glossolalia is the most prominent of these gifts, we will concentrate on it. Our conclusions will serve to evaluate the other gifts as well. The case for glossolalia has been argued throughout the twentieth century by Pentecostal groups, and in more recent years by neo-Pentecostals. Their position, relying heavily upon the narrative passages in the Book of Acts, is a rather straightforward one. The argument usually begins with the observation that subsequent to the episodes of conversion and regeneration recorded in Acts, there customarily came a special filling or baptism with the Holy Spirit, and that its usual manifestation was speaking in an unknown tongue. There is no indication that the Holy Spirit would cease to bestow this gift on the church.[15]

Often an experiential argument also is employed in support of glossolalia. People who have experienced the gift themselves or have observed others practicing it have a subjective certainty about the experience. They emphasize the benefits which it produces in the Christian's spiritual life, especially its value as a means of vitalizing one's prayer life.[16]

In addition, the advocates of glossolalia argue that the practice is nowhere forbidden in Scripture. In writing to the Corinthians, Paul does not censure proper use of the gift, but only perversions of it. In fact, he says, "I thank God that I speak in tongues more than you all" (1 Cor. 14:18).

On the other side of the argument are those who reject the idea that the Holy Spirit is still dispensing the charismatic gifts. They argue that historically the miraculous gifts ceased; they were virtually unknown throughout most of the history of the church.[17] A few who reject the possibility of contemporary glossolalia utilize 1 Corinthians 13:8 as evidence: "as for tongues, they will cease." They argue that tongues, unlike prophecy and knowledge, were not intended to continue until the end time, but have already ceased.[18] Therefore, tongues are not included in the reference to the imperfect gifts which will pass away when the perfect comes (vv. 9–10).[19] Some theologians would argue for the passing of the miraculous gifts on the basis of Hebrews 2:3–4: "salvation . . . was declared at first by the Lord, and it was attested to us by . . . various miracles and by gifts of the Holy Spirit." The thrust of this argument is that the purpose of the miraculous gifts was to attest to and thus authenticate the revelation and the incarnation. When that purpose had been fulfilled, the miracles being unnecessary, they simply faded away.[20]

A second aspect of the negative argument is the existence of parallels to glossolalia which are obviously not to be interpreted as

---

14. Richard Quebedeaux, *The New Charismatics: The Origins, Development, and Significance of Neo-Pentecostalism* (Garden City, N.Y.: Doubleday, 1976), pp. 4–11.

15. Donald Gee, *The Pentecostal Movement, Including the Story of the War Years (1940–47)*, rev. ed. (London: Elim, 1949), p. 10.

16. Laurence Christenson, *Speaking in Tongues and Its Significance for the Church* (Minneapolis: Bethany Fellowship, 1968), pp. 72–79.

17. Anthony Hoekema, *What About Tongue-Speaking?* (Grand Rapids: Eerdmans, 1966), pp. 16–18.

18. The basis of this argument is the distinction in 1 Cor. 13:8 between the verb used with "tongues" and the verb used with "prophecies" and "knowledge." Not only is a totally different word involved, but the middle voice is used in the former instance and the passive in the latter.

19. Stanley D. Toussaint, "First Corinthians Thirteen and the Tongues Question," *Bibliotheca Sacra* 120 (Oct.–Dec. 1963): 311–16; Robert Glenn Gromacki, *The Modern Tongues Movement* (Philadelphia: Presbyterian and Reformed, 1967), pp. 118–29.

20. Benjamin B. Warfield, *Miracles: Yesterday and Today* (Grand Rapids: Eerdmans, 1953), p. 6.

special gifts of the Holy Spirit. It is noted, for example, that similar phenomena are found in other religions. The practices of certain voodoo witch doctors are a case in point. Psychology, too, finds parallels between speaking in tongues and certain cases of heightened suggestibility caused by brainwashing or electroshock therapy.[21]

One particular point of interest in recent years has been the study of glossolalia by linguists. Although some advocates of glossolalia say that the tongues of Corinth and those today are merely utterances of apparently unrelated syllables, others maintain that the tongues of Corinth and of today are, like those at Pentecost, actual languages. The latter group must answer scientific charges that many cases of glossolalia simply do not display a sufficient number of the characteristics of language to be classified as such.[22]

Is there a way to deal responsibly with the considerations raised by both sides of this dispute? Because the issue has a significant effect on the fashion in which one conducts one's Christian life, and even on the very style or tone of the Christian life, the question cannot simply be ignored. While few dogmatic conclusions can be drawn in this area, a number of significant observations can be made.

We begin with the question of the baptism of the Holy Spirit. We note first that the Book of Acts speaks of a special work of the Spirit subsequent to new birth. It appears, however, that the Book of Acts covers a transitional period. Since that time the normal pattern has been for conversion/regeneration and the baptism of the Holy Spirit to coincide. Paul writes in 1 Corinthians 12:13, "For by one Spirit we were all baptized into one body—Jews or Greeks, slaves or free—and all were made to drink of one Spirit."

From verse 12 it is very clear that this "one body" is Christ. Thus Paul appears to be saying in verse 13 that we become members of Christ's body by being baptized into it by the Spirit. Baptism by the Spirit appears to be, if not equivalent to conversion and new birth, at least simultaneous with them.

But what of the cases in Acts where there clearly was a separation between conversion/regeneration and the baptism of the Spirit? In keeping with the observation in the preceding paragraph that Acts covers a transitional period, it is my interpretation that these cases did indeed involve people who were regenerated before they received the Holy Spirit. They were the last of the Old Testament believers.[23] They were regenerate because they believed the Old Testament and feared God. They had not received the Spirit, however, for the promise of his coming could not be fulfilled until Jesus had ascended. (Keep in mind that even the disciples of Jesus, who were certainly already regenerate under the New Testament system, were not filled with the Spirit until Pentecost.) But when on Pentecost those who were already regenerate under the Old Testament system received Christ, they were filled with the Spirit. As soon as that happened, there were no longer any regenerate Old Testament believers. After the events of Pentecost we find no other clear cases of such a postconversion experience among Jews. What happened to the Jews as a group (Acts 2) also happened to the Samaritans (Acts 8) and to the Gentiles (Acts 10). Thereafter, regeneration and the baptism of the Spirit were simultaneous. The case of the disciples of Apollos in Acts 19 appears to be a matter of incompletely evangelized believers, for they had been baptized only into the baptism of John, which was a baptism of repentance, and had not even heard that there is a Holy Spirit. In none of these four cases was the baptism of the Holy Spirit sought by the recipients, nor is there any indication

21. William Sargent, "Some Cultural Group Abreactive Techniques and Their Relation to Modern Treatments," in *Proceedings of the Royal Society of Medicine* (London: Longmans, Green, 1949), pp. 367ff.

22. William J. Samarin, *Tongues of Men and Angels: The Religious Language of Pentecostalism* (New York: Macmillan, 1972), chs. 4–6.

23. For a more complete treatment, see Frederick Dale Bruner, *A Theology of the Holy Spirit* (Grand Rapids: Eerdmans, 1970), pp. 153–218.

that the gift did not fall upon every member of the group. This interpretive scheme seems to fit well with the words of Paul in 1 Corinthians 12:13, with the fact that Scripture nowhere commands us to be baptized in or by the Holy Spirit, and with the record in Acts.

In my judgment it is not possible to determine with any certainty whether the contemporary charismatic phenomena are indeed gifts of the Holy Spirit. There simply is no biblical evidence indicating the time of fulfilment of the prediction that tongues will cease. Nor is the historical evidence clear and conclusive. There is a great deal of evidence on both sides. Each group is able to cite an impressive amount of data which are to its advantage, bypassing the data presented by the other group. This lack of historical conclusiveness is not a problem, however. For even if history proved that the gift of tongues has ceased, there is nothing to prevent God from reestablishing it. On the other hand, historical proof that the gift has been present through the various eras of the church would not validate the present phenomena.

religious experience can be of divine origin, unless God is a very broadly ecumenical and tolerant being indeed, who even grants special manifestations of his Spirit to some who make no claim to Christian faith and may actually be opposed to it. Certainly if demonic forces could produce imitations of divine miracles in biblical times (e.g., the magicians in Egypt were able to imitate the plagues up to a certain point), the same may be true today as well. Conversely, however, no conclusive case can be made for the contention that such gifts are not for today and cannot occur at the present time. Consequently, one cannot rule in an *a priori* and categorical fashion that a claim of glossolalia is spurious. In fact, it may be downright dangerous, in the light of Jesus' warnings regarding blasphemy against the Holy Spirit, to attribute specific phenomena to demonic activity.

In the final analysis, whether the Bible teaches that the Spirit dispenses special gifts today is not an issue of great practical consequence. For even if he does, we are not to set our lives to seeking them. He bestows them sovereignly; he alone determines the recipients (1 Cor. 12:11). If he chooses to

Being filled with the Spirit is not so much a matter of our getting more of the Spirit as it is a matter of his possessing more of our lives.

What we must do, then, is to evaluate each case on its own merits. This does not mean that we are to sit in judgment on the spiritual experience or the spiritual life of other professing Christians. What it does mean is that we cannot assume that everyone who claims to have had a special experience of the Holy Spirit's working has really had one. Scientific studies have discovered enough non-Spirit-caused parallels to warn us against being naively credulous about every claim. Certainly not every exceptional

give us a special gift, he will do so regardless of whether we expect it or seek it. What we are commanded to do (Eph. 5:18) is be filled with the Holy Spirit (the form of the Greek imperative suggests ongoing action). This is not so much a matter of our getting more of the Holy Spirit; presumably all of us possess the Spirit in his entirety. It is, rather, a matter of his possessing more of our lives. Each of us is to aspire to giving the Holy Spirit full control of our lives. When that happens, our lives will manifest whatever gifts God intends for us to have, along with all the fruit and acts of his empowering that he wishes to display through us. It is to be remembered, as we noted earlier, that no one gift is for every Christian, nor is any gift more significant than the others.

Of more importance, in many ways, than receiving certain gifts is the fruit of the Spirit. These virtues are, in Paul's estimation, the real evidence of the Spirit at work in Christians. Love, joy, and peace in an individual's life are the surest signs of a vital experience with the Spirit. In particular, Paul stresses love as more desirable than any gifts, no matter how spectacular (1 Cor. 13:1–3).

But what is proper procedure with regard to an actual case of modern-day public practice of what is claimed to be the biblical gift of glossolalia? First, no conclusions should be drawn in advance as to whether it is genuine or not. Then, the procedure laid down by Paul so long ago should be followed. Thus, if one speaks in tongues, there should be an interpreter so that the group as a whole may be edified. Only one should speak at a time and no more than two or three at a session (1 Cor. 14:27). If no one is present to interpret, whether the speaker or some other person, then the would-be speaker should keep silence in the church and restrict the use of tongues to personal devotional practice (v. 28). We must not prohibit speaking in tongues (v. 39); on the other hand, we are nowhere commanded to seek this gift.

Finally, it is to be noted that the emphasis in Scripture is upon the one who bestows the gifts rather than upon those who receive them. God frequently performs miraculous works without involving human agents. We read, for example, in James 5:14–15 that the elders of the church are to pray for the sick. It is the prayer of faith, not a human miracle-worker, that is said to save them. Whatever be the gift, it is the edification of the church and the glorification of God that are of ultimate importance.

Implications of the Work of the Spirit

1. The gifts that we have are bestowals upon us by the Holy Spirit. We should recognize that they are not our own accomplishments. They are intended to be used in the fulfilment of his plan.

2. The Holy Spirit empowers believers in their Christian life and service. Personal inadequacies should not deter or discourage us.

3. The Holy Spirit dispenses his gifts to the church wisely and sovereignly. Possession or lack of a particular gift is no cause for pride or regret. His gifts are not rewards to those who seek or qualify for them.

4. No one gift is for everyone, and no one person has every gift. The fellowship of the body is needed for full spiritual development of the individual believer.

5. We may rely upon the Holy Spirit to give us understanding of the Word of God, and to guide us into his will for us.

6. It is appropriate to direct prayer to the Holy Spirit, just as to the Father and the Son, as well as to the Triune God. In such prayers we will thank him for, and especially ask him to continue, the unique work that he does in us.

Salvation

30 Conceptions of Salvation

Salvation is the application of the work of Christ to the life of the individual. Accordingly, the doctrine of salvation has particular appeal and relevance, since it pertains to our most crucial need. While the term *salvation* may seem to persons familiar with it to have a somewhat obvious meaning, there are, even within Christian circles, rather widely differing conceptions of what salvation entails. Before examining the more prominent of these conceptions, it will be helpful to look briefly at various details on which they differ. This will give us categories we can employ as we analyze the several views.

Details on Which Conceptions of Salvation Differ

The Time Dimension

There are various opinions as to how salvation is related to time. It is variously thought of as a single occurrence at the beginning of the Christian life, a process continuing throughout the Christian life, or a future event. Some Christians regard salvation as basically complete at the initiation of the Christian life. They tend to say, "We have been saved." Others see salvation as in process—"we are being saved." Yet others think of salvation as something which will be received in the future—"we shall be saved." It is, of course, possible to combine two or all three of these views. In that case, the separate aspects of salvation (e.g., justification, sanctification, glorification) are understood as occurring at different times.

If salvation is thought of as taking place within time, then we must determine the kind of chronological framework that is involved. Because particular actions can take place in a single moment or over a period of time, salvation and its constituent aspects can be conceived of in several different ways:

1. A series of points: . . . . . .
2. A series of discontinuous processes:

   ____ ____ ____ ____

3. A series of overlapping processes:

   _____

   _____

4. A single continuous process with distinguishable components:

   _|___|___|___|___|___

Nature and Locus of the Need

A second question relates to the nature and locus of the need which must be dealt with. In the traditional view, our basic deficiency is thought of as being vertical in nature. The primary human problem is separation from God. What is needed is to restore the broken relationship between God and the creature. This is the evangelical view of salvation. A second view is that the primary human problem is horizontal. This may mean that an individual has difficulty in adjusting to other persons, or that there is a fundamental lack of harmony within society as a whole. Salvation involves the removal of ruptures within the human race, the healing of personal and social relationships. "Relational theology" is concerned with this process on the level of individual maladjustments and small-group problems. Liberation theologies are concerned with the conflicts between different racial or economic classes. A third view is that the primary human problem is internal. The individual is plagued with feelings which must be eradicated—guilt, inferiority, insecurity. "Adjustment," "self-understanding," "self-acceptance," and "growth in self-esteem" are catchwords here.

The Medium of Salvation

The question of how salvation is obtained or transmitted is also highly important. Some views regard the transmission of salvation as virtually a physical process. This is true of certain sacramentalist systems which believe salvation or grace to be obtained by means of a physical object. For example, in traditional Roman Catholicism, grace is believed to be actually transmitted and received by taking the bread of communion into one's body. While the value of the sacrament depends to some extent upon the inward attitude or condition of the communicant, grace is received primarily through the external physical act. Others think that salvation is conveyed by moral action. Here salvation is not so much something possessed by some individual or organization and transmitted to others, as it is something created by altering the state of affairs. This idea of salvation is found in the social-gospel movement and in liberation theologies. Evangelical theologies represent a third idea: salvation is mediated by faith. Faith appropriates the work accomplished by Christ. The recipient is, in a sense, passive in this process.

The Direction of Movement in Salvation

An additional consideration is the direction of movement in salvation. Does God work by saving individuals, effecting a personal transformation which proceeds outward into society and changes the world of which the redeemed are a part? Or does God work by altering the structures of our society and then using these altered structures to change the persons who make it up?

upon individual responses to the grace of God. It maintains that not all will respond affirmatively to God; consequently, some will be lost and some saved. The universalist position, on the other hand, holds that God will restore all humans to the relationship with him for which they were originally intended. No one will be lost. There are two varieties of the universalist position. One might be a universalist by being an optimistic particularist. That is to say, one might hold both that it is necessary to accept Jesus Christ personally in order to be saved, and

> *In the evangelical view, the primary human problem is our separation from God, the Word of God is his means of presenting to us the salvation found in Christ, and faith is our means of accepting that salvation.*

The social-gospel movement of the late nineteenth and early twentieth century was convinced that the basic human problem lies not in a perverted human nature, but in an evil social environment that infects us. So instead of attempting to cure individuals, we must alter the conditions leading to their illness. We might say that the advocates of the social gospel were proposing a sort of spiritual public-health ministry.

The opposite approach has been advocated by those elements within Christianity that emphasize conversion. They hold that human nature is radically corrupt. The evils of society result from the fact that it is composed of evil individuals. Only as there is transformation of these individuals is there any real hope for changing society.

The Extent of Salvation

The extent of salvation is an issue for those who think of salvation as applying to individual persons rather than to society. The question is, Who or how many members of the human race will be saved? The particularist position sees salvation as based

that every individual will do so. Unfortunately, however, it does not appear that everyone in the past has accepted Christ; indeed, countless numbers did not even have the opportunity to do so. It consequently is not feasible to think of all as being saved in this fashion, unless there is some sort of unconscious means by which the conditions for salvation can be fulfilled. The more common universalist position is to assume that in the end God will on some basis simply accept all persons into eternal fellowship with himself.

Current Conceptions of Salvation

Liberation Theologies

One of the vital movements currently propounding its unique view of salvation is the cluster of theologies which may collectively be referred to as "liberation theologies." We might subdivide this movement into black, feminist, and Third World theologies. It is especially the last of these three that is referred to as liberation theology. While there are some significant differences which have

281

occasionally produced conflict among these groups, there is a sufficient commonality among them to enable us to trace some basic features of their view of the nature of salvation.

One of the common emphases here is that the basic problem of society is the oppression and exploitation of the powerless classes by the powerful. Salvation consists in deliverance (or liberation) from such oppression. The method of liberation will be appropriate to the nature of the specific situation.

The liberation theologies' analysis of humanity's predicament stems from two sources. First, there is a consensus that the capitalist or "developmentalist" approach to economic and political matters (all problems will automatically be solved as undeveloped nations advance along the path laid out by the industrial nations) is inherently both wrong and inept. To the liberation theologians it is increasingly apparent that the economic development of the advanced nations, as well as the prosperity of the elite social classes, is achieved at the expense of the less fortunate, who will never extricate themselves from their plight. Second, there is a sense that the Bible identifies with the oppressed. The charge that liberation theology is biased in its approach to the Bible is acknowledged to be true, but it is pointed out by way of response that the biblical writers shared this bias. The history of God's redemptive working is a history of groups of oppressed people. Certainly the people of Israel were oppressed in Egypt. Indeed, the Book of Exodus is one of liberation theology's favorite portions of God's Word. From the fact that much of Scripture is written from the perspective of the powerless, liberation theology concludes that God's message of salvation concerns them in particular.

But what is the specific nature of salvation as viewed by liberation theologies? They do not think of salvation primarily as individual life after death. The Bible, it is contended, concerns itself much more with achieving the kingdom of God in the present age. Even eternal life is usually placed in the context of a new social order, and is regarded as consisting not so much in being plucked out of history as in being a participant in its culmination. The salvation of all persons from oppression is the goal of God's work in history and must therefore be the task of those who believe in him. They will seek to bring about salvation in this sense by every means possible, including political effort and even revolution if necessary.

Existential Theology

A variety of twentieth-century theologies have been existential in the sense of being based upon or constructed from existential philosophy. Perhaps the outstanding representative of existential theology in this sense is Rudolf Bultmann. Bultmann sought to interpret the New Testament and indeed to construct a theology on the basis of the thought of existential philosopher Martin Heidegger. In Heidegger's thought, our aim should be authentic existence, that is, being what we are meant to be, living in such a way as to fulfil the potential which is ours as humans. An example of inauthenticity is failure to exercise one's ability to make choices and act freely. To do something simply because everyone else does it, going along with and conforming to the crowd, is to fail to be one's own person.[1] Another example of inauthenticity is unwillingness to accept the fact that one has acted freely and is therefore responsible. Authenticity, on the other hand, involves accepting responsibility for one's acts.

From Heidegger, Bultmann borrows the concept of authentic and inauthentic existence. In applying these ideas, Bultmann mentions two tendencies in modern humans. There is, on the one hand, a tendency to be guided in life by a self-orientation. Our chief aim is to fulfil our desires for happiness and security, usefulness and profit. Humans are selfish and presumptuous. Not

---

1. Martin Heidegger, *Being and Time* (New York: Harper and Row, 1962), pp. 163–68.

only are they disrespectful of the concerns and needs of others; they are also disobedient to the commands and claims of God upon their lives. They either deny that God exists or, if they do believe, deny that God has legitimate right to their obedience and devotion.[2]

The other tendency mentioned by Bultmann is that modern individuals believe that they can gain real security by their own efforts. The accumulation of wealth, the proliferation of technology, and the quest to wield influence are either individual or collective attempts of humans to guarantee their future. Death, however, inevitably comes, no matter what the human may do. And natural disasters cannot be anticipated or prevented. So human efforts to build security are doomed to failure. Still humans keep on trying. And as they continue to act selfishly and to seek security through their own efforts, they reject or deny all that they are intended to be. This is Bultmann's theological equivalent of inauthentic existence.[3]

What humans are called to by God and by the gospel is their true selves, their true destinies. This is, as it were, authentic existence or salvation. The word of God "calls man away from his selfishness and from the illusory security which he has built up for himself. It calls him to God, who is beyond the world and beyond scientific thinking. At the same time, it calls man to his true self."[4] Construed as obeying God by "turning our backs on self and abandoning all security," salvation is not, then, an alteration in the substance of the soul, as some have tended to understand regeneration, nor is it a forensic declaration that we are righteous in the sight of God, the traditional understanding of justification. Rather, it is a fundamental alteration of our *Existenz*, our whole outlook on and conduct of life.[5]

Secular Theology

The whole cultural milieu within which theology is developed has been changing. The human race's view of reality is undergoing alteration. In earlier periods most people believed in God. His activity was thought to be the explanation of the existence of the world and of what goes on within it, and he was the solver of the problems which humans faced. Today, however, many people put their trust in the visible, in the here and now, and in explanations which do not assume any transcendent or supersensible entities. They have become secular, that is, they have unconsciously come to follow a lifestyle which in practice has no place for God. Part of this secular outlook is the result of a basic pragmatism. Scientific endeavor has succeeded in meeting human needs; religion is no longer necessary or effective. So we live in a post-Christian era.[6]

There are two possible responses which the church can make to this situation. One is to see Christianity and secularism as competitors, alternatives to one another. In recent years, however, a different response has increasingly been adopted by Christian theologians. That is to regard secularism not as a competitor, but as a mature expression of Christian faith. One of the forerunners of this approach was Dietrich Bonhoeffer. In the final years of his life he developed a position which he referred to as "religionless Christianity."[7] God has educated his highest creature to be independent of him. Thus, God has been at work in the process of secularization. Others picked up and elaborated on Bonhoeffer's ideas. John A. T. Robinson in Great Britain and the Death of God theologians in the United States have been

2. Rudolf Bultmann, *Jesus Christ and Mythology* (New York: Scribner, 1958), pp. 39–40.

3. Ibid., p. 45.

4. Ibid., p. 40.

5. Rudolf Bultmann, "New Testament and Mythology," in *Kerygma and Myth*, ed. Hans Bartsch (New York: Harper and Row, 1961), pp. 18–19, 30.

6. Paul Van Buren, *The Secular Meaning of the Gospel* (New York: Macmillan, 1963), pp. 1–20; Langdon Gilkey, *Naming the Whirlwind: The Renewal of God-Language* (Indianapolis: Bobbs-Merrill, 1969), pp. 3–29.

7. Dietrich Bonhoeffer, *Letters and Papers from Prison*, enlarged ed. (New York: Macmillan, 1972), pp. 278–80.

the primary proponents of secular theology.[8]

Secular theology rejects the traditional understanding that salvation consists of removal from the world and reception of supernatural grace from God. Rather, salvation is not so much through religion as from religion. Realizing one's capability and utilizing it, becoming independent of God, coming of age, affirming oneself, and getting involved in the world—this is the true meaning of salvation.

Contemporary Roman Catholic Theology

When we come to examine contemporary Roman Catholic thinking on any subject, we have a difficult task. It is difficult because, whereas at one time there was a uniform, official position within Roman Catholicism on most issues, now there appears to be only great diversity. Official doctrinal standards still remain, but they are now supplemented, and in some cases are seemingly contradicted, by later statements. Among these later statements are the conclusions of the Second Vatican Council and the published opinions of individual Catholic scholars. It is necessary to see some of these statements against the background of the traditional stance of the church.

The official Catholic position has long been that the church is the only channel of the grace of God. This grace is transmitted through the sacraments of the church. Those outside the official or organized church cannot receive it. The church regarded itself as having an exclusive franchise for the distribution of divine grace.

This traditional position that union with the church is necessary for salvation has now been modified. For example, Yves Congar in effect argues for degrees of membership in the church.[9] While the majority of

the human race have no visible and official connection with the church, there is nonetheless such a thing as an invisible membership. The Vatican Council adopted a position similar to Congar's: the people of God are not limited to the visible, hierarchical church. This is not to say, however, that some of the people of God have no involvement with or do not participate in the visible or Catholic church. As a matter of fact, the people of God are divided into three categories in accordance with their degree of involvement with the church:

1. Catholics, who are "incorporated" into the church.
2. Non-Catholic Christians, who are "linked" to the church. While their situation is not as secure as that of Roman Catholics, they have genuine churches and are not completely separated from God.
3. Non-Christians, who are "related" to the church.[10]

The third group includes those whom Karl Rahner refers to as "anonymous Christians." The fact that people are outside the visible Catholic church (or any Christian church for that matter) does not mean that all of them are apart from the grace of God. Christ died for them as well, and we should not deny this grace.

There has also been discussion within the church regarding the nature of salvation. There has been a greater openness to the classical Protestant concept of justification. In this regard, Hans Küng's work on Karl Barth's theology has been particularly significant. In the past, Catholicism merged what Protestants term justification and sanctification into one concept, sanctifying grace. Küng, however, talks about objective and subjective aspects of justification. The former corresponds to what Protestants usu-

8. See, e.g., John A. T. Robinson, *Honest to God* (Philadelphia: Westminster, 1963).

9. Yves Congar, *The Wide World My Parish: Salvation and Its Problems* (Baltimore: Helicon, 1961), pp. 101–4.

10. "Dogmatic Constitution on the Church," in *The Documents of Vatican II*, ed. Walter M. Abbott (New York: Herder and Herder, 1966), pp. 30–35, secs. 13–16.

Figure 5. The Aspects of Salvation

Antecedents	Beginning	Continuation	Completion

| Election
Effectual Calling | Objective Aspects:
Union with Christ
Justification
Adoption

Subjective Aspects:
Conversion
Regeneration | Sanctification——Perseverance——Glorification | |

ally refer to as justification. In this aspect of salvation the human is passive and God is active. The latter corresponds roughly to what Protestants have usually called sanctification; here the human is active.[11] Küng observes that Barth emphasized the former whereas the Council of Trent emphasized the latter. Nonetheless, there is no real conflict between Barth and Trent.[12]

To summarize: the Catholic church has in recent years been more open to the possibility that some outside of the visible church, and perhaps some with absolutely no claim of being Christians, may be recipients of grace. As a result, the Catholic understanding of salvation has become somewhat broader than the traditional conception. In particular, the current understanding includes dimensions which have usually been associated with Protestantism.

Evangelical Theology

The traditional orthodox or evangelical position on salvation is correlated closely with the orthodox understanding of the human predicament. In this understanding, the relationship between the human being and God is the primary one. When that is not right, the other dimensions of life are adversely affected as well.

The Scriptures are understood by the evangelical to indicate that there are two major aspects to the human problem of sin.

11. Hans Küng, *Justification: The Doctrine of Karl Barth and a Catholic Reflection* (New York: Thomas Nelson, 1964), pp. 222–35, 264–74.
12. Ibid., pp. 275–84.

First, sin is a broken relationship with God. The human has failed to fulfil divine expectations, whether by transgressing limitations which God's law has set or by failing to do what is positively commanded there. Deviation from the law results in a state of guilt or liability to punishment. Second, the very nature of the person is spoiled as a result of deviation from the law. Now there is an inclination toward evil, a propensity for sin. Usually termed corruption, this often shows itself in terms of internal disorientation and conflict as well. Beyond that, because we live in the context of a network of interpersonal relationships, the rupture in our relationship with God also results in a disturbance of our relationships with other persons. Sin even takes on collective dimensions: the whole structure of society inflicts hardships and wrongs upon individuals and minority groups.

Certain aspects of the doctrine of salvation relate to the matter of one's standing with God. (For a diagram of the temporal relationships between the various aspects of salvation, see Figure 5.) The individual's legal status must be changed from guilty to not guilty. This is a matter of one's being declared just or righteous in God's sight, of being viewed as fully meeting the divine requirements. The theological term here is *justification*. One is justified by being brought into a legal union with Christ. More is necessary, however, than merely remission of guilt. Remember that the warm intimacy that should characterize one's relationship with God has been lost. This problem is rectified by *adoption*. In adoption one is restored to favor with God and given the opportunity to claim all the benefits provided by the loving Father.

In addition to the need to reestablish one's relationship with God, there is also a need to alter the condition of one's heart. The basic change in the direction of one's life from an inclination toward sin to a positive desire to live righteously is termed *regeneration* or, literally, new birth. An actual alteration of one's character is involved, an infusion of a positive spiritual energy. This, however, is merely the beginning of the spir-

> *Salvation both reestablishes our relationship with God and transforms the radically corrupt nature of our hearts.*

itual life. There also is a progressive alteration of the individual's spiritual condition; one actually becomes holier. This progressive subjective change is referred to as *sanctification* ("making holy"). Sanctification finally comes to completion in the life beyond death, when the spiritual nature of the believer will be perfected. This is termed *glorification*. The individual's maintaining faith and commitment to the very end through the grace of God is *perseverance*.

What, according to the evangelical construction of theology, are the means of salvation or, more broadly put, the means of grace? In the evangelical view, the Word of God plays an indispensable part in the whole matter of salvation. Peter speaks of this instrumental role of the Word of God: "You have been born anew, not of perishable seed but of imperishable, through the living and abiding word of God. . . . That word is the good news which was preached to you" (1 Peter 1:23, 25). Thus the Word of God, whether read or preached, is God's

means of presenting to us the salvation found in Christ; faith is our means of accepting that salvation.[13] Paul put this quite clearly in Ephesians 2:8–9: "For by grace you have been saved through faith; and this is not your own doing, it is the gift of God— not because of works, lest any man should boast." Works, then, are not a means of receiving salvation. Rather, they are the natural result and evidence of genuine faith.[14] Faith that does not produce works is not real faith. Conversely, works that do not stem from faith and a proper relationship to Christ will have no bearing at the time of judgment.

What, in evangelical theology, is the extent of salvation? That is, who will be saved? And specifically, will all be saved? From time to time, the position that all will be saved has been espoused in the church. This position, as we mentioned earlier in this chapter, is known as universalism. The church's usual view throughout history, however, and the view espoused by most evangelicals, is that while some or even many will be saved, some will not. The church took this position not because it did not want to see everyone saved, but because it believed there are clear statements in Scripture to the effect that some will be lost.

As we have done with respect to other issues, we will adopt the evangelical position on salvation. Although God is concerned about every human need, both individual and collective, Jesus made clear that the eternal spiritual welfare of the individual is infinitely more important than the supplying of temporal needs. God's preoccupation with our eternal spiritual welfare, and the biblical picture of sin as being so thoroughgoing that a radical transformation of human nature is required if restoration to favor with God is to be experienced, are compelling evidence for the evangelical view of salvation which we will develop in the following chapters.

13. Edward J. Carnell, *The Case for Orthodox Theology* (Philadelphia: Westminster, 1959), p. 70.

14. Alexander Ross, *The Epistles of James and John* (Grand Rapids: Eerdmans, 1954), pp. 54–55.

31 The Antecedent to Salvation: Predestination

Of all the doctrines of the Christian faith, certainly one of the most puzzling and least understood is the doctrine of predestination. It seems to many to be obscure and even bizarre. It appears to others to be an unnecessary inquiry into something that exceeds the human capacity to understand. Such theological hairsplitting is considered to have little if any practical significance. Perhaps more jokes have been made about this doctrine than about all other Christian doctrines combined. Yet because the biblical revelation mentions it, the Christian has no option but to inquire into its meaning. The fact that it is a difficult and obscure doctrine does not excuse us from the necessity of intensive study and reflection to determine just what the truth is in this matter.

It is necessary to define precisely what is meant by the term *predestination*. Although some use it interchangeably with "foreordination" and "election,"[1] for our purposes here "predestina-

1. E.g., Benjamin B. Warfield took the position that "'foreordain' and 'predestinate' are exact synonyms, the choice between which can be determined only by taste"—"Predestination," in *Biblical Doctrines* (New York: Oxford University Press, 1929), p. 4. Warfield uses "election" to designate what we are here labeling "predestination."

Figure 6. The Terminology of Predestination

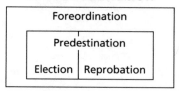

tion" is midway in specificity between "foreordination" and "election." "Foreordination," as seen in Figure 6, is the most inclusive term, denoting God's will with respect to all matters which occur, whether that be the fate of individual human persons or the falling of a rock. "Predestination" refers to God's choice of individuals for eternal life or eternal death. "Election" is the selection of some for eternal life, the positive side of predestination; "reprobation" is the negative side.

Differing Views of Predestination

Calvinism

While the doctrine of predestination has been developed by various theologians from Augustine to Karl Barth, the contrasting formulations of John Calvin and James Arminius most clearly focus the basic issues. What is designated Calvinism has taken many different forms over the years. We shall here examine certain common features found in all of them. A mnemonic aid sometimes used to summarize the complete system is the acronym TULIP: total depravity, unconditional predestination, limited atonement, irresistible grace, and perseverance.[2] While there are somewhat varying interpretations of these expressions, and not all of these concepts are essential to our current considerations, we will regard them as the framework for our examination of the Calvinist view of predestination.

Calvinists think of the whole human race as lost in sin. They emphasize the concept of total depravity: every individual is so sinful as to be unable to respond to any offer of grace. This condition, which we fully deserve, involves both moral corruption (and hence moral disability) and liability to punishment (guilt). All persons begin life in this condition. For this reason it is called "original sin." Sometimes the phrase "total inability" is used to describe the human plight. This terminology stresses that sinners have lost the ability to do good and are unable to convert themselves.[3] Numerous passages indicate both the universality and the seriousness of this condition (e.g., John 6:44; Rom. 3:1–23; 2 Cor. 4:3–4; and especially Eph. 2:1–3).

Calvinism's second major concept is the sovereignty of God. He is the Creator and Lord of all things, and consequently he is free to do whatever he wills.[4] He is not subject to or answerable to anyone. Humans are in no position to judge God for what he does. One of the passages frequently cited in this connection is the parable of the laborers in the vineyard. Those who were hired at the eleventh hour were paid the same amount promised to those hired at the beginning of the day. When those hired earlier complained about this seeming injustice, the master replied to one of them, "Friend, I am doing you no wrong; did you not agree with me for a denarius? Take what belongs to you, and go; I choose to give to this last as I give to you. Am I not allowed to do what I choose with what belongs to me? Or do you begrudge my generosity?" (Matt. 20:13–15). Another significant passage is Paul's metaphor of the potter and the clay. To the individual who complains that God is unjust, Paul responds: "But who are you, a man, to answer back to God? Will what is molded say to its molder, 'Why have you made me

2. See, e.g., Edwin H. Palmer, *The Five Points of Calvinism* (Grand Rapids: Baker, 1972); Duane Edward Spencer, *TULIP: The Five Points of Calvinism in the Light of Scripture* (Grand Rapids: Baker, 1979).

3. Loraine Boettner, *The Reformed Doctrine of Predestination*, 8th ed. (Grand Rapids: Eerdmans, 1958), pp. 61–82.
4. Benjamin B. Warfield, "Perfectionism," in *Biblical Doctrines*, pp. 62–64.

thus?' Has the potter no right over the clay, to make out of the same lump one vessel for beauty and another for menial use?" (Rom. 9:20–21). This concept of divine sovereignty, together with human inability, is basic to the Calvinistic doctrine of election.

Election, according to Calvinism, is God's choice of certain persons for his special favor. It may refer to the choice of Israel as impressively that all of these choices are totally of God and in no way depend on the people chosen. Having quoted God's statement to Moses in Exodus 33:19, "I will have mercy on whom I have mercy, and I will have compassion on whom I have compassion," Paul comments, "So it depends not upon man's will or exertion, but upon God's mercy" (Rom. 9:15–16).[6]

> *An impressive collection of biblical texts suggest that God has selected some to be saved, and that our response to the offer of salvation depends on this prior decision by God.*

God's special covenant people or to the choice of individuals to some special office. The sense which primarily concerns us here, however, is the choice of certain persons to be God's spiritual children and thus recipients of eternal life.[5] One biblical evidence that God has selected certain individuals for salvation is found in Ephesians 1:4–5: "[The Father] chose us in [Jesus Christ] before the foundation of the world, that we should be holy and blameless before him. He destined us in love to be his sons through Jesus Christ, according to the purpose of his will." Jesus indicated that the initiative had been his in the selection of his disciples to eternal life: "You did not choose me, but I chose you and appointed you that you should go and bear fruit and that your fruit should abide" (John 15:16). Furthermore, all who are given to Jesus by the Father will come to him: "All that the Father gives me will come to me; and him who comes to me I will not cast out" (John 6:37).

The interpretation that God's choice or selection of certain individuals for salvation is absolute or unconditional is in keeping with God's actions in other contexts, such as his choice of the nation Israel, which followed through on the selection of Jacob and rejection of Esau. In Romans 9 Paul argues

We have already seen several characteristics of election as viewed by Calvinists. One is that election is an expression of the sovereign will or good pleasure of God. It is not based on any merit in the one elected. Nor is it based upon foreseeing that the individual will believe. It is the cause, not the result, of faith. Second, election is efficacious. Those whom God has chosen will most certainly come to faith in him and, for that matter, will persevere in that faith to the end. All of the elect will certainly be saved. Third, election is from all eternity. It is not a decision made at some point in time when the individual is already existent. It is what God has always purposed to do. Fourth, election is unconditional. It does not depend upon human beings performing a specific action or meeting certain conditions or terms of God. It is not that God wills to save people if they do certain things. He simply wills to save them and brings it about. Finally, election is immutable. God does not change his mind. Election is from all eternity and out of God's infinite mercy; he has no reason or occasion to change his mind.[7]

For the most part, Calvinists insist that election is not inconsistent with free will,

5. Ibid., p. 65.

6. Ibid., p. 53.
7. Louis Berkhof, *Systematic Theology* (Grand Rapids: Eerdmans, 1953), pp. 114–15.

that is, as they understand the term. They deny, however, that humans have free will in the Arminian sense. What Calvinists emphasize is that sin has removed, if not freedom, at least the ability to exercise freedom properly. Loraine Boettner, for example, compares fallen humanity to a bird with a broken wing. The bird is "free" to fly, but is unable to do so. Likewise, "the natural man is free to come to God but not able. How can he repent of his sin when he loves it? How can he come to God when he hates Him? This is the inability of the will under which man labors."[8] It is only when God comes in his special grace to those whom he has chosen that they are able to respond.

One area where there are variations among Calvinists is the concept of reprobation. Some hold to double predestination, the belief that God chooses some to be saved and others to be lost. Others say that God actively chooses those who are to receive eternal life, and passes by all the others, leaving them in their self-chosen sins.[9] The effect is the same in both cases, but the latter view assigns the lostness of the nonelect to their own choice of sin rather than to the active decision of God, or to God's choice by omission rather than commission.

Arminianism

Arminianism is a term which covers a large number of subpositions. It may range all the way from the evangelical views of Arminius himself to left-wing liberalism. Arminianism also includes conventional Roman Catholicism with its emphasis on the necessity of works in the process of salvation. For the most part, we will be considering the more conservative or evangelical form of Arminianism, but we will construe it in a fashion broad enough to encompass the position of most Arminians.

While statements of the Arminian view vary to some degree, there is a logical starting point: the concept that God desires all persons to be saved.[10] Arminians point to some definite assertions of Scripture. That God finds no pleasure in the death of sinners is clear from Peter's statement, "The Lord is not slow about his promises as some count slowness, but is forbearing toward you, not wishing that any should perish, but that all should reach repentance" (2 Peter 3:9). Paul echoes a similar sentiment: "God our Savior . . . desires all men to be saved and to come to the knowledge of the truth" (1 Tim. 2:3–4; see also Ezek. 33:11; Acts 17:30–31).

It is not only in didactic statements, but in the universal character of many of God's commands and exhortations that his desire for the salvation of the entire human race is seen. The Old Testament contains universal invitations; for instance, "Ho, every one who thirsts, come to the waters; and he who has no money, come, buy and eat!" (Isa. 55:1). Jesus' invitation was similarly without restriction: "Come to me, all who labor and are heavy-laden, and I will give you rest" (Matt. 11:28). If, contrary to what these verses seem to imply, it is not God's intent that all persons be saved, he must be insincere in his offer.

A second major conception of Arminianism is that all persons are able to believe or to meet the conditions of salvation. If this were not the case, the universal invitations to salvation would make little sense. But is there room in theology for the concept that all persons are able to believe? There is, if we modify or eliminate the idea of the total depravity of sinners. Or like John Wesley and others, we might adopt the concept of "prevenient grace." It is this latter position that will occupy our attention here.[11]

As generally understood, prevenient grace is grace that is given by God to all persons indiscriminately. It is seen in God's sending

8. Boettner, *Predestination*, p. 62.
9. Augustus H. Strong, *Systematic Theology* (Westwood, N.J.: Revell, 1907), pp. 789–90.

10. Samuel Wakefield, *A Complete System of Christian Theology* (Cincinnati: Hitchcock and Walden, 1869), pp. 387, 392.
11. Richard Watson, *Theological Institutes; or, A View of the Evidences, Doctrines, Morals, and Institutions of Christianity* (New York: Lane and Scott, 1850), vol. 2, p. 377.

the sunshine and the rain upon all. It is also the basis of all the goodness found in people everywhere. Beyond that, it is universally given to counteract the effect of sin. Since God has given this grace to all, everyone is capable of accepting the offer of salvation; consequently, there is no need for any special application of God's grace to particular individuals.

A third basic concept is the role of foreknowledge in the election of persons to salvation. For the most part, Arminians desire to retain the term *election* and the idea that individuals are foreordained to salvation. This means that God must prefer some people to others. In the Arminian view, he chooses some to receive salvation, whereas he merely passes the others by. Those who are predestined by God are those who in his infinite knowledge he is able to foresee will accept the offer of salvation made in Jesus Christ. This view is based upon the close connection in Scripture between foreknowledge and foreordination or predestination. The primary passage appealed to is Romans 8:29: "For those whom he foreknew he also predestined to be conformed to the image of his Son, in order that he might be the first-born among many brethren." A supporting text is 1 Peter 1:1–2, where Peter addresses the "elect, . . . who have been chosen according to the foreknowledge of God the Father" (NIV). Both references represent foreordination as based upon and resulting from foreknowledge.[12]

Finally, the Arminian raises objections to the Calvinistic understanding of predestination as unconditional or absolute. Some of these are practical rather than theoretical in nature. Many of them reduce to the idea that Calvinism is fatalistic. If God has determined everything that is to occur, does it really make any difference what humans do? Ethical behavior becomes irrelevant. If we are elect, does it matter how we live? We will be saved regardless of our actions.

A further objection is that Calvinism negates any missionary or evangelistic impulse. If God has already chosen who will be saved, and their number cannot be increased, then what is the point of preaching the gospel? The elect will be saved anyway, and neither more nor less than the appointed number will come to Christ. So why bother to raise funds, send missionaries, preach the gospel, or pray for the lost? Such activities must surely be exercises in futility.[13]

The last objection is that the Calvinistic doctrine is a contradiction to human freedom. The thoughts that we have, the choices that we make, and the actions that we carry out are not really our doing. They are not free, but are caused by an external force, namely, God. And so we are not really human in the traditional sense of that word. We are automatons, robots, or machines. This, however, contradicts everything that we know about ourselves and the way in which we regard others as well. There is no point in God's commending us for having done good, or rebuking us for having done evil, for we could not have done otherwise.[14]

A Suggested Solution

We must now attempt to arrive at some conclusions regarding the nettlesome matter of the decrees of God with respect to salvation. Note that we are not dealing here with the whole matter of the decrees of God in general. In other words, we are not considering whether God renders certain every event that occurs within all of time and within the entire universe. We are concerned merely with the issue of whether some are singled out by God to be special recipients of his grace.

We begin with an examination of the biblical data. Scripture speaks of election in

12. H. Orton Wiley, *Christian Theology* (Kansas City, Mo.: Beacon Hill, 1958), vol. 2, p. 351.

13. John Wesley, "Free Grace," in *The Works of John Wesley*, 3d ed. (Kansas City, Mo.: Beacon Hill, 1979), vol. 7, p. 376.

14. Wakefield, *Complete System*, pp. 326–35; Wesley, "Free Grace," pp. 376–77.

several different senses. Election sometimes refers to God's choice of Israel as his specially favored people. It occasionally points to the selection of individuals to special positions of privilege and service, and, of course, to selection to salvation. In view of the varied meanings of election, any attempt to limit our discussion to only one of them will inevitably result in a truncation of the topic.

Prior to investigating the Bible's teaching that God has specially chosen some to have eternal life, it is important to consider its vivid picture of the lostness, blindness, and inability of humans in their natural state to respond in faith to the opportunity for salvation. In Romans, especially chapter 3, Paul

Brought back to the question of why some believe, we do find an impressive collection of texts suggesting that God has selected some to be saved, and that our response to the offer of salvation depends upon this prior decision and initiative by God. For example, in connection with Jesus' explaining that he spoke in parables so that some would hear but not understand, we observe that he went on to say to the disciples, "But blessed are your eyes, for they see, and your ears, for they hear" (Matt. 13:16). One might construe this to mean that they were not as spiritually incapacitated as were the other hearers. We can get a better grasp of what is entailed here, however, if we look at Matthew 16. Jesus had asked the disciples

It is not that those who are called must *respond, but that God makes his offer so appealing that they* will *respond.*

depicts the human race as hopelessly separated from God because of their sin. They are unable to do anything to extricate themselves from this condition, and in fact, being quite blind to their situation, have no desire to do so. Calvinists and conservative Arminians agree on this. It is not merely that humans cannot in their natural state do good works of a type that would justify them in God's sight. Beyond that, they are afflicted with spiritual blindness (Rom. 1:18–23; 2 Cor. 4:3–4) and insensitivity.

If this is the case, it follows that no one would ever respond to the gospel call without some special action by God. It is here that many Arminians, recognizing human inability as taught in the Scripture, introduce the concept of prevenient grace, which is believed to have a universal effect nullifying the noetic results of sin, thus making belief possible. The problem is that there is no clear and adequate basis in Scripture for this concept of a universal enablement. The theory, appealing though it is in many ways, simply is not taught explicitly in the Bible.

who men said that he was, and they had recited the varied opinions—John the Baptist, Elijah, Jeremiah, or one of the prophets (v. 14). Peter, however, confessed, "You are the Christ, the Son of the living God" (v. 16). Jesus' comment is instructive: "Blessed are you, Simon Bar-Jona! For flesh and blood has not revealed this to you, but my Father who is in heaven" (v. 17). It was a special action of God which made the difference between the disciples and the spiritually blind and deaf. This is in accordance with Jesus' statements, "No one can come to me unless the Father who sent me draws him" (John 6:44), and "You did not choose me, but I chose you" (John 15:16). Jesus also tells us that this drawing and choosing are efficacious: "All that the Father gives me will come to me; and him who comes to me I will not cast out" (John 6:37); "Every one who has heard and learned from the Father comes to me" (v. 45). The concept that our belief depends on God's initiative also appears in the Book of Acts, where Luke tells us that when the Gentiles at Antioch of Pisidia heard of salvation, "they were glad and glorified the word of God; and as many as were ordained to eternal life believed" (Acts 13:48).

Furthermore, the Arminian argument that God's foreordaining is based upon his foreknowledge is not persuasive. For the Hebrew word *yāda'*, which seems to lie behind the references to "foreknowledge" in Romans 8:29 and 1 Peter 1:1–2 (NIV), signifies more than an advance knowledge or precognition. It carries the connotation of a very positive and intimate relationship. It suggests looking with favor upon or loving someone, and is even used of sexual relations.[15] What is in view, then, is not a neutral advance knowledge of what someone will do, but an affirmative choice of that person. Against this Hebraic background it appears likely that the references to foreknowledge in Romans and 1 Peter are presenting foreknowledge not as the grounds for predestination, but as a confirmation of it.

But what of the universal offers of salvation and the general invitations to the hearers to believe? Arminians sometimes argue that, on Calvinistic grounds, someone might choose to accept salvation, but not be permitted to be saved. But according to the Calvinistic understanding, this scenario never takes place, for no one is able to will to be saved, to come to God, to believe, without special enablements. God sincerely offers salvation to all, but all of us are so settled in our sins that we will not respond unless assisted to do so.

Is there real freedom in such a situation? Here we refer the reader to our general discussion of human freedom in relationship to the plan of God (ch. 12). We must note additionally, however, that we are now dealing specifically with spiritual ability or freedom

of choice in regard to the critical issue of salvation. And here the chief consideration is depravity. If, as we have argued, humans in the unregenerate state are totally depraved and unable to respond to God's grace, there is no question as to whether they are free to accept the offer of salvation—no one is! Rather, the question to be asked is, Is anyone who is specially called free to reject the offer of grace? The position taken herein is not that those who are called *must* respond, but that God makes his offer so appealing that they *will* respond affirmatively.

Implications of Predestination

Correctly understood, the doctrine of predestination has several significant implications:

1. We can have confidence that what God has decided will come to pass. His plan will be fulfilled, and the elect will come to faith.

2. We need not criticize ourselves when some people reject Christ. Jesus himself did not win everyone in his audience. He understood that all those whom the Father gave to him would come to him (John 6:37) and only they would come (v. 44). When we have done our very best, we can leave the matter with the Lord.

3. Predestination does not nullify incentive for evangelism and missions. We do not know who the elect and the nonelect are, so we must continue to spread the Word. Our evangelistic efforts are God's means to bring the elect to salvation. God's ordaining of the end includes the ordaining of the means to that end as well. The knowledge that missions are God's means is a strong motive for the endeavor and gives us confidence that it will prove successful.

4. Grace is absolutely necessary. While Arminianism often gives strong emphasis to grace, in our Calvinistic scheme there is no basis for God's choice of some to eternal life other than his own sovereign will. There is nothing in the individual which persuades God to grant salvation.

15. Francis Brown, S. R. Driver, and Charles A. Briggs, *Hebrew and English Lexicon of the Old Testament* (New York: Oxford University Press, 1955), p. 394; Paul Jacobs and Hartmut Krienke, "Foreknowledge, Providence, Predestination," in *The New International Dictionary of New Testament Theology*, ed. Colin Brown (Grand Rapids: Zondervan, 1975), vol. 1, pp. 692–93.

32 The Beginning of Salvation: Subjective Aspects

The doctrine of salvation encompasses a large and complex area of biblical teaching and of human experience. Consequently, it is necessary to draw some distinctions among its various facets. While we could organize the material in many different ways, we have chosen to utilize a temporal scheme. We will look at salvation in terms of its beginning, continuation, and completion. Chapters 32 and 33 both deal with the inception of the Christian life. They are distinguished, however, by a difference of perspective. Conversion and regeneration (ch. 32) are subjective aspects of the beginning of the Christian life; they deal with change in our inward nature, our spiritual condition. Conversion is this change as viewed from the human perspective; regeneration is this change as viewed from God's perspective. Union with Christ, justification, and adoption (ch. 33), on the other hand, are objective aspects of the beginning of the Christian life; they refer primarily to the relationship between the individual and God.

Effectual Calling

There are certain matters which are pre-liminary to actual salvation. In the preceding chapter we examined the whole complex of issues involved in predestination, concluding that God chooses some persons to be saved and that their conversion is a result of that decision on God's part. Because all humans are lost in sin, spiritually blind, and unable to believe, however, some action by God must intervene between his eternal decision and the conversion of the individual the conversion of Saul (Acts 9:1–19). Sometimes his calling takes a quieter form, as in the case of Lydia: "The Lord opened her heart to give heed to what was said by Paul" (Acts 16:14).

Special calling is in large measure the Holy Spirit's work of illumination, enabling the recipient to understand the true meaning of the gospel. This working of the Spirit is necessary because the depravity which is characteristic of all humans prevents them from grasping God's revealed truth. Com-

---

Effectual calling is God's special work with the elect, enabling them to respond in repentance and faith, and rendering it certain that they will.

---

within time. This activity of God is termed special or effectual calling.

It is apparent from Scripture that there is a general calling to salvation, an invitation extended to all persons. Jesus said, "Come to me, all who labor and are heavy-laden, and I will give you rest" (Matt. 11:28). Further, when Jesus said, "Many are called, but few are chosen" (Matt. 22:14), he was probably referring to God's universal invitation. But note the distinction here between calling and choosing. Those who are chosen are the objects of God's special or effectual calling.

Special calling means that God works in a particularly effective way with the elect, enabling them to respond in repentance and faith, and rendering it certain that they will. The circumstances of special calling can vary widely. We see Jesus issuing special invitations to those who became the inner circle of disciples (see, e.g., Matt. 4:18–22; Mark 1:16–20; John 1:35–51). He singled out Zacchaeus for particular attention (Luke 19:1–10). In these cases, Jesus no doubt presented his claims in a direct and personal fashion which carried a special persuasiveness not felt by the surrounding crowd. We see another dramatic approach by God in menting on 1 Corinthians 2:6–16, George Ladd remarks that

> the first work of the Spirit is to enable men to understand the divine work of redemption. . . . This [the cross] was an event whose meaning was folly to Greeks and an offense to Jews. But to those enlightened by the Spirit, it is the wisdom of God. In other words, Paul recognizes a hidden meaning in the historical event of the death of Christ ("God was in Christ reconciling the world to himself," II Cor. 5:19) that is not evident to the human eye but which can be accepted only by a supernatural illumination. . . . Only by the illumination of the Spirit can men understand the meaning of the cross; only by the Spirit can men therefore confess that Jesus who was executed is also the Lord (I Cor. 12:3).[1]

Special or effectual calling, then, involves an extraordinary presentation of the message of salvation. It is sufficiently powerful to counteract the effects of sin and enable the person to believe. It is also so appealing that the person will believe. Special calling

---

1. George E. Ladd, *A Theology of the New Testament* (Grand Rapids: Eerdmans, 1974), pp. 490–91.

is in many ways similar to the prevenient grace of which Arminians speak. It differs from that concept, however, in two respects. It is bestowed only upon the elect, not upon all humans, and it leads infallibly or efficaciously to a positive response by the recipient.

Conversion

The Christian life, by its very nature and definition, represents something quite different from the way in which we previously lived. In contrast to being dead in sins and trespasses, it is *new* life. While it is of lifelong and even eternal duration, it has a finite point of beginning. "A journey of a thousand miles must begin with a single step," said the Chinese philosopher Lao-tzu. And so it is with the Christian life. The first step of the Christian life is called conversion. It is the act of turning from one's sin in repentance and turning to Christ in faith.

The image of turning from sin is found in both the Old and New Testaments. In the Book of Ezekiel we read the word of the Lord to the people of Israel: "Therefore I will judge you, O house of Israel, every one according to his ways, says the Lord GOD. Repent and turn from all your transgressions, lest iniquity be your ruin. Cast away from you all the transgressions which you have committed against me, and get yourselves a new heart and a new spirit! Why will you die, O house of Israel? For I have no pleasure in the death of anyone, says the Lord GOD; so turn, and live" (Ezek. 18:30–32). In Ephesians 5:14 Paul uses different imagery, but the basic thrust is the same: "Awake, O sleeper, and arise from the dead, and Christ shall give you light." In Acts we find Peter advocating a change in direction of life: "Repent therefore, and turn again, that your sins may be blotted out" (Acts 3:19). While contemporary evangelists frequently plead, "Be converted," it is noteworthy that in the passages we have cited, the command is in the active. What is actually said is, "Convert!"

Conversion is a single entity which has two distinguishable but inseparable aspects: repentance and faith. Repentance is the unbeliever's turning away from sin, and faith is his or her turning toward Christ. They are, respectively, the negative and positive aspect of the same occurrence.[2] In a sense, each is incomplete without the other, and each is motivated by the other. As we become aware of sin and turn from it, we see the necessity of turning to Christ for the provision of his righteousness. Conversely, believing in Christ makes us aware of our sin and thus leads to repentance.

Scripture gives no specifications concerning the amount of time conversion involves. On some occasions (e.g., Pentecost) it appears to have been a cataclysmic decision, with the change taking place virtually in a moment's time. On the other hand, for some people conversion was something more of a process (e.g., Nicodemus; see John 19:39). Similarly, the emotional accompaniments of conversion can vary greatly. Lydia's turning to Christ seems to have been very simple and calm in nature (Acts 16:14). On the other hand, just a few verses later we read of the Philippian jailer, who, still trembling with fear upon hearing that none of the prisoners had escaped after the earthquake, cried out, "What must I do to be saved?" (v. 30). The conversion experiences of these two people were very different, but the end result was the same.

Sometimes the church has forgotten that there is variety in God's ways of working. On the American frontier a certain type of preaching became stereotypical. Life was uncertain and often difficult, and the circuit-riding evangelist came only on infrequent occasions. The general pattern of preaching included a strong emphasis upon the awfulness of sin, a vivid presentation of the death of Christ and its benefits, and then

2. Charles M. Horne, *Salvation* (Chicago: Moody, 1971), p. 55; Fritz Laubach, "Conversion, Penitence, Repentance, Proselyte," in *The New International Dictionary of New Testament Theology*, ed. Colin Brown (Grand Rapids: Zondervan, 1975), vol. 1, p. 354.

an emotional appeal to accept Christ. The hearers were pressed to make an immediate decision.[3] And so conversion came to be thought of as a crisis decision. Although God frequently does work with individuals in this way, differences in personality type, background, and immediate circumstances may result in a very different type of conversion. It is important not to insist that the incidentals or external factors of conversion be identical for everyone.

It is important also to draw a distinction between conversion and conversions. There is just one major point in life when the individual turns toward Christ in response to the offer of salvation. There may be other points when believers must abandon a particular practice or belief lest they revert to a life of sin. These events, however, are secondary, reaffirmations of the one major step that has been taken. We might say that there may be many conversions in the Christian's life, but only one Conversion.

Repentance

The negative aspect of conversion is the abandonment or repudiation of sin. This is what we mean by repentance. It is based upon a feeling of godly sorrow for the evil we have done. As we examine repentance and faith, it should be remembered that they cannot really be separated from one another. We will deal with repentance first because where one has been logically precedes where one is going.

There are two Hebrew terms which express the idea of repentance. One is *nācham*, signifying "to pant, sigh, or groan." It came to mean "to lament or to grieve." When used in reference to an emotion aroused by consideration of one's own character and deeds, it means "to rue" or "to repent."[4] Interestingly, when *nācham* occurs in the sense of

"repent," the subject of the verb is usually God. A prime example is Genesis 6:6: "And the LORD was sorry that he had made man on the earth, and it grieved him to his heart."

The type of genuine repentance that humans are to display is more commonly designated by the word *shûv*. It is used extensively in the prophets' calls to Israel to return to the Lord. It stresses the importance of a conscious moral separation, the necessity of forsaking sin and entering into fellowship with God.[5]

In the New Testament there are also two major terms for repentance. The word *metamelomai* means "to have a feeling of care, concern, or regret."[6] It stresses the emotional aspect of repentance, a feeling of regret or remorse for having done wrong. Jesus used the word in his parable of the two sons. When the first son was asked by his father to go and work in the vineyard, "he answered, 'I will not'; but afterward he repented and went" (Matt. 21:29). The second son said he would go, but did not. Jesus likened the chief priests and Pharisees (whom he was addressing) to the second son and repentant sinners to the first son. The word *metamelomai* is also used of Judas's remorse over his betrayal of Jesus (Matt. 27:3). It appears that *metamelomai* can designate simply regret and remorse over one's actions, as in the case of Judas. Or it can represent true repentance, which involves an actual alteration of behavior as in the case of the first son. It is instructive to contrast the actions of Judas and Peter in response to their sins. Peter returned to Jesus and was restored to fellowship. In the case of Judas, awareness of sin led only to despair and self-destruction.

The other major New Testament term for repentance is *metanoeō*, which literally means "to think differently about something

---

3. W. L. Muncy, Jr., *A History of Evangelism in the United States* (Kansas City, Kans.: Central Seminary, 1945), pp. 86–90.

4. Francis Brown, S. R. Driver, and Charles A. Briggs, *Hebrew and English Lexicon of the Old Testament* (New York: Oxford University Press, 1955), pp. 636–37.

5. Ibid., pp. 996–1000.

6. Otto Michel, μεταμέλομαι, in *Theological Dictionary of the New Testament*, ed. Gerhard Kittel and Gerhard Friedrich, trans. Geoffrey W. Bromiley, 10 vols. (Grand Rapids: Eerdmans, 1964–1976), vol. 4, p. 626.

or to have a change of mind." It was a key term in the preaching of the early church. On Pentecost Peter urged the multitude, "Repent, and be baptized every one of you in the name of Jesus Christ for the forgiveness of your sins; and you shall receive the gift of the Holy Spirit" (Acts 2:38).

As we examine this matter of repentance, we cannot avoid being impressed with its importance as a prerequisite for salvation. The large number of verses and the variety of contexts in which repentance is stressed make clear that it is not optional but indispensable. That people in many different cultural settings were urged to repent shows that it is not a message meant only for a few specific local situations. Rather, repentance is an essential part of the Christian gospel. It was prominent in the preaching of John the Baptist and of Jesus (Matt. 3:2; 4:17). And Paul declared in his message to the philosophers on Mars' Hill: "The times of ignorance God overlooked, but now he commands all men everywhere to repent" (Acts 17:30). This last statement is especially significant, for it is universal: *all* men *everywhere.* There can be no doubt, then, that repentance is an ineradicable part of the gospel message.

It is important for us to understand the nature of true repentance. Repentance is godly sorrow for one's sin together with a resolution to turn from it. There are other forms of regret over one's wrongdoing which are based upon different motivations. One form of regret may be motivated by little more than selfishness. If we have sinned and the consequences are unpleasant, we may well regret what we have done. But that is not true repentance. That is mere penitence. Real repentance is sorrow for one's sin because of the wrong done to God and the hurt inflicted upon him. This sorrow is accompanied by a genuine desire to abandon that sin.

The Bible's repeated emphasis upon the necessity of repentance is an incontrovertible argument against what Dietrich Bonhoeffer called "cheap grace" (or "easy be-

lievism").[7] It is not enough simply to believe in Jesus and accept the offer of grace; there must be a real alteration of the inner person. If belief in God's grace were all that is necessary, who would not wish to become a Christian? But Jesus said, "If any man would come after me, let him deny himself and take up his cross daily and follow me" (Luke 9:23). If there is no conscious repentance, there is no real awareness of having been saved from the power of sin. There may be a corresponding lack of depth and commitment. Any attempt to increase the number of disciples by making discipleship as easy as possible ends up diluting the quality of discipleship instead.

Faith

As repentance is the negative aspect of conversion, turning from one's sin, so faith is the positive aspect, laying hold upon the promises and the work of Christ. Faith is at the very heart of the gospel, for it is the vehicle by which we are enabled to receive the grace of God. Once again it is important to look first at the biblical terminology.

Old Testament Hebrew conveys the idea of faith primarily with verb forms. Perhaps that is because the Hebrews regarded faith as something that one does rather than as something one has. It is an activity rather than a possession. Specifically, the Hebrew idea of faith is a confident resting or leaning upon someone or something, usually God or his word of promise.

When we turn to the New Testament, there is one primary word which represents the idea of faith. It is the verb *pisteuō* together with its cognate noun *pistis.* The verb has two basic meanings. First, it means "to believe what someone says, to accept a statement (particularly of a religious nature) as true."[8] An example is found in 1 John 4:1: "Beloved, do not believe every spirit, but test the spirits to see whether they are of God." A

7. Dietrich Bonhoeffer, *The Cost of Discipleship* (New York: Macmillan, 1963), pp. 45–47.
8. Rudolf Bultmann, πιστεύω, in *Theological Dictionary of the New Testament*, vol. 6, p. 203.

dramatic instance of the verb is Jesus' statement to the centurion, "Go; be it done for you as you have believed" (Matt. 8:13). Greatly impressed, Jesus rewarded the centurion's belief that his servant could be healed. These and numerous other instances (e.g., Matt. 9:28; Mark 5:36) establish that faith involves believing that something is true. Indeed, the author of Hebrews declares that faith in the sense of acknowledging certain truths is indispensable to salvation: "And without faith it is impossible to please him. For whoever would draw near to God must believe that he exists and that he rewards those who seek him" (Heb. 11:6).

At least equally important are the instances in which *pisteuō* and *pistis* signify "personal trust as distinct from mere credence or belief."[9] This sense is usually identifiable through the use of a preposition. In Mark 1:15 the Greek preposition *en* ("in") is used: after the Baptist's arrest Jesus preached in Galilee, saying, "Repent, and believe in the gospel." The preposition *eis* ("in") is used in Acts 10:43: "To him all the prophets bear witness that every one who believes in him receives forgiveness of sins through his name." The same construction is found in Matthew 18:6; John 2:11; Acts 19:4; Galatians 2:16; Philippians 1:29; 1 Peter 1:8; and 1 John 5:10. The apostle John speaks of believing in the name of Jesus: "But to all who received him, who believed in his name, he gave power to become children of God" (John 1:12; see also 2:23; 3:18; and 1 John 5:13). This construction had special significance to the Hebrews, who regarded one's name as virtually equivalent to the individual. Thus, to believe on or in the name of Jesus was to place one's personal trust in him.[10]

On the basis of the foregoing considerations, we conclude that the type of faith necessary for salvation involves both believing that and believing in, or assenting to facts and trusting in a person. It is vital to keep these two together. The God in whom we are to trust reveals himself, at least in part, through communicating information about himself to which we are to assent.

Sometimes faith is pictured as being antithetical to reason and unconfirmable. It is true that faith is not something established on an antecedent basis by indisputable evidence. But it is also the case that faith, once engaged in, enables us to reason and to recognize various evidences supporting it.[11] This means that faith is a form of knowledge; it works in concert with, not against, reason. Pertinent here is Jesus' response to the two disciples whom John the Baptist sent to ask, "Are you he who is to come, or shall we look for another?" (Luke 7:19). Jesus responded by telling them to report to John the miracles which they had seen and the message which they had heard. Jesus in effect said to John, "Here is the evidence you need in order to be able to believe."

We should note that although we have depicted conversion as a human response to divine initiative, even repentance and faith are gifts from God. Jesus made very clear that conviction, which is presupposed by repentance, is the work of the Holy Spirit (John 16:8–11). Jesus also said, "No one can come to me [i.e., exercise faith] unless the Father who sent me draws him; and I will raise him up at the last day" (John 6:44). Thus, both repentance and faith are gracious works of God in the life of the believer.

Regeneration

Conversion refers to our response to God's offer of salvation and approach to humankind. Regeneration is the other side of conversion. It is God's doing. It is God's transformation of individual believers, his giving a new spiritual vitality and direction to their lives when they accept Christ.

9. G. Abbott-Smith, *A Manual Greek Lexicon of the New Testament* (Edinburgh: T. and T. Clark, 1937), pp. 361–62.

10. Ladd, *Theology of the New Testament*, pp. 271–72.

11. Augustine *Letter* 137.15; cf. Ladd, *Theology of the New Testament*, pp. 276–77.

Underlying the doctrine of regeneration is an assumption regarding human nature. Human nature is in need of transformation. The human being is spiritually dead and therefore needs new birth or spiritual birth.[12] Not only are unbelievers unable to perceive spiritual truths; they are incapable of doing anything to alter their condition of blindness and their natural tendency toward sin. When one reads the description of the sinful human in Romans 3:9–20, it is apparent that some radical change or metamorphosis is needed, rather than a mere modification or adjustment in the person.

The Biblical Descriptions

The biblical descriptions of the new birth are numerous, vivid, and varied. Even in the Old Testament, we find a striking reference to God's renewing work. He promises, "And I will give them a new heart, and put a new spirit within them; I will take the stony heart out of their flesh and give them a heart of flesh, that they may walk in my statutes and keep my ordinances and obey them; and they shall be my people, and I will be their God" (Ezek. 11:19–20).

In the New Testament, the term which most literally conveys the idea of regeneration is *palingenesia* ("rebirth"). It appears just twice in the New Testament. One of these instances is Matthew 19:28, where it refers to the "new world" which will be part of the consummation of history. The other is Titus 3:5, which refers to salvation: God our Savior "saved us, not because of deeds done by us in righteousness, but in virtue of his own mercy, by the washing of regeneration and renewal in the Holy Spirit." Here we have the biblical idea of rebirth.

The best-known and most extensive exposition of the concept of the new birth is found in Jesus' conversation with Nicodemus in John 3. Jesus told Nicodemus, "Unless one is born anew, he cannot see the kingdom of God" (v. 3). At a later point in the discussion he made the comment, "Do not marvel that I said to you, 'You must be born anew'" (v. 7). In the same conversation, Jesus spoke of being "born of the Spirit." He had in mind a supernatural work transforming the life of the individual. This work, which is indispensable if one is to enter the kingdom of God, is not something that can be achieved by human effort or planning. It is also spoken of as being "born of God" or "born through the word of God" (John 1:12–13; James 1:18; 1 Peter 1:3, 23; 1 John 2:29; 5:1, 4). Whoever undergoes this experience is a new creation (2 Cor. 5:17). Paul speaks of the renewing in the Holy Spirit (Titus 3:5), of being made alive (Eph. 2:1, 5), and of resurrection from the dead (Eph. 2:6). The same idea is implicit in Jesus' statements that he had come to give life (John 6:63; 10:10, 28).

The Meaning of Regeneration

While it is fairly easy to list instances where the idea of new birth occurs, it is not so easy to ascertain its meaning. We ought not to be surprised that the new birth is difficult to understand, however.[13] Jesus indicated to Nicodemus, who was having great difficulty grasping what Jesus was talking about, that the concept is difficult. It is like the wind: although one does not know where it comes from or where it goes, one hears its sound (John 3:8). Not only is the new birth not perceived by the senses, but the concept itself encounters natural resistance.

Despite the problems in understanding the concept, several assertions can be made about regeneration. First, it involves something new, a whole reversal of the person's natural tendencies. It is not merely an amplification of present traits. For one side of regeneration involves putting to death or crucifying existent qualities. Contrasting the life in the Spirit with that in the flesh, Paul says: "And those who belong to Christ Jesus have crucified the flesh with its passions and desires. If we live by the Spirit, let us also

---

12. Ladd, *Theology of the New Testament*, p. 290.

13. Millard J. Erickson, "The New Birth Today," *Christianity Today*, 16 Aug. 1974, pp. 8–10.

walk by the Spirit" (Gal. 5:24–25). Other references to the death of the individual or of certain aspects of the individual include Romans 6:1–11 and Galatians 2:20; 6:14.

As a putting to death of the flesh, the new birth involves a counteracting of the effects of sin. This is perhaps most clearly seen in Paul's statement in Ephesians 2:1–10. The deadness that requires a transformation is a result of the sin in which we live, being led by the prince of the power of the air. Although regeneration involves something totally new to us, it does not result in anything

the beginning of a process of growth which continues throughout one's lifetime. This process of spiritual maturation is sanctification. Having noted that his readers were formerly dead but are now alive, Paul adds, "For we are his workmanship, created in Christ Jesus for good works, which God prepared beforehand, that we should walk in them" (Eph. 2:10). He speaks in Philippians 1:6 of continuing and completing what has been begun.

New birth is a supernatural occurrence. It is not something which can be accom-

> *Regeneration is God's transformation of individual believers—he reverses their natural tendencies, gives a new spiritual vitality to their lives, and thus restores them to what they were originally intended to be.*

foreign to human nature. Rather, the new birth is the restoration of human nature to what it originally was intended to be and what it in fact was before sin entered the human race at the time of the fall. It is simultaneously the beginning of a new life and a return of the old life and activity.

Further, it appears that the new birth is itself instantaneous. There is nothing in the descriptions of the new birth to suggest that it is a process rather than a single action. It is nowhere characterized as incomplete. Scripture speaks of believers as "born again" or "having been born again" rather than as "being born again" (John 1:12–13; 2 Cor. 5:17; Eph. 2:1, 5–6; James 1:18; 1 Peter 1:3, 23; 1 John 2:29; 5:1, 4). While it may not be possible to determine the precise time of the new birth, and there may be a whole series of antecedents, it appears that the new birth itself is completed in an instant.[14]

Although regeneration is instantaneously complete, it is not an end in itself. As a change of spiritual impulses, regeneration is

14. Augustus H. Strong, *Systematic Theology* (Westwood, N.J.: Revell, 1907), pp. 826–27.

plished by human effort. Jesus made this clear in John 3:6: "That which is born of the flesh is flesh, and that which is born of the Spirit is spirit." It is also important to bear in mind that regeneration is especially the work of the Holy Spirit. Although salvation was planned and originated by the Father and actually accomplished by the Son, it is the Holy Spirit who applies it to the life of the believer, thus bringing to fulfilment the divine intention for humans.

The doctrine of regeneration places the Christian faith in an unusual position. On the one hand, Christians reject the current secular belief in the goodness of the human and the optimistic expectations arising therefrom. The very insistence upon regeneration is a declaration that without external help and complete transformation there is no possibility that genuine good on a large scale will emerge from humankind. On the other hand, despite the pessimistic assessment of the natural powers of the human, Christianity is very optimistic: with supernatural aid humans can be transformed and restored to their original goodness. It was in regard to God's ability to change human hearts, enabling us to enter his kingdom, that Jesus said, "With men this is impossible, but with God all things are possible" (Matt. 19:26).

Implications of Effectual Calling, Conversion, and Regeneration

1. Human nature cannot be altered by social reforms or education. It must be transformed by a supernatural work of the Triune God.

2. No one can predict or control who will experience new birth. It is ultimately God's doing; even conversion depends upon his effectual calling.

3. The beginning of the Christian life requires a recognition of one's own sinfulness and a determination to abandon the self-centered way of life.

4. Saving faith requires correct belief regarding the nature of God and what he has done. Correct belief is insufficient, however. There must also be active commitment of oneself to God.

5. One person's experience of conversion may be radically different from that of another. What is important is that there be genuine repentance and faith.

6. The new birth is not felt when it occurs. It will, rather, establish its presence by producing a new sensitivity to spiritual things, a new direction of life, and an increasing ability to obey God.

33 The Beginning of Salvation: Objective Aspects

Thus far we have examined those aspects of the beginning of the Christian life which involve the actual spiritual condition of the person, that is, the subjective aspects of the beginning of salvation. In this chapter we will be considering the change in the individual's status or standing in relationship to God, that is, the objective dimensions of the beginning of salvation.

Union with Christ

The Scriptural Teaching

In one sense, union with Christ is an inclusive term for the whole of salvation; the various other doctrines are simply subparts.[1] While this term and concept are often neglected in favor

1. John Murray, *Redemption—Accomplished and Applied* (Grand Rapids: Eerdmans, 1955), p. 161.

of concentrating on other concepts such as regeneration, justification, and sanctification, it is instructive to note the large number of references to the oneness between Christ and the believer. The most basic references in this connection depict the believer and Christ as being "in" one another. On the one hand, we have many specific references to the believer's being in Christ; for example, 2 Corinthians 5:17: "Therefore, if any one is in Christ, he is a new creation; the old has passed away, behold, the new has come." There are two such phrases in Ephesians 1:3–4: "Blessed be the God and Father of our Lord Jesus Christ, who has blessed us in Christ with every spiritual blessing in the heavenly places, even as he chose us in him before the foundation of the world, that we should be holy and blameless before him." Two verses later we read of the "glorious grace which he freely bestowed on us in the Beloved. In him we have redemption through his blood, the forgiveness of our trespasses, according to the riches of his grace, which he lavished upon us" (vv. 6–8). Similar expressions occur in 1 Corinthians 1:4–5; 15:22; Ephesians 2:10; and 1 Thessalonians 4:16.

The other side of this relationship is that Christ is said to be in the believer. Paul says, "To [the saints] God chose to make known how great among the Gentiles are the riches of the glory of this mystery, which is Christ in you, the hope of glory" (Col. 1:27). Christ's presence in the believer is also expressed, in a somewhat different way, in Galatians 2:20: "I have been crucified with Christ; it is no longer I who live, but Christ who lives in me; and the life I now live in the flesh I live by faith in the Son of God, who loved me and gave himself for me." There is also Jesus' analogy of the vine and branches, which emphasizes the mutual indwelling of Christ and the believer (John 15:4–5). It is apparent that all that the believer has spiritually is based upon Christ's being within. Our hope of glory is Christ in us. Our spiritual vitality is drawn from his indwelling presence. Other passages we might mention include Jesus' promises to be present with the believer (Matt. 28:20; John 14:23). Finally, there is also a whole host of experiences which the believer is said to share "with Christ": suffering (Rom. 8:17); crucifixion (Gal. 2:20); death (Col. 2:20); burial (Rom. 6:4); quickening (Eph. 2:5); resurrection (Col. 3:1); glorification and inheritance (Rom. 8:17).

Inadequate Models

Although there are numerous references to our union with Christ, we must nevertheless ask what precisely is entailed, for the language is less than lucid. In what sense can Christ be said to be in us, and we in him? Are these expressions completely metaphorical, or is there some literal referent?

Several explanations which have been offered do not accurately convey what this doctrine involves. Among them is the view that our union with Christ is metaphysical. The underlying idea here is the pantheistic concept that we are one in essence with God. This explanation, however, goes beyond the teaching of Scripture.

A second model which has been proposed is that our union with Christ is mystical.[2] The relationship between the believer and Jesus is so deep and absorbing that the believer virtually loses his or her own individuality. In contrast, Scripture makes it clear that strong as is the influence of Christ upon the believer, they remain two. They do not merge into one, nor is one of them submerged into the personality of the other.

A third model sees our union with Christ as being like the union between two friends or between a teacher and student. A psychological oneness results from sharing the same interests and being committed to the same ideals. If the second model errs by making the connection between Christ and

2. Adolf Deissmann, *Paul: A Study in Social and Religious History*, 2d ed. (New York: George H. Doran, 1926), pp. 142–57. In its more extreme forms, which Deissmann terms "unio-mysticism," this view verges on pantheism.

the believer too strong, this third model makes it too weak.

A fourth inadequate model is the sacramental view—the believer obtains the grace of Jesus Christ by receiving the sacraments.[3] Indeed, one actually takes Christ into himself by participating in the Lord's Supper, eating Christ's flesh and drinking his blood. This model is based upon a literal interpretation of Jesus' words in instituting the Lord's Supper, "This is my body. . . . this is my blood" (Matt. 26:26–28; Mark 14:22–24; Luke 22:19–20; see also John 6:53). Taking these passages in the most literal sense seems unwarranted and leads to some virtually ludicrous conclusions (e.g., that Jesus' flesh and blood are simultaneously part of his body and the elements of the Eucharist, as the Lord's Supper is often termed by sacramentalists). A further difficulty with this view is that a human intermediary administers the sacraments. This conception contradicts the statements in Hebrews 9:23–10:25 that Jesus has eliminated the need for mediators and that we may now come directly to him.

Characteristics of the Union

It is not sufficient, however, to point out the deficiencies of the models we have just mentioned. We must ask just what the concept of union with Christ does mean. To gain a grasp of the concept, we will note several characteristics of the union. We must not expect that we will be able to comprehend this matter completely, for Paul said, "This is a great mystery" (Eph. 5:32). He was referring to the fact that knowledge of this union is inaccessible to humans except through special revelation from God.

The first characteristic of our union with Christ is that it is judicial in nature. When the Father evaluates or judges us before the law, he does not look upon us alone. We are in his sight one with Christ. Thus, he does not say, "Jesus is righteous but that human

is unrighteous." He sees the two as one and says in effect, "They are righteous." The believer has been incorporated into Christ and Christ into the believer (although not exclusively so). All of the assets of each are now mutually possessed. From a legal perspective, the two are now one.

Second, the union of the believer with Christ is spiritual. This has two meanings. On the one hand, the union is effected by the Holy Spirit. There is a close relationship between Christ and the Spirit, closer than is often realized. Note the interchangeability of Christ and the Spirit in Romans 8:9–10: "But you are not in the flesh, you are in the Spirit, if the Spirit of God really dwells in you. Any one who does not have the Spirit of Christ does not belong to him. But if Christ is in you, . . . your spirits are alive" (see also 1 Cor. 12:13). John Murray says, "Christ dwells in us if his Spirit dwells in us, and he dwells in us by the Spirit." The Spirit is "the bond of this union."[4]

Not only is our union with Christ brought about by the Holy Spirit; it is a union of spirits. It is not a union of persons in one essence, as in the Trinity. It is not a union of natures in one person, as is the case with the incarnation of Jesus Christ. It is not a physical bonding, as in the welding of two pieces of metal. It is in some way a union of two spirits which does not extinguish either of them. It does not make the believer physically stronger or more intelligent. Rather, what the union produces is a new spiritual vitality within the human.

Finally, our union with Christ is vital. His life actually flows into ours, renewing our inner nature (Rom. 12:2; 2 Cor. 4:16) and imparting spiritual strength. There is a literal truth in Jesus' metaphor of the vine and the branches. Just as the branch cannot bear fruit if it does not receive life from the vine, so we cannot bear spiritual fruit if Christ's life does not flow into us (John 15:4).

Various analogies have been used to illuminate the idea of union with Christ. Sev-

3. Eric Mascall, *Christian Theology and Natural Science: Some Questions on Their Relations* (New York: Longmans, Green, 1956), pp. 314–16.

4. Murray, *Redemption*, p. 166.

---

eral of them are drawn from the physical realm. In mouth-to-mouth resuscitation one person actually breathes for another. An artificial heart performs the vital function of supplying the body cells with blood (and hence with oxygen and various essential nutrients) during heart surgery. And drawing on the realm of psychology, or parapsychology, we find a considerable amount of evidence that thoughts can somehow be transmitted from certain individuals to others. Now since Christ has designed and created our entire nature, including our psyches, it is not surprising that, dwelling within us in some way that we do not fully understand,

who strengthens me" (Phil. 4:13). He also claimed, "The life I now live in the flesh I live by faith in the Son of God, who loved me and gave himself for me" (Gal. 2:20; see also 2 Cor. 12:9).

Being one with Christ also means that we will suffer. The disciples were told that they would drink the cup that Jesus drank, and be baptized with the same baptism as he (Mark 10:39). If tradition serves us correctly, most of them suffered a martyr's death. Jesus had told them not to be surprised if they encountered persecution (John 15:20). Paul did not shrink from this prospect; indeed, one of his goals was to

Justification is God's action pronouncing sinners righteous in his sight; it is a forensic act imputing the righteousness of Christ to the believer.

he is able to affect our very thoughts and feelings. A final illustration, and one with biblical warrant, is that of husband and wife. Not only do the two become one physically, but ideally they also become so close in mind and heart that they have great empathy for and understanding of one another. While none of these analogies in itself can give us an adequate understanding, all of them collectively may enlarge our grasp of our union with Christ.

Implications of Union with Christ

Our union with Christ has certain implications for our lives. First, we are accounted righteous. Paul wrote, "There is therefore now no condemnation for those who are in Christ Jesus" (Rom. 8:1). Because of our judicial union with Christ, we have a right standing in the face of the law and in the sight of God. We are as righteous as is God's own Son, Jesus Christ.

Second, we now live in Christ's strength.[5] Paul affirmed, "I can do all things in him

5. George E. Ladd, *A Theology of the New Testament* (Grand Rapids: Eerdmans, 1974), pp. 492–93.

share Christ's sufferings: "For his sake I have suffered the loss of all things . . . that I may know him and the power of his resurrection, and may share his sufferings, becoming like him in his death" (Phil. 3:8–10).

Finally, we also have the prospect of reigning with Christ. The two disciples who asked for positions of authority and prestige were instead promised suffering (Mark 10:35–39); but Jesus also told the entire group that because they had continued with him in his trials, they would eat and drink at his table in his kingdom, "and sit on thrones judging the twelve tribes of Israel" (Luke 22:30). Paul made a similar statement: "If we endure, we shall also reign with him" (2 Tim. 2:12). Although we often have trials and even suffering here, we are given resources to bear them. And for those who suffer with Christ, a glorious future lies ahead.

Justification

Humankind has a twofold problem as a result of sin and the fall. On the one hand, there is a basic corruption of human nature;

our moral character has been polluted through sin. This aspect of the curse is nullified by regeneration, which reverses the direction and general tendencies of human nature. The other problem remains, however: our guilt or liability to punishment for having failed to fulfil God's expectations. It is to this problem that justification relates. Justification is God's action pronouncing sinners righteous in his sight. It is a matter of our being forgiven and declared to have fulfilled all that God's law requires of us. This is an issue of considerable practical significance, for it deals with the question, How can I be right with God? How can I, a sinner, be accepted by a holy and righteous judge?

Justification and Forensic Righteousness

In order to understand justification, it is necessary first to understand the biblical concept of righteousness, for justification is a restoration of the individual to a state of righteousness. In the Old Testament, the verb *tsādaq* means "to be righteous" or "to conform to a given norm."[6] The particular norm in view varies with the situation. Sometimes the context is family relationships. Tamar was more righteous than Judah, because he had not fulfilled his obligations as her father-in-law (Gen. 38:26). And David, in refusing to slay Saul, was said to be righteous (1 Sam. 24:17; 26:23), for he was abiding by the standards of the monarch-subject relationship. Clearly righteousness is understood to be a matter of living up to the standards set for a relationship. Ultimately, God's own person and nature are the measure or standard of righteousness.

In the Old Testament, the concept of righteousness frequently appears in a forensic or juridical context. A righteous person is one who has been declared by a judge to be

free from guilt. The task of the judge is to condemn the guilty and acquit the innocent:[7] "If there is a dispute between men, and they come into court, and the judges decide between them, acquitting the innocent and condemning the guilty . . ." (Deut. 25:1). God is the Judge of us all (Ps. 9:4; Jer. 11:20). Those who have been acquitted have been judged to stand in right relationship to God, that is, to have fulfilled what was expected of them in that relationship. In the Old Testament sense, then, justification involves ascertaining that a person is innocent and then declaring what is indeed true: that he or she is righteous, that is, has fulfilled the law.

The New Testament advances upon this Old Testament view of justification. Without some addition to the understanding of the concept, it would have been shocking and scandalous for Paul to say, as he did, that God justifies the ungodly (Rom. 4:5). Justice demands that they be condemned; a judge who justifies or acquits the unrighteous is acting unrighteously himself. And so, when we read that, on the contrary, God in justifying the ungodly has shown himself to be righteous (Rom. 3:26), we must also understand that such justification is apart from the works of the law. In the New Testament, justification is the declarative act of God by which, *on the basis of the sufficiency of Christ's atoning death*, he pronounces believers to have fulfilled all of the requirements of the law which pertain to them. Justification is a forensic act imputing the righteousness of Christ to the believer; it is not an actual infusing of holiness into the individual. It is a matter of declaring the person righteous, as a judge does in acquitting the accused.[8] It is not a matter of making the person righteous or altering his or her actual spiritual condition.

There are several factors which support the argument that justification is forensic or declarative in nature:

6. Francis Brown, S. R. Driver, and Charles A. Briggs, *Hebrew and English Lexicon of the Old Testament* (New York: Oxford University Press, 1955), pp. 842–43; J. A. Ziesler, *The Meaning of Righteousness in Paul* (Cambridge: Cambridge University Press, 1972), p. 18.

7. Ladd, *Theology of the New Testament*, p. 440.
8. Ziesler, *Righteousness*, p. 168.

1. The concept of righteousness as a matter of formal standing before the law or covenant, and of a judge as someone who determines and declares our status in that respect.

2. The juxtaposition of "justify" *(dikaioō)* and "condemn" in passages like Romans 8:33–34: "Who shall bring any charge against God's elect? It is God who justifies; who is to condemn? Is it Christ Jesus, who died, yes, who was raised from the dead, who is at the right hand of God, who indeed intercedes for us?" "Justifies" and "condemn" are parallel here. Certainly the act of condemning is not a matter of changing someone's spiritual condition, of somehow infusing sin or evil. It is simply a matter of charging a person with wrong and establishing guilt. Correspondingly, the act of justifying is not a matter of infusing holiness into believers but of declaring them righteous. If condemning is a declarative act, justifying must be also.

3. Passages where *dikaioō* means "to defend, vindicate, or acknowledge (or prove) to be right." In some cases it is used of human action in relation to God. Luke reports that upon hearing Jesus' preaching, "all the people and the tax collectors justified God, having been baptized with the baptism of John" (Luke 7:29; see also v. 35).

We conclude from the preceding data that justification is a forensic or declarative action of God, like that of a judge in acquitting the accused.

Objections to the Doctrine of Forensic Justification

Objections have been raised to the view that justification is forensic in nature. As we deal with them, we will gain a clearer picture of the meaning of justification. William Sanday and Arthur Headlam raised the question of how God could justify the ungodly (i.e., declare them righteous). Is this not something of a fiction in which God treats sinners as if they had not sinned or, in other words, pretends that sinners are something other than what they really are? This interpretation of justification seems to make God guilty of deception, even if it is only self-deception.[9] Vincent Taylor picked up on this idea and contended that righteousness cannot be imputed to a sinner: "If through faith a man is accounted righteous, it must be because, in a reputable sense of the term, he is righteous, and not because another is righteous in his stead."[10]

We respond that the act of justification is not a matter of God's announcing that sinners are something which they are not. There is a constitutive aspect to justification as well. For what God does is actually to constitute us righteous by imputing (not imparting) the righteousness of Christ to us. Here we must distinguish between two senses of the word *righteous*. One could be righteous by virtue of never having violated the law. Such a person would be innocent, having totally fulfilled the law. But even if we have violated the law, we can be deemed righteous once the prescribed penalty has been paid. There is a difference between these two situations, which points up the insufficiency of defining justification simply as God's regarding me "just-as-if-I had never sinned." I am not righteous in the former sense but in the latter. For the penalty for sin has been paid, and thus the requirements of the law have been fulfilled. It is not a fiction, then, that believers are righteous, for the righteousness of Christ has been credited to them. This situation is somewhat analogous to what takes place when two corporations merge. Their separate assets are brought into the union and are thereafter treated as mutual possessions.[11]

9. William Sanday and Arthur C. Headlam, *A Critical and Exegetical Commentary on the Epistle to the Romans*, 5th ed. (Edinburgh: T. and T. Clark, 1958), p. 36.

10. Vincent Taylor, *Forgiveness and Reconciliation* (London: Macmillan, 1952), p. 57.

11. Ziesler, *Righteousness*, p. 169.

One of the objections sometimes raised to the doctrines of substitutionary atonement and forensic justification is that virtue simply cannot be transferred from one person to another. However, Christ and the believer do not stand at arm's length from one another, so that when God looks squarely at the believer, he cannot also see Christ with his righteousness but only pretends to. Rather, Christ and the believer have been brought into such a unity that Christ's spiritual assets, as it were, and the spiritual liabilities and assets of the believer are merged. Thus, when looking at the believer, God the Father does not see him or her alone. He sees the believer together with Christ, and in the act of justification justifies both of them together. It is as if God says, "They are righteous!" He declares what is actually true of the believer, which has come to pass through God's constituting the believer one with Christ. This union is like that of a couple who, when they marry, merge their assets and liabilities. With their property held in joint tenancy, the assets of the one can wipe out the liabilities of the other, leaving a positive net balance.

Justification, then, is a three-party, not a two-party matter. And it is voluntary on the have been saved through faith; and this is not your own doing, it is the gift of God— not because of works, lest any man should boast." Justification is something completely undeserved. It is not an achievement. It is an obtainment, not an attainment. Even faith is not some good work which God must reward with salvation. It is God's gift. It is not the cause of our salvation, but the means by which we receive it. And, contrary to the thinking of some, it has always been the means of salvation. In his discussion of Abraham, the father of the Jews, Paul points out to his readers that Abraham was not justified by works, but by faith. He makes this point both positively and negatively. He affirms that "Abraham 'believed God, and it was reckoned to him as righteousness'" (Gal. 3:6). Then he rejects the idea that we can be justified by works: "For all who rely on works of the law are under a curse. . . . Now it is evident that no man is justified before God by the law" (vv. 10–11). So God has not introduced a new means of salvation. He has always worked in the same way.

Faith and Works

The principle of salvation by grace brings us to the question of the relationship of faith

---

While it is faith that leads to justification, justification must and will invariably produce good works.

---

part of all three. Jesus willingly volunteered to give himself and unite with the sinner. There is also a conscious decision on the part of the sinner to enter into this relationship. And the Father willingly accepts it. That no one is constrained means that the whole matter is completely ethical and legal.

Numerous passages of Scripture indicate that justification is the gift of God. One of the best-known is Romans 6:23: "For the wages of sin is death, but the free gift of God is eternal life in Christ Jesus our Lord." Another is Ephesians 2:8–9: "For by grace you to works. It is apparent from what has been said that works do not produce salvation. Yet the biblical witness also indicates that while it is faith that leads to justification, justification must and will invariably produce works appropriate to the nature of the new creature that has come into being. It is well when we quote the classic text on salvation by grace, Ephesians 2:8–9, not to stop short of verse 10, which points to the outcome of this grace: "For we are his workmanship, created in Christ Jesus for good works, which God prepared beforehand, that we should walk in them." James puts it even more forcefully: "So faith by itself, if it has no works, is dead" (James 2:17; see also v. 26). Despite the fairly common opinion that there is a tension between Paul and James, both make essentially the same point: that the genuineness of the faith that leads to justification becomes apparent in the results which issue from it. If there are no good works, there has been no real faith nor justification.

The Lingering Consequences of Sin

One issue remains: the consequences of sin seem to linger on, even after sin has been forgiven and the sinner justified. An example is David. He was told that his sin in committing adultery with Bathsheba and murdering Uriah had been put away so that he would not die; nevertheless, the child born to Bathsheba would die because of David's sin (2 Sam. 12:13–14). Is such forgiveness real and complete? Is it not as if God in such instances holds back a bit on his forgiveness so that a bit of punishment remains? And if this is the case, is there real grace?

We need to make a distinction here between the temporal and eternal consequences of sin. When one is justified, all of the eternal consequences of sin are canceled. This includes eternal death. But the temporal consequences of sin, both those which fall on the individual and those which fall on the human race collectively, are not necessarily removed. Thus we still experience physical death and the other elements of the curse of Genesis 3. A number of these consequences follow from our sins in a cause-and-effect relationship which may be either physical or social in nature. God ordinarily does not intervene miraculously to prevent the carrying through of these laws. So if, for example, a person in a fit of rage, perhaps a drunken state, kills his family but later repents and is forgiven, God does not bring the family members back to life. The sin has led to a lifetime loss. There is a warning here—although God's forgiveness is boundless and accessible, sin is not something to be treated lightly. Though forgiven, it can still carry heavy consequences.

Adoption

The effect of justification is primarily negative: the cancelation of the judgment against us. Unfortunately, it is possible to be pardoned without simultaneously acquiring positive standing. Such is not the case with justification, however. For not only are we released from liability to punishment, but we are restored to a position of favor with God. This transfer from a status of alienation and hostility to one of acceptance and favor is termed adoption.[12] It is referred to in several passages in the New Testament. Perhaps the best-known is John 1:12: "But to all who received him, who believed in his name, he gave power to become children of God." Paul notes that our adoption is a fulfilment of part of the plan of God (Eph. 1:5). And in Galatians 4:4–5 Paul links adoption with justification: "But when the time had fully come, God sent forth his Son, born of woman, born under the law, to redeem those who were under the law, so that we might receive adoption as sons."

The Nature of Adoption

It is important to note several characteristics of our adoption. First, it occurs at the same time as do conversion, regeneration, justification, and union with Christ. It is, additionally, the condition in which the Christian lives and operates from that time onward. Although adoption is logically distinguishable from regeneration and justification, the event is not really separable from them. Only those who are justified and regenerated are adopted, and vice versa.[13]

Adoption involves a change of both status and condition. In the formal sense, adoption is a declarative matter, an alteration of our legal status. We become God's children. In addition, however, there is the actual experi-

12. Murray, *Redemption*, pp. 132–34.
13. Augustus H. Strong, *Systematic Theology* (Westwood, N.J.: Revell, 1907), p. 857.

ence of being favored of God. We enjoy what is designated the spirit of sonship. The Christian looks affectionately and trustingly upon God as Father rather than as a fearsome slavedriver and taskmaster (John 15:14–15).

It is also significant that through adoption we are restored to the relationship with God which humans once had but lost. We are by nature and creation children of God, but we have voted ourselves out of God's family as it were. God in adopting us, however, restores us to the relationship with him for which we were originally intended.

Thus, adoption introduces a type of relationship with God quite different from that which humans in general have with him. John clearly pointed out this distinction: "See what love the Father has given us, that we should be called children of God; and so we are. The reason why the world does not know us is that it did not know him" (1 John 3:1). The unbeliever simply does not have, and cannot experience, the type of status which the believer experiences.[14]

The Benefits of Adoption

The meaning or significance of adoption becomes most apparent when we examine its results, the effects which it has in and upon the believer's life. One of these is, of course, forgiveness. God delights in forgiving; he is merciful, tenderhearted, and kind (Deut. 5:10; Ps. 103:8–14). He is not to be feared, but trusted. Our adoption means that there is continued forgiveness. In light of the fact that God has forgiven us, Paul urges us to forgive others: "Be kind to one another, tenderhearted, forgiving one another, as God in Christ forgave you" (Eph. 4:32).

Our adoption also involves reconciliation. Not only has God forgiven us, but we also have been reconciled to him. We no longer carry enmity toward him. God has shown his love for us by taking the initiative in restoring the fellowship which was damaged by our sin (Rom. 5:8, 10). In adoption both sides are reconciled to one another.

There also is liberty for the children of God. The child of God is not a slave who obeys out of a sense of bondage or compulsion. As God's children we need not fear the consequences of failing to live up to the law: "For all who are led by the Spirit of God are sons of God. For you did not receive the spirit of slavery to fall back into fear, but you have received the spirit of sonship. When we cry, 'Abba! Father!' it is the Spirit himself bearing witness with our spirit that we are children of God" (Rom. 8:14–16). A similar thought is expressed in Galatians 3:10–11. We are free persons. We are not obligated to the law in quite the way in which a slave or servant is.

This liberty is not license, however. There are always some who pervert their freedom. Paul gave warning to such people: "For you were called to freedom, brethren; only do not use your freedom as an opportunity for the flesh, but through love be servants of one another" (Gal. 5:13). The believer keeps the commandments, not out of fear of a cruel and harsh master, but out of friendship and love for a kindly and loving God (John 14:15, 21; 15:14–15).[15]

Adoption means that the Christian is the recipient of God's fatherly care. Paul noted that "we are children of God, and if children, then heirs, heirs of God and fellow heirs with Christ" (Rom. 8:16–17). As heirs we have available to us the unlimited resources of the Father (Phil. 4:19). The believer can pray confidently, knowing that there is no limitation upon what God is able to do. According to Jesus, the Father who feeds the birds of the air and clothes the lilies of the fields cares even more for his human children (Matt. 6:25–34). His provision is always wise and kind (Luke 11:11–13).

It should not be thought that God is indulgent or permissive, however. He is our

14. Charles M. Horne, *Salvation* (Chicago: Moody, 1971), pp. 76–77.

15. Ladd, *Theology of the New Testament*, pp. 493–94.

heavenly Father, not our heavenly Grand-father. Thus, discipline is one of the features of our adoption. In the letter to the Hebrews there is a rather extended discussion of this subject (Heb. 12:5–11). Quoting Proverbs 3:11–12, the writer comments: "It is for discipline that you have to endure. God is treating you as sons; for what son is there whom his father does not discipline?" (Heb. 12:7). Discipline may not be pleasant at the moment of application, but it is beneficial in the long term. It is to be remembered that love is concern and action for the ultimate welfare of another. Therefore, discipline should be thought of as evidence of love rather than as evidence of lack of love.

Finally, adoption involves the Father's good will. It is one thing for us to be pardoned, for the penalty incurred by our wrongdoing to have been paid. That, however, may simply mean we will not be punished in the future. It does not necessarily guarantee good will. If a criminal's debt to society has been paid, society will not thereafter look favorably or charitably upon him or her. There will instead be suspicion, distrust, even animosity. With the Father, however, there are the love and good will that we so much need and desire. He is ours and we are his, and he through adoption extends to us all the benefits his measureless love can bestow.

34 The Continuation and Completion of Salvation

The beginnings of salvation as we examined them in the preceding two chapters are both complex and profound. Yet they are not the end of God's special working to restore his children to the likeness to him for which they are destined. Having begun this work of transformation, he continues and completes it.

Sanctification

The Meaning of Sanctification

Sanctification is the continuing work of God in the life of the believer, making him or her actually holy. By "holy" here is meant "bearing an actual likeness to God." Sanctification is a process by which one's moral condition is brought into conformity with one's legal status before God. It is a continuation of what was begun in regeneration, when a newness of life was

313

conferred upon and instilled within the believer. In particular, sanctification is the Holy Spirit's applying to the life of the believer the work done by Jesus Christ.

There are two basic senses of the word *sanctification*, which are related to two basic concepts of holiness. The first is holiness as a formal characteristic of particular objects, persons, and places. In this sense holiness refers to a state of being separate, set apart from the ordinary or mundane and dedicated to a particular purpose or use. In the Old Testament, particular places (especially the Holy Place and the Holy of Holies), objects (e.g., Aaron's garments and the Sabbath day), and persons (e.g., the priests and Levites) were specially set apart or sanctified to the Lord.

This sense of sanctification is found in the New Testament as well. Peter refers to his readers as "a chosen race, a royal priesthood, a holy nation, God's own people" (1 Peter 2:9). Here, being sanctified means "to belong to the Lord." Sanctification in this sense is something that occurs at the very beginning of the Christian life, at the point of conversion, along with regeneration and justification. It is in this sense that the New Testament so frequently refers to Christians as "saints," even when they are far from perfect.[1] Paul, for example, addresses the persons in the church at Corinth in this way (1 Cor. 1:2), even though it was probably the most imperfect of the churches to which he ministered.

The second sense of holiness or sanctification is moral goodness or spiritual worth. This sense gradually came to predominate. It designates not merely the fact that believers are formally set apart, or belong to Christ, but that they are then to conduct themselves accordingly. They are to live lives of purity and goodness.[2]

In order to focus more sharply the nature of sanctification, it will be helpful to contrast it with justification. There are a number of significant differences. One pertains to duration. Justification is an instantaneous occurrence, complete in a moment, whereas sanctification is a process requiring an entire lifetime for completion. There is a quantitative distinction as well. One is either justified or not, whereas one may be more or less sanctified. That is, there are degrees of sanctification but not of justification. Justification is a forensic or declarative matter, as we have seen earlier, while sanctification is an actual transformation of the character and condition of the person. Justification is an objective work affecting our standing before God, our relationship to him, while sanctification is a subjective work affecting our inner person.

Characteristics of Sanctification

We need to look now at the characteristics of sanctification. We must first emphasize that sanctification is a supernatural work; it is something done by God, not something we do ourselves. Thus, it is not reform that we are speaking of. Paul wrote, "May the God of peace himself sanctify you wholly; and may your spirit and soul and body be kept sound and blameless at the coming of our Lord Jesus Christ" (1 Thess. 5:23; see also Eph. 5:26; Titus 2:14; Heb. 13:20–21).

Further, this divine working within the believer is a progressive matter. This is seen, for example, in Paul's assurance that God will continue to work in the lives of the Philippians: "And I am sure that he who began a good work in you will bring it to completion at the day of Jesus Christ" (Phil. 1:6). Paul also notes that the cross is the power of God "to us who are being saved" (1 Cor. 1:18). The form of the Greek verb clearly conveys the idea of ongoing activity.

The aim of this divine working is likeness to Christ himself. This was God's intention from all eternity: "For those whom he foreknew he also predestined to be conformed to the image of his Son, in order that he might be the first-born among many breth-

---

1. G. Abbott-Smith, *A Manual Greek Lexicon of the New Testament*, 3d ed. (Edinburgh: T. and T. Clark, 1953), p. 5.
2. Ibid.

ren" (Rom. 8:29). The word translated "to be conformed to" indicates a likeness to Christ which is not just an external or superficial resemblance; it signifies the whole set of characteristics or qualities which makes something what it is. Further, it indicates vital connection with the Son. This is clear evidence that our being made like Christ is not an arm's-length transaction. What we come to have we have *together with* him.

Sanctification is the work of the Holy Spirit.[3] In Galatians 5 Paul speaks of the life in the Spirit: "Walk by the Spirit, and do not gratify the desires of the flesh" (v. 16); "If we live by the Spirit, let us also walk by the Spirit" (v. 25). He also lists a group of qualities which he designates collectively as "the fruit of the Spirit"—"love, joy, peace, patience, kindness, goodness, faithfulness, gentleness, self-control" (vv. 22–23). Similarly, in Romans 8 Paul says much about the Spirit and the Christian. Christians walk according to the Spirit (v. 4), set their minds on the things of the Spirit (v. 5), are in the Spirit (v. 9); the Spirit dwells in them (v. 9); by the Spirit they have put to death the deeds of the body (v. 13); they are led by the Spirit (v. 14); the Spirit bears witness that they are children of God (v. 16); the Spirit intercedes for them (vv. 26–27). It is the Spirit who is at work in the believer, bringing about likeness to Christ.

One might conclude from the preceding that sanctification is completely a passive matter on the believer's part. This is not so, however. While sanctification is exclusively of God, that is, its power rests entirely on his holiness,[4] the believer is constantly exhorted to work and to grow in the matters pertaining to salvation. For example, Paul writes to the Philippians: "Work out your own salvation with fear and trembling; for God is at work in you, both to will and to

work for his good pleasure" (Phil. 2:12–13). Paul urges both practice of virtues and avoidance of evils (Rom. 12:9, 16–17). We are to put to death the works of the body (Rom. 8:13) and present our bodies a living sacrifice (Rom. 12:1–2). So while sanctification is God's work, the believer has a role as well, entailing both removal of sinfulness and development of holiness.

Sanctification: Complete or Incomplete?

One major issue over which there has been disagreement throughout church history is whether the process of sanctification is ever completed within the earthly lifetime of the believer. Do we ever come to the point where we no longer sin? There are sharp differences of opinion upon this matter. Those who answer that question in the affirmative, the perfectionists, hold that it is possible to come to a state where a believer does not sin, and that indeed some Christians do arrive at that point. This does not mean that the person cannot sin, but that indeed he or she does not sin. Nor does this mean that there is no further need for the means of grace or for the Holy Spirit, that there is no longer any temptation or struggle with the innate tendency toward evil, or that there is no room for further spiritual growth.[5] It does mean, however, that it is possible not to sin, and that some believers actually do abstain from all evil. There are ample biblical texts supporting such a view. One of them is Matthew 5:48, where Jesus tells his hearers, "You, therefore, must be perfect, as your heavenly Father is perfect." Paul prays for the Thessalonians, "May the God of peace himself sanctify you wholly; and may your spirit and soul and body be kept sound and blameless at the coming of our Lord Jesus Christ" (1 Thess. 5:23; see also Eph. 4:13; Heb. 13:20–21). These verses certainly seem to offer prima-facie evidence that total sanctification is a possibility for all believers, and a reality for some.[6]

---

3. Otto Procksch, ἅγιος, ἁγιάζω, ἁγιασμός, in *Theological Dictionary of the New Testament*, ed. Gerhard Kittel and Gerhard Friedrich, trans. Geoffrey W. Bromiley, 10 vols. (Grand Rapids: Eerdmans, 1964–76), vol. 1, p. 113.
4. Ibid., p. 111.

5. John Wesley, *A Plain Account of Christian Perfection* (London: Epworth, 1952), p. 28.
6. Charles G. Finney, *Lectures on Systematic Theology* (London: William Tegg, 1851), pp. 604–13.

No less earnest about their convictions are those who maintain that perfection is an ideal which will never be attained within this life. They maintain that as much as we should desire and strive after complete deliverance from sin, sinlessness is simply not a realistic goal for this life. They point to certain passages which indicate that we cannot escape sin.[7] One of the more prominent of these passages is 1 John 1:8–10: "If we say we have no sin, we deceive ourselves, and the truth is not in us. If we confess our sins, he is faithful and just, and will forgive our sins and cleanse us from all unrighteousness. If we say we have not sinned, we make him a liar, and his word is not in us." That this passage was written to believers renders the statement that there is sin in all of us the more cogent.

Another passage which is very frequently alluded to by the nonperfectionist is Romans 7, where Paul describes his own experience. On the assumption that Paul has in view his life after conversion (an assumption which not all scholars accept), this passage appears to be a vivid and forceful testimony to the effect that the believer is not free from sin. Paul puts it powerfully: "For I know that nothing good dwells within me, that is, in my flesh. I can will what is right, but I cannot do it. For I do not do the good I want, but the evil I do not want is what I do" (vv. 18–19). This word came from one of the greatest of all Christians; indeed, many would say he was the greatest Christian of all time. If even he confessed having great difficulty with sin, certainly we must conclude that perfection is not to be experienced in this life.

How shall we untangle all of these considerations and arrive at a conclusion on this difficult but important topic? We begin by noting again the character of sin. It is not merely acts of an external nature. Jesus made it quite clear that even the thoughts and attitudes that we have are

sinful if they are less than perfectly in accord with the mind of the almighty and completely holy God (see, e.g., Matt. 5:21–28). Thus, sin is of a considerably more pervasive and subtle character than we might tend to think.

We also need to determine the nature of the perfection that is commanded of us. The Greek word *teleioi* ("perfect"), which is found in Matthew 5:48, does not mean "flawless" or "spotless." Rather, it means "complete." It is quite possible, then, to be "perfect" without being entirely free from sin.[8] That is, we can possess the fullness of Jesus Christ (Eph. 4:13) and the full fruit of the Spirit (Gal. 5:22–23) without possessing them completely.

The standard to be aimed for is complete freedom from sin. The commands to strive by the grace of God to attain that goal are too numerous to ignore. And certainly, if it is possible by this enablement to avoid giving in to a particular temptation, then it must be possible to prevail in every case. We must also note, however, the forcefulness of passages like 1 John 1. And even beyond these didactic passages there is the confirming fact that Scripture freely portrays the great men and women of God as sinners. Our conclusion is that while complete freedom from and victory over sin are the standard to be aimed at and are theoretically possible, it is doubtful whether any believer will attain this goal within this life.

Certain difficulties attach to assuming such a stance, however. One is that it seems contradictory to repeatedly exhort Christians to a victorious, spotless life unless it is a real possibility.[9] But does this necessarily follow? We may have a standard, an ideal, toward which we press, but which we do not expect to reach within a finite period of time. It has been observed that no one has ever reached the North Star by sailing or flying toward it. That does not change the fact,

7. Augustus H. Strong, *Systematic Theology* (Westwood, N.J.: Revell, 1907), p. 879.

8. James Hope Moulton and George Milligan, *The Vocabulary of the Greek New Testament* (Grand Rapids: Eerdmans, 1974), p. 629.

9. Finney, *Lectures*, pp. 611–13.

however, that it is still the mark toward which we press, our measure of "northernness." Similarly, although we may never be perfectly sanctified within this life, we shall be in the eternity beyond and hence should presently aim to arrive as close to complete sanctification as we can.

Another problem is the presence of teachings like 1 John 3:4–6: "Every one who commits sin is guilty of lawlessness; sin is lawlessness. You know that he appeared to take away sins, and in him there is no sin. No one who abides in him sins; no one who sins has either seen him or known him." Does this not confirm the perfectionist position? It should be noted, however, that the form of

tionship? In other words, will a person who becomes a Christian always remain such? And if so, on what basis? This issue is of considerable importance from the standpoint of practical Christian living. If, on the one hand, there is no guarantee that salvation is permanent, believers may experience a great deal of anxiety and insecurity that will detract from the major tasks of the Christian life. On the other hand, if our salvation is absolutely secure, if we are preserved quite independently of what we do or what our life is like, then there may well be, as a result, a sort of indifference to the moral and spiritual demands of the gospel. Therefore, determining the scriptural teaching concern-

Though sanctification is exclusively of God, the believer is constantly exhorted to work and grow in matters pertaining to salvation.

Is our Salvation secure

the Greek verbs in the phrases "every one who commits sin" and "no one who sins" indicates recurrent action. The meaning here is that everyone who continues in habitual sin is guilty of lawlessness and has never known Christ.

There are important practical implications of our view that though sinlessness is not experienced in this life, it must be our aim. On the one hand, this position means that there need not be great feelings of discouragement, defeat, even despair and guilt when we do sin. But on the other hand, it also means that we will not be overly pleased with ourselves nor indifferent to the presence of sin. For we will faithfully and diligently ask God to overcome completely the tendency toward evil which, like Paul, we find so prevalent within us.

Perseverance

Will the believer who has genuinely been regenerated, justified, adopted by God, and united with Jesus Christ persist in that rela-

ing the security of the believer is worth whatever time and effort may be necessary.

The Calvinist View

Two major positions have been taken on the issue of whether the salvation of the believer is absolutely secure—the Calvinist and the Arminian. These two positions hold certain conceptions in common. They agree that God is powerful and faithful, willing and able to keep his promises. They agree, at least in their usual forms, that salvation is neither attained nor retained by works of the human person. They are agreed that the Holy Spirit is at work in all believers (although there may be some disagreement as to whether the Spirit is more fully present and active in some Christians than in others). Both are convinced of the completeness of the salvation provided by God. They both insist that the believer can indeed know that he or she currently possesses salvation. But with all of these beliefs held in common, there are still significant points of difference between the two.

The Calvinist affirms that since God has elected certain individuals out of the mass of fallen humanity to receive eternal life, and those so chosen will necessarily come to receive eternal life, it follows that there must be a permanence to their salvation. If the elect could at some point lose their salvation, God's election of them to eternal life would not be truly effectual. Thus, the doctrine of election as understood by the Calvinist requires perseverance as well.

It is not logical consistency alone which leads the Calvinist to hold to the doctrine of perseverance. There are numerous biblical teachings which serve independently to support the doctrine. Among them is a group of texts emphasizing the indestructible quality of the salvation which God provides.[10] An example is 1 Peter 1:3–5: "Blessed be the God and Father of our Lord Jesus Christ! By his great mercy we have been born anew to a living hope through the resurrection of Jesus Christ from the dead, and to an inheritance which is imperishable, undefiled, and unfading, kept in heaven for you, who by God's power are guarded through faith for a salvation ready to be revealed in the last time."

Various texts emphasizing the persistence and power of divine love also support the doctrine of perseverance.[11] One such testimony is found in Paul's statement in Romans 8:31–39, culminating in verses 38 and 39: "For I am sure that neither death, nor life, nor angels, nor principalities, nor things present, nor things to come, nor powers, nor height, nor depth, nor anything else in all creation, will be able to separate us from the love of God in Christ Jesus our Lord." Christ does not simply give us eternal life and then abandon us to our human self-efforts. Rather, the work he began in us continues until it is completed (Phil. 1:6). Moreover, Christ constantly intercedes for us to

the Father (Heb. 7:25), who always hears his prayers (John 11:42). Support for the Calvinist position is also afforded by the biblical assurances that, because of God's provisions, we will be able to deal with and overcome whatever obstacles and temptations come our way. Our Master will enable us his servants to stand in the face of the judgment (Rom. 14:4). He provides a way for coping with temptations (1 Cor. 10:13).

The Calvinist finds the greatest source of encouragement concerning this matter, however, in the direct promises of the Lord's keeping. One of the most straightforward is Jesus' statement to his disciples: "My sheep hear my voice, and I know them, and they follow me; and I give them eternal life, and they shall never perish, and no one shall snatch them out of my hand. My Father, who has given them to me, is greater than all, and no one is able to snatch them out of the Father's hand. I and the Father are one" (John 10:27–30). Accordingly, Paul had complete confidence in the Lord's keeping: "But I am not ashamed, for I know whom I have believed and I am sure that he is able to guard until that Day what has been entrusted to me" (2 Tim. 1:12).

In addition, many Calvinists infer their view of perseverance from other doctrines.[12] Among them is the doctrine of union with Christ. If believers have been made one with Christ and his life flows through them (John 15:1–11), it is inconceivable that anything could nullify that connection. The doctrine of the new birth, the Holy Spirit's impartation of a new nature to the believer, likewise lends support to the doctrine of perseverance (1 John 3:9). If salvation could be lost, there would have to be some reversal of regeneration. But can this be? Can spiritual death actually come to someone in whom the Holy Spirit dwells, that is, to someone who has already been given eternal life? This must surely be an impossibility, for eternal life is by definition everlasting. Finally, perseverance is an im-

---

10. John Murray, *Redemption—Accomplished and Applied* (Grand Rapids: Eerdmans, 1955), p. 155.

11. Loraine Boettner, *The Reformed Doctrine of Predestination*, 8th ed. (Grand Rapids: Eerdmans, 1958), p. 185.

12. Strong, *Systematic Theology*, p. 882.

plication of the biblical teaching that we can be assured of salvation. Relevant passages here include Hebrews 6:11; 10:22; and 2 Peter 1:10. Perhaps the clearest of all is found in the Book of 1 John. Having cited several evidences (the testimony of the Spirit, the water, and the blood) that God has given us eternal life in his Son, the apostle summarizes: "I write this to you who believe in the name of the Son of God, that you may know that you have eternal life" (1 John 5:13). That we can have such assurance means that our salvation must be secure.

The Arminian View

A quite different stance is taken by the Arminians. The first class of biblical materials cited by Arminians consists of warnings against apostasy. Jesus warned his disciples about the danger of being led astray (Matt. 24:3–14). Would Jesus have issued such a warning to his disciples if it were not possible for them to fall away and thus lose their salvation? Similarly, Paul, whom Calvinists frequently cite in support of their position, suggested that there is a conditional character to salvation: "And you, who once were estranged and hostile in mind, doing evil deeds, he has now reconciled in his body of flesh by his death, in order to present you holy and blameless and irreproachable before him, provided that you continue in the faith, stable and steadfast, not shifting from the hope of the gospel which you heard" (Col. 1:21–23a). The writer to the Hebrews was especially vehement, calling his readers' attention on several occasions to the dangers of falling away and the importance of being on guard. One notable example is Hebrews 2:1: "Therefore we must pay the closer attention to what we have heard, lest we drift away from it." A slightly different injunction is found in 3:12–14. It is difficult, says the Arminian, to understand why such warnings were given if the believer cannot fall away.[13]

The Arminian also cites texts which urge believers to continue in the faith. An example of these exhortations to faithfulness, which frequently appear in conjunction with warnings such as we have just noted, is Hebrews 6:11–12: "And we desire each one of you to show the same earnestness in realizing the full assurance of hope until the end, so that you may not be sluggish, but imitators of those who through faith and patience inherit the promises."

Arminians also base their view upon passages which apparently teach that people do apostatize.[14] Hebrews 6:4–6 is perhaps the most commonly cited and straightforward instance: "For it is impossible to restore again to repentance those who have once been enlightened, who have tasted the heavenly gift, and have become partakers of the Holy Spirit, and have tasted the goodness of the word of God and the powers of the age to come, if they then commit apostasy, since they crucify the Son of God on their own account and hold him up to contempt." Another instance is Hebrews 10:26–27. These are clear statements about people who, having had the experience of salvation, departed from it.

The Bible does not simply remain on this abstract level, however. It also records concrete cases of specific persons who apostatized or fell away.[15] One of the most vivid is the case of King Saul in the Old Testament. He had been chosen and anointed king of Israel, but eventually proved so disobedient that God did not answer him when he prayed (1 Sam. 28:6). Rejected by God, Saul lost his position as king and came to a tragic death. A striking New Testament instance of apostasy is Judas. It seems inconceivable to the Arminian either that Jesus would have intentionally chosen an unbeliever to be one of his most intimate associates and confidants, or that he made a mistake of judg-

13. Dale Moody, *The Word of Truth: A Summary of Christian Doctrine Based on Biblical Revelation* (Grand Rapids: Eerdmans, 1981), pp. 350–54.

14. I. Howard Marshall, *Kept by the Power of God* (London: Epworth, 1969), p. 141.

15. Samuel Wakefield, *A Complete System of Christian Theology* (Cincinnati: Hitchcock and Walden, 1869), pp. 463–65.

ment in his selection. The conclusion is clear: when chosen, Judas was a believer. Yet Judas betrayed Jesus and ended his own life apparently without any return to faith in Christ. Surely this must be a case of apostasy. Others who are mentioned include Ananias and Sapphira (Acts 5:1–11); Hymenaeus and Alexander, who "by rejecting conscience . . . have made shipwreck of their faith" (1 Tim. 1:19–20); Hymenaeus and Philetus (2 Tim. 2:16–18); Demas (2 Tim. 4:10); the false teachers and those who follow them (2 Peter 2:1–2). In addition to biblical examples, Arminians also point to various extrabiblical cases of persons from history or from their current experience who at one time gave every appearance of being regenerate yet subsequently abandoned any semblance of Christian faith.

Arminians also raise several practical objections to the Calvinistic understanding of perseverance. One of these objections is that the Calvinistic view is in conflict with the scriptural concept of human freedom.[16] If it is certain that those who are in Christ will persevere and not fall away, then it must surely be the case that they are unable to choose apostasy. And if this is the case, they cannot be free. Yet Scripture, the Arminians point out, depicts humans as free beings, for they are repeatedly exhorted to choose God and are clearly portrayed as being held responsible by him for their actions.

A Resolution of the Problem

We have seen two opposed views. How shall we relate them to one another? The advocates of both have cogent arguments which they can appeal to in support of their positions. Is there truth within both, or must we choose one or the other? One way in which we may deal with this dilemma is to examine two key biblical passages which serve, respectively, as the major textual support for each of the two theories. These passages are John 10:27–30 and Hebrews 6:4–6.

Jesus' words in John 10:27–30 constitute a powerful declaration of security. Verse 28 is especially emphatic: "I give them eternal life, and they shall never perish, and no one shall snatch them out of my hand." In the clause "and they shall never perish" John uses a Greek grammatical construction which is a very emphatic way of declaring that something will not happen in the future. A literal translation would be something like, "They shall not, repeat, shall not ever perish in the slightest." This assertion is followed by statements that no one can snatch believers out of Jesus' hand or out of the Father's hand (vv. 28–29). All in all, this passage is as definite a rejection of the idea that a true believer might fall away as could be given.

Arminians argue that Hebrews 6 presents an equally emphatic case for their position. The passage seems clear enough: "For it is impossible to restore again to repentance those who have once been enlightened, who have tasted the heavenly gift, and have become partakers of the Holy Spirit, and have tasted the goodness of the word of God and the powers of the age to come, if they then commit apostasy" (vv. 4–6). The description is apparently of genuinely saved persons who abandon the faith and thus lose their salvation. Because of the complexity of the issue and the material in this passage, however, a number of interpretations have grown up:

1. The writer has in mind genuinely saved persons who lose their salvation.[17] It should be noted that once they have lost their salvation, there is no way they can regain it. The one item that is unequivocal in this passage is that it is impossible to renew them to salvation (v. 4a), a point which many Arminians ignore.
2. The persons in view were never regenerate. They merely tasted of the truth and the life, were but exposed to the

---

16. Ibid., pp. 465–66.

17. Marshall, *Power of God*, pp. 140–47.

word of God; they did not fully experience these heavenly gifts. They do in fact apostatize, but from the vicinity of spiritual truth, not from its center.[18]

3. The people in view are genuinely and permanently saved; they are not lost. Their salvation is real, the apostasy hypothetical. That is, the "if"-clause does not really occur. The writer is merely describing what would be the case if the elect were to fall away (an impossibility).[19]

Upon close examination, the second explanation is difficult to accept. The vividness of the description, and particularly the statement "[those who] have become partakers of the Holy Spirit," argues forcefully against denying that the people in view are (at least for a time) regenerate. The choice must therefore be made between the first and third views.

Part of the difficulty in interpretation stems from the ambiguity of the Greek word translated "if they then commit apostasy" or "if they fall away." This is a legitimate translation of the word, but it could also be rendered in several other ways, including "when they fall away" and "because they fall away." The meaning in cases like this must be determined on the basis of the context. The key element in the present context is found in verse 9: "Though we speak thus, yet in your case, beloved, we feel sure of better things that belong to salvation." It is our contention that the referents in verses 4–6 and verse 9 are the same. They are genuinely saved people who could fall away. Verses 4–6 declare what their status would be if they did. Verse 9, however, is a statement that

they will not fall away. They could, but they will not! Their persistence to the end is evidence of that truth. The writer to the Hebrews knows that his readers will not fall away; he is convinced of better things regarding them, the things that accompany salvation.[20] He speaks of their past work and love (v. 10), and exhorts them to continue earnestly in the same pursuits (v. 11). The full data of the passage would seem to indicate, then, that the writer has in view genuine believers who could fall away, but will not.

We are now able to correlate John 10 and Hebrews 6. While Hebrews 6 indicates that genuine believers *can* fall away, John 10 teaches that they *will not*.[21] There is a logical possibility of apostasy, but it will not come to pass in the case of believers. Although they could abandon their faith and consequently come to the fate described in Hebrews 6, the grace of God prevents them from apostatizing. God does this, not by making it impossible for believers to fall away, but by making it certain that they will not. Our emphasis on *can* and *will not* is not inconsequential. It preserves the freedom of the individual. Believers are capable of repudiating their faith, but will freely choose not to.

At this point someone might ask: If salvation is sure and permanent, what is the purpose of the warnings and commands given to the believer? The answer is that they are the means by which God renders it certain that the saved individual will not fall away.[22] Consider as an analogy the case of parents who fear that their young child may run out into the street and be struck by a car. One way the parents can prevent that from happen-

---

18. John Calvin, *Commentaries on the Epistle to the Hebrews* (Grand Rapids: Eerdmans, 1949), pp. 135–40 (Heb. 6:4–6).

19. Thomas Hewitt, *The Epistle to the Hebrews: An Introduction and Commentary* (Grand Rapids: Eerdmans, 1960), p. 110. Hewitt refers to the three views as, respectively, the "saved and lost theory," the "non-Christian theory," and the "hypothetical theory." See also Brooke Foss Westcott, *The Epistle to the Hebrews* (Grand Rapids: Eerdmans, 1962), p. 165.

20. Westcott, *Hebrews*, pp. 154, 165.

21. This distinction appears to elude Marshall, who regards the "hypothetical theory" as "a thoroughly sophistical theory which evades the plain meaning of the passage. There is no evidence whatsoever that the writer was describing an imaginary danger which could not possibly threaten his readers" (*Power of God*, p. 140).

22. G. C. Berkouwer, *Faith and Perseverance* (Grand Rapids: Eerdmans, 1958), pp. 83–124.

ing is to build a fence around the yard. That would prevent the child from leaving the yard, but would also remove the child's freedom. Try as he or she might, the child could not possibly get out of the yard. Another possibility is for the parents to teach and train the child regarding the danger of going into the street and the importance of being careful. This is the nature of the security which we are discussing. It is not that God renders apostasy impossible by removing the very option. Rather, he uses every possible means of grace, including the warnings contained in Scripture, to motivate us to remain committed to him. Because he enables us to persevere in our faith, the term *perseverance* is preferable to *preservation*.

But what of the claims that Scripture records cases of actual apostasy? When closely examined, these instances appear much less impressive than at first glance. Some cases, such as that of Peter, should be termed backsliding rather than apostasy. It

---

While genuine believers can *fall away, they* will not.

---

is a bit difficult, on the other hand, to know how to classify the situation of King Saul, since he lived under the old dispensation. As for Judas, there were early indications that he was not regenerate. Consider particularly the mention of his thievery (John 12:6). The references to Hymenaeus and Alexander in 1 Timothy 1:19–20 and to Hymenaeus and Philetus in 2 Timothy 2:17–18 need to be seen in the light of Paul's statements in 1 Timothy 1:6–7 about persons who have wandered away into vain discussions. Paul's remark that they do not understand what they are saying may well imply that they are not true believers. The proximity of 1 Timothy 1:6–7 to the reference to Hymenaeus and Alexander (vv. 19–20), and the use of the key word *astocheō* ("to swerve" from the truth) in both 1 Timothy 1:6 and the reference to

Hymenaeus and Philetus (2 Tim. 2:18), may indicate that the two situations were similar. As for the other names (e.g., Demas) cited by the Arminians, there is insufficient evidence to warrant the conclusion that they were true believers who fell away.

Even less reliable are the instances cited of contemporary persons who supposedly were at one time true believers but fell away. The difficulty here is pointed up by the fact that we can also cite instances of persons who by their own testimony were never really Christians, but were thought to be so. Further, we must be careful to distinguish cases of temporary backsliding, such as that of Peter, from real abandonment of the faith. It is necessary to ask regarding someone who seems to have lost the faith, "Is he or she spiritually dead yet?" Beyond that, we must note that the Bible does not justify identifying every person who makes an outward profession of faith as genuinely regenerate (see Matt. 7:15–23).

The practical implication of our understanding of the doctrine of perseverance is that believers can rest secure in the assurance that their salvation is permanent; nothing can separate them from the love of God. Thus they can rejoice in the prospect of eternal life. On the other hand, however, our understanding of the doctrine of perseverance allows no room for indolence or laxity. It is questionable whether anyone who reasons, "Now that I am a Christian, I can live as I please," has really been converted and regenerated. Genuine faith issues, instead, in the fruit of the Spirit. Assurance of salvation, the subjective conviction that one is a Christian, results from the Holy Spirit's giving evidence that he is at work in the life of the individual.

Glorification

The final stage of the process of salvation is termed glorification. In Paul's words, those whom God "foreknew he also predestined to be conformed to the image of his Son. . . . And those whom he predestined he also called; and those whom he called he also justified; and those whom he justified he also glorified" (Rom. 8:29–30). Glorification is the point at which the doctrine of salvation and the doctrine of the last things overlap, for it looks beyond this life to the world to come. The topic is one which receives little treatment in standard theology textbooks, and even less attention in sermons, yet it is rich in practical significance, for it gives believers encouragement and strengthens their hope.

Glorification is multidimensional. It involves both individual and collective eschatology. It involves the perfecting of the spiritual nature of the individual believer, which takes place at death, when the Christian passes into the presence of the Lord. It also involves the perfecting of the bodies of all believers, which will occur at the time of the resurrection in connection with the second coming of Christ.[23] It even involves transformation of the entire creation (Rom. 8:18–25).

The Meaning of "Glory"

To understand the doctrine of glorification, we must first know the meaning of the term *glory*, which translates a number of biblical words. One of them is the Hebrew *kābôd*. It refers to a perceptible attribute, an individual's display of splendor, wealth, and pomp.[24] When used with respect to God, it does not point to one particular attribute, but to the greatness of his entire nature.[25]

Psalm 24:7–10 speaks of God as the King of glory. As King he is attended by his hosts and marked by infinite splendor and beauty.

In the New Testament, the Greek word *doxa* conveys the meaning of brightness, splendor, magnificence, and fame.[26] Here we find glory attributed to Jesus Christ, just as it was to God in the Old Testament. Jesus prayed that the Father would glorify him as he had glorified the Father (John 17:1–5). It is especially in the resurrection of Christ that we see his glory (Acts 3:13–15; 1 Peter 1:21). The second coming of Christ is also to be an occasion of his glory. Jesus himself has drawn a vivid picture of the glorious nature of his return: "they will see the Son of man coming on the clouds of heaven with power and great glory" (Matt. 24:30).

The Glorification of the Believer

It is important to realize that not only Christ, but all true believers as well, will be glorified. What precisely will be entailed in the glorification of the believer? One of its aspects will be a full and final vindication of the believer.[27] The justification which took place at the moment of conversion will be manifested or made obvious in the future. This is the meaning of Romans 5:9–10. In chapter 8, Paul contemplates the future judgment and asks who will bring any charge against the elect; in view of the fact that Christ died for us and now intercedes for us, no one will (vv. 33–34). Neither things present, nor things to come, can separate us from the love of God in Christ Jesus (vv. 38–39). Like a student who is thoroughly prepared for an examination, the Christian regards the last judgment, not with apprehensiveness, but with anticipation, knowing that the result will be positive.

In glorification there will also be a moral and spiritual perfecting of the individual.[28] Several biblical references point to a future completion of the process begun in regener-

---

23. John Murray restricts glorification to the time of the resurrection; in his view all believers will be glorified together at the return of Christ (*Redemption*, pp. 174–75). Bernard Ramm, however, looks upon glorification as occurring in connection with face-to-face knowledge of Christ (*Them He Glorified: A Systematic Study of the Doctrine of Glorification* [Grand Rapids: Eerdmans, 1963], p. 65). The issue here is how to define "glorification." What is its extent; to what events does it apply? The answer will depend in part on one's view of the nature of the intermediate state between death and resurrection (see ch. 38).

24. Francis Brown, S. R. Driver, and Charles A. Briggs, *Hebrew and English Lexicon of the Old Testament* (New York: Oxford University Press, 1955), pp. 458–59.

25. Ramm, *Them He Glorified*, p. 18.

26. William F. Arndt and F. Wilbur Gingrich, eds., *A Greek-English Lexicon of the New Testament*, 4th ed. (Chicago: University of Chicago Press, 1957), pp. 202–3.

27. Ramm, *Them He Glorified*, pp. 67–69.

28. Charles M. Horne, *Salvation* (Chicago: Moody, 1971), pp. 102–6.

ation and continued in sanctification. One of the most direct of these statements is Colossians 1:22: "he has now reconciled [you] in his body of flesh by his death, in order to present you holy and blameless and irreproachable before him." The concept of future flawlessness or blamelessness is also found in Ephesians 1:4; Philippians 1:9–11; and Jude 24. Guiltlessness is mentioned in 1 Corinthians 1:8. Our moral and spiritual perfection will be attained in part through the removal of temptation, for the source of sin and evil and temptation will have been conclusively overcome (Rev. 20:7–10).

The glorification which is to come will also bring fullness of knowledge. In 1 Corinthians 13:12 Paul contrasts the imperfect knowledge which we now have with the perfect which is to come: "For now we see in a mirror dimly, but then face to face. Now I know in part; then I shall understand fully, even as I have been fully understood." Our knowledge will increase because we will see the Lord; we will no longer have to be content with merely reading accounts written by those who knew him during his earthly ministry. As John says, "Beloved, we are God's children now; it does not yet appear what we shall be, but we know that when he appears we shall be like him, for we shall see him as he is" (1 John 3:2).

the Lord Jesus Christ, who will change our lowly body to be like his glorious body, by the power which enables him even to subject all things to himself." In 2 Corinthians 5:1–5 Paul envisions the body that we will have, a body eternal in nature, not made by human hands but coming from God. It is to be our heavenly dwelling. That which is mortal will be swallowed up by life (v. 4). The third passage is 1 Corinthians 15:38–50. Paul draws a comparison between the body which we are to have and our present body:

1. The present body is perishable, subject to disease and death; the resurrection body is incorruptible, immune to disease and decay.
2. The present body is sown in dishonor; the resurrection body will be glorious.
3. The present body is weak; the resurrection body is powerful.
4. The present body is physical; the resurrection body will be spiritual.

Paul notes that the great change which will take place at the time of the coming of Christ will be instantaneous: "Lo! I tell you a mystery. We shall not all sleep, but we shall all be changed, in a moment, in the twinkling of an eye, at the last trumpet. For the trumpet will sound, and the dead will be

When glorified, we will be everything that God has intended us to be.

There is also to be a glorification of the body. This will take place in connection with the resurrection of the believer. At the second coming of Christ, all who have died in the Lord will be raised; and they, together with the surviving believers, will be transformed. Three passages in particular emphasize the change which will be produced in the body of the believer. In Philippians 3:20–21 Paul says, "But our commonwealth is in heaven, and from it we await a Savior,

raised imperishable, and we shall be changed" (vv. 51–52). Bernard Ramm comments: "In short, the four positive attributes of the resurrection body may be equated with the glorification of that body. This glorification is no process, no matter of growth, but occurs suddenly, dramatically, at the end-time."[29]

Finally, we should note the relationship between the believer's glorification and the

29. Ramm, *Them He Glorified,* p. 103.

renewal of the creation. Because humans are part of the creation, their sin and fall brought certain consequences to it as well as to themselves (Gen. 3:14–19). Creation is presently in subjection to futility (Rom. 8:18–25). Yet Paul tells us that "the creation itself will be set free from its bondage to decay and obtain the glorious liberty of the children of God" (v. 21). The nature of the transformation which is to take place is stated more specifically in Revelation 21:1–2: "Then I saw a new heaven and a new earth; for the first heaven and the first earth had passed away, and the sea was no more. And I saw the holy city, new Jerusalem, coming down out of heaven from God, prepared as a bride adorned for her husband." At that time God will declare, "Behold, I make all things new" (v. 5). Part of our glorification will be the provision of a perfect environment in which to dwell. It will be perfect, for the glory of God will be present.

In this life believers sometimes groan and suffer because they sense their incompleteness. Yet they have a sure hope. The doctrine of sanctification continues God's work of justification by conforming us to the very image of Christ. The doctrine of perseverance guarantees that the salvation we possess will never be lost. And the doctrine of glorification promises that something better lies ahead. We will be everything that God has intended us to be. In part our glorification will take place in connection with death and our passage from the limitations of this earthly existence; in part it will occur in connection with the second coming of Christ. That we will thereafter be perfect and complete is sure.

Complete in Thee! no work of mine
May take, dear Lord, the place of Thine;
Thy blood hath pardon bought for me,
And I am now complete in Thee.

Yea, justified! O blessed thought!
And sanctified! Salvation wrought!
Thy blood hath pardon bought for me,
And glorified, I too shall be!

(Aaron R. Wolfe and James M. Gray)

The Church

35

The Nature of the Church

We have discussed to this point the nature of salvation as it pertains to individual Christians. Yet the Christian life is not a solitary matter. Typically, in the Book of Acts, we find that conversion leads the individual into the fellowship of a group of believers. That collective dimension of the Christian life we call the church.

The Basic Meaning of the Term "Church"

The church is one aspect of Christian doctrine on which virtually everyone, believer and unbeliever alike, has an opinion. Part of the reason is that, as an institution of society, the church can be observed and studied by the methods of social science. This presents us with a dilemma, however. We may be tempted to define the church by what it is found to be empirically. Such an approach, however, would confuse the actual with the ideal and thus, interesting though it may be, must be bypassed.

329

The other way of approaching and defining the church is through the same means which we have used in the preceding portions of this book, namely, studying the biblical material. The meaning of the term *church* can best be seen against both the Greek and the Old Testament background. The Greek word which is used in the New Testament for church (*ekklēsia*) referred in classical Greek simply to the assembly of the citizens of a city. The closest Old Testament equivalent (*qāhāl*) is not so much a specification of the members of an assembly as a designation of the act of assembling.

In the New Testament, the word *church* has two senses. On the one hand, it denotes all believers in Christ at all times and places. This universal sense is found in Matthew 16:18, where Jesus promises that he will build his church, and in Paul's image of the church as the body of Christ (e.g., Eph. 1:22–23; 4:4; 5:23). More frequently, however, "church" refers to a group of believers in a given geographical locality. This is clearly the meaning in, for instance, 1 Corinthians 1:2 and 1 Thessalonians 1:1.

The Unity of the Church

Of assistance in understanding the nature of the church is a doctrine clearly taught in the New Testament, the unity of the church. The ideal of unity is emphasized in Jesus' high-priestly prayer (John 17:20–23) as well as in Paul's discussion of the church in Ephesians 4:1–16. It is also reflected in a reference to the local church at Jerusalem (Acts 4:32) and in an appeal to believers to be of one accord and one mind (Phil. 2:2).

Paradoxically, however, the church as it exists in the world today does not seem to be unified. We see countless denominations, sometimes quite similar in teachings, competing with one another. And the relationships between members of the local church are sometimes characterized by aloofness or even outright hostility. Yet we know that as believers we should be pursuing unity, for this is Christ's declared will for the church.

We must ask, then, just what he had in view. In recent years there have been a number of different conceptions of what unity should entail:

Some Christians regard church unity as essentially spiritual in nature. They find unity in the fact that all believers serve and love the same Lord. Although they are not organically connected with other groups of believers and may not cooperate in any outward endeavors, they love one another, even those with whom they have no contact. One day, when the bride of Christ, the church, is gathered, there will be actual unity. Unity, in other words, applies to the universal or invisible church more than to the visible church.

A second view focuses on mutual recognition and fellowship. This approach emphasizes that although congregations and denominations are separate from one another, they are basically of the same faith, and so should strive to give observable expression to this unity in whatever fashion possible. Thus, there will be fellowship between different groups, ready transfers of membership, and pulpit exchanges. Whenever possible, congregations and denominations will work together in their service of the Lord.

A third view promotes conciliar unity. While retaining their individual identity, denominations bind themselves together in a formal association or council. They witness to their own traditions and convictions, but also seek to combine their strengths in action.

Finally, there is the view that church unity means organic unity. Here congregations unite in one large denomination, combining their traditions. The United Church of Canada, which combined Methodists, Presbyterians, and Congregationalists into one fellowship, is an example of such a movement. The ultimate aim is the uniting of all denominations into one group.

In general, the drives toward conciliar and organic unity, especially the latter, have been in considerable decline in recent years. Certainly, believers should desire and seek to bring about spiritual unity and, to the extent possible, mutual recognition and fellowship. Each person and congregation will have to determine the degree to which closer involvement and cooperative activity are consistent with preservation of their biblical convictions and fulfilment of the task given by the Lord.

Biblical Images of the Church

We next need to inquire regarding the qualities or characteristics which are present in the true church. We will approach this topic through an examination of certain of the images which Paul used of the church. While there are a large number of such images,[1] we will examine three in particular. Arthur Wainwright has argued that in much of Paul's writing there is an implicit trinitarianism which shows itself even in the structure with which he organizes his letters.[2] It is also present in the way he understands the church, for he describes it as the people of God, the body of Christ, and the temple of the Holy Spirit.

The People of God

Paul wrote of God's decision to make believers his people: "God said, 'I will live in them and move among them, and I will be their God, and they shall be my people'" (2 Cor. 6:16). The church is constituted of God's people. They belong to him and he belongs to them.

The concept of the church as the people of God emphasizes God's initiative in choosing them. In the Old Testament, he did not adopt as his own an existing nation, but actually *created* a people for himself. He chose Abraham and then, through him, brought into being the people of Israel. In the New Testament, this concept of God's choosing a people is broadened to include both Jews and Gentiles within the church. So Paul writes to the Thessalonians: "But we are bound to give thanks to God always for you, brethren beloved by the Lord, because God chose you from the beginning to be saved, through sanctification by the Spirit and belief in the truth. To this he called you through our gospel, so that you may obtain the glory of our Lord Jesus Christ" (2 Thess. 2:13–14; see also 1 Thess. 1:4).

> *The church is the chosen people of God; they belong to him and he belongs to them.*

Among the Old Testament texts in which Israel is identified as God's people are Exodus 15:13, 16; Numbers 14:8; Deuteronomy 32:9–10; Isaiah 62:4; Jeremiah 12:7–10; and Hosea 1:9–10; 2:23. In Romans 9:24–26 Paul applies the statements in Hosea to God's taking in of Gentiles as well as Jews: God "has called [us], not from the Jews only but also from the Gentiles[.] As indeed he says in Hosea, 'Those who were not my people I will call "my people," and her who was not beloved I will call "my beloved."' 'And in the very place where it was said to them, "You are not my people," they will be called "sons of the living God."'"

The concept of Israel and the church as the people of God contains several implications. God takes pride in them. He provides care and protection to his people; he keeps them "as the apple of his eye" (Deut. 32:10). Finally, he expects that they will be his people without reservation and without dividing their loyalty. Jehovah's exclusive claim on his people is pictured in the story of Hosea's exclusive claim on his unfaithful wife

1. Paul S. Minear, *Images of the Church in the New Testament* (Philadelphia: Westminster, 1960), suggests over one hundred such images.
2. Arthur W. Wainwright, *The Trinity in the New Testament* (London: S.P.C.K., 1962), pp. 256–60.

Gomer. All of the people of God are marked with a special brand as it were. In the Old Testament, circumcision was the proof of divine ownership. It was required of all male children of the people of Israel, as well as of all male converts or proselytes. It was an external sign of the covenant which made them God's people. It was also a subjective sign of the covenant in that it was applied individually to each person, whereas the ark of the covenant served as an objective sign for the whole group.

Instead of this external circumcision of the flesh, found in the administration of the old covenant, we find under the new covenant an inward circumcision of the heart. Paul wrote, "He is a Jew who is one inwardly, and real circumcision is a matter of the heart, spiritual and not literal" (Rom. 2:29; see also Phil. 3:3). Whereas in the Old Testament, or under the old covenant, the people of God had been national Israel, inclusion among the people of God was not, in the New Testament, based upon national identity: "For not all who are descended from Israel belong to Israel" (Rom. 9:6). It is inclusion within the covenant of God that distinguishes the people of God; they are made up of all those "whom he has called, not from the Jews only but also from the Gentiles" (v. 24). For Israel the covenant was the Abrahamic covenant; for the church it is the new covenant wrought and established by Christ (2 Cor. 3:3–18).

A particular quality of holiness is expected of the people of God. God had always expected Israel to be pure or sanctified. As Christ's bride the church must also be holy: "Christ loved the church and gave himself up for her, that he might sanctify her, having cleansed her by the washing of water with the word, that he might present the church to himself in splendor, without spot or wrinkle or any such thing, that she might be holy and without blemish" (Eph. 5:25b–27).

The Body of Christ

Perhaps the most extended image of the church is its representation as the body of Christ. This image emphasizes that the church is the focal point of Christ's activity now, just as was his physical body during his earthly ministry. The image is used both of the church universal (Eph. 1:22–23) and of individual local congregations (1 Cor. 12:27). The image of the body of Christ also emphasizes the connection of the church, as a group of believers, with Christ. Salvation, in all of its complexity, is in large part a result of union with Christ. We observed in chapter 33 several references to the believer's being "in Christ." Here we find an emphasis upon the converse of this fact. Christ in the believer is the basis of belief and hope. Paul writes, "To [the saints] God chose to make known how great among the Gentiles are the riches of the glory of this mystery, which is Christ in you, the hope of glory" (Col. 1:27; see also Gal. 2:20).

There are several aspects to the image of the church as the body of Christ:

1. Christ is the head of this body (Col. 1:18) of which believers are individual members or parts. All things were created in him, through him, and for him (Col. 1:16). He is the beginning, the first-born (v. 15). "All things in heaven and on earth [will be brought] together under one head, even Christ" (Eph. 1:10, NIV). Believers, united with him, are being nourished through him, the head to which they are connected (Col. 2:19). As the head of the body (Col. 1:18), he also rules the church: "For in him the whole fulness of deity dwells bodily, and you have come to fulness of life in him, who is the head of all rule and authority" (Col. 2:9–10). Christ is the Lord of the church. It is to be guided and controlled by his direction and his activity.

2. The image of the body of Christ also speaks of the interconnectedness between all the persons who make up the church. There is no such thing as an isolated, solitary Christian life. In 1 Corinthians 12 Paul develops the concept of the interconnected-

ness of the body, especially in terms of the gifts of the Spirit. Here he stresses the dependence of each believer upon every other.

There is, in this understanding of the body, a mutuality; each believer encourages and builds up the others. In Ephesians 4:11–16 Paul develops this idea of the value of each one's contribution to the others. There is to be a purity of the whole. Members of the body are to bear one another's burdens (Gal. 6:2) and restore those who are found to be in sin (v. 1). In some cases, as here, dealing with sinful members may involve gentle restoration. At times, it may involve barring from the fellowship those who are defiling it. That is to say, it may involve actual exclusion or excommunication. In Matthew 18:8, 17, Jesus spoke of this possibility, as did Paul in Romans 16:17 and 1 Corinthians 5:12–13.

3. The body is to be characterized by genuine fellowship. This does not mean merely a social interrelatedness, but an intimate feeling for and understanding of one another. There are to be empathy and encouragement (edification). What is experienced by one is to be experienced by all. Thus Paul writes, "If one member suffers, all suffer together; if one member is honored, all rejoice together" (1 Cor. 12:26). The church in the Book of Acts even shared material possessions with one another.

4. The body is to be a unified body. Members of the church in Corinth were divided as to what religious leader they should follow (1 Cor. 1:10–17; 3:1–9). Social cliques or factions had been formed and were very much in evidence at the gatherings of the church (1 Cor. 11:17–19). This was not to be, however, for all believers are baptized by one Spirit into one body (1 Cor. 12:12–13; see also Eph. 4:4–6).

5. The body of Christ is also universal. It is for all who will come into it. There are no longer any special qualifications like nationality. All such barriers have been removed, as Paul indicated: "Here there cannot be Greek and Jew, circumcised and uncircumcised, barbarian, Scythian, slave, free man,

but Christ is all, and in all" (Col. 3:11). The same idea, with special reference to eliminating divisions between Jews and Gentiles within the body, is found in Romans 11:25–26, 32; Galatians 3:28; and Ephesians 2:15.

6. As the body of Christ, the church is the extension of his ministry. We ought not press this idea too far in the direction of viewing the church as a literal incarnation of Christ, for the result would be a virtual pantheism. Rather, we should look to Christ's Great Commission. Having indicated that all authority in heaven and on earth had been given to him (Matt. 28:18), he sent his disciples to evangelize, baptize, and teach, promising them that he would be with them always, even to the end of the age (vv. 19–20). He told them that they were to carry on his work, and would do so to an amazing degree (John 14:12). The work of Christ, then, if it is done at all, will be done by his body, the church.

The Temple of the Holy Spirit

Filling out Paul's trinitarian concept of the church is the picture of the church as the temple of the Spirit. It is the Spirit who brought the church into being. This dramatic work of the Spirit occurred at Pentecost, where he baptized the disciples and converted three thousand, giving birth to the church. And he has continued to populate the church: "For by one Spirit we were all baptized into one body—Jews or Greeks, slaves or free—and all were made to drink of one Spirit" (1 Cor. 12:13).

The church is now indwelt by the Spirit, on both an individual and a collective basis. Paul writes to the Corinthians, "Do you not know that you are God's temple and that God's Spirit dwells in you? If any one destroys God's temple, God will destroy him. For God's temple is holy, and that temple you are" (1 Cor. 3:16–17). Elsewhere he describes believers as "a holy temple in the Lord . . . a dwelling place of God in the Spirit" (Eph. 2:21–22).

Dwelling within the church, the Holy Spirit imparts his life to it. Those qualities which are his nature and which are spoken of as the "fruit of the Spirit" will be found in the church: love, joy, peace, patience, kindness, goodness, faithfulness, gentleness, self-control (Gal. 5:22–23). The presence of such qualities is indicative of the activity of the Holy Spirit and thus, in a sense, of the genuineness of the church.

It is the Holy Spirit who conveys power to the church, as Jesus indicated in Acts 1:8. Because of the imminent coming of the Spirit with power, Jesus could give his disciples the incredible promise that they would do even greater works than he had done (John 14:12). Thus Jesus told them, "It is to your advantage that I go away, for if I do not go away, the Counselor will not come to you; but if I go, I will send him to you" (John 16:7). It is the Spirit who does whatever is necessary to convict the world of sin, righteousness, and judgment (v. 8).

The Spirit, being one, also produces a unity within the body. This does not mean uniformity, but a oneness in aim and action. The early church is described as being "of one heart and soul" (Acts 4:32). They even held all their material goods in common (2:44–45; 4:32, 34–35). The Spirit had created in them a stronger consciousness of membership in the group than of individual identity, and so they viewed their possessions not as "mine" and "yours," but as "ours."

The Holy Spirit, dwelling within the church, also creates a sensitivity to the Lord's leading. Jesus had promised to continue to abide with his disciples (Matt. 28:20; John 14:18, 23). Yet he had said as well that he had to go away so that the Holy Spirit could come (John 16:7). We conclude that the indwelling Spirit is the means of Jesus' presence with us. So Paul wrote: "But you are not in the flesh, you are in the Spirit, if the Spirit of God really dwells in you. Any one who does not have the Spirit of Christ does not belong to him. But if Christ is in you, although your bodies are dead because of sin, your spirits are alive because of righteousness" (Rom. 8:9–10). Paul uses interchangeably the ideas of Christ's being in us and the Spirit's dwelling in us.

As the Spirit indwelt Jesus' disciples, he brought to their remembrance the Lord's teachings (John 14:26) and guided them into all truth (John 16:13). This work of the Spirit was dramatically illustrated in the case of Peter. In a vision Peter was told to kill and eat certain unclean beasts which had been let down to earth in something like a great sheet (Acts 10:11–13). Peter's first response was, "No, Lord" (v. 14), for he was well aware of the prohibition upon eating unclean animals. Peter soon realized, however, that the essence of the message of the vision was not that he should eat unclean animals, but that he should bring the gospel to the Gentiles as well as to the Jews (vv. 17–48). The Spirit who dwelt within made Peter both aware that the Lord was leading him to the Gentiles and willing to obey. The Holy Spirit renders believers who are set in their ways responsive and obedient to the leading of the Lord.

The Spirit is in one sense also the sovereign of the church. For it is he who equips the body by dispensing gifts, which in some cases are persons to fill various offices and in other cases are special abilities. He decides when a gift will be bestowed, and upon whom it is to be conferred (1 Cor. 12:11).

Finally, the Holy Spirit makes the church holy and pure. For just as the temple was a holy and sacred place under the old covenant because God dwelt in it, so also are believers sanctified under the new covenant because they are the temple of the Holy Spirit (1 Cor. 6:19–20).

Implications

1. The church is not to be conceived of primarily as a sociological phenomenon, but as a divinely established institution. Accordingly, its essence is to be determined not from an analysis of its activity, but from Scripture.

2. The church exists because of its relationship to the Triune God. It exists to carry

out its Lord's will by the power of the Holy Spirit.

3. The church is the continuation of the Lord's presence and ministry in the world.

4. The church is to be a fellowship of regenerate believers who display the spiritual qualities of their Lord. Purity and devotion are to be emphasized.

5. While the church is a divine creation, it is made up of imperfect human beings. It will not reach perfect sanctification or glorification until its Lord's return.

36 The Role and Government of the Church

The functions of the church are very important topics, for the church was not brought into being by our Lord simply to exist as an end in itself. Rather, it was brought into being to fulfil the Lord's intention for it. It is to carry on the Lord's ministry in the world—to perpetuate what he did and to do what he would do were he still here. Our first consideration in this chapter will be the various functions which the church is charged with carrying out.[1] Then we will look at what is at the heart of the ministry of the church and gives form to all that the church does, namely, the gospel. Finally, we will note several types of church government and try to determine which is best suited to carrying out the Lord's work.

1. J. C. Hoekendijk, *The Church Inside Out* (Philadelphia: Westminster, 1966), part 1.

The Functions of the Church

Evangelism

The one topic emphasized in both accounts of Jesus' last words to his disciples is evangelism. In Matthew 28:19 he instructs them, "Go therefore and make disciples of all nations." In Acts 1:8 he says, "But you shall receive power when the Holy Spirit has come upon you; and you shall be my witnesses in Jerusalem and in all Judea and Samaria and to the end of the earth." This was the final point Jesus made to his disciples. It appears that he regarded evangelism as the very reason for their being.

The call to evangelize is a command. Having accepted Jesus as Lord, the disciples had brought themselves under his rule and were obligated to do whatever he asked. For he had said, "If you love me, you will keep my commandments" (John 14:15). If the disciples truly loved their Lord, they would carry out his call to evangelize. It was not an optional matter for them.

The disciples were not sent out merely in their own strength, however. Jesus prefaced his commission with the statement, "All authority in heaven and on earth has been given to me" (Matt. 28:18). Having all authority, he commissioned the disciples as his agents. Thus they had the right to go and evangelize all nations. Further, Jesus promised his disciples that the Holy Spirit would come upon them and that they would consequently receive power. So they were both authorized and enabled for the task. Moreover, they were assured that he was not sending them off on their own. Although he was to be taken from them bodily, he would nonetheless be with them spiritually to the very end of the age (Matt. 28:20).

Note also the extent of the commission: it is all-inclusive. In Matthew 28:19 Jesus speaks of "all nations," and in Acts 1:8 he gives a specific enumeration: "You shall be my witnesses in Jerusalem and in all Judea and Samaria and to the end of the earth." There was no geographical restriction upon the commission. The disciples were to take the gospel message everywhere, to all nations and every type of people. They could not, of course, accomplish this on their own. Rather, as they won converts, those converts would in turn evangelize yet others. Thus the message would spread in ever-widening circles, and the task would eventually be completed.

Therefore, if the church is to be faithful to its Lord and bring joy to his heart, it must be engaged in bringing the gospel to all people. This involves going to people whom we like and people whom we may by nature tend to dislike. It extends to those who are unlike us. And it goes beyond our immediate sphere of contact and influence. In a very real sense, local evangelism, church extension or church planting, and world missions are all the same thing. The only difference lies in the length of the radius. The church must work in all of these areas. If it does not, it will become spiritually ill, for it will be attempting to function in a way its Lord never intended.

Edification

The second major function of the church is the edification of believers. Although Jesus laid greater emphasis upon evangelism, the edification of believers is logically prior. Paul repeatedly spoke of the edification of the body. In Ephesians 4:12, for example, he indicates that God has given various gifts to the church "for the equipment of the saints, for the work of ministry, for building up the body of Christ." Believers are to grow up into Christ, "from whom the whole body, joined and knit together by every joint with which it is supplied, when each part is working properly, makes bodily growth and upbuilds itself in love" (v. 16). The potential for edification is the criterion by which all activities, including our speech, are to be measured: "Let no evil talk come out of your mouths, but only such as is good for edifying, as fits the occasion, that it may impart grace to those who hear" (v. 29).

There are other passages, for instance, 1 Corinthians 12, where Paul links spiritual gifts to edification. All of the various members of the church have been given gifts. These gifts are not for personal satisfaction, but for the edification (building up) of the body as a whole (14:4–5, 12). While there is diversity of gifts, there is not to be division within the body. Some of these gifts are more conspicuous than others, but they are not therefore more important (12:14–25). No one gift is for everyone (12:27–31); this means, conversely, that no one person has all the gifts.

Moreover, in Paul's discussion of certain controversial spiritual gifts, he brings up the matter of edification. He says, for example, in 1 Corinthians 14:4–5: "He who speaks in a tongue edifies himself, but he who prophesies edifies the church. Now I want you all to speak in tongues, but even more to prophesy. He who prophesies is greater than he who speaks in tongues, unless someone interprets, so that the church may be edified." The importance of edifying others as one exercises controversial gifts is mentioned again, in varying ways, in verses 12, 17, and 26. The last of these references sums up the matter: "Let all things be done for edification." Note that edification is mutual upbuilding by all the members of the body. It is not merely the minister or pastor who is to build up the other members.

There are several means by which members of the church are to be edified. One of them is fellowship.[2] The New Testament speaks of *koinōnia*, literally, a having or holding all things in common. And indeed, according to Acts 5, the members of the early church held even all their material possessions in common. Paul speaks of sharing one another's experiences: "If one member suffers, all suffer together; if one member is honored, all rejoice together" (1 Cor. 12:26). While hurt is reduced, joy is increased by being shared. We are to encourage and sympathize with each other.

The church also edifies its members through instruction or teaching.[3] This is part of the broad task of discipling. One of Jesus' commands in the Great Commission was to teach converts "to observe all that I have commanded you" (Matt. 28:20). To this end, one of God's gifts to the churches is "pastors and teachers" (Eph. 4:11) to prepare and equip the people of God for service. Education may take many forms and occur on many levels. It is incumbent upon the church to utilize all legitimate means and technologies available today. Preaching is a means of instruction that has been used by the Christian church from its very beginning.[4] In 1 Corinthians 14, when Paul speaks of prophesying, he probably is referring to preaching. He comments that prophesying is of greater value than is speaking in tongues, because it edifies or builds up the church (vv. 3–4).

To the end of mutual edification God has equipped the church with various gifts apportioned and bestowed by the Holy Spirit (1 Cor. 12:11). As we noted earlier (p. 270), the New Testament contains four significantly different lists of these gifts. Whenever virtues like faith, service, and giving, which, on biblical grounds, are to be expected of all believers, are represented as special gifts of the Spirit, it appears that the writer has in mind unusual or extraordinary dimensions or degrees of those virtues. The Holy Spirit in his wisdom has given just what is needed, so that the body as a whole may be properly built up and equipped.

Worship

Another activity of the church is worship. Whereas edification focuses upon the believers and benefits them, worship concentrates upon the Lord. The early church came together to worship on a regular schedule, a practice commanded and commended by

2. James E. Carter, *The Mission of the Church* (Nashville: Broadman, 1974), pp. 65–73.

3. Edmund Clowney, "Toward a Biblical Doctrine of the Church," *Westminster Theological Journal* 31.1 (Nov. 1968): 71–72.

4. Karl Barth, *The Word of God and the Word of Man*, trans. Douglas Horton (New York: Harper and Row, 1956), pp. 97–135.

the apostle Paul. His direction to the Corinthians to set aside money on the first day of every week (1 Cor. 16:2) intimates that they regularly gathered for worship on that day. The writer to the Hebrews exhorts his readers not to neglect the assembling of themselves together, as was the habit of some

Social Concern

Cutting across the various functions of the church which we have thus far examined is its responsibility to perform acts of Christian love and compassion for both believers and non-Christians. It is clear that Jesus cared about the problems of the needy and the suffering.[5] He healed the sick and even raised the dead on occasion. If the church is to carry on his ministry, it will be engaged in some form of ministry to the needy and the suffering. That Jesus has such an expectation of believers is evident in the parable of the good Samaritan (Luke 10:25–37). Jesus told this parable to the lawyer who, understanding that one can inherit eternal life by loving God with one's whole being and one's neighbor as oneself, asked who his neighbor was. In answering the question, Jesus also explained what it means to love one's neighbor as oneself. In the same vein, Jesus suggests in Matthew 25:31–46 that the one sign by which true believers can be distinguished from those who make empty professions is acts of love which are done in Jesus' name and emulate his example.

they went forth to reach the lost in the world without.

For spiritual health, the church must carefully balance its major functions—evangelism, edification, worship, social concern.

(Heb. 10:25). Although worship emphasizes God, it is also intended to benefit the worshipers. This we infer from Paul's warning against prayers, songs, and thanksgivings which fail to edify because no one is present to interpret their meaning to those who do not understand (1 Cor. 14:15–17).

It is important at this point to note the particular place of each of the various functions of the church. In biblical times the church gathered for worship and instruction. Then it went out to evangelize. In worship, the members of the church focus upon God; in instruction and fellowship, they focus upon themselves and fellow Christians; in evangelism, they turn their attention to non-Christians. It is well for the church to keep some separation between these several activities. If this is not done, one or more may be crowded out. As a result the church will suffer, since all of these activities, like the various elements in a well-balanced diet, are essential to the spiritual health and well-being of the body. For example, worship of God will suffer if the gathering of the body becomes oriented primarily to the interaction among Christians, or if the service is aimed exclusively at evangelizing the unbelievers who happen to be present. This was not the pattern of the church in the Book of Acts. Rather, believers gathered to praise God and be edified; then

Emphasis on social concern carries over into the Epistles as well. James is particularly strong in stressing practical Christianity. Consider, for example, his definition of religion: "Religion that is pure and undefiled before God and the Father is this: to visit orphans and widows in their affliction, and to keep oneself unstained from

5. Sherwood Wirt, *The Social Conscience of the Evangelical* (New York: Harper and Row, 1968), pp. 19–26.

the world" (James 1:27). He speaks out sharply against showing favoritism to the rich, an evil which occurred even within the church (2:1–11). He denounces verbal encouragement unaccompanied by action: "Suppose a brother or sister is without clothes and daily food. If one of you says to him, 'Go, I wish you well; keep warm and well fed,' but does nothing about his physical needs, what good is it? In the same way, faith by itself, if it is not accompanied by action, is dead" (2:15–17, NIV).

Social concern includes the condemning of unrighteousness as well. Amos and several other Old Testament prophets spoke out emphatically against the evil and corruption of their day. John the Baptist likewise condemned the sin of Herod, the ruler of his day, even though it cost him his liberty (Luke 3:19–20) and eventually even his life (Mark 6:17–29).

The church is to show concern and take action wherever it sees need, hurt, or wrong. Obviously the church has a great deal to do by way of improving its record in this area. Yet it occasionally fails to note just how much has already been accomplished. What percentage of the colleges and hospitals in England and the United States were founded in earlier years by Christian groups? Today many of the charitable and educational functions once carried out by the church are instead managed by the state and supported by taxes paid by both Christians and non-Christians. Consider also that the social needs in developed countries are not nearly as severe as they once were.

Many of the churches which minimize the need for regeneration claim that evangelicals have not participated sufficiently in the alleviation of human needs.[6] When, however, one shifts the frame of reference from the American domestic scene to the world, the picture is quite different. For evangelicals, concentrating their medical, agricultural, and educational ministries in

countries where the needs are most severe, have outstripped their counterparts in the mainline churches in worldwide mission endeavor. Indeed, on a per capita basis, evangelicals have done more than have the liberal churches, and certainly much more than has the general populace.[7]

The Heart of the Ministry of the Church: The Gospel

It is important for us now to look closely at the one factor which gives basic shape to everything the church does, the element which lies at the heart of all its functions, namely, the gospel, the good news. At the beginning of his ministry Jesus announced that he had been anointed specifically to preach the gospel; later he charged the apostles to continue his ministry by spreading the gospel. Without doubt, then, the gospel lies at the root of all that the church does.

Jesus entrusted to the believers the good news which had characterized his own teaching and preaching from the very beginning. It is significant that, in the Book of Mark, the first recorded activity of Jesus after his baptism and temptation is his preaching the gospel in Galilee (Mark 1:14–15). Similarly, Luke records that Jesus inaugurated his ministry in Nazareth by reading from Isaiah 61:1–2 and applying the prophecy to himself: "The Spirit of the Lord is upon me, because he has anointed me to preach good news to the poor. He has sent me to proclaim release to the captives and recovering of sight to the blind, to set at liberty those who are oppressed, to proclaim the acceptable year of the Lord" (Luke 4:18–19).

The key New Testament word with reference to the gospel, *euangelion*, denotes good

6. Robert M. Price, "A Fundamentalist Social Gospel?" *Christian Century* 96.39 (28 Nov. 1979): 1183–86. Note readers' replies in vol. 97.3 (23 Jan. 1980): 78–79.

7. Harold Lindsell, "The Missionary Retreat," *Christianity Today*, 9 Nov. 1971, pp. 26–27 (188–89); William Hordern, *New Directions in Theology Today*, vol. 1, *Introduction* (Philadelphia: Westminster, 1966), pp. 75–76. See also *Yearbook of American Churches*, ed. Herman C. Weber (New York: Round Table), 1933 ed., pp. 300–305; 1939 ed., pp. 6–17; 1941 ed., pp. 129–38.

tidings.[8] It has two basic senses: active proclamation of the message and the content proclaimed. Both senses occur in 1 Corinthians 9:14: "those who proclaim the gospel [the content] should get their living by the gospel [the act of proclaiming it]." It is significant that on many occasions Paul uses *euangelion* without any qualifier; that is, there is no adjective, phrase, or clause to define what he means by "the gospel" (e.g., Rom. 1:16; 10:16; 11:28). Obviously, *euangelion* had a meaning sufficiently standardized that Paul's readers knew precisely what he meant.

The question arises, If Paul and his readers viewed the gospel as involving a certain content, what is that content? While Paul nowhere gives us a complete and detailed statement of the tenets of the gospel, some passages are indicative of what it includes. In Romans 1:3–4 he speaks of "the gospel concerning [God's] Son, who was descended from David according to the flesh and designated Son of God in power according to the Spirit of holiness by his resurrection from the dead, Jesus Christ our Lord." In 1 Corinthians 15 Paul reminds his readers in what terms he had preached the gospel to them (v. 1): "For I delivered to you as of first importance what I also received, that Christ died for our sins in accordance with the scriptures, that he was buried, that he was raised on the third day in accordance with the scriptures, and that he appeared to Cephas . . . to the twelve . . . to more than five hundred brethren at one time . . . to James . . . also to me" (vv. 3–8). A briefer reference is Paul's exhortation in 2 Timothy 2:8: "Remember Jesus Christ, risen from the dead, descended from David, as preached in my gospel."

Paul viewed the gospel as centering upon Jesus Christ and what God has done through him. The essential points of the gospel are Jesus Christ's status as the Son of God, his genuine humanity, his death for our sins, his burial, resurrection, subsequent appearances, and future coming in judgment. We must not think, however, of the gospel as merely a recital of theological truths and historical events. Rather, it relates these truths and events to the situation of every individual believer. Thus, Jesus died. But he died "for our sins" (1 Cor. 15:3). Nor is the resurrection of Jesus an isolated event; it is the beginning of the general resurrection of all believers (1 Cor. 15:20 in conjunction with Rom. 1:3–4). Furthermore, the fact of coming judgment pertains to everyone. We will all be evaluated on the basis of our personal attitude toward and response to the gospel (2 Thess. 1:8).

To Paul, the gospel is all-important. He declares to the church in Rome that the gospel "is the power of God for salvation to every one who has faith, to the Jew first and also to the Greek" (Rom. 1:16). Convinced that only the gospel can bring salvation along with all its attendant blessings, Paul insists that the gospel is absolute and exclusive. Nothing is to be added to or taken from it, nor is there any alternate route to salvation.

Knowing that the gospel is the only route to salvation, Paul is determined to defend it. He writes to the Philippians of his "defense and confirmation of the gospel" (Phil. 1:7). He is prepared to give a reasoned argument for it. It is noteworthy that it is in this particular letter that Paul speaks of his defense of the gospel. There is every likelihood that the jailer who had responded to Paul's presentation of the gospel and become a new creature (Acts 16:25–34) was a member of the church in Philippi. Having witnessed in that very city an earthshaking demonstration of the power of God to salvation, could Paul ever have surrendered the gospel? Yet some people have contended that the gospel needs no defense, that it can stand on its own two feet. This reasoning, however, runs contrary to the pattern of Paul's own activity, for example, his speech in the middle of the Ar-

8. Gerhard Friedrich, εὐαγγελίζομαι, in *Theological Dictionary of the New Testament*, ed. Gerhard Kittel and Gerhard Friedrich, trans. Geoffrey W. Bromiley, 10 vols. (Grand Rapids: Eerdmans, 1964–76), vol. 2, pp. 710–12, 721–25.

eopagus (Acts 17:16–34).[9] The objection to an apologetic approach rests upon a misconception of how God works, a failure to recognize that in creating belief the Holy Spirit makes use of human minds and reason.

But we must not characterize Paul's activity as simply a defense of the gospel. He went on the offensive as well. He was eager to proclaim the good news to all nations. He had a sense of compulsion about his mission: "Woe to me if I do not preach the gospel" (1 Cor. 9:16). It had been entrusted to his stewardship, and he had a sacred obligation to proclaim it.

The gospel not only cuts across all racial, social, economic, and educational barriers (Rom. 1:16; Gal. 3:28), but also spans the centuries of time. A message which does not become obsolete (Jude 3), it is the church's sacred trust today. This good news which the church offers to the world brings hope. In this respect the message and ministry of the church are unique. For in our world today there is little hope. Existentialism has spawned literary works like Jean-Paul Sartre's *No Exit* and Albert Camus's "Myth of Sisyphus." There is little encouraging news, whether social, economic, or political, in the newspapers. In *Herzog* Saul Bellow has captured well the spirit of the entire age: "But what is the philosophy of this generation? Not God is dead, that period was passed long ago. Perhaps it should be stated death is God. This generation thinks—and this is its thought of thoughts—that nothing faithful, vulnerable, fragile can be durable or have any true power. Death waits for these things as a cement floor waits for a dropping light bulb."[10] By contrast, the church says with Peter, "Blessed be the God and Father of our Lord Jesus Christ! By his great mercy we have been born anew to a living hope through the resurrection of Jesus Christ

9. F. F. Bruce, *The Defence of the Gospel in the New Testament* (Grand Rapids: Eerdmans, 1959), pp. 37–48.
10. Quoted in Sam Keen, "Death in a Posthuman Era," in *New Theology No. 5*, ed. Martin E. Marty and Dean G. Peerman (New York: Macmillan, 1968), p. 79.

from the dead" (1 Peter 1:3). There is hope, and it comes to fulfilment when we believe and obey the gospel. Because the gospel has been, is, and will always be the way of salvation, the only way, the church must preserve it at all costs.

Forms of Church Government

Having looked at the basic functions of the church and the centrality of the gospel to its mission, we must now ask what type of structure will best facilitate carrying out the Lord's work in the world. With the twentieth-century emphasis upon ecumenism, this question of organization has risen to special visibility. For if there are to be close fellowship and cooperation, there must be some agreement upon the seat of authority. If, for example, a minister who belongs to one denomination is to preach and officiate at the Lord's Supper in another, there must be

> *An ideal form of church government will fulfil the biblical principles of order and the priesthood of all believers.*

some agreement as to who is a duly ordained minister, which in turn presupposes agreement upon who has the power to ordain. For the question of church government is in the final analysis a question of where authority resides within the church and who is to exercise it. Actually, the advocates of the various forms of church government agree that God is (or has) the ultimate authority. Where they differ is in their conceptions of how or through whom he expresses or exercises it.

Episcopal
Throughout the history of the church there have been several basic forms of church government. Our study will begin

with the most highly structured—the episcopal—and move on to the less structured. After we have surveyed the basic forms, we will attempt to determine whether one is preferable.

In the episcopal form of church government, authority resides in the bishop. There are varying degrees of episcopacy, that is to say, the number of levels of bishops varies. The simplest form of episcopal government is found in the Methodist church, which has only one level of bishops. Somewhat more developed is the governmental structure of the Anglican or Episcopal church, while the Roman Catholic Church has the most complete system of hierarchy, with authority being vested especially in the supreme pontiff, the bishop of Rome, the pope.

Inherent in the episcopal structure is the idea of different levels of ministry or different degrees of ordination.[11] The first level is that of the ordinary minister or priest. In some churches there are steps or divisions within this first level, for example, deacon and elder. The clergy at this level are authorized to perform all of the basic duties associated with the ministry, that is, they preach and administer the sacraments. Beyond this level, however, there is a second level of ordination, which constitutes one a bishop. The role of the bishops is to exercise the power of God which has been vested in them. In particular, as God's representatives and pastors they govern and care for a group of churches rather than merely one local congregation.[12] Among their powers is the ordination of ministers or priests.

Presbyterian

The presbyterian system of church government places primary authority in a particular office as well, but there is less emphasis upon the individual office and office-holder than upon a series of representative bodies which exercise that authority. The key officer in the presbyterian structure is the elder,[13] a position which harks back to the Jewish synagogue. Elders are also found in the New Testament church. In Acts 11:30 we read of the presence of elders in the Jerusalem congregation: the brethren in Antioch provided relief to the believers in Jerusalem, "sending it to the elders by the hand of Barnabas and Saul." The pastoral Epistles also make mention of elders.

It seems that in New Testament times the people chose their elders, individuals whom they assessed to be particularly qualified to rule the church. In selecting elders to rule the church, the people were conscious of confirming, by their external act, the choice which the Lord had already made. In the presbyterian system, the authority of Christ is understood as dispensed to individual believers and delegated by them to the elders whom they select and who thereafter represent them. Once elected or appointed, the elders function on behalf of or in the place of the individual believers. It is therefore at the level of the elders that divine authority actually functions within the church.[14]

This authority is exercised in a series of governing assemblies. At the level of the local church the session (Presbyterian)[15] or consistory (Reformed)[16] is the decision-making group. All the churches in one area are governed by the presbytery (Presbyterian) or classis (Reformed). The next grouping is the synod, made up of an equal number of lay elders and clergy chosen by each presbytery or classis. At the highest level the Presbyterian church also has a General As-

11. Leon Morris, "Church, Nature and Government of (Episcopalian View)," in *Encyclopedia of Christianity*, ed. Gary G. Cohen (Marshalltown, Del.: National Foundation for Christian Education, 1968), vol. 2, p. 483.

12. Leon Morris, "Church Government," in *Baker's Dictionary of Theology*, ed. Everett F. Harrison (Grand Rapids: Baker, 1960), p. 126.

13. R. Laird Harris, "Church, Nature and Government of (Presbyterian View)," in *Encyclopedia of Christianity*, vol. 2, pp. 490–92.

14. *The Constitution of the United Presbyterian Church in the United States of America* (Philadelphia: Office of the General Assembly of the United Presbyterian Church in the United States of America, 1967), vol. 2, *Book of Order*, ch. 9.

15. Ibid., ch. 11.

16. Louis Berkhof, *Systematic Theology* (Grand Rapids: Eerdmans, 1953), pp. 588–89.

sembly, composed again of lay and clergy representatives from the presbyteries. The prerogatives of each of the governing bodies are spelled out in the constitution of the denomination.

The presbyterian system differs from the episcopal in that there is only one level of clergy.[17] There is only the teaching elder or pastor. No higher levels, such as bishop, exist. Of course, certain persons are elected to administrative posts within the ruling assemblies. They are selected (from below) to preside or supervise, and generally bear a title such as stated clerk of the presbytery. They are not bishops, there being no special ordination to such office. There is no special authority attached to the office. Another leveling measure in the presbyterian system is a deliberate coordinating of clergy and laity. Both groups are included in all of the various governing assemblies. Neither has special powers or rights which the other does not have.

Congregational

A third form of church government stresses the role of the individual Christian and makes the local congregation the seat of authority. Two concepts are basic to the congregational scheme: autonomy and democracy. By autonomy we mean that the local congregation is independent and self-governing.[18] There is no external power which can dictate courses of action to the local church. By democracy we mean that every member of the local congregation has a voice in its affairs. It is the individual members of the congregation who possess and exercise authority. Authority is not the prerogative of a lone individual or select group. Among the major denominations which practice the congregational form of government are the Baptists, Congregationalists, and most Lutheran groups.

The principle of autonomy means that each local church calls its own pastor and determines its own budget. It purchases and owns property independently of any outside authorities.[19] The principle of democracy rests on the priesthood of all believers, which, it is felt, would be surrendered if bishops or elders were given the decision-making prerogative. The work of Christ has made such rulers unnecessary, for now every believer has access to the Holy of Holies and may directly approach God. Moreover, as Paul has reminded us, each member or part of the body has a valuable contribution to make to the welfare of the whole.[20]

There are, to be sure, some elements of representative democracy within the congregational form of church government. Certain persons are elected by a free choice of the members of the body to serve in special ways.[21] All major decisions, however, such as the calling of a pastor and the purchase or sale of property, are made by the church as a whole.

Nongovernment

Certain groups, such as the Quakers (Friends) and the Plymouth Brethren, deny that the church has a need for a concrete or visible form of government. Accordingly, they have virtually eliminated all governmental structure. They stress instead the inner working of the Holy Spirit; he exerts his influence upon and guides individual believers in a direct fashion rather than through organizations or institutions.

A System of Church Government for Today

Attempts to develop a structure of church government which adheres to the authority of the Bible encounter difficulty at two points. The first is the lack of didactic ma-

17. Charles Hodge, *The Church and Its Polity* (London: Thomas Nelson and Sons, 1879), p. 119.
18. Franz Pieper, *Christian Dogmatics* (St. Louis: Concordia, 1953), vol. 3, p. 475.

19. Edward T. Hiscox, *The New Directory for Baptist Churches* (Philadelphia: Judson, 1894), pp. 153–59.
20. William Roy McNutt, *Polity and Practice in Baptist Churches* (Philadelphia: Judson, 1935), pp. 21–26.
21. James M. Bulman, "Church, Nature and Government of (Autonomous View)," in *Encyclopedia of Christianity*, vol. 2, p. 478.

terial. There is no prescriptive exposition of what the government of the church is to be like. When we turn to examine the descriptive passages, we find a second problem. There is so much variation in the descriptions of the New Testament churches that we cannot discover an authoritative pattern. We must therefore turn to the principles which we find in the New Testament, and attempt to construct our governmental system upon them.

One principle that is evident in the New Testament, and particularly in 1 Corinthians, is the value of order. It is desirable to have certain persons responsible for specific ministries. Another principle is the priesthood of all believers.[22] Each person is capable of relating to God directly. Finally, the idea that each person is important to the whole body is implicit throughout the New Testament and explicit in passages like Romans 12 and 1 Corinthians 12.

It is my judgment that the congregational form of church government most nearly fulfils the principles which have been laid down. It takes seriously the principle of the priesthood and spiritual competency of all believers. It also takes seriously the promise that the indwelling Spirit will guide all believers. At the same time, the need for orderliness suggests that a degree of representative government is necessary. In some situations leaders must be chosen to act on behalf of the group. Those chosen should always be conscious of their answerability to those whom they represent; and where possible, major issues should be brought to the membership as a whole to decide.

22. Cyril Eastwood, *The Priesthood of All Believers* (Minneapolis: Augsburg, 1962), pp. 238–57.

37

The Ordinances of the Church: Baptism and the Lord's Supper

Baptism: The Initiatory Rite of the Church

Virtually all Christian churches practice the rite of baptism. They do so in large part because Jesus in his final commission commanded the apostles and the church to "go . . . and make disciples of all nations, baptizing them in the name of the Father and of the Son and of the Holy Spirit" (Matt. 28:19). It is almost universally agreed that baptism is in some way connected with the beginning of the Christian life; it is one's initiation into the universal, invisible church as well as the local, visible church. Yet there is also considerable disagreement regarding baptism.

Three basic questions about baptism have sparked great controversy among Christians: (1) What is the meaning of baptism? What does it actually accomplish? (2) Who are the proper subjects of baptism? Is it to be restricted to those who are capable of exercising conscious faith in Jesus Christ, or may it also be administered to children and even infants; and if so, on what basis? (3) What is the proper mode of baptism? Must it be by dipping (immersion), or are other methods (pouring, sprinkling) acceptable? It could be said that these questions have been arranged in decreasing order of significance, since our conclusion as to the meaning and value of the act of baptism will go far toward determining our conclusions on the other issues.

The Basic Views of Baptism

Baptism as a Means of Saving Grace

Before we attempt to resolve these issues, it will be wise for us to sketch the various ways in which Christians interpret baptism. Some groups speak of baptismal regeneration; they believe that baptism actually effects a transformation bringing a person from spiritual death to life. The most extreme form of this view is to be found in traditional Catholicism. We will, however, focus on a classic Lutheran position which shares many features with Catholicism.

Baptism, according to the sacramentalists, is a means by which God imparts saving grace; it results in the remission of sins.[1] In the Lutheran understanding, the sacrament is ineffectual unless faith is already present. The sacrament itself, however, is God's doing rather than something we offer. Baptism is the Holy Spirit's work of initiating people into the church: "For by one Spirit we were all baptized into one body—Jews or

Greeks, slaves or free—and all were made to drink of one Spirit" (1 Cor. 12:13).[2]

In the sacramentalists' view, baptism objectively unites the believer with Christ once and for all (Rom. 6:3–5). The sacrament also has a subjective effect. The knowledge that one has been baptized and therefore is united with Christ in his death and resurrection will be a constant source of encouragement and inspiration to the believer.[3]

The subjects of baptism, according to Lutheranism, fall into two general groups. First, there are adults who have come to faith in Christ. Explicit examples are found in Acts 2:41 and 8:36–38. Second, children and even infants were also baptized in New Testament times. Evidence is seen in the fact that children were brought to Jesus to be touched (Mark 10:13–16). In addition, we read in Acts that whole households were baptized (Acts 11:14 [see 10:48]; 16:15, 31–34; 18:8). It is reasonable to assume that most of these households were not composed exclusively of adults. Children are part of the people of God, just as surely as, in the Old Testament, they were part of the nation of Israel.[4]

That children were baptized in the New Testament is precedent for the practice today. Moreover, the baptism of children is necessary to remove the taint of original sin. Since children are not capable of exercising the faith needed for regeneration, it is essential that they receive the cleansing wrought by baptism.

The Lutheran theologian is aware of the charge of inconsistency between the practice of infant baptism and the insistence upon justification by faith alone. This apparent dilemma is generally dealt with in one of two ways. One is the suggestion that infants who are baptized may possess an unconscious faith. Evidence is found in Matthew 18:6 ("one of these little ones who believe in me"); 19:14; Mark 10:14; and Luke 18:16–17. Another proof is the prophecy

---

1. Franz Pieper, *Christian Dogmatics* (St. Louis: Concordia, 1953), vol. 3, p. 264.

2. Ibid., p. 270.
3. Ibid., p. 275.
4. Ibid., p. 277.

that John the Baptist "will be filled with the Holy Spirit, even from his mother's womb" (Luke 1:15).[5] The second means of dealing with the apparent inconsistency is to maintain that it is the faith of the parents (or even of the church) that is involved when a child is baptized.[6] In Roman Catholicism, this dilemma does not occur. For according to Catholic doctrine, faith is not really necessary. The only requisites are that someone present the child and a priest administer the sacrament properly.[7]

In the Lutheran view, the mode of baptism is not of great importance. Indeed, we are uncertain what method was used in biblical times, or even whether there was only one method. Since there is no essential, indispensable symbolism in the mode, baptism is not tied to one form.

Baptism as a Sign and Seal of the Covenant

The position held by traditional Reformed and Presbyterian theologians is tied closely to the concept of the covenant. They regard the sacraments as signs and seals of God's working out the covenant which he has established with the human race. Like circumcision in the Old Testament, baptism makes us sure of God's promises.

The significance of the sacrament of baptism is not quite as clear-cut to the Reformed and Presbyterian as to the sacramentalist. The covenant, God's promise of grace, is the basis, the source, of justification and salvation; baptism is the act of faith by which we are brought into that covenant and hence experience its benefits. The act of baptism is both the means of initiation into the covenant and a sign of salvation. In the case of adults, the benefits are absolute, while the salvation of infants is conditional upon future continuance in the vows made.

The subjects of baptism are in many ways the same as in the sacramentalists' view. On the one hand, all believing adults are to be baptized. They have already come to faith. On the other hand, the children of believing parents are also to be baptized. While the baptism of children is not explicitly commanded in Scripture, it is nonetheless implicitly taught. God made a spiritual covenant with Abraham *and with his seed* (Gen. 17:7). This covenant has continued to this day. In fact, there has been and is only one mediator of the covenant (Acts 4:12; 10:43). New Testament converts are participants in or heirs to the covenant (Acts 2:39; Rom. 4:13–18; Gal. 3:13–18; Heb. 6:13–18). Thus, the situation of believers both in the New Testament and today is to be understood in terms of the covenant made with Abraham.[8]

A key step in the argument now occurs: as circumcision was the sign of the covenant in the Old Testament, baptism is the sign in the New Testament. Baptism has been substituted for circumcision.[9] It was Christ who made this substitution. He commissioned his disciples to go and evangelize *and baptize* (Matt. 28:19). The two rites clearly have the same meaning. That circumcision pointed to a cutting away of sin and a change of heart is seen in numerous Old Testament references to circumcision of the heart, that is, spiritual circumcision as opposed to physical circumcision (Deut. 10:16; 30:6; Jer. 4:4; 9:25–26; Ezek. 44:7, 9). Baptism is similarly pictured as a washing away of sin (Acts 2:38). Conclusive evidence for the supplanting of circumcision by baptism is found in Colossians 2:11–12: "In him also you were circumcised with a circumcision made without hands, by putting off the body of flesh in the circumcision of Christ; and you were buried with him in baptism, in which you were also raised with him through faith in the working of God, who raised him from the dead."

Two additional observations need to be made here. First, those who hold that baptism is essentially a sign and seal of the covenant claim that it is not legitimate to im-

5. Ibid., vol. 2, pp. 448–49.
6. Ibid., vol. 3, p. 285.
7. Ibid., p. 256.

8. Louis Berkhof, *Systematic Theology* (Grand Rapids: Eerdmans, 1953), pp. 632–33.
9. Ibid., p. 634.

pose upon a child the requirements incumbent upon an adult. Second, those who hold this view emphasize that what really matters is not one's subjective reaction, but one's objective initiation into the covenant with its promise of salvation.[10]

In the Reformed and Presbyterian approach to baptism, the mode is a relatively inconsequential consideration. What was important in New Testament times was the fact and results of baptism, not the manner in which it was administered.

Baptism as a Token of Salvation

The third view we will examine sees baptism as a token, an outward symbol or indication of the inward change which has been effected in the believer.[11] It is an initiatory rite—we are baptized *into* the name of Christ.[12] The act of baptism was commanded by Christ (Matt. 28:19–20). Since it was *ordained* by him, it is properly understood as an *ordinance* rather than a sacrament. It does not produce any spiritual change in the one baptized. We continue to practice baptism simply because Christ commanded it and because it serves as a form of proclamation of our salvation.

The act of baptism conveys no direct spiritual benefit or blessing. In particular, we are not regenerated through baptism, for baptism *presupposes* faith and the salvation to which faith leads. It is, then, a testimony that one has already been regenerated. If there is a spiritual benefit, it is the fact that baptism brings us into membership or participation in the local church.[13]

In the view of those who regard baptism as basically an outward symbol, the question of the proper subjects of baptism is of great importance. Candidates for baptism will already have experienced the new birth on the basis of faith. The baptism of which we are speaking, then, is *believers'* baptism. Note that this is not necessarily *adult* baptism. It is baptism of those who have met the conditions for salvation (i.e., repentance and active faith). Evidence for this position can be found in the New Testament. First, there is a negative argument or an argument from silence. The only people whom the New Testament specifically identifies by name as having been baptized were adults at the time of their baptism.[14] The argument that "there must surely have been children involved when whole households were baptized" does not carry much weight with those who hold to believers' baptism. Further, Scripture makes it clear that personal, conscious faith in Christ is prerequisite to baptism. In the Great Commission, the command to baptize follows the command to disciple (Matt. 28:19). John the Baptist required repentance and confession of sin (Matt. 3:2, 6). In the conclusion of his Pentecost sermon, Peter called for repentance, then baptism (Acts 2:37–41). Belief followed by baptism is the pattern in Acts 8:12; 18:8; and 19:1–7.[15] All these considerations lead to the conclusion that responsible believers are the only people who are to be baptized.

Regarding the mode of baptism, there is some variation. Certain groups, particularly the Mennonites, practice believers' baptism, but by modes other than immersion.[16] Probably the majority of those who hold to believers' baptism utilize immersion exclusively, however, and are generally identified as Baptists. Where baptism is understood as a symbol and testimony of the salvation which has occurred in the life of the individual, it is not surprising that immersion is the predominant mode, since it best pictures the believer's resurrection from spiritual death.[17]

10. Charles Hodge, *Systematic Theology* (Grand Rapids: Eerdmans, 1952), vol. 3, pp. 552–55.

11. H. E. Dana, *A Manual of Ecclesiology* (Kansas City, Kans.: Central Seminary, 1944), pp. 281–82.

12. Edward T. Hiscox, *The New Directory for Baptist Churches* (Philadelphia: Judson, 1894), p. 121.

13. Augustus H. Strong, *Systematic Theology* (Westwood, N.J.: Revell, 1907), p. 945.

14. Ibid., p. 951.

15. Geoffrey Bromiley, "Baptism, Believers'," in *Baker's Dictionary of Theology*, ed. Everett F. Harrison (Grand Rapids: Baker, 1960), p. 86.

16. John C. Wenger, *Introduction to Theology* (Scottdale, Pa.: Herald, 1954), pp. 237–40.

17. Paul King Jewett, "Baptism (Baptist View)," in *Encyclopedia of Christianity*, ed. Edwin H. Palmer (Marshalltown, Del.: National Foundation for Christian Education, 1964), vol. 1, p. 520.

Resolving the Issues

We now come to the issues which we raised at the beginning of this chapter. We must ask ourselves which of the positions we have sketched is the most tenable in the light of all of the relevant evidence.

The Meaning of Baptism

Is baptism a means of regeneration, an essential to salvation? A number of texts seem to support such a position. On closer examination, however, the persuasiveness of this position becomes less telling. In Mark 16:16 we read, "He who believes and is baptized will be saved"; note, however, that the second half of the verse does not mention baptism at all: "but he who does not believe will be condemned." It is simply absence of belief, not of baptism, which is correlated with condemnation. An additional consideration is the fact that the entire verse (and indeed the whole passage, verses 9–20) is not found in the best texts.

Another verse cited in support of the concept of baptismal regeneration, the idea that baptism is a means of saving grace, is John 3:5: "Unless one is born of water and the Spirit, he cannot enter the kingdom of God." However, we must ask what being "born of water" would have meant to Nicodemus, and our conclusion, while not unequivocal, seems to favor the idea of cleansing or purification, not baptism.[18] Further, in view of the overall context, it appears that being born of water is synonymous with being born of the Spirit.

A third passage which needs to be taken into account is 1 Peter 3:21: "Baptism,

which corresponds to this, now saves you, not as a removal of dirt from the body but as an appeal to God for a clear conscience, through the resurrection of Jesus Christ." Note that this verse is actually a denial that the rite of baptism has any effect in itself. It saves only in that it is "an appeal to God," an act of faith acknowledging dependence upon him. The real basis of our salvation is Christ's resurrection.

Then there are the passages in the Book of Acts where repentance and baptism are linked together. Probably the most crucial is Peter's response on Pentecost to the question, "Brethren, what shall we do?" (Acts 2:37). He replied, "Repent, and be baptized every one of you in the name of Jesus Christ for the forgiveness of your sins; and you shall receive the gift of the Holy Spirit" (v. 38). The emphasis in the remainder of the narrative, however, is that three thousand received his word—then they were baptized. In Peter's next recorded sermon (3:17–26), the emphasis is upon repentance, conversion, and acceptance of Christ; there is no mention of baptism. Thus, unlike repentance and conversion, baptism is not indispensable to salvation. It seems, rather, that baptism may be an expression or a consequence of conversion.

Finally, we must examine Titus 3:5. Here Paul writes that God "saved us, not because of deeds done by us in righteousness, but in virtue of his own mercy, by the washing of regeneration and renewal in the Holy Spirit." If this is an allusion to baptism, it is vague. It seems, rather, that "the washing of regeneration" refers to a cleansing and forgiveness of sins. We conclude that there is little biblical evidence to support the idea that baptism is a means of regeneration or a channel of grace essential to salvation.

What of the view that baptism is a supplanting of the Old Testament rite of circumcision as a mark of one's entrance into the covenant? Significant here is Paul's assertion that Old Testament circumcision was an outward formality denoting Jewishness, but the true Jew is one who is a Jew inwardly: "He is

18. Leon Morris, *The Gospel According to John* (Grand Rapids: Eerdmans, 1971), pp. 215–16. An Anglican, Morris comments on the suggestion that Jesus is referring to Christian baptism: "The weak point is that Nicodemus could not possibly have perceived an allusion to an as yet non-existent sacrament. It is difficult to think that Jesus would have spoken in such a way that His meaning could not possibly be grasped. His purpose was not to mystify but to enlighten. In any case the whole thrust of the passage is to put the emphasis on the activity of the Spirit, not on any rite of the church." See also D. W. B. Robinson, "Born of Water and Spirit: Does John 3:5 Refer to Baptism?" *Reformed Theological Review* 25.1 (Jan.–April 1966): 15–23.

a Jew who is one inwardly, and real circumcision is a matter of the heart, spiritual and not literal" (Rom. 2:29). Paul is saying not merely that circumcision has passed, but that the whole framework of which circumcision was a part has been replaced. If anything has taken the place of external circumcision, it is not baptism but internal circumcision.

What, then, is the meaning of baptism? To answer this question, we note, first, that there is a strong connection between baptism and our being united with Christ in his death and resurrection. Paul emphasizes this point in Romans 6:1–11. At a specific moment the believer actually becomes linked to Christ's death and resurrection (vv. 3–5). We note, second, that the Book of Acts often ties belief and baptism together. Baptism ordinarily follows upon or virtually coincides with belief. Baptism is itself an act of faith and com-

The Subjects of Baptism

Who are the proper subjects of baptism? The issue here is whether to hold to infant baptism or believers' baptism (i.e., the position that baptism should be restricted to those who have confessed faith in Christ's atoning work). Note that our dichotomy is not between infant and adult baptism, for those who reject infant baptism stipulate that candidates for baptism must actually have exercised faith. We contend that believers' baptism is the correct position.

We note that the case for baptism of infants rests upon either the view that baptism is a means of saving grace or the view that baptism, like Old Testament circumcision, is a sign and seal of entrance into the covenant. Since both of those views were found to be inadequate, we must conclude that infant baptism is untenable. The meaning of

This isn't on baptism

Baptism is an act of faith and a powerful testimony to the believer's union with Christ.

mitment. While faith is possible without baptism (i.e., salvation does not depend upon one's being baptized), baptism is a natural accompaniment and the completion of faith.

Baptism is, then, a powerful proclamation of the truth of what Christ has done; it is a "word in water" testifying to the believer's participation in the death and resurrection of Christ. It is a symbol rather than merely a sign, for it is a graphic picture of the truth it conveys. There is no inherent connection between a sign and what it represents. It is only by convention, for example, that green traffic lights tell us to go rather than to stop. By contrast, the sign at a railroad crossing is more than a sign; it is also a symbol, for it is a rough picture of what it is intended to indicate, the crossing of a road and a railroad track. Baptism is a symbol, not a mere sign, for it actually pictures the believer's death and resurrection with Christ.

baptism requires us to hold to the position of believers' baptism.

The Mode of Baptism

It is not possible to resolve the issue of the proper mode of baptism on the basis of linguistic data. We should note, however, that the predominant meaning of the Greek word *baptizō* is "to dip or to plunge under water."[19] Even Martin Luther and John Calvin acknowledged immersion to be the basic meaning of the term and the original form of baptism practiced by the early church.[20] There are several considerations which argue that immersion was the biblical procedure. John baptized at Aenon "be-

19. Henry George Liddell and Robert Scott, *A Greek-English Lexicon* (Oxford: Clarendon, 1951), vol. 1, pp. 305–6.
20. *What Luther Says*, comp. Ewald M. Plass (St. Louis: Concordia, 1959), vol. 1, pp. 57–58; John Calvin, *Institutes of the Christian Religion*, book 4, ch. 16, sec. 13.

cause there was much water there" (John 3:23). When baptized by John, Jesus "came up out of the water" (Mark 1:10). Upon hearing the good news, the Ethiopian eunuch said to Philip, "See, here is water! What is to prevent my being baptized?" (Acts 8:36). Then they both went down into the water, Philip baptized him, and they came up out of the water (vv. 38–39).

There is little doubt that the procedure followed in New Testament times was immersion. But does that mean we must practice immersion today? Or are there other possibilities? Those to whom the mode does not seem crucial maintain that there is no essential link between the meaning of baptism and the way in which it is administered. But if, as we stated in our discussion of the meaning, baptism is truly a symbol, and not merely an arbitrary sign, we are not free to change the mode.

In Romans 6:3–5 Paul appears to be contending that there is a significant connection between how baptism is administered (one is lowered into the water and then raised out of it) and what it symbolizes (death to sin and new life in Christ—and beyond that, baptism symbolizes the basis of the believer's death to sin and new life: the death, burial, and resurrection of Christ). In light of these considerations, immersionism seems the most adequate of the several positions. While it may not be the only valid form of baptism, it is the form which most fully preserves and accomplishes the meaning of baptism.

Whatever mode be adopted, baptism is not a matter to be taken lightly. It is of great importance, for it is both a sign of the believer's union with Christ and, as a confession of that union, an additional act of faith which serves to cement the more firmly that relationship.

The Lord's Supper: The Continuing Rite of the Church

While baptism is the initiatory rite, the Lord's Supper is the continuing rite of the visible church. It may be defined, in preliminary fashion, as a rite which Christ himself established for the church to practice as a commemoration of his death.

We immediately encounter a curious fact about the Lord's Supper. Virtually every branch of Christianity practices it. Yet on the other hand, there are many different interpretations. Historically, it has actually kept, and still does keep, various Christian groups apart. So it is at once a factor which unites and divides Christendom.

On occasion the subject of the spiritual or practical value of the Lord's Supper has become lost in the dispute over theoretical issues. The theoretical questions are important (they affect the spiritual considerations), and so they ought not to be too quickly dismissed. If, however, we bog down in the technical issues, and do not move on to deal with the practical meaning, we will have missed the whole point of Christ's having established the Supper. It is not sufficient to comprehend what it means. We must also experience what it means.

Major Views

The Traditional Roman Catholic View

The official Roman Catholic position on the Lord's Supper was spelled out at the Council of Trent (1545–63). While many Catholics, especially in Western countries, have now abandoned some of the features of this view, it is still the basis of the faith of large numbers. Let us note its major tenets.

Transubstantiation is the doctrine that as the administering priest consecrates the elements, an actual metaphysical change takes place. The substance of the bread and wine—what they actually are—is changed into Christ's flesh and blood respectively. Note that what is changed is the substance or the essence, not the accidents. Thus the bread retains the shape, texture, and taste of bread. However, the whole of Christ is fully present within each of the particles of the host.[21] All who participate in the Lord's Supper, or the Holy Eucharist as it is

21. Joseph Pohle, *The Sacraments: A Dogmatic Treatise*, ed. Arthur Preuss (St. Louis: B. Herder, 1942), vol. 2, p. 99.

termed, literally take the physical body and blood of Christ into themselves.

A second major tenet of the Catholic view is that the Lord's Supper involves a sacrificial act. In the mass a real sacrifice is again offered by Christ in behalf of the worshipers. It is a sacrifice in the same sense as was the crucifixion.[22]

A third tenet of the Catholic view is sacerdotalism, the idea that a properly ordained priest must be present to consecrate the host. Without such a priest to officiate, the elements remain merely bread and wine. When, however, a qualified clergyman follows the proper formula, the elements are completely and permanently changed into Christ's body and blood.[23]

In the traditional administration of the sacrament, the cup was withheld from the laity, being taken only by the clergy. The major reason was the danger that the blood might be spilt.[24] For the blood of Jesus to be trampled underfoot would be a desecration. In addition, there were two arguments to the effect that it is unnecessary for the laity to take the cup. First, the clergy act representatively for the laity; they take the cup on behalf of the people. Second, nothing would be gained by the laity's taking the cup. The sacrament is complete without it, for every particle of both the bread and wine contains fully the body, soul, and divinity of Christ.[25]

The Lutheran View

The Lutheran view differs from the Roman Catholic view at many but not all points. Luther retained the Catholic conception that Christ's body and blood are physically present in the elements. What Luther denied was the Catholic doctrine of transubstantiation. The molecules are not changed into flesh and blood. But the body and blood of Christ are present "in, with, and under" the bread and wine. It is not that the bread and wine have become Christ's body and

blood, but that we now have the body and blood in addition to the bread and wine. While some have used the term consubstantiation to denote Luther's concept that body and bread are concurrently present, that blood and wine coexist, it was not Luther's term. Thinking in terms of one substance interpenetrating another, he used as an analogy an iron bar which is heated in fire. The substance of the iron does not cease to exist when the substance of fire interpenetrates it, heating it to a high temperature.[26]

Luther rejected other facets of the Catholic conception of the mass. In particular, he rejected the idea that the mass is a sacrifice. Since Christ died and atoned for sin once and for all, and since the believer is justified by faith on the basis of that one-time sacrifice, there is no need for repeated sacrifices.[27] Luther also rejected sacerdotalism. The presence of Christ's body and blood is not a result of the priest's actions. It is instead a consequence of the power of Jesus Christ.

What of the benefit of the sacrament? Here Luther's statements are not as clear as we might wish. He insists that by partaking of the sacrament one experiences a real benefit—forgiveness of sin and confirmation of faith. This benefit is due, however, not to the elements in the sacrament, but to one's reception of the Word by faith.[28] At this point Luther sounds almost as if he regards the sacrament as simply a means of proclamation to which one responds as to a sermon. If the sacrament is merely a form of proclamation, however, what is the point of the physical presence of Christ's body and blood? At other times Luther appears to have held that the benefit comes from actually eating the body of Christ. What is clear from Luther's disparate statements is that by virtue of taking the elements believers re-

22. Ibid., part 3.
23. Ibid., pp. 256–60.
24. Ibid., p. 252.
25. Ibid., pp. 246–54.

26. Martin Luther, *The Babylonian Captivity of the Church*, in *Three Treatises* (Philadelphia: Muhlenberg, 1943), p. 140.
27. Ibid., pp. 161–68.
28. Ibid., p. 147.

ceive a spiritual benefit which they otherwise would not experience.

The Reformed View

The third major view of the Lord's Supper is the Calvinistic or Reformed view. While the term *Calvinism* usually stirs up images of a specific view of salvation and of God's initiative in it, his choosing and decreeing that certain persons shall believe and be saved, that is not what we have in mind here. Rather, we are referring to Calvin's view of the Lord's Supper.

The Reformed view holds that Christ is present in the Lord's Supper, but not physically or bodily. Rather, his presence in the sacrament is spiritual or dynamic. Using the sun as an illustration, Calvin asserted that Christ is present influentially. The sun remains in the heavens, yet its warmth and light are present on earth. So the radiance of the Spirit conveys to us the communion of Christ's flesh and blood.[29] According to Romans 8:9–11, it is by the Spirit and only by the Spirit that Christ dwells in us. The notion that we actually eat Christ's body and drink his blood is absurd. Rather, true communicants are spiritually nourished as the Holy Spirit brings them into closer connection with the person of Christ.

Further, while the elements of the sacraments signify or represent the body and blood of Christ, they do more than that. They also seal. Louis Berkhof suggests that the Lord's Supper seals the love of Christ to believers, giving them the assurance that all the promises of the covenant and the riches of the gospel are theirs by a divine donation. In exchange for a personal claim on and actual possession of all this wealth, believers express faith in Christ as Savior and pledge obedience to him as Lord and King.[30]

There is, then, a genuine objective benefit of the sacrament. It is not generated by the participant; rather, it is brought to the sacrament by Christ himself. By taking the elements the participant actually receives anew

and continually the vitality of Christ. This benefit should not be thought of as automatic, however. The effect of the sacrament depends in large part upon the faith and receptivity of the participant.

The Zwinglian View

The final position we will examine is the view that the Lord's Supper is merely a commemoration. This view is usually associated with Ulrich Zwingli, who emphasized the role of the sacrament in bringing to mind the death of Christ and its efficacy in behalf of the believer. Thus, the Lord's Supper is essentially a commemoration of Christ's death.[31]

The value of the sacrament lies simply in receiving by faith the benefits of Christ's death. So the effect of the Lord's Supper is no different in nature from, say, that of a sermon. Both are types of proclamation.[32] In both cases, as with all proclamation, there is the absolute essential of faith if there is to be any benefit. We might say, then, that it is not so much that the sacrament brings Christ to the communicant as that the believer's faith brings Christ to the sacrament.

Dealing with the Issues

The Presence of Christ

We must now come to grips with the issues posed by these views and seek to arrive at some resolution. The first issue pertains to whether, and in what sense, the body and blood of Christ are actually present in the elements employed. Several answers have been given to this question:

1. The bread and wine *are* the physical body and blood of Christ (the Roman Catholic view).[33]
2. The bread and wine *contain* the physical body and blood (the Lutheran view).[34]

29. Calvin, *Institutes*, book 4, ch. 17, sec. 12.
30. Berkhof, *Systematic Theology*, p. 651.
31. Hodge, *Systematic Theology*, pp. 627–28.
32. Strong, *Systematic Theology*, pp. 541–43.
33. Pohle, *Sacraments*, p. 25.
34. Pieper, *Christian Dogmatics*, vol. 3, p. 345.

3. The bread and wine *contain spiritually* the body and blood (the Reformed view).[35]

4. They *represent* the body and blood (the Zwinglian view).[36]

The most natural and straightforward way to render Jesus' words, "This is my body," and "This is my blood," is to interpret them literally. However, in this particular case it so happens that there are certain considerations which argue against literal interpretation.

First, if we take "This is my body" and "This is my blood" literally, a problem results. If Jesus meant that the bread and wine were at that moment in the upper room actually his body and blood, he was asserting that his flesh and blood were in two places at once, since his corporeal form was right there beside the elements. This would have been something of a denial of the incarnation, which limited his physical human nature to one location.

Second, there are conceptual difficulties for those who declare that Christ has been bodily present in the subsequent occurrences of the Lord's Supper. Here we face the problem of how two substances (e.g., flesh and bread) can be in the same place simultaneously (the Lutheran conception) or of how a particular substance (e.g., blood) can exist without any of its customary characteristics (the Catholic view). While those who hold to a physical presence offer explanations of their view, their cases rest upon a type of metaphysic which seems very strange to twentieth-century minds, and indeed appears to us to be untenable.

If Jesus' words are not to be taken literally, what did he mean when he said, "This is my body," and "This is my blood"? As he spoke these words, he was focusing attention on his relationship with individual believers. It is noteworthy that on many of the other occasions when he addressed this topic, he used metaphors to characterize himself: "I am the way, and the truth, and the life"; "I am the vine, you are the branches"; "I am the good shepherd"; "I am the bread of life." At the Last Supper he used similar metaphors: "This [bread] is my body"; "This [wine] is my blood," which could be rendered, "This represents [or signifies] my body," and "This represents [or signifies] my blood." This approach spares us from the type of difficulties incurred by the view that Christ is physically present in the elements.

But what of the idea that Christ is spiritually present? As we evaluate this view, it is important to remember that Jesus promised to be with his disciples everywhere and through all time (Matt. 28:20; John 14:23; 15:4–7). Yet he has also promised to be with us especially when we gather as believers (Matt. 18:20). The Lord's Supper, as an act of worship, is therefore a particularly fruitful opportunity for meeting with him. It is likely that Christ's special presence in the sacrament is influential rather than metaphysical in nature. In this regard it is significant that Paul's account of the Lord's Supper says nothing about the presence of Christ. Instead, it simply says, "For as often as you eat this bread and drink the cup, you proclaim the Lord's death until he comes" (1 Cor. 11:26). This verse suggests that the rite is basically commemorative.

How, then, should we regard the Lord's Supper? We should look forward to the Lord's Supper as a time of relationship and communion with Christ. We should come to each observance of it with the confidence that we will therein meet with him, for he has promised to meet with us. We should think of the sacrament not so much in terms of Christ's presence as in terms of his promise and the potential for a closer relationship with him.

The Efficacy of the Rite

What has been said about the presence of Christ has intimated a great deal about the nature of the benefit conferred by the Lord's Supper. It is also apparent from Paul's state-

35. Berkhof, *Systematic Theology*, pp. 653–54.
36. Strong, *Systematic Theology*, pp. 538–43.

ments in 1 Corinthians 11:27–32 that there is nothing automatic about this benefit. Many at Corinth who participated in the Lord's Supper, instead of being spiritually edified, had become weak and ill; some had even died (v. 30). Thus the effect of the Lord's Supper must be dependent upon or proportional to the faith of the believer and his or her response to what is presented in the rite. A correct understanding of the meaning of the Lord's Supper and an appropriate response in faith are necessary for the rite to be effective.

It is therefore important to note what the Lord's Supper symbolizes. It is in particular a reminder of the death of Christ and its sacrificial and propitiatory character as an offering to the Father in our behalf. It further symbolizes our dependence upon and vital

church. It would therefore seem to be in order for the persons who have been chosen and empowered by the church to supervise and conduct its services of worship to superintend the Lord's Supper as well.

The Appropriate Recipients

Nowhere in Scripture do we find an extensive statement of prerequisites for receiving the Lord's Supper. We may infer, however, that if the Lord's Supper signifies, at least in part, a spiritual relationship between the individual believer and the Lord, a personal relationship with God is a prerequisite. In other words, those who participate should be genuine believers in Christ. And while no age qualifications can be spelled out in hard and fast fashion, the communicant should be mature enough to be able to discern the body (1 Cor. 11:29).

> *The Lord's Supper is a reminder of the death of Christ and of its sacrificial character in our behalf, a symbol of our vital connection with the Lord, and a testimony to his second coming.*

connection with the Lord, and points forward to his second coming. In addition, it symbolizes the unity of believers within the church and their love and concern for each other. The Lord's Supper reflects the fact that the body is *one* body.

It is appropriate to explain the meaning of the Lord's Supper at each observance. And every participant should carefully examine his or her own understanding and spiritual condition (1 Cor. 11:27–28). The Lord's Supper will then be an occasion of recommitment of oneself to the Lord.

The Proper Administrator

Scripture gives very little guidance on the matter of who should administer the Lord's Supper. What does appear in the Gospel accounts and in Paul's discussion is that the Lord's Supper has been entrusted to, and is presumably to be administered by, the

We infer another prerequisite from the fact that there were some people whose sin was so grave that Paul urged the church to remove them from the body (1 Cor. 5:1–5). Certainly, the church should, as a first step in discipline, withhold the bread and cup from one known to be living in flagrant sin. In other cases, however, since we do not know what the requirements for membership in the New Testament churches were, it is probably best, once we have explained what the sacrament means and on what basis one should partake, to leave the decision as to whether to participate to the individuals themselves.

The Elements to Be Used

What elements are used will depend on the concerns of the participants. If their chief concern is duplication of the original meal, they will use the unleavened bread of the traditional Passover and the wine, probably diluted with anywhere from one to twenty parts of water for every part of wine.[37] If, however, the participants' chief concern is preservation of the symbolism, they might use a loaf of leavened bread and grape juice. The oneness of the loaf would symbolize the unity of the church; breaking the loaf would signify the breaking of Christ's body. The grape juice would sufficiently represent the blood of Christ.

The use of bizarre substitutes simply for variety should be avoided. Potato chips and cola, for example, bear little resemblance to the original. A balance should be sought between, on the one hand, repeating the act with so little variation that we participate routinely without awareness of its meaning, and, on the other, changing the procedures so severely that we focus our attention upon the mechanics instead of Christ's atoning work.

The Frequency of Observance

How often we should observe the Lord's Supper is another matter concerning which we have no explicit didactic statements in Scripture. We do not even have a precise indication of what the practice was in the

37. Robert H. Stein, "Wine-Drinking in New Testament Times," *Christianity Today*, 20 June 1975, pp. 9–11 (923–25).

early church, although it may well have been weekly, that is, every time the church assembled. In view of the lack of specific information, we will make our decision on the basis of biblical principles and practical considerations.

The Lord's Supper should be observed often enough to prevent long gaps between times of reflection upon the truths which it signifies, but not so frequently as to make it seem trivial or so commonplace that we go through the motions without really thinking about the meaning. Perhaps it would be good for the church to make the Lord's Supper available on a frequent basis, allowing the individual believer to determine how often to partake.

The Lord's Supper, properly administered, is a means of inspiring the faith and love of the believer as he or she reflects again upon the wonder of the Lord's death and the fact that those who believe in him will live everlastingly.

> And can it be that I should gain
> An interest in the Savior's blood?
> Died He for me, who caused His pain?
> For me, who Him to death pursued?
> Amazing love! how can it be
> That Thou, my God, shouldst die for me?
>
> (Charles Wesley, 1738)

Part Twelve

The Last Things

Introductory Matters and Individual Eschatology

Introduction to Eschatology

Eschatology has traditionally meant the study of the last things. Accordingly, it has dealt with questions concerning the consummation of history, the completion of God's working in the world. In many cases it has also been literally the last thing in the study of theology, the last topic considered, the last chapter in the textbook.

In the late nineteenth century and throughout the twentieth century, eschatology has received closer examination than it ever had before. There are a number of reasons for the current attention to eschatology. One is the rapid development of technology and consequent changes in our culture in general. To avoid obsolescence, it is necessary for corporations and public agencies to predict and prepare for the future. This has given rise to a whole new discipline—"futurism." Curiosity as to what homes, transportation, and communication will be like in the next decade or the next century gives rise to speculation and then research. There is a corresponding interest in the future in a broader sense, a cosmic sense. What does the future hold for the whole of reality?

A second major reason for the prominence of eschatology is the rise of the Third World, whose present may be bleak, but whose future holds great promise and potential. As Christianity continues its rapid growth in Third World nations, indeed, more rapid there than anywhere else, their excitement and anticipation regarding the future stimulate greater interest in eschatology than in accomplished history.

Further, the strength of communism or dialectical materialism forced theologians to focus upon the future. Communism has a definite philosophy of history. It sees history as marching on to an ultimate goal. As the dialectic achieves its purposes, history keeps moving from one stage to the next. Ernst Bloch's *Das Prinzip Hoffnung* (*The Principle of Hope*),[1] which represents Marxism as the world's hope for a better future, had great impact on various Christian theologians, such as Jürgen Moltmann, who felt challenged to set forth an alternative, superior basis for hope.

Certain schools of psychology have also begun to emphasize hope. Perhaps the most notable example is Viktor Frankl's logotherapy, a blend of existentialism and psychoanalysis. From his experiences in a concentration camp during World War II, Frankl concluded that humans need a purpose for living. One who has hope, who "knows the 'why' for his existence . . . will be able to bear

almost any 'how.'"[2] In a very real sense, the why, the purpose, of existence is related to the future, to what one anticipates will occur.

Finally, the threat of destruction which hovers above the human race has stirred inquiry regarding the future. The possibility of a nuclear holocaust is a dark cloud over the whole world. And while the effect of the ecological crises we face is less rapid than nuclear war would be, they, too, jeopardize the future of the race. These facts make it clear that we cannot live merely in the present, preoccupied with what is now. We must think of the future.

When we examine what theologians and ministers are doing with eschatology, we find two contrasting trends. On the one hand, there is an intensive preoccupation with eschatology. One pastor is reported to have preached on the Book of Revelation every Sunday evening for nineteen years! Sometimes the teaching is augmented by large detailed charts of the last times. Current political and social events, especially those relating to the nation of Israel, are identified with prophecies in the Scripture. As a result, some preachers have been caricatured as having the Bible in one hand and the daily newspaper in the other. Hal Lindsey's *Late Great Planet Earth* is a noteworthy example of this type of "eschatomania."[3]

There is another variety of eschatomania, very different in orientation and content. This is the approach which makes eschatology the whole of theology.[4] The Christian faith is regarded as so thoroughly eschatological that "eschatological" is attached as an adjective to virtually every theological concept. In the view of those who follow this approach, however, the central subject of eschatology is not the future, but the idea that a new age has begun.

---

1. Ernst Bloch, *Das Prinzip Hoffnung* (Frankfurt am Main: Suhrkamp, 1959).

2. Viktor Frankl, *Man's Search for Meaning* (New York: Washington Square, 1963), p. 127.

3. Hal Lindsey, *The Late Great Planet Earth* (Grand Rapids: Zondervan, 1971).

4. Jürgen Moltmann, *The Theology of Hope* (New York: Harper and Row, 1967).

The opposite of the two varieties of eschatomania might be called "eschatophobia"—a fear of or aversion to eschatology, or at least an avoidance of discussing it. In some cases, eschatophobia is a reaction against those who have a definite interpretation of all prophetic material in the Bible and identify every significant event in history with some biblical prediction. Not wanting to be equated with this rather sensationalistic approach to eschatology, some preachers and teachers avoid discussion of the subject altogether. In other cases, eschatophobia is a reflection of the difficulty and obscurity of many of the issues.

Somewhere between the two extremes of preoccupation with and avoidance of eschatology, we must take our stance. We will find an appropriate mediating position if we keep in mind the true purpose of eschatology. Paul indicates in 1 Thessalonians 4 his reason for writing about the second coming. Some believers whose loved ones had died were experiencing a grief which was, at least to a degree, unhealthy and unnecessary. Paul did not want them to sorrow like unbelievers,

2. The truths of eschatology deserve careful, intense, and thorough attention and study. At the same time, we must guard against exploring these matters merely out of curiosity. Further, we must avoid undue speculation and recognize that because the biblical sources vary in clarity, our conclusions will vary in degree of certainty.

3. We need to recognize that eschatology does not pertain exclusively to the future. Jesus did introduce a new age, and the victory over the powers of evil has already been won, even though the struggle is still to be enacted in history.

4. We must pair with this insight the truth that there are elements of predictive prophecy, even within Jesus' ministry, which simply cannot be regarded as already fulfilled. We must live with an openness to and anticipation of the future.

5. The biblical passages regarding eschatological events are far more than existential descriptions of life. They do indeed have existential significance, but that significance is dependent upon, and an application of, the

---

The purpose of the eschatological truths in God's Word is to comfort and assure us.

---

who have no hope for their departed loved ones (v. 13). After describing the second coming and assuring his readers of its certainty, he counsels, "Therefore comfort one another with these words" (v. 18). It is sometimes easy to forget that the eschatological truths in God's Word, like the rest of his revelation, are intended to comfort and assure us.

As we embark on the study of eschatology, it is important to keep a number of considerations in view:

1. Eschatology is a major topic in systematic theology. Consequently, we dare not neglect it. Nor, since it is but one doctrine among several, should we convert our entire doctrinal system into eschatology.

factuality of the events described. They really will come to pass.

6. We as humans have a responsibility to play a part in bringing about those eschatological events which are to transpire here upon earth and within history. Some see this responsibility in terms of evangelism; others see it in terms of social action. As we carry out our role, however, we must also be mindful that eschatology pertains primarily to a new realm beyond space and time, a new heaven and a new earth. This kingdom will be ushered in by a supernatural work of God; it cannot be accomplished by human efforts.

7. The truths of eschatology should arouse in us watchfulness and alertness in expectation of the future. But preparation for what is going to happen will also entail diligence in the activities which our Lord has assigned to us. We should study the Scripture intensively and watch developments in our world carefully, so that we may discern God's working and not be misled. We must not become so brash, however, as to dogmatically identify specific historical occurrences with biblical prophecy or predict when certain eschatological events will take place.

8. As important as it is to have convictions regarding eschatological matters, it is good to bear in mind that they vary in significance. It is essential to have agreement on such basic matters as the second coming of Christ and the life hereafter. On the other hand, holding to a specific position on less central and less clearly expounded issues, such as the millennium or the tribulation, should not be made a test of orthodoxy or a condition of Christian fellowship and unity. Emphasis should be placed upon the points of agreement, not the points of disagreement.

9. When we study the doctrines of the last things, we should stress their spiritual significance and practical application. They are incentives to purity of life, diligence in service, and hope for the future. They are to be regarded as resources for ministering, not topics for debate.

Death

When we speak of eschatology, we must distinguish between individual eschatology and cosmic eschatology—those experiences which lie, on the one hand, in the future of the individual, and, on the other, in the future of the human race and indeed of the entire creation. The former will occur to each individual as he or she dies. The latter will occur to all persons simultaneously in connection with cosmic events, specifically, the second coming of Christ.

The Reality of Death

An undeniable fact about the future of every person is the inevitability of death. There is a direct assertion of this fact in Hebrews 9:27: "It is appointed to men to die once, and after that comes judgment." The thought also runs through the whole of 1 Corinthians 15, where we read of the universality of death and the effect of Christ's resurrection. While death is said to have been defeated and its sting removed by his resurrection (vv. 54–56), there is no suggestion that we will not die. Paul certainly anticipated his own death (2 Cor. 5:1–10; Phil. 1:19–26).

Although everyone at least intellectually acknowledges the reality and the certainty of death, there nonetheless is often an unwillingness to face its inevitability. At funeral homes, many people pay their formal respects and then seek to get as far away from the casket as possible. We employ a whole series of euphemisms to avoid acknowledging the reality of physical death. Persons do not die—they expire or pass away. We no longer have graveyards, but cemeteries and memorial parks. The Christian, however, will squarely face death's reality and inescapability. Thus, Paul acknowledges that death is ever present in the world: "For while we live we are always being given up to death for Jesus' sake, so that the life of Jesus may be manifested in our mortal flesh. So death is at work in us, but life in you" (2 Cor. 4:11–12).

The Nature of Death

What is death, however? How are we to define it? Various passages in Scripture speak of physical death, that is, cessation of life in our physical body. In Matthew 10:28, for example, Jesus contrasts death of the body with death of both body and soul: "And do not fear those who kill the body but cannot kill the soul; rather fear him who can destroy both soul and body in hell." Several other passages speak of loss of the *psychē* ("life"). An example is John 13:37–38: "Peter said to him, 'Lord, why cannot I follow you now? I will lay down my life for you.' Jesus answered, 'Will you lay down your life for me?'" Finally, death is referred to in Ecclesiastes 12:7 as separation of body and soul (or spirit): "And the dust returns to the earth as it was, and the spirit returns to God who gave it." In the New Testament, James 2:26 also speaks of death as separation of body and spirit. What we are dealing with in these passages is cessation of life in its familiar bodily state. This is not the end of existence, however. Life and death, according to Scripture, are not to be thought of as existence and nonexistence, but as two different states of existence.[5] Death is simply a transition to a different mode of existence; it is not, as some tend to think, extinction.

In addition to physical death, Scripture speaks of spiritual and eternal death. Spiritual death is the separation of the person from God; eternal death is the finalizing of that state of separation—one is lost for all eternity in his or her sinful condition.[6] Scripture clearly refers to a state of spiritual deadness, which is an inability to respond to spiritual matters or even a total loss of sensitivity to such stimuli. This is what Paul has in mind in Ephesians 2:1–2: "And you he made alive, when you were dead through the trespasses and sins in which you once walked." On the other hand, when the Book of Revelation refers to the "second death" (e.g., 21:8), it is eternal death which is in view. This second death is something separate from and subsequent to normal physical death. We know from Revelation 20:6 that the second death will not be experienced by believers: "Blessed and holy is he who shares in the first resurrection! Over such the second death has no power, but they shall be priests of God and of Christ, and they shall reign with him a thousand years." The second death is an endless period of punishment and of separation from the presence of God, the finalization of the lost state of the individual who is spiritually dead at the time of physical death.

Physical Death: Natural or Unnatural?

There has been a great deal of debate as to whether the first humans were created mortal or immortal, whether they would have died had they not sinned.[7] It is our position that physical death was not an original part of the human condition. But death was always there as a threat should they sin, that is, eat of or touch the forbidden tree (Gen. 3:3). While the death which was threatened must have been at least in part spiritual death, it appears that physical death was also involved, since the man and woman had to be driven out of the Garden of Eden lest they also eat of the tree of life and live forever (Gen. 3:22–23). Another evidence of our position is to be found in 1 Corinthians 15, where Paul is clearly referring, at least in part, to physical death when he says, "As by a man came death, by a man has come also the resurrection of the dead" (v. 21). For physical death is one of the evils countered and overcome by Christ's resurrection. This verse, then, is proof that physical death came from human sin; it was not part of God's original intention for humankind.

Since physical death is a result of sin, it seems probable that the first humans were created with the possibility of living forever. They were not inherently immortal, however; that is, they would not by virtue of their nature have lived on forever. Rather, if they had not sinned, they could have partaken of the tree of life and thus have received everlasting life. They were mortal in the sense of being able to die; and when they sinned, that potential or possibility became a reality. We might say that they were created with contingent immortality. They could have lived forever, but it was not certain that they would.

5. Louis Berkhof, *Systematic Theology* (Grand Rapids: Eerdmans, 1953), p. 668.

6. Augustus H. Strong, *Systematic Theology* (Westwood, N.J.: Revell, 1907), p. 982.

7. E.g., Augustine, *Anti-Pelagian Writings*, in *A Select Library of the Nicene and Post-Nicene Fathers of the Christian Church*, vol. 5, ed. Philip Schaff (New York: Scribner, 1902).

The Effects of Death

For the unbeliever, death is a curse, a penalty, an enemy. For although death does not bring about extinction or the end of existence, it cuts one off from God and from any opportunity of obtaining eternal life. But for those who believe in Christ and so are righteous, death has a different character. The believer still undergoes physical death, but its curse is gone. Because Christ himself became a curse for us by dying on the cross (Gal. 3:13), believers, although still subject to physical death, do not experience its fearsome power, its curse (see 1 Cor. 15:54–57).

Looking on death as indeed an enemy, the non-Christian sees nothing positive in it why should not such translation be the experience of all whose faith is placed in Christ?

It is necessary to distinguish here between the temporal and the eternal consequences of sin. We have noted that the eternal consequences of our own individual sins are nullified when we are forgiven, but the temporal consequences, or at least some of them, may linger on. This is not a denial of the fact of justification, but merely an evidence that God does not reverse the course of history. What is true of our individual sins is also true of God's treatment of Adam's sin or the sin of the race as well. All judgment upon and our guilt for original and individual sin are removed, so that spiritual and

---

Death is desirable for believers, for it will bring them into the presence of their Lord.

---

and recoils from it in fear. Paul, however, was able to take an entirely different attitude toward it. He saw death as a conquered enemy, an erstwhile foe which now is forced to do the Lord's will. So Paul regarded death as desirable, for it would bring him into the presence of his Lord. He wrote to the Philippians: "It is my eager expectation and hope that I shall not be at all ashamed, but that with full courage now as always Christ will be honored in my body, whether by life or by death. For to me to live is Christ, and to die is gain. . . . My desire is to depart and be with Christ, for that is far better" (Phil. 1:20–23).

Here the question arises as to why the believer is still required to experience death at all. If death, physical as well as spiritual and eternal, is the penalty for sin, then when we are delivered from sin and its ultimate consequence (eternal death), why should we not also be spared from the symbol of that condemnation, namely, physical death? If Enoch and Elijah were taken to be with the Lord without having to go through death, eternal death are canceled. Nonetheless, we must experience physical death simply because it has become one of the conditions of human existence. It is now a part of life, as much so as are birth, growth, and suffering, which also ultimately takes its origin from sin. One day every consequence of sin will be removed, but that day is not yet. The Bible, in its realism, does not deny the fact of universal physical death, but insists that it has different significance for the believer and the unbeliever.

The Intermediate State

The Difficulty of the Doctrine

The doctrine of the intermediate state is an issue which is both very significant and yet also problematic. It therefore is doubly important that we examine carefully this somewhat strange doctrine. "Intermediate state" refers to the condition of humans between their death and the resurrection. The question is, What is the condition of the individual during this period of time?

It is vital that we have practical answers to this question at the time of bereavement. Many pastors and parents have been asked at a graveside, "Where is Grandma now? What is she doing? Is she with Jesus already? Are she and Grandpa back together? Does she know what we are doing?" These questions are not the product of idle speculation or curiosity; they are of crucial importance to the individual posing them. An opportunity to offer comfort and encouragement is available to the Christian who is informed on the matter. Unfortunately, many Christians do not seize this opportunity because they do not know of a helpful reply.

There are two major reasons why many Christians find themselves unable to minister effectively to the bereaved. The first is the relative scarcity of biblical references to the intermediate state. The second reason is the theological controversy which has developed around the doctrine. Prior to the twentieth century, orthodoxy had a fairly consistent doctrine worked out. Believing in some sort of dualism of body and soul (or spirit) in the human person, the orthodox maintained that a part of the human survives death. The immaterial soul lives on in a conscious personal existence while the body decomposes. At the second coming of Christ, there will be a resurrection of a renewed or transformed body which will be reunited with the soul. Thus, orthodoxy held to both the immortality of the soul and the resurrection of the body.[8]

Liberalism, however, rejected the idea of the resurrection of the body, replacing it with the immortality of the soul. Since those who held this view did not anticipate any future resurrection, they did not believe in a bodily second coming of Christ either.[9] Neoorthodoxy took a quite different view of the matter. The neoorthodox hope for the future lay in an expectation of the resurrection of the body. Underlying this view was the monistic idea of the human person as a radical unity—existence means bodily existence; there is no separate spiritual entity to survive death and exist apart from the body.[10] So whereas liberalism held to immortality of the soul, neoorthodoxy held to resurrection of the body. Both schools were in agreement that their views were mutually exclusive. That is, it was a matter of either/or; they did not consider the possibility of both/and.

Current Views of the Intermediate State

Soul Sleep

We turn now to examine various current understandings of the intermediate state. One view which over the years has had considerable popularity is termed "soul sleep." This is the idea that the soul, during the period between death and resurrection, reposes in a state of unconsciousness. In the sixteenth century, many Anabaptists and Socinians apparently subscribed to this view. A similar position is taken today by the Seventh-Day Adventists.[11] In the case of the Adventists, however, the phrase "soul sleep" is somewhat misleading. Anthony Hoekema suggests instead "soul-extinction," since in the Adventist view one does not fall asleep at death, but actually becomes completely nonexistent, nothing surviving.[12] Hoekema's characterization of the Adventist position as soul-extinction is quite in order as long as we understand that "soul" is here being used, as is often the case, as a synonym for "person."

The case for soul sleep rests in large measure on the fact that Scripture frequently uses the imagery of sleep to refer to death. Stephen's death is described as sleep (Acts 7:60). Paul notes that "David, after he had

8. James Addison, *Life Beyond Death in the Beliefs of Mankind* (Boston: Houghton Mifflin, 1931), p. 202.

9. Harry Emerson Fosdick, *The Modern Use of the Bible* (New York: Macmillan, 1933), pp. 98–104.

10. Emil Brunner, *The Christian Doctrine of the Church, Faith, and the Consummation* (Philadelphia: Westminster, 1962), pp. 383–85, 408–14.

11. *Seventh-Day Adventists Answer Questions on Doctrine* (Washington: Review and Herald, 1957), p. 13.

12. Anthony Hoekema, *The Four Major Cults* (Grand Rapids: Eerdmans, 1963), p. 345.

served the counsel of God in his own generation, fell asleep" (Acts 13:36). Paul uses the same image four times in 1 Corinthians 15 (vv. 6, 18, 20, 51) and three times in 1 Thessalonians 4:13–15. Jesus himself said of Lazarus, "Our friend Lazarus has fallen asleep, but I go to awake him out of sleep" (John 11:11), and then indicated clearly that he was referring to death (v. 14). Literal understanding of this imagery has led to the concept of soul sleep.

Those who subscribe to soul sleep maintain that the person is a unitary entity without components. Thus, when the body ceases to function, the soul (i.e., the whole person) ceases to exist. Nothing survives physical death. There is no tension, then, between immortality of the soul and resurrection of the body. The simplicity of this view makes it quite appealing. Nevertheless, there are several problems.

One of the problems is that there are several biblical references to personal, conscious existence between death and resurrection. The most extended is the parable of the rich man and Lazarus (Luke 16:19–31). Another reference is Jesus' words to the thief on the cross, "Truly, I say to you, today you will be with me in Paradise" (Luke 23:43). In addition, dying persons speak of giving up their spirits to God. Jesus himself said, "Father, into thy hands I commit my spirit!" (Luke 23:46).

The second problem is whether it is legitimate to conclude that Scripture passages which refer to death as sleep are literal descriptions of the condition of the dead prior to the resurrection. It would seem, rather, that "sleep" should be understood simply as a euphemism for the cessation of life. Jesus' use of the image of sleep in reference to Lazarus (John 11:11) and the explanation which follows (v. 14) support this interpretation. If indeed "sleep" is more than a figure of speech, that needs to be substantiated.

Another problem for the theory of soul sleep is the conceptual difficulty attaching to the view that human nature is unitary. If indeed nothing of the person survives death, then what will be the basis of our identity? If the soul, the whole person, becomes extinct, what will come to life in the resurrection? On what basis can we maintain that what will come to life will be the person who died? It would seem that we will identify the postresurrection person with the predeath person on the basis of the body that is raised. Yet this in turn presents two further difficulties. How can the very same molecules come together to form the postresurrection person? The molecules constituting the predeath person may well have been destroyed, have formed new compounds, or even have been part of someone else's body. In this connection, cremation presents a particularly difficult problem. But beyond that, to identify the predeath and postresurrection persons on the basis of the body raised is to hold that human nature is primarily material or physical. For all of the foregoing reasons, the theory of soul sleep must be rejected as inadequate.

Purgatory

Because the doctrine of purgatory is primarily a Roman Catholic teaching, it is necessary to see it in the context of Catholic dogma in general. We begin with the idea that immediately upon death, the individual's eternal status is determined. Those who have died in a state of wickedness go directly to hell, where they immediately realize that they are irrevocably lost.[13] Their punishment, eternal in nature, consists of both the sense of having lost the greatest of all goods and actual suffering. The suffering is in proportion to the individual's wickedness and will intensify after the resurrection.[14] On the other hand, those who are in a perfect state of grace and penitence, who are completely purified at the time of death, go directly and immediately to heaven, which, while it is described as both a state and a

13. Joseph Pohle, *Eschatology; or, The Catholic Doctrine of the Last Things: A Dogmatic Treatise* (St. Louis: B. Herder, 1917), p. 70.
14. Ibid., pp. 52–61.

place, should be thought of primarily as a state.[15] Those who, although in a state of grace, are not yet spiritually perfect go to purgatory. It is purgatory which constitutes the most unusual and most interesting feature of the traditional Roman Catholic teaching regarding the intermediate state. Joseph Pohle defines it as "a state of temporary punishment for those who, departing this life in the grace of God, are not entirely free from venial sins or have not yet fully paid the satisfaction due to their transgressions."[16]

Thomas Aquinas argued that the cleansing which takes place after death is through penal sufferings. In this life, we can be cleansed by performing works of satisfaction, but after death that is no longer possible. To the extent that we fail to attain complete purity through works on earth, we must be further cleansed in the life to come. "This is the reason," said Thomas, "why we posit a purgatory or place of cleansing."[17] There are three means by which the souls in purgatory can be assisted in their progress toward heaven by the faithful still on earth—the mass, prayers, and good works.[18] These three means reduce the period of time necessary for purgatorial suffering to have its full effect. When the soul arrives at spiritual perfection, no venial sin remaining, it is released and passes into heaven.

The Roman Catholic Church bases its belief in purgatory upon both tradition and Scripture. There was an ancient tradition of praying, offering the mass, and giving alms for the benefit of the dead. Tertullian mentions anniversary masses for the dead, a practice which suggests belief in purgatory.[19] The primary biblical authority appealed to is 2 Maccabees 12:43–45:

He [Judas Maccabaeus] also took up a collection, man by man, to the amount of two thousand drachmas of silver, and sent it to Jerusalem to provide for a sin offering. In doing this he acted very well and honorably, taking account of the resurrection. For if he were not expecting that those who had fallen would rise again, it would have been superfluous and foolish to pray for the dead. But if he was looking to the splendid reward that is laid up for those who fall asleep in godliness, it was a holy and pious thought. Therefore, he made atonement for the dead, that they might be delivered from their sin.

The New Testament text most often cited is Matthew 12:32, where Jesus says, "But whoever speaks against the Holy Spirit will not be forgiven, either in this age or in the age to come." Roman Catholics contend that this verse implies that some sins (i.e., sins other than speaking against the Holy Spirit) will be forgiven in the world to come, an interpretation held by Augustine[20] and some other Fathers. Some Catholics also cite 1 Corinthians 3:15: "If any man's work is burned up, he will suffer loss, though he himself will be saved, but only as through fire."

The major points in our rejection of the concept of purgatory are points which distinguish Catholicism and Protestantism in general. The major text appealed to is in the Apocrypha, which Protestants do not accept as canonical Scripture. And the inference from Matthew 12:32 is rather forced; the verse in no way indicates that some sins will be forgiven in the life to come. Further, the concept of purgatory implies a salvation by works. For humans are thought to atone, at least in part, for their sins. This idea, however, is contrary to many clear teachings of Scripture, including Galatians 3:1–14 and Ephesians 2:8–9. Accordingly, the concept of purgatory—and indeed any view which posits a period of probation and atonement following death—must be rejected.

15. Ibid., p. 28.
16. Ibid., p. 77.
17. Thomas Aquinas *Summa contra Gentiles* 4.91.
18. Pohle, *Eschatology*, p. 95.
19. Tertullian *On Monogamy* 10.

20. Augustine *Confessions* 9.13.

Instantaneous Resurrection

A novel and creative conception that has been advanced in recent years is the idea of an instant resurrection or, more accurately, an instant reclothing. This is the belief that immediately upon death, the believer receives the resurrection body that has been promised. One of the most complete elaborations of this view is found in W. D. Davies's *Paul and Rabbinic Judaism*. Davies holds that Paul had two different conceptions concerning our resurrection. In 1 Corinthians 15 Paul is thinking of a future resurrection of the body. In 2 Corinthians 5, however, we have his more advanced under-

ond advent (e.g., Phil. 3:20–21; 1 Thess. 4:16–17). Paul also makes much of the second coming as an occasion of deliverance and glorification (e.g., Rom. 2:3–16; 1 Cor. 4:5; 2 Thess. 1:5–2:12; 2 Tim. 4:8). And Jesus himself laid emphasis upon a future time when the dead will be raised (John 5:25–29). We must conclude that Davies's solution to the problem which, as a result of a faulty presupposition, he has injected into the writings of Paul does little more than create additional problems.

A Suggested Resolution

Is there some way to resolve the numerous problems which attach to the issue of

---

There is between death and resurrection an intermediate state in which believers and unbelievers experience, respectively, the presence and absence of God.

---

standing of the subject. The fear of being unclothed, which he speaks of in verse 3, has been supplanted by the realization that on both this side and the other side of death, he will be clothed.[21] Davies concludes that when Paul wrote 2 Corinthians, he no longer believed in an intermediate state. Rather, upon death there will be an immediate transition into the final state, an instantaneous reception of the heavenly body.

But has Davies solved the problem? He labors under the presupposition that human nature is an absolute unity. The fact is, however, that Paul's anthropology was such that he could hold to both a future resurrection of the body and a disembodied survival. They are not contradictory ideas, but complementary parts of a whole. Nor is Davies's solution as biblical as he seems to think, for there are a number of passages in which Paul ties the transformation of our bodies to a *future* resurrection accompanying the sec-

21. W. D. Davies, *Paul and Rabbinic Judaism* (London: S.P.C.K., 1955), pp. 317–18.

the intermediate state, some means of correlating the biblical testimony regarding resurrection of the body and conscious survival between death and resurrection? Several considerations must be kept in mind:

1. Joachim Jeremias has pointed out that the New Testament distinguishes between Gehenna and Hades. Hades receives the unrighteous for the period between death and resurrection, whereas Gehenna is the place of punishment assigned permanently at the last judgment. The torment of Gehenna is eternal (Mark 9:43, 48). Further, the souls of the ungodly are outside the body in Hades, whereas in Gehenna both body and soul, reunited at the resurrection, are destroyed by eternal fire (Mark 9:43–48; Matt. 10:28). This is a counter to the view of some of the early church fathers that all who die, righteous and unrighteous alike, descend to Sheol or Hades, a sort of gloomy, dreamy state

where they await the coming of the Messiah.[22]

2. There are indications that the righteous dead do not descend to Hades (Matt. 16:18–19; Acts 2:31 [quoting Ps. 16:10]).

3. Rather, the righteous, or at least their souls, are received into paradise (Luke 16:19–31; 23:43).

4. Paul equates being absent from the body with being present with the Lord (2 Cor. 5:1–10; Phil. 1:19–26).

On the basis of these biblical considerations, we conclude that upon death believers go immediately to a place and condition of blessedness, and unbelievers to an experience of misery, torment, and punishment. Although the evidence is not clear, it is likely that these are the very places to which believers and unbelievers will go after the great judgment, since the presence of the Lord (Luke 23:43; 2 Cor. 5:8; Phil. 1:23) would seem to be nothing other than heaven. Yet while the place of the intermediate and final states may be the same, the experiences of paradise and Hades are doubtlessly not as intense as what will ultimately be, since the person is in a somewhat incomplete condition.

There is no inherent untenability about the concept of disembodied existence. The human being is capable of existing in either a materialized (bodily) or immaterialized condition (see pp. 174–75). We may think of these two conditions in terms of a dualism in which the soul or spirit can exist independently of the body. Like a chemical compound, the body-soul, so to speak, can be broken down under certain conditions (specifically at death), but otherwise is a definite unity. Or we may think in terms of different states of being. Just like matter and energy, the materialized and immaterialized conditions of the human are interconvertible. Both of these analogies are feasible. Paul Helm,[23] Richard Purtill,[24] and others have formulated conceptions of disembodied survival that are neither self-contradictory nor absurd. We conclude that the disembodied intermediate state set forth by the biblical teaching is philosophically tenable.

Implications of the Doctrines of Death and the Intermediate State

1. Death is to be expected by all, believer and unbeliever. Unless we are alive when the Lord returns, it will happen to us as well. It is important that we take this fact seriously and live accordingly.

2. Although death is an enemy (God did not originally intend for humans to die), it has now been overcome and made captive to God. It therefore need not be feared, for its curse has been removed by the death and resurrection of Christ. It can be faced with peace, for we know that it now serves the Lord's purpose of taking to himself those who have faith in him.

3. There is between death and resurrection an intermediate state in which believers and unbelievers experience, respectively, the presence and absence of God. While these experiences are less intense than the final states, they are of the same qualitative nature.

4. In both this life and the life to come, the basis of the believer's relationship with God is grace, not works. There need be no fear, then, that our imperfections will require some type of postdeath purging before we can enter into the full presence of God.

---

22. Joachim Jeremias, γέεννα, in *Theological Dictionary of the New Testament*, ed. Gerhard Kittel and Gerhard Friedrich, trans. Geoffrey W. Bromiley, 10 vols. (Grand Rapids: Eerdmans, 1964–76), vol. 1, pp. 657–58.

23. Paul Helm, "A Theory of Disembodied Survival and Re-embodied Existence," *Religious Studies* 14.1 (March 1978): 15–26.

24. Richard L. Purtill, "The Intelligibility of Disembodied Survival," *Christian Scholar's Review* 5.1 (1975): 3–22.

39 The Second Coming and Its Consequents

Among the most important events of cosmic eschatology, as we have defined it in this work, are the second coming and its consequents: the resurrection and the final judgment. These events form the subject matter of this chapter.

The Second Coming

With the exception of the certainty of death, the one eschatological doctrine on which orthodox theologians most agree is the second coming of Christ. It is indispensable to eschatology. It is the basis of the Christian's hope, the one event which will mark the beginning of the completion of God's plan.

The Definiteness of the Event

Many Scriptures indicate clearly that Christ is to return. Jesus himself promises that he will come again. In his great discourse on the end times (Matt. 24–25) he says, "Then will appear the sign of the Son of man in heaven, and then all the tribes of the earth will mourn, and they will see the second coming was part of the apostolic kerygma: "Repent therefore . . . that [God] may send the Christ appointed for you, Jesus, whom heaven must receive until the time for establishing all that God spoke by the mouth of his holy prophets from of old" (Acts 3:19–21). Paul makes a very clear and direct statement in 1 Thessalonians 4:15–16: "For this we declare to you by the word of the Lord, that we who are alive, who are left until the coming of the Lord, shall not precede those who have fallen asleep. For the Lord himself will descend from heaven with a cry of command, with the archangel's call, and with the sound of the trumpet of God." Other direct statements are found in 2 Thessalonians 1:7, 10; and Titus 2:13. Other authors also mention the second coming: He-

---

The second coming is the basis of the Christian's hope, the one event which will mark the beginning of the completion of God's plan.

Son of man coming on the clouds of heaven with power and great glory" (24:30). Several other times in this same speech he mentions the "coming of the Son of man" (vv. 27, 37, 39, 42, 44). Later that week, in his hearing before Caiaphas, Jesus said, "But I tell you, hereafter you will see the Son of man seated at the right hand of Power, and coming on the clouds of heaven" (Matt. 26:64). While Matthew records more than do the other Gospel writers, Mark, Luke, and John also include some of Jesus' comments on the second coming. Mark 13:26 and Luke 21:27, for example, are parallel with Matthew 24:30. And John tells us that in the upper room Jesus promised his disciples, "And when I go and prepare a place for you, I will come again and will take you to myself, that where I am you may be also" (John 14:3).

In addition to Jesus' own words, there are numerous other direct statements in the New Testament regarding his return. The brews 9:28; James 5:7–8; 1 Peter 1:7, 13; 2 Peter 1:16; 3:4, 12; 1 John 2:28. Certainly the second coming is one of the most widely taught doctrines in the New Testament.

The Indefiniteness of the Time

While the fact of the second coming is very emphatically and clearly asserted in Scripture, the time is not. Although God has set a definite time, that time has not been revealed. Jesus indicated that neither he nor the angels knew the time of his return, and neither would his disciples (Mark 13:32–33, 35; see also Matt. 24:36–44). Apparently the time of his return was one of the matters to which Jesus was referring when, just before his ascension, he responded to his disciples' question whether he would now restore the kingdom to Israel: "It is not for you to know times or seasons which the Father has fixed by his own authority" (Acts 1:7). Instead of satisfying their curiosity Jesus told the disciples that they were to be his witnesses worldwide. That the time of his return is not to be revealed explains Jesus' repeated emphasis upon its unexpectedness and the consequent need for watchfulness (Matt. 24:44, 50; 25:13; Mark 13:35).

The Character of the Coming

Personal

That Christ's second coming will be personal in character is assumed throughout the references to his return. Jesus says, for example, "I will come again and will take you to myself, that where I am you may be also" (John 14:3). Paul's statement that "the Lord himself will descend from heaven" (1 Thess. 4:16) leaves little doubt that the return will be personal in nature. The word of the angels at Jesus' ascension, "This Jesus, who was taken up from you into heaven, will come in the same way as you saw him go into heaven" (Acts 1:11), argues conclusively that his return will be just as personal as was his departure.

Physical

There are those who claim that Jesus' promise to return was fulfilled on Pentecost through a spiritual coming. Jesus did, after all, say, "I am with you always, to the close of the age" (Matt. 28:20). He also said, "If a man loves me, he will keep my word, and my Father will love him, and we will come to him and make our home with him" (John 14:23). Some interpreters put a great deal of weight upon the use of the Greek term *parousia* for the second coming. Pointing out that the word basically means "presence," they argue that its force in references to "the coming of the Lord" is that Jesus is present with us, not that he is coming at some future time.

Since Pentecost Christ has indeed been with and in each believer from the moment of new birth on. Several considerations, however, prevent our regarding this spiritual presence as the full meaning of the coming which he promised. While it is true that the basic meaning of *parousia* is "presence," it also means "coming," and this is

the meaning which is most prominent in the New Testament, as can be determined by examining how the word is used in context. Further, there are several other New Testament terms, particularly *apokalypsis* and *epiphaneia*, which clearly do indicate "coming."[1] And the statement in Acts 1:11 that Jesus will return in the same way as he departed implies that the return will be bodily. Perhaps the most persuasive argument, however, is that many of the promises of Jesus' second coming were made after Pentecost, in fact as much as sixty years later, and they still placed the coming in the future.

Visible

The Jehovah's Witnesses maintain that Christ began his reign over the earth on October 1, 1914. This was not a visible return to earth, however, for Jesus has not had a visible body since his ascension. Nor was it even a literal return, since it was in heaven that Christ ascended the throne. His presence, then, is in the nature of an invisible influence.[2]

It is difficult to reconcile the Witnesses' conception of the second coming with the biblical descriptions. Once again we point to Acts 1:11: Christ's return will be like his departure, which was certainly visible, for the disciples watched Jesus being taken into heaven (vv. 9–10). Other descriptions of the second coming make it clear that it will be quite conspicuous; for example, Matthew 24:30: "and they will see the Son of man coming on the clouds of heaven with power and great glory."

Unexpected

Although the second coming will be preceded by several signs—the desolating sacrilege (Matt. 24:15), great tribulation (v. 21), darkening of the sun (v. 29), they will not indicate the exact time of Jesus' return. Consequently, there will be many for whom his re-

1. George E. Ladd, *The Blessed Hope* (Grand Rapids: Eerdmans, 1956), pp. 65–70.
2. *Let God Be True* (Brooklyn: Watchtower Bible and Tract Society, 1952), p. 141.

turn will be quite unexpected. Jesus' teachings suggest that because of a long delay before the second coming, some will be lulled into inattention (Matt. 25:1–13; cf. 2 Peter 3:3–4). When the parousia finally occurs, however, it will happen so quickly that there will be no time to prepare (Matt. 25:8–10). As Louis Berkhof puts it, "The Bible intimates that the measure of surprise at the second coming of Christ will be in an inverse ratio to the measure of their watchfulness."[3]

Triumphant and Glorious

Various descriptions of the return of Christ indicate its glorious character, a sharp contrast to the lowly and humble circumstances of his first coming. He will come on the clouds with great power and great glory (Matt. 24:30; Mark 13:26; Luke 21:27). He will be accompanied by his angels and heralded by the archangel (1 Thess. 4:16). He will sit upon his glorious throne and judge all the nations (Matt. 25:31–46). The irony of this situation is that he who was judged at the end of his stay on earth will be the judge over all at his second coming. Clearly, he will be the triumphant, glorious Lord of all.

The Unity of the Second Coming

A large and influential group of conservative Christians teaches that Christ's coming will actually take place in two stages. These stages are the rapture and the revelation, or the "coming for" the saints and the "coming with" the saints. These two events will be separated by the great tribulation, believed to be approximately seven years in duration. Those who hold this view are termed pretribulationists, and most of them are dispensationalists.

The rapture or "coming for" will be secret; it will not be noticed by anyone except the church. Because it is to precede the tribulation, there is no prophecy which must yet be fulfilled before it can take place. Consequently, the rapture could occur at any mo-

ment or, in the usual terminology, it is imminent. It will deliver the church from the agony of the great tribulation. Then at the end of the seven years, the Lord will return again, bringing his church with him in a great triumphant arrival. This will be a conspicuous, glorious event universally recognized.[4] Christ will then set up his earthly millennial kingdom.

In contrast to pretribulationism, the other views of Christ's second coming hold that it will be a single occurrence, a unified event. They refer all prophecies regarding the second coming to the one event, whereas the pretribulationist refers some of the prophecies to the rapture and others to the revelation.[5]

How are we to resolve this issue? Will the second coming be a single or a dual-stage occurrence? While numerous considerations which bear upon this issue will be examined in the following chapter, there is one crucial consideration which we will examine now. It relates to the vocabulary used to designate the second advent. The three major terms for the second coming are *parousia*, *apokalypsis*, and *epiphaneia*. The pretribulationist argues that *parousia* refers to the rapture, the first stage of the return, the believer's blessed hope of being delivered from this world before the tribulation begins. The other two terms refer to Christ's coming with the saints at the end of the tribulation.

When examined closely, however, the terms which designate the second coming do not support the distinction made by pretribulationists. In 1 Thessalonians 4:15–17, for example, the term *parousia* is used to denote an event which it is hard to conceive of as the rapture: "For this we declare to you by the word of the Lord, that we who are alive, who are left until the coming [*parousia*] of the Lord, shall not precede those who have fallen asleep. For the Lord himself will descend from heaven with a cry of com-

---

3. Louis Berkhof, *Systematic Theology* (Grand Rapids: Eerdmans, 1953), p. 706.

4. John F. Walvoord, *The Return of the Lord* (Findlay, Ohio: Dunham, 1955), pp. 52–53.

5. Ladd, *Blessed Hope*, p. 67.

mand, with the archangel's call, and with the sound of the trumpet of God. And the dead in Christ will rise first; then we who are alive, who are left, shall be caught up together with them in the clouds to meet the Lord in the air; and so shall we always be with the Lord." As George Ladd says, "It is very difficult to find a secret coming of Christ in these verses."[6] In addition, the term *parousia* is used in 2 Thessalonians 2:8, where we read that following the tribulation Christ by his coming will destroy the man of lawlessness, the Antichrist, in a public fashion. Further, Jesus said of the *parousia*: "For as the lightning comes from the east and shines as far as the west, so will be the coming of the Son of man" (Matt. 24:27).[7]

Nor do the other two terms fit the pretribulationists' conception. Whereas it is supposedly the *parousia*, not the *apokalypsis* or *epiphaneia*, that is the blessed hope awaited by the church, Paul is thankful that his readers have been enriched in knowledge as they "wait for the revealing [*apokalypsis*] of our Lord Jesus Christ" (1 Cor. 1:7; see also 2 Thess. 1:6–7). And Peter speaks of the believers' joy and reward in connection with the *apokalypsis*: "But rejoice in so far as you share Christ's sufferings, that you may also rejoice and be glad when his glory is revealed" (1 Peter 4:13). This reference (along with 1:7 and 1:13) suggests that the believers to whom Peter is writing (who are part of the church) will receive their glory and honor at the *apokalypsis* of Christ. According to pretribulationism, however, the church should already have received its reward at the *parousia*.

Finally, Paul also speaks of the *epiphaneia* as the object of the believer's hope. He writes to Titus that believers are to live godly lives, "awaiting [the] blessed hope, the appearing [*epiphaneia*] of the glory of our great God and Savior Jesus Christ" (Titus 2:13). A similar use of *epiphaneia* can be found in 1 Timothy 6:14 and 2 Timothy 4:8. We conclude that the use of a variety of terms is not

an indication that there will be two stages in the second coming. Rather, the interchangeableness of the terms clearly points to a single event.

The Imminence of the Second Coming

An additional question which we must deal with is whether the second coming is imminent. Could it occur at any time, or are there some prophecies which must first be fulfilled?

Some Christians, particularly those who hold to a pretribulational coming for the saints by Christ, believe that the return could happen at any moment. In light of this, we must be prepared at all times for that possibility lest we be caught unaware. Several arguments are used in support of this position:

1. Jesus urged his disciples to be ready for his coming, since they did not know when it would take place (Matt. 24–25). If there are other events which must take place before Christ returns, such as the great tribulation, it is difficult to understand why he spoke of the time as unknown, for we would know at least that the return will not occur until those other events have transpired.[8]

2. There is a repeated emphasis that we are to wait eagerly, for the Lord's coming is at hand. Many passages (e.g., Rom. 8:19–25; 1 Cor. 1:7; Phil. 4:5; Titus 2:13; James 5:8–9; Jude 21) indicate that the coming could be very soon and perhaps at any moment.[9]

3. Paul's statement that we await our blessed hope (Titus 2:13) requires that the next event in God's plan be the coming of the Lord. If the next step were instead to be the great tribulation, we could hardly have hope and anticipation. Instead, fear and apprehensiveness would be our reaction. Since the return of our Lord is the next event on God's timetable, there is no reason why it could not happen at any time.[10]

---

6. Ibid., p. 63.
7. Ibid.

8. J. Barton Payne, *The Imminent Appearing of Christ* (Grand Rapids: Eerdmans, 1962), p. 86.
9. Ibid., pp. 95–103.
10. Walvoord, *Return of the Lord*, p. 51.

When examined closely, however, these arguments are not fully persuasive. Do the commands of Christ to watch for his coming and the warnings that his return will occur at an unlikely time and without clear signs necessarily mean that it is imminent? There has already been an intervening period of almost two thousand years. While we do not know how long the delay will be nor, consequently, the precise time of Christ's coming, we can still know that it is not yet. Not knowing when it will occur does not preclude knowing certain times when it will not occur.

Further, Jesus' statements did not at the time they were expressed mean that the second coming was imminent. He indicated through at least three of his parables (the nobleman who went to a far country, Luke 19:11–27; the wise and foolish virgins, Matt. 25:5; and the talents, Matt. 25:19) that there was to be a delay. Similarly, the parable of the servants (Matt. 24:45–51) involves a period of time for the servants to prove their character. In addition, certain events had to transpire before the second coming; for example, Peter would grow old and infirm (John 21:18), the gospel would be preached to all nations (Matt. 24:14), and the temple would be destroyed (Matt. 24:2). His saying, "Watch!" and "You do not know the hour," is not inconsistent with a delay to allow certain events to happen.

This is not to say that it is inappropriate to speak of imminence. It is, however, the complex of events surrounding the second coming, rather than the single event itself, that is imminent. Perhaps we should speak of this complex as imminent and the second coming itself as "impending."

Resurrection

The major result of Christ's second coming, from the standpoint of individual eschatology, is the resurrection. This is the basis for the believer's hope in the face of death. Although death is inevitable, the believer anticipates being delivered from its power.

The Biblical Teaching

The Bible clearly promises resurrection of the believer. The Old Testament gives us several direct statements, the first being Isaiah 26:19: "Thy dead shall live, their bodies shall rise. O dwellers in the dust, awake and sing for joy! For thy dew is a dew of light, and on the land of the shades thou wilt let it fall." Daniel 12:2 teaches resurrection of the believer and of the wicked as well: "And many of those who sleep in the dust of the earth shall awake, some to everlasting life, and some to shame and everlasting contempt." The idea of resurrection is also asserted in Ezekiel 37:12–14.

In addition to direct statements, the Old Testament intimates that we can expect deliverance from death or Sheol. Psalm 49:15 says, "But God will ransom my soul from the power of Sheol, for he will receive me." While there is no statement about the body in this passage, there is an expectation that the incomplete existence in Sheol will not be our final condition. Psalm 17:15 speaks of awaking in the presence of God.

While we must exercise care not to read too much of the New Testament revelation into the Old Testament, it is significant that Jesus and the New Testament writers maintained that the Old Testament teaches resurrection. When Jesus was questioned by the Sadducees, who denied the resurrection, he accused them of error due to lack of knowledge of the Scriptures and of the power of God (Mark 12:24), and then went on to argue for the resurrection on the basis of the Old Testament: "And as for the dead being raised, have you not read in the book of Moses, in the passage about the bush, how God said to him, 'I am the God of Abraham, and the God of Isaac, and the God of Jacob'? He is not God of the dead, but of the living" (vv. 26–27). Peter (Acts 2:24–32) and Paul (Acts 13:32–37) saw Psalm 16:10 as a prediction of the resurrection of Jesus. Hebrews 11:19 commends Abraham's belief in God's ability to raise persons from the dead.

The New Testament, of course, teaches the resurrection much more clearly. John reports several occasions when Jesus spoke directly of the resurrection. One of the clearest declarations is in John 5: "Truly, truly, I say to you, the hour is coming, and now is, when the dead will hear the voice of the Son of God, and those who hear will live. . . . Do not marvel at this; for the hour is coming when all who are in the tombs will hear his voice and come forth, those who have done good, to the resurrection of life, and those who have done evil, to the resurrection of judgment" (vv. 25, 28–29). Other affirmations of the resurrection are found in John 6:39–40, 44, 54, and the narrative of the raising of Lazarus (John 11, especially vv. 24–25).

The New Testament Epistles also give testimony to the resurrection. Paul clearly believed and taught that there is to be a future bodily resurrection. The classic passage is 1 Corinthians 15, where he discusses the resurrection at great length. The teaching is especially pointed in verses 51 and 52: "Lo! I tell you a mystery. We shall not all sleep, but we shall all be changed, in a moment, in the twinkling of an eye, at the last trumpet. For the trumpet will sound, and the dead will be raised imperishable, and we shall be changed." The resurrection is also clearly taught in 1 Thessalonians 4:13–16 and implied in 2 Corinthians 5:1–10. And when Paul appeared before the council, he created dissension between the Pharisees and Sadducees by declaring, "Brethren, I am a Pharisee, a son of Pharisees; with respect to the hope and the resurrection of the dead I am on trial" (Acts 23:6); he made a similar declaration before Felix (Acts 24:21). John also affirms the doctrine of resurrection (Rev. 20:4–6, 13).

A Work of the Triune God

All of the members of the Trinity are involved in the resurrection of believers. Paul informs us that the Father will raise believers through the Spirit (Rom. 8:11). And there is a special connection between the resurrection of Christ and the general resurrection, a point particularly emphasized by Paul in 1 Corinthians 15:12–14: "Now if Christ is preached as raised from the dead, how can some of you say that there is no resurrection of the dead? But if there is no resurrection of the dead, then Christ has not been raised; if Christ has not been raised, then our preaching is in vain and your faith is in vain." In Colossians 1:18 Paul refers to Jesus as "the beginning, the first-born from the dead." In Revelation 1:5 John similarly refers to Jesus as the "first-born of the dead." This expression does not point so much to Jesus' being first in time within the group as to his supremacy over the group (cf. Col. 1:15, "the first-born of all creation"). The resurrection of Christ is the basis for the believer's hope and confidence (1 Thess. 4:14).

Bodily in Nature

There are several passages in the New Testament which affirm that the body will be restored to life. One of them is Romans 8:11: "If the Spirit of him who raised Jesus from the dead dwells in you, he who raised Christ Jesus from the dead will give life to your mortal bodies also through his Spirit which dwells in you" (see also Phil. 3:20–21). In the resurrection chapter, 1 Corinthians 15, Paul says, "It is sown a physical body, it is raised a spiritual body. If there is a physical body, there is also a spiritual body" (v. 44). Paul also makes clear that the view that resurrection has already occurred, that is, in the form of a spiritual resurrection not incompatible with the fact that the bodies are still lying in their graves, is a heresy. He makes this point when he condemns the views of Hymenaeus and Philetus, "who have swerved from the truth by holding that the resurrection is past already. They are upsetting the faith of some" (2 Tim. 2:18).

In addition, there are inferential or indirect evidences of the bodily nature of the resurrection. The redemption of the believer is spoken of as involving the body, not merely the soul (Rom. 8:22–23). In 1 Corinthians 6:12–20 Paul points out the spiritual significance of the body. Our bodies are members of Christ (v. 15). The body is a temple of the Holy Spirit (v. 19). "The body is not meant for immorality, but for the Lord, and the Lord for the body" (v. 13). In view of the emphasis on the body, the statement which immediately follows is obviously an argument for bodily resurrection: "And God raised the Lord and will also raise us up by his power" (v. 14). The conclusion of the entire passage is: "So glorify God in your body" (v. 20).

Another indirect argument for the bodily character of the resurrection is that Jesus' resurrection was bodily in nature. When Jesus appeared to his disciples, they were frightened, thinking that they were seeing a spirit. He reassured them by saying, "Why are you troubled, and why do questionings rise in your hearts? See my hands and my feet, that it is I myself; handle me, and see; for a spirit has not flesh and bones as you see that I have" (Luke 24:38–39; see also John 20:27). The fact that the tomb was empty and the body was never produced by the opponents of Christ is a further indication of the bodily nature of his resurrection. The special connection which, as we have already noted, exists between the resurrection of Christ and that of the believer argues that our resurrection will be bodily as well.

Our resurrection body will have some connection with and derive from our original body, and yet it will not be merely a resuscitation of our original body. Rather, there will be a transformation or metamorphosis. An analogy here is the petrification of a log or a stump. While the contour of the original object is retained, the composition is entirely different. We have difficulty in understanding because we do not know the exact nature of the resurrection body. It does appear, however, that it will retain and at the same time glorify the human form. We will be free of the imperfections and needs which we had on earth.

Of Both the Righteous and the Unrighteous

Most of the references to the resurrection are to the resurrection of believers. Isaiah 26:9 speaks of the resurrection in a fashion which indicates that it is a reward. Jesus speaks of the "resurrection of the just" (Luke 14:14; see also 20:35). In Philippians 3:11 Paul expresses his desire and hope "that if possible I may attain the resurrection from the dead." Neither the Synoptic Gospels nor Paul's writings make explicit reference to unbelievers being raised from the dead.

On the other hand, there are a number of passages which do indicate a resurrection of unbelievers. Daniel 12:2 says, "And many of those who sleep in the dust of the earth shall awake, some to everlasting life, and some to shame and everlasting contempt." John reports a similar statement of Jesus (John 5:28–29). Paul, in his defense before Felix, said, "But this I admit to you, that according to the Way, which they call a sect, I worship the God of our fathers, believing everything laid down by the law or written in the prophets, having a hope in God which these themselves accept, that there will be a resurrection of both the just and the unjust" (Acts 24:14–15). And since both believers and unbelievers will be present at and involved in the last judgment, we conclude that the resurrection of both is necessary. Whether they will be raised simultaneously or at two different times will be discussed in the following chapter.

> *When Christ returns, our original body will be raised and transformed; our human form will be both retained and glorified.*

The Final Judgment

The second coming will also issue in the great final judgment. This is for many people one of the most frightening prospects regarding the future, and well it might be for those who are apart from Christ and consequently will be judged to be among the unrighteous. For those who are in Christ, however, it is something to look forward to, for it will vindicate their lives. As we study the final judgment, we should keep in mind that it is not intended to ascertain our spiritual condition or status, for that is already known to God. Rather, it will manifest or make our status public.[11]

A Future Event

The final judgment will occur in the future. Of course, God has in some cases already made his judgment manifest, as when he took righteous Enoch and Elijah to heaven to be with him, sent the destructive flood upon the earth (Gen. 6–7), and struck down Ananias and Sapphira (Acts 5:1–11). Friedrich Schelling, among others, maintained that the history of the world is the judgment of the world, that, in other words, the events that occur within history are in effect a judgment upon the world. Yet this is not the whole of what the Bible has to say about judgment. A definite event is to occur in the future. Jesus alluded to it in Matthew 11:24: "But I tell you that it shall be more tolerable on the day of judgment for the land of Sodom than for you." On another occasion he spoke clearly of the judgment which he would execute in connection with the future resurrection (John 5:27–29). There is an extended picture of this judgment in Matthew 25:31–46. The author of the letter to the Hebrews put it clearly and directly: "It is appointed for men to die once, and after that comes judgment" (Heb. 9:27). Other clear references include Acts 17:31; 24:25; Romans 2:5; Hebrews 10:27; 2 Peter 3:7; and Revelation 20:11–15.

Scripture specifies that the judgment will occur after the second coming. Jesus said, "For the Son of man is to come with his angels in the glory of his Father, and then he will repay every man for what he has done" (Matt. 16:27). This idea is also found in Matthew 13:37–43; 24:29–35; 25:31–46; and 1 Corinthians 4:5.

Jesus Christ the Judge

Jesus pictured himself as sitting on a glorious throne and judging all nations (Matt. 25:31–33). Although God is spoken of as the judge in Hebrews 12:23, it is clear from several other references that he delegates this authority to the Son. Jesus himself said, "The Father judges no one, but has given all judgment to the Son . . . and has given him authority to execute judgment, because he is the Son of man" (John 5:22, 27; see also Acts 10:42). Paul wrote to the Corinthians, "We must all appear before the judgment seat of Christ, so that each one may receive good or evil, according to what he has done in the body" (2 Cor. 5:10). Second Timothy 4:1 states that Christ is to judge the living and the dead.

While we are not told the exact details, it appears that believers will share in the judging. In Matthew 19:28 and Luke 22:28–30 Jesus suggests that the disciples will judge the twelve tribes of Israel. We are also told that believers will sit on thrones and judge the world (1 Cor. 6:2–3; Rev. 3:21; 20:4).

The Subjects of the Judgment

All humans will be judged (Matt. 25:32; 2 Cor. 5:10; Heb. 9:27). Paul warns that "we shall all stand before the judgment seat of God" (Rom. 14:10). Every secret will be revealed; all that has ever occurred will be evaluated. Some have questioned whether the sins of believers will be included—that would seem to be unnecessary inasmuch as believers have been justified. But the statements concerning the review of sins are universal. Berkhof's perspective on this matter

11. Gottlob Schrenk, δικαιοσύνη, in *Theological Dictionary of the New Testament*, ed. Gerhard Kittel and Gerhard Friedrich, trans. Geoffrey W. Bromiley, 10 vols. (Grand Rapids: Eerdmans, 1964–76), vol. 2, p. 207.

is probably correct: "Scripture leads us to believe that [the sins of believers] will be [revealed], though they will, of course, be revealed as *pardoned* sins."[12]

In addition, the evil angels will be judged at this time. Peter writes that "God did not spare the angels when they sinned, but cast them into hell [Tartarus] and committed them to pits of nether gloom to be kept until the judgment" (2 Peter 2:4). Jude 6 makes an almost identical statement. The good angels, on the other hand, will participate in the judgment by gathering together all who are to be judged (Matt. 13:41; 24:31).

The Basis of the Judgment

Those who appear will be judged in terms of their earthly lives.[13] Paul said that we will all appear at the judgment, "so that each one may receive good or evil, according to what he has done in the body" (2 Cor. 5:10). Jesus said that at the resurrection all will "come forth, those who have done good, to the resurrection of life, and those who have done evil, to the resurrection of judgment" (John 5:29). While one might infer from Matthew 25:31–46 that it is the doing of good deeds that makes the difference, Jesus indicated that some who claim and who even appear to have done good deeds will be told to depart (Matt. 7:21–23).

The standard on the basis of which the evaluation will be made is the revealed will of God. Jesus said, "He who rejects me and does not receive my sayings has a judge; the word that I have spoken will be his judge on

12. Berkhof, *Systematic Theology*, p. 732.
13. Floyd V. Filson, "The Second Epistle to the Corinthians," in *The Interpreter's Bible*, ed. George A. Buttrick (Nashville: Abingdon, 1978), vol. 10, p. 332.

the last day" (John 12:48). Even those who have not explicitly heard the law will be judged: "All who have sinned without the law will also perish without the law, and all who have sinned under the law will be judged by the law" (Rom. 2:12).

The Finality of the Judgment

Once passed, the judgment will be permanent and irrevocable. The righteous and the ungodly will be sent away to their respective final places. There is no hint that the verdict can be changed. In concluding his teaching about the last judgment, Jesus said that those on his left hand "will go away into eternal punishment, but the righteous into eternal life" (Matt. 25:46).

Implications of the Second Coming and Its Consequents

1. History will not simply run its course, but under the guidance of God will come to a consummation. His purposes will be fulfilled in the end.

2. We as believers should watch for and work in anticipation of the sure return of the Lord.

3. Our earthly bodies will be transformed into something far better. The imperfections which we now know will disappear; our everlasting bodies will know no pain, illness, or death.

4. A time is coming when justice will be dispensed. Evil will be punished, and faith and faithfulness rewarded.

5. In view of the certainty of the second coming and the finality of the judgment which will follow, it is imperative that we act in accordance with the will of God.

Millennial and Tribulational Views

Over the years there has been considerable discussion in Christian theology regarding the chronological relationship between Christ's second coming and certain other events. In particular, this discussion has involved two major questions. (1) Will there be a millennium, an earthly reign of Jesus Christ; and if so, will the second coming take place before or after that period? The view that there will be no earthly reign of Christ is termed amillennialism. The teaching that the return of Christ will inaugurate a millennium is termed premillennialism, while the belief that the second coming will conclude a millennium is postmillennialism. (2) Will Christ come to remove the church from the world before the great tribulation (pretribulationism), or will he return only after the tribulation (posttribulationism)? This second question is found primarily in premillennialism. We shall examine in turn each of the millennial and then the tribulational views.

Millennial Views

Postmillennialism

Postmillennialism rests on the belief that the preaching of the gospel will be so successful that the world will be converted. The reign of Christ, the location of which is human hearts, will be complete and universal. The petition, "Thy will be done, on earth as it is in heaven," will be actualized. Peace will prevail and evil will be virtually banished. Then, when the gospel has fully taken effect, Christ will return. Basically, then, postmillennialism is an optimistic view.

Postmillennialism, therefore, was most popular during periods in which the church appeared to be succeeding in its task of winning the world. Though propounded in the fourth century by Tyconius, and adopted by Augustine, it came to particular popularity in the latter part of the nineteenth century. Bear in mind that this was a period of great effectiveness in world missions as well as a time of concern about and progress in social conditions. Consequently, it seemed reasonable to assume that the world would soon be reached for Christ.

As we have suggested, the major tenet of postmillennialism is the successful spread of the gospel. This idea is based upon several passages of Scripture. In the Old Testament, Psalms 47, 72, and 100; Isaiah 45:22–25; and Hosea 2:23, for example, make it clear that all nations will come to know God. In addition, Jesus said on several occasions that the gospel would be preached universally prior to his second coming (see, e.g., Matt. 24:14). Inasmuch as the Great Commission is to be carried out in his authority (Matt. 28:18–20), it is bound to succeed. Often the idea of the spread of the gospel includes a transforming effect upon social conditions which follows from the conversion of large numbers of hearers. In some cases, the belief in the spread of the kingdom has taken on a somewhat more secularized form, so that social transformation rather than individual conversions is considered the sign of the kingdom. Emphasizing social transforma-

tion, liberals, insofar as they held a millennial view, were generally postmillennialists, but by no means were all postmillennialists liberal. Many of them envisioned an unprecedented number of conversions, with the human race becoming a collection of regenerated individuals.[1]

In postmillennial thought, the kingdom of God is viewed as a present reality, here and now, rather than a future heavenly realm (see Figure 7). Jesus' parables in Mat-

Figure 7. Postmillennialism

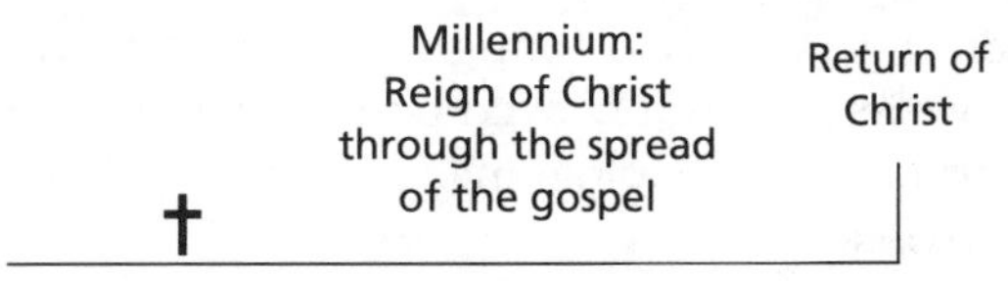

Millennium: Reign of Christ through the spread of the gospel

Return of Christ

†

thew 13 give us an idea of the nature of this kingdom. It is like leaven, spreading gradually but surely throughout the whole. Its growth will be extensive (it will spread throughout the entire world) and intensive (it will become dominant). Its growth will be so gradual that the onset of the millennium may be scarcely noticed by some. The progress may not be uniform; indeed, the coming of the kingdom may well proceed by a series of crises. Postmillennialists are able to accept what appear to be setbacks, since they believe in the ultimate triumph of the gospel.[2]

In the postmillennial view, the millennium will be an extended period, but not necessarily a literal one thousand years. Indeed, the postmillennial view of the millennium is frequently based less upon Revelation 20, where the thousand-year period and the two resurrections are mentioned, than upon other passages of Scripture. The very gradualness of the coming of the kingdom makes the length of the millennium difficult to calculate. The point is that the millen-

1. Charles Hodge, *Systematic Theology* (Grand Rapids: Eerdmans, 1952), vol. 3, pp. 800–812.
2. Loraine Boettner, "Postmillennialism," in *The Meaning of the Millennium*, ed. Robert G. Clouse (Downers Grove, Ill.: Inter-Varsity, 1977), pp. 120–21.

nium will be a prolonged period of time during which Christ, even though physically absent, will reign over the earth. One essential feature which distinguishes postmillennialism from the other millennial views is that it expects conditions to become better, rather than worse, prior to Christ's return. Thus it is a basically optimistic view. Consequently, it has fared rather poorly in the twentieth century. The convinced postmillennialist regards the distressing conditions of the twentieth century as merely a temporary fluctuation in the growth of the kingdom. They indicate that we are not as near the second coming as we had thought. This argument, however, has not proved persuasive to large numbers of theologians, pastors, and lay persons.[3]

Premillennialism

Premillennialism is committed to the concept of an earthly reign by Jesus Christ of approximately one thousand years (or at least a substantial period of time). Unlike postmillennialism, premillennialism sees Christ as physically present during this time; it believes that he will return personally and bodily to commence the millennium. This being the case, the millennium must be seen as still in the future (see Figure 8).

Figure 8. Premillennialism

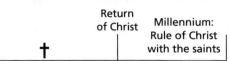

Return of Christ | Millennium: Rule of Christ with the saints

Premillennialism was probably the dominant millennial view during the first three centuries of the church. Much of the millennialism of this period—often termed "chiliasm," from the Greek word for "thousand"—had a rather sensuous flavor. The millennium would be a time of great abundance and fertility, of a renewing of the earth and building of a glorified Jerusalem.[4]

3. Ibid., pp. 132–33.
4. A. J. Visser, "A Bird's-Eye View of Ancient Christian Eschatology," *Numen* 14 (1967): 10–11.

In the Middle Ages, premillennialism became quite rare.

About the middle of the nineteenth century, premillennialism began to grow in popularity in conservative circles. This was partly due to the fact that liberals, insofar as they had a millennial view, were postmillennialists, and some conservatives considered anything associated with liberalism to be suspect. The growing popularity of the dispensational system of interpretation and eschatology also lent impetus to premillennialism. It has considerable adherence among conservative Baptists, Pentecostal groups, and independent fundamentalist churches.

The key passage for premillennialism is Revelation 20:4–6:

> Then I saw thrones, and seated on them were those to whom judgment was committed. Also I saw the souls of those who had been beheaded for their testimony to Jesus and for the word of God, and who had not worshiped the beast or its image and had not received its mark on their foreheads or their hands. They came to life, and reigned with Christ a thousand years. The rest of the dead did not come to life until the thousand years were ended. This is the first resurrection. Blessed and holy is he who shares in the first resurrection! Over such the second death has no power, but they shall be priests of God and of Christ, and they shall reign with him a thousand years.

Premillennialists observe that here is evidence of a thousand-year period and two resurrections, one at the beginning and the other at the end. Premillennialists insist on a literal and consistent interpretation of this passage. Since the same verb—*ezēsan* ("came to life")—is used in reference to both resurrections, they must be of the same type. The amillennialist, or for that matter the postmillennialist, is usually forced to say that they are of different types. The usual explanation is that the first resurrection is a spiritual resurrection, that is, regeneration, while the second is a literal, physical, or bodily resurrection. Thus those who take part in the first resurrection will undergo the second as well. Premillennialists, however, reject this interpretation as untenable. George Ladd says that if *ezēsan* means bodily resurrection in verse 5, it must mean bodily resurrection in verse 4; if it does not, "we have lost control of exegesis."[5]

Context, of course, can alter the meanings of words. However, in this case the two usages of *ezēsan* occur together. Consequently, what we have here are two resurrections of the same type which involve two different groups at an interval of a thousand years. It also appears from the context that those who participate in the first resurrection are not involved in the second. It is "the rest of the dead" who do not come to life until the end of the thousand years.

It is also important to observe the nature of the millennium. Whereas the postmillennialist thinks that the millennium is being introduced gradually, perhaps almost imperceptibly, the premillennialist envisions a sudden, cataclysmic event. In the premillennialist view, the rule of Jesus Christ will be complete from the very beginning of the millennium. Evil will have been virtually eliminated.

According to premillennialism, then, the millennium will not be an extension of trends already at work within the world. Instead, there will be a rather sharp break from conditions as we now find them. For example, there will be worldwide peace. This is a far cry from the present situation, where worldwide peace is a rare thing indeed, and the trend does not seem to be improving. The universal harmony will not be restricted to humans. Nature, which has been "groaning in travail," awaiting its redemption, will be freed from the curse of the fall (Rom. 8:19–23). Even animals will live in harmony with one another (Isa. 11:6–7; 65:25), and the destructive forces of nature will be calmed. The saints will rule together with Christ in this millennium. Although the exact nature of their reign is not spelled out, they will, as a reward for their faithfulness, participate with him in the glory which is his.

Premillennialists also hold that the millennium will be a tremendous change from what immediately precedes it, namely, the great tribulation. The tribulation will be a time of unprecedented trouble and turmoil, including cosmic disturbances, persecution, and great suffering. While premillennialists disagree as to whether the church will be present during the tribulation, they agree that the world situation will be at its very worst just before Christ comes to establish the millennium, which will be, by contrast, a period of peace and righteousness.

One particular premillennial approach, dispensationalism, deserves special mention, for although it is relatively new as orthodox theologies go, it has exerted a considerable influence within conservative circles. Dispensationalism is a unified interpretive scheme. That is to say, each specific part or tenet is vitally interconnected with the others. Thus, the various conclusions in eschatology follow from one another.

Dispensationalists tend to think of their system as being, first and foremost, a method of interpreting Scripture. At its core is the conviction that Scripture is to be interpreted literally. This does not mean that obviously metaphorical passages are to be taken literally, but that if the plain meaning makes sense, one must not look further.[6] In part, this means that prophecy is interpreted very literally and often in considerable detail. Specifically, "Israel" is always understood as a reference to national or ethnic Israel, not the church.

Dispensationalism finds in God's Word evidence of a series of "dispensations" or economies under which he has managed the world. These dispensations are successive stages in God's revelation of his purposes.

5. George E. Ladd, "Revelation 20 and the Millennium," *Review and Expositor* 57.2 (April 1960): 169.

6. John Walvoord, "Dispensational Premillennialism," *Christianity Today*, 15 Sept. 1958, pp. 11–12.

They do not entail different means of salvation, for the means of salvation has been the same at all periods of time, namely, by grace through faith. There is some disagreement as to the number of dispensations, the most common number being seven. Many dispensationalists emphasize that recognizing to what dispensation a given passage of Scripture applies is crucial. We should not attempt to govern our lives by precepts laid down for the millennium, for example.[7]

Dispensationalists also put great stress on the distinction between Israel and the church. Some of them hold that God made an unconditional covenant with Israel; that is to say, his promises to them do not depend upon their fulfilling certain requirements. They will remain his special people and ultimately receive his blessing. Ethnic, national, political Israel is never to be confused with the church, nor are the promises given to Israel to be regarded as applying to and fulfilled in the church. They are two separate entities.[8] God has, as it were, interrupted his special dealings with Israel, but will resume them at some point in the future. Unfulfilled prophecies regarding Israel will be fulfilled within the nation itself, not within the church. Indeed, the church is not mentioned in the Old Testament prophecies. It is virtually a parenthesis within God's overall plan of dealing with Israel. The millennium, then, takes on a special significance in dispensationalism. At that time God will resume his dealings with Israel, the church having been taken out of the world or "raptured" some time earlier (just prior to the great tribulation). The millennium consequently will have a markedly Jewish character. The unfulfilled prophecies regarding Israel will come to pass at that time.

Amillennialism

Literally, amillennialism is the idea that there will be no millennium, no earthly reign of Christ. The great final judgment will immediately follow the second coming and issue directly in the final states of the righteous and the wicked (see Figure 9). Amil-

Figure 9. Amillennialism

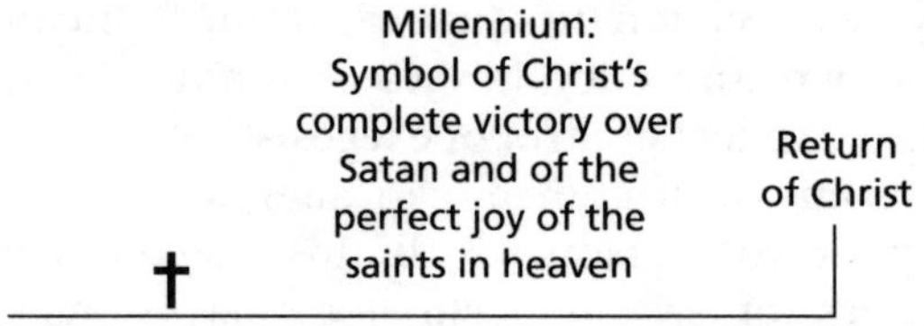

Millennium:
Symbol of Christ's
complete victory over
Satan and of the
perfect joy of the
saints in heaven

Return
of Christ

lennialism is a simpler view than either of the others that we have been considering. Its advocates maintain that it is built on a number of relatively clear eschatological passages, whereas premillennialism is based primarily upon a single passage, and an obscure one at that.

Despite the simplicity of amillennialism and the clarity of its central tenet, it is in many ways difficult to grasp. This is due in part to the fact that, its most notable feature being negative, its positive teachings are not always expounded. It has sometimes been distinguished more for its rejection of premillennialism than for its affirmations. Also, in dealing with the very troublesome passage of Revelation 20:4–6, amillennialists have come up with a rather wide variety of explanations. One wonders at times whether these explanations reflect the same basic view or quite different understandings of eschatological and apocalyptic literature. Finally, it has not always been possible to distinguish amillennialism from postmillennialism, since they share many common features. Indeed, various theologians who have not addressed the particular issues which serve to distinguish the two views from one another—among them are Augustine, John Calvin, and Benjamin B. Warfield—have been claimed as ancestors by both camps. What the two views share is a belief that the "thousand years" of Revelation 20 is to be taken symbolically. Both often hold as well that the millennium is the church age. Where they differ is that the postmillennialist, unlike the amillennialist,

7. Charles C. Ryrie, *Dispensationalism Today* (Chicago: Moody, 1965), pp. 86–90.
8. Ibid., pp. 132–55.

holds that the millennium involves an earthly reign of Christ.

In light of the problems one encounters in trying to grasp amillennialism, its history is difficult to trace. It is likely that postmillennialism and amillennialism simply were not differentiated for much of the first nineteen centuries of the church. When postmillennialism began to fade in popularity in the twentieth century, amillennialism was generally substituted for it, since amillennialism is much closer to postmillennialism than is premillennialism. Consequently, amillennialism has enjoyed its greatest popularity in the period since World War I.

When amillennialists deal with Revelation 20, they usually have the whole book in view. They see the Book of Revelation as consisting of several sections, seven being the number most frequently mentioned. These several sections do not deal with successive periods of time; rather, they are recapitulations of the same period, the period between Christ's first and second comings.[9] It is believed that in each of these sections the author picks up the same themes and elaborates them. If this is the case, Revelation 20 does not refer solely to the last period in the history of the church, but is a special perspective upon the entire history of the church.

Amillennialists also remind us that the Book of Revelation as a whole is very symbolic. They note that even the most rabid premillennialists do not take everything in the Book of Revelation literally. The bowls, seals, and trumpets, for example, are usually interpreted as symbols. By a simple extension of this principle amillennialists contend that the "thousand years" of Revelation 20 might not be literal either. In addition, they point out that the millennium is mentioned nowhere else in Scripture.[10]

The question arises, If the figure of a thousand years is to be taken symbolically rather than literally, of what is it a symbol? Many amillennialists utilize Warfield's interpretation: "The sacred number seven in combination with the equally sacred number three forms the number of holy perfection, ten, and when this ten is cubed into a thousand the seer has said all he could say to convey to our minds the idea of absolute completeness."[11] The references to a "thousand years" in Revelation 20, then, convey the idea of perfection or completeness. In verse 2 the figure represents the completeness of Christ's victory over Satan. In verse 4 it suggests the perfect glory and joy of the redeemed in heaven at the present time.[12]

The major exegetical problem for amillennialism, however, is not the one thousand years, but the two resurrections. Among the variety of amillennial opinions about the two resurrections, the one common factor is a denial of the premillennial contention that John is speaking of two physical resurrections involving two different groups. The most common amillennial interpretation is that the first resurrection is spiritual and the second is bodily or physical. One who has argued this at some length is Ray Summers. From Revelation 20:6 ("Blessed and holy is he who shares in the first resurrection! Over such the second death has no power") he concludes that the first resurrection is a victory over the second death. Since it is customary in eschatological discussions to consider the second death to be spiritual rather than physical, the first resurrection must be spiritual as well. The first death, which is not mentioned but implied, must surely be physical death. If it is to be correlated with the second resurrection as the second death is with the first resurrection, the second resurrection must be physical. The first resurrection, then, is the

9. Floyd Hamilton, *The Basis of Millennial Faith* (Grand Rapids: Eerdmans, 1942), pp. 130–31.

10. William Hendriksen, *More than Conquerors* (Grand Rapids: Baker, 1939), pp. 11–64; Anthony Hoekema, "Amillennialism," in *Meaning of the Millennium*, pp. 156–59.

11. Benjamin B. Warfield, "The Millennium and the Apocalypse," in *Biblical Doctrines* (New York: Oxford University Press, 1929), p. 654.

12. W. J. Grier, "Christian Hope and the Millennium," *Christianity Today*, 13 Oct. 1958, p. 19.

new birth. The second resurrection is the bodily or physical resurrection which we usually have in view when we use the word *resurrection*. All those who participate in the first resurrection also participate in the second resurrection, but not all of those experiencing the second resurrection will have partaken of the first.[13]

The most common premillennial criticism of the view that the first resurrection is spiritual and the second physical is that it is inconsistent in interpreting identical terms (*ezēsan*) in the same context. Some amillennialists have accepted this criticism and have sought to develop a position in which the two resurrections are of the same type. James Hughes has constructed such a view. He suggests that not only is the first resurrection spiritual, but so is the second resurrection. While some commentators infer from Revelation 20:5 ("The rest of the dead did not come to life until the thousand years were ended") that the unjust will come to life at the end of the millennium, Hughes renders this verse, "They did not live during the thousand years, nor thereafter." Having never spiritually come to life, this group will suffer the second death. So unlike the first resurrection, which is the ascension of the just soul to heaven to reign with Christ, the second resurrection is virtually hypothetical. Like the first, however, it is spiritual in nature. Thus Hughes has managed to interpret the two occurrences of *ezēsan* consistently.[14]

Another feature of amillennialism is a more general conception of prophecy, especially Old Testament prophecy, than is found in premillennialism. Amillennialists frequently treat prophecies as historical or symbolic rather than futuristic and literal. As a general rule, prophecy occupies a much less important place in amillennial than in premillennial thought.

13. Ray Summers, "Revelation 20: An Interpretation," *Review and Expositor* 57.2 (April 1960): 176.
14. James A. Hughes, "Revelation 20:4–6 and the Question of the Millennium," *Westminster Theological Journal* 35 (1973): 299–300.

Finally, we should observe that amillennialism usually does not display the optimism that is typically found in postmillennialism. There may be a belief that preaching of the gospel will be successful, but great success in this regard is not necessary to the amillennial scheme, since no literal reign of Christ, no coming of the kingdom before the coming of the King, is expected. This is not to say that amillennialism is like premillennialism in expecting an extreme deterioration of conditions before the second coming. Yet there is nothing in amillennialism to preclude such a possibility. And because no millennium will precede the second coming, the Lord's return may be at hand. For the most part, however, amillennialists do not engage in the type of eager searching for signs of the second coming that characterizes much of premillennialism.

Resolving the Issues

We must now address the question of which millennial view to adopt. The issues are large and complex, but on close analysis can be reduced to a comparative few. We have noted in the course of this treatise that theology, like other disciplines, is often unable to find one view which is conclusively supported by all of the data. What must be done in such situations is to find the view which has fewer difficulties than do the alternatives. That is the approach we will follow here.

The postmillennial view has much less support at the present time than it did in the late nineteenth and early twentieth centuries. Its optimism regarding gospel proclamation has come to seem somewhat unjustified today. In parts of the world the percentage of the population actually practicing the Christian faith is very small. Further, some countries are still closed to Christian missionary endeavor of a conventional type.

There are also strong biblical grounds for rejecting postmillennialism. Jesus' teaching regarding great wickedness and a cooling off of the faith of many before his return seems to conflict quite sharply with postmillennial optimism. That a clear depiction of an earthly reign of Christ without his physical presence is nowhere found in Scripture seems to be another major weakness of this position.

This leaves us with a choice between amillennialism and premillennialism. The issue comes down to the biblical references to the millennium—are they sufficient grounds for adopting the more complicated premillennial view rather than the simpler amillennial conception? It is sometimes contended that the whole premillennial conception rests upon a single passage of Scripture, and that no doctrine should be based upon a single passage. But if one view can account for a specific reference better than can another, and both views explain the rest of Scripture about equally well, then the former view must certainly be judged more adequate than the latter.

We note here that there are no biblical passages with which premillennialism cannot cope, or which it cannot adequately explain. We have seen, on the other hand, that the reference to two resurrections (Rev. 20) gives amillennialists difficulty. Their explanations that we have here two different types of resurrection or two spiritual resurrections strain the usual principles of hermeneutics.

Nor is the premillennialist interpretation based upon only one passage in the Bible. Intimations of it are found in a number of places. For example, Paul writes, "For as in Adam all die, so also in Christ shall all be made alive. But each in his own order: Christ the first fruits, then at his coming those who belong to Christ. Then comes the end, when he delivers the kingdom to God the Father after destroying every rule and every authority and power" (1 Cor. 15:22–24). The particular adverbs translated "then" (*epeita* and *eita*) indicate temporal sequence. Paul could have used an adverb that suggests concurrent events (*tote*), but he did not do so.[15] We should also observe that while the two resur-

rections are spoken of explicitly only in Revelation 20, there are other passages which hint at either a resurrection of a select group (Luke 14:14; 20:35; 1 Cor. 15:23; Phil. 3:11; 1 Thess. 4:16) or a resurrection in two stages (Dan. 12:2; John 5:29). Accordingly, we judge the premillennial view to be more adequate than amillennialism.

Tribulational Views

We come now to the issue of the relation between Christ's return and the complex of events known as the great tribulation. In theory, all premillennialists hold that there will be a great disturbance of seven years' duration (that figure need not be taken literally) prior to Christ's coming. The question is whether there will be a separate coming to remove the church from the world prior to the great tribulation or whether the church will go through the tribulation and be united with the Lord only afterward. The view that Christ will take the church to himself prior to the tribulation is called pretribulationism; the view that he will take the church after the tribulation is called posttribulationism. There are also certain mediating positions which we will mention briefly at the conclusion of the chapter. In practice, these distinctions are drawn only by premillennialists, who tend to devote more attention to the details of the end times than do the advocates of either postmillennialism or amillennialism.

Pretribulationism

There are several distinctive ideas held by pretribulationists. The first concerns the nature of the tribulation. It will be a *great* tribulation unparalleled within history. It will be a period of transition concluding God's dealings with the Gentiles and preparing for the millennium and the events which will transpire therein. The tribulation is not to be understood as in any sense a time for disciplining believers or purifying the church.

A second major idea of pretribulationism is the rapture of the church. Christ will

15. Joseph H. Thayer, *Greek-English Lexicon of the New Testament* (Edinburgh: T. and T. Clark, 1955), pp. 188, 231, 629.

come at the beginning of the great tribulation (or just prior to it, actually) to remove the church from the world. This coming in a sense will be secret. No unbelieving eye will observe it. The rapture is pictured in 1 Thessalonians 4:17: "Then we who are alive, who are left, shall be caught up together with [the dead in Christ] in the clouds to meet the Lord in the air; and so we shall always be with the Lord." Note that in the rapture Christ will not descend all the way to earth, as he will when he comes *with* the church at the end of the tribulation (see Figure 10).[16]

Figure 10. Pretribulationism

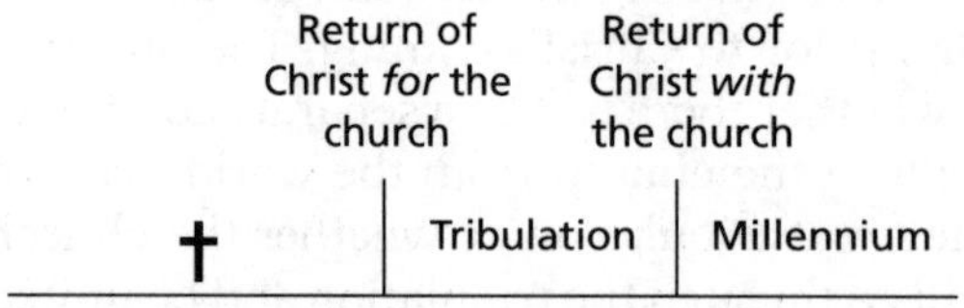

Pretribulationism, then, maintains that there will be two phases in Christ's coming, or one could even say two comings. There will also be three resurrections. The first will be the resurrection of the righteous dead at the rapture, for Paul teaches that believers who are alive at the time will not precede those who are dead. Then at the end of the tribulation there will be a resurrection of those saints who have died during the tribulation. Finally, at the end of the millennium, there will be a resurrection of unbelievers.[17]

The point of the rapture is to deliver the church from the tribulation. We can expect deliverance because Paul promised the Thessalonians that they would not experience the wrath which God will pour out upon unbelievers: "For God has not destined us for wrath, but to obtain salvation through our Lord Jesus Christ" (1 Thess.

5:9); "Jesus . . . delivers us from the wrath to come" (1 Thess. 1:10).

But what of the references in Matthew 24 which indicate that some of the elect will be present during the tribulation? We must understand that the disciples' asking what would be the sign of Jesus' coming and of the end of the age (24:3; cf. Acts 1:6) occurred within a Jewish framework. And accordingly, Jesus' discussion here pertains primarily to the future of Israel. It is significant that the Gospel uses the general term *elect* rather than "church," "body of Christ," or any similar expression. It is elect Jews, not the church, who will be present during the tribulation. This distinction between Israel and the church is a determinative and crucial part of pretribulationism, which is closely allied with dispensationalism. The tribulation is viewed as being the transition from God's dealing primarily with the church to his reestablishing relationship with his original chosen people, national Israel.[18]

There is, finally, within pretribulationism a strong emphasis that the Lord's return is imminent.[19] Since his return will precede the tribulation, nothing remains to be fulfilled prior to the rapture. His coming for the church, then, could occur at any time, even within the next instant.

Jesus urged watchfulness upon his hearers, since they did not know the time of his return (Matt. 25:13). The parable of the ten virgins conveys this message. Just as in the time of Noah, there will be no warning signs (Matt. 24:36–39). The coming of the Lord will be like a thief in the night (Matt. 24:43). Or like the master who returns at an unexpected time (Matt. 24:45–51). There will be sudden separation. Two men will be working in the field; two women will be grinding at the mill. In each case, one will be

16. John F. Walvoord, *The Rapture Question* (Findlay, Ohio: Dunham, 1957), pp. 101, 198.

17. Charles L. Feinberg, *Premillennialism or Amillennialism? The Premillennial and Amillennial Systems of Interpretation Analyzed and Compared* (Grand Rapids: Zondervan, 1936), p. 146.

18. E. Schuyler English, *Re-thinking the Rapture: An Examination of What the Scriptures Teach as to the Time of the Translation of the Church in Relation to the Tribulation* (Neptune, N.J.: Loizeaux, 1954), pp. 100–101.

19. Walvoord, *Rapture Question*, pp. 75–82.

taken and the other left. What clearer depiction of the rapture could there be? Since it can occur at any moment, watchfulness and diligent activity are very much in order.[20]

There is another basis for the belief that Christ's return is imminent. The church can have a blessed hope (Titus 2:13) only if the next major event to transpire is the coming of Christ. If the Antichrist and the great tribulation were the next items on the eschatological agenda, Paul would have told the church to expect suffering, persecution, anguish. But instead he instructs the Thessalonians to comfort one another with the fact of Christ's second coming (1 Thess. 4:18). Since the next event, to which the church is to look forward with hopeful anticipation, is the coming of Christ for the church, there is nothing to prevent it from happening at any time.[21]

Finally, pretribulationism maintains that there will be at least two judgments. The church will be judged at the time of the rapture. It is then that rewards for faithfulness will be handed out. The church will not be involved, however, in the separation of the sheep and goats at the end of the millennium. Its status will have already been determined.

Posttribulationism

Posttribulationists maintain that the coming of Christ for his church will not take place until the conclusion of the great tribulation (see Figure 11). They avoid use of the term

Figure 11. Posttribulationism

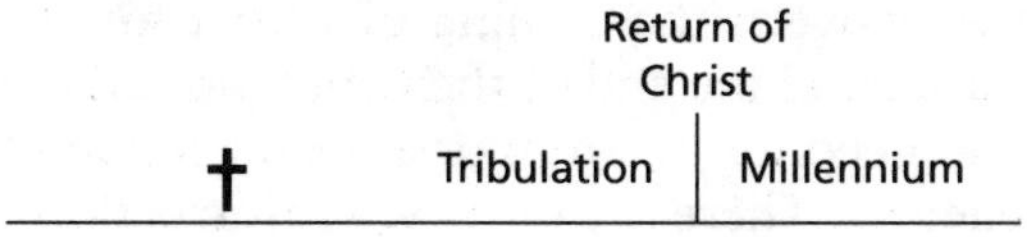

Return of
Christ

† | Tribulation | Millennium

rapture because (1) it is not a biblical expression, and (2) it suggests that the church will escape or be delivered from the tribulation,

a notion which runs contrary to the essence of posttribulationism.

A first feature of posttribulationism is a less literal interpretation of the events of the last times than is found in pretribulationism.[22] For instance, while pretribulationists take the word *shābûa'* ("week") in Daniel 9:27 to be an indication that the great tribulation will be literally seven years in duration, most posttribulationists hold merely that the tribulation will last a substantial period of time. Similarly, pretribulationists generally have a concrete conception of the millennium. In their view, for instance, the millennium will begin when Christ's feet literally stand on the Mount of Olives (Zech. 14:4). The posttribulationist's understanding of the millennium is much more generalized in nature; for example, it will not necessarily be one thousand years in length.

According to posttribulationism, the church will be present during and experience the great tribulation. The term *elect* in Matthew 24 (after the tribulation, the angels will gather the elect—vv. 29–31) should be understood in the light of its usage elsewhere in Scripture, where it means "believers." Since Pentecost, the term *elect* has denoted the church. The Lord will preserve the church during, but not spare it from, the tribulation.

Posttribulationists draw a distinction between the wrath of God and the tribulation. The wrath of God is spoken of in Scripture as coming upon the wicked—"he who does not obey the Son shall not see life, but the wrath of God rests upon him" (John 3:36; see also Rom. 1:18; 2 Thess. 1:8; Rev. 6:16–17; 14:10; 16:19; 19:15). On the other hand, believers will not undergo the wrath of God—"we [shall] be saved by [Christ] from the wrath of God" (Rom. 5:9; see also 1 Thess. 1:10; 5:9).[23] Scripture makes it

20. Gordon Lewis, "Biblical Evidence for Pretribulationism," *Bibliotheca Sacra* 125 (1968): 216–26.

21. John F. Walvoord, *The Return of the Lord* (Findlay, Ohio: Dunham, 1955), p. 51.

22. George E. Ladd, "Historic Premillennialism," in *Meaning of the Millennium*, pp. 18–27.

23. George E. Ladd, *The Blessed Hope* (Grand Rapids: Eerdmans, 1956), p. 122; Robert H. Gundry, *The Church and the Tribulation* (Grand Rapids: Zondervan, 1973), pp. 48–49.

clear, however, that believers will experience tribulation (Matt. 24:9, 21, 29; Mark 13:19, 24; Rev. 7:14). This is not God's wrath, but the wrath of Satan, Antichrist, and the wicked against God's people.[24]

Tribulation has been the experience of the church throughout the ages. Jesus said, "In the world you have tribulation" (John 16:33). Other significant references are Acts 14:22; Romans 5:3; 1 Thessalonians 3:3; 1 John 2:18, 22; 4:3; and 2 John 7. While posttribulationists do not deny a distinction between tribulation in general and the great tribulation, they believe that the difference is one of degree only, not of kind. Since the church has experienced tribulation throughout its history, it would not be surprising if the church also experiences the great tribulation.

Posttribulationists acknowledge that Scripture speaks of believers who will escape or be kept from the impending trouble. In Luke 21:36, for example, Jesus tells his disciples, "But watch at all times, praying that you may have strength to escape all these things that will take place, and to stand before the Son of man." The word here is *ekpheugō*, which means "to escape out of the midst of." A similar reference is found in Revelation 3:10. Posttribulationists argue, then, that the church will be kept from the midst of the tribulation, not that it will be kept away from the tribulation.[25] In this respect, we are reminded of the experience of the Israelites during the plagues on Egypt.

The posttribulationist also has a different understanding of Paul's reference in 1 Thessalonians 4:17 to our meeting the Lord in the air. The pretribulationist maintains that this event is the rapture; Christ will come secretly *for* the church, catching believers up with him in the clouds and taking them to heaven until the end of the tribulation. Posttribulationists like George Ladd, however, in light of the other scriptural usages of the Greek term translated "to meet" (*apantēsis*),

disagree. There are only two other undisputed occurrences of this word in the New Testament (Matt. 27:32 is textually suspect). One of these references is in the parable of the wise and foolish virgins, an explicitly eschatological parable. When the bridegroom comes, the announcement is made, "Behold, the bridegroom! Come out to meet [*apantēsis*] him" (Matt. 25:6). What does the word signify in this situation? The virgins do not go out to meet the bridegroom and then depart with him. Rather, they go out to meet him and then accompany him back to the wedding banquet. The other occurrence of the word (Acts 28:15) is in a noneschatological historical narrative. Paul and his party were coming to Rome. A group of the believers in Rome, hearing of their approach, went out to the Forum of Appius and Three Taverns to meet (*apantēsis*) them. This encouraged Paul, and the group then continued with him back to Rome. On the basis of these usages, Ladd argues that the word *apantēsis* suggests a welcoming party that goes out to meet someone on the way and accompanies him back to where they came from. So our meeting the Lord in the air is not a case of being caught away, but of meeting him and then immediately coming with him to earth as part of his triumphant entourage. It is the church, not the Lord, that will turn around at the meeting.[26]

Posttribulationists have a less complex understanding of the last things than do their pretribulational counterparts. For example, there is in posttribulationism only one second coming. Since there is no interlude between the coming of Christ for the church and the end of the tribulation, there is no need for an additional resurrection of believers. There are only two resurrections: (1) the resurrection of believers at the end of the tribulation and the beginning of the millennium, and (2) the resurrection of the ungodly at the end of the millennium.

Posttribulationists also see the complex of events at the end as having a basic unity.

24. Gundry, *Church and the Tribulation*, p. 49.
25. Ibid., p. 55.

26. Ladd, *Blessed Hope*, pp. 58–59.

They believe that this complex of events is imminent, although they usually do not mean that the coming itself is imminent in the sense that it could occur at any moment. They prefer to speak of the second coming as *impending*.[27] Their blessed hope is not an expectation that believers will be removed from the earth before the great tribulation, but rather a confidence that the Lord will protect and keep believers regardless of what may come.[28]

Mediating Positions

Because there are difficulties attaching to both pretribulationism and posttribulationism, a number of mediating positions have been created. Three major varieties may be noted. The most common is the midtribulational view. This holds that the church will go through the less severe part (usually the first half, or three-and-a-half years) of the tribulation, but then will be removed from the world.[29] In one formulation of this view, the church will experience tribulation but be removed before the wrath of God is poured out (see Figure 12). A second type of mediating position is the partial-rapture view. This holds that there will be a series of raptures. Whenever a portion of believers are ready, they will be removed from earth.[30] The third mediating position is imminent posttribulationism. While the return of Christ will not

Figure 12. Midtribulationism

	Return of Christ *for* the church	Return of Christ *with* the church
†	Tribu|lation	Millennium

ing position is the partial-rapture view. This holds that there will be a series of raptures. Whenever a portion of believers are ready, they will be removed from earth.[30] The third mediating position is imminent posttribulationism. While the return of Christ will not

27. Gundry, *Church and the Tribulation*, pp. 29–43.
28. Ladd, *Blessed Hope*, p. 13.
29. James Oliver Buswell, Jr., *A Systematic Theology of the Christian Religion* (Grand Rapids: Zondervan, 1962–63), vol. 2, pp. 445–57; Norman B. Harrison, *The End: Re-thinking the Revelation* (Minneapolis: Harrison, 1941), p. 118.
30. Robert Govett, *The Saints' Rapture to the Presence of the Lord Jesus* (London: Nisbet, 1852), pp. 126–28; George H. Lang, *The Revelation of Jesus Christ: Select Studies* (London: Oliphant, 1945), pp. 88–89.

take place until after the tribulation, it can be expected at any moment, for the tribulation may already be occurring.[31] None of these mediating positions has had large

> *The Bible does not promise removal from adversities, but ability to endure and overcome them.*

numbers of proponents, particularly in recent years. Accordingly, we will not deal with them in detail.[32]

Resolving the Issues

When all considerations are evaluated, there are several reasons why the posttribulational position emerges as the more probable:

1. The pretribulational position involves several distinctions which seem rather artificial and lacking in biblical support. The division of the second coming into two stages, the postulation of three resurrections, and the sharp separation of national Israel and the church are difficult to sustain on biblical grounds. The pretribulational view that the prophecies concerning national Israel will be fulfilled apart from the church and that, accordingly, the millennium will have a decidedly Jewish character cannot be easily reconciled with the biblical depictions of the fundamental changes which have taken place with the introduction of the new covenant.

2. Several specifically eschatological passages are better interpreted on posttribulational grounds. These passages include the indications that elect individuals will be present during the tribulation (Matt. 24:29–

31. J. Barton Payne, *The Imminent Appearing of Christ* (Grand Rapids: Eerdmans, 1962).
32. The reader who wishes a more thorough examination of these positions is directed to Millard J. Erickson, *Contemporary Options in Eschatology* (Grand Rapids: Baker, 1977), pp. 163–81.

31) but will be protected from its severity (Rev. 3:10), descriptions of the phenomena which will accompany the appearing of Christ, and the reference to the meeting in the air (1 Thess. 4:17).

3. The general tenor of biblical teaching fits better the posttribulational view. For example, the Bible is replete with warnings about trials and testings which believers will undergo. It does not promise removal from these adversities, but ability to endure and overcome them.

This is not to say that there are no difficulties with the posttribulational position. For example, there is in posttribulationism relatively little theological rationale for the millennium. It seems to be somewhat superfluous.[33] But all in all, the preponderance of evidence favors posttribulationism.

33. See, however, George E. Ladd, "The Revelation of Christ's Glory," *Christianity Today*, 1 Sept. 1958, p. 14.

41 Final States

When we speak of the final states, we are in a sense returning to the discussion of individual eschatology, for at the last judgment every individual will be consigned to the particular state which he or she will personally experience throughout all eternity. Yet the whole human race will enter these states simultaneously and collectively, so we are really dealing with questions of collective or cosmic eschatology as well.

Final State of the Righteous

The Term "Heaven"

There are various ways of denoting the future condition of the righteous. The most common, of course, is "heaven." The Hebrew and Greek words for "heaven" (*shāmayim* and *ouranos*) are used in basically three different ways in the Bible. The first is cosmological.[1] The expression "heaven and earth" (or "the heavens and the earth") is used to designate the entire universe. In the creation account we are told, "In the beginning God created the heavens and the earth" (Gen. 1:1). Second, "heaven" is a virtual synonym for God.[2] Among examples is the prodigal son's confession to his father, "I have sinned against heaven and before you" (Luke 15:18, 21).

The third meaning of the word *heaven*, and the one most significant for our purposes, is the abode of God.[3] Thus, Jesus taught his disciples to pray, "Our Father who art in heaven" (Matt. 6:9). He often spoke of "your Father who is in heaven" (Matt. 5:16, 45; 6:1; 7:11; 18:14) and "my Father who is in heaven" (Matt. 7:21; 10:32, 33; 12:50; 16:17; 18:10, 19). Jesus is said to have come from heaven (John 3:13, 31; 6:42, 51).[4] Angels come from heaven (Matt. 28:2; Luke 22:43) and return to heaven (Luke 2:15). They dwell in heaven (Mark 13:32), where they behold God (Matt. 18:10) and carry out the Father's will perfectly (Matt. 6:10). They are even referred to as a heavenly host (Luke 2:13).

It is from heaven that Christ is to be revealed (1 Thess. 1:10; 4:16; 2 Thess. 1:7). He has gone away to heaven to prepare an eternal dwelling for believers (John 14:2–3). As God's abode, heaven is obviously where believers will be for all eternity. Thus, the believer is to make preparation for heaven: "Do not lay up for yourselves treasures on earth, where moth and rust consume and where thieves break in and steal, but lay up for yourselves treasures in heaven, where neither moth nor rust consumes and where thieves do not break in and steal" (Matt. 6:19–20).

The Nature of Heaven

Sometimes, especially in popular presentations, heaven is depicted as primarily a place of great physical pleasures, a place where everything we have most desired here on earth is fulfilled to the ultimate degree. Thus heaven seems to be merely earthly (and even worldly) conditions amplified. The correct perspective, however, is to see the basic nature of heaven as the presence of God; from his presence all of the blessings of heaven follow.

The presence of God means that we will have perfect knowledge. Paul makes the comment that at present "our knowledge is imperfect and our prophecy is imperfect; but when the perfect comes, the imperfect will pass away. . . . For now we see in a mirror dimly, but then face to face. Now I know in part; then I shall understand fully, even as I have been fully understood" (1 Cor. 13:9–12). For the first time we shall see and know God in a direct way (1 John 3:2).

Heaven will also be characterized by the removal of all evils. In being with his people, God "will wipe away every tear from their eyes, and death shall be no more, neither shall there be mourning nor crying nor pain any more, for the former things have passed away" (Rev. 21:4). Not only these afflictions, but also the very source of evil, the one who tempts us to sin, will be gone: "and the devil who had deceived them was thrown into the lake of fire and brimstone where the beast and the false prophet were, and they will be tormented day and night for ever and ever" (Rev. 20:10). The presence of the perfectly holy God and the spotless Lamb means that there will be no sin or evil of any kind.

Since glory is of the very nature of God, heaven will be a place of great glory.[5] The announcement of Jesus' birth was accompanied by the words: "Glory to God in the high-

1. Helmut Traub, οὐρανός, in *Theological Dictionary of the New Testament*, ed. Gerhard Kittel and Gerhard Friedrich, trans. Geoffrey W. Bromiley, 10 vols. (Grand Rapids: Eerdmans, 1964–76), vol. 5, pp. 514–20.

2. Ibid., pp. 521–22.

3. Francis Brown, S. R. Driver, and Charles A. Briggs, *Hebrew and English Lexicon of the Old Testament* (New York: Oxford University Press, 1955), p. 1030.

4. Leon Morris, *The Lord from Heaven* (Grand Rapids: Eerdmans, 1958), pp. 26–29.

5. Bernard Ramm, *Them He Glorified: A Systematic Study of the Doctrine of Glorification* (Grand Rapids: Eerdmans, 1963), pp. 104–15.

est, and on earth peace among men with whom he is pleased!" (Luke 2:14). The second coming of Christ will be in great glory (Matt. 24:30), and he will sit upon his glorious throne (Matt. 25:31). Images suggesting immense size or brilliant light depict heaven as a place of unimaginable splendor, greatness, excellence, and beauty. The new Jerusalem which will come down out of heaven from God is described as made of pure gold (even its streets are pure gold) and decorated with precious jewels (Rev. 21:18–21). It is

> *The basic nature of heaven is the presence of God; our life in heaven will consist of rest, worship, and service.*

likely that while John's vision employs as metaphors those items which we think of as being most valuable and beautiful, the actual splendor of heaven far exceeds anything that we have yet experienced. There will be no need of sun or moon to illumine the new Jerusalem, for "the glory of God is its light, and its lamp is the Lamb" (Rev. 21:23; see also 22:5).

Our Life in Heaven: Rest, Worship, and Service

We are told relatively little about the activities of the redeemed in heaven, but there are a few glimpses of what our future existence is to be. One quality of our life in heaven will be rest.[6] Rest, as the term is used in Hebrews, is not merely a cessation of activities, but the experience of reaching a goal of crucial importance. Thus, there are frequent references to the pilgrimage through the wilderness en route to the "rest" of the

Promised Land (Heb. 3:11, 18). A similar rest awaits believers (Heb. 4:9–11). Heaven, then, will be the completion of the Christian's pilgrimage, the end of the struggle against the flesh, the world, and the devil. There will be work to do, but it will not involve fighting against opposing forces.

Another facet of life in heaven is worship.[7] A vivid picture is found in Revelation 19:

> After this I heard what seemed to be the mighty voice of a great multitude in heaven, crying, "Hallelujah! Salvation and glory and power belong to our God, for his judgments are true and just; he has judged the great harlot who corrupted the earth with her fornication, and he has avenged on her the blood of his servants." Once more they cried, "Hallelujah! The smoke from her goes up for ever and ever." And the twenty-four elders and the four living creatures fell down and worshiped God who is seated on the throne, saying, "Amen. Hallelujah!" [vv. 1–4]

Then a voice from the throne exhorted the multitude to praise God (v. 5), and they did so (vv. 6–8).

There will evidently be an element of service in heaven as well.[8] For when Jesus was in the region of Judea beyond the Jordan, he told his disciples that they would judge with him: "Truly, I say to you, in the new world, when the Son of man shall sit on his glorious throne, you who have followed me will also sit on twelve thrones, judging the twelve tribes of Israel" (Matt. 19:28; see also Luke 22:28–30). We are reminded of the stewardship parable in Matthew 25:14–30, where the reward for work done faithfully is greater opportunity for work. Because that parable occurs in an eschatological setting, it may well be an indication that the reward for faithful work done here on earth will be work in heaven. Note also that Revelation 22:3 tells us that the Lamb will be worshiped by "his servants."

---

6. We are here assuming that our life in heaven will be the personal, conscious, individual existence which appears to be presupposed in all the biblical references. For the view that our future existence will be merely a living on in God's memory, see David L. Edwards, *The Last Things Now* (London: SCM, 1969), pp. 88–91.

7. Ulrich Simon, *Heaven in the Christian Tradition* (New York: Harper, 1958), p. 236.

8. Morton Kelsey, *Afterlife: The Other Side of Dying* (New York: Paulist, 1979), pp. 182–83.

There is, moreover, a suggestion that in heaven there will be some type of community or fellowship among believers: "But you have come to Mount Zion and to the city of the living God, . . . and to the assembly of the first-born who are enrolled in heaven, and to a judge who is God of all, and to the spirits of just men made perfect, and to Jesus, the mediator of a new covenant" (Heb. 12:22–24). Note, too, the reference to "the spirits of just men made perfect"—heaven is a place of perfected spirituality.[9]

Issues Regarding Heaven

One of the disputed questions regarding heaven is whether it is a place or a state. On the one hand, it should be noted that the primary feature of heaven is closeness and communion with God, and that God is pure spirit (John 4:24). Since God does not occupy space, which is a feature of our universe, it would seem that heaven is a state, a spiritual condition, rather than a place.[10] On the other hand, we will have bodies of some type (although they will be "spiritual bodies") and Jesus presumably continues to have a glorified body as well, a factor which seems to require place. In addition, parallel references to heaven and earth suggest that, like earth, heaven must be a locale. The most familiar of these references is, "Our Father who art in heaven, Hallowed be thy name. Thy kingdom come, Thy will be done, On earth as it is in heaven" (Matt. 6:9–10).[11] We must be mindful, however, that heaven is another realm, another dimension of reality. It is probably safest to say that while heaven is both a place and a state, it is primarily a state. The distinguishing mark of heaven will not be a particular location, but a condition of blessedness, sinlessness, joy, and peace.[12] Life in heaven, accordingly, will be more real than our present existence.

A second issue concerns the question of physical pleasures. Jesus indicated that there will be in the resurrection, presumably the life hereafter, no marrying or giving in marriage (Matt. 22:30; Mark 12:25; Luke 20:35). Since sex is in this life to be restricted to marriage (1 Cor. 7:8–11), we have here an argument that there will be no sex in heaven. The high value Paul places upon virginity (1 Cor. 7:25–35) suggests the same conclusion.[13] What of eating and drinking? Revelation 19:9 refers to the "marriage supper of the Lamb." In view of the fact that the references to Christ and the church as bridegroom and bride are symbolic, the marriage supper of the Lamb is presumably symbolic as well. Although Jesus ate with his resurrection body (Luke 24:43; cf. John 21:9–14), it should be borne in mind that he was resurrected but not yet ascended, so that the transformation of his body was probably not yet completed. The question arises, If there is to be no eating nor sex, will there be any pleasure in heaven? It should be understood that the experiences of heaven will far surpass anything experienced here (1 Cor. 2:9–10). It is likely that heaven's experiences should be thought of as, for example, suprasexual, transcending the experience of sexual union with the special individual with whom one has chosen to make a permanent and exclusive commitment.[14]

A third issue relates to the question of perfection. Within this life we gain satisfaction from growth, progress, development. Will not, then, our state of perfection in heaven be a rather boring and unsatisfying situation?[15] Bear in mind here that the contention that we cannot be satisfied unless we grow is an extrapolation from life as now constituted, and an illegitimate one at that!

9. J. A. Motyer, *After Death: A Sure and Certain Hope?* (Philadelphia: Westminster, 1965), pp. 74–76.

10. W. H. Dyson, "Heaven," in *A Dictionary of Christ and the Gospels*, ed. James Hastings (New York: Scribner, 1924), vol. 1, p. 712.

11. Alan Richardson, *Religion in Contemporary Debate* (London: SCM, 1966), p. 72.

12. Austin Farrer, *Saving Belief* (London: Hodder and Stoughton, 1967), p. 144.

13. Simon, *Heaven*, p. 217.

14. C. S. Lewis, *Miracles* (New York: Macmillan, 1947), pp. 165–66. Lewis uses the term *transsexual* with much the same meaning as we have here attached to "suprasexual."

15. Alfred, Lord Tennyson, "Wages."

Frustration and boredom occur within this life whenever there is an arresting of development at a finite point, whenever one has stopped short of perfection. If, however, one were to fully achieve, if there were no feeling of inadequacy or incompleteness, there would probably be no frustration. Now heaven is not a fixed state short of one's goal, but a state of completion beyond which there can be no advance. Therefore, we will not grow in heaven. We will, however, continue to exercise the perfect character which we will have received from God. John Baillie speaks of "development *in* fruition" as opposed to "development *towards* fruition."[16]

There also is the question of how much the redeemed in heaven will know or remember. Will we recognize those close to us in this life? Much of the popular interest in heaven stems from expectation of reunion with loved ones. Will we be aware of the absence of relatives and close friends? Will there be an awareness of sinful actions taken and godly deeds omitted in this life? If so, will not all of this lead to regret and sorrow? With regard to these questions we must necessarily plead a certain amount of ignorance. It does not appear, from Jesus' response to the Sadducees' question about the woman who had outlived seven husbands, all of them brothers (Luke 20:27–40), that there will be family units as such. On the other hand, the disciples were evidently able to recognize Moses and Elijah at the transfiguration (Matt. 17:1–8; Mark 9:2–8; Luke 9:28–36). This fact suggests that there will be some indicators of personal identity by which we will be able to recognize one another.[17] But we may infer that we will not recollect past failures and sins and missing loved ones, since that would introduce a sadness incompatible with "he will wipe away every tear from their eyes, and death shall be no more, neither shall there be mourning nor crying nor pain any more, for the former things have passed away" (Rev. 21:4).

A fifth question is whether there will be varying rewards in heaven. That there apparently will be degrees of reward is evident in, for example, the parable of the pounds (Luke 19:11–27).[18] Ten servants were each given one pound by their master. Eventually they returned differing amounts to him and were rewarded in proportion to their faithfulness. Supporting passages include Daniel 12:3 and 1 Corinthians 3:14–15.

The differing rewards or differing degrees of satisfaction in heaven are usually pictured in terms of objective circumstances. For instance, we might suppose that a very faithful Christian will be given a large room in the Father's house; a less faithful believer will receive a smaller room. But if this is the case, would not the joy of heaven be reduced by one's awareness of the differences and the constant reminder that one might have been more faithful? In addition, the few pictures which we do have of life in heaven evidence no real difference: all are worshiping, judging, serving. A bit of speculation may be in order at this point. May it not be that the difference in the rewards lies not in the external or objective circumstances, but in the subjective awareness or appreciation of those circumstances? Thus, all would engage in the same activity, for example, worship, but some would enjoy it much more than others. Perhaps those who have enjoyed worship more in this life will find greater satisfaction in it in the life beyond than will others. An analogy here is the varying degrees of pleasure which different people derive from a concert. The same sound waves fall on everyone's ears, but the reactions may range from boredom (or worse) to ecstasy. A similar situation may well hold with respect to the joys of heaven, although the range of reactions will presumably be narrower. No one will be aware of the differences in range of enjoyment, and thus there

16. John Baillie, *And the Life Everlasting* (New York: Scribner, 1933), p. 281.

17. Motyer, *After Death*, p. 87.

18. S. D. F. Salmond, "Heaven," in *A Dictionary of the Bible*, ed. James Hastings (New York: Scribner, 1919), vol. 2, p. 324.

will be no dimming of the perfection of heaven by regret over wasted opportunities.

Final State of the Wicked

Just as in the past, the question of the future state of the wicked has created a considerable amount of controversy in our day. The doctrine of an everlasting punishment appears to some to be an outmoded or sub-Christian view.[19] Part of the problem stems from what appears to be a tension between the love of God and his judgment. Yet, however we regard the doctrine of everlasting punishment, it is clearly taught in Scripture.

The Bible employs several images to depict the future state of the unrighteous. Jesus said, "Then [the King] will say to those at his left hand, 'Depart from me, you cursed, into the eternal fire prepared for the devil and his angels'" (Matt. 25:41). He likewise described their state as "outer darkness" (Matt. 8:12). The final condition of the wicked is also spoken of as eternal punishment (Matt. 25:46), torment (Rev. 14:10–11), the bottomless pit (Rev. 9:1–2, 11), the wrath of God (Rom. 2:5), second death (Rev. 21:8), eternal destruction and exclusion from the face of the Lord (2 Thess. 1:9).

If there is one basic characteristic of hell, it is, in contrast to heaven, the absence of God or banishment from his presence. It is an experience of intense anguish, whether it involve physical suffering or mental distress or both.[20] Other aspects include a sense of loneliness, of having seen the glory and greatness of God, of having realized that he is the Lord of all, and then of being cut off. There is the realization that this separation is permanent. Similarly, the condition of one's moral and spiritual self is permanent. Whatever one is at the end of life will continue for all eternity. There is no basis for expecting change for the better. Thus, hopelessness comes over the individual.

The Finality of the Future Judgment

It is important to recognize the finality of the coming judgment. When the verdict is rendered at the last judgment, the wicked will be assigned to their *final* state.[21] To some, this seems contrary to reason, and even perhaps to Scripture. Here we encounter the concept of universalism, that is, the view that all will eventually be saved. Some even contend that those who in this life reject the offer of salvation will, after their death and Christ's second coming, be sobered by their situation and will therefore be reconciled to Christ.[22]

This matter is not easily resolved. The biblical texts appear contradictory. Some passages seem to assert or imply that salvation is universal, that is, that no one will be lost. Paul says, for example, "At the name of Jesus every knee [shall] bow, in heaven and on earth and under the earth, and every tongue confess that Jesus Christ is Lord, to the glory of God the Father" (Phil. 2:10–11). Further, in Christ "all the fulness of God was pleased to dwell, and through him to reconcile to himself all things, whether on earth or in heaven, making peace by the blood of his cross" (Col. 1:19–20). Additional verses cited in support of universalism include Romans 5:18; 11:32; and 1 Corinthians 15:22. Many other texts appear to contradict universalism, however; for instance, "And they will go away into eternal punishment, but the righteous into eternal life" (Matt. 25:46). Also cited are Matthew 8:12; John 3:16; 5:28–29; Romans 2:5; and 2 Thessalonians 1:9.

Can the apparent contradictions be reconciled? A fruitful endeavor here is to interpret the universalistic passages in such a way as to fit with the restrictive ones. For example, Philippians 2:10–11 and Colossians

19. Nels Ferré, *The Christian Understanding of God* (New York: Harper and Brothers, 1951), pp. 233–34.

20. Charles Hodge, *Systematic Theology* (Grand Rapids: Eerdmans, 1952), vol. 3, p. 868.

21. J. A. Motyer, "The Final State: Heaven and Hell," in *Basic Christian Doctrines*, ed. Carl F. H. Henry (New York: Holt, Rinehart and Winston, 1962), p. 292.

22. Origen *De principiis* 1.6.2; 3.6.3. For a contemporary statement of universalism, see John A. T. Robinson, *In the End, God* (New York: Harper and Row, 1968), pp. 119–33.

1:19–20 do not say that all will be saved and restored to fellowship with God. They speak only of setting right the disrupted order of the universe, the bringing of all things into subjection to God. But this could be achieved by a victory forcing the rebels into reluctant submission; it does not necessarily point to an actual return to fellowship.

In passages which draw a parallel between the universal effect of Adam's sin and of Christ's saving work, there are elements which serve to qualify the universal dimension as it applies to Christ's work. In the case of Romans 5:18 ("Then as one man's trespass led to condemnation for all men, so one man's act of righteousness leads to acquittal and life for all men"), verse 17 specifies that *"those who receive* the abundance of grace and the free gift of righteousness reign in life through the one man Jesus Christ" (italics added). Furthermore, the term "many" rather than "all" is used in verses 15 and 19.

> *Whatever one is morally and spiritually at the end of life will continue for all eternity.*

Paul similarly restricts the meaning of "all" in 1 Corinthians 15:22 ("in Christ shall all be made alive"). For in the next verse he adds: "But each in his own order: Christ the first fruits, then at his coming *those who belong to Christ"* (italics added). In fact, he had earlier made it clear that he is speaking about believers: "If Christ has not been raised . . . those also who have fallen asleep in Christ have perished" (vv. 17–18).

One universalistic passage remains. Romans 11:32 seems to suggest that God saves all: "God has consigned all men to disobedience, that he may have mercy upon all." In actuality, however, the mercy which God has shown is his providing his Son as an atonement and extending the offer of salva-

tion to all. God's mercy is shown to all humans, but only those who accept it will experience and profit from it. Thus, although salvation is universally available, it is not universal.

Finally, we must note that Scripture nowhere gives indication of a second chance. Surely, if there is to be an opportunity for belief after the judgment, it would be clearly set forth in God's Word. What we find instead are definite statements to the contrary. A finality attaches to the biblical depictions of the sentence rendered at the judgment; for example, "Depart from me, you cursed, into the eternal fire prepared for the devil and his angels" (Matt. 25:41). The parable of the rich man and Lazarus (Luke 16:19–31), although it relates to the intermediate rather than the final state, makes it clear that there is an absoluteness about their condition. It is not even possible to travel between the different states (v. 26). We must therefore conclude that restorationism, the idea of a second chance, must be rejected.

The Eternality of Future Punishment

Not only is the future judgment of unbelievers irreversible, but their punishment is eternal. We do not reject merely the idea that all will be saved; we also reject the contention that none will be eternally punished. The school of thought known as annihilationism, on the other hand, maintains that although not everyone will be saved, there is only one class of future existence. Those who are saved will have an unending life; those who are not saved will be eliminated or annihilated. They will simply cease to exist. While granting that not everyone deserves to be saved, to receive everlasting bliss, this position maintains that no one deserves endless suffering.

There are different forms of annihilationism.[23] The form most deserving of the title sees the extinction of the evil person at

23. See Benjamin B. Warfield, "Annihilationism," in *Studies in Theology* (New York: Oxford University Press, 1932), pp. 447–50.

death as a direct result of sin. Humans are by nature immortal and would have everlasting life but for the effects of sin. There are two subtypes of annihilationism proper. The first sees annihilation as a natural result of sin. Sin is self-destruction. After a certain length of time, perhaps proportionate to the sinfulness of the individual, those who are not redeemed wear out as it were. The other type of pure annihilationism is the idea that God cannot and will not allow the sinful person to have eternal life. Because punishment need not be infinite, God will, after a sufficient amount has been endured, simply destroy the individual self. It should be noted that in both subtypes of annihilationism proper, the soul or self would be immortal but for sin.[24]

The problem with annihilationism is that it contradicts the teaching of the Bible. Both the Old and New Testaments refer to unending or unquenchable fire. Jesus borrows the imagery of Isaiah 66:24 to describe the punishment of sinners in hell: "their worm does not die, and the fire is not quenched" (Mark 9:48). Such passages make it clear that the punishment is unending. It does not consume the one upon whom it is inflicted and thus simply come to an end.

In addition, there are several instances where words like "everlasting," "eternal," and "forever" are applied to nouns designating the future state of the wicked: fire or burning (Isa. 33:14; Jer. 17:4; Matt. 18:8; 25:41; Jude 7), contempt (Dan. 12:2), destruction (2 Thess. 1:9), chains (Jude 6), torment (Rev. 14:11; 20:10), and punishment (Matt. 25:46). The parallelism found in Matthew 25:46 is particularly noteworthy: "And they will go away into eternal punishment, but the righteous into eternal life." If the one (life) is of unending duration, then the other (punishment) must be also.

A problem arises from the fact that Scripture speaks not merely of eternal death (which one might interpret as meaning that

the wicked will not be resurrected), but of eternal fire, eternal punishment, and eternal torment as well. What kind of God is it who is not satisfied by a finite punishment, but makes humans suffer for ever and ever? The punishment seems to be out of all proportion to the sin, for, presumably, all sins are finite acts against God. How does one square belief in a good, just, and loving God with eternal punishment? The question must not be dismissed lightly, for it concerns the very essence of God's nature.

We should note, first, that whenever we sin, an infinite factor is invariably involved. All sin is an offense against God, the raising of a finite will against the will of an infinite being. It is failure to carry out one's obligation to him to whom everything is due. Consequently, one cannot consider sin to be merely a finite act deserving finite punishment.

Further, if God is to accomplish his goals in this world, he may not have been free to make humans unsusceptible to endless punishment. God's omnipotence does not mean that he is capable of every conceivable action. He is not capable of doing the logically contradictory or absurd, for example. He cannot make a triangle with four corners.[25] And it may well be that those creatures that God intended to live forever in fellowship with him had to be fashioned in such a way that they would experience eternal anguish if they chose to live apart from their Maker. Humans were designed to live eternally with God; if we pervert this our destiny, we will experience eternally the consequences of that act.

We should also observe that God does not send anyone to hell. He desires that none should perish (2 Peter 3:9). It is the choice of humans to experience the agony of hell. Their sin sends them there, and their rejection of the benefits of Christ's death prevents their escaping. As C. S. Lewis has put it, sin is a person's saying to God throughout

24. *Seventh-Day Adventists Answer Questions on Doctrine* (Washington: Review and Herald, 1957), p. 14.

25. C. S. Lewis, *The Problem of Pain* (New York: Macmillan, 1962), p. 28.

life, "Go away and leave me alone." Hell is God's finally saying to that individual, "You may have your wish." It is God's leaving one to oneself, as he or she has chosen.[26]

Degrees of Punishment

We should observe, finally, that Jesus' teaching suggests that there are degrees of punishment in hell. He upbraided those cities which had witnessed his miracles but failed to repent: "Woe to you, Chorazin! woe to you, Bethsaida! . . . For if the mighty works done in you had been done in Sodom, it would have remained until this day. But I tell you that it shall be more tolerable on the day of judgment for the land of Sodom than for you" (Matt. 11:21–24). There is a similar hint in the parable of the faithful and faithless stewards: "And that servant who knew his master's will, but did not make ready or act according to his will, shall receive a severe beating. But he who did not know, and did what deserved a beating, shall receive a light beating. Every one to whom much is given, of him will much be required; and of him to whom men commit much they will demand the more" (Luke 12:47–48).

The principle here seems to be, the greater our knowledge, the greater is our responsibility, and the greater will be our punishment if we fail in our responsibility. It may well be that the different degrees of punishment in hell are not so much a matter of objective circumstances as of subjective awareness of the pain of separation from God. This is parallel to our conception of the varying degrees of reward in heaven. To some extent, the different degrees of punishment reflect the fact that hell is God's leaving sinful people with the particular charac-

26. Ibid., pp. 127–28.

ter that they fashioned for themselves in this life. The misery they will experience from having to live with their wicked self eternally will be proportionate to their degree of awareness of precisely what they were doing when they chose evil.

Implications of the Doctrine of the Final States

1. The decisions which we make in this life will govern our future condition not merely for a period of time, but for all eternity. So we should exercise extraordinary care and diligence as we make them.

2. The conditions of this life, as Paul put it, are transitory. They fade into relative insignificance when compared with the eternity to come.

3. The nature of the future states is far more intense than anything known in this life. The images used to depict them are quite inadequate to fully convey what lies ahead. Heaven, for example, will far transcend any joy that we have known here.

4. The bliss of heaven ought not to be thought of as simply an intensification of the pleasures of this life. The primary dimension of heaven is the presence of the believer with the Lord.

5. Hell is not so much a place of physical suffering as it is the awful loneliness of total and final separation from the Lord.

6. Hell should not be thought of primarily as punishment visited upon unbelievers by a vindictive God, but as the natural consequences of the sinful life chosen by those who reject Christ.

7. It appears that although all humans will be consigned either to heaven or to hell, there will be degrees of reward and punishment.

Conclusion

Ideas have a profound impact upon the behavior of groups and individuals. Francis Schaeffer has pointed out how obscure the idea of dialectic must have seemed when Georg Hegel first propounded it.[1] Yet it has made a major difference in the lives of the millions and possibly even billions of people who have been under the control of an ideology derived from it.

The doctrines we hold will, either consciously or unconsciously, affect our attitudes, our outlook on life, the way we treat other humans, and the way we respond to God. The type of persons and Christians we are and will become in the years ahead is rightly viewed as resulting, at least in part, from our doctrinal beliefs.

Doctrine also helps to make our Christianity something we can live today. Unlike Noah, we are not called to build an ark, but to believe that God is still a holy God who continues to judge sin. We are not called upon like Abraham to offer a loved one as a sacrifice, but to serve a God who, as the Supreme Being, expects and deserves that we love him more than anything or anyone else. Doctrine is the point of continuity between the Bible's past events and teachings and our present situation.

May the study of Christian doctrine be a continuing endeavor for each of us. For it is part of the fulfilment of God's command (Deut. 6:5), as interpreted by Jesus (Matt. 22:37; Mark 12:30; Luke 10:27), to love him with our whole being, which includes the mind.

1. Francis Schaeffer, *The God Who Is There* (Downers Grove, Ill.: Inter-Varsity, 1968), p. 20.

Scripture Index

(The letters *a* and *b* refer, respectively, to the left and right column of the page cited. The letter *n* refers to the footnotes.)

Genesis

1—165b, 166b, 167b
1–2—146a
1–3—158b
1:1—82b, 120, 123a, 396a
1:2—123a, 266a
1:10—124a
1:12—124a
1:18—124a
1:20—159a
1:21—124a, 159a
1:24—159a
1:25—124a
1:26—99b, 163a, 164a, 165b, 167a, 225b
1:26–27—157b, 163a
1:27—99b, 163a, 169a
1:27–28—165b
1:28—44b, 158a, 183a, 188a
1:31—124a, 161a
2:7—54b, 158a, 158b, 159a
2:15–17—247b
2:16–17—180b
2:17—90b, 142ab, 189b
2:24—29a, 57a, 100a
3—83b, 149a, 310a
3:2–3—142b
3:3—365b
3:4–5—183b
3:8—44b, 186a
3:11—192b
3:12—192b
3:14—158b
3:14–19—325a
3:16—142b
3:17—142b
3:17–19—39b
3:18—142b
3:19—142b, 158b, 159a, 189b, 190a
3:22—190b, 225b
3:22–23—365b
4:26—83b
5:1—163a
5:1–2—169a
5:2—163a
6—113b, 189a
6–7—380a
6:5—195a, 197a
6:6—113b, 143b, 297b
8:21—195a
9:6—163a, 169a, 188b
11:7—225b
17:1—85b
17:7—348b
18:25—90a
35:18—173a
38:26—307a
41:8—173a
41:38—266b

Exodus

3:6—57a
3:14—45a, 82a, 83a
3:14–15—209a
3:44—57a
12:40–41—63a
15:11—89a
15:13—331b
15:16—331b
19—147b
20:2–3—97b, 125a
20:3—83b, 181a
20:4—97b
20:5—186b
20:7—83b
20:8–11—208b
20:14—143b
23:22—186b
31:3–5—266b
33:19—289b
34:6—93b

Leviticus

1:3–4—248b
4:35—251b
11:44–45—89b
24:16—209a

Numbers

14:8—331b
23:19—86b, 92a

Deuteronomy

4:42—196a
5:10—93b, 311a
6—97b
6:4—97b, 100a
6:5—97b, 405

6:6—97b
6:7—97b
7:7–8—92b
7:10—186b
10:16—348b
18:15—239a
25:1—307b
25:13–15—91b
30:6—348b
32:9–10—331b
32:10—331b
32:35—189a
33:2—146b, 147b

Joshua

9:16–21—92a
10:12–14—136b

Judges

6:34—266b
6:36–40—134b

1 Samuel

2:6–7—132a
8:3—91a
13:14—195a
15:23—181a
15:29—91b
16:13—266b
18:10—63a
24:17—307a
26:23—307a
28:6—319b

Name and Subject Index

(The letters *a* and *b* refer, respectively, to the left and right column of the page cited. The letter *n* refers to the footnotes.)

Abelard, Peter, 242b
Abortion, 169b
Absence of God, hell as the, 400a, 403b
Absolute inerrancy, 61a
Accidental occurrences, 132a
Acts of God as special revelation, 47ab, 48b
Adam, 142a, 158a, 167b; sin of, 198b–203b
Adam and Eve, 44ab, 142b, 180b, 183b, 186a, 189b–191a, 192b, 220b, 365b; as true humans, 162, 222b, 229b
Administration as a gift of the Holy Spirit, 266b
Administrator of the Lord's Supper, 356ab
Adoption, 286a, 294, 310b–312b
Adoptionism, 227ab
Adult baptism, 349b, 351b
Affirmations, inerrancy of, 63b–64a
Agapē, 92b
Age of the earth, 126ab
Alexander, 320a, 322a
All-inclusiveness: of creation, 122b–123a; of God's governing activity, 133a; of God's plan, 110b–111b, 112b; of the Great Commission, 337ab
Althaus, Paul, 211b
Amillennialism, 382, 384b, 386a–388b, 389ab

Anabaptists, 367b
Analogical nature of special revelation, 46a–47a
Analysis of the meanings of biblical teachings (step in theology), 20a
Angel of the Lord, 147b–148a
Angels, 145–151b, 381a; activities of, 147a–148b; capacities of, 147a; guardian, 148ab; nature of, 146b; numbers of, 146b; origin of, 146a; powers of, 147a; status of, 146b
Anger of God. *See* Wrath of God
Anglican church, 343a
Animal nature as source of sin, 181b
Animals, humans as, 156ab
Annihilationism, 401b–402a
Anonymous Christians, 284b
Anselm, 36b, 244b
Anthropic nature of special revelation, 45b–46a
Anthropological argument, 36b
Anthropomorphisms, 82a, 86b, 113b
Anthropopathisms, 86b
Anxiety caused by finiteness (as source of sin), 181b
Apokalypsis, 374b, 375b–376a
Apollinarianism, 218b–219a, 231b
Apollinarius, 172b
Apologetic approach, 342a
Apologetics, 71a
Apostasy, warnings against, 319a–322b
Approximations in the Bible, 65a
Arianism, 212b–213a, 231b, 261a
Arminianism, 114ab, 116b–117a, 140b, 189n, 199b, 200a, 290a–291b, 292a, 293a, 293b, 317b, 319a–320a, 320b
Ascension, 237b–238b

Asceticism, 124b, 176b, 223b
Assertions, inerrancy of, 63b–64a
Athanasius, 102a
Atonement, 28b, 30a, 95b, 222b, 241a–255b, 309a; basic meaning of, 251a–253b; infinite value of, 255a; limited, 288a; necessity of, 253b–254a
Attributes of God, 76a, 79a–95b; classification of, 80ab; essence and, 79b; nature of, 79a–80a
Augustine, 104ab, 200b, 243b, 288a, 369b, 383a, 386b
Aulen, Gustaf, 243b
Authentic existence, salvation as, 282b–283a
Authority, 67–71b; church government and, 342b; Jesus' claim to, 208b; objective and subjective components of, 70ab; rejection of, 193b; religious, 67–68a
Autonomy in the congregational form of church government, 344ab
Axhead, floating, 136b, 137a
Azusa Street meetings, 271b

Backsliding, 322a, 322b
Baillie, John, 399a
Baptism, 28b–29a, 346–352b; basic views of, 347a–349b; of the Holy Spirit, 271b, 272a, 273a–274a; of Jesus, 101b, 102a, 212a, 227b, 263b, 267b; meaning of, 350a–351b; mode of, 348a, 349a, 349b, 351b–352a; subjects of, 347b, 348ab, 349ab, 351b
Baptismal regeneration, 347a, 350ab, 351b
Baptist churches, 344a, 349b, 384b

415